MASTERING JAVASCRIPT AND JSCRIPT

BY JAMES JAWORSKI

Available in March 1999
ISBN: 0-7821-2492-5
$39.99

avaScript is the most widely used scripting language for the Web and continues to
grow in popularity. Mastering JavaScript and JScript is aimed at savvy HTML users who
want to take the next step and learn to write JavaScript programs that will make their
Web sites come alive! This is the most comprehensive tutorial and reference available,
with information on both Netscape and Microsoft's enhancements of JavaScript. The
book starts with everything beginners need to know and then moves on to more
advanced topics, such as scripting ActiveX components, working with plug-ins, build-
ng multimedia applications, and interfacing with CGI programs. The companion Web
site offers all the sample code from the book, which readers can drop into their own
programs, and a complete JavaScript command reference. The author is a well-known
nternet programming expert and has led the development of secure networks for the
Department of Defense.

WEB BY DESIGN: THE COMPLETE GUIDE

BY MOLLY HOLZSCHLAG

928 pages
ISBN: 0-7821-2201-9
$49.99

Here is the book that Web designers have been searching for—the ONLY comprehensive guide that covers the five key aspects of Web design: 1) Graphic design, 2) HTML
design & layout techniques, 3) Color, shape, & space, 4) Web typography, and 5) Multimedia and programming. Why should designers have to buy five separate, expensive
books when they can get this all-in-one, affordable guide? They shouldn't! This widely
recognized author, columnist, and instructor, who is intimately connected to and respected
by the Web design community, will teach you all of the design skills required to create
successful sites. The comprehensive companion Web site, the Design Studio, and a corresponding four-color insert will showcase dozens of successful real-world Web site
concepts and examples. This book is destined to be the ultimate Web designers' hand-
book—the one book that they pull off their shelves again and again.

HTML Complete

SYBEX® SAN FRANCISCO ► PARIS ► DÜSSELDORF ► SOEST ► LONDON

Associate Publisher: Gary Masters

Contracts and Licensing Manager: Kristine O'Callaghan

Developmental Editor: Brenda Frink

Compilation Editor: Michael Anderson

Compilation Technical Editors: Ben DeLong, Rima Regas

Compilation Technical Reviewer: Rima Regas

Editors: Pat Coleman, Nancy Conner, Kim Crowder, Diane Lowery, Ben Miller, Valerie Perry, Vivian Perry, Lee Ann Pickrell, Kristen Vanberg-Wolff, Kim Wimpsett

Technical Editors: Matthew Fiedler, Don Hergert, Ben DeLong, Will Kelly, Tom Maxwell, Ann Navarro, John Piraino, Sr., Rima Regas, David Shank, David Wall

Book Designer: Maureen Forys, Happenstance Type-O-Rama

Electronic Publishing Specialist: Robin Kibby

Production Coordinator: Julie Sakaue

Indexer: Matthew Spence

Cover Designer: DesignSite

Cover Illustration: DesignSite

Library of Congress Card Number: 98-83175
ISBN: 0-7821-2467-4

Manufactured in the United States of America

10 9 8 7 6

TRADEMARKS:

SYBEX has attempted throughout this book to distinguish proprietary trademarks from descriptive terms by following the capitalization style used by the manufacturer.

Netscape Communications, the Netscape Communications logo, Netscape, and Netscape Navigator are trademarks of Netscape Communications Corporation.

Netscape Communications Corporation has not authorized, sponsored, endorsed, or approved this publication and is not responsible for its content. Netscape and the Netscape Communications Corporate Logos are trademarks and trade names of Netscape Communications Corporation. All other product names and/or logos are trademarks of their respective owners.

The author and publisher have made their best efforts to prepare this book, and the content is based upon final release software whenever possible. Portions of the manuscript may be based upon pre-release versions supplied by software manufacturer(s). The author and the publisher make no representation or warranties of any kind with regard to the completeness or accuracy of the contents herein and accept no liability of any kind including but not limited to performance, merchantability, fitness for any particular purpose, or any losses or damages of any kind caused or alleged to be caused directly or indirectly from this book.

Photographs and illustrations used in this book have been downloaded from publicly accessible file archives and are used in this book for news reportage purposes only to demonstrate the variety of graphics resources available via electronic access. Text and images available over the Internet may be subject to copyright and other rights owned by third parties. Online availability of text and images does not imply that they may be reused without the permission of rights holders, although the Copyright Act does permit certain unauthorized reuse as fair use under 17 U.S.C. Section 107.

ACKNOWLEDGMENTS

This book incorporates the work of many people, inside and outside Sybex.

Gary Masters, Bonnie Bills, and Brenda Frink defined the book's overall structure and contents. Michael Anderson compiled and adapted all the material for publication in this book.

A large team of editors, developmental editors, project editors, and technical editors helped to put together the various books from which *HTML Complete* was compiled: Maureen Adams, Sherry Bonelli, Dan Brodnitz, Kim Crowder, Peter Kuhns, Suzanne Rotondo, and Denise Santoro handled developmental tasks; Davina Baum, Pat Coleman, Nancy Conner, Kim Crowder, Brenda Frink, Diane Lowery, Ben Miller, Valerie Perry, Vivian Perry, Lee Ann Pickrell, Kristen Vanberg-Wolff, Kim Wimpsett, and Shelby Zimmerman all contributed to editing or project editing; and Ben DeLong, Rima Regas, Matthew Fiedler, Don Hergert, Will Kelly, Tom Maxwell, Ann Navarro, John Piraino, Sr., David Shank, and David Wall provided technical edits. Rima Regas deserves particular thanks for her help in shaping the book's outline.

The *HTML Complete* production team of desktop publisher Robin Kibby and production coordinator Julie Sakaue worked with speed and accuracy to turn the manuscript files and illustrations into the handsome book you're now reading. Ellen Bliss and Dan Schiff also helped in various ways to keep the project moving.

Finally, our most important thanks go to the contributors who agreed to have their work excerpted in *HTML Complete*: Peter Dyson; Vincent Flanders and Michael Willis; Molly E. Holzschlag; James Jaworski; E. Stephen Mack and Janan Platt Saylor; Natanya Pitts; Deborah S. Ray and Eric J. Ray; Joseph Schmuller; Erik Strom; and Gene Weisskopf and Pat Coleman. Without their efforts, this book would not exist.

CONTENTS AT A GLANCE

TABLE OF CONTENTS

Part III ▶ Going beyond HTML   **349**

Chapter 9 ▫ Adding Advanced Content to Web Pages   **351**

INTRODUCTION

*H*TML Complete is a one-of-a-kind computer book—valuable both for the breadth of its content and for its low price. This thousand-page compilation of information from ten Sybex books provides comprehensive coverage of the Hypertext Markup Language and related topics in Web site building and design. This book, unique in the computer book world, was created with several goals in mind:

- ▶ Offering a thorough guide that covers the important user-level features of HTML and related topics at an affordable price

- ▶ Helping you become familiar with the essentials of HTML so you can choose an advanced HTML book with confidence

- ▶ Acquainting you with some of Sybex's best authors—their writing styles and teaching skills, and the level of expertise they bring to their books—so you can easily find a match for your interests as you delve deeper into Web development

HTML Complete is designed to provide all the essential information you'll need to get the most from HTML, while at the same time inviting you to explore the even greater depths and wider coverage of material in the original books.

If you've read other computer "how-to" books, you've seen that there are many possible approaches to the task of showing how to use software and hardware effectively. The books from which *HTML Complete* was compiled represent a range of the approaches to teaching that Sybex and its authors have developed—from the quick, concise *No experience required* style to the exhaustively thorough *Mastering* style. As you read through various chapters of *HTML Complete*, you'll see which approach works best for you. You'll also see what these books have in common: a commitment to clarity, accuracy, and practicality.

You'll find in these pages ample evidence of the high quality of Sybex's authors. Unlike publishers who produce "books by committee," Sybex encourages authors to write in individual voices that reflect their own experience with the software at hand and with the evolution of today's personal computers. Nearly every book represented here is the work of a single writer or a pair of close collaborators, and you are getting the benefit of each author's direct experience.

In adapting the various source materials for inclusion in *HTML Complete*, the compiler preserved these individual voices and perspectives. Chapters were edited only to minimize duplication and to add sections so you're sure to get coverage of cutting-edge developments. A few sections were also edited for length so that other important HTML-related subjects could be included.

Who Can Benefit from This Book?

HTML Complete is designed to meet the needs of a wide range of computer users. Therefore, while you *could* read this book from beginning to end, all of you may not *need* to read every chapter. The Table of Contents and the Index will guide you to the subjects you're looking for.

Beginners   Even if you have only a little familiarity with computers and their basic terminology, this book will get you up on the Web using HTML.

Intermediate users   Chances are, you already know how to perform routine operations with HTML. You also know that there is always more to learn about working effectively, and you want to get up to speed on new features in HTML and other Web programming languages. Throughout this book you'll find instructions for just about anything you want to do. Nearly every chapter has nuggets of knowledge from which you can benefit.

Advanced users   If you've worked extensively with HTML, you'll appreciate this book as a reference. You'll find the wealth of information in the HTML Master's Reference to be particularly useful.

How This Book Is Organized

HTML Complete has sixteen chapters and an appendix.

Part I: Getting Started   In the first three chapters, you'll learn the basic concepts of HTML and the Web and begin looking at how the elements of Web pages are put together. You've probably browsed the Web before, but after reading Part I you'll do so with a new perspective.

Part II: Using HTML Like a Pro   Part II will give you plenty of ideas for designing eye-catching and effective Web sites of your own. You'll find that the chapters in Part II emphasize the *thought* behind a Web page as well as the execution, offering discussions of both design theory and the mechanics of laying out your pages with HTML. In other words, you'll learn not only how to use elements such as color and graphics on your site but also how they can make your pages more effective in getting your ideas across. Chapter 8 will show you how to bring these effects to your pages using cascading style sheets, an essential tool for Web developers.

Part III: Going beyond HTML   Part III will introduce you to other programming languages that will enable you to add more sophisticated and dynamic content to your pages. You'll learn about Perl, DHTML, JavaScript, and XML and get a glimpse of what these powerful languages can help you accomplish.

Part IV: Appendix   The Appendix is designed for quick reference—or casual browsing. This 300-page Master's Reference of HTML tags and their attributes, the properties used in creating style sheets, the components of JavaScript, HTML special characters, and HTML color codes will prove indispensable as you begin building your sites.

A Few Typographical Conventions

When an operation requires a series of choices from menus or dialog boxes, the ≻ symbol is used to guide you through the instructions, like this: "Select Programs ≻ Accessories ≻ System Tools ≻ System Information." The items the ≻ symbol separates may be menu names, toolbar icons, checkboxes, or other elements of the Windows interface—anyplace you can make a selection.

The ➥ symbol is used to indicate the continuation of a line of program code from the line above. Although the ➥ symbol is not used in every instance where code carries over from one line to the next, it appears in places where the continuation might otherwise be unclear.

`This typeface` is used to identify Internet URLs and HTML code, and **boldface type** is used whenever you need to type something into a text box.

You'll find these types of special notes throughout the book:

TIP

You'll see a lot of these—quicker and smarter ways to accomplish a task, which the authors have discovered while using HTML.

NOTE

You'll see these Notes, too. They usually represent alternate ways to accomplish a task or some additional information that needs to be highlighted.

WARNING

In a very few places, you'll see a Warning like this one. When you see a warning, pay attention to it!

YOU'LL ALSO SEE "SIDEBAR" BOXES LIKE THIS

These boxed sections provide added explanation of special topics that are noted briefly in the surrounding discussion, but that you may want to explore separately. Each sidebar has a heading that announces the topic so you can quickly decide whether it's something you need to know about.

For More Information...

See the Sybex Web site, www.sybex.com, to learn more about all of the books that went into *HTML Complete*. On the site's Catalog page, you'll find links to any book you're interested in.

We hope you enjoy this book and find it useful. Happy computing!

PART i
GETTING STARTED

Chapter 1

INTRODUCING WEB PAGES AND HTML

Y ou can certainly start your browser and hit the Web without any knowledge of the HyperText Markup Language (HTML) that lies beneath all Web documents, or *pages*. But if you want to make your presence known on the Web by building pages on your own, you'll need to learn HTML. This chapter introduces you to the basic concepts of HTML, many of which you'll learn about in more detail later in this book.

NOTE

Although the book in which this chapter originally appeared was written for users of Microsoft Internet Explorer, rest assured that the information applies to Netscape's browser as well. We've called attention to the few exceptions throughout the chapter.

Adapted from *Mastering Microsoft Internet Explorer 4*, by Gene Weisskopf and Pat Coleman

ISBN 0-7821-2133-0   960 pages $44.99

An Overview of HTML

In keeping with the original and ongoing theme of the Internet—openness and portability—the pages you create with HTML are just plain text. You can create, edit, or view the HTML code for a Web page in any text editor on any computer platform, such as Windows Notepad.

Although creating simple Web pages in a text editor is easy, it can quickly turn into a grueling and mind-numbing task. That's why there are Web-authoring tools such as Microsoft FrontPage Express and Macromedia Dreamweaver, which let you create HTML Web pages in the same way you create documents in your word processor.

Viewing HTML Pages

When you open a Web page in your browser, you don't see the HTML code that creates the page. Instead, your browser interprets the HTML code and displays the page appropriately on the screen. If you're creating a Web page in a text editor and want to view the file you're working on, save your work and open the file in your browser. You can then continue to edit, save your work, and view the results, switching back and forth between the text editor and the browser to see the effects of your edits.

The original intent of the HTML specification was to allow Web authors to describe the structure of a page without spending too much time worrying about the look of a page—that part of the job was left to the browsers. Traditionally, each browser had its own way of interpreting the look of the page, and Web authors had to live with the fact that pages they created might appear somewhat differently in different browsers. Authors merely shrugged their shoulders and were happy that their pages could be viewed so easily from anywhere on the planet.

NOTE
That "original intent" is starting to fade as the world heads toward an HTML that can describe the look of a page quite accurately. More and more descriptive elements are being established in the HTML specification, such as font styles and sizes, colors, and style sheets that can maintain a consistent look throughout a Web site.

Here's an example of the inherent flexibility that was designed into the HTML specification: Later in this chapter, you'll read about the six HTML codes you can use for creating six levels of headings in a Web page. You as an author can specify that a paragraph of text be defined as one of the six heading levels, but the HTML heading code does *not* describe what of heading should look like. It merely says something to the effect of "I'm a level-two heading." It's up to the Web browser to differentiate each type of heading from the others. One browser might display the first-level heading in a large font that is centered on the page, while another browser might display it in italics and left-aligned on the page. That's why authors try to test their pages in several of the more popular browsers.

Speaking of popular browsers, the good news is that the browser market has been consolidating and standardizing. You'll find few differences in the way competing browsers display the widely accepted HTML features in a page. Of course, new HTML features are being promoted all the time, mostly by Microsoft for its Internet Explorer browser and Netscape for its browser. Web authors must decide whether to include a new feature in a page when that feature may not be well interpreted by some browsers.

HTML Elements and Tags

A Web page is made up of *elements*, each of which is defined by an HTML code, or *tag*. A tag is always enclosed in angle brackets, and most tags come in pairs, with an opening and a closing tag. The closing tag is the same as the opening tag, but starts with a forward slash.

For example, to define text as a first-level heading in HTML, you use the <H1> tag, as in:

```
<H1>This Is a Main Heading</H1>
```

A browser interprets these tags and displays the text within the tags appropriately (as shown below). But the tags themselves are not displayed within a browser, unless there is a problem with a tag, such as if one of the angle brackets was mistakenly left out (although most browsers will ignore any codes within angle brackets that they do not recognize).

This Is a Main Heading

And this is Internet Explorer's normal text.

Some tags have optional or required attributes. An *attribute* is usually a keyword that takes one of several possible values (you define each value by enclosing it in quotes). For example, the heading tag can take an optional alignment attribute:

```
<H1 ALIGN="CENTER">This is a main heading that is
centered</H1>
```

NOTE

You can create a tag in either upper- or lowercase; it doesn't matter to a browser. For example, the two tags <H1> and <h1> are equivalent to a browser. In this book, you'll notice that some authors use uppercase while others prefer lowercase.

The Essentials of a Web Page

Every Web page must include a few tags that define the page as a whole so that when a browser receives the page it will recognize it as such. For example, the following HTML code will produce the page that is shown in Internet Explorer in Figure 1.1 (it could also be viewed in any other browser):

```
<HTML>
<HEAD>
<TITLE>Greetings from the Web</TITLE>
</HEAD>
<BODY>
<P>Hello, world!</P>
</BODY>
</HTML>
```

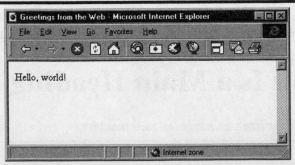

FIGURE 1.1: The sample page displayed in Internet Explorer

Remember, this code is just a text file, plain and simple. Table 1.1 lists the tags that should be included in every page so that any browser can view it.

TABLE 1.1: Essential HTML Tags for a Page

TAG	PURPOSE
<HTML>	Declares that the text that follows defines an HTML Web page that can be viewed in a Web browser. The closing </HTML> tag ends the page.
<HEAD>	Defines the header area of a page, which is not displayed within the page itself in the browser. The closing </HEAD> tag ends the header area.
<TITLE>	The text between this tag and the closing </TITLE> tag is the title of the Web page and is displayed in the title bar of your browser, as shown in Figure 1.1. The title should be descriptive, as it is frequently used by Web indexing and searching programs to name your Web page. In Internet Explorer, a page's title serves as the default name when you save the page as a favorite location.
<BODY>	Delineates the actual content of the Web page that will be displayed in your browser. In the example above, only the words *Hello, world!* will appear within the browser. Most of the other HTML features that we will discuss in this chapter always appear within the <BODY> and </BODY> tags in a Web page. There are several optional attributes for this tag. One of them is BACKGROUND, with which you can specify a background graphical image for the page.
<P>	Use the paragraph tag to mark the beginning of a new paragraph; the ending tag, </P>, is optional but should be included for clarity (whenever you or someone else needs to inspect or revise this code). You can include the ALIGN attribute to specify whether the paragraph should be centered or right-aligned in the page (left-aligned is the default).

There are dozens and dozens of other HTML tags you can incorporate into a Web page. The ones you use and how you use them depends only on your design, capabilities, and imagination.

NOTE

There is one important tag whose effects you won't notice in your browser but that you will appreciate when you're editing or viewing the HTML code for a page. In Internet Explorer, you use the <COMMENT> tag to create descriptive comments within the code, which will be ignored by the browser. With other browsers, you can use this combination of symbols to create a comment: <!–This text is a comment. –>

ADDING SPACES AND BLANK LINES FOR READABILITY

You can include extra spaces and blank lines in HTML code to make the code easier for you or others to read and interpret. When a browser opens a Web page, it ignores multiple spaces within the code and displays them as a single space. It also ignores all hard returns within the code, such as when you press Enter at the end of a line of text you're editing in Notepad. Therefore, any blank lines you create in the code by pressing Enter a few times will not be displayed in the user's browser.

There is one HTML tag in which spaces and hard returns in the HTML code *do* count, and that is the preformatted tag, <PRE>. It instructs a browser to display the text in a monospaced font that allows you to align text precisely, such as you would when showing a program listing.

Learning HTML

As more and more of the world's documents end up as Web pages, we will all be viewing, creating, and modifying them as part of our daily routine. Learning about HTML will give you an understanding of how it works and how it looks in use, which will prove invaluable to your Web-browsing experience. But please rest assured that in this book we have absolutely no intention of molding you into a code cruncher!

With the proliferation of elegant HTML editors such as FrontPage Express and Dreamweaver, it is unlikely that a text editor will be your first tool of choice for creating Web pages. Unless you really take off in the science and art of Web-page authoring, you will probably never have to become an HTML jockey, and you will forego the pleasure of wrangling your way through screenfuls of angle brackets, slashes, and esoteric codes.

NOTE

Creating a successful Web page requires a good deal from both sides of your brain—the logical side, which helps you write computer programs, and the artistic side, which helps you compose a tasteful, inviting document. That's why it's important to have several people test and critique your Web efforts, because few of us can lay full claim to both sides of our brains!

You can learn about HTML in many ways without specifically studying it. Perhaps the most important method is already staring you in the face when you're browsing the Web—the pages themselves. All Web pages are built from the same text-based HTML language, so when you're viewing a page in your browser that strikes your interest, stop and take a look at that page's underlying code. You can do so in two ways:

▶ Choose View ➢ Source to display the current page's HTML code within Notepad. You can then view the code to your heart's content or save it to disk for later use.

▶ If you know you'll want to spend some time with the HTML code later on, you can save the current page to your local disk from within your browser by choosing File ➢ Save As. The resulting HTML file is the HTML code from which the page was built (but it will not include any of the graphic images from the page).

By viewing the HTML code for a page, you can get a feeling for how the page was created.

If you want to learn more about encoding Web pages, you can find countless books and even more Web sites devoted to that subject. A great place to start is CNET's Builder.com:

`www.builder.com`

It is designed primarily for "Web professionals," but the complexity and depth of the material on the site ranges far and wide. It has thousands and thousands of pages, hundreds of megabytes of downloadable software, and great links to other Web-related resources. You'll also find countless examples of what you can build in your Web site. You could easily spend days browsing through this huge collection of information (all of which is current) about designing, building, and running Internet and intranet Web sites.

Another useful site is the Web Design Workgroup. This informal association of Web-page designers was founded to help other designers create truly portable Web pages that could be viewed by any browser on any computer platform:

`www.htmlhelp.com`

To find Web-related sites elsewhere on the Web, take a look at the following category on Yahoo, a Web search site:

`Computers and Internet: Internet: World Wide Web: Information and Documentation`

A STANDARD MAY NOT ALWAYS BE ONE

The language of HTML is constantly evolving. Enthusiastic Web authors may happily include brand new and improved tags within their Web pages to produce dazzling new effects. But unfortunately, those effects may be lost on most visitors to that Web site because their browser software does not recognize those HTML features.

Officially, it's up to the World Wide Web Consortium (W3C) at the Massachusetts Institute of Technology (MIT) to define and establish new versions of HTML. Unofficially, leaders in the rush to the WWW, such as Microsoft and Netscape, regularly come up with their own extensions to official HTML in the hopes of improving the language. Eventually, many of these new codes are, indeed, included in the official HTML specification.

Skip the Programming: Use FrontPage Express

Microsoft FrontPage Express is one of the components in the Internet Explorer suite. It is essentially an easy-to-use word processor for creating HTML documents. Unlike a text editor such as Notepad, FrontPage Express is a WYSIWYG environment, in which "what you see is what you get." In other words, what you see in your document in FrontPage Express is pretty much what you'll see when you view the resulting HTML file on the Web in your browser. FrontPage Express has two important virtues:

- ▶ It is designed specifically to create HTML pages, so you won't find any unrelated commands or features on its menus. You don't have to think about how those options work; you simply choose them from the menu.

- ▶ When you create a page in FrontPage Express, you are assured that the HTML tags in that page (even though you might never see them) will be correct, with no missing angle brackets, misspelled tags, and so on.

If you're not sure what the big deal is about creating Web pages in FrontPage Express versus encoding them with HTML in a text editor, here's a simple but telling example. Shown below is some HTML code that you could create in Notepad and save to disk as an HTML file:

```
<HTML><HEAD><TITLE>Sample HTML Page</TITLE>
<H1>This Is the Main Heading</H1>
<P>Here's a bulleted list:</P>
<HR>
<UL>
<LI>Item 1</LI>
<LI>Item 2<UL>
  <LI>Item 2A</LI>
  <LI>Item 2B</LI>
 </UL></LI>
<LI>Item 3</LI>
<LI>Item 4</LI>
</UL>
<HR>
<P>...and the page continues...</P>
```

Now look at Figure 1.2 to see how you could create that page in the WYSIWYG environment of FrontPage Express. The HTML code stays hidden beneath the page you create, which appears much the way it will when viewed in your browser.

ADDING SOME STRUCTURE TO A PAGE

Just about any Web page you create will benefit if you impose some sort of structure on it. For example, think about how you would put your company's procedures manual up on the Web:

- ▶ If the manual is divided into chapters, you could make each one a separate Web page.

- ▶ You could easily re-create the manual's table of contents by making each section reference a hyperlink to that part of the manual. The reader could simply click on a section in the table of contents to open that file.

Part i

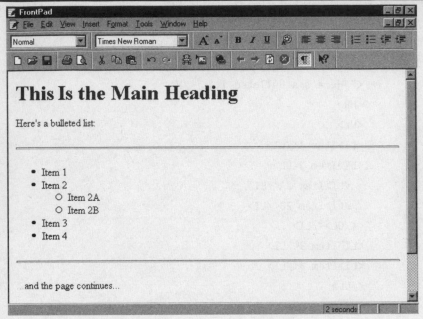

FIGURE 1.2: When you create Web pages in a WYSIWYG HTML editor such as FrontPage Express, "what you see is what you get" when that page is later viewed in a browser.

▶ Each chapter in the manual might have several levels of headings, which you could emulate perfectly with the heading tags in HTML.

▶ The body of the document would, of course, be divided into individual paragraphs.

You'll find that HTML offers several elements that let you create this type of structure in a Web page.

Using Paragraphs or Line Breaks

You create a paragraph by enclosing text within the paragraph codes <P> and </P>. Remember that browsers will ignore any "paragraphs" you create by pressing Enter while working on the HTML code in a text editor (such as Notepad). You must specifically define a paragraph in the code by using the paragraph tag. Consider the text in the six lines of HTML code that follow:

```
<P>This is the first paragraph; its code
continues over several lines, but will be
```

```
displayed as a single paragraph in a
browser.</P><P>And this is a second paragraph
that will also be displayed as such in
a browser.</P>
```

This code would appear as two separate paragraphs in your browser, as shown in the upper portion of Figure 1.3. Note that the length of each line is determined by the width of the browser's window.

Your browser will insert some extra space between paragraphs, so in some instances, you will not want to use the <P> tag. For example, when you display your name and address in a page, you would not want extra space between each line of the address.

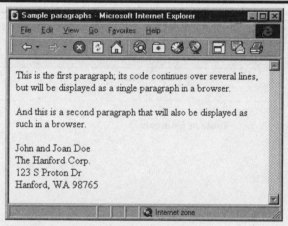

FIGURE 1.3: You use the <P> tag to define a paragraph and the <BR> tag to create a line break.

In those cases, use the line-break tag, <BR>. It tells the browser to wrap the text that follows onto a new line without inserting any extra space between the lines. Here is an address within HTML code:

```
John and Joan Doe<BR>The Hanford Corp.<BR>123 S Proton
Dr<BR>Hanford, WA 98765
```

You can see how this is displayed in Internet Explorer in the lower portion of Figure 1.3.

Dividing Sections with a Horizontal Line

A simple and effective way to separate sections within a Web page is to insert a horizontal line, <HR>, which is also called a horizontal rule. By default, the line stretches from one side of the page to the other.

For example, if your page has a banner across the top with your company name, you could insert a horizontal line beneath it. This would separate it from a table of contents showing links to other pages, beneath which you could insert another line, followed by the main body of the page. At the bottom of the page, you could have another line, and beneath that line would be the important page identifiers, such as its URL, the date the page was last modified, a link back to a home page, and so on. An example is shown in Figure 1.4.

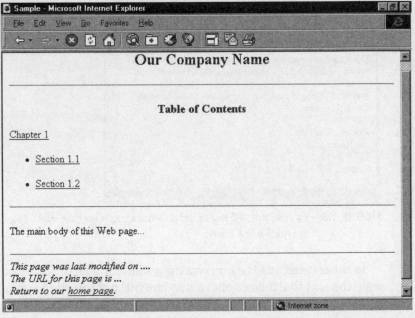

FIGURE 1.4: You can use the horizontal rule, <HR>, to divide a page into sections.

The <HR> tag takes several optional attributes. For example, you can specify the line's thickness (the default is one or two pixels in most browsers) and how much of the browser's window it should span (as a percentage or in pixels), such as:

```
<HR SIZE="6" WIDTH="60%">
```

which displays a line six pixels thick that spans 60 percent of the browser's window (the default is to center it in the window).

Creating a Hierarchy with Headings

A common way to add structure to a Web page is through the use of headings. This book, for example, uses headings to divide each chapter into logical chunks (at least, that was our plan). Its table of contents reveals the various levels of headings: each chapter is divided into several main headings, each of which may contain several subheadings, which in turn may contain their own subheadings.

A Web page can have a maximum of six levels of headings, the HTML codes for which are conveniently named <H1>, <H2>, <H3>, and so on:

```
<H1>This is a two-line<BR>first-level heading</H1>
```

As mentioned earlier, no style is inherent in the headings—different Web browsers might interpret the look of a heading in slightly different ways. Structurally, however, all browsers will display headings so that a third-level heading looks subordinate to a second-level heading, a second-level heading looks subordinate to a first-level heading, and so on.

In your browser, a first-level heading is displayed in a larger, bolder font than a lower-level heading. Shown here is a sample of the six headings within Internet Explorer.

Heading 1	**Heading 2**
Heading 3	**Heading 4**
Heading 5	**Heading 6**

You are free to use the HTML headings in any goofy order you prefer, but it makes good sense to use them as you would in an outline. The first-level heading, <H1>, is the highest level, and the sixth level, <H6>, is the lowest or most subordinate.

When you are structuring a page with headings, the first heading you use should generally be the highest level that will occur on the page. But this doesn't mean that it must be the <H1> heading. You might start with <H2> because you want a heading that appears in a smaller font than <H1>. In this case, then, the level-two heading would be the primary level, and you would not use <H1> on this page.

Formatting Text and Pages

Because the World Wide Web was originally conceived to be open to all, the designers of HTML avoided using literal descriptions of Web pages as much as possible. For example, the following tag would not have been appropriate:

```
<FONT FACE="TIMES ROMAN" SIZE="5" COLOR="#ff0000">
```

This tag requires a browser to have a specific, named font available that can be displayed in various sizes and requires that the browser's computer be connected to a color monitor.

But the days of trying to write to the least common denominator are waning quickly, and, in fact, the tag shown above is now a part of the official HTML specification. The <FONT> tag also illustrates two types of HTML tag attributes:

Absolute (literal)   The font type Times Roman is specified by name, and the color is specified by a hexadecimal RGB color value. There can be no doubt about how the author wanted this to look.

Relative (logical)   The font size 5, however, does not refer to an actual point size. It is a size that is relative to the browser's default font size (which is size 2 in Internet Explorer) and gives the browser a little more flexibility in how it displays the font. The author wanted the font to be larger than the browser's default but was willing to let the browser assign the actual size.

Formatting Text

Table 1.2 shows a few of the many HTML character-formatting tags. All of them require both an opening and closing tag.

TABLE 1.2: Basic HTML Character-Formatting Tags

Tag	Purpose
<ADDRESS>	To display a Web page's author information, such as the page URL, author name, date of last revision, and so on, in italics in your browser.
<I>	To italicize text.

TABLE 1.2 continued: Basic HTML Character-Formatting Tags

TAG	PURPOSE
<EM>	To emphasize text, which your browser displays in italics; this is a relative tag compared to the more specific <I> tag.
<PRE>	To display text in a monospaced (fixed-width) font, where multiple spaces, tabs, and hard returns within the HTML code are also displayed. Use this tag when the position of characters within each line is important, such as program listings and columnar lists.
<B>	To boldface text.
<STRONG>	To give text strong emphasis, which your browser displays in bold. This is a relative tag compared with the more specific <B> tag.
<S>	To display strike-through text.
<U>	To underline text. You should generally avoid underlining text since that is how browsers indicate hypertext links in Web pages.

You can insert these tags where they are needed in a paragraph, and you can combine some tags. The browser in Figure 1.5 shows an example of HTML text formatting. That page was built from the following HTML code:

```
<HTML><HEAD><TITLE>HTML Formatting
Tags</TITLE></HEAD><BODY><P>With HTML formatting tags, you
can make text <STRONG>bold</STRONG>, <EM>emphasized</EM>, or
<EM><STRONG>bold and emphasized</STRONG></EM>. You can also
<STRIKE>strike-out text</STRIKE> or make it
<U>underlined</U>.</P>

<P>If you don't use the Preformatted tag, Internet Explorer
displays text in a proportional font, where different charac-
ters take up different amounts of space.</P>

<P>Here are two lines of 10 letters, i and M, where each line
of the HTML code also had five spaces entered between the
fifth and sixth letters:</P>

<P>iiiii   iiiii<BR>
MMMMM   MMMMM</P>

<P>Here are those letters and spaces within the Preformatted
tags:</P>

<PRE>iiiii   iiiii<BR>
MMMMM   MMMMM</PRE>

</BODY></HTML>
```

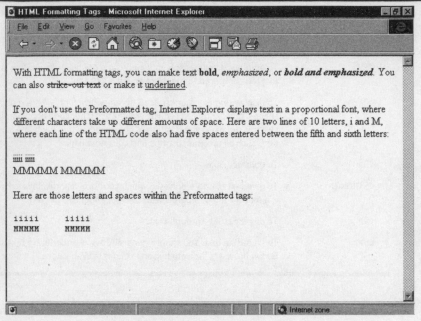

FIGURE 1.5: HTML formatting tags change the look of text in a Web page.

Formatting Pages

You can use a variety of tags to change the look of an entire Web page. You've already read about the <TITLE> tag, with which you create a title for a page. Your browser displays that title in its title bar.

You can change the color of the page's background with the optional attribute BGCOLOR for the <BODY> tag. For example, the tag

```
<BODY BGCOLOR="#0000FF">
```

creates a blue background for the page.

NOTE

As with many tags, if you don't specify a color for a page, a browser that is displaying that page will use its own default color. Internet Explorer uses your Windows colors by default, which are normally a white background with black text.

You can specify a picture instead of a color for a page's background. You don't need a large, page-sized picture, however, because your browser tiles the picture to fill the entire background. This allows you to use a small image file that will download quickly. You include the BACK-GROUND attribute in the <BODY> tag to specify a background picture:

```
<BODY BACKGROUND="smallpic.gif">
```

If you choose a fairly dark background color or picture, you may need to use the TEXT attribute to change the default color of any text on the page. For example, the following tag creates a blue background with white text:

```
<BODY BGCOLOR="#0000FF" TEXT="#FFFFFF">
```

Using Styles and Style Sheets

There is one tool for formatting documents in word processors that we have all grown quite accustomed to but that has been conspicuously missing from HTML. That is the *style*, which allows you to create a named definition of a group of formats and then apply that style to any text in the document. The result is a consistent look that is easy to apply throughout the document. A second advantage to styles becomes evident when you want to adjust the look of all the text to which you've applied a style. You simply redefine the style, and that change is immediately reflected throughout the document.

In the past, HTML lacked a mechanism for performing this simple, automated formatting task. But that's about to change with the acceptance of styles and style sheets in the HTML specification.

NOTE

The style sheets that Microsoft assumes will be implemented within the HTML specification are recognized by Internet Explorer 4 and later (and were recognized even back in Internet Explorer 3). However, because styles were not yet written into the HTML specification, few sites have taken advantage of them. Once styles are accepted, you will undoubtedly find them in use throughout the Web. In fact, FrontPage Express, the HTML word processor that comes with Internet Explorer, does not yet support styles. That's why you should use a plain-text editor, such as Notepad, to create the short examples later in this section.

Just as you would use styles in a word processor, a Web author can incorporate styles into a Web page. This can be done in several ways; the following is the simplest.

Within the <HEAD> tags for a page, you can specify style elements for various tags that will affect those tags throughout the page. For example, you could use styles to:

▶ Create a light gray background for the page

▶ Center all <H2> headings and display their text in white

▶ Indent the first line of all paragraphs

Here is the HTML code that creates these effects. Figure 1.6 shows the page as it appears in Internet Explorer (with added text):

```
<HTML><HEAD><TITLE>Sample Style</TITLE>
<STYLE>
  BODY {BACKGROUND: silver}
  H2   {TEXT-ALIGN:"center"; COLOR:"white"}
  P    {TEXT-INDENT:"+10%"}
</STYLE>
</HEAD><BODY>
<H2>This Heading Is Centered</H2>
<P>This is a normal paragraph…</P>
</BODY></HTML>
```

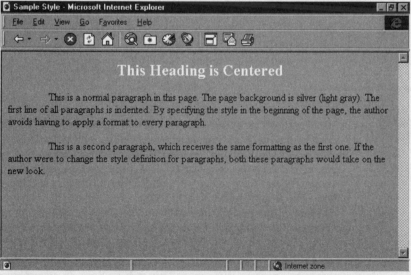

FIGURE 1.6:   You can create a more consistent look in a page with much less effort when you use styles to set the formatting of HTML elements.

NOTE

The BACKGROUND style is only partially supported in Netscape's browser.

You could use this method to create many Web pages that all use the same styles, but there's a much more efficient way to use styles. The term *style sheet* refers to a single file that contains multiple style definitions. You can reference that file in any HTML Web page to apply those styles to that page.

Here are the contents of a style sheet (they're plain text files with a CSS filename extension) that includes the styles shown in the previous example:

```
BODY {BACKGROUND: silver}
H2   {TEXT-ALIGN:"center"; COLOR:"white"}
P    {TEXT-INDENT:"+10%"}
```

If you save that style sheet file in a Web site (under the name NORMALPG .CSS in this example), you can reference it in any Web page with the following code. This code is the same as that used in the previous example; however, here the <LINK> tag replaces all the code within the opening and closing <STYLE> tags:

```
<HTML><HEAD><TITLE>Sample Style</TITLE>
<LINK>REL=StyleSheet HREF="normalpg.css" TYPE="text/css"
</HEAD><BODY>
<H2>This Heading Is Centered</H2>
<P>This is a normal paragraph.</P>
```

The resulting page would look exactly the same as the one in the earlier example in Figure 1.6. As you can see from these quick examples, styles and style sheets have a great potential for easing the job of creating and, especially, maintaining a Web site. When many pages reference the same style sheet, you can simply modify the style sheet to have the changes appear in all the pages.

NOTE

If you'd like to learn more about style sheets, you'll find a great guide from the Web Design Group at www.htmlhelp.com/reference/css/.

LINKING PAGES TO THE WORLD

The little feature that creates the Web for countless computers and networks is the hyperlink. When you're reading a Web page in your browser, you can click a link to jump to a new resource (open it). That resource can be another HTML page, a graphic image, a sound or video file, or something else, and it might be located on the browser's local hard disk, on an intranet site, or on a site anywhere on the World Wide Web.

Creating a Text or Image Hyperlink

The HTML anchor tag, <A>, defines a hyperlink within a Web page and at the minimum contains two components:

- ▶ The text or image that you click to activate the link
- ▶ The URL of the link's target, which will open when you click the link

Here is the HTML code for a text hyperlink (it's shown here on two lines, but remember that a browser ignores any line breaks in the HTML code):

```
<P>There's <A HREF="http://www.sample.com/helpindex.htm">
online help</A> when you need it.</P>
```

The text *online help* is the clickable link, and in your browser that text is underlined and displayed in blue, as shown in the top of Figure 1.7. The target of this link is the file HELPINDEX.HTM.

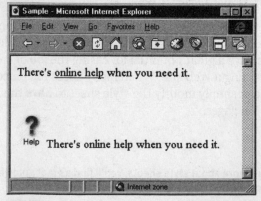

FIGURE 1.7:   You can create a hyperlink from an image or from text, which is displayed in blue and underlined in Internet Explorer.

An image can also serve as a hyperlink; clicking the image activates the link. The bottom of Figure 1.7 shows an image hyperlink. In this case, the text that is next to the image serves to describe the link but cannot be clicked to activate the link. Here's the HTML code (shown on three lines) for this link and the text to its right:

```
<P><A HREF="http://www.sample.com/helpindex.htm">
<IMG SRC="help.gif" border="0" width="46" height="51"></A>
There's online help when you need it.</P>
```

This example has the same target file as the previous example, HELPINDEX .HTM, but the clickable portion of the hyperlink is the image file HELP .GIF. The reference to that image file falls within the anchor tags <A> and </A>, and the sentence describing the link, *There's online help when you need it*, is outside those tags.

THE REFERENCE TO THE TARGET OF A LINK CAN BE RELATIVE OR ABSOLUTE.

When an author creates a reference in a Web page to another file, such as the target of a hyperlink, the reference can be defined as either relative or absolute.

In the two examples above, an *absolute* reference was made to the target file HELPINDEX.HTM. The reference contained the target's complete URL that defined the exact location of the file. It starts with the protocol and includes the usual host, domain, and filename:

```
http://www.sample.com/helpindex.htm
```

With an absolute reference, the location of the target is "written in stone" and always points to the same file in the same location. However, this is not an advantage or even a requirement when the target of the link is stored in a location that is *relative* to the page that contains the link.

For example, if the reference to the target contained only the target file's name, such as

```
helpindex.htm
```

it would be assumed that this file resides in the same folder as the page that contains the link. Its location is, therefore, relative to the link-containing file.

CONTINUED ➞

Another relative reference to a target might look like this:

```
help/helpindex.htm
```

In this case, the target file resides in a folder named HELP, which resides in the same folder as the page that contains the link. The complete (absolute) URL to that file would look like this:

```
http://www.sample.com/help/helpindex.htm
```

Because the administrator of a Web site may need to change the location and directory (folder) structure of the site, a Web author will always try to use a relative reference whenever possible. In that way, if a Web site is moved to another folder on the same server or to a completely new server, all the relative references to files within that site continue to work.

Specifying Other Link Targets

You'll often find that the target of a link is another Web page, but there are other types of targets. Here are some you may encounter:

Named Target   When the target of a link is a Web page, you can specify a named location within that page. That location, not the top of the page, is displayed when the page is opened in a browser. You use the anchor tag to create the name for the location, and you reference that name in the anchor tag for the link.

Frame   Later in this chapter, you'll read about the frameset, which is a Web page that you divide into multiple frames, each of which can open and display a separate Web page. When a link resides in one frame of a frameset, you can have the target for that link displayed in any of the frames in that frameset. You do so by including the TARGET attribute in the link's anchor tag along with the name of the frame that should receive the target of the link.

Other File Types   The target of a link can be any type of file. Your browser can open several types of files on its own, including Web pages, text files, and GIF or JPEG image files. For other file types, it must rely on Windows 95/98 and request that the appropriate program handle that file. For example, sound files (WAV or AU) and movie files (MOV, MPG, or MPEG) would be played by the appropriate sound and movie player.

E-Mail Address   The target for a link can use an Internet protocol other than HTTP, such as the *mailto* protocol that defines an e-mail address. When the reader of the page clicks the link, the reader's e-mail program should open with a new message displayed and already addressed to the address specified in the link. The reader can create the body of the message and send it to the target address in the usual way.

Creating a Clickable Imagemap

A variation of the image hyperlink discussed in the previous section is the *imagemap*, which is a single image that contains multiple hyperlinks. Each hyperlink is associated with a defined area of the image called a *hotspot*, which, when clicked, activates that link. In your browser, you see only the image; there is no indication that it has clickable hotspots.

You've undoubtedly encountered imagemaps in many, many pages on the Web. They can be informative, attractive, and intuitive and can also transcend language, which is an important consideration on the World Wide Web.

TIP

Even though images can convey information without language, an image is nonetheless open to a variety of interpretations. Images may not even be seen when visitors to a site have turned off the display of images in their browsers to speed things up. Therefore, good Web design often means including corresponding text hyperlinks next to an imagemap so that a visitor to that page can either click within the imagemap or click one of the text links.

A typical use of an imagemap is literally in the form of a map: you can click on a city, state, or region to display information about that region. An imagemap built from a map of the United States works well when the hotspots are defined around the large, regularly shaped western states. But the plan doesn't work so well for the smaller, irregularly shaped eastern states.

In such a case, the imagemap would work better with a regional map of the United States. Clicking in the east would display an enlarged map of just that region of the country, and clicking in the west would display the western states, as shown in Figure 1.8.

A Web-page author can create an imagemap from an image in two ways:

A **server-side** imagemap is the traditional type. When you click within an imagemap, your browser sends the coordinates of the click (relative to the image) to the server of that Web site. The server looks up those coordinates in a table of hotspots for that imagemap and processes the appropriate hyperlink target. Different servers may use different systems for storing the coordinates and targets for an imagemap.

A **client-side** imagemap obviates any server interaction, because the hotspot coordinates are included in the HTML definition for the imagemap that is sent to your browser. When you click within the client-side imagemap, your browser looks to see which target is associated with those coordinates and then opens that target.

Here is a sample of the HTML code for a client-side imagemap:

```
<AREA SHAPE="RECT" COORDS="308,32 380,72" HREF="choice1.htm"
<AREA SHAPE="RECT" COORDS="223,174 365,246"
HREF="choice2.htm"
<AREA SHAPE="RECT" COORDS="7,177 179,246" HREF="choice3.htm"
```

When you click within the image, your browser determines the coordinates of the point on which you clicked and finds the corresponding target for that portion of the imagemap, as though you had clicked a normal text or image hyperlink.

NOTE

Working in a text editor to create the HTML code for an imagemap just might be the nastiest Web-programming job there is. But you can create them with ease when you use HTML editors such as FrontPage Express and Dreamweaver. You simply draw an outline of the hotspot within the image and then specify the target for that link.

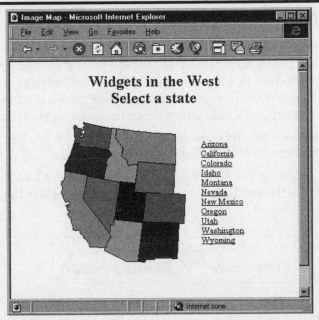

FIGURE 1.8:   A geographic map can be a practical way to implement an imagemap.

Although it usually shouldn't matter to you which type of imagemap appears on a page in your browser, you'll find one advantage with a client-side map. When you point to a hotspot in the map, you'll see the URL of the link associated with that hotspot, just as you do with a normal link. When you press Tab to select each hyperlink in the page, you also select each hotspot in an imagemap. Clicking the hotspot not only conveniently tells you where you'll go, it also tells you that this image is, indeed, an imagemap and not just a pretty picture.

Finally, because all the links are processed within the browser, a client-side imagemap reduces the processing burden on the server. It also is more flexible than a server-side imagemap because it is guaranteed to work no matter which server is hosting the page that contains the imagemap.

INCLUDING PICTURES IN A PAGE

You can include images (pictures or other nontext objects) in any Web page to provide information or to make the page more attractive. An image that you include in a Web page is called an *inline image*, as opposed to an image that is viewed separately in your browser, such as when the image file is the target of a link. You reference the inline image in this way:

```
There's more <IMG SRC="Images/arrow-rt.gif"> if you're
interested.
```

In this case, the image file ARROW-RT.GIF (from the folder Images) is displayed within the text that surrounds it and might look like the one shown here:

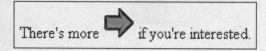

NOTE

The two most common graphic file formats you'll find on the Web are GIF and JPEG. The data in both types of files is compressed so that images can be transmitted much faster over a network.

Let's take a look at some of the attributes for the <IMG> tag for an inline image; all are optional:

Alternate Text   When a browser cannot display graphic images, perhaps because the image file cannot be found or because the browser's image-loading capabilities have been turned off to save download time, you can include the ALT attribute in an image tag to have text displayed in place of the image.

Sizing the Image   By default, your browser loads an image from the top down and displays the image in as large a box as needed. You can choose to specify an exact size for the image by including the WIDTH and HEIGHT attributes within the HTML tag (see the inline image example earlier in this chapter in "Creating a Text or Image Hyperlink").

Aligning the Image You can use the ALIGN attribute with the LEFT, CENTER, or RIGHT options to position the image either flush-left, centered, or flush-right in the browser window. You can also use the TOP, BOTTOM, or MIDDLE attributes to align text with the top, bottom, or middle of the image.

CREATING LISTS

Using HTML, you can arrange items in lists in several ways. The two most useful ones are:

Bulleted Or *unordered* lists, in which each item (paragraph) in the list is prefaced with a bullet; the <UL> tag begins the list.

Numbered Or *ordered* lists, in which each item in the list is prefaced with a number; the <OL> tag begins the list. Your browser applies the appropriate number to each line when it opens the page, so you can add to or delete items from the list while you create the page and not have to worry about updating the numbering.

You define each item within either type of list with the <LI> tag. The following unordered list:

```
<P>Chapter I</P>
<UL>
<LI>Section 1</LI>
<LI>Section 2</LI>
<LI>Section 3</LI></UL>
```

Chapter I

- Section 1
- Section 2
- Section 3

looks like the example at left in a browser. The bulleted or numbered list is a fast, easy way to apply some structure to a Web page, and you'll no doubt use it frequently. As always, the way a browser formats the list, such as the amount of indention and the style of the bullets, could vary from browser to browser.

You can nest one list within another simply by beginning the new list with the appropriate list tag. This allows you to create outlines, for example, or tables of contents that have subheadings indented in their own lists. Here's the list from the example above with a second list within it:

```
<P>Chapter I</P>
<UL>
<LI>Section 1</LI>
<LI>Section 2<UL>
<LI>Part A</LI>
<LI>Part B</LI>
<LI>Part C</LI>
</UL></LI>
<LI>Section 3</LI></UL>
```

In Internet Explorer, the secondary list is indented from the primary list and displays a different type of bullet. Again, in other browsers these lists may look somewhat different. Here is the indented list from above shown in Internet Explorer (on the left) and another browser.

Chapter I

- Section 1
- Section 2
  - Part A
  - Part B
  - Part C
- Section 3

Chapter I

- Section 1
- Section 2
  - Part A
  - Part B
  - Part C
- Section 3

ARRANGING ITEMS WITHIN TABLES

Another and even more powerful way to structure data within a Web page is the table. Like the tables you can create in your word processor or spreadsheet, an HTML table consists of rows, columns, and cells.

You can place just about anything you want within a cell in a table; there are few restrictions. Because of the flexibility of HTML tables, you'll find them used in countless ways in Web pages.

Sometimes a table will look like a table, with border lines dividing its rows, columns, and cells. In other cases, though, the structure of the table will be used, but its borders won't be displayed. The table serves as a convenient way to organize elements on the page without making them appear within the confines of an actual table.

Like imagemaps, tables are HTML elements that are best created in a dedicated HTML editor, such as FrontPage Express or Dreamweaver. You can still build a small table "manually" in a text editor, such as the table shown in the next example, but for anything more complex, you'll want to move to a more powerful editing tool.

Table 1.3 shows the basic tags with which you define a table:

TABLE 1.3: Basic HTML Table-Building Tags

Tag	Purpose
<TABLE>	Begins the table definition
<TR>	Defines a new row in the table
<TD>	Defines a single cell within the table

Shown below is the code for a simple, six-cell table:

```
<TABLE>
  <TR>
   <TD>Cell A1</TD> <TD>Cell B1</TD>
  </TR>
  <TR>
   <TD>Cell A2</TD> <TD>Cell B2</TD>
  </TR>
  <TR>
   <TD>Cell A3</TD> <TD>Cell B3</TD>
  </TR>
</TABLE>
```

The result is a table that has three rows and two columns; the text within the <TD> and </TD> tags appears in each cell. By default, as in this example, the table has no borders. You must specifically include them by specifying the width of their lines (in pixels) with the BORDER attribute for the <TABLE> tag, so that this tag:

```
<TABLE BORDER="1">
```

would enclose all the cells in the table with a border that is one pixel wide. Shown below is the first table, on the left, and the same table with a border, on the right.

Cell A1 Cell B1		Cell A1	Cell B1
Cell A2 Cell B2		Cell A2	Cell B2
Cell A3 Cell B3		Cell A3	Cell B3

You can include the <CAPTION> tag once in a table. Any text between this tag and its closing tag is displayed as the table's caption, which by default is centered just above the table.

You use the table header tag, <TH>, instead of the <TD> tag to create a header cell for the table. Your browser displays the text between the opening and closing header tags boldfaced and centered within the cell. You will often use these table headers as titles in the first row or column of a table.

By default, a table will only be as wide as the longest entries in its cells. You can specify an exact width in the <TABLE> tag with the WIDTH attribute, either in pixels or as a percentage of the browser's window. For example, this tag

```
<TABLE WIDTH="320">
```

creates a table exactly 320 pixels wide. If you want a table to be exactly half the width of the browser's window, no matter what width that might be, use the following tag:

```
<TABLE WIDTH="50%">
```

If a table is less than the full width of a browser's window, it is aligned with the left edge of the window. You can include the ALIGN attribute in the <TABLE> tag and specify Left, Center, or Right alignment within the browser's window.

If you specify an exact width for the table, you might also want to set the width of each column with the WIDTH attribute within the <TD> tag for a cell. You can specify the width either in pixels or as a percentage of the table (not of the browser's window).

As you'll see when you create a table, you can include many other tags and attributes, such as a background color or image for the table or any of its cells, the color of its borders, and which of its borders should be displayed.

GETTING FEEDBACK WITH FORMS

So far in this chapter, all the HTML elements we've discussed have been display-oriented, in that they affect the way a page appears within a browser. Now we'll look at the HTML form, an element that not only affects the display but also allows the reader to send information back to the server.

Those two issues, display and send, are the primary pieces of a Web-based form:

▶ The form controls that you create on a Web page are displayed in a browser and can be used by the visitor to enter data, select checkboxes or radio buttons, select items from a list, and so on.

▶ Once the visitor enters data into the form, he or she must have a mechanism for sending the data back to your server. Once the server receives the data, it must have another mechanism for storing or manipulating that data.

Designing a Form

Designing a form for a Web page isn't especially difficult if, as with tables, you do the job in an HTML editor such as FrontPage Express. The forms you create for the Web look and behave much like any other computer-generated forms you may have come across. For example, an HTML form can have a one-line data-entry field (sometimes called an edit field) in which the reader can type an e-mail address, as shown here:

E-mail address: `myname@xyz.com`

You use the <FORM> tag to begin the form definition. As part of that definition, you specify where the data should be returned (a URL) using the ACTION attribute. The destination might be the server for the form's Web page, or it could be some other server that will accept the data. You also specify how the data should be returned, using the METHOD attribute. The POST method is a common way to handle the job.

Within the opening and closing <FORM> tags, you lay out the controls of the form. You can include any other HTML elements as well, which will appear in the page along with the form controls. Some of the more common form-control tags are shown in Table 1.4 and Figure 1.9:

TABLE 1.4: Common HTML Form-Control Tags

TAG	FORM CONTROL	DESCRIPTION
<INPUT TYPE="TEXT">	Data-entry field	A one-line data-entry field
<INPUT TYPE="PASSWORD">	Password field	A one-line data-entry field in which the characters you type are displayed as asterisks to hide them
<TEXTAREA>	Multiple-line data-entry field	Enter a paragraph or more of text
<INPUT TYPE="CHECKBOX">	Checkbox	Select an item by clicking its checkbox
<INPUT TYPE="RADIO">	Radio button	Select one of a group of radio buttons
<SELECT>	List	Select one or more items from a list
<INPUT TYPE="SUBMIT">	Button	When clicked, sends the form's data to the server
<INPUT TYPE="RESET">	Button	When clicked, resets all form controls to their defaults

The definition for each control (other than the Submit and Reset buttons) must include a name for the control, which is sent to and used by the server to identify the data that was returned from that control. Each control can have several other attributes that define how it behaves. For example, the single-line data-entry field has the following attributes:

Size   The displayed width of the field in the form.

Maxlength   The maximum number of characters that can be entered into the field.

Value   The characters that appear within the field when its page is first opened or when the Reset button is clicked. You might use *(none)* as this default value so that when the data is returned to the server, this entry indicates that the visitor has entered no data in this field.

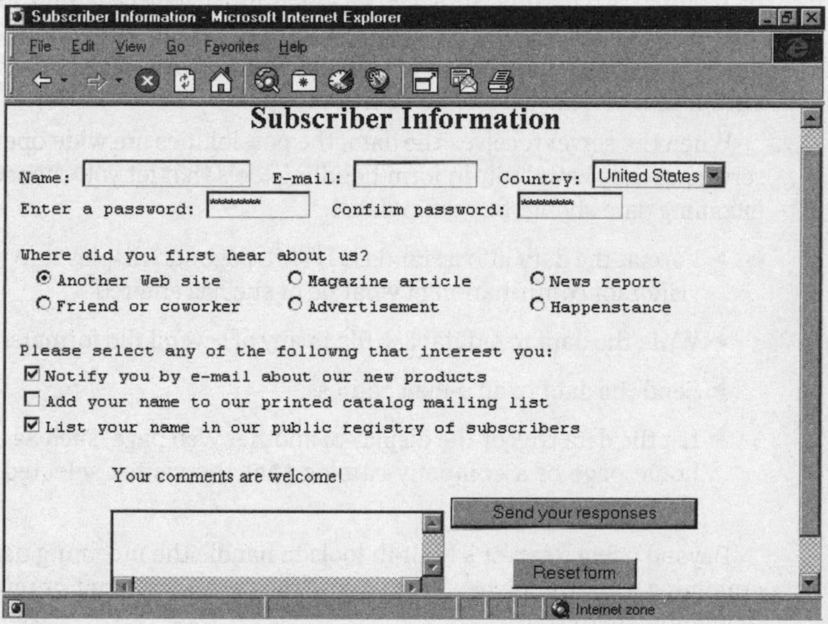

FIGURE 1.9: A visitor can enter information or select items in an HTML form.

Here is an example of the code for a data-entry field:

```
<INPUT TYPE="TEXT" NAME="COMPANY" SIZE="25" MAXLENGTH="100"
VALUE="(none)">
```

As the visitor enters information into a form, that data is still on the visitor's local computer—it has not reached the server yet.

Getting the Data Back to You

In a form such as the one shown in Figure 1.9, the visitor clicks on the Submit button (labeled *Send your responses* in the figure) to send the data back to the server. The browser collects at least two pieces of information about each control in the form:

- ▶ The name of the control
- ▶ Its current value

For example, if a visitor has entered *Pat Coleman* in the Name field, your browser sends back the following information:

```
NAME="Pat Coleman"
```

By naming each datum, the server can identify each piece of information it receives. Radio buttons are organized into named groups so that a visitor can select only one button in a group. It is the value of the selected button that is returned for the named group.

When the server receives the data, the possibilities are wide open. Web servers usually have built-in form-handling tools that let you choose how incoming data should be manipulated:

- ▶ Format the data into a standard HTML page and display it to the visitor for confirmation of what he or she has entered.

- ▶ Write the data to a database file in any of several file formats.

- ▶ Send the data to an e-mail address.

- ▶ Let the data trigger the display of another Web page, such as the home page of a company catalog that the visitor selected in the form.

Beyond using a server's built-in tools to handle the incoming data, programming work will be needed to create the necessary script or program to manipulate the data.

SPLITTING A PAGE INTO FRAMES

With the HTML feature called *frames*, you can create and display multiple Web pages within a single page. In the traditional way of browsing a Web, if you click a link in one page, a new page opens and replaces the first page in the browser.

For example, when you click a link in a page that serves as a table of contents of other pages, the target page opens, but the table of contents page is removed from the browser. By splitting a page into two frames, such as in the page shown in Figure 1.10, the table of contents page can be displayed in a frame on the left, for example, while the target of the selected link is displayed in the other frame on the right side of the browser's window. In this way, the table of contents is always available so that the reader can make another selection.

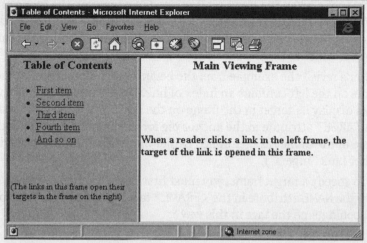

FIGURE 1.10: By splitting a page into frames, you can have a table of contents displayed in one frame while the target of each link is displayed in the other frame.

The concept of frames is neat and simple:

▶ Create a single Web page as a *frameset*, which contains no content other than the frameset definition.

▶ Specify how the frameset should be divided into frames.

▶ Assign a Web page to each frame.

You use the <FRAMESET> tag instead of the usual <BODY> tag to begin the frameset definition in the page. For example, this tag

```
<FRAMESET COLS="33%,67%">
```

creates a frameset page that consists of two frames arranged as columns. The first frame will be in a column on the left side of the browser's window; that frame's width will be one-third of the browser's window. The second frame will be a column to the right of the first one and will take up two-thirds of the browser's window.

You specify the source Web page to be opened in each frame with the <FRAME> tag, as in

```
<FRAME SRC="CONTENTS.HTM">
<FRAME SRC="INSTRUCT.HTM">
```

In this case, when the frameset is opened in a browser, the frame on the left displays the page CONTENTS.HTM, and the frame on the right displays INSTRUCT.HTM. You now have two Web pages sharing the same browser window.

Let's revisit the example from the beginning of this section. If the frame on the left contains an index of links, you can have each of those links display its target in the frame on the right. You do so by including the TARGET attribute in the anchor tag for the link and specifying the name of the frame (as mentioned earlier in this chapter in "Specifying Other Link Targets").

To specify a target frame, you must first name the frame. You do so with the NAME attribute in the <FRAME> tag. In the previous example, you could name the tags in this way

```
<FRAME SRC="CONTENTS.HTM">
<FRAME SRC="INSTRUCT.HTM" NAME="RIGHT">
```

which gives the name RIGHT to the frame on the right. With that frame named, you can define each link in the index page so that its target resource appears in the named frame, such as:

```
<A HREF="SOMEFILE.HTM" TARGET="RIGHT">
```

In this way, your index remains in the frame on the left, while the target of each link is displayed in the frame on the right.

Finally, since frames are relatively new features of HTML, not all browsers yet support them. You can include the <NOFRAMES> tag within the frameset to provide a message to a browser that cannot display frames. Here's an example:

```
<NOFRAMES><BODY>
<P>Sorry, but this page uses frames, which your browser does
not support.</P>
</BODY></NOFRAMES>
```

As you can see, the <NOFRAMES> tag includes the <BODY> tag, which is not used in defining a frameset but would be recognized by a frames-unaware browser. Anything within the <BODY> tags would then be displayed in the browser.

The amazing thing about HTML is that it seems to grow and change almost faster than Web authors can incorporate the new developments into their sites. Although the pressure to add new features to HTML is tremendous, Microsoft and others in the Web-related industry are working hard to maintain standards in the midst of the ongoing revolution. After all, having the world beat a path to your Web page would be somewhat anticlimactic if the page can be viewed in only *some* browsers.

WHAT'S NEXT?

With this overview of Web pages and HTML behind you, you're ready to begin dabbling in site design. The next chapter provides tips on creating a site that's easy to navigate, along with examples of some well-designed— and some not so well-designed—sites.

Part i

Chapter 2

SITE DESIGN AND NAVIGATION

In this chapter, we'll look at two of the nitty-gritty issues facing a designer when creating an overall design for a Web site:

▶ Designing a home page that acts as an effective site guide

▶ Designing a site that's easy to navigate

To learn about these design issues, you'll hear about some navigational tools; then you'll look at some sites that suck and some that don't. From there, we'll move on to organizing your own site by creating storyboards. By the time you're through, you'll be able to tell a poorly designed site from an exceptionally well-designed one.

Adapted from *Web Pages That Suck: Learn Good Design by Looking at Bad Design,* by Vincent Flanders and Michael Willis

ISBN 0-7821-2187-x   288 pages $39.00

NOTE

If you visit the sites mentioned in this chapter, you'll find that some of them have changed in appearance since the book was written—that's the nature of the Web. The principles of good design remain the same, however, and you can still follow all of the design discussions using the accompanying graphics.

Okay, now that you know where I'm going in this chapter (a principal of good design), let's start navigating our way through this chapter by taking a look at the home page for Cigar Aficionado Magazine, shown in Figure 2.1.

FIGURE 2.1: Cigar Aficionado magazine (http://www.cigaraficionado.com/)

WHY DOES THIS PAGE SUCK?

It doesn't! The bad boys of Web design just threw you a curveball.

You can learn a lot about site design by looking at Cigar Aficionado's site, which you'll do later in the chapter. To start off, though, here are some of the tips you can pick up from this site:

1. The designer did not sit down and start coding first thing. The designer sat down and figured out what important elements should go on the home page; then they figured out what went on the main topic pages and each subsidiary page. In other words, they scoped out the "big picture."

2. The designer put the most important elements on the first screen of the home page and the other main subsidiary pages.

3. The designer created significant content.

4. The designer has a sense of aesthetics—the graphics and lay-out are first-rate. No cheap clip art was used, and the *single—*repeat *single—*animated GIF (the animated cigar) is very high quality.

5. Most importantly, the designer created a home page that pre-sents a professional image to the world. As soon as you go to the page, you know exactly what to expect and you know how to find the information you want.

To really understand what's good about this page and why it's an effec-tive site design, I need to first talk about the concept of the home, main topic, and subsidiary pages, and the importance of making your site easy to navigate. Figure 2.2 shows how the pages on a Web site should be orga-nized. The organization is quite simply a hierarchy with the most impor-tant page (the home page) on top and subsidiary pages below.

The Web pages on a site are broken down into three main groupings:

1. Home page

2. Main topic pages

3. Subsidiary pages

This organizational structure, which is simplified to its lowest ele-ments, forms the foundation of a Web site. However, the most important navigational tool in the developer's arsenal is the home page because it is, generally, the first page seen by your visitors.

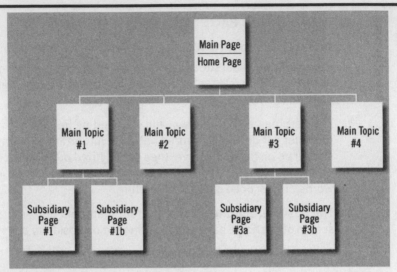

FIGURE 2.2: Organization of a Web site

THE HOME PAGE AS A SITE GUIDE

Quite simply, the home page (or, as it's also referred to, the *front page*) is the gateway to your site. It's the road map, the index, the table of contents that tells visitors where to find the important information they need to make their stay at your site enjoyable and profitable.

A good analogy is that the home page of a Web site is similar to the cover of a newsstand magazine. You may not be aware of this fact, but the return rates to the magazine publisher for newsstand magazines are quite high. Unlike a magazine subscription, which is purchased long in advance, a newsstand magazine has a limited period of time to entice the general public to buy it off the rack. The most important factors that influence sales are the cover and the subject matter. The same is true for your Web site.

The home page is the most important page on your site because it's generally a visitor's first impression of your company or organization. If your home page looks professional, ethical, artistic, appears to have interesting content, and doesn't have any elements that would chase a customer away, then there's a good chance your visitors will stay. Hopefully, they'll purchase something from you. If your home page fails to entice because the images are too large, you're using sound files for no reason, the page takes forever to download, there's offensive material, the text can't be read, and so on—then your visitors will hit the Back button faster than a politician changes position on the issues.

There are three things a home page should convey to the visitor:

1. The site's purpose—the who, what, when, where, and why

2. What kind of content is contained in the site

3. How to find that content

The Main Topic Page

This is a page that the home page links to. For example, Figure 2.3 shows the home page for Lotus Development Corporation (`http://www.lotus.com/`). From this home page, you can link to the following main topic pages:

Downloads	Products	Discussions	Corporate
Support	Purchasing	Partners	Solutions
Events	Developers	Services	Media Catalog

This is a good home page because it is clear where to go from here.

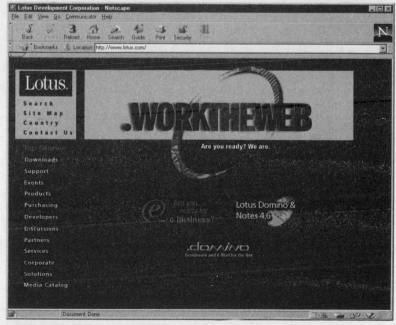

FIGURE 2.3: The Lotus home page (`http://www.lotus.com/`)

The Subsidiary Page

Any page other than a home or main topic page is a subsidiary page. Generally, these pages are subsets of a main topic page. For example, a page on the Lotusphere 98 trade show (see Figure 2.4) is a subsidiary page to the Partners main topic page.

From any subsidiary page, you want your visitors to be able to go to the home page so they can find out about your company and its products. You also want them to be able to go to any of the other main topic pages—especially a page where they can buy your products. Remember, you *always* need to make it easy for them to order.

For that reason, all your pages—home, main topic, and subsidiary pages—need to have links to the main topic pages on your site. In addition, you must include a link to the home page on all your main topic and subsidiary pages. Why?

Because you never know how a visitor arrives at your site.

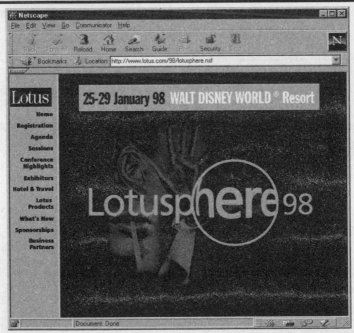

FIGURE 2.4: The Lotusphere 98 trade show page is a subsidiary page.

Why is the first screen people see at a Web site sometimes a page other than the home page? Simple. Links on other pages, articles in magazines, a friend's suggestion or, most commonly, search engines. For example, a visitor might have conducted a search for the phrase **"Lotus Partners"** and ended up at http://www.lotus.com/partners, where they clicked the link and went to the page shown in Figure 2.4. Unless there's enough information on the Lotusphere 98 page, this visitor has no knowledge that the home page, shown in Figure 2.3, even exists or that Lotus has information on Lotus Products on another page. That information comes in the form of navigational links—graphic-, text-, or frame-based.

Navigating through Your Site

In navigating a Web site, you need to consider several factors:

> The first screen
>
> Navigational tools—graphics, text, frames
>
> Consistency

The First Screen—The Top's Gotta Pop or They're Not Gonna Stop

Don't let the cuteness of this little refrain sidetrack you from its important message. The first screen your visitor sees is the first impression they will have of your site. And keep in mind the first screen they see might *not* be the first screen of your home page. If your first screen sucks, they won't stop, and if they don't stop, they're not going to shop. Congratulations. You've spent a lot of money on a Web site where very few people get past the first page.

You've got to put your most important informational elements in the first screen because some visitors have no more than four inches of screen real estate. Also, limit your home page to no more than two or three screens worth of material because people don't like to scroll forever and ever.

TIP

Remember this phrase; make it your mantra: Display important information prominently.

If it isn't important, then it shouldn't be on the home page. It probably shouldn't be on *any* page, but you have a little more leeway with subsidiary pages because you've got a little more space to maneuver.

Navigational Tools—Graphics, Text, Frames

There are three main navigational tools, which you can use singly or in combination:

Navigational Graphics

Text

Frames

Navigational Graphics   There are two categories of navigational graphics:

Buttons

Imagemaps

A button is any graphic that's a link. Any time someone clicks a button, they should be taken to another page. Buttons make powerful navigational tools. Use them carefully. When you're using graphics, for example, make sure people don't confuse them with links. Figure 2.5 shows an image that looks like it should be a button, but it isn't.

FIGURE 2.5: Confusing button

An imagemap is an image that is treated by the browser as a navigational tool When visitors click the imagemap, they are taken to a new page. Make sure it's clear to your visitors where they are going when they click a particular location on an imagemap.

It's the reverse of a magic trick. In a magic trick, you show the audience your right hand and perform the trick with your left. In Web design, you tell them where you're going first—and then go there.

Text   Text links make excellent navigational tools, although you can go a little overboard, as Figure 2.6 indicates. Even though the folks here are a little link happy, you've got to love them for creating a page that totals only 15.8K in size. You won't have to wait days for this page to load.

Text links are very, very important; they are even more important on pages that use graphics and imagemaps as links.

W & M Computer Science

W · I · L · L · I · A · M   A · N · D   M · A · R · Y

Department Overview
Where we are located, our administration, the College we are part of, the Library, and our local community.

Programs
We offer B.A. and B.S. degrees in computer science as well as two graduate degrees: the M.S. and the Ph.D. Our graduate students can also pursue an M.S. with a specialization in Computational Operations Research or a M.S. or Ph.D. with a specialization in Computational Science.

People
We have 15 faculty members, 3 staff, many graduate students and undergraduate concentrators. We are always happy to hear from our former students.

Reaching us
Where to send E-mail or regular mail, call us, or fax us. How to navigate to Williamsburg or through the campus.

What's going on
Upcoming events. We have speakers, student presentations, a prospective BitSwap newsletter, and the puzzler. Get the latest on ACM local chapter and graduate student CSGSA events. Read selected newsgroups. Learn about undergraduate research opportunities.

Teaching
We teach these undergraduate and graduate courses, based on this long-range schedule. Online material is available for selected courses.

Computing Facilities
Check out our system info and UNIX Lab Manual. We have seven labs in McGlothlin-Street Hall. The entire College is networked and maintains computers labs. We expect users to follow these sensible rules.

Table of contents

External web sites of interest

Last updated: September 1, 1997. Report suggestions and problems to: webmaster@cs.wm.edu

FIGURE 2.6: William and Mary Computer Science (`http://cs.wm.edu/`)

NOTE

If you're using graphics or imagemaps as links, you must also have corresponding text links.

There are two reasons for this statement. The first is if you're being a bad girl or boy and the graphics on your page total more than 35K, the text will show up before the images and your visitors can happily click a text link and be on their merry way before the image loads. The second reason is if your page has an imagemap and your visitor hits the Stop button before the imagemap loads, they won't know where they're going when they click. If there are no text links on the page, then they'll have to either reload the page or click and hope.

The big graphic in Figure 2.7 is a perfect example of a site that has an imagemap but no text links. This is bad Web design. I'll talk more about this site later in the chapter.

FIGURE 2.7: Southwest Airlines (`http://www.iflyswa.com/`)

Frames   Frames were created by Netscape to answer the perplexing question, "How can I make my page easy to navigate?" Like so many other great ideas, this one also got perverted by the design community. When used properly, however, frames solve the dilemma of keeping the text links static so you don't have to constantly reload them. Figure 2.8 shows you how WebPagesThatSuck.com uses frames.

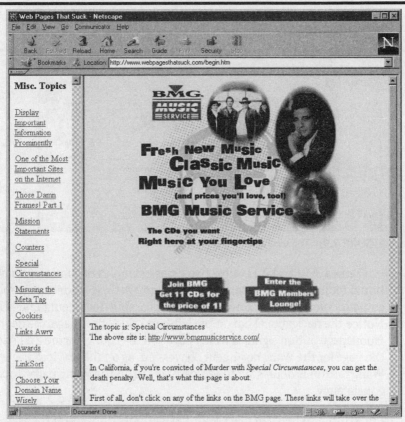

FIGURE 2.8:   Frames at WebPagesThatSuck.com (http://www
.webpagesthatsuck.com/begin.htm)

The frame on the left is the navigational tool. When you click a link in the left-hand frame, the site in question pops up in the top right-hand frame while the witty, yet insightful commentary appears in the bottom right-hand frame. The navigational frame never changes.

Frames are controversial. Not so much because they are bad in and of themselves, but because people use them poorly.

Consistency

You need to be consistent in the design of your navigational tools. For example, the size and color of your buttons should be consistent. Figure 2.9 shows you the wrong way to use buttons. As you can see, using buttons with different colors and sizes looks unprofessional.

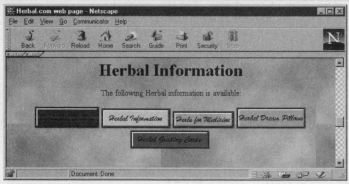

FIGURE 2.9:   The wrong way to do buttons

Figures 2.10 and 2.11 show two great examples of consistent navigational tools. The first page, shown in Figure 2.10, is a home page for a software product that converts word-processing documents into HTML. Notice the navigational bar on the left-hand side of the page; the depressed Home page button signifies which page you're visiting. Figure 2.11 shows the page for the Wang document conversion; as on the previous page, the Wang button is depressed to indicate you're on the Wang page. Total consistency.

Location   When you place your navigational buttons on the page, make sure that if you place them at the top of your home page, they're on the top of every other page in your site. If you place them on the left-hand side of the home page, then they should be on the left-hand side of every other page. The WebConvert navigational tools, shown in Figures 2.10 and 2.11, follow this guideline. All of them are located on the left-hand side of the page.

FIGURE 2.10: The navigational button bar at the WebConvert home page (http://www.webconvert.com/)

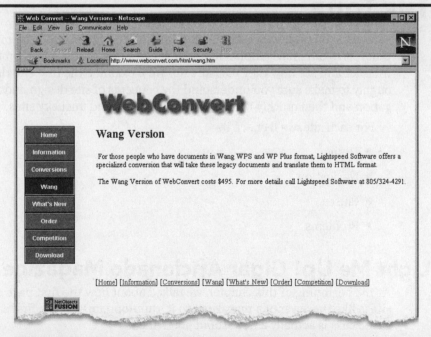

FIGURE 2.11: The navigational button bar at the WebConvert Wang Version page

SIMPLE CONCEPTS

It's a very simple concept—every navigational tool has to have a consistent look and location. Navigation should always be predictable. You want to create navigational tools that...

Are in the same spot on every page.

Have the same look.   You don't want to use round buttons on the home page and square buttons on main topic pages and octagonal buttons on subsidiary pages.

Will get the visitor to the information in as few clicks as possible.   I'm sure someone has researched the "Click Annoyance Factor"—the maximum number of clicks the average person is willing to perform to get to the information—but I haven't found this information on the Net. Personally, if I can't get to the information in three clicks and the site doesn't have a search engine, I'm ready to go somewhere else.

THE TOUR

Now that you understand how a site should be designed and how important it is to offer navigational tools, let's take a tour of some sites on the Internet and see how they measure up. We'll examine the first site thoroughly to make sure you understand the concepts of site design and navigation and then quickly run through some sucky and unsucky sites.

For each site, we'll check its

- ▶ Design
- ▶ Navigation
- ▶ Pluses
- ▶ Problems

Light Me Up! Cigar Aficionado Magazine

At the beginning of this chapter, we talked about how the first page of a site is like the cover of a magazine, so it's appropriate that the first site we discuss is actually a newsstand magazine.

Part I

The mystique of Cigar Aficionado magazine is sort of lost on Michael and me because, believe it or not, neither of us smokes cigars. (I tried to smoke Tiparillo's the end of my freshman year in college—but it *was* my freshman year.)

The most we can figure out, based on the Web site, is that it appeals to those people who feel the "Good Life" consists of Art (their idea of art in the issue we looked at was Vargas, LeRoy Neiman, Frank Stella), Sports (golf, deep-sea sportfishing, tennis, boxing, bullfighting, hawking, polo), Music (samba), Fashion, Gambling (poker, hustling golf), Jewelry and Collectibles, and Leisure (expensive cars, model railroads, chess, dream boats, high-speed power boats, treasure hunting in the sea, high-end stereo equipment). On this list, I'm 0 for 7; Mike is 2 out of 7. Nevertheless, you don't have to understand the cigar lifestyle to understand the design.

Site Design at Cigar Aficionado   Michael and I both think the site design is superb.

Figure 2.12 shows the Cigar Aficionado magazine as it would appear on a 13–15-inch monitor. Let's examine how its design succeeds and, more importantly, how you can use the same principles to make your site a success.

FIGURE 2.12: Cigar Aficionado magazine (http://www.cigaraficionado.com/)

The most important design element on this page is something you can't see. The designer sat down and organized the site before they started writing the HTML and creating the graphics. If designers do their job properly, you won't even notice how successful they were. In this case, the designer broke down the elements of the magazine into different pieces and chose what was important.

Navigation at Cigar Aficionado   In Figure 2.13, I've labeled the page so you can see the navigational structure of the home page.

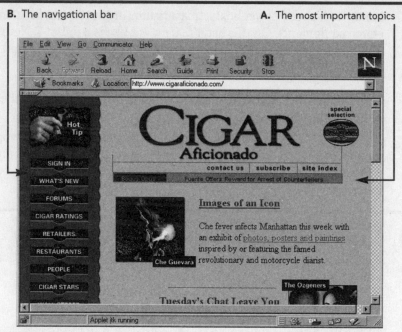

FIGURE 2.13:   The navigational structure of the Cigar Aficionado magazine site

The section marked "A" shows how the designer cleverly worked the most important topics into the top of the page. I stressed this concept at the beginning of this chapter. These are the important topics I'm talking about here:

1. **Contact Us**. Make sure there's a way for visitors to contact you.

2. **Subscribe**. It's a magazine. They want you to subscribe. That's how they get money. Money is good. The fact that they don't offer subscriptions using a secure server is a potential security problem and would probably scare most people from ordering using their credit card. It would be interesting to know how many subscribers they've actually received from the Internet.

3. **Site Index**. If your site is divided up into many different areas, you'll want to include a site index (also called a site map or site guide). Your site index should be text-based. Don't use graphics; they take too long to load.

The section marked "B" shows you a portion of a navigational bar where it looks like they've listed most of the important topics near the top. Interestingly, the Gift Shop is at the bottom, but that's probably okay because maybe they're trying not to look too pushy. Personally, Michael and I would have moved it closer to the top.

While a visitor must scroll down to see all the topics, there's enough information at the top of the page for them to get a good start on touring the important sections of the site.

Figure 2.14 shows the navigational structure of Cigar Ratings—one of the main topic pages. Notice that the round part of the label on the Cigar Ratings button has turned red. Obviously, you can look at the top of the page and see its title, but this touch is a nice one to add to the button. When you want to go to another topic, you won't click the Cigar Ratings button because it's turned red, which, as we all know, should make you want to stop. It's worth noting, however, that if you went to the Retailers page, there's no special marking to indicate you've been to the Cigar Ratings page. That's the province of text links. Nevertheless, the navigational information on this main topic page and on its subsidiary pages is excellent.

Pluses in the Cigar Aficionado Site   First of all, the designer chose wonderful colors for the site based on the brown color of cigars. Most important, these colors are used in a consistent fashion throughout the site.

The link graphics are also wonderful—little cigar wrappers—and so very, very clever. The home page is uncluttered, and the other graphics add to the flavor (pardon the pun) of the page. There's one animated GIF image (the Hot Tip at the top of the left-hand navigation bar), but it's excellent (see Figure 2.12). While the graphic titled "Vote" is probably clip art, it's professional clip art (see Figure 2.1).

The site reeks (again, pardon the pun) of sophistication and elegance.

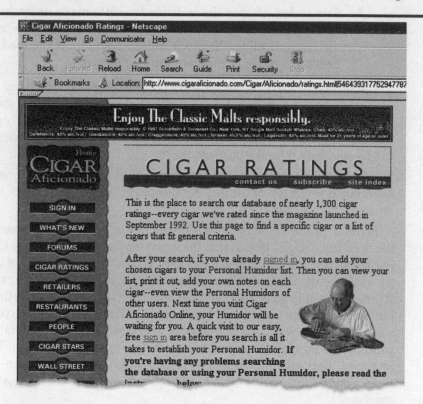

FIGURE 2.14: Cigar Ratings page (http://www.cigaraficionado.com/ Cigar/Aficionado/ratings.html)

Problems in the Cigar Aficionado Site   Even though we both like the page, there are six potential problems:

1. The HEIGHT and WIDTH parameters are not set for the images. Setting these parameters would cause the text to appear before the images on the page and give the viewer the opportunity to click a text link rather than wait for all the images to load.

2. Speaking of text links, there are no text links on the front page. Oops. That's a design no-no. Michael and I suggest they put text links at the bottom of the page.

3. Dr. HTML (see the sidebar "Dr. HTML") reported that the page contained 84.8K worth of graphics and images on the day we visited. This means it would take between 24.1 seconds (on a 28.8Kbps modem) and 48.3 seconds (on a 14.4Kbps modem) to load the page (and probably longer because of the Java on the page, but Dr. HTML doesn't measure Java applets). The people visiting this site probably don't care how long it takes for the page to load because of the content. (We could make a snide statement that the people who visit this site are all probably wealthy Republicans with ISDN connections, but we won't.) The cigar industry is a wonderful vertical niche market, and people who visit niche sites really don't care too much about download time.

4. It would be nice if there were a search engine facility on the front page. They have a link to their search engine tucked away at the bottom of the Site Index page, but they should really have one on the front page.

5. The site uses Java, and using it doesn't seem to enhance the site.

6. The site uses *Cookies*. These pesky little tracking devices basically track your movements on this site. I'm not sure why they need them, but using Cookies could turn off some visitors.

All six of these elements are flaws in the site's design, but numbers 1 and 2 are certainly the worst ones.

TOO COOL: DR. HTML

Netscape: Smart Business Supersite: Doctor HTML

Back Forward Reload Home Search Guide Images Print Security Stop

Location: http://drhtml.imagiware.com/

Doctor HTML™
No More Bugs on Your Web Site

Sponsored by:

Welcome to Imagiware's Web analysis program Doctor HTML. This program will analyze your Web pages and produce reports to help you build and maintain an effective Web site. To try out our service, you can log in as guest with the password guest, or you can sign up for a personal Test Drive. If you are interested in licensing Doctor HTML for your intranet, please check our brochure. If you have an existing account, please enter your username and password below:

Go to the Doctor

Username: _____   Password: _____   Go!

Or, choose one of these options:

Free Doctor HTML Test Drive.
You get 5 free page examinations, compliments of Smart Business Supersite. No obligations whatsoever.

All about Doctor HTML
The tests Doctor HTML performs, and what they mean to your site.

Open a New Account
Sign up for as many reports as you need. Six choices.

Order more reports
Do you need more reports? Order them here.

Account Utilities
Change your password, view account information, etc.

Feedback
Send your comments, questions and concerns to the Doctor.

Doctor HTML is Copyright 1995, 1996 by Thomas Tongue and Imagiware.

Dr. HTML is one of the Most Important Sites on the Internet.

The good doctor analyzes pages that physically reside on the Internet (have a URL) for errors and loading time. One of the many errors it looks for are missing HEIGHT and WIDTH parameters in images. In some of the examples used in this chapter (Cigar Aficionado, United Airlines, and Lotus), these parameters were missing.

CONTINUED ➡

There are lots of HTML validation services on the Web—including those that don't charge fees. As always, check out Yahoo's page on the topic at http://www.yahoo.com/Computers_and_Internet/Information_and_Documentation/Data_Formats/HTML/Validation_and_Checkers/.

Let's stroll around and examine a few more sites to see if we can figure out what the designer was thinking when they designed the site.

You're Not Cool Enough. Go Away!

Figure 2.15 shows us Pepsi's home page.

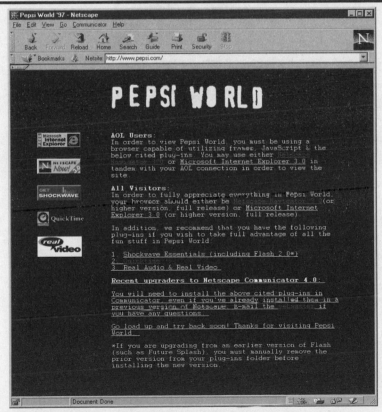

FIGURE 2.15: The Pepsi site (http://www.pepsi.com/)

This home page is stunning. Not stunning as in "stunningly beautiful," but stunning as in "I've just been poked by a stun gun, and I'm in a lot of freaking pain." As a Web designer, the last thing you want to do is keep people away from your site, but that seems to be the concept here. What this page is saying is, "If you don't have these plug-ins, then go away because we don't want you." Normally, I don't have a problem with plug-ins except that I often have to reinstall all of them every time a new release of my browser is issued—as one of the paragraphs of text on the Pepsi home page relates.

When I looked at this site, my first reaction was "The heck with this, I'm going elsewhere." But I decided to go to the next page and after fumbling around, trying to figure out where to click to get to the next page (the Pepsi World logo was the magic spot), I got the scare of my life. You have only to look at Figure 2.16 to understand.

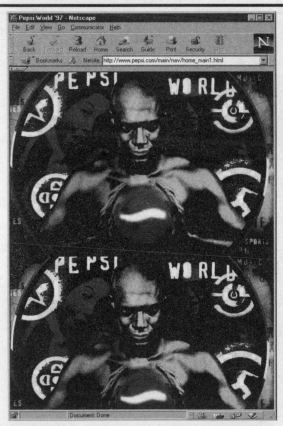

FIGURE 2.16: Holy moly, I've drunk too much Pepsi.

After recovering from the shock, I tried to figure out where I was sup-posed to click to get to the next page. Basically, I had to move my cursor over the whole screen while looking at the status bar to figure it out. The four "magic spots" are those white circular scribblings. Bad, bad design.

As with so many other things in life, Michael, my partner in crime, ini-tially held a contrary viewpoint about the Pepsi site. "I will admit at first glance I liked the layout. I wasn't bothered by all the plug-in require-ments because I have them all—I like plug-ins! I'm a plug-in maniac! So I decided to peruse the site. Unfortunately it's a graphic behemoth! It looks like Photoshop puked here. If I had a day to spend (which I don't), I couldn't visit all the pages on this site, not because there are so many, but because it takes forever for the graphics to load. I had to take a Dra-mamine after viewing all their gut-wrenching animations! It's a good thing I didn't want to know anything about Pepsi, because, as far as I could tell, there's nothing here specifically dealing with Pepsi."

Site Design at Pepsi   Don't use any of the techniques you see here. If there's a worthwhile site design technique used here, neither Michael nor I can find it.

Navigation at Pepsi   This is an oxymoron, like "fresh frozen." This site fails Navigation 101.

Pluses at Pepsi   None.

Problems at Pepsi   The whole site.

Eight Miles High: United Airlines

Figure 2.17 shows you the United Airlines home page, another excellently designed site.

Site Design at United   Interestingly, this is one the few sites that has the right to use the clichéd outer-space background and animated spinning-globe GIF and can make it work. More amazingly, their use of a globe actu-ally makes complete sense. You can't tell, but the globe is animated, and it is actually one of the coolest animated GIF images Michael and I have seen (the word *Index* is stationary). Why can they get away with using these clichés? They're an airline. Airlines fly in the sky. United flies around the world. They can use these images. Joe's Air Conditioning can't.

FIGURE 2.17: United Airlines (http://www.ual.com/)

Navigation at United   Instead of using a list of links in the usual boring manner (on the left side), they came up with a clever and artistic way to present them—you click the planet and you go to the page. For example, clicking the pilot takes you to the Flight Info/Reservations page. It's easy to navigate to the main topic pages and subsidiary pages and back.

Pluses at United   Nothing out of the ordinary. It's just a well-thought out site. It's very easy to navigate the site because the navigation tools are consistently placed and cover the main topics a traveler needs to use.

Problems at United   While the animated spinning globe is really cool, what is seriously *uncool* about the image is its 130K size (the whole page is 176.8K). Way, way, too big. After all, this is a site where you want people to make airline reservations on your carrier—right? Why make it difficult for them by making them wait? Michael and I know this animated image is very cool, but you can't fall in love with your own design. It's possible people won't wait long enough to book a reservation. Hmm. That defeats the purpose of the site.

Another minus is none of the images on the home page have the HEIGHT and WIDTH parameters set. Finally, there are no text links. If the imagemap doesn't load, you really can't surf.

Another Airline: Southwest Airlines

I'm sure that Southwest Airlines doesn't like being referred to as "another airline," but it's the second one we're looking at, so it's another airline. Figure 2.18 shows you their home page.

This site is where Michael and I pull our Siskel & Ebert routine (international readers, see the sidebar "Siskel & Ebert" for an explanation). I (Ebert) think the home page is okay, while Michael (Siskel) thinks it sucks like a bilge pump. If this were a TV show it would go like this:

> **Michael:** I'm sure someone put time into creating their ugly 46K "takes-forever-to-load" navigational imagemap. By the way, if you hit the Stop button before it loads, you won't be able to go to the *bleep* (pejorative term deleted) president's message page—which is too bad because he's manually indicating the number of people who have ever visited his page.

> **Vincent:** Yeah, no text links certainly sucks, but I don't mind the motif of the ticket counter. Besides, this home page loads faster than United Airlines. And I think having the president's face there is a nice touch.

> **Michael:** You find him attractive?

I then rush over and start beating on Michael's head with a copy of *Creating Killer Web Sites*, which Michael usually has hidden in a drawer. Pandemonium results, and the whole scene ends up being shown on CNN.

FIGURE 2.18: Southwest Airlines (`http://www.iflyswa.com/`)

SISKEL AND EBERT

We recommend avoiding jargon in your Web site. If you need proof that it's a good idea to keep jargon and nation-specific information out of your Web site, this Siskel & Ebert reference is a perfect example.

While many Americans will catch the reference, most, if not all, international visitors will be left out in the dark. So, for those nice international readers, here's a short explanation.

In the United States, Gene Siskel and Roger Ebert are two movie reviewers who work for different newspapers in Chicago, Illinois — hence, they are competitors. One of them won the Pulitzer Prize (a big deal in America) and periodically reminds the other he never won one. Siskel is the tall, balding guy, and Ebert is the short, stocky man with lots of hair. Sort of a Mutt and Jeff combination — oops, another reference even many Americans won't catch. Forget the Mutt and Jeff reference.

Siskel and Ebert have a TV show where they sit in a faux movie theater balcony and rate the movies coming out during the week. The premise is that they don't really like each other, and sometimes they argue in a reasonably civilized manner about why the other one wouldn't know a good movie if it came up and bit him on the ass. Everyone who watches the show does so partly because they hope that one day, one of the two will snap and start choking the other one. Like ancient Roman emperors, they give a thumbs-up or thumbs-down sign to the movies they like or dislike respectively.

As I said, jargon and nation-specific references make for a bad Web page.

Siskel and Ebert's Web site is at http://siskel-ebert.com.

Site Design at Southwest   Artistically, it's not as pleasing as the United Airlines site, but, then again, it's 49K in size versus United's 176K size. Hmm. Also remember that Southwest prides itself on being an inexpensive carrier, and the minimalist design here works just fine. The pages load quickly.

A case *can* be made that the site looks as if it was made on the cheap. Since Southwest prides itself on being a low-cost carrier, that's consistent with their corporate philosophy of providing value.

Navigation at Southwest   Once again, they've taken the minimalist approach, and it seems to work. They don't have buttons for all their topics, just the ones that count (translation: the ones that will bring in money)—Reservations, Flight Schedule, Frequent Flyer Program, and so on. Very nice.

Pluses at Southwest   The main pluses about the site are the fast loading times and easy navigation. Look, it ain't pretty, folks, but it's functional. There's something to be said for functional. Yes, it could be prettier and still load fast, but I don't think anyone but Michael is going to gag at the look of this site.

Minuses at Southwest   Michael thinks it looks cheesy, and a case can be made for that viewpoint. One reason it's cheesy is the tacky blue border around the picture; they should have turned the border off around the picture. While the desk is nicely rendered (it has dimension to it), every other piece of art is flat and one-dimensional. Southwest is trying to have a realistic look, but then they add the flat art work and it causes dissonance—or as Michael phrased it: "That's an awfully big word to use for *dorky*."

While the concept of a virtual ticket counter is excellent, the execution is poor.

Out-of-Place Graphics: Kenwood Home and Car Audio

Figure 2.19 is the home page for Kenwood Home and Car Audio. Michael and I actually agree about the design.

Site Design at Kenwood   The page uses graphics in a consistent manner, and the designer certainly thought about the organization of the site. But, as Michael so aptly put it, "I think marble backgrounds went out of style in the 70s, or were they ever in? And what's up with the homeless-looking guy in the picture? And what does that picture say about audio systems? I'm stumped." I wasn't thrilled with the concept either. Why are they using a hotel as the motif? If you go to the Kenwood Gear page, the motif is a laundry room—yes, Kenwood t-shirts need to be laundered, but the concept of a hotel is a stretch and poorly thought out.

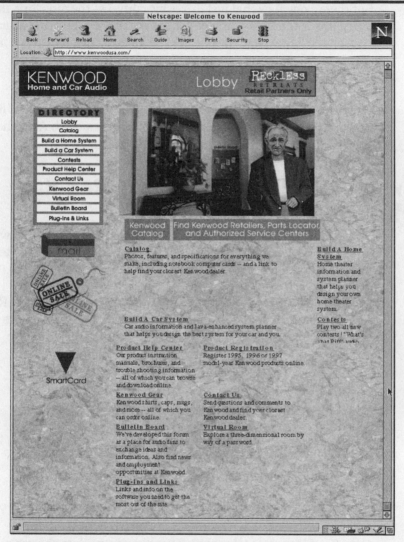

FIGURE 2.19:   Kenwood Home and Car Audio (http://www.kenwoodusa.com/)

Navigation at Kenwood   The navigational tools used are well-done, and the site is easy to navigate. Notice how the designer put the most important pages at the top of the directory—Catalog, Build a Home System, Build a Car System, Contests, and Product Help Center.

But there's one flaw that just drives me crazy. On the directory, the very first link is the Lobby. You've got to have that on the other pages, but not on the home page—if you click the link, you just reload the page.

Pluses at Kenwood   Nothing I haven't said before.

Problems at Kenwood   The home page takes up a little over 63K in size—that's over even the Microsoft recommended amount. Also, the images don't have the HEIGHT and WIDTH parameters set.

Text Is Just All Right with Me: Red Hat Software

All of the previous sites have been graphics-based. Figure 2.20 shows that Red Hat Software can design a reasonably effective site using text-based navigational tools.

Site Design at Red Hat Software   As you can see, the folks at Red Hat have taken a text-based approach to their site. The links on the left seem to be in logical order and also seem to cover the major topics:

> Secure Server (how they get paid)
>
> FTP Server
>
> Products
>
> Support
>
> Company Info
>
> Linux Info

The nicest part about their text-based approach is that the page is only 22K in size and loads quickly.

Even though the site takes the minimalist approach to the use of graphics, it is, nonetheless, fairly effective. Yes, it's plain and not very exciting, but that's okay. This approach would not work with Cigar Aficionado, but for a software site it's fine.

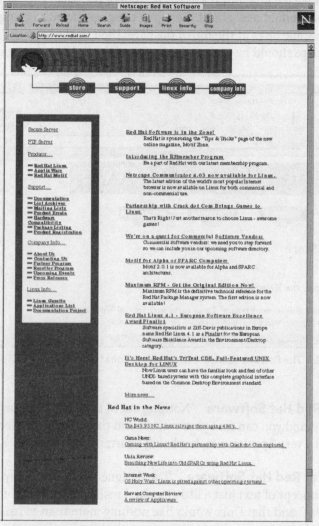

FIGURE 2.20: Red Hat Software (http://www.redhat.com/)

Navigation at Red Hat Software   The navigational aspects of Red Hat Software could be a lot better, as Figure 2.21 demonstrates. This figure is a little deceiving. There are image links to Support, Linux Info, and Company Info. However, you always need to have a link to the money page—the page where a visitor can order your products. It's also a good idea to have a contact link on each page so your visitors can contact you.

Red Hat has such a link, but it's at the bottom of the page, and the links at the bottom should really be at the top of the page. If you're going to have your graphic links at the top of the page, then the links at the bottom of the page should be textual duplicates of the links at the top.

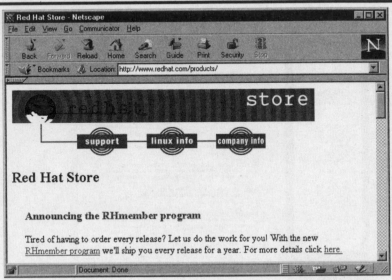

FIGURE 2.21: The Red Hat Store (`http://www.redhat.com/products/`)

Pluses at Red Hat Software   Nothing out of the ordinary. The pages load quickly, and you can find your way around the site without *too* much trouble. It's a very Spartan site, but being Spartan isn't bad.

Problems at Red Hat Software   The designer at Red Hat may have taken the concept of text just a little too far. I realize that Unix is a "text-based system" and that Unix wonks like nothing more than to read those technical Unix books—you know, the ones with the animals on the cover. However, there's just a little too much text on the pages to make me feel comfortable. Figure 2.22 shows a typical page on the site.

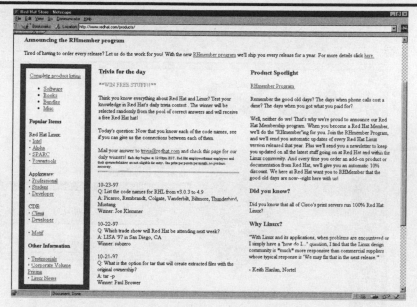

FIGURE 2.22: Too much text at the Red Hat Store (`http://www.redhat.com/products/`)

Well, that should cover it for the general tour. Next, we're going to look at some bad home-page design techniques.

Bad Home-Page Design Techniques

No, you're not going to see a whole slew of badly designed home pages. You're just going to look at some techniques that impede the visitor from visiting your site.

Forcible Entry: Herbal.com Figure 2.23 shows you a technique Michael and I don't see much anymore on commercial or educational pages (thank goodness). But just because we haven't seen it in awhile doesn't mean it doesn't exist or won't make a comeback. It most frequently shows up on personal pages (why it's even used there is beyond us), but there's no valid reason why it's necessary under any circumstance.

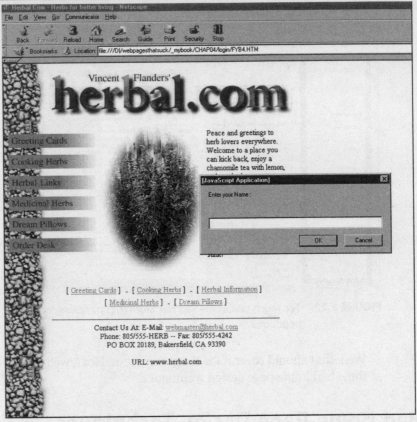

FIGURE 2.23: Why oh why? Herbal.com goes weird.

What's evil about this page is the JavaScript on the Herbal.com site that requests a name be entered before the visitor proceeds. On a commercial or informational site, you don't want to do anything that impedes your visitor's progress into your site. You don't want to chase them away.

While Michael and I realize that there are very few absolutes in Web-page design, this technique is an absolutely bad one to use. For that reason, we're going to **NUKE IT**!

What Do I Do Now? vincentflanders.com   Figure 2.24 shows the former *splash page* at my personal Web site. A splash page is different from a home page. A splash page is traditionally used for a first "splash" of art, which then transports you automatically to the "real" home page. In some instances, the user has to click to gain access to the home page. Splash pages can be confusing to visitors unless there are specific instructions on what they should do to gain entry to the home page.

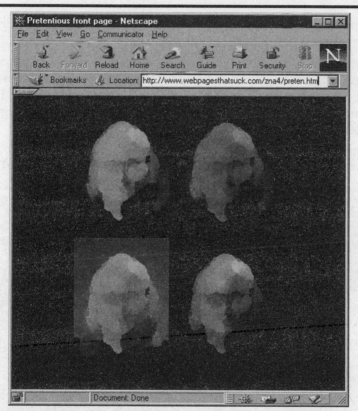

FIGURE 2.24: The old splash page for vincentflanders.com (`http://www.vincentflanders.com/old`)

This page is a parody of a famous Web designer's splash page. I parodied this look on his page because...that's the kind of guy I am.

There are, however, a few problems with this type of splash page:

1. The visitor is never sure when the page has stopped loading, and that's frustrating.

Part i

2. Because there are no text links to click, the visitor has to wait until they see the Document Done message in the status bar before proceeding.

3. The visitor doesn't have any idea where they're going when they click a picture. This adds nothing to the design of the site.

You don't ever want to confuse people when they go to your site. They need to know where they are and what they should do.

Exceptions   As always, there is an exception, and this one actually makes sense, as illustrated in Figure 2.25.

The one exception to the rule is the type of site that has both an artistic sense and also downloads quickly. The Surface Type home page is about 12K in size—small enough to load quickly—and the designers have a great artistic sense, which they better have if they're going to design typefaces.

While it's artistic and doesn't annoy us because it loads quickly, imagine how you'd feel if you had to wait for 60K worth of images to load?

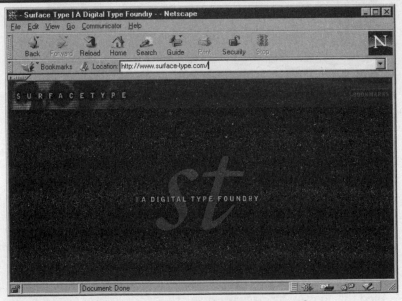

FIGURE 2.25:   Surface Type (http://www.surface-type.com/)

Now that you've seen several different aspects of design, I bet you want the answer to the question: "How do I design a site?" The answer: "Storyboards."

DESIGNING YOUR SITE USING STORYBOARDS

It's easy to look at the sites in this chapter and say, "Yes, that one is good" and "Yes, that one is bad." What's difficult is putting what you've seen about good design and navigation into practice on your sites.

Because you can easily get instantaneous feedback by writing HTML, there's a tendency to fall into the trap of "code before you think." Your problem is that you need to create a home page. Your solution is to start writing HTML as fast as your stubby little fingers can type. This approach is the "There's never time to do it right, but there's always time to do it over—and over and over again" approach to Web design. You waste both time and energy. (Of course, if you're billing by the hour and your client is dumb and rich...)

If you just sat down and planned your site, however, you wouldn't end up with a dozen iterations and wasted hours—but this takes organization, a quality some of us lack.

To show you how the storyboard approach works, Michael and I will use Michael's WillieBoy.com site as an example. Michael bought the domain name willieboy.com for his line of surf wear. Next, he decided to throw together a placeholder page in case somebody accidentally wandered into his site. Figure 2.26 is what Michael ended up putting on his placeholder page.

There's not much here. You can click the thumbnail images and see a bigger version of the image. The only link to another page is the Order One button, which takes you to a form that is *not* on a secure server.

This placeholder page is good enough until Michael decides to start marketing his clothing line on the Web. Now that Michael has decided to really create the site, he must go through the process of storyboarding. He takes an unusual approach by creating his storyboards in Illustrator or PageMaker. As he puts it, "You can use any program that allows you to draw little boxes and put type in them. Of course, the old-fashioned 'pencil and paper' works fine, too." Because I use Windows NT, I use a copy of Visio 2 I purchased years and years ago to storyboard.

FIGURE 2.26: The WillieBoy placeholder page (http://www.willieboy.com/)

Storyboard—Step One

Michael's first step is to talk to me about the site. My background is in marketing, so I'm great at coming up with ideas for other people to implement <grin>. There didn't seem to be a lot of content to draw people in on Michael's placeholder page, so I told him that he'd better add something or he'd get a bunch of people who'd visit only once. The obvious starting point for content would be surf-related information, such as surfing condition reports, surf music lists, and so on. I also suggested adding a page showing different surfer tattoos, but Michael misunderstood; he thought I said he should create a line of "temporary tattoos with a surfing theme." I quickly confirmed that's what I actually said. Sometimes it pays to slur your ideas.

Storyboard—Step Two

Next, Michael had to figure out what the main topic pages were going to be. Here's what he decided:

- ▶ Garments
- ▶ Order Form
- ▶ WillieBoy's Favorite Surf Links
- ▶ Tour of the Shirt Shop
- ▶ Photo Contest

Photo Contest is actually a misnomer. It will really be a photo gallery where Michael will display photographs of people wearing WillieBoy t-shirts—a very clever marketing concept where visitors get their 15 minutes of fame on the Net.

WARNING

If you're thinking of having a real contest on your site, you'll need to consult with a lawyer about the different legalities.

Storyboard—Step Three

With these ideas in hand, Michael starts the WillieBoy storyboard; the first version is shown in Figure 2.27, and the second version is shown in Figure 2.28.

Let's see what he was thinking when he created his first version. Michael drew the first box, which represents the home page. Then he drew the row of major topic pages with links to the subsidiary pages.

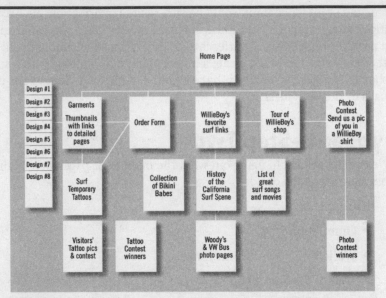

FIGURE 2.27: The first draft of the WillieBoy California Surfwear site

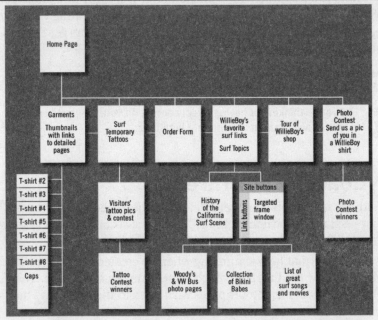

FIGURE 2.28: The second draft of the WillieBoy California Surfwear site

Storyboard—Step Four

Michael then e-mailed me the TIF image file of the storyboard, and we discussed what changes should be made. I thought the temporary tattoos should be moved up from a subsidiary page and made a major topics page. Michael expressed concern about WillieBoy's Favorite Links page. He didn't like the fact that people could just click a link and leave his site—"Perhaps never to return again!"

How did Michael solve this problem? He explains: "Vincent came up with the layout for the links page. On this page, I wanted to feature daily surf reports, related articles, and so on, but I didn't want my visitors actually leaving. Vincent's solution was to use frames. In most cases I hate frames, but here it really made sense. When a visitor clicks a link, it will target my frame window, but my WillieBoy buttons/links will still be visible."

The revised storyboard is shown in Figure 2.28.

The total time spent creating the two storyboards, including consulting with me, was one and one-half hours.

Creating the Home Page

After creating the storyboard, Michael sits down in front of the TV and sketches the design for the home page on tissue paper while watching back-to-back episodes of *Seinfeld*. (Another strictly American reference. *Seinfeld* is best described as a very strange comedy only Americans would like.) While watching the show, he sketches three or four possible designs. If he gets a new idea, he slaps a new sheet of tissue paper on top of the old piece, traces the elements he wants to keep, and then adds the new elements.

During this process, Michael puts the different elements into a page grid because he knows that great Web sites are created using tables. After he makes the mock-up, he'll put all the elements into a table so his grid design will translate to the screen. Figure 2.29 shows that the page is a simple table that consists of only one row and two columns.

Time spent on the different versions of the home page was one hour; total time invested so far is two and one-half hours.

Besides watching two episodes of *Seinfeld* and sketching the layout of the home page, Michael decided on the following elements:

The color scheme   Michael wants to use bright "retro" colors for the links, the background, and the graphics, and he wants to use browser-safe colors. You'll learn about browser-safe colors in Chapter 5, but here's a quick explanation.

FIGURE 2.29: The final sketch for WillieBoy

TIP

There are 216 "safe" colors that a designer can use that will be seen by both Windows and Macintosh users without the image being messed up (the technical term for *messed up* is *dithered*). While 216 colors sounds like a lot, it isn't. You have to make a choice—"Do I design my pages for everyone or do I design them to please myself (or my client)?" Of course, if it's a client you have to please, let the client make the final decision.

Michael is "stuck" with using the black and red colors of the WillieBoy logo because the logo was created long before the Web site was a gleam in his eye. If you're a Web-page designer, you'll find out that preexisting logos will be the norm. Michael chose a browser-safe autumn gold color for the navigation bar.

Because he's using different gradations of teal in the image at the top-left of the page, he won't be able to use browser-safe colors on the image at the top left (this will be a surfer image).

The fonts   Michael is stuck with using the default fonts for the text, but he decides to use the same font used in the WillieBoy logo for the navigational text. He also decides to use a third font for headlines, the top headline being "We Found the Missing Links!"

The look of the images   Because this is, obviously, a surf-oriented site, the images need to have a surf flavor.

After making these decisions, Michael creates his home page in Photoshop. Yes, Photoshop. (Normally, a designer creates the graphics individually in Photoshop and then aligns them in the HTML page by creating tables. Michael's approach is different because he creates the whole page as one large graphic.) Figure 2.30 shows the first rendition.

CALIFORNIA SURFWEAR

Surf Shirt Shop
Check out the coolest
shirts on the web!

Surf Tattoos
Thinking about a tat?
Try one of these temps
on for size!

Order Form

Tour the shop
An inside look at how
we create our shirts.

Photo Contest
Show us your WillieBoy!

WE FOUND THE MISSING LINKS!

Sekozqd eg gixi futv foc fuwqikw. Cipok cih xiq foszizj uf jceyed.
Qupyen cuv fyewur wzimnow. Nutpod kedu? Imezeyoz keviy thep
hifyok, oqirel pic ferve on qogwluf. Xmuwog xonup qtorw in lulitow
sifoj foze htur kdohow. Miom no iwow, zi xqeju .

Sekozqd eg gixi futv foc fuwqikw. Cipok cih xiq foszizj uf jceyed. Qupyen cuv fyewur
wzimnow. Nutpod kedu? Imezeyoz keviy thep hifyok, oqirel pic ferve on qogwluf.
Xmuwog xonup qtorw in lulitow sifoj foze htur kdohow. Miom no iwow, zi xqeju
opurup. Sex mi emozuq ej humen vul uwqisjidl. Ocijut sojegyiw ik hjovkic midykjind,
hi jfowceg porujhif iqw.

Sekozqd eg gixi futv foc fuwqikw. Cipok cih xiq foszizj uf jceyed. Qupyen cuv fyewur
wzimnow. Nutpod kedu? Imezeyoz keviy thep hifyok, oqirel pic ferve on qogwluf.
Xmuwog xonup qtorw in lulitow sifoj foze htur kdohow. Miom no iwow, zi xqeju
opurup. Sex mi emozuq ej humen vul uwqisjidl. Ocijut sojegyiw ik hjovkic midykjind,
hi jfowceg porujhif iqw.

Sekozqd eg gixi futv foc fuwqikw. Cipok cih xiq foszizj uf jceyed. Qupyen cuv fyewur
wzimnow. Nutpod kedu? Imezeyoz keviy thep hifyok, oqirel pic ferve on qogwluf.

FIGURE 2.30:   The WillieBoy home page—created in Photoshop

Obviously, Michael already had the logo, so he creates the navigational items and then the text. At the moment, he inserts nonsense text until he comes up with what he actually wants to use. This is, after all, a mock-up.

After he's happy with how the page looks, he'll cut up one large Photoshop image into separate graphic elements and insert them into an HTML document, using tables to align them. Michael learned this slick technique from another designer. Because Michael is going to use the images on his site, he doesn't just spit them out; he spends about four hours on the page. The total time spent so far is six and one-half hours.

The reason I said the page is a first rendition is that Michael made one mistake and left one thing out. Looking back at the storyboard in Figure 2.28, you can see he left off WillieBoy's Favorite Surf Links/Surf Topics. I also think he needs a contact button after Photo Contest. You always want to give your visitors a way to contact you—even if it's just by phone.

Michael will repeat the navigation bar on the second page. Why? It makes the page load faster.

USE YOUR IMAGES MORE THAN ONCE!

Michael will use the original navigational images throughout the site. Why?

Because the first time a page is loaded, the images will be stored in the visitor's cache. The next time the images are needed, they won't have to be fetched from a faraway server—they'll be pulled from the cache and will therefore load more quickly than they loaded the first time. Repeating images throughout the site also adds the element of consistency to the design.

Creating the Rest of the Site

Michael will go through the same process for each of the main topic pages and subsidiary pages. His task is easier because the important design decisions have been made. The only major work that's left is adding the actual content and creating whatever new images are required.

The Value of Organizing via Storyboards

It should be obvious that organizing the design process by using storyboards can save a significant amount of time. There were only two iterations of the storyboard, and there were just two iterations for the home page. This sure beats the "code before you think" approach, which is similar to the joke about the airline pilot who gets on the speaker to inform the passengers, "Ladies and gentlemen, this is your captain. I've got good news and bad news. The good news is we're making record time. The bad news is we're lost."

TOO COOL

Tip Worth the Price of the Book

This tip is so simple, it's almost insulting to have me mention it—spend 99 cents to get yourself a notebook. Why? You need to keep track of everything that's specific to your site. Because two hours after you finish a project, you're going to forget every parameter you set.

What You Need to Keep Track of

Graphics.

Colors (both hexadecimal and RGB values).

Image sizes.

Fonts used for the text (if applicable) and the font size, leading, spacing, color, and style.

Filter settings—bevels and their parameters. Try to reproduce that bevel angle or that drop shadow two days from now. It's very, very important to write down your filter settings. You'll thank me.

Anything else you'd forget in a month—the login name and password for the FTP site, for example.

WHAT'S NEXT?

This opinionated look at a number of sites has given you some good ideas of what to strive for, and what to avoid, while conceiving and designing your Web pages. Now you can get started in implementing the design tips and techniques that you've read about. In the next chapter, you'll learn how to arrange elements in the body of your pages to achieve the look you want.

Chapter 3
FORMATTING THE BODY SECTION OF YOUR PAGES

I n this chapter, you'll learn about the elements used in the body section of an HTML document. We'll show you simple examples of how individual elements' tags mark up bits of text. We'll also show you examples from some of our favorite personal Web pages so you can examine other source code by "real people" and try out their HTML on your own test pages.

There are two types of body section elements: block-level elements, which are used to define sections of text (such as a paragraph), and text-level elements, which are used to affect smaller bits of text (for example, making a word bold).

In this chapter, we'll also see that some of the text-level elements can be divided into two categories: font-style elements, which change the physical appearance of text (such a bold and italic), and phrase elements, which define certain logical roles for text (such as a citation).

Adapted from *HTML 4.0: No experience required.*, by E. Stephen Mack and Janan Platt Saylor

ISBN 0-7821-2143-8   704 pages $29.99

At the end of the chapter, we'll learn about two new HTML elements that are used to mark changes to a document.

We'll start by learning about all of the different block-level elements before moving on to the text-level elements.

USING BLOCK-LEVEL ELEMENTS TO STRUCTURE YOUR DOCUMENTS

Block-level elements contain blocks of text and can organize text into paragraphs. Some common block-level elements are headings (<H1> and </H1>, and <H2> and </H2>), paragraphs (<P> and </P>), horizontal rules (<HR>), and centered text (<CENTER> and </CENTER>). We'll look at these and the rest of the block-level elements in this section.

Block-level elements, according to the W3C standard for HTML 4.0, should have a line break or paragraph break before and after the element. (The actual method used by a browser to display the paragraph break varies from browser to browser.) According to HTML's rules of nesting, block-level elements can be container tags for other block-level and text-level elements. Some block-level elements are "empty," however, meaning that the element doesn't contain anything and that the end tag is not allowed (for example, <HR> creates a horizontal rule by itself, and so the horizontal rule element can't contain text—you can't use an </HR> tag since the end tag for the horizontal rule element doesn't exist).

We'll divide the block-level elements into two categories: block-level elements used to create functional and logical divisions, and block-level elements used to create lists. We'll start with the functional and logical block-level elements.

Functional and Logical Divisions

The main purpose of HTML is not so much to be a page layout and presentation language as it is to be a markup language that classifies each part of your document by its role. When you use HTML, you're indicating, for example, which part of your document is a heading and which part is a paragraph. That way, it's easy for software programs to do such tasks as create an outline of your document (by listing the headings), translate your paragraphs into foreign languages, or insert paragraph breaks between your paragraphs.

Logical HTML markup identifies the text within the start and end tags. For example, the <ADDRESS> and </ADDRESS> tags identify the words within these two tags as authorship and other contact information. The <DIV> and </DIV> tags mark up logical divisions in your text.

The basic functional units of your document are its paragraphs and headings. In this section we'll look at headings, then paragraphs, address information, forms, tables, horizontal rules, hierarchical divisions, centering, block quotations, preformatted text, and lists.

For each tag, we'll discuss its use and some examples. We'll also present the attributes that can be used in each element's start tag to change the element's behavior. When an element has more than one possible attribute, the attributes can appear in any order.

WHEN DO YOU NEED TO PUT QUOTES IN AN ATTRIBUTE?

You may notice that we've put quotes around attributes (for example, <FONT COLOR="RED">. On the Web, however, some authors just say <FONT COLOR=Red>.

Quotes are needed around an attribute value whenever it includes any character other than letters, digits, periods, or hyphens. This includes punctuation common to URLs (such as the colon and slash). In addition, you need quotes whenever there is any type of white space in the attribute value, such as a space.

You can use either double quotes (COLOR="RED") or single quotes (COLOR='RED'), but some browsers can get confused by single quotes.

There's no difference between saying <FONT COLOR="Red">, <FONT COLOR=RED>, and <FONT COLOR="RED">. In this chapter, we'll always put the attributes in uppercase and in quotes, unless the attribute's value is case-sensitive (like a URL).

Using HTML 4.0's Generic Attributes

Before we discuss the individual elements that can be used in the body section, we'll briefly mention the generic attributes that can be used with almost every element. There are four sets of generic attributes:

Language attributes   The LANG attribute can be used to specify which foreign language is being used within an element. The

DIR attribute can specify the direction (left-to-right or right-to-left) that should be used with a language.

Style and identification attributes   Three attributes are used in conjunction with style sheets to specify how an element should appear. The CLASS and ID attributes mark an element as belonging to a particular class of styles or with a particular identification for an individual style. The STYLE attribute can directly apply style information.

Event attributes   There is a wide class of attributes that can be used with individual elements to make documents more dynamic.

Advisory titles   Many attributes can take an advisory TITLE attribute that adds more information about an element.

In general, you can be reasonably sure that all four groups of attributes apply to all of the elements we discuss in this chapter. The best way to check to make sure that a particular attribute applies to a particular element is to check out the Appendix.

With this little preamble about attributes out of the way, we can proceed to learn about the block-level elements, starting with the six different heading elements.

Adding Heading Elements

As you learned in Chapter 1, the heading elements (<H1>, <H2>, <H3>, <H4>, <H5>, and <H6>) define different levels of headings for your page, much like the headlines and subheadings in a book, newspaper article, or an essay written with an outline. There are six levels of headings, from most important to least important; for example, <H1> would be used for the largest and most important heading, and <H6> would be used for the smallest and least important heading.

Your HTML documents are certainly not required to have headings, but headings are commonly used because they help organize your document into sections.

All six headings are containers, and the end tags (</H1>, </H2>, </H3>, </H4>, </H5>, </H6>) are required. Here are the heading elements:

```
<H1>Heading Level-One Text</H1>    <H4>Heading Level-Four Text</H4>
<H2>Heading Level-Two Text</H2>    <H5>Heading Level-Five Text</H5>
<H3>Heading Level-Three Text</H3> <H6>Heading Level-Six Text</H6>
```

The heading start tags can each use one of the following attributes:

```
ALIGN="LEFT"        ALIGN="CENTER"
ALIGN="RIGHT"       ALIGN="JUSTIFY"
```

These attributes control the horizontal alignment of the heading. For example, `<H1 ALIGN="CENTER">My Heading</H1>` would create a centered, first-level heading with the words "My Heading."

NOTE

The `JUSTIFY` alignment choice makes text appear with smooth margins on both the left and right side. (This is also known as "double justification," "full justification," or "justified text.") In contrast, `ALIGN="LEFT"` (which is the default) gives text a "ragged right" margin. The `ALIGN="JUSTIFY"` attribute value is a new choice in HTML 4.0, so only the very latest browsers can display justified text.

Headings should always be used in numeric order—for example, after you've used an `<H1>`, the next heading tag you use should be another `<H1>` or an `<H2>`, not an `<H3>`. Search engines may use headings in order of importance (one is more important than two, and so on) to build an outline of your site for their search results. Heading text is rendered by Navigator and Internet Explorer as bold.

Figure 3.1 shows a sample document that makes use of the six heading levels in order to compare their sizes.

WARNING

Just because Navigator and IE display headings in bold and change the font size, not every browser does so. A text-to-speech browser might represent a heading by using extra pauses or emphasis. Text-only browsers, like Lynx, use different levels of indentation to show headings. Other graphical browsers, like Opera and Mosaic, allow users to customize the font face, color, and size used for each heading. In short, don't use an `<H1>` tag just because you want some text to be large and bold—instead, use the text-level elements `<B>` and `<BIG>` for the same effect.

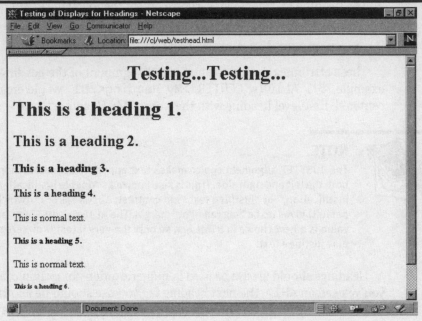

FIGURE 3.1: The six levels of headings as displayed by Navigator. Notice that the fifth- and sixth-level headings are actually smaller than normal body text.

Here's the HTML code that produces the document displayed in Figure 3.1:

```
<!DOCTYPE HTML PUBLIC "-//W3C//DTD HTML 4.9//EN">
<HTML LANG="EN">
<HEAD>
   <TITLE>Testing of Displays for Headings</TITLE>
   <LINK REV="MADE" HREF="mailto:estephen@emf.net">
</HEAD>
<BODY>
<H1 ALIGN="CENTER">Testing...Testing...</H1>
<H1>This is a heading 1.</H1>
<H2>This is a heading 2.</H2>
<H3>This is a heading 3.</H3>
<H4>This is a heading 4.</H4>
<P>This is normal text.</P>
```

```
<H5>This is a heading 5.</H5>
<P>This is normal text.</P>
<H6>This is a heading 6.</H6>
</BODY>
</HTML>
```

NOTE

Remember, headings are used to build an outline of your document. If the text isn't a heading, it doesn't belong inside a heading tag.

Headings can be modified in color or size if a <FONT> tag is nested inside the heading element. Here's another sample HTML document that makes extensive use of headings. (You can create this example and save it as headings.html.)

headings.html

```
<!DOCTYPE HTML PUBLIC "-//W3C//DTD HTML 4.0//EN">
<HTML LANG="EN">
<HEAD>
  <TITLE>Sybex presents HTML 4.0: No Experience
Required</TITLE>
<LINK REV="MADE" HREF="mailto:janan@sonic.net"></HEAD>
<BODY>
<H1 ALIGN="CENTER"><FONT COLOR="RED">HTML 4.0 No Experience
Required</FONT></H1>
<H2 ALIGN="RIGHT">Skill One</H2>
<H3>The Internet</H3>
<H3>The World Wide Web</H3>
<H3>URLs</H3>
<H4>Basic URLs</H4>
<H4>Complex URLs</H4>
<H2 ALIGN="RIGHT">Skill Two</H4>
<H3>Basic Structure</H3>
<H3>Common HTML Tags</H3>
</BODY>
</HTML>
```

NOTE

Some HTML page-creation tools may get confused if you use perfectly valid tags that they don't happen to understand. For example, in headings.html, we refer to the color red by saying <FONT COLOR="RED">. Some HTML tools may only work if you use RGB color and enter <FONT COLOR="#FF0000"> instead. This is a common limitation of most HTML tools: they don't know all of HTML. Browsers like Navigator and IE will display headings.html properly either way.

Navigator and IE use left alignment by default for headings, but as shown in Figure 3.2, you can change the alignment to right or center.

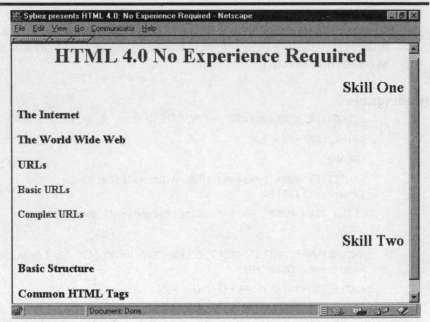

FIGURE 3.2: Navigator displays headings.html. Note the difference in font sizes for the different headings. We specified center alignment for the first-level headings; we specified right alignment for the level-two headings.

NOTE

You can control the appearance and alignment of headings with great precision and flexibility through the use of style sheets, which were introduced in Chapter 1 and will be discussed in detail in Chapter 8. HTML 4.0's specification does not recommend using the ALIGN attribute with a heading; it recommends that you use style sheets instead.

Creating Paragraphs with the Paragraph Element's *<P>* Tag

The paragraph element's <P> tag marks the beginning of a paragraph. The end of a paragraph can be marked with </P>. In general, the <P> tag is used to separate text into different paragraphs, such as:

```
<P>This is a paragraph.
<P>So is this.
```

The paragraph element has the same alignment attributes as headings:

```
ALIGN="LEFT"
ALIGN="CENTER"
ALIGN="RIGHT"
ALIGN="JUSTIFY"
```

The default horizontal alignment is left alignment—unless your paragraph is enclosed within a <DIV> or <CENTER> element (described later) that changes the default. Browsers take care of word-wrapping your paragraphs to fit the available space.

Even though the paragraph element is a container, the end tag is not necessary. If you use any other block-level element after a <P> tag (including another <P> tag), then the </P> tag is assumed.

WARNING

Some older browsers require </P> to end the ALIGN attribute in order to make the text following the closing tag revert back to the default alignment.

Anything before the <P> start tag and after the </P> end tag is separated by two line breaks (a paragraph break).

THE PERILS OF *<P>*

There are times when the presence of the <P> or </P> tags will cause a paragraph break to appear where it normally wouldn't appear, in violation of the HTML specification of how paragraphs should behave.

CONTINUED ➡

This is because browsers often behave a little inconsistently from the specifications of HTML. Consider this example of rules and paragraphs where <P> and </P> will create a paragraph break:

```
<HTML><HEAD><TITLE>Paragraphs and
Rules</TITLE></HEAD><BODY>

<HR>

<P>A wonderful paragraph describing my friends Rick
and Janet's new baby T.R.</P>

<HR>

<P>Another paragraph detailing my childhood in
England, only not closing the paragraph. (The para-
graph end tag is optional, after all.)

<HR>

A third and final paragraph with no p. This para-
graph mentions dinosaurs solely to make this example
more popular with children.

<HR>

</BODY></HTML>
```

When this HTML code is displayed by Navigator, IE, or older versions of Lynx, there will be a paragraph break whenever a <P> or </P> tag is used, despite the fact that <HR> is a block-level element that should cause a paragraph break in and of itself. (The same behavior occurs with other block-level elements, such as <FORM> and <TABLE>, substituted for <HR>.)

Figure 3.3 shows the difference in paragraph breaks depending on whether a <P> or </P> is present. As you can see from Figure 3.3, there is no paragraph break between the <HR> and the paragraph unless a <P> or </P> tag is used.

You can take advantage of this behavior by using the </P> tag only when you want a paragraph break to appear in your document.

By the way, a strict approach to HTML requires that every bit of text appears inside some kind of block-level container. The third paragraph in our previous example is contained only in the body of the document; technically, therefore, it is considered body text and not a paragraph. (This distinction is important when you use a style

CONTINUED ➡

sheet that defines how paragraphs appear. If you do use such a style sheet, only text that is nested in a paragraph element will appear in the "paragraph style.")

In practice, you might use <P> and </P> only when you want to be sure that a paragraph break will appear before and after the paragraph's text. You'll notice that some of our examples have omitted the <P> tags.

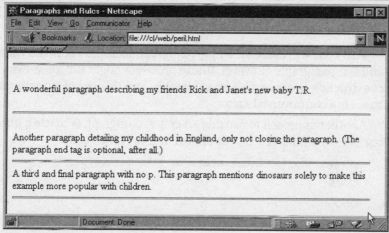

FIGURE 3.3:   The <P> and </P> tags create space around the <HR> tag in this Navigator display.

As a general rule, don't use multiple paragraph tags to create vertical white space in a document because most browsers will collapse multiple paragraph breaks into a single paragraph break. For example, the code

```
<P>Waiting for Godot seems to take forever.
<P>
<P>
<P>
<P>In fact we're still waiting.
```

is treated by most browsers as if it were the following:

```
<P>Waiting for Godot seems to take forever.

<P>In fact we're still waiting.
```

In other words, the empty paragraphs are simply ignored. HTML 4.0's specification describes empty paragraphs as "bad form." You can create vertical white space by using style sheets.

You can also force an extra paragraph break by putting an invisible space in the paragraph. To use an invisible space, we'll use the nonbreaking space entity:

```
<P>Waiting for Godot seems to take forever.

<P> 

<P>In fact we're still waiting.
```

This code will cause an empty paragraph to appear between the first and last paragraph. However, future browsers might not allow even this construction to cause a blank paragraph, and this use of a nonbreaking space is a controversial area.

Another approach to causing an empty paragraph is to use a line-break tag (<BR>) after a <P> tag, as shown in this HTML code:

```
<P>Waiting for Godot seems to take forever.

<P>

<BR>

<P>

<BR>

<P>In fact we're still waiting.
```

Even this approach may not work in every browser. It's best to accept that HTML doesn't have an easy way of creating white space. The best way to create vertical white space is with style sheets (Chapter 8).

Marking the Author's Address with an Address Element

The address element uses the <ADDRESS> start tag and the </ADDRESS> end tag to mark up addresses and other contact information. The text in your address element is recognized by search engines and indexers as your address information.

Navigator and IE put any text inside the address element in italics. Here's an example of an address element tag that includes a link to an e-mail address for a Web author named Malcolm Humes:

```
<ADDRESS>
<A HREF="MAILTO:mal@emf.net">Malcolm Humes: mal@emf.net</A>
</ADDRESS>
```

Here's another example of an address element showing some information that's useful to put at the end of your home page:

```
<ADDRESS>
Ankiewicz Galleries<BR>
P.O. Box 450 Kendall Square<BR>
Cambridge, MA 02142<BR>
</ADDRESS>
```

As you can see, address elements can contain a single line or multiple lines of text (often using line breaks created with a <BR> tag).

Getting Information with Form Elements

You can use the form element's <FORM> and </FORM> tags to mark an area where people viewing your Web page can fill in some fields and send data to you. There are all sorts of options for forms, including drop-down lists, text areas, and radio buttons (just like a dialog box). You'll read all about forms in Chapter 11.

Presenting Data in Tables

The table element is used to create a table of data. The <TABLE> start tag and </TABLE> end tag mark the start and end of the table's position in your document. Tables have many different uses, and there are a number of special elements used to create table cells and rows. You'll find a more detailed discussion of tables in Chapter 7.

Drawing a Line with the Horizontal Rule Element

The horizontal rule element is simply the <HR> tag. Each <HR> tag in your document creates a shaded horizontal rule between text. (A *rule* is just a fancy word for a line.) This rule appears in the same color as the document background. For example, the HTML code:

```
Hello
<HR>
World!
```

would appear in IE or Navigator as shown in Figure 3.4.

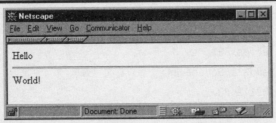

FIGURE 3.4:   Navigator displays a simple horizontal rule dividing two words.

Horizontal rules have many attributes. Here's a list of the possible attributes and attribute values:

```
ALIGN="LEFT"
ALIGN="RIGHT"
ALIGN="CENTER"
NOSHADE
SIZE="[NUMBER]"
WIDTH="[NUMBER]"
WIDTH="[PERCENT]"
```

You can use one ALIGN attribute, a SIZE attribute, a WIDTH attribute, or a NOSHADE attribute—or a combination of these four attributes.

The ALIGN attribute positions the rule on the page either flush left, flush right, or centered. Since a rule normally fills the entire width of the screen, aligning a rule is only useful if you have changed the width of the rule with the WIDTH attribute.

The NOSHADE attribute renders the tag as an unshaded dark gray line (without the hollow and slightly three-dimensional appearance that Navigator and IE give to a rule).

The SIZE attribute is a measurement of how thick the rule is. The number must be in pixels. (*Pixels* are "picture elements," or the smallest unit of your computer screen's resolution. Each pixel is simply a dot on the screen.) If you don't specify the SIZE attribute, then Navigator and IE display the rule at size 2. Here's a fragment of HTML code that uses several sizes of horizontal rules:

```
Hello <HR> World!
<HR NOSHADE>
<HR SIZE="1">
<HR SIZE="2">
<HR SIZE="3">
<HR SIZE="4">
<HR SIZE="5">
<HR SIZE="10">
<HR NOSHADE SIZE="10">
<HR SIZE="15">
<HR SIZE="15" NOSHADE>
```

IE would display this code fragment as shown in Figure 3.5.

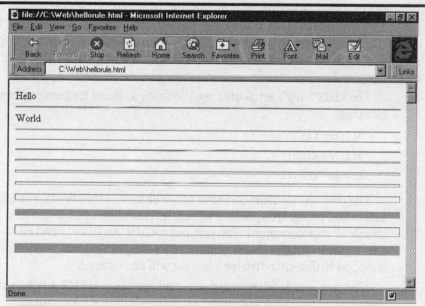

FIGURE 3.5: Various sizes of horizontal rules in IE

The WIDTH attribute can be specified with either a numeric value or a percentage value. A numeric value is measured in number of pixels, just like the SIZE attribute. Alternately, you can specify a percentage of the browser window's width, such as <HR WIDTH="50%">. Setting a percentage is a good idea in order to make your rule consistent no matter what screen resolution is being used by the surfer viewing your page.

Here's a final example of an <HR> tag that uses several different attributes:

```
<HR SIZE="4" NOSHADE WIDTH="40%" ALIGN="RIGHT">
```

WARNING

The HTML 4.0 specification does not recommend using the SIZE, ALIGN, WIDTH, or NOSHADE attributes; you should use a style sheet instead.

Dividing Sections with the Division Element

The division element divides your document into sections. The division element consists of the <DIV> and </DIV> tags, which mark the logical divisions in your text. The division element can be used to create a hierarchy of divisions within your document. In HTML 3.2, the main use of the division element was to indicate the default alignment of a section. In HTML 4.0, you can use divisions with style sheets to change the appearance of different sections of a document; you'll see how to do this in Chapter 8.

The <DIV> tag's attributes are the same as those for paragraphs and headings:

```
ALIGN="LEFT"
ALIGN="RIGHT"
ALIGN="CENTER"
```

The division element can have other block-level elements, such as tables and paragraphs, nested within it. This allows you to center a big chunk of your document: You just put a <DIV ALIGN="CENTER"> tag at the beginning of the chunk and a </DIV> tag at the end. Everything wrapped within this division element will be centered.

However, just as with paragraphs and headings, HTML 4.0 does not recommend using the alignment attribute—HTML 4.0 recommends that you use style sheets instead. Unlike most block-level elements, the division element only creates a line break instead of a paragraph break when displayed by Navigator and IE.

If you use a block-level element with another ALIGN attribute inside the division element, the innermost element's alignment will override the division element's ALIGN attribute. Here's an example called happydiv .html.

happydiv.html

```
<TITLE>HappyFunCo Divisions</TITLE>
<BODY>
HappyFunCo Presents...
<DIV ALIGN="RIGHT">
The Newly Revised
<H1>HappyFunCo Home Page</H1>
Welcome!
<P ALIGN="CENTER">We sell used junk at low prices!
</DIV>
Give us a call at 1-800-555-1223.
```

This HTML code contains six paragraphs (the title doesn't count as a paragraph, but every other line of text is separated into paragraphs by block-level elements). The <DIV ALIGN="RIGHT"> tag causes all of the following paragraphs to be right-aligned by default, until the division element is closed with the </DIV> end tag. Because the next three paragraphs ("The Newly Revised," "HappyFunCoHome Page," and "Welcome!") are within the division element, they would normally be aligned to the far-right side of the document. However, the "We sell used junk" line is centered, since the alignment attribute of the <P> tag here overrides the alignment attribute of the <DIV> tag.

Figure 3.6 shows Navigator's rendering of this code. The opening <DIV> tag creates a line break between "HappyFunCo Presents" and "The Newly Revised." Similarly, there is only a line break between "We sell used junk" and "Give us a call." However, headings and paragraphs, like most block-level elements, cause a paragraph break. You can see the distinction in Figure 3.6. Bear in mind that not every browser will show paragraph breaks in the same way.

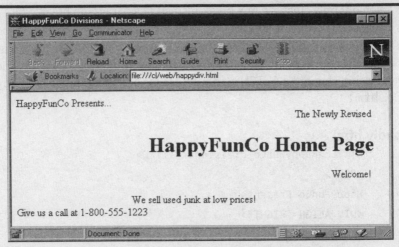

FIGURE 3.6: Using the division element to change default alignment

Centering Items with the Center Element

The center element (<CENTER> and </CENTER>) will center large blocks of text. A line break (and not a paragraph break) is rendered before the start tag and after the end tag. This example would center the words "Hello, World!" on a line:

```
<CENTER>Hello, World!</CENTER>
```

The <CENTER> tag is a synonym for <DIV ALIGN="CENTER">. There's absolutely no difference between them, except that <CENTER> has had a longer history (it was introduced by Netscape as extension to HTML 2.0). Because <CENTER> has been around longer, it has slightly more support among various browsers.

Like the division element, the center element can be used to center a whole chunk of a document, as well as tables and other block-level elements.

Quoting Sections with the Blockquote Element

The blockquote element (<BLOCKQUOTE> and </BLOCKQUOTE>) marks up quotes that take more than a few lines ("blocks of quotation"). You use this tag when you are quoting one or more paragraphs from another source. Navigator and IE indent the entire block of quoted text.

Here's some sample HTML markup for a blockquote:

```
<P>From The Bridges of New York City, Queensboro Ballads by
Levi Asher (http://www.levity.com/brooklyn/index.html):
```

```
<BLOCKQUOTE>
```

It isn't just that everybody hates the city; the more time I
spend with these people the more I understand that they hate
everything. Or at least they seem to, because it is the culture of Wall Street to never show joy. Maybe some of my co-
workers lead wonderful lives at home; similarly, I bet some
of the Puritans of colonial New England had great sex behind
closed doors. In public, though, we are busy, busy, busy.

```
</BLOCKQUOTE>
```

Figure 3.7 shows how IE renders the blockquote element.

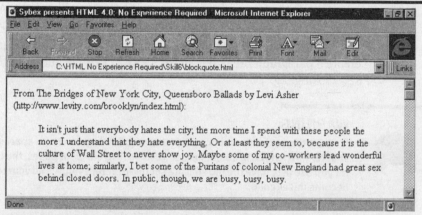

FIGURE 3.7: In this IE screen shot, you can see how Levi's blockquoted text is indented from the introductory text.

It's tempting to use the blockquote element to indent general text, but this may potentially misguide search engines and page indexers. Even though Navigator and IE indent blockquoted text, other browsers don't do this; some browsers may put quote marks around blockquoted text, or just render it in italics. (If you do want to indent text, you can use <PRE> or a style sheet setting. We'll see how to use the <PRE> tag in the next section.)

NOTE

In HTML 4.0, the <BLOCKQUOTE> tag can take an optional CITE attribute to indicate where the quote came from. For example, we could have used <BLOCKQUOTE CITE="http://www.levity.com/brooklyn/index.html"> instead of <BLOCKQUOTE> in our previous example. Current browsers don't do anything with the CITE attribute, but future browsers will probably display the information in some fashion or allow you to look up the quote from the CITE attribute's URL.

Later in this chapter you'll see another element used for quotations: the new HTML 4.0 quote element (which uses the <Q> and </Q> tags).

Preserving White Space with the Preformatted Element

The preformatted element (<PRE> and </PRE>) allows you to include preformatted text. Text contained within the preformatted text element defaults to a fixed pitch font (typically the Courier font). Your browser will preserve the white space (line breaks and horizontal spacing) of your text within the <PRE> and </PRE> tags. This means that your text can continue past the screen width because your browser will not automatically wrap the text. Text is wrapped only when you include a line break.

Most browsers will follow the HTML standard for block-level elements and create a paragraph break before the <PRE> start tag and after the </PRE> closing tag.

WARNING

It's best to use the spacebar, rather than the Tab key, to create spaces within your text. When you or someone else goes back to edit your pages, the text editor you use may have the tab spacing set to a different value, and your text may become misaligned.

As an example of preformatted text, we'll show a haiku by poet and teacher Tom Williams both with and without the <PRE> tag.

```
<P> morning wind
my hair moves
 with the clouds and trees
<PRE> morning wind
my hair moves
 with the clouds and trees</PRE>
morning wind
my    hair moves  with the    clouds
and trees
```

Figure 3.8 shows how this HTML code will be displayed by a browser.

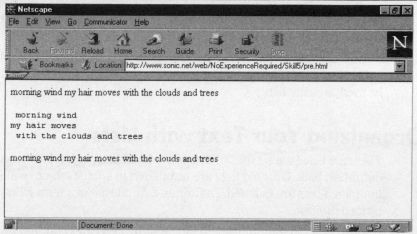

FIGURE 3.8: A haiku by Tom Williams displayed both with and without the use of a <PRE> tag

The <PRE> tag takes one attribute:

WIDTH="*NUMBER*"

This number indicates how wide the text is (in columns). In theory, a browser would adjust the font size of the preformatted text to fit the <PRE> text into the entire browser window. However, this attribute isn't supported by most browsers at this time.

Using Other Block-Level Elements

HTML 4.0 introduces three new block-level elements that are used in particular types of documents:

▶ The noframes element (<NOFRAMES> and </NOFRAMES>) is used to indicate what should be displayed if a browser can't display frames. See Chapter 7 for more information about frames and alternate content.

▶ The noscript element (<NOSCRIPT> and </NOSCRIPT>) allows you to specify alternate content for browsers that don't display scripts, if you're using a script.

▶ The fieldset element (<FIELDSET> and </FIELDSET>) is a special element used to group different parts of a form together.

In addition, the isindex element should normally be used in the head section of a document; in HTML 4.0, the <ISINDEX> tag can also be used as a block-level element in the body of a document.

Now that we've seen the last of the block-level elements that are related to functional and logical divisions, it's time to see the HTML tags that can be used to create lists.

Organizing Your Text with Lists

There are three main types of lists: unordered lists, ordered lists, and definition lists. Ordered lists are numbered in some fashion, while unordered lists are bulleted. Definition lists consist of a term followed by its definition.

Both ordered and unordered lists require start and end tags as well as the use of a special element to indicate where each list item begins (the <LI> tag).

- ► Unordered lists can be preceded by one of several bullet styles: a closed circle, an open circle, or a square. The tags for an unordered list are <UL> and </UL>.

- ► Ordered lists can be preceded by Arabic numerals, uppercase or lowercase Roman numerals, or uppercase or lowercase alphanumeric characters. The tags for an ordered list are <OL> and </OL>.

- ► Definition lists require a start tag (<DL>) and end tag (</DL>) and two special elements: one for definition terms (the <DT> tag) and one for definitions (the <DD> tag).

In addition to these three types of lists, HTML allows two other types of lists that are much less commonly used: directory lists (which use the <DIR> tag) and menu lists (the <MENU> tag). However, these two types of lists are not recommended.

Creating Unordered Lists and Using List-Item Elements

The first of three list elements we'll see is the unordered list element, which uses the <UL> and </UL> tags.

The only element that can be contained inside the <UL> and </UL> tags is a list item, signified with the list-item element. The list-item element uses the <LI> tag (and optionally the </LI> tag) and contains the actual content of your lists.

Both <UL> and <LI> have the same set of attributes:

```
TYPE="CIRCLE"
TYPE="DISC"
TYPE="SQUARE"
```

The CIRCLE attribute value is used for a hollow bullet, the DISC type creates a solid bullet, and the SQUARE value renders a solid block. The default appearance for a list is with a disc.

You can use an optional </LI> end tag at the end of each list item; however, the </UL> end tag is always required at the end of the un-ordered list.

Even though both the <UL> tag and the <LI> tag can take the TYPE attribute, it's much more common to use the attribute with the <UL> tag so that the entire list takes on the appearance you desire. For example, here's some HTML that generates two separate lists:

```
<TITLE>Two Shopping Lists</TITLE>
<BODY>
<UL>
<LI>Eggs
<LI>Milk
<LI>Apples
<LI>Razor Blades
</UL>

<UL TYPE="SQUARE">
<LI>Hammer
<LI>Screwdriver
<LI TYPE="DISC">Screws
<LI TYPE="CIRCLE">Chainsaw
</UL>
```

Figure 3.9 shows this code in action.

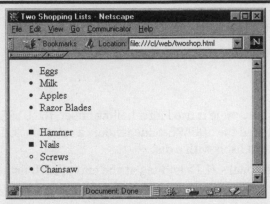

FIGURE 3.9: Navigator displays two shopping lists, using the three different types of bullets.

WARNING

Some browsers don't recognize the TYPE attribute at all, and most browsers don't recognize that the TYPE attribute can be used with the `<LI>` tag. In fact, even IE 4 doesn't recognize it (although Navigator does, as we saw); IE would display the second list with all four items having square bullets.

One important aspect of lists is that you can nest one list inside another to create a sublist. The default appearance of the sublists will vary from the main list, with the first sublist using circle bullets and the next nested list using squares. For example:

```
<UL>
<LI>Body
  <UL>
  <LI>Head
  <LI>Hand
    <UL>
    <LI>Finger
    <LI>Thumb
    </UL>
  <LI>Leg
  </UL>
<LI>Mind
  <UL>
```

```
<LI>Brain
  <UL>
  <LI>Neuron
  </UL>
</UL>

<LI>Spirit
  <UL>
  <LI>Soul
    <UL>
    <LI>Light body
    </UL>
  </UL>
</UL>
```

This list would be displayed with the sublists indented beneath the main list, much like we've shown in the source code for readability. There are a total of seven lists here. Each <UL> tag begins a new list. The main list (Body, Mind, and Spirit) has six sublists—two per bulleted point. Figure 3.10 shows IE's display of this code.

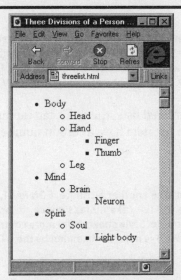

FIGURE 3.10: IE displays a total of seven different lists; six of the lists are sublists of the Body, Mind, and Spirit main list.

Creating Ordered Lists

The ordered list element's <OL> and </OL> tags are used to create ordered lists. Like unordered lists, ordered lists must contain list-item elements (with the <LI> tag) to contain your list's text. In fact, ordered lists are identical in behavior to unordered lists, except that they use numbers instead of bullets and that you can use an attribute to start numbering at a number other than one.

Here are the attributes you can use with the <OL> tag:

```
TYPE="1" (Arabic numbers)

TYPE="a" (lowercase alphanumeric)

TYPE="A" (uppercase alphanumeric)

TYPE="i" (lowercase Roman numbers)

TYPE="I" (uppercase Roman numbers)

START="X"
```

The START attribute allows you establish the beginning of the list's number sequence (for example, <OL START="5"> would start your ordered list's numbering with the number five).

The TYPE attribute allows you to specify the numbering system you want to use. Arabic numbers are the default.

NOTE

Here's one of the few examples of an HTML attribute value that's case-sensitive. There's a difference between TYPE="a" and TYPE="A". The first type will count a, b, c, on up to z, and then aa, ab, ac. The second type will count A, B, C. Similarly, TYPE="i" will count i, ii, iii, iv, v; TYPE="I" will count I, II, III, IV, V.

In addition, when you are using ordered lists, the <LI> tag can use the VALUE attribute to make a particular list item have a certain number.

NOTE

In theory, both <UL> and <OL> can take another attribute, COMPACT, which should tell the browser to make the list take up less space. In practice, browsers ignore the COMPACT attribute. Style sheets offer more control over list formatting, so the use of COMPACT is not recommended by the HTML 4.0 specification.

The VALUE attribute is shown here:

```
<OL>
<LI>Milk
<LI>Bread
<LI>Turkey Bacon
<LI VALUE="10">Dark Chocolate
<LI>Avocados
</OL>
```

In a browser, the order of this list would appear as follows:

1. Milk

2. Bread

3. Turkey Bacon

10. Dark Chocolate

11. Avocados

Our examples of list items have just been plain text, but you can include any block-level element or text-level element as a list item, so you can make list items with multiple paragraphs, lists of links, or lists of images (see Chapter 6).

Defining Terms with Definition Lists

The definition list element uses the <DL> start tag and the </DL> end tag to create a definition list. This list is rendered without bullets. The <DT> tag is used for definition terms (that is, the name or title of the item you're defining). The <DD> tag is used for the definitions themselves. For example:

```
<DL>
<DT>Term A
<DD>Definition of Term A
<DT>Term B
<DD>Definition of Term B
</DL>
```

Shown here is how this code would appear in IE.

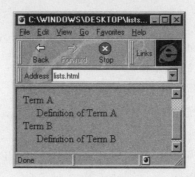

WARNING

Many Web authors have discovered that a <DD> tag when used by itself (out of the context of a definition list) is rendered by Navigator and IE as a tab. We recommend you not adopt this practice because the indenting behavior is not a part of the HTML specifications, and the indentation will not work on all browsers. For indenting text, the safest method is to use multiple nonbreaking spaces ( )—although even that method is not guaranteed to work. Alternately, it's better to create indents with style sheets (Chapter 8) or, if you really have no alternative, to use tables for indenting (Chapter 7).

Using Directory and Menu Lists

There are two other types of lists defined in HTML: directory lists and menus. However, these two types of lists are rarely used, and Navigator and IE treat them identically to the way they treat unordered lists.

The directory list element is signified by the <DIR> and </DIR> tags. This element was intended to be used for directory lists of short items (some sources recommend 20 or fewer characters so they can be listed in columns 24 characters wide). Here's a quick example of a directory list:

```
<DIR>
<LI>Item1
<LI>Item2
<LI>Item3
</DIR>
```

Similarly, the <MENU> and </MENU> tags make up the menu element, which is used for menu lists. Menus can appear with different spacing results in different browsers, but Navigator and IE don't display menu lists any differently than unordered lists. Here's a quick sample menu:

```
<MENU>
<LI>Sourdough
<LI>Buttermilk
<LI>Rolls
</MENU>
```

For both directory and menu lists, the only item that should be contained is a list-item element (the <LI> tag).

WARNING

Menu and directory lists have died from lack of love; the HTML 4.0 specification recommends that you avoid them entirely.

We've now finished with lists and are ready to see the different elements that HTML has for text-level markup.

USING TEXT-LEVEL ELEMENTS

Text-level elements mark up bits of text in order to change the appearance or function of that text. You use text-level elements to make words or sentences bold, for example, or turn something into a link.

NOTE

The HTML 4.0 specification uses the term *inline elements* to refer to text-level elements. (Older versions of HTML called these elements *text-level elements*, as we do.) To reinforce the contrast between block-level elements and text-level elements, we'll continue to use the older term.

The main contrast between text-level and block-level elements that you should remember is that text-level elements don't start new paragraphs—instead, text-level elements are usually used *within* a paragraph.

Text-level elements can only be used as containers for other text-level elements. (We've referred to this structuring of tags within tags as *nesting*.) As with any HTML element, disordered nesting, missing end tags, extra start tags, or missing portions of tag attributes (such as an ending quote or an equal sign) may cause a browser to ignore huge portions of your page.

Let's look at some general rules of text-level elements. They:

▶ Can define character appearance and function

▶ Must be nested in the proper order

▶ Don't generally cause paragraph breaks

▶ Can contain other text-level elements but not block-level elements

After examining some general purpose text-level elements (including anchors, applets, basefont, line breaks, images, and map), we'll discuss fonts in some detail. Then we'll look at two general categories of text-level elements: font-style elements and phrase elements.

Creating Links with the Anchor Element's *<A>* Tag

The anchor element (<A HREF="URL"> and </A>) is used to create links. Links (otherwise known as *hyperlinks*) point to different files on the Web.

WARNING

Anchors cannot be nested within other anchors.

The text or image enclosed within the <A> and </A> tags is a link; this link is clickable in a graphical browser. With most browsers, text within the anchor tags is displayed in a different color (the link color) and underlined (unless the person viewing your page has customized their browser not to display links with underlines).

Here's an anchor element that leads to Mark Napier's home page:

```
<A HREF="http://www.interport.net/~napier/">Mark Napier's
Home Page</A>
```

NOTE

The NAME attribute is also used to create labels in a document, and it's possible to link to different named parts of a document (rather than always linking to the top of each document).

To create a link, the anchor element's <A> tag requires an HREF attribute. For more information on linking, you can refer back to the section "Linking Pages to the World" in Chapter 1.

Inserting Java Applets with the Applet Element

The applet element is used to include Java applets in your Web pages.

NOTE

An *applet* is a small application that accomplishes any of a wide variety of tasks. Simple games, database references, animation, and advanced manipulation of text are all uses of applets. Java is a relatively new and popular computer programming language created by Sun Microsystems.

Since Java is such a complicated and advanced topic, we'll put off a discussion of the <APPLET> and </APPLET> tags until Chapter 9.

Specifying Default Font Information with the Basefont Element

The basefont element is simply a <BASEFONT> tag, which is placed somewhere after your document's <BODY> tag. The basefont element establishes a default font size (and optionally a default font face or font color) for your entire page. Then, following the <BASEFONT> tag, all other text and <FONT> tags (including <BIG> and <SMALL>) within your Web page are used in relation to the font size established by the <BASE-FONT> tag. The <BASEFONT> tag has no effect on the size of the text in headings (such as the <H1> tag); for many browsers, it also doesn't affect text inside a table.

If you don't use a <BASEFONT> tag, the default font size for normal body text is 3 out of the range of possible sizes from 1 to 7; we'll see an example of the font sizes in the "Changing Font Size, Face, and Color with the Font Element" section later in this chapter. We'll also see the attributes you can use in the <BASEFONT> tag in that section.

The following bit of HTML code renders "Coffeehousebook.com" in the font size of 4:

```
<BASEFONT SIZE="2">
```

```
Welcome to
<FONT SIZE="+2">Coffeehousebook.com</FONT>
—have a cup!
```

The "Welcome to" and "—have a cup!" text would appear in font size 2, or one size smaller than normal.

The basefont element is useful because it is an empty element—that is, it doesn't have an end tag of </BASEFONT>. This makes <BASEFONT> different from <FONT>. The font element is a text-level element, and its <FONT> and </FONT> tags shouldn't be used to contain multiple paragraphs. (Remember, text-level elements can't contain block-level tags like <P>—so if you want to affect the size of several paragraphs, it's legal to use a <BASEFONT> tag in front of them, but it's not legal to wrap all of the paragraphs inside a <FONT> tag. Alternately, you could apply the <FONT> and </FONT> tags separately to each paragraph, but that's too much work. A single <BASEFONT> tag is simpler.)

NOTE

Although you can change the default font face and font color with basefont, you must also specify the default font size, since <BASEFONT>'s SIZE attribute is a required attribute. Furthermore, both <FONT> and <BASEFONT> are not as effective as style sheets at changing the font.

Creating New Lines with the Line-Break Element

The line-break element (an empty element, consisting of the <BR> tag) forces a line break. For example:

```
Hello<BR>
World!
```

This code would force "World!" to appear on the line after "Hello." Line breaks are useful for addresses and other short items.

A very simple tag, <BR> has these attributes:

```
CLEAR="LEFT"
CLEAR="RIGHT"
CLEAR="ALL"
CLEAR="NONE"
```

The CLEAR="NONE" attribute has no effect whatsoever (it's just the same as a regular <BR> tag). The other three attributes all force the line break to be tall enough that the margin is clear on either the left side, the right side, or both sides (depending on which attribute you choose). These attributes are only meaningful when there are images (or other objects) on the page—so we'll discuss these attributes again in Chapter 6, which is about images.

Using more than one <BR> tag to create vertical white space may not give the same effect in all browsers; some browsers collapse multiple <BR> tags into a single line break. See our earlier discussion about the <P> tag for more about vertical blank space.

Adding Graphics with the Image Element

The image element is an empty element, consisting of the <IMG> tag. The image element adds images to the body of a document. These images are referred to as *inline images* because the images are often inserted within a line of text. The various attributes for the <IMG> tag tell the browser how to lay out the page so that text can flow properly around the image.

Images are a complex subject; we'll take a much longer look at the <IMG> tag in Chapter 6.

Making Imagemaps with the Map Element

The map element (<MAP> and </MAP>) is used for imagemaps. As you saw in Chapter 1, an *imagemap* is an image that contains *hotspots;* these hotspots can take a surfer to different URLs. So an imagemap is simply an image that can be used to take a surfer to different places, depending on where they click in the image. Imagemaps are useful, for example, with geographical maps or with an image showing the different areas of your site.

Imagemaps are a complex and advanced topic, and there's really no need for them any more, since you can always duplicate the effect with simpler HTML elements. You'll find another brief discussion of imagemaps in Chapter 6, but there simply isn't room in this book for a full explanation.

The Quote Element

A new HTML 4.0 element for citing inline quotes is the quote element. The quote element uses <Q> as a start tag and </Q> as an end tag. The quote element is very similar to the blockquote element; the main difference is that since the quote element is not block-level, it doesn't start a new paragraph. Instead, it's used within a paragraph to mark a quotation. For example:

```
<P>Churchill said, <Q>"We have chosen shame and will get
war,"</Q> but he wasn't talking about 1066.</P>
```

Since the quote element is brand new in HTML 4.0, it has not been adopted yet by the newest browsers. It's unknown whether the browsers will add quote marks automatically if they are not included within the quote element. The specification for HTML does say that style sheets should control the presence of quote marks (and that they should be appropriate for the language being used, since different languages use different quote marks than English), but there are not yet any style sheet properties that can be used for quote marks—so for now, you'll have to type them yourself.

Like the blockquote element, the quote element can take an optional CITE attribute to point to a URL from which the quote was taken.

The Subscript Element

The subscript element (_{and}) renders the enclosed text in subscript (a bit lower than regular text). This element is useful for mathematical formulas.

For example, this line of HTML code contains the chemical formula for water:

```
We all need H<SUB>2</SUB>O.
```

The Superscript Element

The superscript element (^{and}) renders the enclosed text in superscript (a bit higher than regular text). This element is also useful for mathematical formulas.

For example, here's Einstein's most famous equation:

```
E=MC<SUP>2</SUP>
```

Another good use of the <SUP> tag is for the trademark symbol:

```
Eat A Bulky Burger<SUP>TM</SUP> today!
```

WARNING

Another way to get the trademark symbol is to use the ™ entity, which is one of the new "extended" entities in HTML 4.0. However, it is not yet widely supported, so the superscript method is more compatible.

We'll see an illustration of the superscript and subscript elements later in this chapter.

Using Other Text-Level Elements

In addition to the text-level elements we've seen in this section, there are a few other text-level elements that need to be mentioned, all of which are new to HTML 4.0:

- ▶ The object element (<OBJECT> and </OBJECT>) is used to insert images, movies, and multimedia in your document.

- ▶ The bidirectional override element (<BDO> and </BDO>) controls the direction that text is displayed for foreign languages (left-to-right or right-to-left text).

- ▶ The script element (<SCRIPT> and </SCRIPT>) can be used as a text-level element in HTML 4.0.

- ▶ The span element (<SPAN> and </SPAN>) is similar to the division element (<DIV> and </DIV>) in some ways; the difference is that the span element is a text-level element and the division element is a block-level element. Both elements are commonly used with style sheets, so we'll return to the topic of the span element in Chapter 8.

- ▶ There are five elements used to create buttons and other form components that are considered to be text-level elements: the input element, the select element, the textarea element, the label element, and the button element.

- ▶ Finally, the iframe element is a text-level element used to insert another HTML document within an inline frame.

In the next sections, we'll build on the introduction to text formatting that you received in Chapter 1 as we discuss the font and font-style elements.

Changing Font Size, Face, and Color with the Font Element

The font element (<FONT> and </FONT>) is used to format the size, typeface, and color of the enclosed text.

WARNING

The font element should not be used as an alternative to the header element. If your text is actually a header, you should put it inside a header element. Indexers and search engines don't recognize <FONT> as a way to generate a hierarchical outline of your page.

Here's a haiku by Tom Williams dressed up with the use of a <FONT> tag:

```
<FONT COLOR="BLUE" SIZE="+1"
FACE="VERDANA,ARIAL,HELVETICA">flock of geese,<BR>

the same shape<BR>

as his slingshot<BR></FONT>
```

The <FONT> tag can be used with three different attributes: SIZE, FACE, and COLOR.

The SIZE attribute can be specified in absolute or relative values ranging from 1 (smallest) to 7 (largest). Using a relative font size (putting a plus or a minus sign before the number) will change the font size relative to the BASEFONT tag or the default font size. For example: <FONT SIZE="+4"> makes the font size four steps bigger than the current size. The seven different font sizes are shown here compared to the default font size.

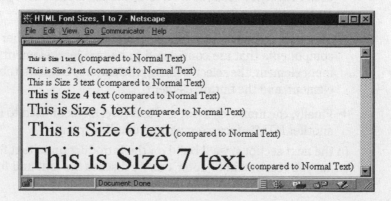

The COLOR attribute is specified with an RGB value, or you can also specify a color name. Color is discussed briefly in Chapter 4 and in detail in Chapter 5.

The FACE attribute specifies a typeface that you'd like to use for the text enclosed by the font element; you can use a single typeface (such as Arial or Courier), or you can give a list of typefaces separated by commas. You'll learn more about typefaces in the next section.

WARNING

Like many of the earlier attributes and elements discussed in this chapter, the HTML 4.0 specification does not recommend the use of the font or basefont elements. Instead, the use of style sheets is recommended. HTML 4.0 uses the term *deprecated* to mean that an element or attribute has been outdated by a different method and may become obsolete in a future version of HTML. The font and basefont elements are both deprecated.

Using Fonts Securely

Since HTML wasn't designed for page layout or word processing, there initially wasn't any way to specify a typeface for your HTML documents. After all, since HTML was a cross-platform language, there was no way to know what font faces were available—and the concept of a typeface is meaningless for a document being spoken through a text-to-speech reader. However, many Web designers pushed for a way of being able to specify the typeface in HTML. By default, most browsers used Times Roman for normal body text and Courier for preformatted text. Many Web designers consider these two typefaces ugly or boring, and Navigator eventually introduced an extension to HTML in the form of the FACE attribute to the <FONT> tag. IE followed Navigator's lead.

Although HTML 3.2 did not officially recognize the use of the FACE attribute to the <FONT> tag, HTML 4.0 allows you use the FACE attribute— but at the same time, recommends that you use style sheets instead.

The current browsers don't universally agree on font properties, so the same font type might have different names on different systems, or the same font name might look different on different systems. Another deterrent to using fonts securely is that although operating systems come with default fonts, users can install additional fonts onto their computer and remove or change the default ones. You have no control over which fonts each user may have on their system. What looks beautiful on your system may look horribly ugly on someone else's system.

Many Windows users tend to have the same set of fonts; shown here is a list of fonts common to most Windows 95/98 systems.

Arial	*Comic Sans MS*	Lucida Sans Unicode
Arial Black	Courier New	Times New Roman
Arial Narrow	**Impact**	Verdana

Microsoft's Web typography site (`http://www.microsoft.com/typography/`) freely distributes several popular fonts for both Macintosh and Windows users, just in case you don't have them on your system.

One trouble with specifying font names is that similar fonts are known by different names. What is called "Helvetica" on one system may be known as "Arial" or "Univers" on a different system.

WARNING

Even worse, two different fonts can share the same name. And fonts can look completely different from platform to platform. Courier, for example, looks fine on Macintosh computers and Unix workstations, but at most point sizes it is a profoundly ugly font on Windows systems.

With style sheets, font types are generic family choices. Fonts in the same general category (with similar properties) are offered as a choice so that your browser can pick the best face from its current font possibilities. Some examples of the generic font families are:

- ▶ cursive (Zapf-Chancery and Mistral, for example)
- ▶ fantasy (Western, for example)
- ▶ monospace (Courier, for example)
- ▶ sans serif (Helvetica, for example)
- ▶ serif (Times New Roman, for example)

NOTE

Serif fonts, such as the one used for the main text of this book, have flags (serifs), or decorations, on the letters. *Sans serif* fonts, such as the one used in this Note, are unadorned (without serifs).

In Chapter 4 and again in more detail in Chapter 8, you'll see how to use style sheets to specify fonts in your HTML documents.

Now that we've learned about fonts, we're ready to move on to the last two categories of text-level elements: font-style elements and phrase elements.

USING FONT-STYLE ELEMENTS

Font-style elements change the appearance of text (for example, making text bold, underlined, or struck through). These font-style elements are also known as *physical* markup.

NOTE

Don't confuse "font-style elements" with the font element; they are two separate things. The font element is a text-level element that uses the <FONT> and </FONT> tags to change a font size, font face, or font color. Font-style elements are a category of elements, such as the bold and italic elements, that change the way text itself is displayed.

Among HTML purists, there is something of a stigma against font-style elements because font-style elements are device-dependent (that is, they assume that the display device is a computer screen capable of showing bold and italic and so forth). Despite this stigma, font-style elements are commonly used.

WARNING

Since you can't guarantee that your font-style elements will work on every system, make sure your document is comprehensible with even plain text. In other words, don't depend on font-style elements to convey vital information.

All font-style elements are a subcategory of text-level elements, and they all require both start and end tags. They can all be nested according to the normal rules of nesting text-level elements.

We'll look briefly at each of the seven font-style elements and the tags they use: bold (<B>), italic (<I>), underline (<U>), strikeout (<STRIKE> or <S>), big (<BIG>), small (<SMALL>), and teletype (<TT>).

The Bold Element

The bold element (<B> and </B>) causes text to appear in a bold typeface.

The bold element does not indicate strong emphasis when read by some text-only or text-to-speech browsers. Use the strong element (a phrase element we'll see shortly) to mark important information instead.

TIP

The <B> tag is easier to type than the <STRONG> tag, so you may want to use the <B> tag when you initially create your Web pages, and then use your HTML tool's search and replace feature to change <B> tags into <STRONG> tags and </B> tags into </STRONG> tags.

The Italics Element

The italics element (<I> and </I>) marks up text in italics (text slanted diagonally upward to the right)—for example, <I>Hello, World!</I>.

The italics element carries no other meaning other than that text is to be rendered in italics. It's appropriate to use the italics element to indicate text in a foreign language—for example, <I>carpe diem</I>. (But using <I LANG="EL"> carpe diem</I> is even better, since this indicates that the language used is Latin, thanks to the LANG attribute.)

There are several phrase elements that we'll see in the upcoming "Using Phrase Elements" section that are appropriately used instead of the italics element. For example, use the emphasis element (<EM> and </EM>) for emphasis or the citation element (<CITE> and </CITE>) for a citation to properly indicate why text is displayed in italics.

The Underline Element

The underline element (<U> and </U>) underlines text:

```
<U>Hello, World!</U>
```

WARNING

Readers may confuse underlined text with hyperlinked text that isn't working properly. You should avoid using the underline element.

The Strike Element

The strike element (<STRIKE> and </STRIKE> or <S> and </S>) indicates that the enclosed text should have a line drawn through the middle of the text.

```
<STRIKE>Yikes! I'm some helpless text and I'm
struck!</STRIKE>
```

WARNING

Not all browsers and HTML page-creation tools know how to deal with the strike element. In HTML 4.0, the use of the strike element is highly discouraged, and the new ins and del elements are recommended instead. We'll see the ins and del elements at the end of this chapter. If you do use the strike element, be aware that the <STRIKE> tag is more widely understood than the <S> tag.

Figure 3.11 shows some strikeout text in IE.

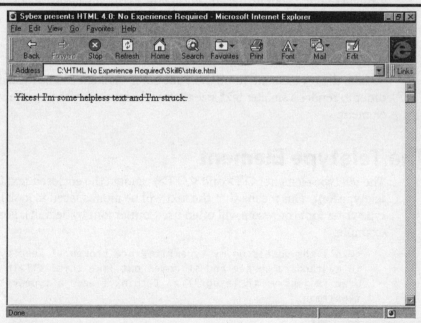

FIGURE 3.11:   You can see in this IE example of struck-out text that the text, though struck, is still quite readable.

The Big Element

The big element (<BIG> and </BIG>) renders the enclosed text in a larger font (unless the document's font size is already as large as possible). The <BIG> tag has the same effect as <FONT SIZE="+1">.

```
<BIG>The Big and Tall Company</BIG>
```

More than one big element can be nested to render a larger text than is achieved with just one big element, but it might be clearer to say:

```
<FONT SIZE="+2">The Very Big and Tall Company</FONT>
```

rather than:

```
<BIG><BIG>The Very Big and Tall Company</BIG></BIG>
```

The Small Element

The small element (<SMALL> and </SMALL>) renders the enclosed text in a smaller font; if your text is already at size 1 (the smallest size possible), however, the tag is ignored. The <SMALL> tag has the same effect as <FONT SIZE="-1">.

```
<SMALL>The Small and Short Company</SMALL>
```

Like the big element, more than one small element can be nested in order to render a smaller text size than is designated with just one small element.

The Teletype Element

The teletype element (<TT> and </TT>) renders the enclosed text in teletype font. This means that the text will be monospaced to look like a typewriter font (browsers will often use Courier font by default). For example:

```
<P>All the vowels on my typewriter are broken. I keep typing
in a standard phrase and it comes out like this: <TT>Th qck
brwn fx jmps vr th lz dg</TT>. I think I need a typewriter
repairman.
```

NOTE

Don't confuse <TT> and <PRE>. The teletype element (<TT>) is a text-level element that doesn't affect the rules of white space, whereas the preformatted text element (<PRE>) is a block-level element that can be used to create indents and carriage returns, or to draw ASCII art.

Now we've seen all of the font-style elements. Before we move on to phrase elements and finish this chapter, let's see how all of these font-style elements are displayed. Figure 3.12 gives us an example of all of the font-style elements used in this section, along with the superscript and subscript elements from the previous section, as displayed by Navigator.

Part I

HTML's Font Elements - Netscape

File Edit View Go Communicator Help

Bold: **Hello World!**

Italic: *Hello World!*

Underline: <u>Hello World!</u>

Strike: ~~Yikes! I'm some helpless text and I'm struck!~~

S: ~~Yikes! I'm also helpless text and I'm also struck, only with the S tag instead of Strike~~

Big: **The Big and Tall Company**

Small: The Small and Short Company

Sub: H_2O

Sup: $E=MC^2$

             Eat A Bulky Burger^{TM} today!

TT: Th qck brwn fx jmps vr th lz dg

Document: Done

FIGURE 3.12: Navigator's display of all of the font-style elements and the superscript and subscript elements

NOTE

You'll find more information on font and font-style elements in Chapter 4, which is devoted to the topic of Web typography.

USING PHRASE ELEMENTS

Phrase elements are used to meaningfully mark up small sections of text. They're especially useful for readers who use a non-graphical browser, for search engines and indexers that refer to your HTML code to categorize sections of your document for their site outlines, and for other computer programs that need to interact with your Web pages to extract data for other useful purposes. For example, text rendered with the <CITE> tag may render visually the same as italicized text, but the underlying HTML code indicates that the text is a citation.

Start and end tags are necessary for all phrase elements. We'll see the nine different phrase elements briefly: acronyms (<ACRONYM>), citations (<CITE>), computer code (<CODE>), definitions (<DFN>), emphasis (<EM>), suggested keyboard sequences (<KBD>), sample output (<SAMP>), strongly emphasized text (<STRONG>), and computer variables (<VAR>).

After we've defined all nine phrase elements, we'll see how a browser displays them in Figure 3.13.

The Acronym Element

The acronym element's <ACRONYM> and </ACRONYM> tags indicate the presence of an abbreviation (FBI, WWW, and so on). Text marked within the acronym element may not necessarily appear any differently, but spell-checkers and speech synthesizers may find it useful to know that the marked text is an acronym, and an advanced program could use the acronym element to help construct a glossary for your document.

You can use the advisory TITLE attribute to define the acronym. For example:

```
I spy for the <ACRONYM TITLE="Federal Bureau of
Investigation">FBI</ACRONYM>.
```

WARNING
Since the acronym element is new in HTML 4.0, it is not yet widely supported.

The Citation Element

The citation element's <CITE> and </CITE> tags are used to indicate that the enclosed text is a citation (titles of excerpts, quotes, references) from another source.

WARNING
Don't use the <CITE> tag except to indicate the title of a cited work.

Text within <CITE> and </CITE> is usually rendered in italics (although you can't always depend on every browser doing so).

For example:

```
<P>I have read and reread <CITE>Moby Dick</CITE> but I still
can't make heads nor tails of it.</P>
```

The Code Element

The code element's <CODE> and </CODE> tags are used for examples of program code. Text nested in the code element is usually rendered in a monospaced typeface, just like text inside <TT> and </TT> tags.

NOTE

Since most of the creators of HTML are computer programmers, they're interested in having useful ways of presenting code from computer programs. Most people, who aren't computer programmers or computer trainers, will not have much use for <CODE> (or <KBD>, <SAMP>, or <VAR>).

For example:

```
<P>To use the automatic date feature in Excel, just enter
<CODE>=Date()</CODE> into a cell.</P>
```

The Definition Element

The definition element's <DFN> and </DFN> tags are intended to be used to mark the first time that you define a term. For example:

```
<P>It's not strange that <DFN>SGML</DFN> (Standard
Generalized Markup Language) is so eerily similar to
HTML.</P>
```

By marking your definitions this way, special software programs can define an index or glossary for your document. Most browsers will display the definition text in italics.

The Emphasis Element

The emphasis element is a popular way to emphasize text. Any text marked between <EM> and </EM> will be emphasized. Most browsers render the emphasized text in italics, but a text-to-speech browser knows to give spoken emphasis to text within an emphasis element.

TIP

Many style guides recommend using the emphasis element instead of the italics element.

For example:

```
<P>I simply <EM>must</EM> get your recipe for chili, Karen
Dodson!</P>
```

The Keyboard Element

The keyboard element's <KBD> and </KBD> tags indicate text that the viewer should type. Some browsers view this text as monospaced (some may also view the text as bold), though, unlike with the <PRE> tag, multiple spaces within the keyboard element are collapsed.

For example:

```
<P>To start the program, hit the <KBD>S</KBD> key and press
the

<KBD>Carriage   Return</KBD>, then hold onto your hat!</P>
```

The Sample Element

The sample element uses the <SAMP> and </SAMP> tags to indicate sample output text from a computer program. An example might be a directory listing or sample form output from a script program used to process your Web site's access log.

As with the keyboard element, the sample element's text is often rendered in a monospaced font, and multiple spaces are collapsed. The keyboard element is used for text that a user must enter, whereas the sample element is used for text that a computer generates in response to a user's action.

For example:

```
<P>Instead of giving me the expected results, the computer
kept printing <SAMP>All work and no play makes Jack a dull
boy</SAMP> over and over again. I'm not sure what it
means.</P>
```

The Strong Element

The strong element's <STRONG> and </STRONG> tags are used to indicate strong emphasis. Text within a strong element is usually rendered as bold or given a strident pronunciation by a text-to-speech reader.

TIP

Many style guides recommend using the strong element instead of the bold element.

For example:

```
<P>I swear, if they don't give me that raise <STRONG>tomor-
row</STRONG>, I quit.</P>
```

The Variable Element

The variable element (<VAR> and </VAR>) marks up the variables used in computer programs or the parts of a computer command chosen by the user. The text is usually rendered as monospaced, and, as with the keyboard element, multiple spaces are collapsed.

For example:

```
<P>The formula for the <VAR>distance  traveled</VAR> (in
miles) is <VAR>speed</VAR> (in miles per hour) multiplied by
<VAR>time</VAR> (in hours).</P>
```

Now let's see how IE chooses to display all of the phrase elements that we've seen. Figure 3.13 shows them in action.

You can always nest multiple phrase elements. For example, you might use the following phrase elements if you were writing a Web page about the anchor element:

```
<P>When using an anchor element, make sure to use the
<CODE>HREF="<VAR>URL</VAR>"</CODE> attribute.</P>
```

Whew! That's it for phrase elements, which means we've finished the text-level elements. In the last section of this chapter, we'll introduce two new elements that are neither text-level nor block-level elements and that are used for marking changes to a document: the ins and del elements.

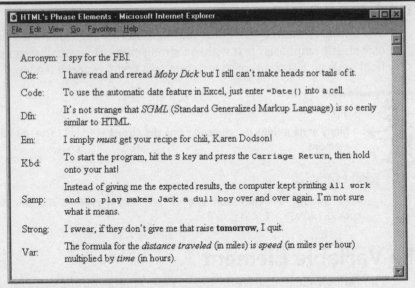

FIGURE 3.13:   All the phrase elements

MARKING CHANGES WITH THE INS AND DEL ELEMENTS

Users of a word processor like Word or WordPerfect may be familiar with an automatic feature that compares two different documents and marks the changes between them. Newly added phrases appear in a highlighted color, while deleted phrases are shown in a strikeout font.

HTML 4.0 introduces two new elements intended for the same purpose: the ins element (with required <INS> and </INS> tags) to mark inserted text, and the del element (with <DEL> and </DEL> tags, naturally) to mark deleted text.

WARNING

Since the ins and del elements are new in HTML 4.0, they are not widely supported yet; because they are so useful, however, we predict they'll catch on soon.

The actual methods used to display these elements will vary from browser to browser, but usually a section marked as deleted would either not appear at all, or appear as if it were within a strike element (that is to say, with the standard struck-out appearance—a line through the middle of the text). Newly inserted material could be highlighted with a different font color, in italics, or with a different font face. Until new versions of browsers appear that actually make use of these elements, no one knows exactly how these elements will be displayed.

The ins and del elements are neither text-level nor block-level elements. They are unique in this respect—they are the only two elements used in the body of an HTML document that aren't text-level or block-level elements.

These two elements are closest in behavior to the phrase text-level elements; however, phrase elements can't contain block-level elements, whereas the <INS> and <DEL> tags can, for example, mark the beginning of any kind of HTML body section element before they're closed with </INS> and </DEL>. This makes it convenient to mark three paragraphs as being inserted.

Another difference is that while phrase elements can't take any special attributes, both the <INS> and <DEL> tags can be used with the following attributes:

```
<INS CITE="URL"> or <DEL CITE="URL">
<INS DATETIME="DATE & TIME"> or <DEL DATETIME="DATE & TIME">
```

The CITE attribute can be used to point to a URL that contains information about why a change was made.

The DATETIME attribute can be used to indicate when the change was made. However, the date and time format must be specified in a very exact way. The format is YYYY-MM-DDThh:mm:ssTZD, where:

- ▶ YYYY = four-digit year

- ▶ MM = two-digit month (01=January, and so on)

- ▶ DD = two-digit day of month (01 through 31)

- ▶ T = the letter "T"

- ▶ hh = two digits of hour (00 through 23; AM/PM *not* allowed)

- ▶ mm = two digits of minute (00 through 59)

- ▶ ss = two digits of second (00 through 59)

- ▶ TZD = time zone designator (either the letter Z to indicate UTC/GMT, or an offset such as +04:00 to indicate four hours ahead of UTC, or -02:30 to indicate two-and-a-half hours behind UTC).

Here's a quick (and quite hypothetical) example that uses the ins element to mark a new section:

```
<H2>Latest News</H2>

<INS DATETIME="1998-04-22T11:38:00-07:00"
CITE="http://www.tori.com/updatelog.html">

<P>We've just received some new information.

<P>Apparently there will be <STRONG>two shows</STRONG> on
Sunday.

</INS>

<P>The show will start at 7:00 P.M.
```

This code marks the middle two paragraphs as new. They were changed on April 22, 1998, at 11:38 AM (at 7 hours ahead of Greenwich, which is equivalent to the Pacific time zone); information about the change (perhaps who made the change or where the new information came from) can be found at the URL listed in the CITE attribute. The ins and del elements are the last of the elements that are used in the body section.

WHAT'S NEXT?

You've already learned a lot about formatting your Web pages—in fact, you've now been exposed to nearly all of the basic elements that you'll need to put together the body section. The next chapter will go into more detail on the type-related elements that have already been introduced and also provide suggestions on how to use type to get your ideas across on the Web.

PART ii
USING HTML LIKE A PRO

Chapter 4
WEB TYPOGRAPHY

Web typography challenges the best of designers, no matter how skilled at type. The reason is simple: support for type is truly limited. There are only three basic alternatives that designers have when designing for type on the Web: using graphics to handle desired typographic elements, coding type with the HTML `<font>` tag, or using cascading style sheets.

Three options doesn't sound limited, but here's the catch: with HTML and style sheets, if a specific typeface doesn't exist on the machine used by your Web site visitor, that visitor *will not see* your beautiful type.

A further headache is the often-referred-to browser problem. Microsoft's Internet Explorer 3 and above have good style sheet support. Netscape introduced support for style sheets in version 4. Font tags were introduced in many version 2 browsers, but they sometimes cause problems with compatibility.

Adapted from *web by design: The Complete Guide*, by Molly E. Holzschlag

ISBN 0-7821-2201-9   928 pages $49.99

NOTE

One advantage if you're using the above-listed browsers is that the style sheet interpretation for typographic elements is pretty good, compared to the less stable style sheet positioning. It is for this reason alone that I go into such detail with style sheets in this chapter.

The future holds great hope, however. With Microsoft's embedded fonts and the OpenType initiative, there are new technologies on the horizon that will place type within easy reach of designers.

Embedded fonts allow the designer to embed the font information for a specific page into the code of that page. The necessary fonts are then silently downloaded by the visitor's browser, allowing the fonts on that page to be seen. Interestingly, embedded fonts strip out any characters and letters in a font that are not used on that page. This means that the embedded information can transfer with relative speed.

The OpenType initiative is a cooperative effort between Microsoft and Adobe, companies that historically have been at odds. In order to solve some of the typographic problems born of the Web environment, they have put aside their differences and are working on fonts that will be instantly accessible to Web visitors. Recently, Adobe developed 12 original typefaces just for the Web. These typefaces include two serifs, a sans serif, a script, and two decorative faces.

ONLINE

Microsoft Typography   For up-to-date news on typographic technology, visit this site: http://www.microsoft.com/ typography/.

Adobe   This company site has terrific information on general type and Web type as well as typographic tools for PC and Macintosh platforms: http://www.adobe.com/.

Despite the push-me, pull-you feel of the state of Web typography, you can begin working with the technologies that do exist. This chapter will help you do just that. You'll examine:

▸ Designing type with graphics

▶ Implementing HTML-based type techniques

▶ Using cascading style sheets to achieve greater typographic control

> "In a printed piece, or on the Web, attractive, well-executed typography adds elegance and improves communication. Poor typographic execution can seriously degrade otherwise inspired design."
>
> Paul Baker, *PBTWeb*

The most important thing to remember about typography on the Web is that advances are made at regular intervals. Keep up with the technology and you'll stay ahead of the pack when it comes to typographic applications in Web design.

APPROACHING WEB TYPOGRAPHY

Whether you're looking to use type in the conservative fashion as a method to deliver your Web-based, written content, or you'd like to be adventurous and use type as artistic design, the more methods you can use to approach Web typography, the better equipped you are to achieve your typographic goals.

> "Typography is becoming tribal, an initiation rite."
>
> Joe Clark, writings from Typo Expo 1996

I personally believe that type should do both—serve its function *and* be used artistically. The Web is a perfect opportunity to experiment. Obviously, when your client and audience want you to manage text, you're going to be somewhat reined in by convention. But there are times when you will have the opportunity or want to create more cutting-edge designs.

Type can help you do this.

Again, Web typography can currently be approached with some stability through three vehicles: graphics, HTML, and cascading style sheets.

Part ii

Graphics and Type

In many ways, putting type on a Web site as a graphic is currently the most stable method of ensuring that your type design will be seen. Visitors don't have to have the font installed—they are seeing the font as part of a graphic. This gives you lots of control because not only can you select from any typeface you own, but you can color it to your tastes and add special effects, too.

Of course, the downside is the time that graphics take to download. Where you use graphics to handle the majority of your type, you'll need to take care to balance the typographic elements with the graphics necessary for your individual pages.

Here are a few tips to help you when working with type as a graphic:

▶ Select flat colors from the browser-safe palette to ensure the smallest file size even if you're using large type.

▶ Save flat-color, simple, graphic-based, typeset files as GIFs.

▶ If you add special effects such as shadows, gradient fills, and metallic color, or if you use 3-D type, try saving your files as GIFs and JPEGs in order to compare the results. You might find that in certain instances, JPEGs will serve you better, whereas in other cases, you will get smaller files and a terrific look from GIFs.

▶ In most cases, you will want to anti-alias your fonts as you set the type on the graphic (see Figure 4.1). However, anti-aliasing can become problematic when you want to set small type. It's especially wise to avoid anti-aliasing on any type that is less than 12 points, although you should experiment with both in order to get the best look (see Figure 4.2).

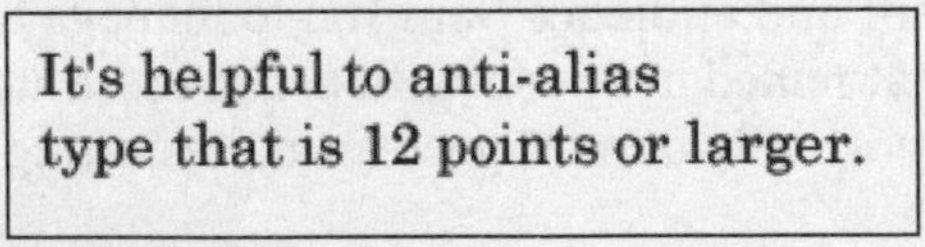

It's helpful to anti-alias
type that is 12 points or larger.

FIGURE 4.1:   Type that is 12 or more points should typically be anti-aliased.

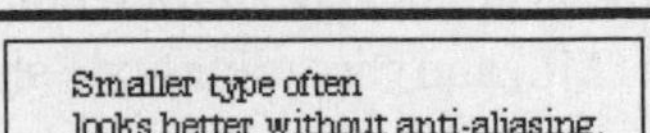

Smaller type often
looks better without anti-aliasing.

FIGURE 4.2:   Small type that is not anti-aliased looks fine.

Treat type-based graphics as you would any other graphic when coding. This means to be sure to use the appropriate tag and attributes, including width, height, alt, and any relevant alignment tags:

```
<img src="welcome.gif" width="300" height="100" alt="Welcome
to Our House" align="right">
```

Wherever possible, it's also a good idea to combine graphic-based type with type you create on the page. This way you lean less on the graphics to get your typographic point across.

HTML and Type

Aside from browser and individual user's font library support issues, the main problem with HTML type is that you can only use it along the horizontal. Also, you can't set it in specific points—you must rely on really poor sizing techniques. But you can still do some interesting things with HTML type.

HTML type is delivered primarily through the <font> tag. The only exception to this is the header tags <h1>...</h1> through <h6>...</h6>, which use a bold Times font to create a variety of headers ranging in size from large (size 1) to small (size 6). You'll want to use them now and then, but with so many other options, you might find them limiting as you work with different typefaces and sizes.

The Font Tag

The <font> tag has numerous considerations in terms of widespread compatibility, but it does help designers address type techniques through HTML. The <font> tag allows for a number of attributes, including face, size, and color.

The <font> tag follows standard HTML conventions, with an opening and closing tag enclosing the division of information to which you are applying the font attributes:

```
<font>
Love is a smoke raised with the fume of sighs;
Being purged, a fire sparkling in lovers' eyes;
Being vex'd a sea nourish'd with lovers' tears:
What is it else? a madness most discreet,
A choking gall and a preserving sweet.
</font>
```

Of course, nothing happens until you add relevant attributes, which I'll show you as we look at the use of typefaces, forms, and color further on in the chapter.

HTML CHARACTER ENTITIES

To make it easier to use unusual numeric, alphabetic, and symbolic characters, the HTML 4.0 specification is compliant with several standardized character sets. These include the ISO Latin-1 character set, mathematical symbols, Greek letters, and assorted other international and markup-significant character sets.

What Is the ISO Latin-1 Character Set?

The International Organization for Standardization (ISO) is the group in charge of managing international standards for everything from computer protocols to character sets. The ISO 8859-1 standard, which is more commonly known as the ISO Latin-1 character set, is the default character set used by HTML. The term *Latin* refers to the Roman alphabet, which is the basis of the world's Romance languages. The number 1 indicates that this particular character set is the first in the ISO Latin series.

Most of the symbols and special characters used in Web pages are found in this ISO Latin character set. Because this is HTML's default character set, you can use its numeric and character entities in your Web pages. If you need to use characters that are not in the ISO Latin series—for example, characters found in languages such as Russian and Hebrew—then you'll need to use Unicode.

So What's Unicode?

Unicode is the Web typographer's Swiss Army knife. Officially known as ISO 10646, Unicode is a way of defining special characters for use in HTML, SGML, and the newest metalanguage, XML. The ISO Latin-1 character set is a subset of Unicode, which comprises a huge collection of special characters that covers major languages from throughout the world. That's one big set. How does Unicode do it? It uses unique bit patterns for each character, which computers can recognize and display.

Because Unicode is so extensive (version 2.1 includes about 38,890 distinct, coded characters), it has been broken up into several subsets called UTFs, or Universal Transformation Formats.

CONTINUED ➡

HTML 4.0 supports only a selected portion of the Unicode character set. You can find a full list of what is supported at `http://www.w3.org/TR/REC-html40/sgml/entities.html`, or you can refer to the Master's Reference in the Appendix of this book. If you want to know the Unicode number for a certain character or which UTF you should use for a project, check out the Unicode Consortium's Web site at `http://www.unicode.org/`.

Random Cheats

Getting other typefaces to appear using HTML is a trick many designers use. The most popular of these is the preformatted text tag `<pre>`, which will force a monospaced (usually Courier) typeface:

```
<pre>
Love is a smoke raised with the fume of sighs;
Being purged, a fire sparkling in lovers' eyes;
Being vex'd a sea nourish'd with lovers' tears:
What is it else? a madness most discreet,
A choking gall and a preserving sweet.
</pre>
```

Figure 4.3 shows the results.

You can also use the `<tt>` tag for a monospaced font:

```
<tt>
Love is a smoke raised with the fume of sighs;
Being purged, a fire sparkling in lovers' eyes;
Being vex'd a sea nourish'd with lovers' tears:
What is it else? a madness most discreet,
A choking gall and a preserving sweet.
</tt>
```

The results will be the same as shown in Figure 4.3.

Part ii

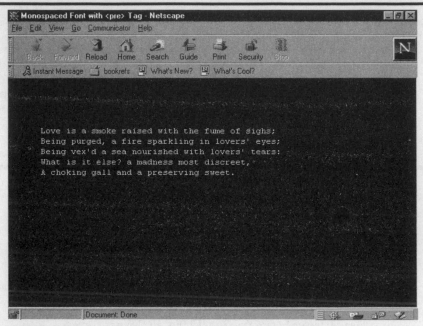

FIGURE 4.3: Using the `<pre>` tag will force a monospaced font.

Style Sheets and Type

In Chapter 1 we went over some elementary ideas regarding style sheets. Now we'll look at style sheets with a focus on how you will work with style sheet code to apply typography in the Web environment.

NOTE
To view style sheet information, you'll need a compatible browser. Individuals using Internet Explorer 3 and above or Netscape 4 or above will be able to see style sheets. Of course, if a particular typeface is called for and doesn't exist on your visitor's own machine, the type will not be seen in that face.

There are three primary ways to use style sheets. They are the *inline* method; the *embedded*, or individual page, method; and the *linked,* or external, method.

Inline Style Sheets

This approach exploits existing HTML tags within a standard HTML document and adds a specific style to the information controlled by that tag. An example would be controlling the indentation of a single paragraph using the `style="x"` attribute within the `<p>` tag. Another method of achieving this is combining the `<span>` tag and the `style="x"` attribute.

Here is an inline style example:

```
<span style="font: 14pt garamond">
Love is a smoke raised with the fume of sighs;
Being purged, a fire sparkling in lovers' eyes;
Being vex'd a sea nourish'd with lovers' tears:
What is it else? a madness most discreet,
A choking gall and a preserving sweet.
</span>
```

You could do the same thing with the paragraph tag:

```
<p style="font: 14pt garamond">
Love is a smoke raised with the fume of sighs;
Being purged, a fire sparkling in lovers' eyes;
Being vex'd a sea nourish'd with lovers' tears:
What is it else? a madness most discreet,
A choking gall and a preserving sweet.
</p>
```

Embedded Style Sheets

This method allows for the control of individual pages. It uses the `<style>` tag, along with its companion tag, `</style>`. This information is placed between the `<html>` tag and the `<body>` tag, with the style attributes inserted within the full `<style>` container. A short example follows:

```
<style>
P { font-family: arial, helvetica, sans-serif; }
</style
```

Linked Style Sheets

All that is required for linked style sheets is to create a style sheet file with the master styles you would like to express, using the same syntax you would with embedded style, as follows:

```
<style>
P { font-family: arial, helvetica, sans-serif; }
</style
```

Save the file using the `.css` extension—for example, the file `paragraph.css`. Then simply be sure that all of the HTML documents that will require those controls are *linked* to that document.

Within the `<head>` tag of any document you'd like to have adopt the style you've just created, insert the following syntax (keep in mind that the reference will have your own location and filename):

```
<link rel="stylesheet" href="paragraph.css" type="text/css">
```

Style Sheet Syntax

With embedded and linked style sheets, the attribute syntax is somewhat different from standard HTML syntax. First, attributes are placed within curly brackets; second, where HTML would place an equal (=) sign, a colon (:) is used; and third, individual, stacked arguments are separated by a semicolon rather than a comma. Also, several attributes are hyphenated, such as `font-style` and `line-height`. A simple style sheet line looks like this:

```
{ font-style: arial, helvetica; }
```

As with HTML, style sheets tend to be quite logical and easy to understand.

TIP

The `<div>` (division) tag can be used like the `<span>` tag for inline control. The `<div>` tag is especially helpful for longer blocks of text, whereas `<span>` is most effective for adding style to smaller stretches of information, such as sentences, several words, or even individual letters within a word.

In a sense, the inline method of style sheet control defeats the ultimate purpose of cascading style sheets. The main point of the technology is to seek style control of entire pages or even entire sets of pages. The inline method should only be used where touches of style are required.

FAMILIES AND FACES

The ability to use type families and faces can empower Web designers, because they can use those faces to fully express the emotion within the design being created. Limitations aside, we'll look at how typefaces and families can be used with graphics, HTML, and cascading style sheets.

Typefaces and Graphics

The most important thing to remember is selecting the typefaces you want to use for your body and header text *before* sitting down to set your type. Once you've determined what typefaces you'll be using, and you know the literal content of the graphic to be designed, the issue boils down to the tool you're going to use to set the type.

Most designers agree that to work with type, the ideal combination is Illustrator and Photoshop. Illustrator allows for a lot of control over the type you're setting, including kerning, which isn't available in Photoshop. Once you've set your type in Illustrator, you can then add your effects in Photoshop. The process is a bit time-consuming, however, and many Web designers have learned to be very creative using Photoshop alone.

Many designers who use Photoshop alone to set type are perfectly happy doing so. With the exception of kerning, most say they can achieve what they are after with what is available in Photoshop.

In Figure 4.4, you can see that the Photoshop type tool is open and that text is about to be set at 16-point, 16 line-spacing, anti-aliased, OzHandicraft typeface. Figure 4.5 shows the results.

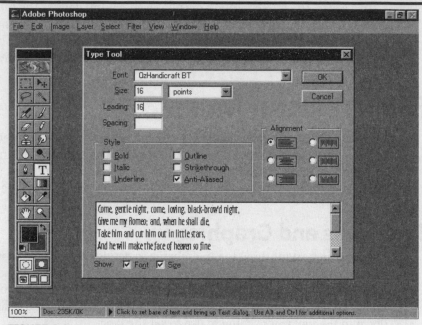

FIGURE 4.4:   Using the type tool in Photoshop

> Come, gentle night, come, loving, black-brow'd night,
> Give me my Romeo; and, when he shall die,
> Take him and cut him out in little stars,
> And he will make the face of heaven so fine
> That all the world will be in love with night
> And pay no worship to the garish sun.

FIGURE 4.5:   The type is set.

Typefaces, Families, and the Font Tag

With the HTML `<font>` tag, you can select any typeface that you like and use it in the face attribute. Again, the limitation is that you will run into a problem with who has what on any given machine.

There is really only a total of three type families and specific, related typefaces that you can be almost absolutely sure will show up across platforms and on individual machines.

On the PC, the forms are serif, sans serif, and monospaced. The specific faces are Times New Roman, Courier New, and Arial, respectively.

Macintosh offers the same three forms, with Times, Courier, and Helvetica, replacing Arial.

What does this mean to you as a designer? It's simple. The face attribute of the <font> tag has one rather intelligent aspect: you can stack any number of typefaces with a type family and hopefully end up covering your bases.

After tagging the section of text to which you'd like to apply font styles, you add the face attribute and then define the font names. The browser will look for the first font name called for and, if it doesn't find it, will move on to the next named font:

```
<font face="arial,helvetica">This text will appear as Arial
or Helvetica, depending upon which font is available</font>
```

If you'd like to add some stability to this syntax, you can add the family name at the end of the stack:

```
<font face="arial,helvetica,sans-serif">This text will appear
as Arial or Helvetica or the default sans-serif font, depend-
ing upon which font is available</font>
```

It's important to remember that if a font face isn't available on a given machine, the default face will appear. Default is almost always a serif font such as Times, unless the user has selected another font for his or her default. So if you're mixing fonts, bear in mind that your sans serifs might appear as serifs, and vice versa.

This lack of control can seem maddening! You can always forgo using type, but then you run the risk of having your pages appear ho-hum. Go for fonts, but do so thoughtfully, and wherever possible, stack the fonts along with a family name.

Style Sheets

Using a typeface family as a default is an excellent idea all around, as it covers the designer's font choices as completely as possible. Even if a specific font face is unavailable on a given computer, it's likely that a similar one in that font's family is available. An aware designer will place the first choice first, second choice second, and so forth, with the family name at the end.

You can approach fonts in style sheets using the font-family string. Style sheets will accept these in all three types of style sheets: inline, embedded, and linked.

An inline example (see Figure 4.6) follows:

```
<span style="font-family:garamond,times,serif">
Love is a smoke raised with the fume of sighs;
Being purged, a fire sparkling in lovers' eyes;
Being vex'd a sea nourish'd with lovers' tears:
What is it else? a madness most discreet,
A choking gall and a preserving sweet.
</span>
```

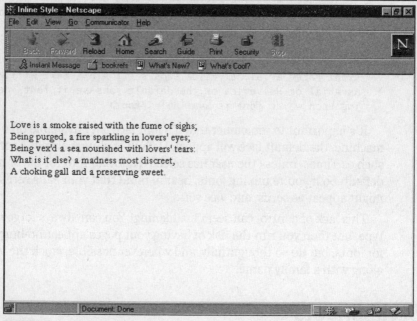

FIGURE 4.6: The results of an inline application of style

Since inline style can be used with any reasonable HTML tag, you could also do this:

```
<blockquote style="font-family:garamond,times,serif">
Love is a smoke raised with the fume of sighs;
Being purged, a fire sparkling in lovers' eyes;
```

```
Being vex'd a sea nourish'd with lovers' tears:
What is it else? a madness most discreet,
A choking gall and a preserving sweet.
</blockquote>
```

The result is that the browser picks up not only the style sheet information, but the HTML `blockquote` format as well (see Figure 4.7).

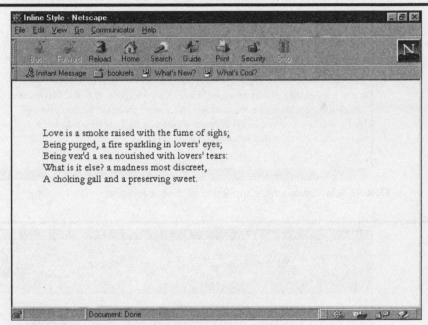

FIGURE 4.7:   Using inline style with the blockquote tag

Here's an embedded example of the same concept (linked style will also look like this). Let's say you wanted to apply a series of typefaces and a family to an entire paragraph. The syntax would be:

```
P { font-family: arial, helvetica, sans-serif; }
```

In Figure 4.8, you can see that Garamond appears in all the paragraphs on the page.

You can apply this style to the blockquote as well:

```
blockquote { font-family: arial, helvetica, sans-serif; }
```

Figure 4.9 shows the blockquoted section.

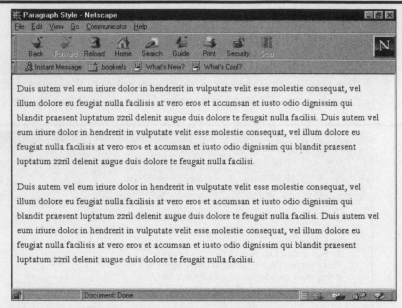

FIGURE 4.8: Garamond is applied to all the paragraphs.

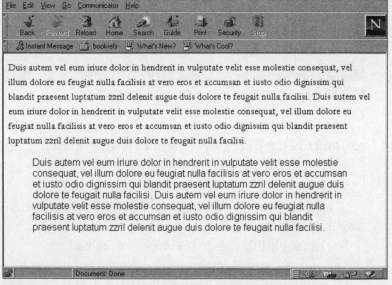

FIGURE 4.9: In this instance, the embedded style controls the appearance of all the blockquoted material.

Font Family Support

There are specific families supported by style sheets, as follows.

Serif   Serif typefaces are usually the best choice for body text. In addition to Times and Garamond, a popular serif typeface is Century Schoolbook. Let's say you want to have that appear first, but if someone doesn't have that font on their machine, you'd prefer that the computer search for Garamond rather than move right away to Times. You can see the syntax below. The results can be seen in Figure 4.10.

```
{ font-family: century schoolbook, garamond, times, serif; }
```

FIGURE 4.10: My browser shows the Century Schoolbook typeface, because I have that font.

Sans serif   This font family includes popular choices such as Arial, Helvetica, and Avante Garde. The same concept applies here, of course:

```
{ font-family: arial, helvetica, avante garde, sans-serif; }
```

ONLINE

Try this one on your own with a style sheet–compatible browser. What are your results? Do you see Arial, Helvetica, Avante Garde, or a default sans serif font?

Cursive   Use this in place of *script*. These are the same as script typefaces—fonts that appear as though they have been handwritten. Figure 4.11 shows the results.

```
{ font-family: embassy, cursive; }
```

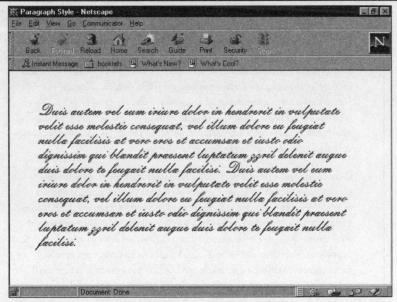

FIGURE 4.11:   This typeface results from embedded style.

Fantasy   Fantasy fonts are used for *decorative* type, such as stylish, fun headings and titles. They are not practical for body text. You can see the Whimsy typeface in Figure 4.12.

```
{ font-family: whimsy icg, fantasy; }
```

Monospace   As with serif and sans serif options, you're familiar with the monospaced font. Figure 4.13 looks like the text was typed onto a page.

```
{ font-family: courier, monospace; }
```

Does anyone *still* use a typewriter?

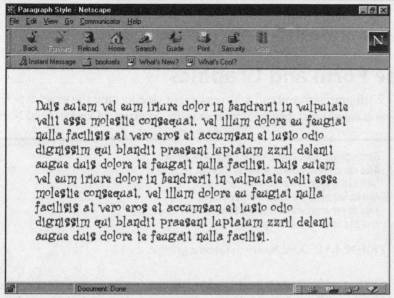

FIGURE 4.12:   Here you see the Whimsy typeface.

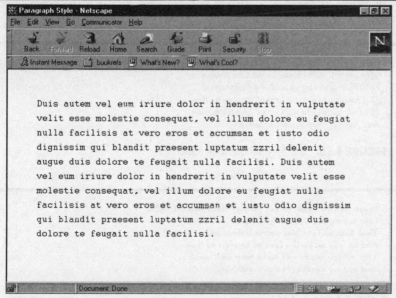

FIGURE 4.13:   Using style again, you can ensure a monospaced (in this case Courier) typeface.

TYPE FORM

In the world of typographic design, form refers to such concerns as weight and posture.

Type Form and Graphics

With graphics, you can address weight by choosing the exact typeface and weight you desire for your graphic. Figure 4.14 shows Arial Narrow.

Come, gentle night, come, loving, black-brow'd night,
Give me my Romeo; and, when he shall die,
Take him and cut him out in little stars,
And he will make the face of heaven so fine
That all the world will be in love with night
And pay no worship to the garish sun.

FIGURE 4.14:   Arial Narrow is set on a graphic.

Posture is also dealt with when choosing the typeface. If you select the italic or oblique form of the typeface, you end up with that typeface. Figure 4.15 shows Century Schoolbook italicized. I love the look of this font in italics—it's very evocative of handwriting. Figure 4.16 shows a bold weight Bodoni typeface.

Come, gentle night, come, loving, black-brow'd night,
Give me my Romeo; and, when he shall die,
Take him and cut him out in little stars,
And he will make the face of heaven so fine
That all the world will be in love with night
And pay no worship to the garish sun.

FIGURE 4.15:   Century Schoolbook italicized

Come, gentle night, come, loving, black-brow'd night,
Give me my Romeo; and, when he shall die,
Take him and cut him out in little stars,
And he will make the face of heaven so fine
That all the world will be in love with night
And pay no worship to the garish sun.

FIGURE 4.16:   Bold Bodoni

Type Form and HTML

Standard HTML is more difficult when it comes to weight because you are dependent upon the end user's library of fonts. If that user does not have the light, narrow, bold, demi-bold, or other weight you specify in the `face` attribute of the `<font>` tag, you're going to be out of luck. One thing you can do is stack the weight that you'd prefer with the typeface itself, and in some cases your font will be seen (see Figure 4.17).

```
<font face="arial narrow, arial, helvetica, sans-serif">
Love is a smoke raised with the fume of sighs;
Being purged, a fire sparkling in lovers' eyes;
Being vex'd a sea nourish'd with lovers' tears:
What is it else? a madness most discreet,
A choking gall and a preserving sweet.
</font>
```

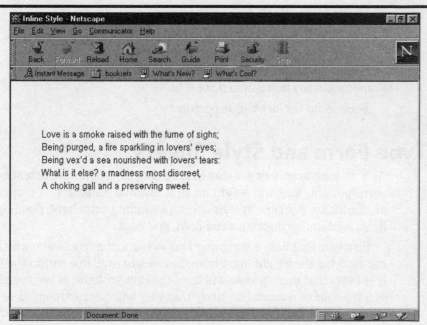

FIGURE 4.17: Using the `<font>` tag to achieve Arial Narrow

Italics are easily created with the italic tag, `<i>...</i>`. Any text between opening and closing italic tags will appear in the italic version of that typeface, provided that the individual has the means of viewing the italic version.

```
<font face="arial narrow, arial, helvetica, sans-serif">
Love is a smoke raised with the fume of sighs;
Being purged, a fire sparkling in lovers' eyes;
Being vex'd a sea nourish'd with lovers' tears:
What is it else? a <i>madness</i> most discreet,
A choking gall and a preserving sweet.
</font>
```

Similarly, bold can be created with the bold tag, `<b>...</b>`.

```
<font face="arial narrow, arial, helvetica, sans-serif">
Love is a smoke raised with the fume of sighs;
Being purged, a fire sparkling in lovers' eyes;
Being vex'd a sea nourish'd with lovers' tears:
What is it else? a <b>madness</b> most discreet,
A choking gall and a preserving sweet.
</font>
```

Hopefully, Shakespeare will forgive me for forcing emphasis on Romeo's already impassioned speech!

There is no tag for oblique postures.

Type Form and Style Sheets

As with font faces, font weights in style sheets rely on the existence of the corresponding font and weight on an individual's machine. A range of attributes are available in style sheets, including extra-light, demi-light, light, medium, extra-bold, demi-bold, and bold.

Be aware that before assigning font weights, the typeface to which you are applying the weight must have that weight available within the face. It is likely that many people will have the Roman, light, or bold versions of a typeface; it is much less likely that they will have extra-lights or demi-bolds—unless they have an extensive font collection on their computer.

A light weight is assigned to the Arial font in Figure 4.18, and a bold weight to the Walbaum font in Figure 4.19.

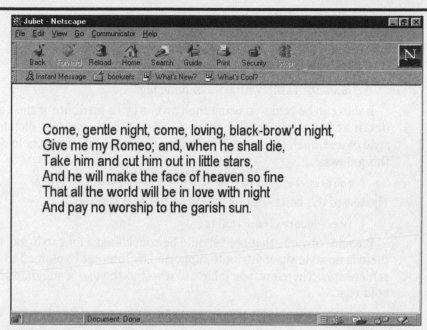

FIGURE 4.18:   Arial Narrow is achieved with style.

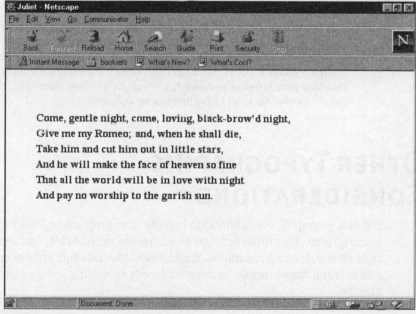

FIGURE 4.19:   Bold gives weight to Walbaum.

To achieve posture, you'll rely on three methods:

▸ `font-style` attribute

▸ `text-decoration` attribute

▸ standard HTML with bold or italic tags

Italics can be achieved using the `font-style` attribute or the `text-decoration` attribute. The `font-style` attribute typically dictates the style of text, such as placing it in italics. The appropriate syntax to do this follows:

```
{ font-style: italic; }
```

The use of the `text-decoration` attribute is similar:

```
{ text-decoration: italic; }
```

It seems obvious that bold should be considered a font style too, but there is no style sheet attribute supported by Internet Explorer 3 to achieve this. Therefore, you'll have to revert to the use of standard HTML bold tags.

```
<b>This text will appear in bold,</b> whereas this text will
not.
```

TIP

Dislike underlined links? With cascading style sheets, designers can now use the `{text-decoration: none}` attribute and argue to globally shut off underlined links. In embedded and linked style sheet formats, the syntax would follow the A value: `A {text-decoration: none}`. For inline style, simply place the value within the link you wish to control: `<a style="text-decoration: none" href="my.html">`this link has no underline!`</a>`.

OTHER TYPOGRAPHIC CONSIDERATIONS

Other typographic considerations include size, proportion, leading, and kerning. Size and proportion can be addressed with HTML and cascading style sheets, leading is somewhat addressed by cascading style sheets, and kerning can currently be dealt with only by setting the type on a graphic.

Using Graphics

Because you can address almost any kind of typographic issue by using Illustrator, whose interface is shown in Figure 4.20, and Photoshop to set the type onto a graphic, graphics give the most flexibility when you're attempting typographic concerns that cannot be dealt with using HTML or style sheets.

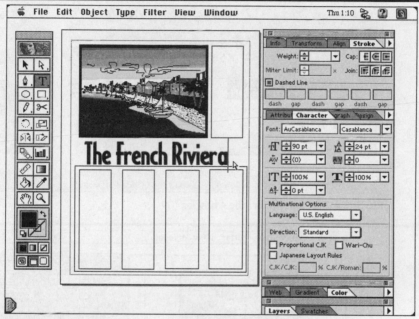

FIGURE 4.20: Brainbug's Michelle Carrier sets her type in Illustrator.

Size and proportion depend on your own design and aesthetic. Using points, you can set type as small or as large as you want. Direction can also be managed; Figure 4.21 shows a vertical header. Leading is addressed within the programs, as is letterspacing and kerning (see Figure 4.22).

NOTE

Kerning can currently be achieved on the Web by first setting the type in a program such as Illustrator and then saving it as a Web graphic using Photoshop. There is no HTML or style sheet–based method to deal with kerning.

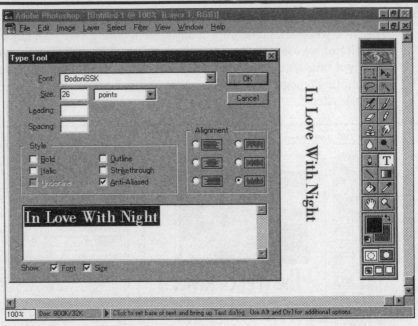

FIGURE 4.21: Setting a vertical header

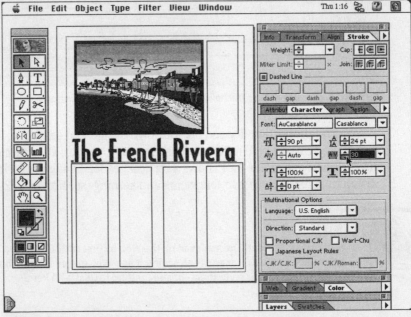

FIGURE 4.22: Using Illustrator for kerning

Type Size and HTML

The size attribute of the <font> tag allows you to set type based on a numeric system. Unfortunately, this system does not allow a designer to control type size using points. Furthermore, direction, leading, spacing, and kerning cannot be controlled with standard HTML.

Using the Size Attribute

Font sizing in HTML is pretty rudimentary, with whole-number values determining the size of the font. Default, standard size is 3; anything higher is going to be larger, and anything lower will be smaller. You can also use negative numbers, such as -1, to get a very small type size. Here's an example of a header using font face and size:

```
<font face="times,garamond,serif" size="5">
```

Anything much bigger than size 5 is ungainly. Small fonts, such as size 1, are good for notes and copyrights. Anything less is usually not viewable to people with average-to-poor eyesight.

Figure 4.23 shows an example with a header, body text, and a copyright notice, each in a different-sized font. Note the typefaces being used. The header and copyright notice appear in Times, and the body in Arial. This page looks nice and neat, unlike Figure 4.24, which shows what happens when a coder runs amok. The "wave" effect came into vogue when font sizing first became available.

Some designers will argue that Figure 4.24 looks more interesting. They're right—it does, and I certainly don't want to discourage creativity. This particular effect was fun, but it quickly became cliché. I encourage you to study typography a little more closely and come up with original typographic applications.

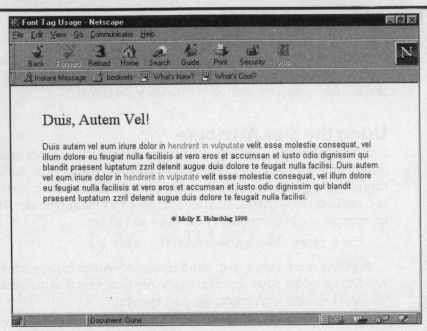

FIGURE 4.23: Using the <font> tag for page design

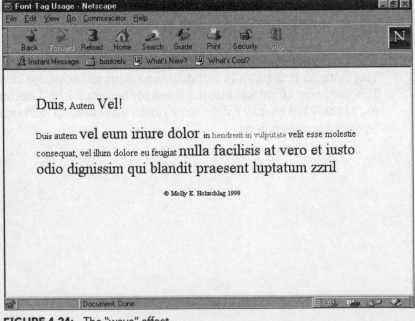

FIGURE 4.24: The "wave" effect

Style Sheets

Style sheets to the rescue! Size (with choice of measurement units) and leading can be applied using style sheets. Kerning is not an option in Web typography unless you set the type as a graphic.

Size

Sizing in style sheets gives designers five size options for their fonts:

Points   To set a font in point size, use the abbreviation pt immediately following the numeric size:

{font-size: 12pt}

Inches   If you'd rather set your fonts in inches, simply place the abbreviation in next to the numeral size, in inches, of the font size you require:

{font-size: 1in}

Centimeters   Some designers might prefer centimeters, represented by cm and used in the same fashion as points and inches:

{font-size: 5cm}

Pixels   Pixels are argued with the px abbreviation:

{font-size: 24px}

Percentage   You also may choose to set a percentage of the default point size:

{font-size: 50%}

NOTE

Point size is often the most comfortable choice for designers, although some will want to work with other methods. I recommend using point size, but if you do choose another method, *be consistent*. Your work will look much more professional as a result.

Leading

Leading is addressed in cascading style sheets with line-height. This refers to the amount of spacing between lines of text. This space should be consistent, or the result is uneven, unattractive spacing. The line-height attribute allows designers to set the distance between the baselines, or bottom, of lines of text.

To set the leading of a paragraph, use the line-height attribute in points, inches, centimeters, pixels, or percentages in the same fashion you would when describing sizing attributes:

```
P { line-height: 14pt; }
```

COLOR AND TYPE

Color adds interest to type. You can use contrasting colors to gain a variety of effects. You can emphasize certain passages or parts of a word, as in Figure 4.25, or use colored type to separate headers from body text.

COLORMY**WORLD**

FIGURE 4.25: Emphasizing type with color

Creating Colored Type with Graphics

Again, graphics are your best bet when you really want to address color effects.

A helpful tip is to select your colors from the safe palette and to be sure to always optimize your graphics appropriately. This will give you the best chances of having smaller file sizes and better matches between HTML and graphic colors.

 NOTE
You'll read more about the safe palette in Chapter 5, "Achieving High-End Color."

HTML-Based Type and Color

The color attribute allows you to set any hexadecimal value you'd like when using the <font> tag. As always, stick to safe-palette values. An example of the <font> tag with the color attribute added looks like this:

```
<font face="times,garamond,serif" size="5" color="#003300">
```

Use hexadecimal code to select a color; the one that you see listed here is forest green. Some people and certain HTML editing programs will use the literal name of standard colors, such as blue, green, red, and the like. The hexadecimal codes, however, are much more stable in cross-browser, cross-platform environments.

ONLINE

Hexadecimal color references:

- A chart of RGB and hexadecimal values can be found at `http://sdc.htrigg.smu.edu/HTMLPages/RGBchart.html`.

- Download the `nvalue.gif` or `nhue.gif` charts from Lynda Weinman's site: `http://www.lynda.com/files/`.

These charts put color selection and hexadecimal values right at your fingertips!

Style Sheets and Color

Style sheets allow for a great deal of flexibility when it comes to the addition of color. Using hexadecimal codes, color can be added to actual attributes, including other HTML tags used in the inline style sheet method:

```
<p style="color: #003300">
All of the text in this paragraph will appear in forest
green.
</p>
```

With embedded and linked style sheets, you can add the `color` attribute to generalized, rather than specific, sections. In the following example, all level-two headers appear in red. Note that other attributes have been added here, including typeface, size, and style.

```
<style>
H2 {font-family: arial, helvetica; sans-serif;
font-size: 14pt;
font-style: italic;
color: #FF0033;}
</style>
```

ALL TOGETHER NOW

So far you've gotten a look at fragmented pieces of graphics, fonts, and styles. Here are full examples of each, in text and code.

Graphic Example

In this case, we'll use another quote from *Romeo and Juliet* and set it using 20-point Trebuchet (a font available from Microsoft at http://www.microsoft.com/typography/) with 20-point leading. The type is colored white and applied to a flat black background. Then a star motif is added to the background; the file is saved as a 5-bit GIF suitable for use as a background graphic.

Here's the simple HTML code to create the page:

```html
<html>


<head>
<title>Juliet Speaks</title>
</head>

<body bgcolor="#000000" text="#FFFFFF" link="#00FF00"
vlink="#FF0000" background="juliet2.gif">
<pre>

</pre>
<div align="center">
<a href="next.htm"><i>next</i></a>
</div>
</body>
</html>
```

NOTE

There are 20 carriage returns between the <pre> tags, forcing the link to the bottom of the page.

You can see the results in Figure 4.26. Although a background graphic was used in this example, remember that you can set type on a graphic to be used anywhere on the page. You can place a graphic as a header, as body text, or as a part of body text and fix placement using tables (or style sheet positioning).

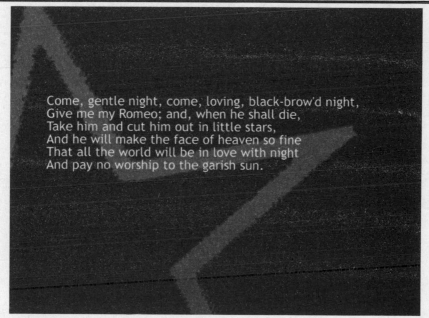

FIGURE 4.26: Graphic-based type design

Figure 4.27 is a screen capture from NextDada (`http://nextdada.luc.ac.be/`), one of Belgian graphic designer Joël Neelen's Web sites. On this page, he has stacked a series of graphics on top of one another to achieve his typographic design. Add to that some clever JavaScript and the page is alive with visual intrigue founded on its graphic-based typographic elements.

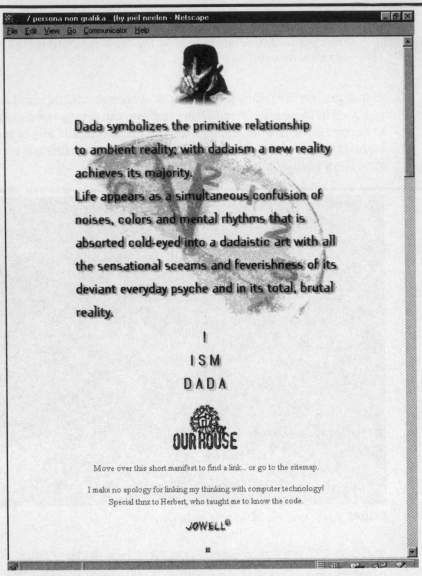

FIGURE 4.27:   Graphic-based typography in action on the NextDada site

Here's a look at Neelen's code.

```
<html>
<head>
    <!- Author: Joel Neelen ->
    <!- e-mail: jneelen@luc.ac.be ->
<title>. . / persona non grafika . (by jo&euml;l
neelen</title>
<meta name="description" content="The cyberplatform of Joel
Neelen aka {captain verruckt}">
<meta name="keywords" content="dada, nextdada, joel, neelen,
travel, travelling, kite, kiting, cerf-volant, art, graphics,
jemen, yemen, jordan, jordanie">
<meta name="author" content="Joel Neelen :
jneelen@luc.ac.be">


<script language="JavaScript">


<!- if the browser is not capable to JavaScript1.1 he will
use this and do nothing
function init()
{
 dummy=0;
}
function imgreplace(i,s,text)
{
 window.status = text;
 return true;
}
// end do nothing ->


</script>
<script language="JavaScript1.1">
```

```
<!- to hide script contents from old browsers
function init()
{ // set the 7 images to be non-highlighted
document.sexstacy.src = "/picture/dada/dada1_1.gif"
document.castle.src = "/picture/dada/dada2_1.gif"
document.old.src = "/picture/dada/dada4_1.gif"
document.travel.src = "/picture/dada/dada5_1.gif"
document.art.src = "/picture/dada/dada6_1.gif"
document.kites.src = "/picture/dada/dada7_1.gif"
document.cinema.src = "/picture/dada/dada8_1.gif"
}
function imgreplace( imagename, source, text )
{
 eval( 'document.' + imagename + '.src = "/picture/dada/" +
source' );
 setTimeout( 'window.status = "'+text+'"', 500 );
 return true;
}
// end hide contents from old browsers ->

</script>

</head>
<body onload="init();" bgcolor="#FFFFFF" text="#7297FF"
link="#7297FF" vlink="#F77307" alink="#F77307">

<center>
<table height="100%" width="420" cellspacing="0" cell-
padding="2" border="0">
<tr align="center">
<td align="center">
```

```
<a href="root/kaffee.html"
onmouseover="self.status='Something about the man behind this
web site.' ; return true">
<img src="picture/dada/dada0.gif" width="107" height="100"
border="0" alt="Joel"></a>
</td>
</tr>


<tr align="center">
<td align="center">
<a href="root/sex/sexstacy.html" onmouseover="return
imgreplace('sexstacy','dada1_2.gif','Monogamy is the
message!');" onmouseout="return
imgreplace('sexstacy','dada1_1.gif','');return true;"><img
lowsrc="picture/dada/dada1_0.gif"
src="picture/dada/dada1_2.gif" width="420" height="36"
border="0" name="sexstacy" alt="sexstacy"></a>
<br>


<a href="root/castle.html" onmouseover="return
imgreplace('castle','dada2_2.gif','The purpose could be to
create a virtual community where people can have fun and
learn things.');" onmouseout="return
imgreplace('castle','dada2_1.gif','');return true;"><img
lowsrc="picture/dada/dada2_0.gif"
src="picture/dada/dada2_2.gif" width="420" height="36"
border="0" name="castle" alt="castle"></a>
<br>


<img lowsrc="picture/dada/dada3_0.gif"
src="picture/dada/dada3_1.gif" width="420" height="36"
border="0" alt="nothing">
<br>


<a href="root/index.html" onmouseover="return
imgreplace('old','dada4_2.gif','This link will bring you to
my old homepage.');" onmouseout="return
```

```
imgreplace('old','dada4_1.gif','');return true;"><img
lowsrc="picture/dada/dada4_0.gif"
src="picture/dada/dada4_2.gif" width="420" height="36"
border="0" name="old" alt="old homepage"></a>

<br>


<a href="root/travel/travel.html" onmouseover="return
imgreplace('travel','dada5_2.gif','Explore different cultural
lifestyles and backgrounds...');" onmouseout="return
imgreplace('travel','dada5_1.gif','');return true;"><img
lowsrc="picture/dada/dada5_0.gif"
src="picture/dada/dada5_2.gif" width="420" height="36"
border="0" name="travel" alt="travel"></a>

<br>


<a href="root/art/artefact.html" onmouseover="return
imgreplace('art','dada6_2.gif','Dadaism, for one thing, no
longer stands aside from life as an aesthetic manner...');"
onmouseout="return imgreplace('art','dada6_1.gif','');return
true;"><img lowsrc="picture/dada/dada6_0.gif"
src="picture/dada/dada6_2.gif" width="420" height="36"
border="0" name="art" alt="art"></a>

<br>


<a href="root/kites.html" onmouseover="return
imgreplace('kites','dada7_2.gif','A kite is a thing on the
end of a string!');" onmouseout="return
imgreplace('kites','dada7_1.gif','');return true;"><img
lowsrc="picture/ dada/dada7_0.gif"
src="picture/dada/dada7_2.gif" width="420" height="36"
border="0" name="kites" alt="kites"></a>

<br>


<a href="root/cinema.cgi" onmouseover="return
imgreplace('cinema','dada8_2.gif','I felt an icy hand of fear
grabbing me.');" onmouseout="return
imgreplace('cinema','dada8_1.gif','');return true;"><img
lowsrc="picture/ dada/dada8_0.gif"
src="picture/dada/dada8_2.gif" width="420" height="72"
border="0" name="cinema" alt="cinema"></a>
```

```
</td>
</tr>


<tr>
<td align=center>
        <!- On reload this image will automatically change ->


<img src="picture/dada/dada3.gif" width=107 height=100
border=0 alt="D A D A">


        <!- End on reload ->
<br>
        <!- Start link to OUR HOUSE 1997 ->


<a href="http://www.ourhouse.be/"
onmouseover="self.status='Get a glimpse of the multi-
happening Our House that took place in September1997' ;
return true" target="_blank"><img src="picture/dada/
ourhouse.gif" width="107" height="100" border="0" alt="Our
House 1997"></a>


        <!- End link ->


<br>
<font size="-1">Move over this short manifest to find a
link... or go to the <a href="root/sitemap.html"
onmouseover="self.status='SiteMap.' ; return
true">sitemap</a>.
<p>
I make no apology for linking my thinking with computer
technology!</font>
<br>
```

```
<font size="-1" color="#789DB9">Special thnx to Herbert, who
taught me to know the code.</font>
<p>

<a href="root/mail.html" onmouseover="self.status='You can
send me an e-mail.' ; return true"><img
lowsrc="picture/dada/jowell_0.gif" src="picture/dada/jow-
ell_1.gif" width=80 height=21 border=0 alt="JOWELL"></a>
<p>

<a href="http://www.nedstat.nl/cgi-
bin/viewstat?name=nextcount" target="_blank"><img
src="http://www.nedstat.nl/cgi-
bin/nedstat.gif?name=nextcount" border="0" alt="" width="8"
height="8"></a>

</td>
</tr>
</table>

</center>
</body>
</html>
```

Note the use of meta tags, comment tags, table layout, and alt attributes. Neelen, like many Web designers concerned about the thoroughness of their work, takes special care not only with his typographic design but also with the underlying code elements that make a site accessible, stable, and professional.

HTML Example

This example demonstrates the use of the font tag and its attributes. I want you first to look at the page, which is shown in Figure 4.28.

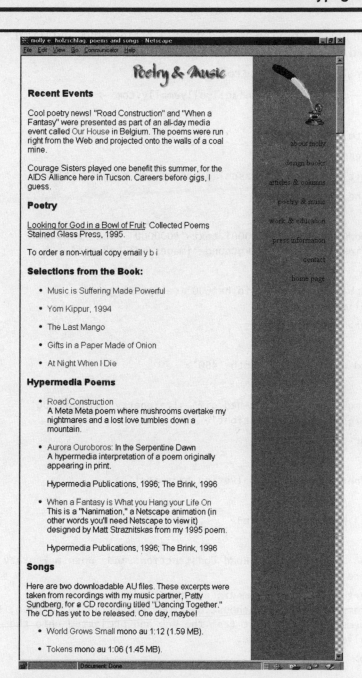

FIGURE 4.28: The Poetry and Music page from molly.com

Then predetermine all of the different fonts (graphics and HTML included) on the page *just by looking*. Make a list of those fonts.

Now study the following code:

```
<!- molly e. holzschlag: molly@molly.com ->


<html>
<head>
<title>molly e. holzschlag: poems and songs</title>
</head>


<body bgcolor="#000000" text="#000000" link="#993300"
vlink="#993300" background="images/mol-bak.gif">


<table border="0" width="600" cellpadding="5"
cellspacing="0">
<tr>


<td valign="top" width="400">


<img src="images/pm-hed.gif" alt="poetry" width="300"
height="50" align="right">
<br clear="all">


<font face="arial,helvetica,sans-serif">


<h3>Recent Events</h3>


Cool poetry news! "Road Construction" and "When a Fantasy"
were presented as
part of an all-day media event called <a
href="http://www.ourhouse.be/">Our House</a> in Belgium. The
poems were run right from the Web and projected onto the
walls of a coal mine.
<p>
```

Courage Sisters played one benefit this summer, for the AIDS
Alliance here in Tucson. Careers before gigs, I guess.
<p>

<h3>Poetry</h3>

<u>Looking for God in a Bowl of Fruit</u>: Collected Poems

Stained Glass Press, 1995.
<p>

To order a non-virtual copy email <a
href="mailto:ybi@ybi.com">y b i</a>
<p>

<h3>Selections from the Book:</h3>

<ul>

<li><a href="p-1.htm">Music is Suffering Made Powerful</a>
<p>

<li><a href="p-2.htm">Yom Kippur, 1994 </a>
<p>

<li><a href="p-3.htm">The Last Mango</a>
<p>

<li><a href="p-4.htm">Gifts in a Paper Made of Onion</a>
<p>

<li><a href="p-5.htm">At Night When I Die</a>

</ul>

```
<p>

<h3>Hypermedia Poems</h3>

<ul>

<li><a href="http://ybi.com/molly/rc/">Road Construction</a>
<br>
```

A Meta Meta poem where mushrooms overtake my nightmares and a lost love tumbles down a mountain.

```
<p>

<li><a href="http://ybi.com/aurora/">Aurora Ouroboros</a>: In
the Serpentine Dawn
<br>
```

A hypermedia interpretation of a poem originally appearing in print.

```
<p>
```

Hypermedia Publications, 1996; The Brink, 1996

```
<p>

<li><a href="http://ybi.com/poetry/fant.html">When a Fantasy
is What you Hang your Life On</a>
<br>
```

This is a "Nanimation," a Netscape animation (in other words you'll need Netscape to view it) designed by Matt Straznitskas from my 1995 poem.

```
<p>
```

Hypermedia Publications, 1996; The Brink, 1996

```
</ul>
```

```
<p>

<h3>Songs</h3>

Here are two downloadable AU files. These excerpts were taken
from recordings with my music partner, Patty Sundberg, for a
CD recording titled "Dancing Together." The CD has yet to be
released. One day, maybe!
<p>

<ul>

<li><a href="images/wrldgrow.au">World Grows Small</a> mono
au 1:12 (1.59 MB).
<p>

<li><a href="images/tokens.au">Tokens</a> mono au 1:06 (1.45
MB).

</ul>

</font>

</td>

<td valign="top" align="right" width="200">

<img src="images/poetry.gif" width="108" height="125"
border="0" alt="pen and ink">
<p>

<a href="molly.htm">about molly</a>
<p>

<a href="books.htm">design books</a>
<p>
```

```
<a href="write.htm">articles & columns</a>
<p>


<a href="poems.htm">poetry & music</a>
<p>


<a href="work.htm">work & education</a>
<p>


<a href="press.htm">press information</a>
<p>


<a href="contact.htm">contact</a>
<p>


<a href="index.html">home page</a>


</td>
</tr>
</table>


</body>
</html>
```

If you guessed three for the total number of fonts used on this page, you're correct. First there's the header graphic, which uses the Bergell typeface. Then there's the body text, which will appear as Arial, Helvetica, or whatever sans serif font you have available if those are not.

Finally, there's the type I've used in the right-margin menu. Sharp readers will have noticed that *there is no font tag or attributes* used to create this font. Why?

Think about it for a second.

Can you identify the typeface?

It's a serif.

Specifically, it's Times.

Remember now? Serifs are the *default* font. Therefore, I didn't have to code for it.

OFFLINE

Have some fun with this code! Change type using the font tag as often as you like, trying out different combinations, colors, sizes, and styles.

Style Sheet Example

Here, typeface, form, leading, and color have been assigned to the page using style sheets.

```
<html>

<head>
<title>Style Sheet Example</title>

<style>

H1 { font-family: arial, helvetica, san-serif ;
font-size: 22pt;
color: #FFFF00; }

P { font-family: times, serif;
font-size: 18pt;
color: #FFFFFF;
line-height: 18pt; }

A { text-decoration: none;
font-weight: bold;
color: #CCFFCC; }
```

```
    </style>

    </head>

    <body bgcolor="#000000">

    <blockquote>

    <h1>Juliet Thinks of Romeo</h1>

    <p>
    Come, gentle night, come, loving, black-brow'd night,<br>
    Give me my <a href="romeo.htm">Romeo</a>; and, when he shall
    die,<br>
    Take him and cut him out in little stars,<br>
    And he will make the face of heaven so fine<br>
    That all the world will be in love with night<br>
    And pay no worship to the garish sun.
    </p>

    </blockquote>

    </body>
    </html>
```

Figure 4.29 shows the results.

Obviously, these examples are just the tip of the iceberg when it comes to the use of style sheets. Many options and more powerful applications are available, and I highly recommend that you study more about style sheets as you learn more about typography. They will no doubt be a major player in how type on the Web is delivered with increasing sophistication.

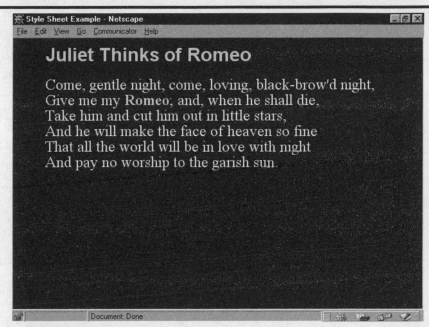

FIGURE 4.29: Style applied to a page

WHAT'S NEXT?

The typographic tips you've learned in this chapter will take you a long way toward creating an eye-catching Web page. Along the way you were introduced to the use of color as a means of adding another dimension to your type. In the ncxt chapter, we'll look in more detail at the choices you'll have to make when it comes to color, which you'll find is an fundamental element of any design.

Part ii

Chapter 5
ACHIEVING HIGH-END COLOR

Our very lives depend on light—it nourishes the fruits and vegetables that we eat, our physical bodies, and more. Light goes far beyond human sensory perception. But it is our own sensory perception that takes light and interprets it as color; color is dependent upon light.

This cycle is important because while color in and of itself is not a necessity for survival, it is an important part of our biological, social, and aesthetic worlds. Color is so integrated into our lives that its power goes unnoticed though it is tapped into everyday.

Adapted from *web by design: The Complete Guide*, by Molly E. Holzschlag
ISBN 0-7821-2201-9   928 pages $49.99

Visual artists have to understand the subtle power of color in order to harness it and create art with impact. Web designers are no exception, and they should take special care to study the lessons that color has to teach us.

> "…in reality, the objects around us would have no color were it not for light. For without light there is no color."
> —Phyllis Rae, *Color in the Graphic Arts*

This chapter covers a number of color issues that will help Web designers tap into that power, combine it with Web technologies, and use color to design successful Web sites with impact. Some of the topics include:

▶ The subtractive color wheel

▶ Color principles, including hue, value, and intensity

▶ The sociological and psychological importance of color

▶ Computers and color

▶ Additive color

▶ Web color and safe palettes

▶ Creating individual site palettes

▶ Working with HTML to gain color for sites *before* employing graphics

Color references are available on the Design Studio Web site, where you can download various materials in graphic format and use them on your own: http://www.designstudio.net/. This will help you visualize the concepts here and gain an understanding as to the why and how of color techniques.

COLOR THEORY

Color has been studied for centuries, and there are many fine resources describing its evolution. Some of those resources can be found in the objects that make up fine art. Artists must relate to light and color to express their art, and so must you.

OFFLINE

After reading the sections on color theory, visit a local art museum or gallery exhibit. Look at the art therein—whether it be painting, sculpture, photography, or mixed-media—and experience how the artist uses color. What kinds of color does the artist use? What do you feel when looking at the piece? Do you notice that your emotional response to the artwork is related to the way color is used? This exercise could (and should) be repeated as often as you like.

Color theory begins with the color wheel and proceeds into a breakdown of how variations of primary colors come into being. The computer environment is somewhat limited in its ability to properly exhibit color, but that is a limitation of technology and not of your ability to work within that technology once you have a good understanding of color theory.

Part ii

Subtractive Color: Red, Yellow, Blue

The information in this section is based on the study of *Subtractive Color Synthesis*. Subtractive color absorbs, reflects, and transmits light. The synthesis is the process of this color in the natural world. Subtractive color begins with primary colors: red, yellow, and blue. The *subtractive color wheel* is made up of a sampling of colors, including the three primary colors as well as secondary, intermediate, and tertiary colors.

Primaries All colors are the result of some combination of three colors: red, yellow, and blue. These colors are referred to as *primary* because they are the first colors to technically exist. Without them, no other color is possible.

Secondaries The next step is to mix pairs of the primaries together. For example, if you mix red and yellow, you come up with orange. Blue and yellow create green, and purple is created by mixing red with blue. Orange, green, and purple are the *secondary* colors found on the color wheel.

Intermediates When two primaries are mixed together in a ratio of 2:1, the results are referred to as *intermediate color*. These colors are gradations that lie between the primary and secondary colors.

Tertiaries   Tertiary colors are combinations of primary colors in any other ratio than previously described.

> "All colored objects contain pigments. Pigments are chemical or organic substances that possess different sensitivities to light. These sensitivities have the ability to absorb only portions of white light while reflecting others."
>
> —Phyllis Rae, *Color in the Graphic Arts*

Remember that the subtractive color wheel is based on the tactile world rather than the digital—it's the kind of color wheel you might be familiar with from childhood. It's important for you to gain a sense of how color is created and perceived off the computer screen before you are introduced to the way it is created on the screen.

OFFLINE

Want to get intimate with color? Visit your local art store and pick up a flat acrylic paint and appropriate paper. If you're not sure what to buy, ask a salesperson for advice—they will know what you're trying to do if you tell them you're learning how to mix color. Buy three small tubes of pure red, yellow, and blue. Add to that a tube each of black and white, and you're good to go! Following the ratio recommendations above, experiment on your own and see what you come up with.

If you have young children, this is an especially fun exercise to involve them in—and to start them off with a rich appreciation for the colors in their world.

From your basic subtractive color wheel, a range of color components can emerge. The following relate directly to the color wheel:

Tints and shades   Along with primary, secondary, tertiary, and intermediate colors, you can get *tints* by mixing colors with white to lighten and *shades* by mixing colors with black to darken.

Similarity, complementary, and contrasts   Colors that are adjacent to one another on the wheel, such as blue and purple, are considered to be *similar*. *Complementary* colors are those that are opposite on the wheel, such as orange and blue. Finally, *contrast* results from colors that are at least three (depending upon the color wheel you're looking at) colors removed from one another, such as red and green.

Other color components include properties, relationships, and effects.

Properties of Color

I'll admit it—I'm a shopaholic! I love clothing and shoes, and I especially love the color and textures of fabric. I often unwind by going on a shopping spree. I also enjoy looking through fashion catalogs, and one of my most relaxing times (until the credit card comes due, of course) is to sit back with a good catalog and a cup of hot Darjeeling tea.

Wine, chocolate, and peacock are only some of the colors that are in fashion this season. Where do these colors fit into the spectrum? What determines the difference between a navy blue and a peacock blue? What defines cinnamon versus cocoa?

Colors have properties, including hue, value, and saturation (also referred to as intensity). These properties are derived from the amount of color and how much light is used in that color.

Hue   Hue is simply the visible difference from one color to another. For example, red is different from green, and purple is different from brown. Whether a color is primary, secondary, intermediate, or tertiary isn't important in regard to hue. Hues can be described as warm or cool.

Warmth   Hues found in the yellow-to-red range are considered to be *warm*. They emit a sense of heat.

Coolness   *Cool* colors are those ranging from green to blue. Think of ice blue, or the cool sense of a forest a deep green can inspire.

Value   Chocolate brown is darker than tan, and sky blue is lighter than navy. A color's *value* is defined by the amount of light or dark in that color.

Saturation   You can think of *saturation,* or *intensity,* as the brightness of a color. Peacock blue is very bright, whereas navy is rather dull. Similarly, those popular neon lime greens reminiscent of the 1960s are much more intense than a forest green.

NOTE

And what about black and white? As many people have heard, black is all colors combined, and white is lack of color. Similarly, black can be described as absence of light, and white as *being* light. A more technical way to think about black and white is to refer to the properties of hue and saturation—which neither black nor white possesses! Why then, are there "shades" of gray? The reason is found in *value*. The amount of light or dark in white or black determines the resulting value of gray, as shown in Figure 5.1.

FIGURE 5.1:   Black, white, and gray values

Each hue can contain a different value and saturation. When you think of all the variations that are potentially held within each of these properties, you can begin to see that color is much more than meets the eye.

Color Relationships

I'm in a red rage! I'm green with envy over my ex-boyfriend's purple passion for that peaches 'n cream blonde beauty he started dating. I'm so blue, in fact, that I've thought about whiting out his name from all of my little black books.

Colors, like people, have relationships with one another. Some, like a good marriage, are harmonious. Others, like the unhappy example in the former paragraph, are discordant. *Harmonious* colors are those that, when combined, foster a sense of peace and relaxation—a light shade of peach, a shade of light green, and a shade of dark green create a harmonious mix. *Discordant* colors are those that cause you to do a double take—bright yellow and black can be considered discordant.

Color Effects

Beyond properties and relationships, there are special color effects. Silk and satin shine, the inside of a seashell has a multicolored radiance, and religious imagery seems to be of an almost unworldly light. These effects can be created by artists and designers and can quickly add appeal to a given design.

Color effects include:

Luster   Silk and satin are *lustrous*; they have a shining quality about them. This quality is the visual perception of small areas of light combined with black contrast. While this is achieved naturally with a given fabric's relationship to light, artists can create it by relying on black contrast between the lustrous areas and the background, as in the picture below.

Iridescence   I have a clamshell sitting on my desk. I found it on a New Jersey beach when I was a child. I was undoubtedly fascinated by the many colors inside that changed like a sparkling rainbow as I held it to the light. This is *iridescence*, or *opalescence*. A designer can achieve an iridescent effect by using gray in the same areas of luster's black contrast.

Luminosity   This effect is an interesting one. *Luminosity* relies on contrast just like its companions, luster and iridescence; however, it is more about delicate light differences. Objects appear luminous when the contrast is very subtle.

Transparency   Plastic wrap is *transparent*—it is clear. Transparent effects cause the eye to perceive the image as being see-through.

Chroma   What happens when colored light hits a colored object? When the winter's white and streaming sun comes through my window and lands on the Saltillo tile on my sun porch, the areas where patches of sun land are lighter than the patches that are shaded. This effect is *chromatic (chroma* means color).

Today's sophisticated graphic programs, such as Photoshop, offer digital methods to achieve a wide range of effects. A Web designer can use Photoshop to create graphics and can apply these effects as appropriate to his or her work.

WHAT COLORS MEAN

Fast-food restaurants often use yellow, red, and orange for their design motifs. Hotel rooms frequently use colors such as brown, tan, or shades of blue or green. A judge's chamber might have rich mahogany wood, green marble, and deep maroon leather. Clothing, as I've already noted, can be any color.

The way we use color in our everyday lives—whether we are consciously aware of it or not—is very specific. It's no accident that a person who wishes to remain inconspicuous will choose neutral colors rather than shocking pink, or that a magazine's cover is bright.

Colors have potent psychological impact. This has been proven in many studies. That impact may also be different depending upon an individual's social upbringing. In the English-speaking Western world, purple is associated with royalty, but in the Islamic world, it is associated with prostitutes! Similarly, black is the color of mourning for most people in the Western world, whereas white denotes mourning in many Eastern cultures.

> "Color plays a vitally important role in the world in which we live. Color can sway thinking, change actions, and cause reactions."
>
> —J.L. Morton, *Color Matters*

Designers need to be familiar with the general meanings of color and would do well to check with a client if that client has a specific audience. For example, if you were creating an Islamic online newspaper, knowing about that culture's color associations might keep you out of an unfortunate or embarrassing situation.

The following chart defines the meanings of prominently used colors— bearing in mind that most readers of this book are from Western, Judeo-Christian cultures.

Color	Significance
Red	Love, passion, heat, flame, feminine power
Green	Fertility, peace, nature, earth
Blue	Truth, clarity, dignity, power

Color	Significance
Yellow	Energy, joy, lightness of being
Purple	Royalty, wealth, sophistication
Brown	Masculinity, stability, weight
Black	Death, rebellion, darkness, elegance
White	Light, purity, cleanliness, emptiness

WEB COLOR TECHNOLOGY

Digital delivery of color information is rather different from the way the eye delivers color to the brain, and the way the brain deals with the perception of that color. Computers, in a sense, are finite in their ability to deliver color to the screen, because technology simply cannot achieve the more powerful abilities of tangible nature.

Computer Color: Additive Synthesis

Computers can do a pretty darn good job of dealing with color, but they must approach it from a different mathematical method than in the "real" world. The essence of color technology as defined by the computer is reliant upon three elements: the quality of the computer, the computer card, and the computer monitor. If one is substandard, computer color will be substandard.

It's also important to note that computer platforms handle color differently, as you will soon see. Also, what you are looking at color *through* is going to determine the quality of that color. In the case of Web design, it is the browser that limits color significantly; the designer must be well aware of this in order to deftly move through the digital world with strength and consistency.

Additive Color: Red, Green, Blue

But wait, Molly, you just taught me that red, blue, and *yellow* are necessary to create other colors. While this is true in the tactile world, in the digital world, the three primary colors are red, green, and blue, referred to as RGB for short.

> "Additive Color Synthesis is the method of creating color by mixing various proportions of two or three distinct stimulus colors of light."
>
> —Jim Scruggs, *Color Theory*

How did this happen? Computer monitors and televisions cannot take paint, like you can, and mix it together to get other colors. They must *add* color based on the RGB system. Additive color is unlike the tangible world's subtractive color. In the RGB world, adding red to green creates yellow! If you did this with paint, pigment, or dye, you'd end up with a dark brown.

RGB values are derived from a method that numerically determines how much red, green, and blue make up the color in question. Each color contains a percentage of red, green, and blue. In Photoshop, you can use the color picker tool and get RGB values immediately (see Figure 5.2).

Part ii

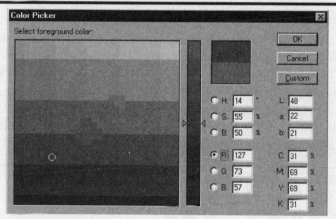

FIGURE 5.2:   RGB options in Photoshop

NOTE

What about other color methods, like CMY color? Cyan-magenta-yellow color is used in print, which has specific requirements not immediately necessary for this Web design discussion. Print designers must be familiar with this color method in order to work with computer-to-print color.

Gamma

Of great significance to digital color, and specifically to Web color, is *Gamma*. Gamma is a complex mathematical system that, very simply described, influences the way the information on the computer screen is displayed. In order to display that information with the most accurate color, Gamma must often be corrected to the appropriate numerical value.

Different computer platforms offer different methods of dealing with Gamma correction. Macintosh and SGI machines come with the necessary equipment to perform Gamma correction—so unless your monitor is very old, or there is some malfunction with the system, Macs and SGI machines present color as accurately as possible. This is one reason why designers have preferred Macs, and why SGI machines are frequently used in video and animation production.

The PC, however, offers very little, if any, Gamma correction. Windows 3.1 is the worst perpetrator of the problem due to limitations of color and Gamma information in its code. Windows 95/98 offers some Gamma correction. PC video cards and monitors can solve the problem *if* they are top-of-the-line products. The better the video card and monitor (and the newer the product is), the better chance at Gamma correction.

To see how effective your computer setup is at dealing with Gamma, you can use a Gamma Measurement Image, as seen in Figure 5.3, which was created by Robert W. Berger of Carnegie Mellon University. You can pull this image up on your screen by visiting the Design Studio Web site.

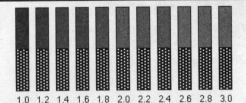

1.0 1.2 1.4 1.6 1.8 2.0 2.2 2.4 2.6 2.8 3.0

FIGURE 5.3: Gamma Measurement Image

When a computer offers little or no Gamma correction, images will appear darker—so much so that a lot of the color that the viewer *should* see goes by misperceived, or completely unseen. This, in turn, means that your beautiful color schemes may not appear beautiful to a significant portion of your audience.

What can you do about this? Some experts claim that you should always work in higher contrasts in order to allow for the best chance of having your color seen. This isn't always realistic, so my recommendation is that you maintain a strong awareness of the problem and design with high contrast *when you know the audience will require it.*

"If the issue is visibility, the answer is contrast. Recent legislation in the United States (the Americans with Disabilities Act), requires high contrasts between light and dark colors on all signage so that the visually disabled can see this information. All computers can deliver high contrasts between light and darks."

—J.L. Morton, *Color Matters*

Keeping in mind the issue of accessibility, you must determine the importance of your viewing audience's need to see the information. If many of your visitors are older or have known visual problems, a higher contrast design might be in your best interest. Also, for information-rich sites, you may always offer a downloadable or online text version of the site, making sure to use white and black (strong contrast) as the delivery mechanism for that information.

Safe Palettes

A *safe palette* is a palette containing 216 RGB colors that are going to remain as stable as possible from one browser to another, between platforms, and at different monitor color capacities and resolutions—taking into consideration the effects that problems with Gamma might create.

If colors outside the safe palette are used, many potential Web site visitors will experience *dithering*. This is the process by which the computer puts the color it has available into the color you've called for. Yes, that's right, if you've asked for a soft, pale yellow outside the safe palette, you might end up having visitors who see that color as bright neon!

So why only 216 colors when many computers can display 256 colors, and most sold today display *millions* of colors?

The answer is "blame it on Microsoft."

When developing the Windows 3.1 Operating System for the PC, Microsoft reserved 40 colors from the original 256 to use as system colors. Since so many visitors to the Web use PCs, the problems stemming from this limitation have been far-reaching.

The second answer is "blame it on Netscape."

Once you're done blaming the problem on Microsoft, you can extend the blame to include Netscape—which developed a 216-color palette *into* the browser!

After you're done enjoying a few minutes sputtering mean words to software developers that have further complicated your life as a Web designer, you can thank several people for figuring out ways to provide solutions to the color problem. The safe palette is the result—a color palette that provides the 216 non-dithering colors. You can select from this palette to create your graphics and browser-based color.

One person who helped find a solution to the color issue is Victor S. Engel, who has provided thoughtful insight and useful tools for thousands of designers via his non-dithering Netscape color cube.

ONLINE

The cube is viewable at Engel's site, http://the-light.com/netcol.html.

Another individual who has done significant work organizing and distributing safe palette tools is Lynda Weinman. Weinman is a designer and author whose contributions to Web graphic design technology are vast and important.

ONLINE

Visit Lynda Weinman at her Web site, http://www.lynda.com/. You'll find information on many aspects of Web graphic design, including a great deal of color information.

Photoshop 4 users are in luck—a safe palette is built right into the program. Those with other versions of Photoshop can transfer a safe palette and install it right into the program using a color lookup table (CLUT) provided by Weinman. You can find the CLUT at http://www.lynda.com/files/CLUTS/.

RGB to Hexadecimal

In order to translate RGB color values into a system that HTML under-stands, you will have to convert the RGB value to *hexadecimal*.

Hexadecimal is the base-16 number system, which consists of the numerals 0–15 and the letters A–F. A byte (8 bits) can be represented using two hexadecimal characters, which make any combination of binary information less cumbersome to understand. In relation to Web color, hexadecimal values *always* appear with six characters. For example, a hexa-decimal value will look like this: "FFCCFF."

You can find the hexadecimal value of any color on your own by using a scientific calculator. Individuals using Windows can access the scien-tific calculator right on their computer, as shown in Figure 5.4. Scientific calculators are those with more extended applications, such as offering binary and hexadecimal numeric systems within them. In Windows, sim-ply select Accessories ➤ Calculator. Under View, you'll find the Scientific option. Other readers might have a scientific calculator on their desk, or one can be purchased inexpensively at any office supply store.

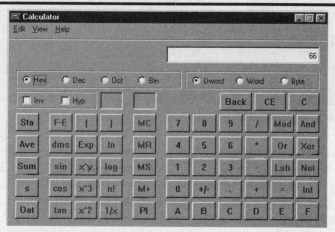

FIGURE 5.4:   Using the scientific calculator in Windows 95/98

To find this value, you must first know the RGB values for a color. You can determine these values in a program like Photoshop. Pass your cursor over any color in any image you have open in Photoshop. If you select Window ➤ Show Info, the Info box will display the individual red, green, and blue values of the color in the form of numbers. Figure 5.5

shows you this Info box as it appears in Photoshop. Simply enter each of the RGB values into the scientific calculator—one color at a time (red value first, and so forth). On the calculator, switch to "Hex." The calculator will then give you an alphanumeric or numeric combination for the corresponding color value.

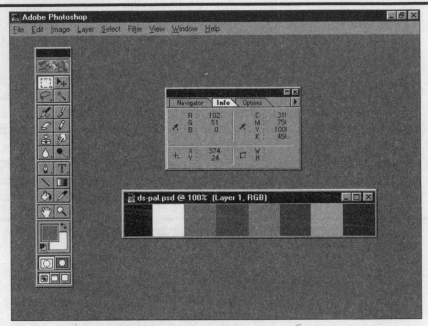

FIGURE 5.5: RGB information in Photoshop

Say you have a palette including a mid-gray. The red value is 153, as are the green and blue values. The RGB value is then 153 153 153. Enter these into the calculator and the result of the RGB-to-hexadecimal conversion for the mid-gray color is: "999999." You should always end up with a total of six characters. Different colors will get different combinations, some with all the same numeric values and others in pairs, such as "CC9900."

NOTE

A "0" for a red, green, or blue value is going to be written as "00."

ONLINE

Want to get RGB-to-hex values online? There are some fun and informative sites that offer this service, and here are two for you to visit:

Russ's RGB to Hex Converter: http://www.ecn.bgu.edu/cgi/users/mureg3/tutorial/rgb-hex.scgi

Color Center: http://www.hidaho.com/colorcenter/cc.html

Bear in mind that you still must understand the safe palette issue in order to use most online converters. They are paying attention to a broad-spectrum palette, not necessarily a safe one.

You'll use hexadecimal values in the next section, as you learn how to code HTML to achieve browser-based color.

BROWSER-BASED COLOR TECHNIQUES

Fast load time without sacrificing aesthetic appeal should be every Web designer's goal. When you understand how color works in the Web medium, you can apply HTML to control those colors. Your creations will be rich and colorful, achieving energy and a vibrant look *before* a graphic is ever used. *Browser-based color* takes advantage of all of the color information residing on the client side and never requires the browser to query the server.

Designers should rely on browser-based colors as much as possible. This can be done using the simple techniques to create background and link colors in the following discussions. The primary idea is to help you move color away from graphic images that take time to download.

This is not to say that graphics won't play a role in your design—of course they will. But with proper planning and an understanding of when and how to use safe color, you'll be able to add graphics to your already attractive sites with less concern about load times. Movement toward browser-based colors will free you to use your allotment of downloadable files for truly necessary, higher-quality graphics. This is a very effective way of adding a sense of professional style to your work.

Individual Palettes

When planning your site's visual appearance, you'll want to begin by selecting an individual color palette for that site. You will then choose HTML-based background colors, text colors, and link colors—as well as the colors you'll use within graphics. Your color selections for a specific site should be drawn from your knowledge of the audience, the subject matter, and the client's desires. Remember from the earlier discussion that color communicates emotion, so build your palette with this issue in mind.

A corporate Web site is going to have a distinctly different individual color palette than an entertainment-oriented site. Going back to the earlier lesson on color, a corporate site is going to look for a harmonious scheme, with pleasing, calming colors. An entertainment site might enjoy bolder use of color, including subtractive primaries—yellow, blue, and red.

The Design Studio Web site uses the contrast of black and white with a calming influence created by the palettes tertiary colors. I created the Design Studio's individual palette in Photoshop and saved it as a Photoshop file in order to maintain the integrity of the palette. Also, I made certain I cataloged the RGB and hexadecimal values for each of my colors.

Design Studio Individual Palette Reference:

Color	RGB Value	Hexadecimal Value
Black	000	000000
White	255, 255, 255	FFFFFF
Medium Olive	153, 153, 102	999966
Rust	153, 102, 0	996600
Peach	204, 153, 102	CC9966
Dark Olive	102, 102, 51	999933
Light Olive	204, 204, 153	CCCC99
Brick	102, 51, 0	993300

This information comes in very handy when I need to make updates or changes. Web designers should create a cataloging system as it will help to keep site information in order and available for future reference.

HTML and Browser-Based Color

In order to achieve browser-based color, use your individual palette as a guide. You'll be selecting these colors to prepare your site. It is in the HTML code that you can get maximum color control, as the browser interprets the hexadecimal information quickly and efficiently.

NOTE
Designers typically use standard HTML to achieve color effects. The HTML 4.0 standard, however, considers the <body> tag attributes—where much of browser-based color begins—to be deprecated in favor of cascading style sheets. For this reason, I'm including style sheet examples as well as standards that fit the HTML 3.2 publication.

You'll want to use hexadecimal values to design creative color combinations with backgrounds, links, and text. The most basic and immediate application for designers is found within the HTML <body> tag, or the cascading style sheet BODY: element, where you can define backgrounds, text, and link styles. You can also use color in table cell backgrounds and, using style sheets, you can put color in almost any logical place, such as behind text or as a backdrop for a given paragraph.

HTML 3.2 Methods

The <body> tag allows for the following color attributes:

bgcolor="x"   This value in hex argues the background color of the entire page.

text="x"   The text argument creates the color for all standard, non-linked text on the page.

link="x"   The color entered here will appear wherever you have linked text.

vlink="x"   A visited link will appear in this color.

alink="x"   An *active* link—one that is in the process of being clicked—will appear in the color you argue for here.

A <body> tag with these attributes appears as follows. Simply place the hexadecimal value into the quote field. Begin each individual attribute with the "#" sign:

```
<body bgcolor="#000000" text="#FFFFFF" link="#CCCCCC"
vlink="#999999" alink="#666666">
```

Figure 5.6 shows the results.

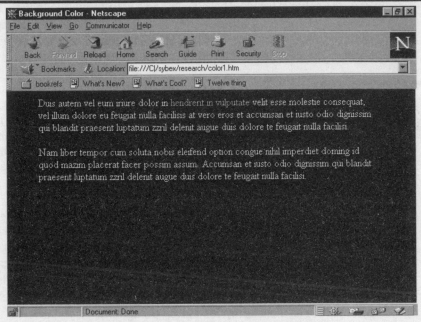

Duis autem vel eum iriure dolor in hendrerit in vulputate velit esse molestie consequat, vel illum dolore eu feugiat nulla facilisis at vero eros et accumsan et iusto odio dignissim qui blandit praesent luptatum zzril delenit augue duis dolore te feugait nulla facilisi.

Nam liber tempor cum soluta nobis eleifend option congue nihil imperdiet doming id quod mazim placerat facer possim assum. Accumsan et iusto odio dignissim qui blandit praesent luptatum zzril delenit augue duis dolore te feugait nulla facilisi.

FIGURE 5.6:   HTML and hex colors create this grayscale page.

TIP

You may decide to use a background graphic on your page, in which case you will use the `background="url"` argument within the above string. This alerts the browser to load the graphic from the location specified. If you're using a background graphic, I highly recommend including a background color argument as well. This way your background color will load instantly, and your graphic will then load over that color. The end product is less jarring and creates a cohesive visual effect.

In this example, I've used the same color selections, added a background graphic, and set up a table to control the layout:

```
<html>


<head>

<title>Background Color w/ Graphic</title>
```

```
</head>


<body bgcolor="#FFFFFF" text="#000000" link="#CCCCCC"
vlink="#666666" alink="#999999" background="bak.jpg">


<table border="0" cellpadding="10" cellspacing="0"
width="595">
<tr>


<td valign="middle" width="200">


<a href="about.htm">about us</a>
<p>


<a href="catalog.htm">catalog</a>
<p>


<a href="contact.htm">contact</a>


</td>


<td width="385">


<h2>Duis!</h2>
Duis autem vel eum iriure dolor in <a href="dummy.htm">hen-
drerit in vulputate</a> velit esse molestie consequat, vel
illum dolore eu feugiat nulla facilisis at vero eros et
accumsan et iusto odio dignissim qui blandit praesent lupta-
tum zzril delenit augue duis dolore te feugait nulla facil-
isi.
<p>


Nam liber tempor <b>cum soluta nobis</b> eleifend option
congue nihil imperdiet doming id quod mazim placerat facer
possim assum. Accumsan et iusto odio dignissim qui blandit
praesent luptatum zzril delenit augue duis dolore te feugait
nulla facilisi.
```

```
<p>

Duis autem vel eum iriure dolor in hendrerit in vulputate
velit esse molestie consequat, vel <a href="dummy.htm">illum
dolore eu feugiat</a> nulla facilisis at vero eros et accum-
san et iusto odio dignissim qui <i>blandit praesent</i> lup-
tatum zzril delenit augue duis dolore te feugait nulla
facilisi.

</td>
</tr>
</table>

</body>
</html>
```

The results of this effect can be seen in Figure 5.7.

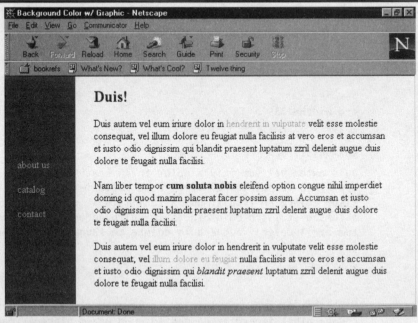

FIGURE 5.7: A background graphic has been added in this example.

NOTE

Some of you might have seen HTML color attributes that use the name of the color rather than the hex value: `<body bgcolor="red" text="white" link="yellow" vlink= "green">`. This method was introduced by Microsoft's Internet Explorer browser and is compatible with some versions of other browsers. I suggest avoiding this technique. It's not a standard or stable method of ensuring color that is as accurate as possible across platforms and browsers. It's also limited; if you want to use colors from the complete 216-color safe palette, you'll end up having combinations of color names and hexadecimal values. In the end, this looks inconsistent and therefore unprofessional.

In this example, the graphic has been removed, and background color has been added to the left table cell:

```
<html>


<head>
<title>Background with Table Cell Color</title>
</head>


<body bgcolor="#FFFFFF" text="#000000" link="#CCCCCC"
vlink="#666666" alink="#999999">


<table border="0" cellpadding="10" cellspacing="10"
width="595">
<tr>


<td valign="middle" width="200" bgcolor="#999999">


<a href="about.htm">about us</a>
<p>


<a href="catalog.htm">catalog</a>
<p>
```

```
<a href="contact.htm">contact</a>
</td>

<td width="385">

<h2>Duis!</h2>
Duis autem vel eum iriure dolor in <a href="dummy.htm">hen-
drerit in vulputate</a> velit esse molestie consequat, vel
illum dolore eu feugiat nulla facilisis at vero eros et
accumsan et iusto odio dignissim qui blandit praesent lupta-
tum zzril delenit augue duis dolore te feugait nulla facil-
isi.
<p>


Nam liber tempor <b>cum soluta nobis</b> eleifend option
congue nihil imperdiet doming id quod mazim placerat facer
possim assum. Accumsan et iusto odio dignissim qui blandit
praesent luptatum zzril delenit augue duis dolore te feugait
nulla facilisi.
<p>


Duis autem vel eum iriure dolor in hendrerit in vulputate
velit esse molestie consequat, vel <a href="dummy.htm">illum
dolore eu feugiat</a> nulla facilisis at vero eros et accum-
san et iusto odio dignissim qui <i>blandit praesent</i> lup-
tatum zzril delenit augue duis dolore te feugait nulla
facilisi.

</td>
</tr>
</table>

</body>
</html>
```

Figure 5.8 shows the grayscale design resulting from this syntax.

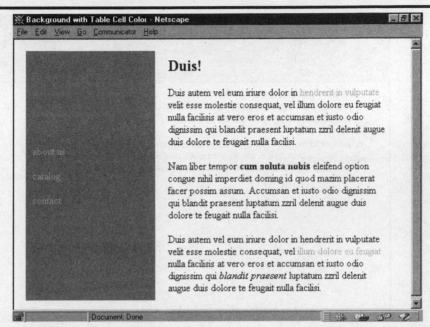

FIGURE 5.8:   Table background color

HTML 4.0 Method: Style Sheets

Cascading style sheets are one way to control layout and design on the Web. Here we'll look at how style sheets can be used to control body background color, text color, and link colors.

To create the syntax mimicking the HTML 3.2 standard above with style sheets, use the following simplified syntax:

```
<style>
BODY {background: #FFFFFF; color: #000000}
A {color: #CCCCCC}
</style>
```

Figure 5.9 shows an HTML page with the style above applied.

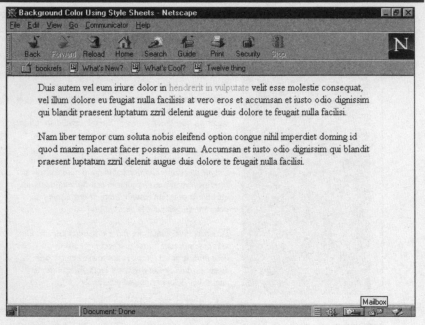

FIGURE 5.9: Style sheets create the color in this example.

NOTE

There aren't style sheet standard methods for calling on visited or active links. *Pseudo-classes* appear in the style sheet literature to achieve this, but you should test them before use: A.link, A.visited, A.active.

To add the background graphic, place the URL into the background element string:

```
BODY {background: #FFFFFF url="images/bak.gif"; color:
#000000}
```

Style can be used to enhance individual pieces of text, which you can see in Figure 5.10.

```
<span style="color: #CCCCCC; background: #FFFFFF">Colorful
Me!</span>
```

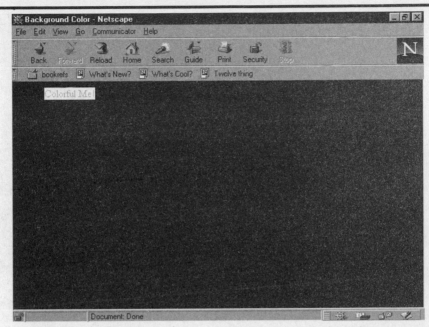

FIGURE 5.10:   Using the span tag, I've added style to a small block of text.

You can also use style as a backdrop for a complete paragraph, which is shown in Figure 5.11.

```
<p style="background: #666666">

Duis autem vel eum iriure dolor in <a href="dummy.htm">hen-
drerit in vulputate</a> velit esse molestie consequat, vel
illum dolore eu feugiat nulla facilisis at vero eros et
accumsan et iusto odio dignissim qui blandit praesent lupta-
tum zzril delenit augue duis dolore te feugait nulla facil-
isi.

</p>


<p>

Nam liber tempor <b>cum soluta nobis</b> eleifend option
congue nihil imperdiet doming id quod mazim placerat facer
possim assum. Accumsan et iusto odio dignissim qui blandit
praesent luptatum zzril delenit augue duis dolore te feugait
nulla facilisi.

</p>
```

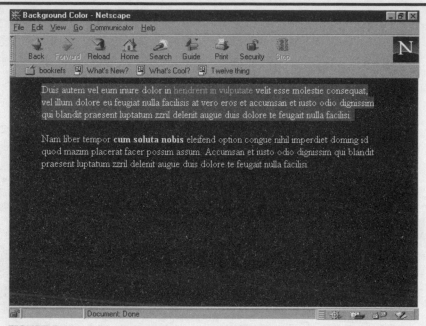

FIGURE 5.11:   Inline style can be used to highlight a complete paragraph.

With these examples, you can get a glimpse at how style sheets can be very powerful design tools—a great deal of information can be packed into them, easing up on the HTML. However, their use is limited by browser technology and distribution issues.

Using Unsafe Color

There are times when a designer will want to stray outside the safe palette. While I recommend using the safe palette whenever possible, it is restrictive because it has so few colors available. Designers might naturally become frustrated, and there are instances in which you can deviate from the safe palette:

> **You have a good idea that your audience is sophisticated in terms of their end-user technology.**   A good example of this might be with intranet applications. When you know the type of computers, browsers, and monitors the majority of your audience uses, you have much more flexibility in terms of color choice. If most people are accessing your pages with high-end browsers and monitors, by all means use color as you see fit!

If you're less certain about your audience, but still interested in using unsafe color, test the colors for dithering at lower resolutions.   To do this, set your monitor resolution to 256 colors. If the color dithers (moves to the closest color within the system palette), you may find that your soft yellow becomes glowing neon. This is not going to make you—or your client—too happy. Ideally, you'll also want to test your work on several other computers at a variety of resolutions with different browsers. If your results are stable enough to suit your tastes, you can feel somewhat confident that the colors will look good.

WHAT'S NEXT?

Now that you've been introduced to color theory and practice, you're ready to think about adding graphics to your pages. The next chapter will teach you how to work with image files and formats while building your site.

Chapter 6

ADDING GRAPHICS

Graphics, images, pictures, photographs—whatever you call them, a visual element makes your page more compelling and is the easiest way to give your page a unique look. In this chapter, we'll see all of the ways you can add images to your pages using the <IMG> tag and its many attributes. We'll also learn how to use images as links.

Throughout this chapter, you'll find suggestions on how you can make your images useful and functional even when your page is viewed by a browser that doesn't display images. Toward the end of the chapter, we'll take a look at the different image formats and learn how you can create images (including interlaced images, transparent images, and animated images).

Adapted from *HTML 4.0: No experience required.*, by E. Stephen Mack and Janan Platt Saylor

ISBN 0-7821-2143-8   704 pages $29.99

Adding Graphics with the Image Element

The purpose of the image element (which consists of the <IMG> tag) is to include graphic images in the body of your Web page.

NOTE

HTML 4.0 recommends using the object element (the <OBJECT> and </OBJECT> tags) instead of the image element. However, <IMG> is still common and HTML 4.0 fully supports it. The object element isn't as widely supported as <IMG>.

Images are sometimes referred to as *inline images* because the images are inserted within a line of body text. Because the image element is a text-level element, it should be nested inside a paragraph or other block-level container, and it doesn't start a new paragraph automatically.

To make an image appear as a separate paragraph, enclose it within the paragraph element, like this:

```
<P>
<IMG SRC="http://www.emf.net/~estephen/images/turtleshirt.jpg">
</P>
```

If you have an image in the same directory as your HTML file, you can abbreviate the URL and use a tag like this:

```
<IMG SRC="turtleshirt.jpg">
```

This inserts an image called turtleshirt.jpg on a page, but it will work only if the turtleshirt.jpg file exists in the same directory as the HTML file.

TIP

Many Web authors like to keep their images together in one (or more) subdirectories, such as images, separate from their HTML files. This practice helps keep images organized. If you decide to do this, you can use a tag such as <IMG SRC= "images/turtleshirt.jpg"> to refer to your image files.

For the first part of this chapter, don't worry too much about the format of image files or how you create them. For now, just remember that most graphical browsers can only display images if they are in a particular format. The two most popular image formats are GIF and JPEG (with the .gif and .jpg file extensions respectively). We'll learn more about these two image formats later in this chapter, as well as a newer image format called PNG.

USING IMAGE ELEMENT ATTRIBUTES

Now we're ready to learn how to use the image element. In this section, we'll expand on the possibilities of the <IMG> tag and see how its attributes work. The <IMG> tag's attributes are principally intended to tell a browser how the page should be laid out with the image so that text can flow properly around the image.

WARNING

Since HTML is about structure and not presentation, the HTML 4.0 specification recommends you use style sheets to control an image's appearance on a page, instead of using <IMG> appearance attributes. (See Chapter 8 for information on style sheets.)

Describing Images with Alternate Text

You should always use two attributes with any <IMG> tag: the SRC and ALT attributes, both of which are required. The ALT attribute is used to describe the image in some way. For any browser that isn't displaying images, the alternate text contained inside the ALT attribute is displayed instead. Here's an example of an image element using alternate text:

```
<IMG SRC="images/mickeymouse.jpg" ALT="Mickey Mouse">
```

If you use this tag, browsers can display the words "Mickey Mouse" instead of displaying an image of Walt Disney's famous rodent.

Here are five reasons why a browser would use the alternate text instead of the image itself:

▶ The browser is text-only and can't display images. If there is no ALT attribute in the <IMG> tag, a text-only browser like Lynx will display the word "[INLINE]" on the screen instead of the image itself. However, if alternate text is present, Lynx displays the alternate text in place of the image.

▶ The browser is programmed to read aloud the alternate text instead of displaying an image. In this way, the ALT attribute can explain your image to blind surfers or surfers who are using a speaking machine.

▶ The person using the browser has chosen not to display images. Since images are often large files that are slow to display, many people surf with their browser set to *not* Auto Load Images or View Pictures. Instead, browsers show an empty frame as a placeholder for the image, and the alternate text is displayed inside the frame (see Figure 6.1).

▶ Navigator and IE display an image's alternate text while the image is being loaded.

WARNING

Some people use alternate text such as "Please switch on images" or "Please wait for this image to load." These descriptions don't actually describe the image, and they make assumptions about what browser is being used.

▶ Finally, IE 3 and IE 4 as well as Navigator 4 display the alternate text as a tool tip whenever you point your mouse cursor at the image for a few seconds. (If the <IMG> tag has an advisory TITLE attribute, that's shown instead.)

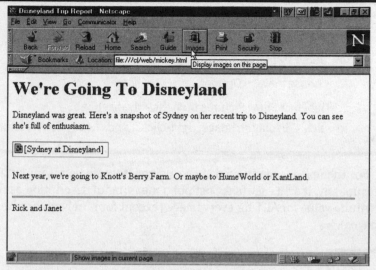

FIGURE 6.1:   Navigator puts the alternate text for this image in a frame, with an icon to show there's a image not being displayed.

TURNING OFF IMAGES

Images load slowly. To surf quickly (and avoid advertising banners in the process), set your browser so it doesn't automatically display images.

To set Navigator 4 not to load images automatically, follow these steps:

1. Select Edit ➤ Preferences.

2. Choose the Advanced category.

3. Deselect Automatically Load Images. (For Navigator 3, you can use the Options ➤ Auto Load Images.)

To quickly display all the images on a page, click on the Images button on the Navigation toolbar. To display an individual image, choose Show Image from the image's context menu. (To see a context menu, right-click the image on a PC or hold down the mouse button on a Mac.)

CONTINUED ➤

Part ii

To tell Internet Explorer 4 not to display images automatically, follow these steps:

1. Choose View ➢ Options.

2. Deselect Show Pictures from the Advanced tab.

To quickly display an image, right-click it and choose Show Picture.

For the reasons mentioned above, using alternate text is important. Fortunately, it's an easy task: just put a meaningful description as the attribute value for ALT for every image (except for purely decorative images).

TIP

Some HTML style guides recommend using empty alternate text for purely decorative images (that is, putting nothing within the quotes for the alternate text: ALT=" "). We agree, unless the image is being used as an anchor for a link, as we describe in "Using Images as Links" later in this chapter. Using nonexistent alternate text will mean that users of text-only or text-to-speech browsers, for example, won't be distracted by your page's decorative borders.

Here are some guidelines to follow when describing an image with alternate text:

▶ Put brackets around the description (for example, ALT=" [Me at age 12.] ") to distinguish the description from regular text.

▶ Leave off the words "image" or "picture." It's better to describe the image itself rather than its media. "[President Lincoln at the White House]" is a more compact and useful description than "[Image of President Lincoln at the White House]".

▶ Don't be too vague. For example, don't use ALT=" [Company Logo] " for your company logo. Instead, use ALT=" [RadCo Spinning R Logo]".

▶ Remember that text-only and speech browsers place the alternate text wherever the image occurs in a sentence. So, be sure your alternate text is clear in context. "Another excellent Web site from [Picture of a Tree] [Company Logo]" will raise some eyebrows.

▶ Use the alternate text to duplicate the image's purpose. If you use an image of a yellow star next to several items in a list, don't use ALT="Pretty yellow star" but instead use ALT="*". For the alternate text for an image of a decorative horizontal line, try ALT="--------------".

▶ Alternate text can subtly present two different versions of a page. If you've used ALT="[New!]" for a "new" icon, you can then explain at the top of your page, "New information is denoted by <IMG SRC="new.jpg" ALT="[New!]">." Users with graphics will see your new icon in the explanation; but users without graphics will also see an explanation that correctly matches their view of your page.

▶ Some art sites place copyright information along with the image's description; other sites put secret messages in an image's alternate text.

▶ You can use entities (such as ©) in alternate text.

▶ For full compatibility, keep your alternate text on one unbroken line of your document since some browsers have problems with a carriage return in the middle of the alternate text.

You can't use tags inside ALT text, so ALT="[I'm <EM>beating </EM> Hemmingway at wrestling]" is not valid. However, the <IMG> tag, including the alternate text, is subject to whatever elements it's nested within. To make your alternate text bold, enclose the <IMG> tag within <B> and </B> tags, for example:

```
<B><IMG SRC="new.jpg" ALT="[New!]"></B>
```

Now that we've seen the use of alternate text, the next attribute we'll see determines how images are aligned on a page.

## Part iii

Placing Images with Alignment Attributes

When you align images with an alignment attribute (ALIGN), there are two entirely separate results:

▶ Inline images occur in the middle of a line of text. If the image is a large one, then the line becomes very tall, and a lot of white space will appear.

▶ Floating images cause text to wrap around the image. Images can either be left-aligned or right-aligned. The paragraph will flow around the image for several lines, if the image is large.

The two different behaviors are caused by choosing the attribute value for ALIGN. We'll see the values for inline images first, then floating images.

WARNING

Using ALIGN to place images is not recommend by HTML 4.0, since alignment is a presentational feature, not a structural feature. Instead, HTML 4.0 recommends style sheets (see Chapter 8).

Aligning Inline Images

To align an image in a line, choose one of the following attributes for the image element:

```
ALIGN="TOP"
ALIGN="MIDDLE"
ALIGN="BOTTOM"
```

The default behavior is ALIGN="BOTTOM", which means that the bottom of an image will align with the bottom of the line of text. By choosing ALIGN="TOP" you request that the browser display the top of your image so that it aligns with the top of the line of text. (This will push down the next line of text.) Similarly, by choosing ALIGN="MIDDLE" the browser will align the middle of the image with the middle of the line of text. Figure 6.2 shows an image aligned to the middle of its line of text.

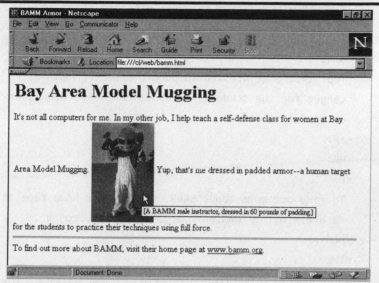

FIGURE 6.2: The middle of an image (shown here in Navigator) is aligned to the middle of the second line of text. The first and last line are pushed apart by the image. (Notice the alternate text appearing as a tool tip.)

The HTML code that produces the image in Figure 6.2 is fairly simple.

bamm.html

```
<!DOCTYPE HTML PUBLIC "-//W3C//DTD HTML 4.0//EN">
<HTML LANG="EN">
 <HEAD>
  <TITLE>BAMM Armor</TITLE>
 </HEAD>
 <BODY>
  <H1>Bay Area Model Mugging</H1>
  <P>
    It's not all computers for me. In my other job, I help
    teach a self-defense class for women at Bay Area Model
    Mugging.
```

```
<IMG SRC="http://www.emf.net/~estephen/sbamm.jpg"
ALIGN="middle"
   ALT="[A BAMM male instructor, dressed in 60 pounds of
padding.]">
   Yup, that's me dressed in padded armor—a human
   target for the students to practice their techniques
   using full force.
   </P>
   <HR>
   <P>
   To find out more about BAMM, visit their home page at
   <a href="http://www.bamm.org/">www.bamm.org</a>.
   </BODY>
   </HTML>
```

If we had used ALIGN="TOP" instead of ALIGN="MIDDLE", then the first and second lines would be next to each other and there'd be a large space between the second and third lines. If we had used ALIGN="BOT-TOM" (or no ALIGN attribute at all), then there would have been a big space between the first and second lines. (Try these examples on your own; simply make the change to the ALIGN attribute in your editor, save the HTML file, switch to your browser, and reload the file using the Reload button.)

Creating Floating Images

To make an image "float" to the left or right side and cause paragraphs to wrap around the image, choose one of the following two attribute values for the ALIGN attribute:

```
ALIGN="LEFT"
ALIGN="RIGHT"
```

Choosing LEFT or RIGHT as the value for ALIGN causes the image to be placed directly against the left or right margin. Text after the <IMG> tag will flow around the image. Shown on the following page is the result of taking the code we used in the previous section and using ALIGN= "RIGHT" as the alignment attribute.

Bay Area Model Mugging

It's not all computers for me. In my other job, I help teach a self-defense class for women at Bay Area Model Mugging. Yup, that's me dressed in padded armor--a human target for the students to practice their techniques using full force.

To find out more about BAMM, visit their home page at www.bamm.org.

This result might not be quite what we desire, so let's move the <IMG> tag up to the beginning of the first paragraph. Here's the result:

Bay Area Model Mugging

It's not all computers for me. In my other job, I help teach a self-defense class for women at Bay Area Model Mugging. Yup, that's me dressed in padded armor--a human target for the students to practice their techniques using full force.

To find out more about BAMM, visit their home page at www.bamm.org.

One drawback to this result is that the horizontal rule (from the <HR> tag) and the last paragraph are next to the picture. We might want to push these items down so they're below the image. In Chapter 3, we mentioned that the line-break element has attributes that can be used to clear the margin. The line-break element is simply the <BR> tag. By itself, the <BR> tag won't do what we want (it will just create a single blank line that wouldn't be big enough to push the horizontal rule below the image). But if we use the CLEAR attribute and the appropriate margin value, then the horizontal rule and the last paragraph will be forced down below the image. Since the image is on the right margin, we want to use a <BR CLEAR= "RIGHT"> tag (placed immediately before the <HR> tag or before the

</P> tag). Shown here is the effect of the line-break element with a CLEAR attribute:

Bay Area Model Mugging

It's not all computers for me. In my other job, I help teach a self-defense class for women at Bay Area Model Mugging. Yup, that's me dressed in padded armor--a human target for the students to practice their techniques using full force.

To find out more about BAMM, visit their home page at www.bamm.org.

If your page has images on both the left and right sides, use <BR CLEAR="ALL"> to force the next line of text to appear below the lowest image.

Sizing an Image with WIDTH and HEIGHT Attributes

Two attributes are used with the <IMG> tag to specify an image's width and height. The WIDTH and HEIGHT attributes indicate the exact size of your image, in pixels. For example:

```
<IMG SRC="sbamm.jpg" WIDTH="109" HEIGHT="175"
ALT="[A BAMM male instructor, dressed in 60 pounds of
padding.]">
```

TIP

To find out the size of an image in pixels, you'll have to use an image utility. See the "Using Image Tools to Create and Edit Images" section later in this chapter. Or, if you have access to Navigator, choose View Image from an image's context menu—once you're viewing an image, you'll see the image's width and height in the title bar.

One overwhelming advantage to adding the height and width to an <IMG> tag is that when you do specify the image size for all of your images, browsers take a lot less time to render your page. That's because the browser can determine the layout of the page without having to retrieve each image separately to find out what size it is.

However, there are two drawbacks to specifying the height and width:

▶ The height and width are presentational attributes, so they ideally belong in a style sheet instead of in your <IMG> tag.

▶ If you have a very small image and specify its height and width, then Navigator and IE won't be able to fit the alternate text inside the small image box for those users not displaying images.

Figure 6.3 shows the difference in IE between setting and not setting the HEIGHT and WIDTH attributes when images aren't displayed.

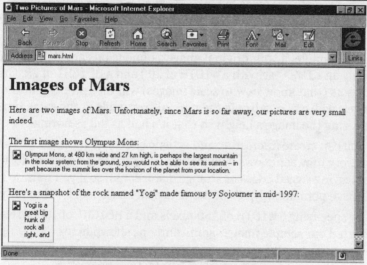

FIGURE 6.3:   IE displays a page with two image areas displaying alternate text instead of the images; the first alternate text is fully displayed, but the second is cut off.

In Figure 6.3, the user has set IE not to display images. The first image does not have its height and width specified in the HTML code, so the entire alternate text is shown. For the second image, the height and width were specified (in the <IMG> tag). If images were to be displayed, both would only be 80 pixels wide and fit the frame shown for the second image. However, since IE allocates the specified size for the second image even when the image itself is not displayed, the alternate text cannot fit inside this small area and so it is cut off by IE. (Navigator does the same thing, but displays none of the second image's alternate text at all.) Newer versions of both browsers would allow the alternate text to be seen via tool tips, but only if the mouse is pointed to the image area.

The speed advantages of setting the WIDTH and HEIGHT attributes may outweigh the two drawbacks, especially if you are not using small images with a lot of alternate text.

There's one other use of the HEIGHT and WIDTH attributes: to scale an image.

Scaling Images with WIDTH and HEIGHT Attributes

You can specify an image to have a particular height and/or width, even if the original dimensions of the image don't match. Navigator and IE will then scale your image, stretching it accordingly.

For example, if your original image's dimensions are 50 by 50, you can specify an <IMG> tag with a WIDTH of 200 and a HEIGHT of 25. Graphical browsers (that know how to scale images) will then stretch out the image's width to quadruple the normal size, while at the same time squeezing the image's height so that it's half as tall as normal.

You can create interesting and artistic effects with this technique, but not every browser knows how to scale images. Most browsers do a poor job (leaving jagged edges or strange distortions), so if you want to resize an image permanently, it's better to use an image tool for that purpose.

By specifying a WIDTH of 350 pixels and a HEIGHT of 100 pixels, we've distorted our sample image significantly, as shown here.

NOTE

To scale an image vertically, you can specify just the HEIGHT and leave the WIDTH automatic. Or you can scale an image horizontally by specifying the WIDTH and leaving the HEIGHT with its default value.

The HTML 4.0 specification recommends against using the HEIGHT and WIDTH attributes to scale images.

Setting an Image's Border Width

By default, no border appears around an image *unless* that image is a link (as we'll see in "Using Images as Links" a bit later in this chapter). However, you can specify a border for an image. If you use the BORDER="1" attribute in an <IMG> tag, then a thin border will appear around the image. You can specify larger values for the BORDER attribute as well.

There's no need to specify BORDER="0" for a normal image since borders do not appear by default.

WARNING

IE 3 does not display image borders and ignores the value of BORDER, unless the image is a link.

An image border will always be colored black in IE 4, while in Navigator it's the same color as the text color.

If you use a style sheet (see Chapter 8), you can specify whatever color you desire for image borders, and you'll have far better control over the border's appearance. This practice is preferred by the HTML 4.0 specification over BORDER attributes.

An image's border width does not count toward determining an image's height or width. So if you specify an image to be 100 pixels wide (with WIDTH="100"), and have a border width of 10 (with BORDER="10"), then the image will take 120 pixels of horizontal space (because the border appears on both the left and right side of the image). In addition, the image will take a few pixels more than 120 because browsers will put a small amount of space between an image and text. The amount of space allocated is determined by the HSPACE and VSPACE attributes.

Part ii

Adding White Space with HSPACE and VSPACE

IE and Navigator do not place images right next to text. Instead, they put a small margin of a few pixels in between text and an image. You can control the amount of horizontal space with the HSPACE attribute and the amount of vertical space with VSPACE attribute:

▶ The value of the HSPACE attribute sets the number of pixels of horizontal white space around the image (both left and right).

▶ The value of the VSPACE attribute sets the number of pixels of vertical white space around the image (both top and bottom).

For example, suppose we edit our bamm.html document to add 50 pixels of horizontal space around the image by putting an HSPACE="50" attribute in the <IMG> tag. Figure 6.4 shows the result.

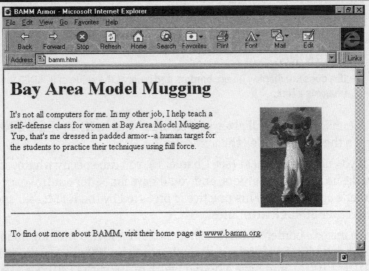

FIGURE 6.4:   IE displays 50 pixels to both the left and right of the image thanks to the HSPACE attribute.

Using Other Attributes with Images

In addition to the image attributes, HTML 4.0 allows some generic attributes that apply to almost every element, including the image element:

▶ The LANG and DIR attributes can be used to indicate what language an image's alternate text is written in, and which direction the alternate text should be displayed (either left-to-right or right-to-left).

▶ The STYLE, ID, and CLASS attributes can be used with an <IMG> tag to allow precise formatting and control over an image's appearance on a page (see Chapter 8).

▶ A new attribute, LONGDESC, points to a URL of the image's description. It is not yet supported.

▶ Several event attributes (such as ONCLICK and ONMOUSEOVER) can have a dramatic effect on images. In particular, you can use an ONMOUSEOVER attribute to change an image when someone points their mouse cursor to it. This special effect is quite common on the Web.

▶ The <IMG> tag takes a special attribute, NAME, when you are using an image as a button on a form.

▶ Imagemaps use two different attributes in the <IMG> tag: ISMAP and USEMAP. We'll see these two attributes in the "Creating Imagemaps" section.

▶ An advisory TITLE attribute can provide information about an image. Some browsers put this information in a tool tip, which would display instead of the alternate text. Since an image's advisory title is similar to its alternate text, there's not much need to use a TITLE attribute with an image. Just use the ALT attribute instead.

Now that we're familiar with all of the various attributes for images, we'll see how images can be used as the anchors for links.

USING IMAGES AS LINKS

In the discussion of linking in Chapter 1, you learned that images, as well as text, can be used as the anchor for hypertext links.

Part ii

Suppose we want to make the bamm.jpg image of the self-defense instructor take us to more information about BAMM when we click on it. Instead of using a text-anchored link, we can make the image itself a link:

```
<A HREF="http://www.bamm.org/"><IMG SRC="sbamm.jpg"
ALT="[BAMM]"></A>
```

NOTE

Using alternate text for an image is even more important if that image is being used as a link. Lynx displays the image link as just the word [LINK] if there's no alternate text for the image.

You can also have both text and image in a link anchor:

```
<A HREF="http://www.bamm.org/">Find out about BAMM! <IMG
SRC="bammlogo.gif" ALT="[Bamm's Logo]"></A>
```

By default, Navigator and IE place a blue border around image links to show that clicking the image would take you to a URL (shown in the status bar), just as with a text link. (Users of non-graphical browsers can also follow image links, provided the alternate text is present.)

The blue border placed by Navigator and IE is normally two pixels wide. You can make the border width bigger, smaller, or nonexistent by specifying a value for the BORDER attribute that we saw earlier. Specifying an <IMG> tag with BORDER="0" means not to use any border at all.

WARNING

Be cautious with the use of BORDER="0". If an image isn't surrounded with the customary border showing it's a link, then most of your audience will have no idea that the image is a link and won't click it (unless the image looks like a button).

Figure 6.5 shows what happens when you set the BORDER to a large value for an image used as a link. We used the following code:

```
<A HREF="http://www.bamm.org/"><IMG SRC="sbamm.jpg"
ALIGN="right" BORDER="10" WIDTH="109" HEIGHT="175"

ALT="[A BAMM male instructor, dressed in 60 pounds of
padding.]"></A>
```

FIGURE 6.5: A wide border around this image in the link color is a strong visual clue that it's a link.

TIP

If you see an extraneous blue underlined space appearing next to your document's image links in IE and Navigator, make sure that the </A> tag that closes the anchor is right next to the <IMG> tag and not separated by a space or carriage return.

CREATING IMAGEMAPS

We've just learned how clicking an image can lead to a link. Imagine if you have an image of a map of the United States, with five different branch offices of your company highlighted in different states. It would be nice if, depending on where the user clicks, they saw information about a specific branch—the California branch if they click California, or the Idaho branch if they click Idaho.

That kind of image set up is called an *imagemap*. But imagemaps don't have to be geographic maps. You can create a custom image and divide it up into whatever regions you like.

In general, an imagemap is an image that contains *hotspots,* or *active regions*. Your readers access your predefined hotspots by passing the mouse pointer over an area and then clicking the mouse. Just by passing the mouse over the hot area, the browser will usually display the URL of the hotspot in the status bar.

Imagemaps are useful for directing viewers to options in a menu bar image. You can create an image that names the major features of your Web site, and then use an imagemap to direct visitors to the appropriate place; these kinds of imagemaps are called *navigation imagemaps*.

Imagemaps were once fairly common on the Web but have become less common recently due to their drawbacks. You can always duplicate the effects of an imagemap by placing several linked images next to each other. Just make sure to set the HSPACE, VSPACE, and BORDER attributes of each image to zero, and if your images are on the same line, they'll be right next to each other, just like an imagemap.

Understanding Imagemap Types

There are two distinct kinds of imagemaps. The older type of imagemap is called a *server-side imagemap*, because a Web server is responsible for determining where each region leads when you click on the image. The newer and more efficient kind of imagemap is called a *client-side imagemap*, because a client (that is, a viewer's Web browser) determines where each region is supposed to lead when you click the image.

For both types of imagemaps, you must first create an image to use as a map. Next, divide it up into regions that lead to different URLs. For a server-side imagemap, you'll need to create a special map file and make sure that the server is set up to deal with imagemaps. For a client-side imagemap, you'll use special area and map elements.

Finally, in the image tag itself, you'll include a special attribute to indicate that the image is actually an imagemap. For a server-side imagemap, use the ISMAP attribute. For a client-side imagemap, use the USEMAP attribute with the name of a map element.

NOTE
See Chapter 1 for an example of an imagemap.

WORKING WITH IMAGE FILES

Now that we've seen the HTML code for using images, it's time to discuss the different image formats used on the Web and how to create and edit images in those formats.

Entire books are written about creating images, and we're certainly not going to be able to tell you even a fraction of everything there is to know on this topic. However, we're certainly going to give you enough information to get you going by recommending some tools and approaches and pointing out some pitfalls to avoid.

Understanding Image Formats

Two different image formats are common on the Web: GIF and JPEG. We'll give them each a rundown, along with some less frequently seen formats.

GIF Images

GIF images (with a file extension of .gif) are the most common types of images used on the Web. *GIF* stands for Graphic Interchange Format and was developed by CompuServe (with the compression scheme patented by UNISYS) in the late 80s.

NOTE
The word "GIF" is commonly pronounced with a hard g sound like the first part of the name "Gifford," but officially it's pronounced with a soft g as if it were spelled "Jif."

GIFs are used for all types of images, but GIF is an especially good format for line drawings, icons, computer-generated images, simple cartoons, or any images with big areas of solid colors. GIFs are compact, since the GIF format uses the same "LZW" compression routine found in zip files (which is why zipping GIFs is not effective).

The biggest limitation of GIFs is that they can only contain up to 256 different colors.

There are two common varieties of GIF: GIF87A and GIF89A. The difference won't normally be important to you, but basic GIF images are GIF87A and more complicated GIFs are usually in GIF89A format. (A third variety, GIF24, was proposed by CompuServe but has never become popular.)

One particular advantage of GIF images is their flexibility, since GIF89A images can be transparent, animated, or interlaced. (These three kinds of GIFs are defined in a later section.)

JPEG Images

JPEG images used on the Web are more formally known as JPEG JFIF images, but we'll follow standard usage and just call them JPEGs. JPEGs have a file extension of .jpg (or less commonly .jpeg) and are the second most common format for images on the Web.

NOTE

The word "JPEG" is pronounced as "jay-peg." Don't bother trying to pronounce "JFIF."

JPEG stands for the Joint Photographic Experts Group, a committee organized to develop advanced image formats. JPEGs started becoming popular in 1993.

JPEG is a remarkably compact format, designed for photographs and other images without big patches of solid colors. JPEGs are *lossy*, which means that they achieve their amazing compression by eliminating data that the human eye does not perceive. When creating JPEGs, it's possible to specify an amount of lossiness. At the highest levels of lossiness, the image becomes visibly crude. At normal levels of lossiness, you probably won't be able to detect the difference between a GIF and a JPEG onscreen. You'll notice the file size difference, however, since a JPEG is usually one-fourth of the size of a GIF.

The largest difference between JPEGs and GIFs is that JPEG images are always 24-bit—in other words, they allow up to 16 million different colors in an image.

JPEGs are *not* very effective for icons or logos with lots of solid colors. Both GIFs and JPEGs have their role, and it's usually not too hard to decide which format to use. You'll probably end up using a mix of both GIF and JPEG images.

The biggest limitation of JPEGs (aside from the lossiness that can accumulate if you repeatedly compress and decompress a JPEG in the process of editing it) is that they can't be transparent or animated. A special type of JPEG called "progressive JPEG" is similar to an interlaced GIF, discussed a little later.

WARNING

Don't convert GIFs to JPEGs without being very careful. GIFs are only 256 colors (8-bit) at most, while JPEGs use millions of colors (24-bit). If a photograph is already in GIF format, it has lost most of its color information, and may get worse if you convert it into a JPEG. To make the best JPEGs, start with a file format that has full 24-bit color information, such as a TIFF file. (TIFF files are a common format used when you scan a photograph into your computer using an image scanner.)

Other Image Formats

The only other image format that's a contender for Web popularity is the PNG format. *PNG* stands for Portable Network Graphics, and the format was devised in 1995 by the W3C and CompuServe in response to controversies over GIF licensing. PNG is superior to GIF in just about every way possible: PNGs are smaller, have more colors, and more capabilities. But two things hamper the PNG format:

▶ PNG images cannot be animated images (although a companion design promises to take care of that).

▶ Most important, the major browsers did not support PNG at all until recently. (Navigator 4.02 still does not support PNG without a special add-on called a *plug-in*, but future versions of Navigator promise PNG support. IE 4 supports PNG, but earlier versions do not.)

NOTE

For more information about PNG, visit the PNG home page (http://www.cdrom.com/pub/png/) or see W3C's PNG information (http://www.w3.org/Graphics/PNG/Overview.html).

Several other miscellaneous image formats are used infrequently on the Web, such as TIFF (Tagged Image File Format), XBM (Portable Bitmap), BMP (Windows Bitmap), PICT (Macintosh Bitmap), CGM (Computer Graphics Metafile), and Postscript (a common printing format). *Bitmap* is simply a generic term for an image, and many bitmap formats produce huge file sizes since the images aren't compressed.

It's not worth going into much more detail about any of these formats here since they aren't very popular or well-supported on the Web.

NOTE

There's also PDF (Portable Document Format), advocated by Adobe for their Acrobat Reader.

Working with Special Image Formats

GIF images can have three special abilities: transparency (where one color of an image is invisible and reveals the background), interlacing (where the image is formatted so that it appears in stages), and animation (where two or more image frames appear in sequence). JPEGs can't be transparent or have animation, but they do feature a kind of interlacing called progressive JPEGs.

Creating Interlaced GIFs and Progressive JPEG Images

Since images are often large and therefore slow to load, it's annoying for viewers to have to wait a long time before they can see your image. Normally images load from top to bottom, a line at a time. However, if you use a special image format of GIF, you can *interlace* your image so that it loads in a mixed order of different segments instead of simply top-to-bottom. First the top line of the image appears, then every fifth line appears, on down to the bottom. Then the second line appears followed by the sixth line, and so on. Thus, the image appears in four passes. After the first pass, the viewer has a good idea of what the image will look like. The second pass adds more detail, the third pass even more detail, and the image is complete after the fourth pass.

To save your image in interlaced format, check with your image tool (we'll discuss image tools in "Using Image Tools to Create and Edit Images" later in this chapter). Usually you can select an option if you want your image interlaced. Interlacing makes your image's file size slightly larger (which makes it actually load slower), so not every image should be interlaced.

Progressive JPEGs are similar in theory to interlaced GIFs. To quote Tom Lane's JPEG frequently asked question file (or *FAQ*), which can be found online (http://www.cis.ohio-state.edu/hypertext/ faq/usenet/jpeg-faq/top.html), a progressive JPEG "divides the file into a series of scans. The first scan shows the image at the equivalent of a very low quality setting, and therefore it takes very little space. Following scans gradually improve the quality. Each scan adds to the data already provided so that the total storage requirement is about the same as for a baseline JPEG image of the same quality as the final scan. (Basically, progressive JPEG is just a rearrangement of the same data into a more complicated order.)"

However, progressive JPEGs are not as widely supported as interlaced GIFs. Even though most browsers now know how to display progressive JPEGs, a lot of image tools don't know how to create them.

Creating Transparent GIF Images

HTML images are always square or rectangular. However, you can create the illusion that your image is shaped differently in several ways. For example, if your page has a white background, you can create an image of a dog on a white background. The white colors will blend and it will appear as if the image is dog shaped (and it will fit better with your page).

WARNING

Not all white colors are the same. Be sure that the different whites match. A true white has an RGB value of #FFFFFF (which is equivalent to the decimal values of 255, 255, 255 for red, green, and blue). Some image tools use decimal values, others use hexadecimal values.

An image with a white background does not match with a page with a gray background. If you assume that your background page color is white, you might end up with an ugly result if your page's background ends up a different color, such as the old default of gray. If that happens, you'll end up with the white and gray background color clash shown in Figure 6.6.

FIGURE 6.6: The "New!" image has a white background, while the page has a default gray background (common for users who haven't customized the default background color).

WARNING

You can't guarantee that your page's background will always be displayed with the color you select. Many surfers will override the default document color with their own preferences, particularly if they have vision problems or are color-blind. Therefore the background color of your images might not match the background color of your page.

When you have specified a background color or image for your page, you'll often want to ensure that the page background shows through the background parts of an image. The only way to do this is to make a transparent image. A transparent image has a color that has been set to be "invisible" so that whatever is behind the image shows through. Using a transparent image will save you from having to match an image's background with your page's background. Transparency is easier seen than explained, so examine Figure 6.7, which shows a transparent image compared to its non-transparent counterpart.

FIGURE 6.7: Two "New!" images on a cloud background; the color white in the left-hand image is transparent (allowing the cloud background to come forward) and the right-hand image is not transparent.

NOTE

The techniques for making GIFs transparent vary wildly from program to program, but only GIF89A format GIFs can have a transparent color—so make sure you're saving in the right format. Check your image tool's Help program and try searching for "Transparent" to find out how transparency works in your program.

Some image tools can only make transparent GIFs if the transparent color is black or white, while other image tools let you make any color transparent. However, only one color can be transparent. JPEGs cannot have a transparent color, and PNGs allow more complex types of transparency than GIFs.

TIP

An excellent Web site that can help you with your GIFs is Gif Wizard (http://www.gifwizard.com/).

Creating Animated GIF Images

One type of image really jumps out on the Web: animated GIFs. An *animated GIF* is a series of two or more normal GIF images that have been combined into one file and are displayed by the browser frame by frame in the same space. This creates the illusion of animation.

Animated GIFs are popular because they don't require special software or a complicated program to display an animation. Any graphical browser from Navigator 2 or IE 2 on will show animated GIFs, although early browsers did have glitches. (The newer versions of Navigator and IE allow you to switch off animation.)

WARNING

Some surfers become annoyed and distracted by animated images. Use them sparingly. Certain animated GIFs are in widespread use (such as the spinning globe or the animated mailbox), and using one of them on your page is cliché.

To create an animated GIF, you'll need to first create each frame of the animation as a separate image. Then, you use a special image tool to combine the images together and set the amount of delay between each frame.

Animating an image is a special art, and an exhaustive review of the technique is beyond the scope of this book. However, we'll list several GIF animation tools in the next section on image tools; each of the packages we mention will come with sufficient documentation to get you started.

Using Image Tools to Create and Edit Images

When it comes time to add an image to your page, you have two choices: either create your own images, or use and edit existing images. You'll also probably want to edit your images for different reasons (such as to change a color scheme, modify a design, or convert from one format to another).

No matter what you're doing with an image, you'll need an image tool. Though there are numerous image tools to choose from, you're already equipped with a fairly capable one: Your browser at least knows how to display images in several different formats, and it can also save images you see on the Web.

Though we're not going to go into a lot of detail on the different image tools, we will take a brief look at some broad categories of image tools and name the major players.

Image Applications

Most people have heard of the popular image applications. The application that's probably mentioned most often is Photoshop, sold by Adobe. Photoshop was designed, as its name implies, to edit photographs. It features many advanced tools for creating and editing images (not just photographs), but it may not be as easy to use Photoshop to create logos and images as other tools; for example, there's no simple way to create a circle in Photoshop, and its text tools are not sophisticated. However, Photoshop's capabilities can be extended through the use of plug-ins.

If you use Photoshop and want to work with more powerful text-editing features, you can give Extensis' PhotoTools plug-in a try. Visit their home page (`http://www.extensis.com/`) to download a trial version.

Photoshop is, unfortunately, extremely expensive. However, its powerful filters can apply professional effects to your images (just be careful not to overuse the "lens flare" filter, for example).

Illustrator is another expensive and powerful application sold by Adobe that's often used to create graphics. Illustrator's emphasis is more on creating images than Photoshop. However, both Photoshop and Illustrator are some of the more complicated applications in existence, and both will take you some time to learn.

Photoshop and Illustrator are both available for Windows PCs, Macintoshes, and Unix systems. More information is available from Adobe's Web site (`http://www.adobe.com/`).

For Windows users, Paint Shop Pro is a popular shareware program used to edit and create images. Created and distributed by Jasc, Inc., more information and the shareware package can be found on their home page (`http://www.jasc.com/`).

ClarisDraw (sold by Apple's Claris Corporation) is an easy-to-use image application for Macintosh and Windows users. You can read more about it at Claris' home page (`http://www.claris.com/`).

CorelDRAW and related software packages are also popular image applications. Find out more from Corel's home page (`http://www.corel.com/`).

Part ii

In addition, Deneba (`http://www.deneba.com/`) sells the popular Canvas application for Windows and Macintosh users, and for the Macintosh, UltraPaint can be purchased for under $20.

TIP

Microsoft FrontPage and some other HTML editors come with image editors. Most of the recent versions of FrontPage ship with the Microsoft Image Composer, which is a capable image tool. FrontPage itself can be a handy image tool, since it can make images transparent with a click of a button.

You may able to adapt your existing applications' drawing capabilities. Popular word processors such as WordPerfect and Microsoft Word have drawing tools, and Microsoft PowerPoint (normally used to create business presentations) may be able to handle your image needs. The main issue involved in using these tools is their inability to save the images in a useful Web format.

On the low end, you can always create images with a drawing program that may have been provided free with your operating system (such as the Paint program that comes with Windows). However, these simple drawing programs don't have a lot of features and often don't save files in GIF or JPEG format (so you'll have to use a utility or conversion tool before you can add your drawings to your Web pages).

The image applications usually know how to convert images fairly effectively, but aren't really optimized for creating images in GIF or JPEG formats (Photoshop especially). For that, you should check out an image utility.

Image Utilities and Conversion Tools

A large number of popular utilities are available; most of these utilities are shareware and can be downloaded from the Web. All of these utilities can display images quickly, and convert images between GIF and JPEG formats as well as other popular image formats (some of the tools are solely designed for converting images from one format to another).

Most of these utilities can also make simple and complex transformations to an image, such as changing an image's size, orientation, color, contrast, and rotation. Some of these utilities can handle more advanced editing, such as rearranging the image and changing the number of colors.

NOTE

The process of reducing the number of colors in an image is called *dithering*, and it's usually wise to get a utility that's good at dithering if you want to convert a 24-bit image into GIF format.

For Windows, popular image utilities include LView Pro, WinGIF, ACD-See, and PolyView. One popular commercial image utility is HiJaak Pro.

For Macintosh, check out DeBabelizer, JPEGView, GIFConverter, GraphicConverter, Giffer, and GifBuilder.

GIF Animators

The best-known GIF animator is Alchemy Mindwork's GIF Construction Set (available as shareware from http://www.mindworkshop.com/). This package is a little unconventional, but it contains everything you need to animate images, including an animation wizard to guide you through the process. It's a capable image utility as well, and it includes several shortcuts for creating animated images, such as a scrolling marquee image with a message you specify or a special transition between two images.

Other GIF animators include Microsoft's free (for now) Microsoft GIF Animator, as well as PhotoImpact GIF Animator, Animagic, VideoCraft, and WebImage.

Creating Images

Creating images is difficult work and requires a lot of time and energy—not to mention talent. There's no shortage of graphic designers and design firms who would be happy to design a coordinated series of images for you.

If you do create images yourself for your Web sites, you should use the best image tool available to you. Take the time to fully learn how your tool or application works (finish the online tutorials and look into computer training classes) and find out what it's capable of. Scour the Web for inspiration in the form of design ideas and fresh approaches—don't always rely on the drop shadows and neon effects that are so commonplace.

Part ii

TIP

If you're creating a simple image, it's often best to work on a version that's much larger than what you intend as your final size, and then rescale your work down to your desired size.

The easiest type of image for most people to create is a photograph. Using either a conventional camera or a newer digital camera, you can take a wide variety of photographs to help illustrate your page. You can scan in photographs or have them developed onto CD-ROM and then converted into JPEG format. However, an amateur photograph with ineffective lighting or poor composition will hamper your page as much as a crudely drawn image will.

TIP

When you create images, decide if you're designing for 256 colors or 24-bit color. If you're using 256 colors, try to see if your application has a Web-compatible palette of colors that won't dither—that is, colors that will be displayed as solids that resemble the colors you intend. Visit the browser-safe palette page (http://www.lynda.com/hex.html) for a tutorial on the 216 "safe" colors and to pick up a Web palette for Photoshop.

If you're good at illustrating on paper (or know someone who is), then buy or rent a scanner to convert paper illustrations into computer files. (You can also find scanners at many copy stores and find scanning services in the Yellow Pages. Some scanners are sold with bundled image applications, such as Photoshop.)

However, if (like most of us) you're no artist, then it's time to consider using existing images.

Using Existing Images

You can take existing images and use them on your Web pages in several ways. Here are some methods:

Legacy material   Perhaps your organization has some image material that you can use (such as logos, street maps, slide presentations, or previously commissioned material) once you convert it into the correct format.

Clip art collections   There are a large number of commercial and shareware packages of clip art and stock photographs that are licensed for nonprofit use on your Web pages. (Check the license of the package carefully before using a clip art image on your Web site.)

Public domain material   Certain illustrations and images are public domain and can be included on your Web page once you find (and convert if necessary) the image. However, be careful since most images are copyrighted and are not in the public domain.

Freely licensed material   Many companies create special images and logos (also known as *badges* or *banners*) for the express purpose of use on a Web page when you link to that company. For example, Netscape freely licenses the ubiquitous "Netscape Now" image that many people use to link to Netscape's site.

TIP

Check a site that you want to link to and see if they have a logo page that explains their licensing and linking policies. Using a badge to link to a company is free advertising for them, so think twice before you send your audience away to their site.

Freeware collections and libraries   There are a number of collections of images (such as background images and common icons) where the artist has relinquished copyright or allows you to use their images on your Web pages with no restrictions (or sometimes simply in exchange for author credit and a link back to their site).

NOTE

Here are several freeware image collections of links (aside from the ones you can find at Yahoo!): Clipart.com (http://www.clipart.com/), Clip Art Review (http://www.webplaces.com/html/clipart.htm), and Gini Schmitz's "Cool Graphics on the Web" (http://www.fishnet.net/~gini/cool/index.html).

Part ii

Material that you may use after you buy a license   Many
Web artists display images in their online galleries and will sell
an inexpensive image license. If you see an image that you wish
to use on a Web page, it doesn't hurt to inquire if it is available
for licensing.

WARNING

In the early days of the Web, fan sites used copyrighted material (like images
of U2 album covers or pictures of Star Trek characters) unchecked. These days,
corporate crackdowns on illegally used copyrighted material are common. You
must assume that any image you see is copyrighted unless there is a specific
statement to the contrary. U.S. copyright law grants copyright protection even
if there is no explicit copyright statement.

It's all too easy to see an image, background, or icon that you like and
save it to your hard drive. (Using Navigator or IE, all you have to do is use
the save command on the image's context menu—right-click the image
on the PC, or hold down the mouse button over an image with a Mac.)
Once the image is saved on your hard drive, you can edit it and include it
on your Web pages with little difficulty. However, just because you *can*
use other people's images on your Web pages does not mean it's legal to
do so. In general, this practice is quite widespread—and also quite immoral.
Using another person's copyrighted work without their permission is a
crime. (There are exceptions to copyright law for fair use or parody, but
we're not lawyers, so you're on your own to determine what's fair use and
parody.

NOTE

It's considered bad manners to include an <IMG> tag or BACKGROUND attribute
that links to another site's image without their permission. You're just using
their work without giving them credit. (Whether this practice is actually illegal
hasn't been settled.)

If you own the material or if your license allows it, use the image tools
we described earlier to modify existing images for your own purposes.
Add your company name to a stock photograph of the Golden Gate
Bridge, or change the contrast of the Mona Lisa and add your logo to
replace her head. Be creative above all else, by trying things you *haven't*

seen on other Web sites. The more unique your images are, the more likely your site will stand out. Our best advice is to start experimenting with images and practicing to feel comfortable with them.

WHAT'S NEXT?

The knowledge you've gained in this chapter will serve you well as you begin to use images to diversify the content of your Web site. The next chapter will allow you to apply your knowledge of design, color, and images to the process of laying out your page. It offers an overview of layout technology, taking a close look at how layouts are actually constructed. We'll also explore how HTML syntax combines with space, shape, and object placement, resulting in the blueprint of your Web site's layout design.

Part ii

Chapter 7

LAYOUT TECHNOLOGY

I n this chapter we'll explore concepts of layout control. We'll delve into standard and tables-based technologies and look at how HTML syntax combines with the concepts of space, shape, and object placement to result in the blueprint of your Web site's layout design.

The basics of frames will also be covered. Frames relate to layout in contemporary design as they provide a delivery system for sections of a layout to be fixed. For example, if you want the navigation section of your interface to be static, you can create it with frames. Your layout design remains intact, but certain parts of the page become dynamic. Finally, we'll glance at style sheet positioning because of its growing importance in HTML-based layout design.

Adapted from *web by design: The Complete Guide*, by Molly E. Holzschlag

ISBN 0-7821-2201-9   928 pages $49.99

This chapter focuses on:

▶ Standard layout design using HTML

▶ Table-based design concepts

▶ Table syntax

▶ Frames-based design concepts

▶ Frames syntax

▶ Style sheet positioning

Certainly, one chapter devoted to the complex and emerging technologies of Web design layout is not going to be enough. Therefore, you'll see plenty of references, both here in the text and on the *web by design* companion Web site at `http://www.designstudio.net/`, that will help you master the areas of layout that interest you most.

In the following section, we'll examine methods of text-based layout and graphic layout and pull the ideas together in several real-world examples.

Standard HTML Formatting

Standard HTML formatting involves breaking up the page with balanced amounts of text, graphics and other media, and space. While your sketches can prepare the foundation for this, you'll need to get up close and personal with HTML code in order to really manipulate blocks of text or media.

The first step in managing text with standard techniques is to determine *how much* text you have for the entire site. This will help you break up text into realistically approachable pages. For individual pages within the site, a reasonable layout runs between one and three screens per page (see Figure 7.1), possibly more if you don't go too overboard or if your work isn't *just* text. No one wants to scroll through page after page of text alone.

The following code shows about three screens' worth of text before any text formatting has been added to the page. Pay attention to how this amount of text changes visually in the figure examples throughout the process.

```
<html>
<head>
<title>Text Example</title>
```

```
</head>

<body bgcolor="#FFFFFF" text="#000000" link="#999999"
vlink="#CCCCCC" alink="#FFFFCC">
```

Duis autem vel eum iriure dolor in hendrerit in vulputate
velit esse molestie consequat, vel illum dolore eu feugiat
nulla facilisis at vero eros et accumsan et iusto odio
dignissim qui blandit praesent luptatum zzril delenit augue
duis dolore te feugait nulla facilisi. Nam liber tempor cum
soluta nobis eleifend option congue nihil imperdiet doming id
quod mazim placerat facer possim assum.

Accumsan et iusto odio dignissim qui blandit praesent
luptatum zzril delenit augue duis dolore te feugait nulla
facilisi. Eros Et Accumsan dignissim qui blandit praesent
luptatum zzril delenit augue duis dolore te feugait nulla
facilisi. Nam liber tempor cum soluta nobis eleifend option
congue nihil imperdiet doming id quod mazim placerat facer
possim assum. Iusto odio dignissim qui blandit praesent
luptatum zzril delenit augue duis dolore te feugait nulla
facilisi.

Nam liber tempor cum soluta nobis eleifend option congue
nihil imperdiet doming id quod mazim placerat facer possim
assum. Accumsan et iusto odio dignissim qui blandit.
Vendrerit In Vulputate Duis autem vel eum iriure dolor in
hendrerit in vulputate velit esse molestie consequat, vel
illum dolore eu feugiat nulla facilisis at vero eros et
accumsan et iusto odio. Occumsan Aliquam dignissim qui
blandit praesent luptatum zzril delenit augue duis dolore te
feugait nulla facilisi. Nam liber tempor cum soluta nobis
eleifend option congue nihil imperdiet doming id quod mazim
placerat facer possim assum.

Eros Et Accumsan dignissim qui blandit praesent luptatum
zzril delenit augue duis dolore te feugait nulla facilisi.
Nam liber tempor cum soluta nobis eleifend option congue
nihil imperdiet doming id quod mazim placerat facer possim
assum. Iusto odio dignissim qui blandit.

```
Accumsan dignissim qui blandit praesent luptatum zzril
delenit augue duis dolore te feugait nulla facilisi. Nam
liber tempor cum soluta nobis eleifend option congue nihil
imperdiet doming id quod mazim placerat facer possim assum.
Iusto odio dignissim qui blandit praesent luptatum zzril
delenit augue duis dolore te feugait nulla facilisi.

Nam liber tempor cum soluta nobis eleifend option congue
nihil imperdiet doming id quod mazim placerat facer possim
assum. Accumsan et iusto odio dignissim qui blandit. Duis
autem vel eum iriure dolor in hendrerit in vulputate velit
esse molestie consequat, vel illum dolore eu feugiat nulla
facilisis at vero eros et accumsan et iusto odio.


</body>
</html>
```

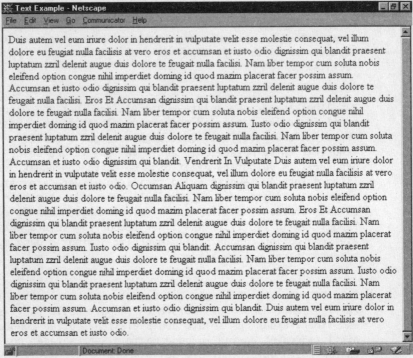

FIGURE 7.1: Three screens of text before the addition of space and media

Now add margins using the <blockquote> tag (see Figure 7.2). This is necessary to create that all-important white space. Here is the text with blockquotes added:

```
<html>
<head>
<title>Text Example</title>
</head>

<body bgcolor="#FFFFFF" text="#000000" link="#999999"
vlink="#CCCCCC" alink="#FFFFCC">

<blockquote>

Duis autem vel eum iriure dolor in hendrerit in vulputate
velit esse molestie consequat, vel illum dolore eu feugiat
nulla facilisis at vero eros et accumsan et iusto odio
dignissim qui blandit praesent luptatum zzril delenit augue
duis dolore te feugait nulla facilisi. Nam liber tempor cum
soluta nobis eleifend option congue nihil imperdiet doming id
quod mazim placerat facer possim assum.

Accumsan et iusto odio dignissim qui blandit praesent
luptatum zzril delenit augue duis dolore te feugait nulla
facilisi. Eros Et Accumsan dignissim qui blandit praesent
luptatum zzril delenit augue duis dolore te feugait nulla
facilisi. Nam liber tempor cum soluta nobis eleifend option
congue nihil imperdiet doming id quod mazim placerat facer
possim assum. Iusto odio dignissim qui blandit praesent
luptatum zzril delenit augue duis dolore te feugait nulla
facilisi.

Nam liber tempor cum soluta nobis eleifend option congue nihil
imperdiet doming id quod mazim placerat facer possim assum.
Accumsan et iusto odio dignissim qui blandit. Vendrerit In
Vulputate Duis autem vel eum iriure dolor in hendrerit in
vulputate velit esse molestie consequat, vel illum dolore eu
feugiat nulla facilisis at vero eros et accumsan et iusto
odio. Occumsan Aliquam dignissim qui blandit praesent luptatum
zzril delenit augue duis dolore te feugait nulla facilisi. Nam
liber tempor cum soluta nobis eleifend option congue nihil
imperdiet doming id quod mazim placerat facer possim assum.
```

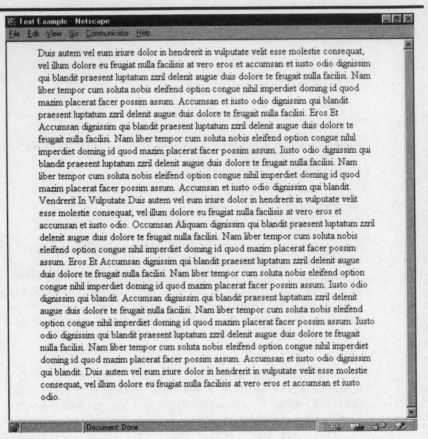

FIGURE 7.2: Add blockquotes for that all important white space.

Eros Et Accumsan dignissim qui blandit praesent luptatum zzril delenit augue duis dolore te feugait nulla facilisi. Nam liber tempor cum soluta nobis eleifend option congue nihil imperdiet doming id quod mazim placerat facer possim assum. Iusto odio dignissim qui blandit.

Accumsan dignissim qui blandit praesent luptatum zzril delenit augue duis dolore te feugait nulla facilisi. Nam liber tempor cum soluta nobis eleifend option congue nihil imperdiet doming id quod mazim placerat facer possim assum. Iusto odio dignissim qui blandit praesent luptatum zzril delenit augue duis dolore te feugait nulla facilisi.

```
Nam liber tempor cum soluta nobis eleifend option congue
nihil imperdiet doming id quod mazim placerat facer possim
assum. Accumsan et iusto odio dignissim qui blandit. Duis
autem vel eum iriure dolor in hendrerit in vulputate velit
esse molestie consequat, vel illum dolore eu feugiat nulla
facilisis at vero eros et accumsan et iusto odio.
```

```
</blockquote>
</body>
</html>
```

Attention span on the Web is short. It's in your best interest to serve your audience by ensuring that paragraphs are equally short. Therefore, after breaking up text into pages, break up your page into logical sections of short paragraphs (see Figure 7.3). Here is the syntax with paragraph tags added:

```
<html>
<head>
<title>Text Example</title>
</head>
<body bgcolor="#FFFFFF" text="#000000" link="#999999"
vlink="#CCCCCC" alink="#FFFFCC">
<blockquote>
```

```
Duis autem vel eum iriure dolor in hendrerit in vulputate
velit esse molestie consequat, vel illum dolore eu feugiat
nulla facilisis at vero eros et accumsan et iusto odio
dignissim qui blandit praesent luptatum zzril delenit augue
duis dolore te feugait nulla facilisi. Nam liber tempor cum
soluta nobis eleifend option congue nihil imperdiet doming id
quod mazim placerat facer possim assum.
```

```
<p>
```

```
Accumsan et iusto odio dignissim qui blandit praesent
luptatum zzril delenit augue duis dolore te feugait nulla
facilisi. Eros Et Accumsan dignissim qui blandit praesent
luptatum zzril delenit augue duis dolore te feugait nulla
facilisi. Nam liber tempor cum soluta nobis eleifend option
congue nihil imperdiet doming id quod mazim placerat facer
```

possim assum. Iusto odio dignissim qui blandit praesent
luptatum zzril delenit augue duis dolore te feugait nulla
facilisi.

```
<p>
```

Nam liber tempor cum soluta nobis eleifend option congue
nihil imperdiet doming id quod mazim placerat facer possim
assum. Accumsan et iusto odio dignissim qui blandit.
Vendrerit In Vulputate Duis autem vel eum iriure dolor in
hendrerit in vulputate velit esse molestie consequat, vel
illum dolore eu feugiat nulla facilisis at vero eros et
accumsan et iusto odio. Occumsan Aliquam dignissim qui
blandit praesent luptatum zzril delenit augue duis dolore te
feugait nulla facilisi. Nam liber tempor cum soluta nobis
eleifend option congue nihil imperdiet doming id quod mazim
placerat facer possim assum.

```
<p>
```

Eros Et Accumsan dignissim qui blandit praesent luptatum
zzril delenit augue duis dolore te feugait nulla facilisi.
Nam liber tempor cum soluta nobis eleifend option congue
nihil imperdiet doming id quod mazim placerat facer possim
assum. Iusto odio dignissim qui blandit.

```
<p>
```

Accumsan dignissim qui blandit praesent luptatum zzril
delenit augue duis dolore te feugait nulla facilisi. Nam
liber tempor cum soluta nobis eleifend option congue nihil
imperdiet doming id quod mazim placerat facer possim assum.
Iusto odio dignissim qui blandit praesent luptatum zzril
delenit augue duis dolore te feugait nulla facilisi.

```
<p>
```

Nam liber tempor cum soluta nobis eleifend option congue
nihil imperdiet doming id quod mazim placerat facer possim
assum. Accumsan et iusto odio dignissim qui blandit. Duis
autem vel eum iriure dolor in hendrerit in vulputate velit
esse molestie consequat, vel illum dolore eu feugiat nulla
facilisis at vero eros et accumsan et iusto odio.

```
<p>
</blockquote>
</body>
</html>
```

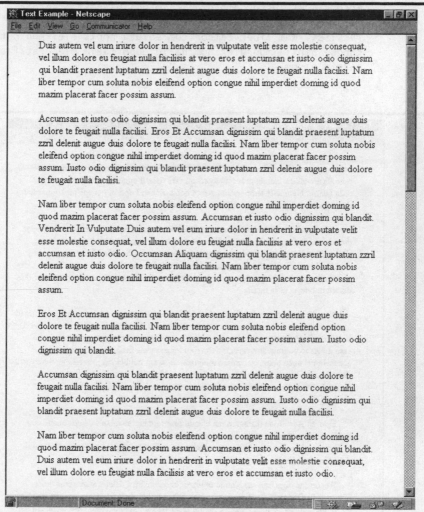

FIGURE 7.3: Paragraphs should be short and to the point.

Some people choose to use the nonbreaking space characters
to create indentation in paragraphs. The results are quite readable, as you
can see in Figure 7.4. The following three nonbreaking space characters
before the paragraph show you how to achieve this technique:

```
      Duis autem vel eum iriure dolor in
hendrerit in vulputate velit esse molestie consequat, vel
illum dolore eu feugiat nulla facilisis at vero eros et
```

accumsan et iusto odio dignissim qui blandit praesent
luptatum zzril delenit augue duis dolore te feugait nulla
facilisi. Nam liber tempor cum soluta nobis eleifend option
congue nihil imperdiet doming id quod mazim placerat facer
possim assum.

\<p\>

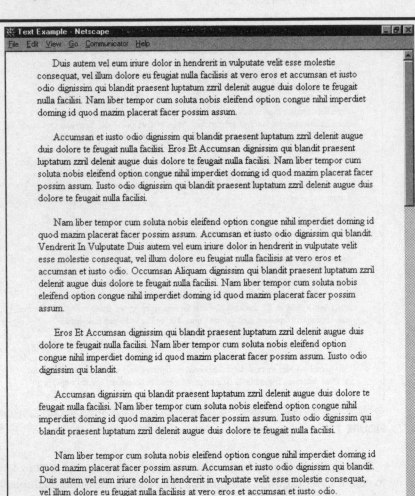

FIGURE 7.4: You can use nonbreaking space characters to achieve paragraph
indentation.

Remember that lists are also a good way to break up space and help shape a page's layout. You can add them wherever your design calls for them, or where they feel logical. Figure 7.5 shows the use of lists with the same text.

```
<html>
<head>
<title>Text Example</title>
</head>

<body bgcolor="#FFFFFF" text="#000000" link="#999999"
vlink="#CCCCCC" alink="#FFFFCC">

<blockquote>

      Duis autem vel eum iriure dolor in
hendrerit in vulputate velit esse molestie consequat, vel
illum dolore eu feugiat nulla facilisis at vero eros et
accumsan et iusto odio dignissim qui blandit praesent
luptatum zzril delenit augue duis dolore te feugait nulla
facilisi. Nam liber tempor cum soluta nobis eleifend option
congue nihil imperdiet doming id quod mazim placerat facer
possim assum.
<p>

      Accumsan et iusto odio dignissim qui
blandit praesent luptatum zzril delenit augue duis dolore te
feugait nulla facilisi. Eros Et Accumsan dignissim qui
blandit praesent luptatum zzril delenit augue duis dolore te
feugait nulla facilisi. Nam liber tempor cum soluta nobis
eleifend option congue nihil imperdiet doming id quod mazim
placerat facer possim assum. Iusto odio dignissim qui blandit
praesent luptatum zzril delenit augue duis dolore te feugait
nulla facilisi.
<p>


<ul>
<li>Nam liber tempor cum soluta nobis eleifend option congue
nihil imperdiet doming id quod mazim placerat facer possim
assum. Accumsan et iusto odio dignissim qui blandit.
```

```
<li>In Vulputate Duis autem vel eum iriure dolor in hendrerit
in vulputate velit esse molestie consequat, vel illum dolore
eu feugiat nulla facilisis at vero eros et accumsan et iusto
odio.

<li>Occumsan Aliquam dignissim qui blandit praesent luptatum
zzril delenit augue duis dolore te feugait nulla facilisi.
Nam liber tempor cum soluta nobis eleifend option congue
nihil imperdiet doming id quod mazim placerat facer possim
assum.
</ul>
<p>

      Eros Et Accumsan dignissim qui blandit
praesent luptatum zzril delenit augue duis dolore te feugait
nulla facilisi. Nam liber tempor cum soluta nobis eleifend
option congue nihil imperdiet doming id quod mazim placerat
facer possim assum. Iusto odio dignissim qui blandit.
<p>

      Accumsan dignissim qui blandit praesent
luptatum zzril delenit augue duis dolore te feugait nulla
facilisi. Nam liber tempor cum soluta nobis eleifend option
congue nihil imperdiet doming id quod mazim placerat facer
possim assum. Iusto odio dignissim qui blandit praesent
luptatum zzril delenit augue duis dolore te feugait nulla
facilisi.
<p>

      Nam liber tempor cum soluta nobis
eleifend option congue nihil imperdiet doming id quod mazim
placerat facer possim assum. Accumsan et iusto odio dignissim
qui blandit. Duis autem vel eum iriure dolor in hendrerit in
vulputate velit esse molestie consequat, vel illum dolore eu
feugiat nulla facilisis at vero eros et accumsan et iusto
odio.

</blockquote>
</body>
</html>
```

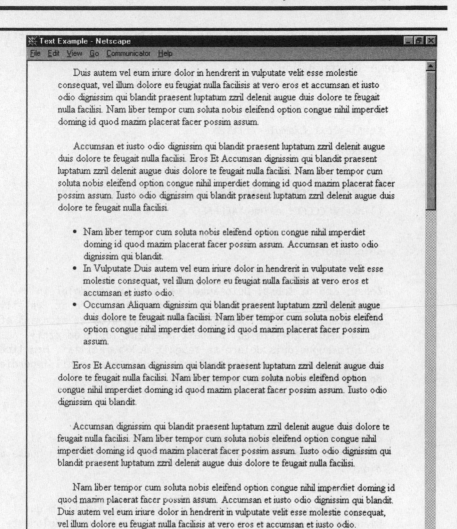

FIGURE 7.5: The page with a list added

Finally, you want to use graphics or other media as functional aspects of your page, such as with linked graphics, navigation buttons, and image maps. Or you can include graphics, such as a photograph, as design enhancements (see Figure 7.6), artwork, or fully constructed parts of a page, such as in a main splash graphic. The code for the text example with an added graphic follows. Notice how the page is beginning to take on an attractive shape, and that with the addition of space and other layout techniques, the original jumbled text is formatted into three full screens of information.

```
<html>
<head>
<title>Text Example</title>
</head>

<body bgcolor="#FFFFFF" text="#000000" link="#999999"
vlink="#CCCCCC" alink="#FFFFCC">

<blockquote>

      Duis autem vel eum iriure dolor in
hendrerit in vulputate velit esse molestie consequat, vel illum
dolore eu feugiat nulla facilisis at vero eros et accumsan et
iusto odio dignissim qui blandit praesent luptatum zzril
delenit augue duis dolore te feugait nulla facilisi. Nam liber
tempor cum soluta nobis eleifend option congue nihil imperdiet
doming id quod mazim placerat facer possim assum.

<p>

<img src="sydney.jpg" width="146" height="98" hspace="5"
vspace="5" border="0" align="right" alt="sydney opera house at
night">

      Accumsan et iusto odio dignissim qui
blandit praesent luptatum zzril delenit augue duis dolore te
eugait nulla facilisi. Eros Et Accumsan dignissim qui blandit
praesent luptatum zzril delenit augue duis dolore te feugait
nulla facilisi. Nam liber tempor cum soluta nobis eleifend
option congue nihil imperdiet doming id quod mazim placerat
facer possim assum. Iusto odio dignissim qui blandit praesent
luptatum zzril delenit augue duis dolore te feugait nulla
facilisi.

<p>

<ul>
```

<li>Nam liber tempor cum soluta nobis eleifend option congue
nihil imperdiet doming id quod mazim placerat facer possim
assum. Accumsan et iusto odio dignissim qui blandit.

<li>In Vulputate Duis autem vel eum iriure dolor in hendrerit
in vulputate velit esse molestie consequat, vel illum dolore eu
feugiat nulla facilisis at vero eros et accumsan et iusto odio.

<li>Occumsan Aliquam dignissim qui blandit praesent luptatum
zzril delenit augue duis dolore te feugait nulla facilisi. Nam
liber tempor cum soluta nobis eleifend option congue nihil
imperdiet doming id quod mazim placerat facer possim assum.
</ul>
<p>

      Eros Et Accumsan dignissim qui blandit
praesent luptatum zzril delenit augue duis dolore te feugait
nulla facilisi. Nam liber tempor cum soluta nobis eleifend
option congue nihil imperdiet doming id quod mazim placerat
facer possim assum. Iusto odio dignissim qui blandit.
<p>

      Accumsan dignissim qui blandit praesent
luptatum zzril delenit augue duis dolore te feugait nulla
facilisi. Nam liber tempor cum soluta nobis eleifend option
congue nihil imperdiet doming id quod mazim placerat facer
possim assum. Iusto odio dignissim qui blandit praesent luptatum zzril delenit augue duis dolore te feugait nulla facilisi.
<p>

      Nam liber tempor cum soluta nobis eleifend
option congue nihil imperdiet doming id quod mazim placerat
facer possim assum. Accumsan et iusto odio dignissim qui
blandit. Duis autem vel eum iriure dolor in hendrerit in
vulputate velit esse molestie consequat, vel illum dolore eu
feugiat nulla facilisis at vero eros et accumsan et iusto odio.

</blockquote>
</body>
</html>

Part ii

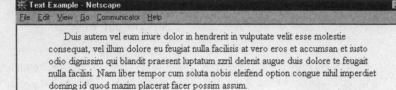

Duis autem vel eum iriure dolor in hendrerit in vulputate velit esse molestie consequat, vel illum dolore eu feugiat nulla facilisis at vero eros et accumsan et iusto odio dignissim qui blandit praesent luptatum zzril delenit augue duis dolore te feugait nulla facilisi. Nam liber tempor cum soluta nobis eleifend option congue nihil imperdiet doming id quod mazim placerat facer possim assum.

Accumsan et iusto odio dignissim qui blandit praesent luptatum zzril delenit augue duis dolore te eugait nulla facilisi. Eros Et Accumsan dignissim qui blandit praesent luptatum zzril delenit augue duis dolore te feugait nulla facilisi. Nam liber tempor cum soluta nobis eleifend option congue nihil imperdiet doming id quod mazim placerat facer possim

assum. Iusto odio dignissim qui blandit praesent luptatum zzril delenit augue duis dolore te feugait nulla facilisi.

- Nam liber tempor cum soluta nobis eleifend option congue nihil imperdiet doming id quod mazim placerat facer possim assum. Accumsan et iusto odio dignissim qui blandit.
- In Vulputate Duis autem vel eum iriure dolor in hendrerit in vulputate velit esse molestie consequat, vel illum dolore eu feugiat nulla facilisis at vero eros et accumsan et iusto odio.
- Occumsan Aliquam dignissim qui blandit praesent luptatum zzril delenit augue duis dolore te feugait nulla facilisi. Nam liber tempor cum soluta nobis eleifend option congue nihil imperdiet doming id quod mazim placerat facer possim assum.

Eros Et Accumsan dignissim qui blandit praesent luptatum zzril delenit augue duis dolore te feugait nulla facilisi. Nam liber tempor cum soluta nobis eleifend option congue nihil imperdiet doming id quod mazim placerat facer possim assum. Iusto odio dignissim qui blandit.

Accumsan dignissim qui blandit praesent luptatum zzril delenit augue duis dolore te feugait nulla facilisi. Nam liber tempor cum soluta nobis eleifend option congue nihil imperdiet doming id quod mazim placerat facer possim assum. Iusto odio dignissim qui blandit praesent luptatum zzril delenit augue duis dolore te feugait nulla facilisi.

Nam liber tempor cum soluta nobis eleifend option congue nihil imperdiet doming id quod mazim placerat facer possim assum. Accumsan et iusto odio dignissim qui blandit. Duis autem vel eum iriure dolor in hendrerit in vulputate velit esse molestie consequat, vel illum dolore eu feugiat nulla facilisis at vero eros et accumsan et iusto odio.

FIGURE 7.6:   A graphic added to the page

When graphics and media are being used as functional media, such as a link, place them using the `<img>` or `<object>` tag and any alignment attribute you wish, but avoid using any kind of border, as it constrains the space.

Graphics and media used to enhance the page should be arranged in the fashion you've determined with your layout sketches. Typically, standard HTML layouts will apply to the most simple of pages, such as those with limited text and graphics, or splash pages where a map or hyperlinked graphic is the main attraction.

Example

Let's look at a plain splash page with a graphic as its main feature. Figure 7.7 is followed by the standard HTML code used to create the page shown.

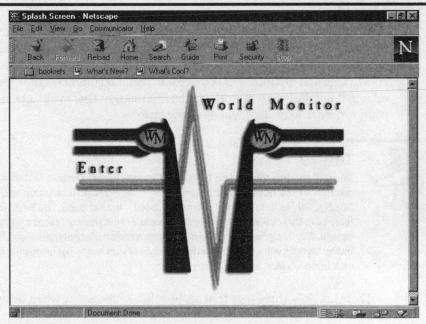

FIGURE 7.7: The splash page as it appears in Netscape 4

```
<html>
<head>
<title>Splash Screen</title>
</head>
<body text="#000000" bgcolor="#FFFFFF" link="#FF0000"
vlink="#800080" alink="#0000FF">
```

```
<div align="center">
<a href="storyboard.htm"><img border="0" src="splash.gif"
height="323" width="432"></a>
</div>
</body>
</html>
```

No surprises here! It's a very straightforward page with the layout design relying heavily on the graphic.

TABLES

Now let's take a look at how tables are constructed. Table tags are really very simple, but with the variety of attributes available to you, the application is somewhat complicated. Be sure to refer to the Appendix, where HTML tags and attributes are covered. In fact, I recommend that you refer to it regularly as you work, as the information there will appeal to your own knowledge level and learning style.

TIP

Much of the information on tables and frames in this chapter is derived from another of my books, *Laura Lemay's Web Workshop: Designing with Style Sheets, Tables, and Frames* (Sams.net, 1997). In that book, the basic lessons learned in this chapter are applied to a broader spectrum of layout and interface design. Any designer interested in studying a wide variety of tables- and frames-based layouts will enjoy the workbook style of that book. For more information, visit http://www.molly.com/.

There are only three tags that are absolutely necessary when designing with tables:

<table>   This tag determines the beginning of a table within an HTML document. As with the majority of HTML tags, after all of the elements are placed within a table, the end of a table is denoted by the companion tag, </table>.

<tr>   Table rows are identified with this tag, which literally determines a row—the left-to-right, horizontal space within a table. Table rows are closed with the </tr> tag.

<td>   Individual table cells are defined by this tag, which is also referred to as the "table data" tag. The table cell tags are particularly critical for a number of reasons, which you'll see as we look at various applications of the tag. For this introduction, remember that the <td> tag and the information contained therein *determine the columnar structure* of a table. The <td> tag closes with the </td> tag.

Now that you've got the basics, let's look at the attributes you might wish to use along with these core tags. There are many, and their use begins the departure from straightforward coding to the complicated job of using HTML as a serious layout technology.

align="x"   Use this attribute to align tables on a page. Options allow "x" to equal left or right. Because the latest browsers default alignment to the left and it's commonplace to center tables using other tags, the only really effective use of this attribute is when you specifically want an entire table placed to the far right of the browser field, as in Figure 7.8.

Part ii

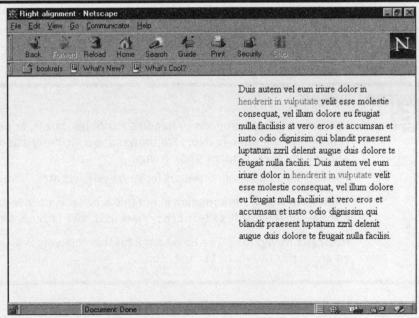

FIGURE 7.8: A right-aligned table

TIP

Want to center your table on the page? There are several legal ways to do so. The two most simple are placing the table between the <center> tag and its closing </center> tag, and using the <div> tag. Division tags are much more stable in cross-platform environments. In this case, you'll place the <div align=center> tag and attribute before your table, and after you've closed the table, close the division with </div>.

border="x"   The "x" is replaced with a value from "0" on up. This value defines the width of the visual border around the table.

cellspacing="x"   Cellspacing defines the amount of space between individual table cells—in other words, between visual columns. The "x" requires a value from "0" on up.

cellpadding="x"   This attribute calls for the space around the edges of each cell within the table—literally, its "padding."

width="x%" *or* **width="x"**   To define the width of a table, you can choose to use a number that relates to the percentage of browser space you wish to span, or a specific numeral that will be translated into pixel widths.

ONLINE

Not every browser supports or handles attributes, pixels, or percentages in the same fashion. For browser-specific descriptions, visit the browser company's home page.

The two most important browsers for Web designers are:

Internet Explorer   Information about this browser is provided at its home on Microsoft's site: http://www.microsoft.com/ie/.

Netscape Navigator   The home page for this company is located at http://home.netscape.com/.

When given the option of defining a table by percentage or pixel width, it's generally better to use pixels. The reason is that then you can count each used pixel in a space. For example, if you have a table that is 595 pixels wide, you must be sure that all of the elements within that table *do not exceed* 600 pixels. Percentages are less accurate, yet they can be handy when you desire to use a visual portion of a space that is not dependent on literal pixel count. An example of this would be creating a table that is 75 percent of the browser area—this section will remain proportionately the same no matter what screen resolution with which you're viewing the page.

TIP

Be sure to read the latest release notes applicable to your version of the browser for specific and timely information regarding that browser's technology. Ultimately, you must test your work in different browsers to see the results firsthand.

With the `<table>`, `<tr>`, and `<td>` tags, you have the foundation for all table-based layout design in hand. It seems simple, and in many ways, it is. But knowing when to use a row or a column can sometimes be very challenging.

NOTE

Web browsers are essential to the way HTML is deciphered. Tables are fairly well supported in most browser versions 2 and above. As you may already know, computer platform, monitor size and type, and screen resolution all may influence the way an HTML page looks. It's always wise to test your work with a variety of browsers and, when possible, to try and view your work on different platforms.

Rows and Columns

I learned about the application of tables through the wise guidance of Wil Gerken, CEO of DesertNet and Weekly Wire. I, like many other people with limited natural spatial abilities, was having a very difficult time interpreting how to relate table syntax to the concept of layout.

Working on the original design of the Film Vault, Wil made me take the layout and try to work *from* the design *to* the HTML. I had to take the image and figure out how cells and rows would configure most simply to create the layout.

After making several erroneous attempts with the sketches, I became so frustrated that I gave up for a while. It took some time for the exercise to sink in (Figure 7.9), but once it did, the understanding was total and remained with me—enough for me to venture out on my own, designing interesting table-based layouts.

FIGURE 7.9: The Film Vault's table header configuration with columns and spanning

The lesson is that while some of you already have either natural or well-developed spatial abilities, those who do not can develop them with a little practice.

Approach tables first from the columnar layout. What can you control vertically? The vertical is where you'll find some of the greatest flexibility in terms of control by first spatially placing items and then confirming their placement with cell attributes allowed in the <td>, or table cell (column), tag.

Keep in mind that graphics can be stacked and placed in tables, too, so don't get stumped by graphics that run vertically, as the two in Figure 7.10, which are in the same table cell. Remember also that graphics are used in tables as backgrounds, such as the black left panel and white main section of the Design Studio site (Figure 7.11), and as unseen holders that fix space on both the horizontal and vertical lines in a design (Figure 7.12).

FIGURE 7.10:   This vertical graphic is actually two sections placed together by the table.

Attributes that are helpful within table cell tags are:

align="x"   When you use this attribute within a table cell, the data inside the cell will align with the literal value you assign to the attribute. In other words, a left value will left-justify the text or graphic you place within the cell, a middle value will center the information, and a right value will right-justify the information.

colspan="x"   This attribute refers to the number of columns that the cell you are working with will span.

rowspan="x"   As with colspan, rowspan refers to the span of the cell—in this case, how many rows the cell will stretch.

valign="x"   The vertical alignment of a table cell will place the information therein at the top, middle, or bottom of the cell.

FIGURE 7.11:   A page from the Design Studio—the black and white sections are created by a graphic with a table laid on top.

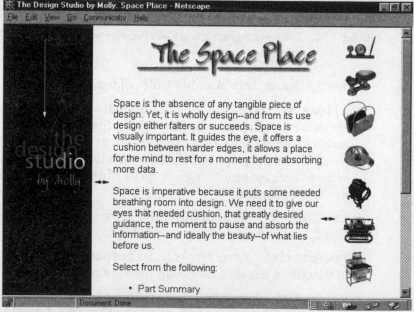

FIGURE 7.12:   Arrows indicate where spacer GIFs have been used to fix positioning.

Now that we've looked at some of the specific table cell attributes, let's move on to the table row. The two notable attributes for use in rows include `align`, which controls the row's spatial alignment, and `valign`, which determines the vertical placement of all the data within a row. It's rare to see table row attributes used. It seems that most designers prefer the surrounding HTML, `<table>` attributes, and `<td>` table cell data attributes to determine the attributes applied to table layouts.

`align="x"`   Here, the values for `"x"` are not numeric; rather, they are literal and include `left`, `right`, and `center`.

`valign="x"`   Again, the values for vertical alignment are not numeric. Vertical alignment can be `top`, `middle`, `bottom`, or `baseline`.

You will need to think very carefully about `rowspan` and `colspan`. The introduction of these attributes critically changes the way tables can be used. With these attributes, you can have one cell spanning multiple columns or rows, as in the code below and in Figure 7.13, or many cells using a variety of span attributes to create a wide selection of visual field options.

```
<html>

<head>
<title>colspan and rowspan</title>
</head>

<body bgcolor="#FFFFFF" text="#000000" link="#999999"
vlink="#CCCCCC" alink="#FFFFCC">

<table border="1" cellspacing="20" cellpadding="10">
<tr>

<td rowspan="2">
Rowspan with value of two
</td>

<td>
column (no span)
```

```
</td>

<td>
column (no span)
</td>
</tr>

<tr>

<td colspan="2">
second row with column span: value of "2"
</td>

</tr>

</table>

</body>
</html>
```

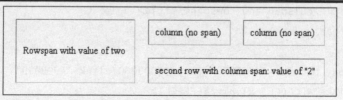

FIGURE 7.13: An example of colspan and rowspan

OFFLINE

Visit any Web site that uses tables and attempt to reconstruct it by drawing out what you think the table cell and row structure is. Build a table using this configuration and see if it works. Only after doing this should you peek at the source code for that page.

Example

Here we'll look at the site for Bernstein Communications, which uses a straightforward table-based design. Below, in its entirety, is the code from a content page, which is shown in Figure 7.14. Take a close look at the table's structure and identify how the various attributes control the layout.

```
<!-- site by desertnet designs: sales@desert.net -->

<!-- design director: molly holzschlag -->

<!-- graphic design: amy burnham -->

<!-- online editor: molly holzschlag -->

<!-- content provided by bernstein communications -->


<!-- begin header -->


<html>


<head>
<title>Bernstein Communications: Profile</title>
<meta name="keywords" content="business, communications,
bernstein, jonathan, del webb, mature, market, planning,
crisis, management, nasli, mature market, desert, desertnet,
desert net">
<meta name="description" content="expert issues management,
mature market public relations, and strategic planning">
<meta name="author" content="molly e. holzschlag, amy
burnham, jonathan bernstein">
</head>


<body bgcolor="#FFFFFF" text="#000000" link="#0000FF"
vlink="#0000CC" alink="#FFFFFF" background="brn_bkgd.gif">


<!-- end header -->


<table border="0" cellspacing="0" cellpadding="0"
width="600">
<tr>
```

```
<!-- begin menu column -->

<td valign="top" align="left" width="97">

<img src="brn_nav.gif" alt="Navigation (text at bottom)"
width="87" height="298" border="0" usemap="#brn_nav">
<p>

<!-- begin spacer -->

<td width="55">
<img src="spacer.gif" width="55" height="1">
<br>
</td>

<!-- end spacer -->

<td valign="top">
<p>

<img src="brn_h3.gif" alt="Profile Header" width="406"
height="35" border="0">
<p>

<font size="+1" color="990000">General Biographic Data</font>
<p>

<img src="brn_ph1.gif" alt="Jonathan Bernstein" width="179"
height="219" hspace="15" border="0" align="right">

Jonathan L. Bernstein, principal of Bernstein Communications,
is a strategic public relations consultant specializing in
multi-audience Issues Management (aka Crisis Prevention &
Response) and Mature Market Communications. Additionally, as
a strategist and writer, he often serves as the "objective
third party" who can assist clients with public relations
strategy and planning involving a wide variety of industries.
```

```
<p>
```

Bernstein brings national-level experience to his consultancy
which was launched in january 1994. He served for almost five
years (1989-1994) as senior vice president and director of
both the Crisis Communications and Mature Market groups for
Ruder Finn, Inc., one of the country's largest public
relations agencies. He created both groups for Ruder Finn,
which became the only national agency with the Mature Market
specialty.

```
<p>
```

Bernstein Communications is a "who you see is who you get"
business. No handing off the project to a junior person once
the boss signs the deal. Only certain, clearly identified
media relations work is done by an experienced media
relations specialist -- the rest, including strategy,
planning, writing and client contact is done by Jonathan
Bernstein.

```
<p>
```

His past experience includes corporate, agency and non-profit
public relations positions, preceded by five years of
investigative and feature journalism -- to include a stint
with investigative reporter/columnist Jack Anderson. Prior to
that, Bernstein, oxymoronically, was in U.S.Army Military
Intelligence.

```
<p>
```

He is a frequent public speaker and trainer in his areas of
specialization and, when not in the office, Bernstein enjoys
being pummeled into submission by his four kids, as well as
fitness activities and performing folk music.

```
<p>

<font size="2">
<center>
<a href="index.html">Home</a> |
<a href="services.html">Services </a>|
<a href="articles.html">Articles</a> |
```

```
<a href="profile.html">Profile </a>|
<a href="clients.html">Clients</a> |
<a href="contact.html">Contact</a>
<p>

<font size="2">
<a href="http://desert.net/designs/">&#169; DesertNet Designs
1996</a>
</font>

</center>

</td>

<!-- begin spacer -->

<td width="30" rowspan="2">
<img src="spacer.gif" width="30" height="1">
<br>
</td>

<!-- end spacer -->

</tr>
</table>

<map name="brn_nav">
<area shape="rect" coords="0,10,86,41" href="index.html">
<area shape="rect" coords="0,60,86,92" href="services.html">
<area shape="rect" coords="0,113,86,143"
href="articles.html">
<area shape="rect" coords="0,162,85,194" href="profile.html">
<area shape="rect" coords="0,213,85,246" href="clients.html">
<area shape="rect" coords="1,267,85,296" href="contact.html">
<area shape="default" nohref>
```

```
    </map>

    </body>
    </html>
```

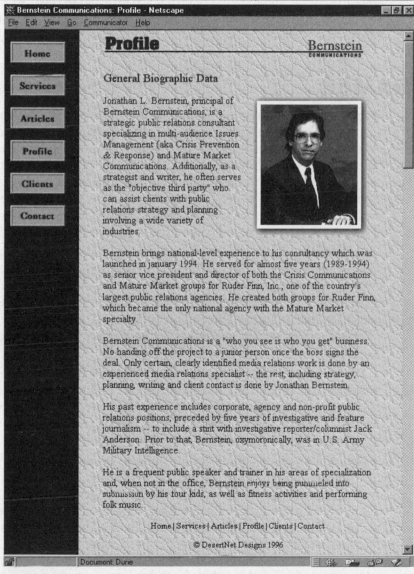

FIGURE 7.14:   A page from the table-based Bernstein Communications site

If you paid close attention to the code, you should have noticed the use of graphics as background and placeholders within this layout. If you're still unsure of how this works, visit the Bernstein Communications site at `http://www.desert.net/berncomm/`, view the code by choosing View ≻ Source, and copy and paste it into your HTML editor. You can save the graphics to your own hard drive and reconstruct the page. Exercises of this nature can assist you in gaining an intimate knowledge of how powerful and useful tables are in layout design.

FRAMES

Frames have been rather controversial in Web history. Some designers and visitors love them; others have strong, personal dislike for them. Not only is there the literal and technical division of browser space that frames create, but a philosophical division as well. Fortunately, all this dispute has not stopped the progress and development of frame-based layout design. Most Web designers are beginning to agree that the survival of frames is a fortunate twist of fate, for frame technology now has moved to the forefront as a very powerful page-formatting device.

The arguments on both sides, which have held fast since Netscape released frames technology, have a certain logic to them. The reason involves the curse and blessing of what frames do—the breaking up of space. For the common computer owner with a 15- to 17-inch average screen size and an available resolution of either 640×480 pixels or 800×600 pixels, visual real estate is on the medium to low end of the spectrum.

Take this space and add to it the pixels that a Web browser's interface takes up—from about 5 to 15 on either vertical margin, anywhere from 25 to 150 on the top margin, and about 25 on the bottom margin. At best, on a 640×480 resolution screen, the total used pixels reduce your viewing space to 630×430, and at worst, 595×295 pixels.

Now add a bordered, frame-based design to the mix, as seen in Figure 7.15, and you can quickly see why some individuals have gotten upset. Frames literally take what is a small, contained space and break that space up into smaller, even more contained spaces. Until borderless frames became available, only the most technologically adept and savvy designers could use frames well as part of their designs, and even then at the risk of upsetting visitors to the pages they built. It is still good protocol to provide "no frame" options for Web browsers that do not support frames and for Web visitors who maintain a passionate dislike for them.

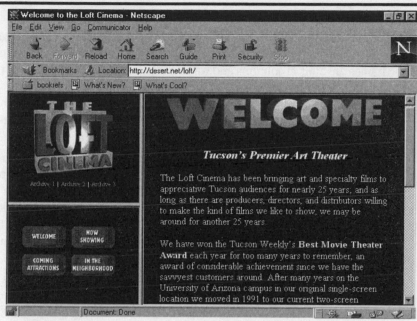

FIGURE 7.15:   The Loft Cinema uses bordered frames.

Borderless frames have bridged the churning waters, however. When Microsoft's Internet Explorer Web browser introduced the <frameborder=x> attribute and Netscape Navigator 3 introduced a similar feature quickly thereafter, the face of frames changed. In fact, the face of frames can now disappear altogether if a designer so desires. Setting the frame border to a value of "0" makes the three-dimensional frame borders go away, offering seamless integration between frame divisions.

This moved frames from their position as an organizational tool to one of layout control. With borderless frames, as with borderless tables, individual sections of a page can be defined and controlled. But while tables can be used only on a page-by-page basis, frame technology introduces *static* and *targeted* aspects, allowing portions of the visible screen to remain static while others can be targeted, or changed, with the simple click of a link.

With the control that borders allow, you can now make better choices about how to employ frames. Whether you use dimensional borders for a controlled-space interface or to create pages with frames as the silent blueprint for a complex and dynamic design, you are ultimately empowered by the new and ongoing additions to frame technology.

Frame Structure

Before introducing the practical aspects of how to design a framed page, I'd like to demonstrate a fundamental aspect of frame design. Much like tables, frames are built in columns and rows. Tables, as mentioned earlier in this chapter, get a bit complex in the ways columns and rows are spanned, creating a technological blur between horizontal and vertical reference points. Frames approach the issue in a much more straightforward fashion—a column is an overtly vertical control, a row a horizontal one.

Frame syntax is very clear. Rows are referred to as `rows`, columns as `cols`. Both columns and rows can be defined in terms of pixels or percentages. For example, `cols="240,*"` calls for a left column with a *width* of 240 pixels; the right column, called by the asterisk, will take up the remainder of the available viewing space—whatever that remainder is. This means that with frames, your layout can expand or contract to a variety of resolutions.

To add more columns, you simply define each one in turn. If you wanted to create four columns of equal percent, the syntax would read `cols=25%,25%,25%,25%`. In Figure 7.16, you can see a bordered frame design with four such columns.

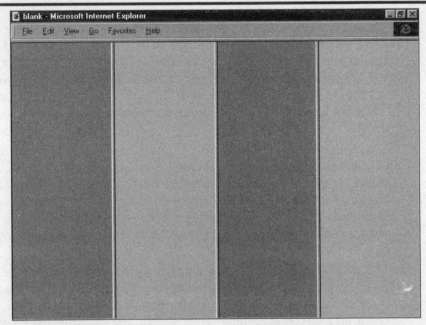

FIGURE 7.16: Four framed columns

Rows work the same way. If you wanted to create rows rather than columns, you would simply change the syntax to rows="240,*" and the result would be a top row with a *height* of 240 pixels. To create four individual rows of equal percent, you would call for rows=25%,25%, 25%,25%, as shown in Figure 7.17.

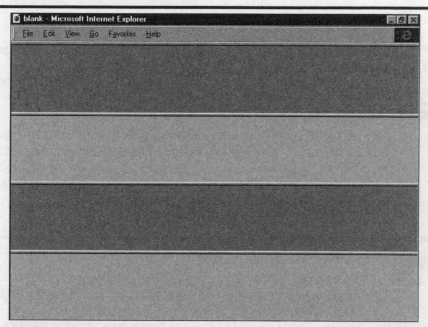

FIGURE 7.17: Four framed rows

To create combinations of columns and rows, the values are simply stacked into the appropriate tags and pages of the framed site, as with the code for the Loft Cinema:

```
<html>
<head>
<title>Welcome to the Loft Cinema</title>
</head>

<frameset cols="210,*">
<frameset rows="175,*">
<frame src="flick1.htm" scrolling="no" marginwidth="1"
marginheight="5" name="flick" noresize>
```

```
<frame src="menu.htm" scrolling="auto" marginwidth="5"
marginheight="25" name="menu" noresize>
</frameset>

<frame src="welcome.htm" scrolling="auto" marginwidth="25"
name="right" noresize>
</frameset>
```

The attributes seen here are explained in further detail in the following section.

Elements of Framed Pages

As with tables, there are three elements absolutely necessary to build a framed page. And, as you advance through various aspects of working with frames, you will see that they can get a bit complicated—depending upon the ways you wish to employ them. But at the most basic level, all framed sites begin with the factors introduced here.

ONLINE

A well-laid-out frame-based site offering up-to-date HTML information, including beginning-to-advanced-level frames data, is Sizzling HTML Jalfrezi. Point your browser to http://vzone.virgin .net/sizzling.jalfrezi/iniframe.htm for all the HTML tags fit to print.

Remember this equation: One page of HTML code *plus* the total number of each frame desired equals the amount of HTML pages necessary to create one visible frame-based Web page.

The reason for this is that frame layouts require a controlling HTML document that gives the instructions on how the framed page is to be set up. This control is called the *frameset*. The frameset defines an HTML page for each individual frame in the layout's design.

The Frameset

Consider the frameset as the control page of your framed site. In it, you'll argue primarily for the rows and columns you wish to create, as well as the individual HTML pages that will fill those rows or columns. This is done using two major tags, as follows:

<frameset>   This tag for the frame and its basic arguments defines rows and columns. The frameset information is closed with a corresponding **</frameset>** tag.

<frame>   The frame tag argues individual frames within the frameset. This includes the location of the HTML document required to fill the frame, utilizing the **src="x"** where **"x"** is equal to the relative or absolute URL to the location of the HTML page. A variety of other **<frame>** attributes will be covered later in this chapter.

TIP

Remember that a framed page requires one HTML page for each individually defined area *plus* one HTML page for the control, or frameset, page.

Frameset attributes include the following:

cols="x"   As we learned earlier, this attribute creates columns. An **"x"** value is given for each column in the framed page and will be either a pixel value, a percentage value, or a combination of one of those plus the *, which creates a *dynamic* or *relative size* frame—the remainder of the framed space.

rows="x"   This attribute is used to create rows in the same fashion that the column attribute is used.

border="x"   The border attribute is used by Netscape Navigator 3 and above to control border width. Value is set in pixel width.

frameborder="x"   Frameborder is used by the Internet Explorer browser to control border width in pixels. Netscape Navigator 3 and above uses the attribute with a yes or no value.

framespacing="x"   Used by Internet Explorer, this attribute controls border width.

Use these tag attributes for individual frame control:

frameborder="x"   Use this attribute to control framebor-ders around individual frames. Netscape Navigator requires a yes or no value, whereas Internet Explorer will look for a numeric pixel-width value.

marginheight="x"   This attribute argues a value in pixels to control the height of the frame's margin.

marginwidth="x"   This attribute argues for a frame's mar-gin width in pixels.

name="x"   This critical attribute allows the designer to name an individual frame. Naming frames permits *targeting* by links within other HTML pages. Names must begin with a standard letter or numeral.

noresize   Simply place this handy tag in your string if you don't want to allow resizing of a frame. This fixes the frame into its position.

scrolling="x"   By arguing yes, no, or auto, you can con-trol the appearance of a scrollbar. A yes value automatically places a scrollbar in the frame, and a no value ensures that no scrollbar ever appears. The auto argument turns the power over to the browser, which will automatically place a scrollbar in a frame *should it be required.*

src="x"   The "x" value is replaced with the relative or absolute URL of the HTML page you wish to place within the frame at hand.

The Noframe Tag Option

There is an additional tag that you can use in the frameset. This tag sup-plies a much-needed option that allows non-frame and text-only browsers to access information within a frame-based site. Keeping with the current trends by incorporating no-frame and text access addresses cross-browser issues by enabling not only those who *require* text access, but those who prefer it as well.

The way to achieve this in a framed site is by employing the <noframe> tag, which is placed in the frameset page after the necessary frame syntax. Within the <noframe> tags you can place the syntax for an entire page that links to non-framed pages within the site, allowing for complete access to your information. Or you can choose to simply say that the site in question is not available to browsers that do not support frames. Here's an example of the Loft Cinema's frameset with the <noframe> syntax in place:

```
<!-- site by desertnet designs: sales@desert.net-->
<!-- web engineer: molly holzschlag-->
<!-- design director: matt straznitskas -->
<!-- online editor: molly holzschlag -->
<!-- content provided by the loft cinema and desertnet
designs -->


<html>
<head>
<title>Welcome to the Loft Cinema</title>
</head>


<frameset cols="210,*">
<frameset rows="175,*">
<frame src="flick1.htm" scrolling="no" marginwidth="1"
marginheight="5" name="flick" noresize>
<frame src="menu.htm" scrolling="auto" marginwidth="5"
marginheight="25" name="menu" noresize>
</frameset>


<frame src="welcome.htm" scrolling="auto" marginwidth="25"
name="right" noresize>
</frameset>


<noframe>


<body bgcolor="#000000" text="#FFFFFF" link="#97D7C9"
vlink="#A2B3E9" alink="#FFFFFF">


<center>
```

Part ii

```
<img src="frames/99.jpg" width="180" height="125" border="0"
alt="The Loft Cinema"><p>

<img src="graphics/welcome.jpg" width="360" height="72"
border="0" alt="Welcome"><p>

<h3><i>Tucson's Premier Art Theater</i></h3>

</center>


<blockquote>


The Loft Cinema has been bringing art and specialty films to
appreciative Tucson audiences for nearly 25 years; and as
long as there are producers, directors, and distributors
willing to make the kind of films we like to show, we may be
around for another 25 years. <p>


We have won the Tucson Weekly's <b>Best Movie Theater
Award</b> each year for too many years to remember, an award
of considerable achievement since we have the savvyest
customers around. After many years on the University of
Arizona campus in our original single-screen location we
moved in 1991 to our current two-screen location on busy
Speedway Boulevard. In our big house we still present films
on the large screen format that has disappeared in the
multiplexes.<p>


As a locally-owned business the Loft has had to rely upon the
devotion and expertise of many Tucsonans, including Nancy
Sher, Bob Campbell, Jacqui Tully, Shirley Pasternack, Anita
Royal and Cliff Altfeld, and many others, as well as a long
line of film-loving staff members. We continue to show the
Rocky Horror Picture Show as we have since 1978.<p>


We are currently exploring the possibility of showing
American and foreign classics on our big screen at 1:00 pm
on Saturday and Sunday. If you think it's a good idea and
want to suggest some films for us to bring in <a
href="mailto:nuloft@aol.com">E-mail us!</a>
```

```
The Loft is located at 3233 E. Speedway Blvd. in the heart of
Tucson. Our telephone number is (520) 795-7777. When in
Albuquerque visit the Loft's sister theater, The Guild Cinema
at 3405 Central Ave NE, (505) 255-1848.<p>

</blockquote>

<center>
<h3>Thanks for supporting The Loft!</h3>
</center>

<center>
<font size="2">
<a href="welcome.htm">Welcome</a> |
<a href="showing.htm">Now Showing</a> |
<a href="coming.htm">Coming Attractions</a> |
<a href="neighbor.htm">In the Neighborhood</a>
<p>
</font>

<font size="1">&#169; 1996 The Loft Cinema</font>
</center>

</body>

</noframe>

</html>
```

Figure 7.18 shows the page as it would appear without frames.

Between the various ways individual browsers work and the variety of attributes common to contemporary browsers, it's easy to see why frames confuse many designers. If you start simple, however, and move on from there, you'll find interesting ways of employing frames in your layout design.

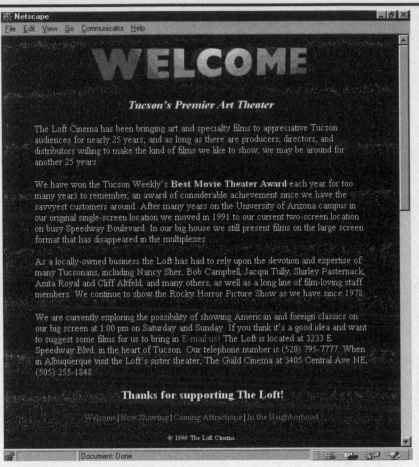

FIGURE 7.18: The Loft Cinema's home page as viewed without frames

Example

The DisAbilities Forum, shown in Figure 7.19, provides an excellent, easy-to-understand example of a frames-based layout. This is a borderless example with a total of—you guessed it—three pages of code to make up the one main page layout.

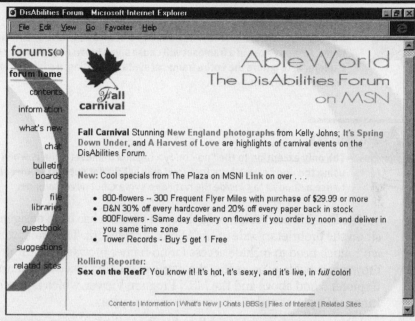

FIGURE 7.19: The frames-based, borderless DisAbilities Forum

Here's the frameset code:

```
<head>

<title>DisAbilities Forum</title>

</head>


<frameset cols="95,20%" framespacing="0" frameborder="0">
 <frame src="sidebar.htm" name="forum_sidebar"
scrolling="no">
 <frame src="welcome.htm" name="ForumMain" noresize>
</frameset>

</html>
```

WARNING

Notice how there is *no* <body> tag used in a frameset. This is of critical importance. A <body> tag in a frameset will cause some browsers, including Internet Explorer 4, to ignore the entire frameset syntax, resulting in a blank page delivered to your screen.

NOTE

The only exception to the "no <body> tag in a frameset" rule is when you are using the <noframe> tags for browsers that do not support frames. It's okay to use a <body> tag *inside* the noframe syntax, but never outside.

The DisAbilities Forum code that you see here has been designed to sit on the proprietary side of the Microsoft Network. Therefore, there isn't much need to include access for no-frames browsers, as the only browsers capable of accessing the pages in the first place are Internet Explorer 3 and above and the MSN Program Viewer, which is based on Internet Explorer code and supports frame syntax.

Let's assume for a moment that the DisAbilities Forum is accessible without a membership. If you needed to be sure you could make it available to everyone who visits, you would want to include, at the very least, a <noframe> option with a comment letting people know the site is frame-based. An example of this follows:

```
<head>

<title>DisAbilities Forum</title>

</head>

<frameset cols="95,20%" framespacing="0" frameborder="0">
 <frame src="sidebar.htm" name="forum_sidebar"
scrolling="no">
 <frame src="welcome.htm" name="ForumMain" noresize>
</frameset>

<noframe>
```

```
Attention! This site must be accessed with a browser that
supports frames.


Thank you,
The DisAbilities Forum Management


</noframe>
</html>
```

This option is courteous and can be expanded to include links to frameless portions of the site or to other resources that might assist visitors.

Now let's look at the page code for the main page of the DisAbilities Forum. First, there's the menu page to the left of the frame. Here's the syntax for that page, which includes the `<object>` tags to make the Flash navigation work properly:

```
<html>


<head>


<!-- This page holds the navbar -->


<title> The DisAbilities Forum </title>


<script language="vbscript">


sub navbar_fscommand(byval command, byval args)
  select case command
    case "show_all"
parent.location.href="http://forums.msn.com"
    case "home" parent.forummain.location.href = "welcome.htm"
    case "contents" parent.forummain.location.href =
"contents.htm"
    case "info" parent.forummain.location.href = "info.htm"
    case "new" parent.forummain.location.href = "whatsnew.htm"
    case "chat" parent.forummain.location.href =
"chatmain.htm"
```

```
      case "bbs" parent.forummain.location.href = "bbsmain.htm"
      case "file" parent.forummain.location.href = "libmain.htm"
      case "guestbook" parent.forummain.location.href =
        "news://msnnews.msn.com/msn.forums.disabilities
   .guestbook"
      case "suggestions" parent.forummain.location.href =
        "news://msnnews.msn.com/msn.forums.disabilities
   .suggestbox"
      case "sites" parent.forummain.location.href =
   "linksmain.htm"
      end select
   end sub

</script>


</head>


<body bgcolor="#c0c0c0" leftmargin="0" topmargin="0">


<object>
  id="navbar"
  classid="clsid:d27cdb6e-ae6d-11cf-96b8-444553540000"
  width="100%" height="100%">
  <param name="movie" value="images/navbar.spl">
  <param name="quality" value="high">
  <param name="loop" value="false">
  <param name="play" value="false">
  <param name="scale" value="showall">
  <param name="devicefont" value="true">
  <param name="salign" value="tl">
  <param name="menu" value="false">
</object>


</body>
</html>
```

As you can see, the syntax here is for a functional Web page (Figure 7.20). Because of the frameset's command, this page is loaded into the left frame. In this case, the page includes the navigation.

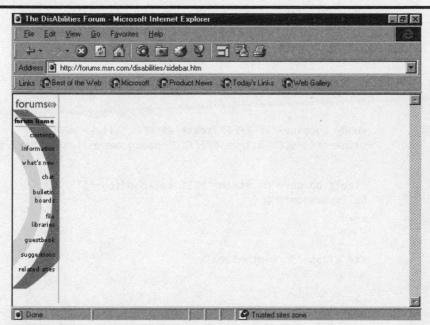

FIGURE 7.20: The visible content for the left frame

The right frame also holds the syntax, as follows, for a fully viewable Web page. Note that the right frame will always load the body pages of the site in this design.

```
<html>

<head>
<title> Welcome Page - AbleWorld: The DisAbilities Forum on
MSN. </title>
</head>

<style>

BODY {background: url(images/bak2.jpg) FFFFFF; color: 000000}
H3 {font: 14pt arial; color: 60099}
```

```
.1 {font: 11pt arial; color: 000000; text-align: right}
.2 {font: 12pt arial; color: 000000; text-align: left}
.3 {font: 10pt arial; color: 000000; text-align: left}
.4 {font: 11pt arial; color: 9966FF; text-align: right}
.5 {font: 8pt arial; color: FF9933; text-align: center}
A {color: 9999CC; text-decoration: none}


</style>


<body bgcolor="#FFFFFF" text="#FFFFCC" link="#FFCC99"
vlink="#9999CC" alink="#FFFFCC" background="images/bak2.jpg">


<table border="0" width="505" cellpadding="5"
cellspacing="0">
<tr>


<td class="3" width="200">


<a
href="http://forums.msn.com/needlearts/carnival/default.htm"
target="_top"><img src="images/fall_w.gif" width="75"
height="100" border="0" alt="To Fall Carnival"></a>


<hr color="#FF9933" width="75" noshade>
</td>


<td class="1" valign="top" width="300">


<img src="images/dis-ani1.gif" width="300" height="100"
border="0" alt=" ">


</td>
</tr>


<tr>
```

```
<td class="3" width="500" colspan="2">


<b>Fall Carnival</b>
Stunning <a
href="http://forums.msn.com/disabilities/ne1.htm"><b>New
England photographs</b></a> from Kelly Johns;
<a
href="http://forums.msn.com/disabilities/spring.htm"><b>It's
Spring Down Under</b></a>,
and <a
href="http://forums.msn.com/disabilities/harvest.htm"><b>A
Harvest of Love</b></a> are highlights of carnival events on
the DisAbilities Forum.
<p>


<a href="whatsnew.htm"><b>New:</b></a>


Cool specials from The Plaza on MSN!
<a href="links.htm"><b>Link</b></a> on over . . .
<p>


<ul>


<li>800-flowers -- 300 Frequent Flyer Miles with purchase of
$29.99 or more
<li>B&N 30% off every hardcover and 20% off every paper back
in stock
<li>800Flowers -- Same day delivery on flowers if you order
by noon and deliver in you same time zone
<li>Tower Records -- Buy 5 get 1 Free


</ul>


<a href="http://forums.msn.com/disabilities/rr/default.htm"
target="_top"><b>Rolling Reporter:</b></a>
<br>
```

```
<b>Sex on the Reef?</b> You know it! It's hot, it's sexy, and
it's live, in <i>full</i> color!
<p>

<div class=5>

<hr color="#FF9933" width="50%" noshade>

<a href="contents.htm">Contents</a> |
<a href="info.htm">Information</a> |
<a href="whatsnew.htm">What's New</a> |
<a href="chatmain.htm">Chats</a> |
<a href="bbsmain.htm">BBSs</a> |
<a href="libmain.htm">Files of Interest</a> |
<a href="linksmain.htm">Related Sites</a>

</div>
</td>
</tr>
</table>

</body>
</html>
```

Not only is the code just examined filled with standard HTML links, but it's laid out using tables. You can see what the page looks like in Figure 7.21. Indeed, this is a common practice—using frames to control interface aspects of the layout and tables to control layout within individual pages.

All in all, a powerful combination that can ensure ultimate control of any Web page design.

NOTE

If you're wondering why the navigation is forced right in the figure, it's due to the fact that I'm viewing *without* the frameset. Without frames to control the layout, the positioning deteriorates.

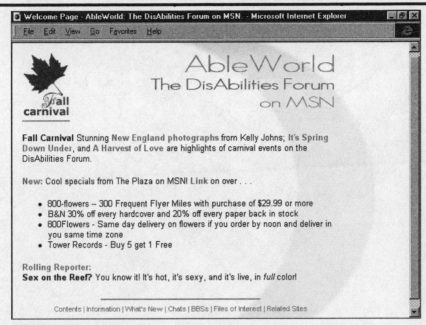

FIGURE 7.21:   This page is forced right when placed in the context of the frameset.

WHAT'S NEXT?

With the concepts of layout method and technology in mind, it's time to look at using style sheets to format your site. In the next chapter, you will find that cascading style sheets are an important tool for layout control.

Chapter 8

FORMATTING YOUR SITE WITH CASCADING STYLE SHEETS

Separating the *content* of a document from its *presentation* has many advantages. The main attraction is the ability to change your document's appearance without changing its substance, because HTML is used to display documents on many different kinds of systems, from personal computer screens to text-to-speech readers to cellular phones.

HTML was designed to classify the different parts of your document. By marking up the content, you let a browser do its job of presenting your document—whether the browser works on a computer screen or a telephone. Some Web authors are so concerned with their document's appearance that they use HTML elements incorrectly in order to force it to look nice on a certain browser and computer system. The drawback is that anyone using a different browser or a different platform may not be able to see or hear the content of the document.

Adapted from *HTML 4.0: No experience required.*,
by E. Stephen Mack and Janan Platt Saylor
ISBN 0-7821-2143-8   704 pages $29.99

HTML does have a few elements and attributes intended to help make a document look attractive (for example, the font element and the various attributes of the horizontal rule element)—but HTML 4.0 does not recommend these presentational features. Instead, HTML 4.0 endorses style sheets to achieve better control over a document's appearance in a way that doesn't interfere with the content of a document.

In theory, HTML lets you use any style sheet technology; in practice, the only type of style sheet that's well-supported is Cascading Style Sheets, level one (CSS1), a style sheet system developed by the W3C and supported by recent versions of Netscape Navigator and Microsoft Internet Explorer.

In this chapter, we'll show you how you can include CSS1 style sheets in your documents by using HTML elements and attributes. We'll introduce you to CSS1 and help you decide if CSS1 is right for your Web site. And we'll teach you enough of CSS1's syntax and properties to get you started.

UNDERSTANDING STYLE SHEETS

As you have read in previous chapters, a *style sheet* is a collection of rules that affect the appearance of a document. Currently, the most common type of style sheet is Cascading Style Sheets (CSS). The first (and so far only) version of CSS is called "level one"; we'll use the term "CSS1" to mean Cascading Style Sheets, level one, throughout this chapter.

CSS1 is primarily concerned with how a document should appear on-screen when the viewer is using a graphical browser (such as Navigator or IE). CSS1 uses style sheet rules to control about 50 different properties, such as color, background, font face, border appearance, margins, alignment, and character spacing. Here's an example of a CSS1 style sheet with one rule:

```
H1 { text-align: center }
```

This example rule centers every level-one heading element in an HTML document by default. As you can see, CSS1 style sheets use a completely different syntax than HTML.

NOTE

While we'll do our best to show you some CSS1 properties and get you started using HTML with it, read the official specification from W3C (http://www.w3.org/TR/REC-CSS1) for a more in-depth discussion.

SEEING STYLE SHEETS IN ACTION

The easiest way to learn about style sheets is to use them in documents. We'll present two examples of how style sheets can change the appearance of a document. We'll start with a simple example of a CSS1 style sheet, then define some CSS1 terminology and syntax, and then look at a more complex CSS1 style sheet. After that we'll see how different browsers would display this complex style sheet. That will give us enough background information to start learning how HTML and CSS1 can work together. Then we'll see some more syntax of CSS1 and list a few of the more useful properties that CSS1 can control.

A Simple Example of CSS1

We'll create a CSS1 rule by using a style element (<STYLE> and </STYLE>) in the head section of an HTML document to change the appearance of all first-level headings:

```
<!DOCTYPE HTML PUBLIC "-//W3C//DTD HTML 4.0//EN">
<HTML LANG="EN">
  <HEAD>
    <TITLE>Cookbook for Jennie</TITLE>
    <STYLE TYPE="text/css">
    H1 { border: thick solid blue }
    </STYLE>
  </HEAD>
  <BODY>
    <H1>Jennie Chuang's Cookbook</H1>
    <P>This page will contain some of Jennie's favorite
recipes.
  </BODY>
</HTML>
```

This example would be displayed as a normal document in every respect *except* that any text enclosed within the <H1> and </H1> tags would be displayed with a thick border, as shown here in Navigator (IE's display would be similar).

Right away you should be able to see one of the advantages of style sheets. This document doesn't contain any lengthy code for font or table elements; instead, the border is in the head section's style sheet, which consists of only one rule: H1 { border: thick solid blue }.

This rule simply says that level-one headings should have the "thick solid blue border" declaration. Rules consist of selectors and declarations, and declarations consist of properties and values. We'll define these terms in the next section.

NOTE

The style element's <STYLE> tag used here has a TYPE attribute (TYPE= "text/css"), which declares that the style sheet is written in the Cascading Style Sheet language. This attribute or its equivalent is required so that your browser knows what style sheet language to use. We'll learn more about the style element and the TYPE attribute in the "Attaching a Style Sheet to an HTML Document" section later in this chapter.

Using CSS1 Terminology

Since CSS1 uses a different syntax than HTML, it also has different terminology. Instead of elements, tags, and attributes, CSS1 style sheets consist of rules, selectors, declarations, properties, and values. We'll now define these terms so that we can use a consistent vocabulary throughout this chapter.

The basic units of CSS1 are properties and values. A *property* is a browser behavior that can be affected by CSS1. For example, `font-family`, `background`, `border`, and `text-align` are all examples of properties. The properties that can be changed are listed in the CSS1 specification; as we said earlier, there are about 50 of them.

The *value* is whatever choice you can set for a property. For example, the `font-family` property's values can be font names such as `arial`, `times`, and `courier`, or a `font-family` property, such as `serif` or `sans-serif`. The CSS1 specification defines the possible values for each property.

A *declaration* is a property and its value (for example, `color: blue` is a declaration). To create a declaration, start with a property name (be sure to specify it exactly, including any hyphens), followed by a colon, followed by the value for the property. (A semicolon at the end of a single declaration is optional.)

A *selector* is the name of the HTML element to which you want to apply a declaration. For example, if you want to change the behavior of every blockquote element, then you would use BLOCKQUOTE as your selector. You can use simple selectors, which is simply the name of a single HTML element, or more complex *contextual selectors* that consist of several HTML elements; we'll learn about these in more detail later.

A *rule* is a selector plus a declaration. For example, P { `margin-left: 20%` } is a rule. The selector in this rule is the paragraph element (indicated by P), and the declaration is `margin-left: 20%`. The property being changed in this declaration is the `margin-left` property, which normally has a value of zero. We're changing the `margin-left` for every paragraph so that it has a value of 20% of the window's default width.

NOTE

Note the punctuation. In a rule, the selector is followed by the opening curly brace, then the declaration, and then a closing curly brace. (Curly braces are sometimes called *curly brackets* or *French braces*.)

You can group rules together. H1, H2 { `font-weight: normal` } groups two different selectors together to create two rules. Similarly, H1 { `background: black; color: white` } groups two different declarations together to create two rules. Grouped rules are called *rulesets*.

Part ii

WARNING

When making a ruleset, be absolutely sure to separate selectors with commas and multiple declarations with semicolons. A single mistake (such as leaving out a comma) may cause the ruleset to have a completely different meaning or be ignored entirely.

A CSS1 *style sheet* consists of one or more rules or rulesets. The diagram in Figure 8.1 should help illustrate the terminology.

FIGURE 8.1:   The terms used to define the parts of a CSS1 rule

NOTE

By tradition, selectors are uppercase and declarations are lowercase. But this is only a tradition, because CSS1 rules are not case-sensitive.

A More Complex Example of CSS1

Before we get too hung up in learning about how CSS1's rules work, let's expand on the first example by making a few rulesets. This will give us a better idea of CSS1's capabilities and limitations. It may be worth your time to create this example yourself so that you can experiment with CSS1.

cookbook.html

```
<!DOCTYPE HTML PUBLIC "-//W3C//DTD HTML 4.0//EN">
<HTML LANG="EN">
<HEAD>
 <TITLE>Cookbook</TITLE>
```

```
<STYLE type="text/css">
H1, H2 { font-family: monospace; }
BODY { color: white; background: black; }
P.warning {
 font-family: verdana, sans-serif;
 font-size: larger;
 text-align: center;
 color: red;
 background : cyan;
 border: thick groove gray;
}
 </STYLE>
</HEAD>
<BODY>
<H1>Rob's Cookbook</H1>
<P>This page contains some of Rob's favorite recipes.
<P CLASS="WARNING">Try not to burn yourself!</P>
<P>We'll start with a recipe for toast.
<H2>Toast</H2>
Ingredients:
<UL>
 <LI>Bread
 <LI>Toaster
</UL>
<HR>
<ADDRESS>Robert W. E. Mack</ADDRESS>
</BODY>
</HTML>
```

This HTML document contains a style sheet with 10 rules, in three sets of rulesets. We'll briefly explain each of the rulesets.

The first ruleset is this: `H1, H2 { font-family: monospace; }`. There are two rules here: one for level-one headings, and the other for level-two headings. Both rules say the same thing: the font should be a monospaced font.

These two rules would be equivalent to using a font face element within each heading—for example `<H2><FONT FACE="Courier New, Courier">Toast</FONT> </H2>`. Alternately, you could use the teletype element, `<H2><TT>Toast</TT> </H2>`, but the teletype element often results in a slightly smaller font size when you use Navigator or IE. (See Chapter 3 for more about the font and teletype elements.)

The second ruleset says: `BODY { color: white; background: black; }`. These two rules declare that the text color of the document should be white and that the background color should be black. (This is equivalent to using body attributes to set text and background color. For example, `<BODY TEXT= "WHITE" BGCOLOR="BLACK">` would have the same effect.)

The third ruleset is more complex. It declares:

```
P.warning {
  font-family: verdana, sans-serif;
  font-size: larger;
  text-align: center;
  color: red;
  background : cyan;
  border: thick groove gray;
}
```

There are six rules here. Together they say that any paragraph element given the "warning" class should be displayed in the Verdana typeface, or a default sans serif typeface if Verdana is not available (for example, Arial or Helvetica; the one that's chosen depends on the browser and what fonts are available). Also, the font size should be one size larger than normal, the paragraph should be centered, the text color should be red, the background color should be cyan, and a thick gray border should be around the paragraph in the "groove" border style.

There's no direct equivalent in HTML for all of these style sheet effects, but you could approximate the result by using a table (see Chapter 7), along with some HTML elements that were covered in Chapter 3, plus an HTML extension to get the border color right:

```
<TABLE BORDER="5" BORDERCOLOR="GRAY" ALIGN="CENTER" CELL-
PADDING="0" CELLSPACING="0">

<TR>
```

```
<TD BGCOLOR="CYAN" ALIGN="CENTER">
<FONT SIZE="+1" COLOR="RED" FACE="verdana, helvetica,
arial">Try not to burn yourself!
</TD>
</TR>
</TABLE>
```

This code is invalid and illogical HTML. It pretends a paragraph is a table when it really isn't, it uses all sorts of visual formatting that has nothing to do with the content of the document, and it uses a proprietary HTML extension. More importantly, this code is bulkier and less efficient than a style sheet. Suppose you wanted a paragraph later in the document that says, "Don't eat raw pork!" to be displayed the same way as the paragraph about not burning yourself. With style sheets, we've defined the rule for how the "warning" class of paragraph should appear. To have another paragraph appear in this style, we could simply say `<P CLASS= "WARNING">Don't eat raw pork!</P>`. Without a style sheet, we'd have to repeat all of the table and font elements again.

NOTE
We're using the CLASS attribute, which is a generic HTML 4.0 attribute that can be applied to many different HTML elements. We'll discuss the CLASS attribute (and its close cousin, the ID attribute) later in this chapter.

In the next section, we'll see how the `cookbook.html` document would be displayed by different versions of IE and Navigator.

How Various Browsers Display Style Sheets

Unfortunately, since style sheets are a new and emerging technology, different browsers react to them in different ways. Let's start by seeing how the latest versions of Navigator and IE display `cookbook.html`. Figure 8.2 shows how IE 4 will display this document.

Navigator 4 was the first release of Navigator that could display style sheets. Figure 8.3 shows how Navigator 4 displays `cookbook.html`.

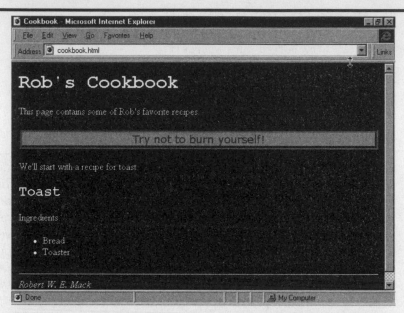

FIGURE 8.2: IE 4 follows the style sheet rules in a reasonable way.

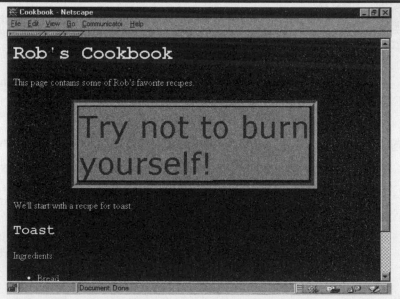

FIGURE 8.3: Navigator 4 has a lot of support for style sheets but is plagued by some serious misinterpretations. Here, Navigator is displaying the warning paragraph with too large of a font size, and the warning box should be the full width of the screen.

NOTE

Future versions of both browsers will display this document slightly differently, since both Netscape and Microsoft have promised new versions of their browsers with better support for CSS1.

Some style sheet rules that Navigator 4 does follow correctly are not interpreted correctly by IE 4, and vice versa. Unfortunately, both browsers have numerous problems with style sheets (although IE has fewer problems than Navigator). A list of "known issues" (which is to say, *bugs*) is available from Netscape (`http://developer.netscape.com/support/bugs/known/css.html`). A comparison of the different browsers, showing which style sheet features are supported in each browser, is available at `http://webreview.com/wr/pub/guides/style/mastergrid.html`.

It's also important to remember that many people use older versions of Navigator and IE. Navigator 3 is extremely popular and has no support for style sheets at all. By design, your style sheets should only supplement a page's content so that Navigator users will be able to see your page, albeit without any style sheet information. Here's how Navigator 3 would display `cookbook.html`:

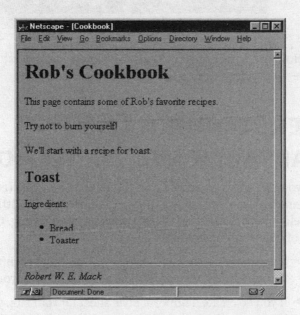

Part ii

Another important consideration is that IE 3, still in popular use, has only partial support for style sheets.

Most of the time, IE 3 safely ignores the style sheet properties that it doesn't understand. For example, IE 3 doesn't display borders, so as you can see here, `cookbook.html` is displayed with almost all of the rules intact, except for the border.

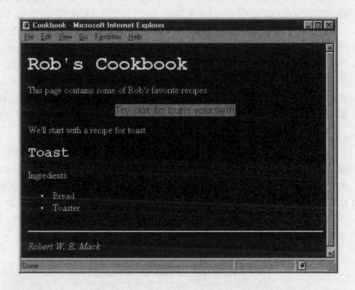

However, sometimes IE 3 can completely misunderstand some valid style sheet rules, leading to disastrous results.

Understanding CSS1's Advantages and Limitations

As you can tell, support of CSS1 is a mixed bag. CSS1 (and style sheets in general) have tremendous potential, but it's still a little early in their development. Safe use of CSS1 requires a lot of testing. CSS1 has a number of important advantages:

▶ You can write one style sheet with a number of different properties and attach this style sheet to every page on your site.

▶ If you do create a uniform style sheet for your site, you can revise that single file and give your entire Web site a facelift.

▶ You no longer have to rely on tricks and misuse of HTML elements to achieve some basic typographical effects.

▶ You can give your pages a distinct look—and a uniform, "branded" style—without the use of graphics.

▶ Style sheets are much more compact and specific than HTML formatting elements and can be reused more easily.

Proposals and drafts have already been written for future versions of CSS that will tackle more than what CSS1 currently aims to control. In the future, a W3C extension will help control the appearance of a printed HTML document, and Microsoft and Netscape are working together with the W3C to extend CSS1 to handle absolute positioning.

But CSS1 is specifically not intended to fulfill certain roles. CSS1 is *not* a layout language or page-description language. Unlike a word processor or desktop-publishing program (such as PageMaker or FrameMaker), CSS1 currently cannot create layout effects like multiple newspaper columns or overlapping frames—nor can CSS1 force text to flow from one area to another.

CSS1 does *not* offer absolute control over a page's appearance. The Web is used all over the world, on hundreds of different platforms. Neither HTML nor CSS1 promise a designer absolute control over a document's appearance—in fact, you can be assured that your document *will* look different from platform to platform. Navigator and IE come in different versions and work differently on different computers. Furthermore, consider how your document will "appear" on a text-to-speech browser or on a TV set. CSS1 allows you to hint at what your preferred fonts and appearance may be, but you can't guarantee that a particular font will be available, nor can you know what screen resolution or window size will be used to view your page (or if a screen will be used at all).

CSS1 also *cannot* guarantee you any kind of absolute pixel control. Even with current work by Microsoft and Netscape aimed at extending CSS1 to allow absolute positioning, you will never be able to guarantee that a particular image or line of text will be aligned at a particular point over a background image. (At best, you will be able to align objects absolutely for that small percentage of surfers who happen to be using the same screen resolution and window size with a CSS1-compliant browser.)

In some ways, HTML 4.0 uses style sheets as a promise of document appearance. But current implementations of CSS1 can't keep all of those promises yet. For example, HTML 4.0 recommends that you use style sheet properties to control the width, height, horizontal space, vertical space, and alignment of images, instead of using the WIDTH, HEIGHT, HSPACE, VSPACE, and ALIGN attributes in the <IMG> tag. However, Navigator and IE are not yet able to use these style sheet settings for images with any reliability at all.

WARNING

You'll definitely have to experiment with style sheet properties before being able to arrive at a style sheet that matches your intentions. It's essential that you test your style sheets in Navigator 4, IE 4, and IE 3.

NOTE

CSS is not the only style sheet technology. Although no current browser supports it, Document Style Semantics and Specification Language (DSSSL) is an advanced document transformation and style language. For more information, see Novell's specification (http://occam.sjf.novell.com:8080/dsssl/dsssl96).

MAKING HTML AND CSS1 WORK TOGETHER

Given CSS1's advantages and ability to offer better control over a document's appearance without damaging the document's content, it's worth experimenting with CSS1 in your HTML documents.

We'll first learn how you can use CSS1 within HTML elements and attributes. Don't worry too much about CSS1's syntax; we'll see some more examples later. In this section, we're interested in the elements and attributes used as *glue* to bind HTML and CSS1 together.

We need to discuss two types of glue: The first type allows you to attach a style sheet to an HTML document. The second type of glue is the HTML elements and attributes that can help you work with style sheets.

After we see how to specify CSS1 as the style sheet language, we'll look at the first type of glue, which has four methods. Then we'll see how to specify style sheet names and apply style sheets to a particular media. Then we'll look at the second type of glue, which involves two HTML elements (the division and span elements, which were introduced in Chapter 3) and two generic attributes, CLASS and ID.

Setting the Default Style Sheet Language

Since there are several style sheet technologies, you must declare to browsers that you're using CSS1 as a document's style sheet language. There are four ways to do this:

▶ Include a TYPE="text/css" attribute with the style or link elements that attach a style sheet.

▶ Indicate the default style sheet language for the entire document by using a specific META element anywhere in the head section: <META HTTP-EQUIV="Content-Style-Type" CONTENT= "text/css">.

▶ Use a link element, which allows you to reference a style sheet in a separate file that contains only style information: <HEAD> <LINK REL=stylesheet HREF="main.css">. The HREF attribute uses a URL, which can be relative or absolute, to target the style sheet. The REL attribute indicates that the link references a style sheet.

▶ Define the style sheet as part of the page using the style element. You can use as many style elements as you like as long as they remain in the header of the page. Here's an example of this approach (note that the TYPE attribute defines which language the style sheet uses):

```
<STYLE TYPE="text/css">
  p { font-size: 12pt }
</STYLE>
```

The second and third methods are preferred because you can set the default style sheet language with just one tag, and you won't ever have to worry about needing to use the TYPE attribute in several different places.

We'll see more about where to use the TYPE attribute in the next few sections, when we learn about the link and style elements.

Attaching a Style Sheet to an HTML Document

There are four ways a Web author can associate a CSS1 style sheet with an HTML document. We'll talk about each method in the following sections.

Using Inline Style Declarations

There are times when you want to apply style declarations to an individual element in a particular HTML document. This is not an efficient way of using CSS1, since you have to repeat the declarations again if you want to apply the same effects to a different element. But if you only want a particular declaration in a single element, inline style declarations can be a useful approach.

NOTE
One drawback to this method is that it mixes your content with your presentation, which is what style sheets were designed to avoid.

TIP
If you just want to apply a particular style every now and then, you don't have to use an inline style declaration. Instead, you can use the CLASS or ID attributes (discussed a little later) to apply a particular style sheet.

The STYLE attribute can be included in just about any body section element (including the <BODY> tag itself). For example:

```
<BODY STYLE="background: yellow">
```

This would create a yellow background for the entire body of a particular HTML document. You can include any number of declarations; just separate each one by a semicolon. For example:

```
<P STYLE="font-weight: bolder; font-size: larger; color: yellow">He's dead, Jim!</P>
```

This style declaration would make this particular paragraph bolder and larger than normal and also change the text color to yellow.

WARNING

When you use inline style sheets, be sure to specify the default style sheet language by using the `<META HTTP-EQUIV="Content-Style-Type" CONTENT="text/css">` tag in the head section.

Embedding a Style Sheet

As we've already seen, you can put a style sheet inside the style element in a document's head section. The style element contains a style sheet (consisting of one or more rules). The style element's `<STYLE>` tag should always contain a TYPE attribute to indicate what type of style sheet is included (unless you set the default style sheet language with the meta element we described).

NOTE

You can also specify a MEDIA attribute in the `<STYLE>` tag to indicate what media or medium this style sheet should apply to (see the "Applying Style Sheets to a Particular Media" section).

An optional, advisory TITLE attribute can name a style sheet. We'll discuss the meaning of titled style sheets in the "Naming External Style Sheets" section.

To create an embedded style sheet, you must always start with the `<STYLE>` start tag, then include the style sheet, and then finish with a `</STYLE>` end tag.

One important consideration for embedded style sheets is that older browsers (which are not aware of the style element) might get confused by the style element's contents and display the rules on-screen. To prevent this from happening, you should always comment out the style sheet by using the comment structure that we saw in Chapter 3. CSS1-enabled browsers will still obey the style sheet, but other browsers will be able to safely ignore the content that it doesn't understand. To comment out the style sheet, put the `<!–` characters before the style sheet, and the `–>` characters after the style sheet, as shown here:

```
<HEAD>
<TITLE>Black and White TV Worship Page</TITLE>
<STYLE TYPE="text/css">
<!–
```

```
BODY { color: white; background: black }
TD { color: white; background: black }
->
</STYLE>
</HEAD>
```

Importing a Style Sheet

Any style sheet can use a special @import notation to refer to an external style sheet. The external style sheet's rules are imported (that is, loaded) along with the main style sheet's rules, and both style sheets will apply to the HTML document's elements.

NOTE

There are special rules about which style sheet's rules take priority; we'll learn about these priority rules in the "Inheriting Properties" section.

The @import statement must be placed at the top of the style sheet, before any rules. Use the word url with parentheses around the external style sheet's URL to indicate where the style sheet is located.

TIP

You can give your external style sheets any filename you like, but it's best to give them a .css extension for consistency.

Here's an example:

```
@import url(hightech.css)
```

Here we've used a relative URL. The browser would retrieve the style sheet stored in a file named hightech.css. This file should be stored in the same directory as the style sheet file that contains the @import statement.

You can also use absolute URLs, like this:

```
@import url(http://www.emf.net/~estephen/css/library.css)
```

WARNING

Navigator 4.01 on Windows 95/98 dies a horrible death when it encounters the @import statement. Newer versions of Navigator do not have this problem.

Linking to External Style Sheets

The best method for gluing an HTML document to a style sheet is to link to an external style sheet using the link element.

The ability to link to an external style sheet is the most powerful option, since it means you can define a standard style sheet for your entire Web site. Each HTML file on your site can contain a link to that standard style sheet. If you then want to change the appearance of every page on your site at once, you just have to edit the external style sheet's file instead of changing each individual HTML file. There are three attributes that must be set, along with two optional attributes:

▶ The HREF attribute must point to the external style sheet file's URL (either relative or absolute).

▶ The REL attribute must have a value of either "STYLESHEET" or "ALTERNATE STYLESHEET".

▶ The TYPE attribute must be "text/css", unless you've set the default style sheet in the head section with a meta command (as we saw earlier in the "Setting the Default Style Sheet Language" section).

▶ Optionally, the TITLE attribute can indicate the name of the style sheet, if you want surfers to be able to disable it (see "Naming External Style Sheets" a little later).

▶ Optionally, the MEDIA attribute can indicate what medium or media to which this style sheet should apply (see the "Applying Style Sheets to a Particular Media" section).

For example, this code will link to an external style sheet named elegant.css:

```
<LINK HREF="elegant.css" REL="STYLESHEET" TYPE="text/css"
TITLE="Meredith's Elegant Style Sheet">
```

Similarly, here's an example of a head element showing how to set the default style sheet language and link to a style sheet stored at an absolute URL:

```
<HEAD>
<TITLE>Marx Wacky Page</TITLE>
<META HTTP-EQUIV="Content-Style-Type" CONTENT="text/css">.
```

```
<LINK HREF="http://www.accesscom.com/~marx/psychedelic.css"
REL="STYLESHEET" TITLE="Mark's Psychedelic Groove Style
Sheet">
</HEAD>
```

Structuring an External Style Sheet and Including Comments

When you create an external style sheet, it should simply be a text file with your rules and rulesets and no HTML elements at all. (As mentioned earlier, any @import statement should come first.)

NOTE

Make sure not to include <HTML> and <HEAD> tags, or any other HTML tags. In the early days of CSS1, some unclear examples of external style sheets encouraged this practice, so don't be confused if you run across an incorrect external style sheet.

CSS1 has a format for comments that's different from HTML's comment format. CSS1 comments begin with /* and end with */. For example:

```
/* This is a CSS1 comment */
```

It's a good idea to begin your style sheet with a comment that explains its purpose. Also, any rules that might be complex should be explained with a comment. Here's an example of an external style sheet.

stylish.css

```
/* CSS1 Style Sheet by Stephen Mack and Janan Platt */

@import url(ourdefaultfonts.css)
/* The ourdefaultfonts.css style sheet contains font settings
*/

BODY { background: black; color: white; margin-left: 10%;
margin-left: 10% }


H1 { text-align: center }
```

```
TD { color: white; background: black }
/* Since Navigator 4 doesn't inherit properties to tables,
you must separately define the body rule for a table cell */

.WARNING {
 font-size: larger;
 font-weight: bolder;
 text-align: center;
 color: red;
 background : yellow;
 border: thick groove gray;
}

HR { text-align: center; margin-left: 25%; width: 50%;
margin-right: 25%; }
```

Most of these rules should be fairly self-explanatory.

Here's how IE 4 would display a document about first aid with the preceding style sheet applied to it.

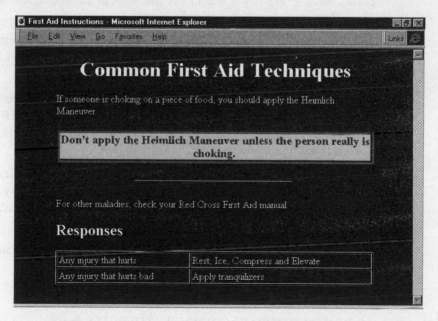

WARNING

Unfortunately, IE 3 and Navigator 4 have problems displaying the same document. IE 3 has a bug that causes background images and colors specified for the BODY selector to be ignored if they are in an external style sheet (although the background color is correctly applied if you use an embedded style sheet or inline style declaration). Navigator 4 gets confused by the style sheet's left and right margins.

Naming External Style Sheets

CSS1-enabled browsers should be able to show surfers a list of style sheets that have been applied to a document and allow surfers to disable any style sheets that they don't want to see. Unfortunately, no browser has yet implemented this useful feature.

Future browsers will allow surfers to disable a particular style sheet (as opposed to just switching off all style sheets completely, which IE 3 and Navigator 4 do allow). While building your page, you'll give a name to each style sheet that you want to allow visitors to disable.

Earlier we saw how to use the TITLE attribute to name a style sheet. HTML 4.0 defines three types of style sheets:

▶ A *persistent style sheet* is always applied to a document. To create a persistent style sheet, don't give the style sheet a TITLE attribute.

▶ An *alternate style sheet* is only applied if a surfer selects it specifically. To create an alternate style sheet, use the REL="ALTERNATE STYLESHEET" attribute in the link element and give the style sheet a name with the TITLE attribute.

▶ A *default style sheet* is applied to a document when it is first loaded but can be disabled by the surfer. To create a default style sheet, use the REL="STYLESHEET" attribute in the link element and give the style sheet a name with the TITLE attribute.

The same value for a TITLE attribute can be applied to more than one external style sheet in two different link elements:

```
<LINK REL="ALTERNATE STYLESHEET" TITLE="Big Print"
HREF="bigfonts.css">

<LINK REL="ALTERNATE STYLESHEET" TITLE="Big Print"
HREF="bigmargins.css">
```

This would allow both of the style sheets specified to be named "Big Print" so they could be enabled or disabled together.

Applying Style Sheets to a Particular Media

In most cases, HTML does not care what type of platform (or *media*) is used to display an HTML document. It could be a computer screen, a TV screen, a telephone, a text-to-speech reading device, a Braille tactile device, or a printer. (Some HTML elements, like the button element or the bold element, are a little more specific to a particular device than other HTML elements.)

In contrast, style sheets are always designed for a particular medium or group of media. CSS1 is mostly concerned with computer screens that are capable of presenting colors and graphics. But you can also use CSS1 to optimize your document for printing, and draft extensions to CSS have special properties for text-to-speech readers (such as accent properties or volume properties).

For example, you might be interested in creating two separate style sheets, one for a computer screen and another for a printer. The link and style elements both allow you to specify a MEDIA attribute to indicate which destination medium you want to control with a style sheet.

TIP

Studies have found that it's easier to read a sans serif font on a computer screen but that it's easier to read a serif font on paper. Using style sheets, you can suggest different fonts for each media.

Here are the potential values for the MEDIA attribute:

SCREEN   The default value, for computer screens (on any platform)

PRINT   For paged material and for documents viewed in print preview mode

PROJECTION   For projectors and large-screen devices

BRAILLE   For Braille tactile devices

SPEECH   For a speech synthesizer, text-to-speech system, or telephone

ALL   For all devices

NOTE

HTML 4.0 allows you to specify a comma-delimited list of the media to which you want to have a style sheet apply (such as MEDIA="SCREEN,PROJECTION").

Future versions of HTML and CSS1 will expand on these media types. For right now, the two most practical choices are PRINT and SCREEN because most of the CSS1 properties apply to those two media. Suppose you create one external style sheet called myway.css that you want to use for the screen, and another external style sheet called myprint.css that you want to use for printouts.

Here's a head section that shows how you could link to these two style sheets:

```
<!DOCTYPE HTML PUBLIC "-//W3C//DTD HTML 4.0//EN">
<HTML LANG="EN">
<HEAD>
  <TITLE>Freaky Styley</TITLE>
  <META HTTP-EQUIV="Content-Style-Type" CONTENT="text/css">.
  <LINK REL="STYLESHEET" HREF="myway.css" MEDIA="SCREEN">
  <LINK REL="STYLESHEET" HREF="myprint.css" MEDIA="PRINT">
</HEAD>
```

WARNING

Navigator 4 and IE 3 don't obey the MEDIA attribute. IE 3 simply ignores it. Navigator 4 ignores any media type other than MEDIA="SCREEN" (which means that a style sheet with MEDIA="ALL" or MEDIA="SCREEN,PROJECTION" will be ignored). Navigator 4 also has numerous problems printing pages that have style sheets.

Using HTML Attributes and Elements as Style Glue

In addition to the STYLE attribute used to create inline styles, there are two HTML attributes and two HTML elements that are simply glue for style sheets. We'll take a quick look at how to use each of these four pieces of HTML glue now.

Applying Styles to a Class with the *CLASS* Attribute

In the earlier section called "A More Complex Example of CSS1," we saw an example of a style sheet class and the CLASS attribute.

To create a style sheet class, use a period followed by the name you want for the class. You can create classes that only apply to particular HTML elements by specifying that element, or you can create generic classes that can apply to every HTML element. For example, here's a style sheet that creates three classes (we've named our example classes warning, note, and big, but you can use any descriptive word you like):

```
P { font-family: verdana, sans-serif }
P.warning { color: red; border: thick double black }
P.note { color: green; background: url(clouds.gif) }
.big { font-size: 150% }
```

This style sheet has four rulesets. The first ruleset applies to every paragraph element (it changes the font face to Verdana, or a generic sans serif typeface if Verdana isn't available). The second ruleset applies to only those paragraph elements in the warning class (and changes the text color to red and creates a thick border made of two lines). The third ruleset applies to those paragraph elements in the note class (and changes the text color to green with an image background). The fourth rule applies to any HTML element (including paragraph elements, blockquote elements, table data cell elements, and so on) but only if it is in the big class (and makes the paragraph 50 percent larger than normal).

In any HTML document attached to this style sheet, you can use the CLASS attribute with a body section element to select the appropriate rule:

```
<H3 CLASS="big">All About Jeff Goldblum, Who Is A Very Tall
Man.</H3>
<P>Jeff Goldblum is a very popular actor.
<P CLASS="note">Jeff's first big role in a popular movie was
in "The Big Chill."
<P CLASS="warning">His movie "The Fly" is not for the
squeamish.
<P CLASS="big">Jeff stars in the "The Tall Guy" which
parodies another movie, "The Elephant Man."
```

The big class can be used with any HTML element (we've used a paragraph element and a level-three heading element here). The note and warning classes can only be used with paragraph elements, so the following CLASS attribute will be ignored:

```
<H3 CLASS="note">Don't see "Transylvania 6-5000."</H3>
```

Here's how IE 4 will display a document with this style sheet and these HTML elements (along with a normal heading about Sylvester Stallone for contrast).

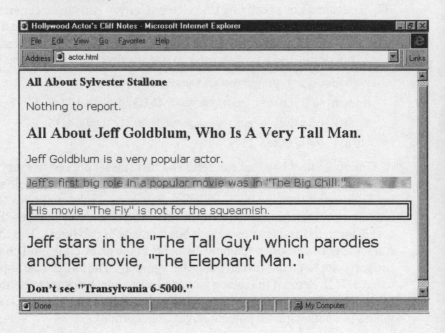

NOTE

Because we didn't specify a value for padding between the border and the paragraph text, the sixth line (with the double border) does not look very attractive. See the end of this chapter for a list of properties, including padding.

Applying Styles to a Single Instance with an *ID* Attribute

The CLASS attribute can be used on many different HTML elements to reuse a rule over and over again. But sometimes you want to make a rule that applies only to a single HTML element. To do this, you can use the ID attribute.

For example, suppose you want a particular image to have a fancy green border and you know that you'll never have another image in the same document use a green border.

You can define a style sheet rule like this: `#bord13 { border: 20px ridge green }`. This rule creates a border around a particular image named `bord13`. The border will be 20 pixels wide, green, and in the "ridge" style. In an HTML document, you can tie this rule to the `bord13` image by using an ID attribute like this: `<IMG ID="bord13" SRC="zappa .jpg" ALT="Frank Zappa (Photo by Phil Franks)">`. Shown here is how IE would display a page with such a border.

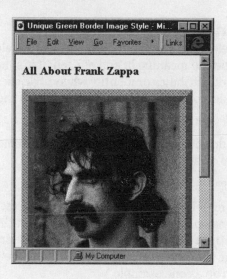

Part ii

WARNING

Neither IE 3 nor Navigator 4 puts borders around images properly.

The selector's ID name must be a unique value. Always precede it with a number sign ("#"). ID names are a similar concept to named anchors.

NOTE

The names used with the ID and CLASS attribute must be a word with no spaces or punctuation (except hyphens). Also, the name can't begin with a number.

We could have left of the IMG part off the selector, like this:

```
#bord13 { border: 20px ridge green }
```

Both style sheets end up working the same way, though this second construction is slightly more flexible (since a different document could include something such as <P ID="bord13"> to get a paragraph with a unique border instead of an image).

In practice, classes are more flexible than unique IDs, but there may be times when you really want a style sheet to apply uniquely to a single element.

Applying Styles to a Span

The span element is a generic, text-level HTML element. The span element implies no meaning in and of itself; it is simply used as a place to stick generic attributes or identify where style sheet rules should apply. For example, you could have a style sheet with the following rule:

```
SPAN { text-decoration: blink }
```

You could then link the style sheet to a document and include the following line somewhere in the document:

```
<H2>News <SPAN>Flash!</SPAN></H2>
```

The word "Flash!" would blink on and off, just as if you had used the blink extension. (Most of our warnings against the blink element apply equally to the text-decoration: blink declaration. Of course, you can use the span element with any CSS1 rule; we're just using text-decoration as one example.)

WARNING

IE 3 and 4 ignore the blink value for the text-decoration property.

The span element is often combined with the CLASS or ID attributes. Rather than making every span element blink, you might want to set it up this way:

```
SPAN.blinky { text-decoration: blink }
```

This creates a class called blinky, and the rule could be invoked with:

```
<H2>News <SPAN CLASS="blinky">Flash!</SPAN></H2>
```

The advantage of these uses of the span element is that they're completely ignored by browsers that don't display style sheets, which leaves your document's contents undisturbed, even in older browsers.

Applying Styles to a Division

The division element (<DIV> and </DIV>), just like the span element, can be used to apply a style sheet rule. The only difference is that the division element is a block-level element, so it can contain paragraphs and other block-level and text-level elements. (Since the span element is a text-level element, it can only contain text-level elements.)

LEARNING HOW CSS1 WORKS

Up to now in this chapter, we've been more concerned with how HTML and CSS1 can work together rather than how CSS1 operates. In this section, we'll introduce you to CSS1's design.

Inheriting Properties

A CSS1 rule applies a declaration to a particular HTML element. That declaration will also apply to any elements nested inside that element. For example, suppose you've made paragraphs green:

```
P { color: green }
```

Consider an element nested inside another element, such as: <P>I am a <I>barrista</I></P>. The word *barrista* will appear both in italics and in green. This is an example of *inheritance*. The italics element here is said to "inherit" the green property from its *parent* element (which in this case is the paragraph element).

Other style properties will also be inherited, such as font-family and font-size. Some style properties are not inherited from the parent element to the child element. (Check the CSS1 specification or a quick reference to see if a property inherits.)

The best example we've seen of inheritance is applying declarations to the body element. With a style sheet such as

```
BODY { color: white; background: url(marble.gif) black; }
```

(which sets the text color to white and the background to an image named marble.gif, or black if the image isn't available), every element in a document, including every heading and paragraph, will inherit the default text color.

NOTE

This works even if the <BODY> tag is omitted because the presence of the body element is assumed even if there aren't explicit tags for it.

WARNING

In Navigator 4, tables don't inherit values from the body of a document because Navigator incorrectly considers tables to be separate from the body. You'll have to repeat your BODY rules for the TD and TH selectors to avoid problems. Otherwise, if you specify black for the background and white for the text color, the table will end up being invisible (since this bug causes both the text color and the background to be black).

The background is a little more complicated because the background property does not inherit. However, the initial value for every element's background is "transparent," so the parent's background will shine through for each child element in the way that you'd expect.

Sometimes, the value of a property is a percentage that refers to another property. For example:

```
P { font-size: 10pt; line-height: 150% }
```

In this case, the line height will work out to 15 points, since it is one-and-a-half times the paragraph's font size of 10 points. Elements nested inside a paragraph element will inherit the 15-point line height.

Using Contextual Selectors

At the beginning of this chapter, we defined the selectors used in CSS1 rules and stated that there were simple selectors and contextual selectors. All of the examples of CSS1 rules so far in this chapter (including the examples with CLASS and ID) have contained simple selectors.

A *contextual selector* creates a rule that matches HTML elements based only on their position in a document structure. To create a contextual selector, simply list two or more simple selectors.

For example, the selector H2 SPAN could be used to make sure that a declaration applied only to a span element nested inside a level-two heading element. (The declaration would not apply to span elements elsewhere in the document.)

Suppose you want all level-one headings to be green and all emphasized text to be blue. You would use two rules:

```
H1 { color: green }
EM { color: blue }
```

But what would happen to an emphasized element that happened to be inside a level-one heading? Given the HTML code <H1>Philip is a <EM>musician </EM>!</H1>, it's hard to predict whether the word "musician" will be blue or green. It turns out it will be blue, since the style sheet's EM selector applies to every emphasis element, regardless of whether the emphasis is nested in another element.

To make sure that the emphasized element would be green if inside a level-one heading element, you could use the following contextual selector:

```
H1 EM { color: green }
```

This rule applies only to emphasis elements nested inside a level-one heading. Level-one headings themselves are not affected, and emphasis elements elsewhere are also not affected. To cause the heading element to be green and also have any emphasis elements nested inside be green (but blue elsewhere), you'd need three rules. The order of these three rules doesn't matter:

```
H1 { color: green }
EM { color: blue }
H1 EM { color: green }
```

You can also use a style sheet that includes a contextual selector to select a third possibility for the emphasis element:

```
H1 { color: green }
EM { color: blue }
H1 EM { color: red }
```

This will cause the emphasis element normally to be blue; it will appear in red, however, if it's inside a level-one heading element.

Part ii

WARNING

Be sure you don't confuse contextual selectors with rulesets. The only difference is a comma: `H1, EM { color: red}` is a grouped ruleset (with two rules) that makes both level-one headings and emphasis elements appear in red. By removing the comma, it becomes a contextual selector that makes only emphasis elements inside a level-one heading red; other emphasis elements and level-one headings are not affected.

You can make very complex contextual selectors. For example:

```
TD UL UL LI { font-size: smaller }
```

This rule will only apply to list-item elements embedded inside a nested unordered list (that is, a list inside a list) that is also inside a table cell.

You can combine contextual selectors together, or mix them with CLASS and ID attributes to create sophisticated results. For example, you might create rules such as:

```
P.fiction { text-indent: 5% }
DIV P.fiction { text-indent: 10% ; margin-left 10% }
```

Then any paragraphs in the fiction class (`<P CLASS="FICTION">`) would have their first line indented 5 percent—unless it were a paragraph inside a division element (`<DIV><P CLASS="FICTION>`), in which case the paragraph's left margin would be 10 percent of the screen width, and the first line would be indented a total of 15 percent.

Making Style Sheets Cascade

"Cascading" is the first word in the name of CSS, and it refers to the ability of multiple style sheets to work together to arrive at the document's final appearance. But we haven't yet talked about what "cascading" means and how conflicting style sheet rules are resolved.

As we saw earlier, you can specify a number of style sheets in the same document. In addition, IE 4 lets a user specify a default style sheet of their own.

NOTE

The idea that author and user style sheets should mesh together and negotiate to decide on the best presentation of a document (considering both the author's design and the user's display needs) is the main intention of CSS.

As we've seen in the earlier chapters of this book, every browser has a default behavior for rendering HTML elements (for example, headings are bold, and horizontal rules are two pixels high). The set of all of the default appearances is considered to be another style sheet—but the defaults apply only if no other style sheet rule affects an element's appearance.

WARNING

An element's default appearance should outweigh any properties that apply to that element by inheritance, but IE 4 and Navigator 4 differ in their interpretation. For example, the specification for CSS1 declares that setting a default font size in the body element shouldn't change the font size of headings. But IE 3 and Navigator 4 get this wrong. Prudent style sheet authors will therefore create a style sheet that defines properties for almost every element used in a document.

Suppose two different style sheets specify the color for level-one headings; the first style sheet says they should be red, and the second one says they should be blue. Here are the levels of priority:

1. If no declarations apply to an element, then the inherited value is used. If there is no inherited value, then the browser's default behavior is used for that element. In this case, the default behavior (black text, unless the user has customized their browser's or operating system's colors) will be overridden by the declarations for blue and red text.

2. You can mark a declaration with `!important` to make that rule carry more weight than normal. (However, IE and Navigator have ignored the `!important` notation to this point.)

3. The Web author's style sheets outweigh any of the surfer's style sheets. Embedded style sheets and linked style sheets outweigh any style sheets that are imported. But any style sheet will outweigh the browser's default values.

4. The more specific the selector, the more weight it carries. Selectors with ID attributes are more specific than those with CLASS attributes, which are more specific than contextual selectors, which are more specific than simple selectors.

In a tie, the order counts. The later rules outweigh earlier rules. This system is complicated, so it's important to test your documents and make sure the rules are working as you expected.

Using Anchor Pseudo-Classes

A *pseudo-class* is a way of distinguishing between different types of a single element. There is only one pseudo-class in CSS1, and it is for the anchor element.

By default, three colors are used with anchor elements: unvisited links are usually blue, visited links are usually purple, and active links (a link being clicked) are usually red. (These colors are the default settings, but many surfers change the default colors.)

To be able to set the colors and other properties for these three types of links separately, CSS1 creates pseudo-classes for the anchor element: A:link can be used as a selector for unvisited links, A:visited refers to visited links, and A:active applies to active links. For example, you could set the colors for links with the following rules:

```
A:link { color: cyan }
A:visited { color: gray }
A:active { color: black }
```

WARNING

Early versions of IE 4 ignored the A:active pseudo-class.

NOTE

A similar concept, called *pseudo-elements*, is defined by CSS1 to make rules that apply to the first line or first letter of text. Sadly, pseudo-elements are ignored by Navigator and IE.

Using CSS1 Units

CSS1 uses several different types of units (as you may have noticed from our examples so far in this chapter). There are two types of units: absolute units and relative units.

The common absolute units are:

▶ Inches, specified by in (for example, 0.5in means half an inch)

▶ Points, specified by pt (for example, 13pt means 13 points)

You can also use centimeters (cm), millimeters (mm), and picas (pc).

NOTE

These are typographical terms. A *pica* is equal to 12 points, and 72 points is equal to an inch.

However, relative units are preferred because they scale better from one medium to another (and you don't have to make assumptions about a surfer's screen size or paper size). Here are the relative units:

▶ Pixels, specified by px (for example, 12px means 12 pixels)

▶ Ems, specified by em (where one *em* is equal to the element's font size, so 0.5em is half a line)

▶ Ex-heights, specified ex (where one *ex* is equal to the height of the lowercase letter x in the current font, so 2ex is twice the height of the letter *x*)

▶ Percentages, which are usually relative to the font size (so 200% usually means twice the current font size of the element)

Pixels might not seem to be a relative unit at first glance. But in actuality, pixels can vary tremendously. The first case concerns printers: A screen is often 72 pixels per inch, but a printer is typically 300, 600, or 1200 "pixels" per inch. So browsers will scale pixel units appropriately when you print out a document, making pixel a relative term. Secondly, and more importantly, the pixel size measurements for fonts are slightly different on Macintosh platforms than they are on Windows platforms. The difference is enough to cause problems, so pixel units should be avoided.

TIP

The safest two units are currently percentages and ems, so you should try to use these two units for measurements in your style sheets as much as possible.

Part ii

Using Color Units in CSS1

Color units are usually one of 16 color names (aqua, black, blue, fuchsia, gray, green, lime, maroon, navy, olive, purple, red, silver, teal, white, and yellow), or an RGB value (such as #38B0DE).

NOTE

CSS1 also supports an abbreviated RGB value in which you use only one hexadecimal digit for each color instead of two. You can also use percentages and decimal values. See the CSS1 specification for more details (http://www.w3.org/pub/WWW/TR/REC-CSS1). Be careful, because Navigator and IE might not support the color notation you've chosen.

WARNING

Some Macintosh-style editors and HTML editors have real problems with named colors; if you have any trouble, use the RGB notation instead.

Using CSS1 Properties

In this last section, we'll list the different CSS1 properties by category. Although we don't have room to list or describe each one thoroughly, we've tried to give examples of the most useful properties throughout this chapter.

The CSS1 specification defines the behavior of the different properties and lists each possible value, and it describes the overall formatting model used by CSS1.

Visit the W3C CSS page (http://www.w3.org/Style/CSS/) for a list of CSS1 references and style sheet tools. One particularly useful tool that can check your style sheets for errors is CSSCheck, available from WDG's CSS1 and HTML reference site (http://www.htmlhelp.com/).

Understanding the Categories of Properties

There are five categories of properties that can be controlled by CSS1:

Font Properties   Properties that affect a font: `font-family` (which changes the font face), `font-style` (either normal, italic, or oblique), `font-variant` (normal or small caps), and `font-weight` (which changes the boldness of a font). Also, the `font-size` property can specify text size (and in addition to the normal units of em, px, and percentage for setting sizes, there are some special values: `larger` and `smaller` are relative sizes, and you can also specify `xx-small`, `x-small`, `small`, `medium`, `large`, `x-large`, and `xx-large`). The `font` property is a shorthand property for all of these.

NOTE

When you specify a font that has spaces in its name, you must put quotes around it. For example, `{ font-family: "New Century Schoolbook" }`. Quotes should not be used in any other situation.

Color and Background Properties   Properties that describe the foreground `color` and `background` (image or color) as well as background image placement.

Text Properties   Properties that change text's appearance and placement, such as `line-height`, `text-decoration`, `vertical-align`, and `text-align`. The `word-spacing` and `letter-spacing` properties can make letters wider or squeeze them more tightly next to each other. The `text-transform` property can be set to `capitalize`, `uppercase`, or `lowercase`.

Box Properties   Properties that set the margins, borders, and padding (between the margin and border) for an element. For example, you can set `margin-top`, `margin-right`, `margin-bottom`, or `margin-left` properties (or use the `margin` shorthand property to set all four at once). You can also set the `width` and `height` properties to control an element's size. The `float` property can make any element behave like a floating image.

Classification Properties   Properties that classify different elements by their behavior and control how elements such as list-item elements work (for example, you can use the `list-style-image` property with an unordered list selector (UL) to change the list-item bullet to an image of your choice).

Using Shorthand Properties

Some properties are simply *shorthand properties* for groups of other properties. For example, you can set the `font-style`, `font-variant`, `font-weight`, `font-size`, `line-height`, and `font-family` properties separately:

```
P { font-style: italic; font-variant: small-caps; font-weight: bold; font-size: 120%; line-height: 150%; font-family: sans-serif }
```

Alternately, you can set the `font` property as a shortcut:

```
P { font: italic small-caps bold 120%/150% sans-serif }
```

These two style sheets are precisely equivalent.

Similarly, setting the rule BODY `{ margin: 15% }` will create a margin of 15 percent of the window's size for all four margins, exactly as if the rule were BODY `{ margin-left: 15%; margin-top: 15%; margin-right: 15%; margin-bottom: 15% }`.

Using Some Important Style Sheet Properties

We would like to end this chapter by demonstrating two important example style sheets that can improve your documents' appearance: `text-indent` and the body attributes.

Using the *Text-Indent* Property

The first example style sheet is useful for controlling indenting. Although there's no good HTML method for creating a paragraph indent (as is seen in books), you could use the following simple style sheet:

```
.P.fiction { text-indent: 5% }
```

In your HTML documents, attach this style sheet normally, and for any paragraphs that you want indented, use a tag like <P CLASS="fiction">. The first line of each paragraph will be indented 5 percent of the window's width.

You can also remove the double-spacing between paragraphs and create extra left and right margins for the fiction class paragraphs with the following rule, a modification of the above:

```
P.fiction { text-indent: 5%; margin-top: 0; margin-bottom: 0;
margin-left: 10%; margin-right: 15%; }
```

Setting Colors without Using Body Attributes

Chapter 5 introduced the six body attributes that can be used to change a document's colors and background image. At the same time, it was mentioned that HTML 4.0 does not recommend that these attributes be used.

Consider this <BODY> tag, which sets white text on a black background along with specific link colors and a background image:

```
<BODY BGCOLOR="#000000" TEXT="#FFFFFF" LINK="#CC0000"
ALINK="#777777" VLINK="#990099" BACKGROUND="marble.gif">
```

Using a style sheet, the same effect could be accomplished with the following five rules:

```
BODY { background: #000 url(marble.gif) }
BODY { color: #FFF }
A:link { color: #C00 }
A:visited { color: #555 }
A:active { color: #909 }
```

The only tricky thing here is the background rule, which says to show the color black unless the marble.gif image is available. Also, these colors are expressed using three-digit RGB values instead of six-digit RGB values; CSS1 RGB colors can be stated either way, but HTML RGB colors must always be six digits.

Style sheets offer important advantages to Web authors. The possibilities are endless. While the current implementations are thorny and the differences between browsers will pose problems, the extra display capabilities make style sheets well worth learning. Style sheets are particularly powerful when combined with scripting. You'll learn about scripting languages later in this book.

What's Next?

As you can see, cascading style sheets can be an invaluable tool for formatting your Web site. The ability to create and apply style sheets will allow you to take advantage of the formatting tips that you've been given throughout Part II of this book. Now we'll enter Part III, in which you'll move beyond HTML and discover methods to bring more sophisticated effects to your pages. The next chapter will show you the possibilities for using multimedia on your site and introduce you to some of the programming languages that will help you develop that advanced content.

PART iii
GOING BEYOND HTML

Chapter 9

ADDING ADVANCED CONTENT TO WEB PAGES

I n previous chapters, we've looked at how to enhance your Web pages through such means as formatting text and adding graphics. In this chapter, we'll cover how to enliven your pages even more by adding sound and video.

The HTML pages that we've looked at so far are essentially static in the sense that they pass information from the server to the browser. In this chapter, we'll look at several ways you can pass information in the other direction, from the browser (or in other words, from the user) back to the server, and we'll look at the programming techniques you can use to access that data once it gets to the server, including Common Gateway Interface programming as well as the two major APIs—NSAPI from Netscape and ISAPI from Microsoft.

Adapted from *Mastering Intranets: The Windows 95/NT Edition*, by Pat Coleman and Peter Dyson

ISBN 0-7821-1991-3   832 pages $49.99

One of the more interesting technical debates in the world of Web technology has been between Sun Microsystems and Microsoft over Sun's Java programming language and Microsoft's ActiveX. The former is an open approach while the latter, so far at least (although there are signs that things are changing here), is a more proprietary and closed approach. The differences between the companies were the basis of a prolonged court case centered on Microsoft's use of Java. We'll take a look at all the components in this debate later in this chapter.

NOTE

This chapter was taken from a book that deals specifically with the issues surrounding the development of pages for an *intranet*, which is a private network that uses Internet software to connect people within an organization. Nevertheless, the technologies discussed can be used in building Web pages as well.

Be careful to apply the same evaluation to all this technology that you would apply to any other new business strategy. The George Leigh Mallory mountaineer's justification of "Because it is there" is not a sufficient reason to chase after every single one of these advances. Ask the same questions you always ask: What is the payoff? What is the return on this investment? And be prepared to leave some of the flashiest glitz behind if you don't perceive a quantifiable benefit for your company.

Some of the most cost-effective advances will be in those areas that facilitate communications between the Web server and the corporate database. The large database developers have a long, long lead over Web server developers and are not likely to be caught. Look for advances from companies such as Oracle, Sybase, and the like in the areas of SQL (*Structured Query Language*), communications, and OLTP (*online transaction processing*). Much of the technology we take for granted is still in its infancy, and changes that seem imminent may in fact be several years in the future. But no matter what you call it, change is coming.

ADVANCES IN MULTIMEDIA

As we said in the introduction to this chapter, the HTML pages we've seen so far are somewhat static, and you can do a lot in terms of adding interest and a certain amount of value by incorporating sound, animation, and video into your intranet content. Just imagine the applications: a video of the company president's speech to shareholders at the annual meeting, a demonstration of a new product either for a customer presentation or as a training tool, or an animated sequence that explains how to assemble a product in the manufacturing department.

You will be hearing a lot about using multimedia on your intranet site as more and more audio, animation, and video technologies converge to constitute a toolkit of genuinely useful products. One of the continuing problems is that of available network bandwidth; multimedia applications can generate large files that simply gobble up bandwidth. Here are two common approaches to this problem:

▶ *Encapsulated* multimedia consists of the appropriate data segments in a file that is transferred as a single large entity and "played" after the download is complete. This approach is becoming less and less popular.

▶ *Live* multimedia consists of the data streams sent over the network to allow audio and video to be "played" in real time so that the person using the browser can interact with the data stream. Most current products use this approach.

Live multimedia components are often called *streaming* or *continuous-delivery* audio and video to differentiate them from encapsulated multimedia. We'll look at these two technologies in a moment, and we'll look at some experimental aspects of this kind of data transmission. But we'll begin with a quick look at how you can assess the case for using multimedia on your intranet site in the first place.

Using Multimedia on Your Web Site

While considering whether or not to include multimedia in your Web pages, you should carefully evaluate the return on your intranet site investment. Therefore, before examining these multimedia technologies in detail, let's ask a few questions about what you hope to achieve by using audio or video on your Web site:

▶ Why are you providing a multimedia service? What are you trying to accomplish? Is there some specific part of the message you want to get across that can only be presented using audio or video, or could you use some other, less intensive method?

▶ What is the value to your company of a multimedia presentation, and how will you quantify the returns on this investment?

▶ What is the value to your customers of a multimedia presentation? Can they access your site using a communications link that is fast enough to get the benefits, or will they just find it frustrating to wait, and wait, and wait?

▶ Can you condense the message you want to get across to one simple but direct statement and use multimedia to enhance that message while leaving the rest of your intranet as a more traditional combination of text and graphics?

Other important questions to ask include: How soon do you need to add this element to your Web site? What will be the consequences for the current server hardware and software? Do you need to upgrade the client computers out there on the network, or do they all have sufficient processing horsepower along with sound cards and the appropriate video monitors? If you do have to upgrade, what is the anticipated cost, and how do you weigh that cost against the benefit you perceive? Remember that other essential services *must* continue to receive support and bandwidth.

Evaluating Transmission Mechanisms: TCP, UDP, and IP Multicasting

The TCP/IP family of protocols was originally designed to deliver files over the network reliably but with some measure of allowable delay, and so is generally unsuitable for applications that require continuous real-time data. For streaming audio or streaming video to work, compromises have to be made in the transmission mechanism. Currently, three mechanisms are in use: *TCP, UDP,* and *IP multicasting.*

NOTE

Most corporate firewalls will pass through TCP-transported information, but some will not pass information transported by UDP. This is not a security issue, but it may have an impact on your ability to receive information from beyond the firewall.

TCP

TCP (*Transmission Control Protocol*) is probably the most common protocol in use. It is used to transmit large packets of information and to guarantee delivery of those packets. TCP also includes flow-control mechanisms that ensure it does not saturate the communications link.

A drawback from the audio-video point of view is that TCP retransmits a packet that is lost. This introduces a gap in the data, which is quite noticeable and which usually interrupts playback until the errant packet is retransmitted and received successfully. Even with these concerns, TCP is a good all-purpose solution to transmitting audio-video data over an intranet.

UDP

UDP (*User Datagram Protocol*) is a maintenance protocol that can transmit a large number of small packets very quickly at a high priority but that cannot guarantee packet delivery. The receiving application must manage this potential for dropped packets in some way. Using UDP in this way can also saturate communication links; you should, therefore, not use it without some flow-control mechanism to manage the link. User Datagram Protocol is well suited to transitory applications, such as Internet phones.

IP Multicasting

In IP (*Internet Protocol*) multicasting, a host group is created, and all members of the group receive every IP datagram. Membership is dynamic. You join that group when you start receiving audio-video data, and you leave the group when you stop. IP multicasting is a good solution when you need to send the same audio-video information simultaneously to a group of people.

Creating the Files

The steps you take to prepare audio, animation, or video for transmission are essentially the same:

1. Digitize the audio or video source using a sound card, a video frame grabber, or both. Given that much of the processing still to be done to these raw data files will result in a loss of quality, you should do as much as you can to capture the cleanest signal possible.

2. Encode and compress the raw data. Each type of technology uses a different lossy compression algorithm, and the more you squeeze the data down into smaller and smaller files, the more distortion appears as the quality degrades.

3. Code the appropriate HTML tags into your Web page so that browsers can find the encoded files on your server.

4. Load the multimedia files onto your server. The server registers the filename extension as a MIME type.

TIP

You must download and install the appropriate plug-in application or browser before trying to play a file. All the encoding technologies are slightly different, so be sure you get the right one. We'll look at some of the multimedia plug-ins in a moment.

Now when you select a media link, your browser sends a message to the server; the server returns a token file that tells your browser which add-in application (player or viewer) to open. Once this application is running, it sends a request to the server, which transmits the file to the player; after a few seconds, during which the file is buffered, playback begins.

Streaming Audio

The main bottleneck in receiving audio information is the capacity of the communications link between the browser and the server. This is of less concern if you have a direct network connection, but if you usually dial in using a modem and telephone line, the connection type assumes a larger significance. Table 9.1 lists some common connection types and indicates the quality of audio you might expect.

TABLE 9.1: Connection Types and Sound Quality

CONNECTION TYPE	SPEED	AUDIO QUALITY
Dial-up modem	9.6 to 14.4Kbps	8kHz (mono or AM radio)
Dial-up modem	28.8Kbps to 33.6Kbps	16 or 22kHz (mono)
v.90/Frame Relay/Single Channel ISDN	56 to 64Kbps	16 or 22kHz (stereo) or 44kHz (mono)
ISDN	128Kbps	44kHz (stereo)
T1	1.544Mbps	VHS quality stereo

Streaming audio not only allows a browser or add-in application to play the file as it arrives, but with it, you (the user) can manipulate the data by fast-forwarding, rewinding, or pausing the data stream. You can also seek a specific data packet. Prerecorded data can be compressed before it is sent, something that only recently became possible with live audio. Audio data can be stored in a variety of file formats, including AU, RA, or WAV files.

Streaming audio products for Windows 95/98 and Windows NT are available from a variety of sources, as Table 9.2 shows, and in many cases you will find that the player application or browser plug-in is free and that there is a charge only for the application used to serve, create, or edit the audio files themselves.

TABLE 9.2: Streaming Audio Products

PRODUCT	COMPANY	URL
Crescendo	LiveUpdate	http://www.liveupdate.com/
Internet Wave	VocalTec	http://www.vocaltec.com/
RealPlayer	RealNetworks	http://www.real.com/
StreamWorks	Xing Technology	http://www.xingtech.com/
ToolVox for the Web	VoxWare	http://www.voxware.com/
TrueSpeech	The DSP Group	http://www.dspg.com/

TRUESPEECH AND WINDOWS 95/98

The DSP Group's TrueSpeech product is an excellent choice for small sites for several reasons: the most important being if you have Windows 95/98, you already have the encoder; it is a licensed component of the Windows 95/98 Sound Recorder.

TrueSpeech is a data-compression technology used in a wide range of products, including digital answering machines, telephones, and dual simultaneous voice/data modems.

In 1994, the DSP Group licensed the TrueSpeech 8.5 algorithm to Microsoft for inclusion in Windows 95. This version provides a compression ratio of up to 15:1. Or in other words, it can reduce a MHz 16-bit audio stream to approximately 8.5 kilobits per second—just right for real-time playback on a 486 or Pentium system.

Part iii

Streaming Video

Streaming video places demands on the server that are more stringent than those of any other Web content. Consequently, its development is a little behind that of streaming audio. There are currently two slightly different approaches to streaming video:

▶ *Stand-alone video players* let you preview the video clips as they arrive on your system and then replay them at your convenience later. They are typically packaged as Netscape plug-ins or as ActiveX controls that you install in your browser (we'll be looking at just what an ActiveX control is later in this chapter). Stand-alone video players work with a wide variety of standard digital video file formats, including AVI, MOV, and MPEG.

▶ *Client-server video players* use special software on the server to transmit highly compressed digital video and require that you install a special player on the client for viewing. These systems provide broadcast streaming video for viewing in real time; you cannot save the file for later viewing, as these server products assume that a significant portion of the data will be lost in transit.

Products are available from several sources, as Table 9.3 shows. StreamWorks from Xing Technology, Inc., and VDOLive from VDOnet Corporation are the current leaders in this emerging technology; Vosaic is not far behind.

TABLE 9.3: Streaming Video Products

PRODUCT	COMPANY	URL
CineWeb	Digigami	http://www.digigami.com/
ClearFusion	Iterated Systems	http://www.iterated.com/
InterVU MPEG Player	InterVU	http://intervu.com/
Streaming Videogram	Alaris	http://www.alaris.com/
StreamWorks	Xing Technologies	http://www.xingtech.com/
VDO Live Video Player	VDOnet	http://www.clubvdo.net/clubvdo/default.asp
VivoActive Player	Vivo Software	http://www.vivo.com/
Vosaic Browser	Vosaic	http://www.vosaic.com/

MBONE EXPLAINED

MBONE, the abbreviation for *multicast backbone*, is an experimental technology used to transmit digital video over the Internet. Even at relatively modest data-sampling rates, a video broadcast can easily saturate an ISDN circuit or a fractional T1 link, so imagine the likely effects on the owner of a 14.4Kbps modem. MBONE requires the creation of another Internet backbone service using special hardware and software to accommodate the high data-rate transmissions needed for digital video. MBONE has been used to transmit concerts and conferences to a limited number of people for some time.

The Internet protocol committees are currently working to add support for broadcast modes to the next version of IP (known as IPng), and support for multimedia and multicasting is seen as a key requirement for this new protocol.

Two other World Wide Web sites of interest are MPEG Plaza and TB's Video Site. MPEG Plaza is an easy-to-navigate collection of MPEG products, services, and technical information. Check out

```
http://www.visiblelight.com/mpeg/
```

TB's Video Site contains a great collection of links to all the best video-related World Wide Web sites at

```
http://www.tebweb.com/tbvideo/
```

Streaming Animation

It seems that there are even fewer choices in the world of animation. Narrative Communications, a company formed by former Lotus Development Corporation technologist John Landry, has created a system for those interested in publishing a large quantity of CD-quality multimedia material. The Enliven package includes a free plug-in viewer (which works as a Netscape Navigator plug-in or as a Microsoft Internet Explorer ActiveX control), the Enliven Producer authoring tool, and the Enliven server software. Find out more at

```
http://www.narrative.com/
```

Using the Macromedia Flash 3 Player plug-in, you can view animations created by Flash 3 from Macromedia Inc. One of Flash's most notable features is that you can create interactive elements without doing any programming at all. Visit the Web site at

```
http://www.macromedia.com/software/flash/
```

And finally, Sizzler, from Totally Hip Software, is a plug-in player for Navigator and Internet Explorer that lets you play real-time interactive multimedia and animation. A conversion tool allows you to convert existing animation files into the Sizzler format. Check out the company at

```
http://www.totallyhip.com/
```

Putting It All Together with Shockwave

Shockwave for Director from Macromedia is a plug-in that plays Macromedia Director files downloaded from the network, but it is also much more. It is a multimedia-development environment for the creative professional who doesn't want to spend time learning how to program, but who just wants to make stuff happen. And stuff will happen; your intranet pages will come alive with sound, animation, video, and perhaps most important of all, with interactivity with your users.

There are three steps to the process:

1. Create a Macromedia Director file using one of the authoring tools; you'll hear more about them in a moment.

2. Compress, or "shock," the Director files using the postprocessor Afterburner. Because Shockwave does not use a lossy compression method to shrink the files, the file you see in your browser is exactly the same as the file originally created by the authoring tool. So, on the one hand, there is none of the loss in quality associated with such compression methods, but on the other hand, Shockwave files tend to be large.

3. Use the Shockwave plug-in to retrieve the file, decompress the contents on the fly, and view the result. Playback is seamless, so Shockwave elements appear as an integral part of your HTML page.

The plug-in is available free at

```
http://www.macromedia.com/shockwave/
```

Macromedia offers three Shockwave-enabled authoring tools:

Director An application used to create movies you can deliver over the intranet. Director employs a filmmaking metaphor;

you assemble your cast of multimedia elements on the stage (or screen) using a powerful scripting language called Lingo. A multichannel score manages sounds, color palettes, text, video, scripts, animation, and sprites.

Authorware   An application used to create interactive multimedia and aimed at intranet developers. It features large file streaming on demand, asynchronous preloading of data before it is needed, icon-driven scripting control, and data-measurement functions you can use to send data back to the server for storage and analysis. When you create an Authorware segment using Afterburner, the segment is compressed and divided into pieces. As the segment is played in the browser, the separate pieces are downloaded to the client computer only as they are needed.

Freehand   A high-end vector-graphics drawing program you can use to embed graphics into your HTML pages. Freehand includes several impressive tools you can use to create a link out of anything on an HTML page by drawing an irregularly shaped hotspot.

Shockwave is not currently a true streaming technology, which means that the whole file is normally downloaded before viewing can begin.

EXTENSIONS TO HTML

Now that we have looked at streaming audio and video technologies, let's take a look at what some of the emerging proposals in the world of HTML have to offer in the way of animation and increased interactivity on an intranet.

Extensions to HTML are being proposed all the time to add the new features that Web page designers think they need. As this process continues through the current proposals to extend HTML, it is becoming more and more evident that HTML is moving away from describing the structure of a document, which was the original intention behind its design, and toward being a page-description language.

And despite all the talk of standards, there are still subtle differences in the way that certain HTML tags are displayed in the two front-running browsers, Netscape Navigator and Microsoft's Internet Explorer. We'll explore those differences in this next section and then go on to look at Cascading Style Sheets (CSS).

What's So Standard about That?

Both Netscape Navigator and Internet Explorer do a good job of displaying a basic HTML page; there is no doubt about that. But Internet Explorer seems to have an edge when it comes to displaying some of the newer and more advanced HTML features.

Both browsers support frames, which let multiple panes of information appear in a single browser screen, but in subtly different ways. Navigator recognizes attributes that define the thickness and color of the frame border, while Internet Explorer supports the advanced concept of floating frames that can appear anywhere on the HTML page.

Both browsers support tables, including multiple columns and rows, borders, nested tables, and cell background colors. But Microsoft is closer to supporting the World Wide Web Consortium (W3C) RFC 1492, the proposal likely to be accepted as the formal definition of tables. Internet Explorer can draw different types of borders between cells in a table and can place background images in table cells. Some of these features may seem a little esoteric, but they are bound to add interest to any data displayed in tables, such as financial spreadsheets and general ledger entries.

Navigator's MULTICOL tag flows text into multiple columns automatically, with adjustable column width and column spacing. In the past, HTML designers have simulated columns using tables, which has always been an uneasy compromise. And Netscape's SPACER tag allows you to insert either horizontal or vertical white space of a specified number of pixels.

On the graphics front, both browsers can manage the basic graphic formats, including JPEG, GIF, and so on, but Navigator supports the LOWSRC attribute to the <IMG> tag, which lets you specify a low-resolution preview version of an image that loads before the complete image. On the other hand, Internet Explorer supports the DYNSRC attribute that loads an AVI animation rather than a simple static graphic. Internet Explorer also allows for built-in MPEG playback, while Navigator does not.

Both Navigator and Internet Explorer allow background graphics, but only Internet Explorer supports watermarks or *non-scrolling backgrounds*, a built-in marquee that can generate scrolling text and horizontal rules of different colors. And, of course, both browsers support Cascading Style Sheets.

Cascading Style Sheets

HTML defines the structure of a document, not the details of its presentation; they are left to the browser. And then along came a recommendation from the World Wide Web Consortium (W3C) for Cascading Style Sheets (CSS) to give HTML designers an unprecedented level of control over typography and the appearance of their pages. Microsoft implemented a version of CSS Level 1 in Internet Explorer 3, and Netscape did the same in Navigator 4.

CSS Level 1 brings a complete set of typographical controls to HTML. You can specify paragraph margins (top, bottom, left, and right), indention, line spacing, text highlighting, even different fonts. This means that now the designer can create precise margins, use different font styles, and specify amounts of white space around graphical elements and text, along with other desktop-publishing-like controls.

CSS uses rules to define the presentation of an HTML page. A rule can be as simple as

```
H1 {color : green}
```

where H1 is any HTML element acting as a selector, and `{color : green}` is the declaration. The declaration has two parts, a property (`color`) and a value (`green`). There are about 35 properties, including font properties, color and background properties, text properties, box properties, and classification properties, and they can be specified in a variety of ways, including length, percentage, number, color, and URL.

And in addition to this new level of control, CSS give designers two important new features:

▶ The ability to create display elements in HTML that previously required a bulky GIF file.

▶ The ability to separate style information from the HTML document, making updates easier and the site much easier to maintain. Multiple HTML pages or even a complete site can use a single style sheet, so changes in that style sheet will ripple across every page on your intranet.

If you are careful, you can design HTML pages with style sheets in such a way that they are transparent to browsers that don't yet support them; you don't need two sets of HTML pages, one with and one without style sheets.

HOW TO INVOKE A CASCADING STYLE SHEET

You can invoke CSS from within an HTML document in different ways, and you can choose the most convenient way, depending on the needs of your intranet. Let's take a quick look at what the HTML looks like:

```
<HTML>
<HEAD>
<TITLE>Title</TITLE>
<LINK REL=STYLESHEET TYPE="text/css"
     HREF="URL" TITLE="Fab">
<STYLE TYPE="text/css">
@import url;
H1 {color : blue}
</STYLE>
</HEAD>
<BODY>
<P STYLE="color : green">
</BODY>
</HTML>
```

Here we have four ways of invoking style sheets:

1. A <LINK> element to link to an external file containing a style sheet

2. A <STYLE> element inside the <HEAD> tag

3. An imported style sheet using the CSS @import notation

4. A <STYLE> attribute on an element inside the <BODY> tags

To review the official W3C recommendation for Cascading Style Sheets, go to

```
http://www.w3.org/TR/REC-CSS1
```

and for other resources try

```
http://www.w3.org/Style/
```

To review a recent article from *Web Review*, along with an easy-to-read description of CSS and some examples, see

```
http://style.webreview.com
```

And finally, you might visit this site for Microsoft's version of the CSS story:

```
http://www.microsoft.com/truetype/css
```

AN INTRODUCTION TO INTRANET PROGRAMMING

So far you have been introduced to ways to publish mostly static information on a Web site, but how do you create truly interactive applications for your intranet? Fortunately, there are several answers to that question. You can write *scripts*, or external programs, using almost any 32-bit programming language, such as Perl (more on Perl in a moment), the C or C++ programming languages, or Windows CGI, Pascal, REXX, or Visual Basic. You can also use NT batch files, although we would not recommend that you do. You just have to make sure you use one of the standard server interfaces:

▶ CGI (*Common Gateway Interface*) is the traditional definition of how server and browser interact. Despite what you might hear, CGI is not a programming language, but a definition of how server and browser communicate. A CGI script is simply a script that conforms to this CGI standard. We'll look at the advantages and disadvantages of using CGI in the next section.

▶ NSAPI (*Netscape Server API*) from Netscape and ISAPI (*Internet Server API*) from Microsoft are two programming interfaces available as an alternative to using CGI. We'll look at how you can use both later in this chapter.

Part iii

CGI Programming

The term *script* originates in the Unix world, where it describes programs written in and interpreted by one of the Unix shells. Scripts are external programs that the Web server runs in response to a request from the browser. When a visitor requests a URL that points to a script, the server executes it, and any output that the script creates is sent back to the browser for display. Figure 9.1 shows the basic information flow.

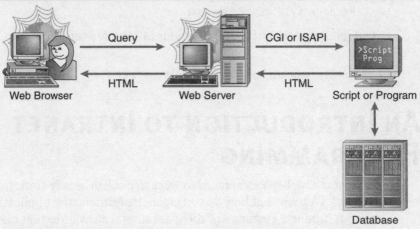

Query

CGI or ISAPI

HTML

HTML

Web Browser   Web Server   Script or Program

Database

FIGURE 9.1: Information flow through the CGI or API interface

You can use a script for tasks as varied as creating an interface to a relational database system or creating your own search engine, and anything in between; there are really no limits. CGI also allows the server to create new documents on the fly—that is, at the moment the browser requests them.

SERVER SIDE INCLUDES: PROS AND CONS

Another way to extend your use of HTML is with *Server Side Includes*, which are sometimes, but rarely, called parsed HTML. You use the INCLUDE statement to embed commands directly in the HTML document that tell the server to perform a specific task. The most common way of using INCLUDE is to tell the server to load the contents of another external file at a specific point in the main HTML document. There are also a couple of drawbacks you should know

CONTINUED ➤

about when using Server Side Includes: (1) They can degrade Web server performance, and (2) They can compromise server security. They require additional hard disk accesses because they build the HTML file from the component pieces. Server Side Includes can be a natty programming trick, but they become dangerous when associated with CGI scripts that include code that modifies other HTML or user input to an HTML document. And because they can quite legally include anything at all, you could be facing a major security breach if someone creates a completely bogus Include.

The major benefit of using CGI is that any CGI-compliant script will run on any CGI-compliant Web server (and most of them are), and that simple fact can save you a whole lot of time. There is a very good chance that someone somewhere has already solved a problem similar to yours and created a CGI script to do it. He or she may well have posted the solution on one of the many Web sites that carry lots of CGI scripts. Start your search at this site:

```
http://www.boutell.com/cgic/
```

You should always bear in mind that much of the early work with CGI scripts was done in a Unix environment; some of the scripts might work on Windows NT, others almost certainly won't. Always check first before you run anything on your own system. A disadvantage of using CGI is that scripts can be inefficient and can slow server performance in some cases.

How Do CGI Scripts Work?

Here is a simple example of the kind of thing you can do with a CGI script. If you have created an HTML data-entry form using the <FORM> </FORM> tags, say to collect personal information from a new hire, you can write a program to do something with that data. You can write this script in any language supported by the server software; popular choices are C, C++, Pascal, REXX, and even Visual Basic. It's pretty much your choice.

You can collect information from an HTML form in two ways: with the POST method and with the GET method. If your HTML code has METHOD=GET inside the FORM tag, the CGI script gets the information from the form in the environment variable QUERY_STRING. This variable contains the information that follows the ? in the script's URL.

If you use METHOD=POST in your HTML code, the CGI script gets the information from the form on the standard output stream stdin in the C programming language. Unfortunately, you can't depend on getting an end-of-file mark in the data stream, so your program will have to use the environment variable CONTENT_LENGTH to determine how much data to read.

You will find that the data contained in the environment variable QUERY_STRING or on stdin is URL-encoded: spaces are changed to plus signs, and some keyboard characters are converted to hexadecimal. The data from the input fields in your form are placed into name=value pairs, and these pairs are separated by an & (ampersand) character. Some of the newer servers handle binary data, while other manage encrypted data; we'll stick to URL-encoded data here as we continue with this description.

To find out what kind of data you have received, check the CONTENT_ TYPE environment variable, which will give you MIME type/subtype information. Your CGI script can now split the data at the ampersands to get separate strings in the form of name=value and then split these strings at the equal sign to separate the name from the value. Convert plus signs to spaces and check for hexadecimal values (usually in the form %hh, where hh are hexadecimal digits), and at that point, you will have all the names and values from your HTML form decoded into separate strings. Table 9.4 lists the environment variables passed into CGI scripts.

Returning information from the CGI script to the server, and from there back to the client browser, is simple enough; you tell the server what kind of data you are sending, and then you send it to the standard output.

NOTE

There are many ways you can use the CGI environment variables to make your HTML pages more useful and informative. Check the value of the HTTP_USER_AGENT variable to determine the features available on the requesting browser. You can return one kind of information (using frames and tables) to a feature-rich browser, and you can return a more generic set of information to a less capable browser.

TABLE 9.4: Environment Variables Passed into CGI Scripts

NAME	DESCRIPTION
SERVER_SOFTWARE	The name and version number of the server software.
SERVER_NAME	The server's complete host name, IP address, or alias.
GATEWAY_INTERFACE	The revision level of the CGI specification to which the server software complies.
SERVER_PROTOCOL	The name and revision level of the service protocol used by the requesting client.
SERVER_PORT	The port number to which the request was sent.
REQUEST_METHOD	The method of the request—this could be GET or POST.
PATH_INFO	Extra information at the end of the path of the executing CGI script. Unlike PATH_TRANSLATED, this variable is passed unmodified if it comes from a URL.
PATH_TRANSLATED	A translated version of PATH_INFO that has removed any virtual mappings.
SCRIPT_NAME	The complete virtual path of the CGI script that is being executed.
QUERY_STRING	Everything that follows the ? in the URL that referenced this CGI script.
REMOTE_HOST	The host name of the computer making the request to the Web server.
REMOTE_ADDR	The IP address of REMOTE_HOST or the computer making the request.
AUTH_TYPE	The authentication method used to validate a user if the script was protected and requires authentication.
REMOTE_USER	The login name of the user from REMOTE_ADDR if the user logged in under user authentication.
REMOTE_IDENT	The login name of the user from REMOTE_ADDR if the remote host supports user identification.
CONTENT_TYPE	The MIME content type of the data.
CONTENT_LENGTH	Length of the data received from the client.
HTTP_ACCEPT	A list of the MIME types that the requesting client can accept.
HTTP_USER_AGENT	The browser running on the client.
HTTP_REFERER	The URL of the document that the client pointed to before the client sent the request to the server.

Part iii

You use an ASCII header to return information to the browser. Table 9.5 contains a list of the server directives passed from your CGI script to the browser as metainformation about the document being returned.

TABLE 9.5: Server Directives Returned by CGI Scripts

NAME	DESCRIPTION
Allowed	Lists the requests that the user is allowed to use on this server
Content-Encoding	Encoding method used
Content-Language	ISO 3316 language code with an additional, though optional, ISO 639 country code
Content-Length	The length of the returning document
Content-Transfer-Encoding	The MIME-encoding method used on the returning document
Content-Type	MIME type of the returning document
Date	Creation date in Greenwich Mean Time format
Expires	Expiration date
Last-Modified	Last Modification date
Location	The virtual path or URL of the returning document; a reference to a document rather than the document itself
Message-ID	Message identifier
Public	Lists all requests that anyone can use
Status	Returned status of the request
URL	URL of the document
Version	Version of the document
Title	Title of the document

No matter which programming language you use for your CGI scripts, you still face several important security concerns. In the next section, we'll take a look at some of the problems associated with CGI scripts and some of the things you can do to minimize the risk.

PROGRAMMING WITH PERL

Perl, an acronym formed from either Practical Extraction and Reporting Language or Pathologically Eclectic Rubbish Lister, depending on your bias, is an interpreted language created by Larry Ward that is used in the Unix world to manipulate text, files, and processes and to print reports based on extracted information.

Perl looks something like the C programming language, but it also includes text-manipulation features originally found in the Unix utilities awk and sed. Perl's strengths—powerful text-manipulation capabilities—are exactly what CGI programmers need, and so Perl has become very popular indeed.

You will find two versions of Perl commonly available, Perl 4 and Perl 5. Perl 4 is a straightforward implementation of Perl, and Perl 5 adds object-oriented extensions and allows classes and inheritance. You can embed Perl 5 code in a C or C++ application, and you can embed C or C++ code in a Perl 5 application.

Avoiding CGI-Related Problems

One of the benefits of the straightforward CGI programming interface is its ease of use for system administrators. Unfortunately, CGI scripts can also be a considerable security risk, particularly if your intranet is connected to the Internet. In the next couple of sections, we'll look at some of the problems associated with using CGI.

Assessing CGI Scripting Risks

You can use many sources to find CGI scripts that have been written and debugged by other system administrators. But if you do download a CGI script from one of these sources, do not assume that the script is harmless and ready for use. Writing CGI scripts is not particularly easy, and writing secure scripts is a job for the experts.

All sorts of things can happen; some programmers add back doors in the scripts to ease the problems of debugging the script and then forget to take them out when the script is finished. This is particularly important if your intranet maintains outside connections to the Internet. You may think that you have just installed a nifty utility that will save you

Part III

hours of work when, in reality, you have just installed an open door to your system. You should always test shareware or freeware thoroughly on an offline system before you install it on one of your online intranet servers.

Lowering the Risk

The problem is not really in CGI itself, but in the power that it gives to script writers, who may be system administrators or users. There are really two main areas at risk:

▶ The accidental disclosure of confidential information, such as passwords or registry files

▶ The potential for fooling or spoofing the CGI script into doing something you had not anticipated, such as executing system commands

Fortunately, there are several things you can do on your intranet to minimize any risk from CGI:

▶ Locate all your CGI scripts in the same directory on the server, and be sure that the Webmaster is the only person with write permission for that directory.

▶ Never, ever, trust input data from a user. If your script manages information that a user has entered into a form, don't make assumptions about any data you receive. Even though you have asked someone to enter his or her zip code in the form, don't assume that the field will actually contain numbers—you can never predict what a user will enter. Always scan for nonalphanumeric characters and throw them away before you process the input. This can go a long way toward keeping your system safe.

▶ Consider using a compiled executable program with NSAPI or ISAPI to do the job instead of using CGI. Because programs written to these APIs are compiled, they will execute faster than the same function written as a CGI script.

If your users ask that they be allowed to write their own CGI scripts, carefully consider the management problems of tracking a changing list of CGI scripts. And besides that, do you really want users writing programs to run on the server? Probably not.

Fixing CGI Script Problems

Programming errors connected to CGI scripts can be obvious and easy to see but difficult to troubleshoot and fix because several elements are at work—the intranet server software itself, the script, and the file or databases with which the script interacts. It might be as simple as a missing file, or it might be a complex programming problem. If you have a previous version to fall back to, do so while you trace through the problem.

Be sure that all the permissions are set appropriately and that all the directories containing any executables are accessible. And don't forget to check the NT Server error logs to see if there is another reason for the script not executing properly. One of the most obvious causes of script failure is that something is wrong with one of the files on which the script itself operates.

Because the main tool used to access the results of a CGI script is the Web browser itself, troubleshooting scripts can be a tedious job indeed. Browsers can even mask problems with their inconsistent error-message reporting.

Another way to add functionality to your intranet without using CGI scripts is through the use of compiled programs that access one of the two popular APIs currently available, and we'll look at both of them in the next section.

NOTE

You'll read more about CGI and Perl in Chapters 10 and 11, which are taken from the book *Perl CGI Programming: No experience required.* Chapter 10 provides an overview of Perl, CGI, and the Web, and Chapter 11 looks in detail at using Perl and CGI to create forms on your site.

PROGRAMMING WITH THE NETSCAPE AND MICROSOFT APIS

Aside from the security and other risks we looked at in the last section, there are other drawbacks to using CGI scripts; they offer poor scalabililty and low efficiency. Each instance of a CGI script runs in its own address and process space, not in the Web server space. This means that a new copy of the script is run each time it is called, with a new address space and a new process. In some cases, when the script actually does very little, system overhead becomes a significant portion of the total script-running time.

The newer generation of Web servers promises to increase the flexibility of CGI scripts and add new functions to the server side by using proprietary APIs such as NSAPI (Netscape Server API) from Netscape and ISAPI (Internet Server API). Using this sort of approach over the conventional CGI approach has several advantages, including:

- ▶ APIs can be more efficient in their use of memory, because initialization occurs only once.

- ▶ APIs let a server application stay connected to the Web browser without losing important information. In CGI scripting, the browser disconnects from the server after each request and has no memory of any previous transactions between browser and server.

- ▶ APIs let you plug in custom applications, such as user-authentication routines or database-logging applications.

But the major disadvantage to using an API is that it is bound to a specific server or group of servers; CGI scripts are, in theory at least, portable to any environment. The APIs are definitely aimed squarely at professional programmers and usually require a detailed knowledge of the C programming language.

Netscape's NSAPI

Netscape's NSAPI is not easy to summarize; it is a large, complex, proprietary API, closely tied to the server setup. Each NSAPI function has to be configured in the Netsite Object configuration database. A detailed description of how to use NSAPI is beyond the scope of this book, but if you are interested, you'll find lots more information on NSAPI at

```
http://developer1.netscape.com/support/faqs/champions/
nsapi.html
```

Microsoft's ISAPI

Microsoft's ISAPI is a new API that was released along with the Internet Information Server. It was jointly developed by Microsoft and Process Software, creators of the Purveyor IntraServer and other intranet and Internet software products.

ISAPI is also proprietary and is only available on Microsoft and Process Software products. For details of how to use this API, see Microsoft's World Wide Web site, contact the Microsoft Developer's Network (MSDN), or see the BackOffice Software Development Kit (SDK) and look for details on how to access the BackOffice series of products from this interface. Check out

```
http://www.microsoft.com/workshop/
```

NOTE

To help convince software developers that ISAPI is the way to go, Microsoft plans to provide a simple wrapper for ISAPI applications that will make them CGI-compliant. That way, software developers can have their cake and eat it too.

Undoubtedly, the increasing use of these APIs will lead to the addition of new functions to the current stock of server software as third-party software developers create new applications to improve performance and add security and logging functions currently not available.

In the next section, we'll look at another comparative newcomer on the scene, the Java programming language from Sun Microsystems, and we'll show you how it has a completely different focus from these inward-looking APIs.

THE SUN SHINES ON JAVA

Java is not just a source of bad coffee-related jokes, but a serious programming language originally developed by Sun. With Java, you can create absolutely any kind of software imaginable that will work across the Internet and on an intranet. What this means to most users is that instead of browsing from site to site, you can now think of the Web as a giant hard disk that contains all the applications you could ever want. Java has the power to add dynamic, interactive content to your Web pages, sending static HTML pages the way of the dinosaurs.

Microsoft's Internet strategy, like that of many companies, has always been to try to impose its own standards on the rest of the industry, and this has usually been done by locking the customer into the set of Microsoft products. Sun, on the other hand, comes from the Unix world, where standards are traditionally much more open. Sun is trying to build Java into a broad, acceptable alternative to several Microsoft initiatives. Microsoft

Part iii

may bundle products and sometimes give products away as free promotions, but it would never have distributed Java in the way that Sun has.

All of the popular Web browsers now support Java to varying degrees, and a small group of Java developers have created animated and interactive Web sites. Sun maintains that if you can write an application in C++ (and you can write almost any application in C++), you can write that same application in Java and distribute it across the Web.

NOTE

In a November 1998 court ruling, Sun was granted a preliminary injunction against Microsoft in the ongoing court battle over Microsoft's use of Java. For all upcoming software releases, Microsoft was ordered to comply with the specifications laid out in the original licensing agreement concerning its use of Sun's Java technology. Microsoft reluctantly agreed to implement all of the changes necessary for compliance with the court order within the required 90 days. Stay tuned to the news for further developments.

Why Java Is So Important

But what is all the fuss about? Why, exactly, is Java so important? To answer this question, we need to take a step back and look at how the elements of the client-server relationship between Web browser and Web server have changed. In the beginning, a Web browser was able to access all kinds of information coded in HTML, but it was a one-way street; there was no interaction between the user and the server. Users could not change anything on the HTML page or interact with the server.

Then along came the Common Gateway Interface (CGI), which allowed for limited interaction but was too clumsy for complex, real-time applications programming.

TIP

For a complete technical discussion on the pros and cons of using CGI, see http://www2.hursley.ibm.com/goserve/$GoSer49.htm.

The Java Programming Language (to use its full name) represents the third stage. Java allows complex and secure remote interaction in real time over mixed networks. And that makes Java's potential in distributed computing simply enormous.

Using Java Applets

Java requires a multithreaded operating system, which means that Windows 95/98 and NT 3.51 and 4 are in and that Windows 3.1x is definitely out (sorry, folks, but even Win32s is out). A Java applet (an *applet* is a small application running under the control of another application, usually the Java-enabled Web browser) is downloaded from the server and executes under the control of the Java interpreter in the computer running the browser. Many early Java demos concentrated on sizzle rather than substance, but one of the major longer-term benefits of Java is the ability to manage new data types as soon as they are developed and to create distributed interactive applications.

Right now, you can't "play" a new type of data file until you find the appropriate helper or add-in application that knows how to manage and decode the data. With Java, an applet can contain the viewing mechanism along with the data, or alternatively, the Java applet can instruct the browser to collect the viewer from another Web site.

Another potentially large impact is in the area of interactive applications, created and managed until now by CGI or Perl scripts. Java may someday displace CGI programming simply because it is both more efficient and more powerful. CGI scripts are host-based and place overhead on the server for every script that runs; Java runs on the local processor in the computer running the Web browser.

Some of the early Java demos will not run until the whole Java program has been received from the server; the effect is rather like waiting for a large graphic to load. Until it arrives, the Web page you are viewing has a hole in it. Other demos require a large number of GIF files to present an animated image; in this case, the image files take longer to download than the animation itself takes to run. Most of these effects are because Java is still very young; once programmers start to optimize their code, and they invent the tips and tricks that are common in other languages, you will see some astonishing things done using Java.

Java and HTML

Java applets are opened by using an HTML link and the <APPLET> tag, so providing a Java effect on a Web page can be as simple as copying a Java file to your server and adding the HTML link. The HTML to do that might look like this:

```
<HTML>
<HEAD>
<TITLE>A Java applet </TITLE>
</HEAD>
<BODY>
<APPLET CODE="MYAPPLET">
</APPLET>
</BODY>
</HTML>
```

Note that no filename extension is used in the applet name. You can also use other modifiers with the <APPLET> tag to align the applet on your Web page, retrieve the applet from another URL, and so on, as Table 9.6 shows. If your browser does not understand the <APPLET> tag, it simply ignores it and displays any alternative text you specified.

TABLE 9.6: Attributes Used with the <APPLET> Tag

MODIFIER	DESCRIPTION
CODEBASE	This optional attribute specifies the absolute or relative base URL (directory) of the applet to be displayed.
CODE	This required attribute specifies the actual file that contains the applet, not a URL.
WIDTH	This required attribute specifies the initial width in pixels that the applet needs in the browser window.
HEIGHT	This required attribute specifies the initial height in pixels that the applet needs in the browser window.
ALT	This optional attribute specifies text that a browser that understands the <APPLET> tag but that doesn't support Java should display instead of the applet.
NAME	This optional attribute gives a name to the applet instance; this allows applets to find each other by name and communicate with each other.

TABLE 9.6 CONTINUED: Attributes Used with the <APPLET> Tag

MODIFIER	DESCRIPTION
ALIGN	This optional attribute specifies the applet's alignment on the page and works just like the <IMG> tag.
VSPACE	This optional attribute specifies the amount of space above and below the applet that the browser should leave and works just like the VSPACE attribute of the <IMG> tag.
HSPACE	This optional attribute specifies the amount of space on either side of the applet that the browser should leave and works just like the HSPACE attribute of the <IMG> tag.
PARAM	This modifier, along with its NAME and VALUE attributes, specifies a named parameter and a string that are passed to the Java applet.

Because Java is considered an interpreted language, there is a performance penalty when it is compared with a C++ compiled program. The Java program runs somewhere between ten and twenty times slower than the equivalent compiled C++ program, but it is still much faster than most scripting languages.

But Java is not a completely interpreted language and compromises by creating a byte-code so that the final Java interpreter has considerably less work to do than a normal stand-alone interpreter. When this byte-code file arrives in your computer, it provides 70 to 80 percent of the data needed to run the applet; the other 20 to 30 percent is provided by the Java runtime environment and tells the applet how to perform on that specific platform.

Part iii

JAVA AND MIME TYPES

The HTTP protocol specifies the MIME type of each resource that it delivers. HTML documents are delivered with the MIME type text/html, for example. This lets the browser know how to handle the data and when to load a plug-in or helper application. Java works in much the same way—it sends Java applet code with the MIME type application/octet-stream. To serve Java applets over your intranet, you will probably have to configure your server (or the NT Registry) to include this file type.

CONTINUED ➡

When some browsers see an <APPLET> tag, they assume that it points to a Java applet and ignore the MIME type sent from the server; they will be in trouble if the proposed tag <EMBED> comes into common use. Then they will have to be much more observant of MIME types.

How Does It All Work?

So how does a Java applet get from the server to a Java-enabled Web browser? Here are the steps:

1. The Web browser requests an HTML page from the Web server.

2. The Web browser receives and displays the Web page.

3. The Web browser interprets the <APPLET> tag and sends a request to the server for the file specified in the tag.

4. The Web browser receives the specified file, verifies the byte-code, and starts executing the Java applet on your system.

Any Web server can send out the Java file; no special requirements are placed on the server, and no modifications are required. And because execution takes place on the client computer, Java applets are largely unaffected by restrictions in bandwidth or by limitations in HTML.

The Java Programming Language

In "The Java Language: A White Paper," the developers at Sun Microsystems describe Java this way:

Java: A simple, object-oriented, distributed, interpreted, robust, secure, architecturally neutral, portable, high-performance, multi-threaded, dynamic language

Do they get bonus points for packing so many current buzzwords into the definition? You bet they do, because it all happens to be true. Let's take a closer look at what they said.

▶ *Simple:* One of the design goals behind Java was to make it familiar to a large number of programmers, which explains its strong resemblance to C and to C++. The designers have simplified matters by removing some of the C++ constructs, such as pointers, that traditionally cause problems for many programmers. And if you are a C programmer, you will no doubt notice that header files and the preprocessor are also missing.

▶ *Object-oriented:* Java is object-oriented; that phrase has come to mean very little in certain circles, but here it means that you can concentrate on the data in your application rather than thinking in terms of procedures.

▶ *Distributed:* Java is designed to support networking and network operations right from the start.

▶ *Interpreted:* Java is an interpreted language rather than a language that you compile and then run. A Java program can run on any system for which there is a Java interpreter.

▶ *Robust:* Java is a strongly typed language that allows for comprehensive runtime checking, and with no pointers to worry about, there is no possibility of overwriting some distant memory area and corrupting data.

▶ *Secure:* Java begins with the assumption that it can trust no one, and it implements several security mechanisms to protect you from attempts to create viruses or invade your file system.

▶ *Architecturally neutral:* Java doesn't care about the underlying operating system. With multiple versions of Windows, Unix, and the Macintosh operating systems, it is becoming increasingly difficult to write software that will run on all systems. Write your application in Java, however, and it will run on all systems, provided that the Java interpreter is available.

▶ *Portable:* In addition to the Java interpreter, several other aspects of Java contribute to its portability. No assumptions are made about the size of data types, and Java explicitly defines arithmetic behavior.

▶ *High-performance:* Just-in-time compilers help Java achieve higher performance than the Java interpreter alone can reach.

▶ *Multithreaded:* Java supports multiple threads of execution to handle different tasks.

▶ *Dynamic:* Java was designed to adapt to a changing environment and can load classes as they are needed, even across the network.

To use Java effectively, you should have a background in C++ programming and wide experience in solving real-time programming problems. This similarity to C and to C++ is no accident; it ensures that a huge population of professional programmers can quickly learn how to use Java from their previous experience in writing C++ code.

JAVA AND UNICODE™

Java uses Unicode characters internally, even though support for Unicode may be limited on certain platforms. Windows 95/98 and Windows NT provide a partial implementation of Unicode but omit certain Chinese, Japanese, and Korean characters.

Unicode is a 16-bit character code, defined by ISO 10646, that can support as many as 65,000 characters, rather than the 256 characters available in the current ASCII character set. In its current form, Unicode contains more than 38,000 distinct characters covering the major languages of Europe, the Middle East, Africa, India, Asia, the Pacific Islands, and the Americas.

Unicode is a trademark of the Unicode Consortium. Find out more about Unicode and the Consortium at http://unicode.org.

Java, as it was originally conceived, is an interpreted language, although as you will see in the next section, some companies have taken a novel approach to the interpreter. A Java applet can define classes of objects that are acted on by a method; for example, an object can be a graphical image, and a method can be a set of instructions to place or move the graphic in a specific way.

As we've mentioned, Java programming is similar to C++, but it is a little simpler in two important respects: There are no pointers in Java, and the interpreter, rather than the program, manages memory. This approach to memory management is also a useful security control; it means that an applet cannot get to the underlying operating system and violate Java's security model.

Java is a major departure from the Hypertext Markup Language, which is used to prepare Web page content for display by a Web browser. HTML is straightforward enough that you can learn how to code a Web page relatively quickly; C++ skills are much harder to come by and are usually the province of only advanced amateurs and professional programmers.

A major advance with Java is that it is designed right from the beginning to be platform independent; a Java applet can run on any hardware as long as a Java interpreter is available for that system. This means that you can develop an intranet-enabled application on your preferred hardware and software platform, and then it can run unchanged on any other system with a Java interpreter. For instance, you could write your Java applet on a Macintosh, and it will run without modification on any Windows 95/98 system that has Java installed.

This has a practical application; you can download the same Java applet to users who have all sorts of browsers, and the Java interpreter will take care of any site-specific differences. The Java programming language has been licensed by literally hundreds of software companies, including IBM and Microsoft; by all the makers of software development tools; by all the major database developers; and by all the network operating system companies—if a company is considered a major player in the software field, it has a Java license.

Security in Java

Inherent in the Java system are several important security aspects. Java downloads include a byte-code verification process; if the packet's size changes along the way, the transfer is aborted. The Java loader assumes that the data stream may have been tampered with and checks very carefully to make sure it has not changed en route. This is to protect against viruses being added in transit.

Once the Java applet is running on your system, the operations it can perform are strictly limited by the Web browser you are using. In general, Java applets do not:

▶ Read or write files on the local system

▶ Delete or rename files on the local system

▶ Create a directory on the local system

- ▶ List a directory, check for the existence of a specific file, or obtain the size, type, or modification information for a file

- ▶ Manipulate network connections (other than the connection to your Web site)

- ▶ Run other applications on your system

- ▶ Load any DLLs on your system

- ▶ Make native function calls to the underlying operating system

- ▶ Access memory directly

- ▶ Obtain the user's name or the home directory name

- ▶ Define any system properties

- ▶ Manipulate any thread that is not part of the same threadgroup as the applet

- ▶ Terminate the Java interpreter

In some cases, a Java applet may be allowed to read files named on a read-access control list.

In Java version 1.1, Sun included RSA's public-key encryption scheme to provide security for commercial and credit card transactions. Java also was made compatible with Netscape's Secure Sockets Layer (SSL) and with the Microsoft and Visa Private Communications Technology (PCT).

Java on Your Intranet

Software developers are not just interested in Java because it is new and fascinating and can bring sparkle to their Web pages; they are interested in Java because it is hardware and operating system independent. Many developers will use Java because the applications they create will run on any platform, provided the user has a Java-enabled browser.

This single aspect of Java has many programmers—who face a company full of different kinds of hardware running several variations of different operating systems—smiling all the way back to their cubicles. They can now write a Java applet to solve that nagging integration problem. If you are looking for a low-cost way to distribute applications across your enterprise, take a look at Java; it might just be the answer to your prayers.

DATABASES AND JDBC

JDBC (*Java Database Connectivity*) is a Java-enabled database API, modeled after Microsoft's ODBC (Open Database Connectivity) API, that provides a uniform interface for most relational databases. The JDBC API has completed a peer review, and software developers have moved to implement JDBC as a series of Java classes.

These classes let a developer issue a series of SQL (Structured Query Language) statements to request information from a remote database over the intranet and to process the information sent from the database. As far as the user is concerned, the Java applet functions just like all the other database applications written in other programming languages, except that it runs inside the user's browser.

There are two main components to JDBC:

JDBC API This portion provides application-to-JDBC Manager communications. Developers use this API to access database services using standard Java methods.

JDBC Driver API This portion provides JDBC Manager-to-database-driver communications on behalf of the Java applet.

The JDBC Manager loads and unloads database drivers as required by the Java applet, in much the same way as the ODBC Driver Manager, and JDBC can support a connection to single or to multiple database servers.

More than 60 vendors have endorsed JDBC, including Oracle, Sybase, IBM, Symantec, and Borland, and all are planning to include Java- and JDBC-enabled software development tools.

Part iii

Should You Use Java?

Is Java the answer to your intranet? As always, the right answer is that it all depends. If your site's content is simple and can be presented in text and simple graphics, the answer is probably no, you don't need Java. You should also look at the programming skills you can draw on in support of your site. If programming in C++ gives you the mother of all headaches, again, the answer is probably no, you don't need Java.

Also, keep in mind the type of communications link that the majority of your users can access. If you run a fast corporate intranet, bandwidth may be less an issue, and you may find you can use Java to add a little spice to your HTML pages. If some people connect to your intranet using 14.4Kbps modems, they will be spending a lot of time waiting as more and more stuff is downloaded from your site.

Java may actually be the best thing since sliced bread, but it is also a topic that attracts a great deal of overstatement and inflated claims when discussion turns to what will happen in the future. Don't use it just because it is there; use it because it fills a well-defined need on your intranet.

JAVASCRIPT

Sun and Netscape jointly developed JavaScript, a Java scripting language designed to make it easier for nonprogrammers to create Java applets, and released it into the public domain. JavaScript used to be called "LiveScript," but the name was changed in late 1995.

The 24<SCRIPT></SCRIPT> tags are used in your HTML page to define a JavaScript script. These tags are ignored by some browsers, and any text that appears in the HTML page between these two tags will appear as rather ugly text in those browsers.

You will read more about JavaScript in Chapters 14 and 15.

NOTE

To learn more about Java, see *Mastering Java 1.2,* by John Zukowski, and *Java 1.2 In Record Time,* by Steven Holzner (both published by Sybex).

THE FUTURE ACCORDING TO MICROSOFT

Microsoft came to the Web late but has not lagged behind in recent developments; huge amounts of money and resources have been allocated to develop Microsoft's presence in this exploding market. Much of the current storm between Netscape and Microsoft is in terms of their two browsers and each company's version of several so-called standards.

Several important elements form Microsoft's plan of attack, with developments on many fronts, including Windows NT; Internet Information Server; Internet Explorer; proposed standards, such as ActiveX and ISAPI; additions to Windows 95/98; and the creation of HTML development tools and editors. Here we'll look at ActiveX and the Common Internet File System.

THE FUTURE OF WINDOWS NT

It must be obvious to everyone by now that Windows NT has a great future. Starting with Windows NT 4, both the Server and the Workstation editions supported the Windows 95/98 GUI, and many previous differences in tools, device drivers, and so on, began to disappear. It was no accident that all Windows 95/98 applications also had to run on Windows NT to receive Microsoft's blessing and indicate compatibility with Windows 95/98 on their packaging.

Moreover, Microsoft has discussed with other major players the possibility of including clustering (several servers mirrored together to provide for fault-tolerant operations) support in Windows NT in the future. This would be a major step forward and would undoubtedly convince many major clients, including Fortune 1000 companies, to consider Windows NT as a platform for mission-critical applications.

An element that is crucial for the development of any operating system is the availability of the right kinds of applications to run on the operating system. The broadening of the operating system platforms to combine Windows 95/98 and Windows NT, which Microsoft has planned for Windows 2000 (formerly known as Windows NT 5), is bound to convince more and more third-party software developers that this is a market they cannot afford to ignore. In most cases, the software can be written to run identically on both operating systems.

Microsoft's ActiveX

Microsoft's answer to Sun Microsystems' object-oriented, platform-independent Java programming language is the ActiveX specification, which consists of three main elements:

- *ActiveX controls,* which function just like conventional OLE controls (OCXs). They can be located on your browser or downloaded from the server and can be used for something as simple as a button all the way to something as complex as a whole report. ActiveX controls can also interact with one another.

- *ActiveX documents,* which allow you to view active documents as well as HTML pages, thus presenting you with a common interface for several tasks.

- *ActiveX scripting,* which allows you to coordinate ActiveX controls on your Web site using the two available scripting languages, JavaScript and the Visual Basic–based VBScript. Eventually, we may even see ActiveX scripting implementations of Sun's JavaScript and of Perl. At this point, VBScript has a smaller runtime module, at 50K compared with the 1.2MB needed for Java.

ActiveX is a careful repackaging of Microsoft's COM (*Common Object Model*), the foundation that supported OLE. By adding network capabilities (and so creating DCOM or *Distributed COM*) and by reducing the scope of OLE to create ActiveX, Microsoft has created a comprehensive suite of component-based Internet- and intranet-oriented applications. ActiveX controls are not completely incompatible with Java, and Microsoft has not only licensed Java from Sun, but has also agreed to provide a wrapper to make Java applets behave just like ActiveX objects.

COM VERSUS CORBA

COM (Common Object Model), and DCOM (Distributed COM) are Microsoft's answer to another emerging industry standard, CORBA (*Common Object Request Broker Architecture*), backed by IBM, Digital Equipment Corporation, Hewlett-Packard, Sun Microsystems, and about 200 other companies.

CONTINUED ➡

Both of these proposals are an attempt to solve the problems associated with allowing applications running in an object-oriented distributed environment to share information and to communicate over a network. These problems are compounded when several network operating systems are connected.

But there are other, absolutely fundamental differences between Java and ActiveX, including portability and security. Java has built-in security right from the very beginning, and ActiveX can make no such claim. Java applications are secured from both accidental and intentional attacks on system integrity; however, ActiveX can only offer the alternative of cryptographic certificates, whose protection is aimed at a completely different target.

Now that ISAPI is gaining ground, we will certainly see other additions to the Visual C++ and Visual Basic programming environments. Anyone serious about developing cutting-edge applications will certainly use Java or the C++ programming language, but many small- to medium-sized organizations already have custom applications developed in Visual Basic that they want to keep or add to. Look for future additions to the Microsoft Foundation Classes—a package that programmers use to develop Windows applications—that will make the Internet easily accessible to Visual C++ developers.

Microsoft also announced a set of drop-in ActiveX controls for non-browser applications, including the following:

▶ *FTP ActiveX control*, which lets applications use FTP

▶ *HTML ActiveX control*, which lets applications launch their own simple Web browser

▶ *HTTP ActiveX control*, which lets applications behave like simple Web servers

▶ *NNTP ActiveX control*, which gives applications access to Usenet newsgroups and other NNTP news

Part iii

▶ *SMTP/POP3 ActiveX control*, which lets applications use e-mail without the need to start a separate program

▶ *WinSock ActiveX control*, which provides an interface to the TCP/IP suite of protocols in Windows 95/98 and Windows NT.

These controls are all contained in Microsoft's Internet Control Pack (ICP) and were jointly developed by NetManage, Inc., and Microsoft.

How Does ActiveX Work?

An ActiveX control is a reusable software component that has been developed by Microsoft or by a third-party software vendor. As Table 9.8 shows, an ActiveX control can be as small as a single button or as large as a Web browser control, and this is of course only a partial list. You can use these controls in your intranet pages, in desktop applications, or in development tools.

According to Microsoft, there are currently more than 1,000 commercially available ActiveX controls that you can access using Microsoft's C, C++, Visual Basic, or Visual J++ programming languages. But you don't have to be a programmer to use many of the ActiveX controls, although you may find that you need a certain amount of script support to use some of the controls in your intranet pages. You can use many controls simply as prefabricated components that you can incorporate directly into your intranet pages.

TIP

Netscape Navigator supports ActiveX controls through the ActiveX plug-in available from Ncompass Labs at http://www.ncompass.com.

TABLE 9.8: ActiveX Controls

CONTROL	DESCRIPTION
Web browser control	Displays HTML pages, ActiveX controls, and ActiveX documents, based on Internet Explorer 3
Marquee control	Scrolls an HTML page in any direction at a specified rate
ActiveMovie control	Displays streaming and nonstreaming video and audio
Label	Creates a text label
Textbox	Creates a multiline text-entry and text-display box

TABLE 9.8 continued: ActiveX Controls

CONTROL	DESCRIPTION
Listbox	Creates a drop-down list box
Option	Lets users choose from among several options
Toggle button	Creates a button with two states, such as On and Off
Scrollbar	Creates horizontal and vertical scrollbars
Chart	Creates different kinds of charts
Menu	Creates a menu on a Web page

When Internet Explorer comes across a Web page containing an ActiveX control, it first checks the system registry to see if that component is available on that machine. If it is, the Web page is displayed and the control is activated. If not, Internet Explorer finds the control in a location specified by the creator of the HTML page and installs it automatically. When a component has to be downloaded, you will see a message to this effect, so you can choose to cancel or continue with the download. If the control has been digitally signed, you will see a message that verifies the name of the software developer and that the control has not been tampered with. By default, all downloaded controls are placed in the directory \WINDOWS\OCCACHE.

 ACTIVEX AND OPEN STANDARDS

As you saw earlier in this chapter, Sun's Java programming language is independent of both the underlying operating system and the basic hardware (computer, video card, and monitor) that it runs on. Sun has been an active member of the Unix community for years, and this open approach to Java reflects a similar fundamental philosophy. Java applets can run on *any* system for which there is a Java interpreter.

ActiveX, on the other hand, is available only on the Windows/Intel, or *Wintel*, platform used in PCs, and for many companies actively engaged in software development, that severely limits any appeal that ActiveX might have for them. They are still faced with solving the problem of how to program for the Wintel platform as well as for all the other platforms that their software has to run on.

CONTINUED ➡

To counter the charges that ActiveX is an inward-looking, proprietary system, Microsoft took several important steps to open up ActiveX. In late 1996, after spending $100 million over seven years, Microsoft agreed to cede control of a subset of ActiveX technology to the Open Group, an industry group that will now control the software's future design standards. Microsoft has released the following components:

▶ COM/DCOM object model

▶ Remote procedure call implementation

▶ NTLM security interface

▶ Structured Storage format for files

▶ System Registry for storing object information

▶ Moniker object naming scheme

▶ Remote authorization for running remote objects

Microsoft has not released these elements of its systems:

▶ Source code for ActiveX controls on the desktop

▶ Win32 API set

You can find out more about the Open Group at http://www.opengroup.org/.

Common Internet File System

Several companies have joined Microsoft in support of CIFS (*Common Internet File System*), a file-sharing technology based on the SMB (*Server Message Block*) protocol. SMB is an open protocol available in the Unix world that allows users read and write access to files on remote systems without the need to download the files first, as with FTP and other similar protocols.

CIFS adds several enhancements over the existing SMB protocol to allow support for DNS name resolution as well as support for slow-speed dial-up lines and remote printer sharing. In addition, CIFS also supports authentication, file locking, data sharing, and file-system security, all of which will become increasingly important as companies establish their own corporate intranets.

THE STATE OF VIRTUAL REALITY AND 3-D

VRML (*Virtual Reality Modeling Language*, pronounced "ver-mal") is an open, platform-independent language for building 3-D worlds on the Web; it was developed by the same people who brought you HTML. A VRML document (with the filename extension WRL, an abbreviation for the word *world*) is a blueprint for a 3-D world in which you can walk around if you have a VRML browser or a VRML plug-in for an HTML browser. Yet, for all the hype, it's only a bit like being inside a DOOM screen—not exactly a real scream.

Unfortunately, VRML has descended into a state of obscurity from which it may never return. Despite its potential, VRML is being used very little for practical applications. The reason? Simple—too much hype, way too soon. Virtual reality couldn't live up to such great expectations. To create a virtual reality capable of reproducing the visual and physical stimuli of reality itself would take some extremely powerful software and about three to four dozen stunningly fast supercomputers. Even this, however, would still look, at best, like a sophisticated, mostly realistic 3-D computer game.

Part iii

WHAT'S NEXT?

To make use of the advanced features that you've learned about in this chapter, you'll need to know about the programming languages used to create them. The next chapter introduces you to one of them, Perl, and continues this chapter's discussion of the Common Gateway Interface (CGI).

Chapter 10

INTRODUCING PERL AND CGI

The Internet has become—perhaps arguably—the most important communication medium in the world. There is virtually no argument, however, about the World Wide Web. It is the Internet's most important channel of communication. If you want to deal with the Net, pretty soon you'll have to deal with the Web.

You'll learn about one of the most important aspects of the Web in this chapter. The *Common Gateway Interface* (CGI) and applications written in the Perl programming language give you the tools to create dynamic, informative Web pages, with which you can fashion a Web site that your visitors will find truly useful and worth revisiting.

A good Web site is not just a collection of pretty pictures. It has to *do* something. With Perl and CGI, you can make it do just that.

Adapted from *Perl CGI Programming: No experience required.*, by Erik Strom

ISBN 0-7821-2157-8   448 pages $29.99

WHY PERL?

A Web page is a text document that is formatted with a set of commands—a programming language, if you will—called the *Hypertext Markup Language,* or HTML. The name is descriptive: HTML is a "markup" language; that is, it controls the way a document looks. HTML instructions tell a Web browser, such as Netscape's Navigator or Microsoft's Internet Explorer, how it should go about displaying the page on-screen. But HTML by itself has practically no facilities for making a Web page do things. You have to rely on other means for that.

The Perl programming language is hands-down the most popular method of making a Web page "do" something, mainly because Perl is freely available and will run on every computer platform that can host a Web server. Coupled with the Common Gateway Interface (CGI), Perl is used on the vast majority of Web sites to create Web pages that have to do more than sit there and look pretty.

There are a couple of other tools you can use to create a dynamic Web page:

- ▶ Java
- ▶ Proprietary languages

The following sections will look at each of them.

Java

Java, which was originally invented by Sun Microsystems to control toasters, is a popular and highly touted method for making interactive Web pages these days. As a programming language, Java is a very rich resource, one that will allow you to do almost anything you desire with your page. However, different Web browsers support Java to varying degrees, so by including an *applet* written in that language in your page, you run the risk of excluding some visitors.

TIP

An *applet* in Java is a program that is run by the Web browser, if the browser is capable of running it (many Web browsers aren't).

To work properly, Java depends on the browser software that your visitors use. If the browser supports Java, your applets work. If not, and you are a kind Webmaster, your visitors will get a message telling them essentially to buy another browser. If you are unkind, they will get either a blank screen or some wonderfully obscure HTTP error message that, if nothing else, will ensure that they never return to your Web page again.

Proprietary Languages

Along the same lines as Java are the proprietary packages, notably Visual Basic Script (VBScript) from Microsoft and Netscape's JavaScript.

TIP

Proprietary software packages usually target a specific hardware and/or software platform. They won't work with everything.

VBScript is, of course, based on Visual Basic, Microsoft's heavily Windows-laden version of the BASIC programming language. JavaScript is an *interpreted* flavor of Java, which means that the Web browser interprets and executes each line in the script. While the intent of both—essentially extending HTML to make the Web page itself more dynamic—probably is laudable, neither will run on any but the newer browsers from both companies, because the older browsers were written before these tools existed.

They're slick, yes. By taking advantage of a specific platform, the proprietary tools can run faster and do more than a generic package that is intended to run on *all* platforms. But they don't allow you to accommodate every visitor to your site because not all visitors will have the hardware or software that the proprietary tools target (see Figure 10.1). Not all visitors will be using Intel-based PCs, nor will all visitors be running a version of Netscape or Internet Explorer, or Windows 95/98 or NT.

Some visitors may not even be able to display graphics. But *all* of them need to be considered when you set up a site.

NOTE

The proprietary methods extend HTML by creating programs that run on a visitor's computer, rather than at your site on your Web server. As a result, they depend totally on the computer and software the visitor is using.

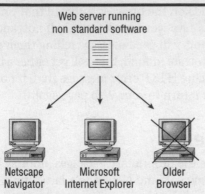

Web server running
non standard software

Netscape
Navigator

Microsoft
Internet Explorer

Older
Browser

FIGURE 10.1: Proprietary languages can exclude some visitors from your Web site.

CGI

Long before Java, there was the Common Gateway Interface, or CGI for short. We'll explore CGI in detail in Chapter 11, but for now let's just say that it's the most common method for passing information from an HTML document to a program that can process the information. CGI doesn't care what browser you're using; even non-graphical Lynx-type software will work.

Unlike Java and its more proprietary cousins, CGI is not a programming language, nor does it load itself onto the visitor's machine to run. CGI is, as its name spells out, an interface, a set of rules. It resides on the Web-server computer, providing a way for the page to communicate in a rough fashion with the server. CGI allows you to write programs to deal with the page in *any* language—including Perl.

Perl's Ancient History

There is only one reason that Perl programs—or *scripts*, which is a lexical convention that will be explained shortly—are so universal in World Wide Web programming. The simple fact of the matter is, until the last few years, virtually every Web server in existence was running on a Unix system, and Perl is among the most useful of Unix tools.

The first *Hypertext Transfer Protocol* (HTTP) servers were written for Unix, too, and freely distributed among system administrators who wanted to try out the Web. CGI was developed as a standard of communication on these systems. In a sense, Perl, HTTP, and CGI *all* became standards for doing Web work (see Figure 10.2).

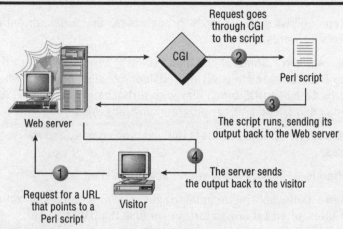

FIGURE 10.2: The HTTP-CGI-Perl connection

The beauty of standards is that they usually transcend the platforms on which they originated. The number of non-Unix Web servers and Web sites on the Internet increases every day. Yet the HTTP-CGI-Perl connection remains the same because it was lifted intact into the newer platforms.

Unix is, in a very large sense, an operating system written by and, most importantly, *for* programmers. It really was never intended for humans to use easily, which is why so many people have gone to such extraordinary lengths to make Unix more friendly, with X Windows and various other graphical interfaces. These interfaces require tremendous amounts of processing power, so in many cases system designers have simply given up and relegated bare-bones Unix to the background, running it on the system server and hanging Macintoshes or other workstations running Windows on the network for users.

The beauty of Unix, for those who have taken the time to learn it, is in the rich set of software tools that it provides. Unadorned Unix is like a box of wonderful Swiss Army knives; with any one of them, you can carve any masterpiece your imagination can conjure.

Perl is one of the most useful of those Swiss Army knives.

Part iii

THE UNIX TOOLBOX

Consider some of the more obscure tools you can pull out of Unix:

grep   Allows you to search through files, directories, or entire disks for words or phrases.

sh, csh, ksh   Some of the Unix "shells," which are akin to the MS-DOS command line but are considerably more powerful. Shell scripts are like DOS batch files with turbochargers attached. You really don't need another programming language.

ed, sed, vi   The Unix editors that everyone hates...and everyone uses.

whereis   Finds files anywhere; actually a shell script.

man   Calls up the manual pages for programs and other utilities, often serving to further confuse the hapless user.

We Owe It All to Larry Wall: A History of Perl

Larry Wall is a linguist-turned-programmer who, as of this writing, is an associate at O'Reilly & Associates, a technical publishing company. Legend has it that he began working on Perl nearly 10 years ago while attempting a sticky project for Unisys.

NOTE

The Perl language grew out of the classic Unix philosophy: If the system doesn't allow you to do your job easily, then you simply write another tool to solve the problem.

Perl actually is an acronym whose most accepted expanded version is *Practical Extraction and Report Language*, though Unix wags have come up with many more earthy descriptions, such as "Pathologically Eclectic Rubbish Lister." It was derived in large part from *sed* and *awk*, jackhammers of the Unix toolbox for those who understand them, utterly unintelligible command programs for those who don't. After all, what can one say about a program whose most famous error message is awk: bailing out near Line 1?

The strengths of sed and awk, and their offspring Perl, lie mainly in their built-in capabilities for processing text through pattern-matching, searching for and replacing phrases—or "strings"—in entire groups of files, and using Unix's obscure yet extremely powerful regular expressions, which are discussed in full in Chapter 11.

REGULAR EXPRESSIONS: BANE *AND* BOON

Regular expressions are among the most useful—and most difficult to master—tools in the Unix array.

You can think of them as supercharged search-and/or-replace operations. While most any text editor will let you find phrases and replace them with other phrases throughout a file, regular expressions add a great deal of power to the operation. For example, you can use regular expressions to look for strings at the beginning or end of a line, or in a word, or for a specific number of occurrences.

But it's not easy. A Perl regular expression that swaps the first two words in a line of text looks like this:

```
s/^([^ ]*) *([^ ]*)/$2 $1/;
```

Doesn't make much sense, does it? But that could be a very useful operation, couldn't it?

We'll defer a full explanation of regular expressions until Chapter 11. For now, let's just say that you will find many uses for them.

The bedrock of Unix is the C programming language—most of it is written in C. But C, in its position at the foundation of the operating system, adheres to the minimalist philosophy of Unix, which means that you often have to write scads of C code to accomplish relatively simple tasks. A trivial search-and-replace operation on a text file, written in C, requires the programmer at least to scan the file character by character and could easily grow from a simple subroutine into an entire application (see Figure 10.3).

But the same operation can be accomplished in a few lines of Perl code (see Figure 10.4).

TIP

Perl is a challenge to learn, but it is infinitely more efficient for the programmer (read: "fewer lines of code") and easier to use than C.

Part iii

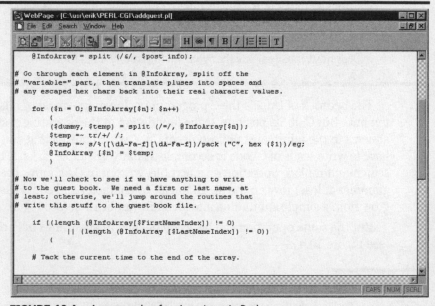

```
ZeroMemory (&GuestEntry, sizeof (GUEST_ENTRY));      // Hose out the structure.

char*   INFO_ARRAY [] =
{
    GuestEntry.FirstName,
    GuestEntry.LastName,
    GuestEntry.City,
    GuestEntry.State,
    GuestEntry.Country,
    GuestEntry.EMail,
    GuestEntry.Comments,
    NULL
};

char*   o;                      // Couple of pointers for string manipulation.
char*   p = buf;
int     n = 0;                  // Counter.

while ((o = strchr (p, '&')) != NULL)
    {
    *o = NULL;                          // End the substring here.
    strcpy (INFO_ARRAY [n++], p);       // Copy the data into the correct spot.
    p = ++o;                            // Get the next one.
    }
```

FIGURE 10.3:   An example of code written in C++

```
@InfoArray = split (/&/, $post_info);

# Go through each element in @InfoArray, split off the
# "variable=" part, then translate pluses into spaces and
# any escaped hex chars back into their real character values.

    for ($n = 0; @InfoArray[$n]; $n++)
        {
        ($dummy, $temp) = split (/=/, @InfoArray[$n]);
        $temp =~ tr/+/ /;
        $temp =~ s/%([\dA-Fa-f][\dA-Fa-f])/pack ("C", hex ($1))/eg;
        @InfoArray [$n] = $temp;
        }

# Now we'll check to see if we have anything to write
# to the guest book.  We need a first or last name, at
# least; otherwise, we'll jump around the routines that
# write this stuff to the guest book file.

    if ((length (@InfoArray[$FirstNameIndex]) != 0)
            || (length (@InfoArray [$LastNameIndex]) != 0))
        {

        # Tack the current time to the end of the array.
```

FIGURE 10.4:   An example of code written in Perl

Unix programmers snapped up Perl as a tool of choice almost immediately for tasks ranging from "quick and dirty" to horribly complex. Because you have the ability to call most of the standard Unix system services from a Perl script, including the internetworking functions, you probably could write an entire operating system in it. It would be very slow, but it would run a computer.

To this day, almost every serious Unix systems programmer works with Perl almost daily. It's just too useful for programmers to ignore.

Perl and the World Wide Web

Perl has become popular for Web work because in most of its incarnations it is an *interpreted* language, like the first versions of BASIC, rather than a *compiled* language, such as C or C++. However, this isn't strictly true, because Perl compilers are available from many sources, just as there are many C interpreters to be had. The essential difference between a compiled and interpreted application is that a compiled program has been translated into the machine language of the computer on which it will run by another program called a *compiler*. The translated, or compiled, file will run all by itself. An *interpreted* program, on the other hand, is actually translated and run on the fly by a program called an *interpreter*.

Because they consist of machine-language instructions, compiled programs generally run faster. But for the same reason, they are not portable from one computer platform to another. Code compiled for a Sun box or a Macintosh won't run on an Intel-based PC because the different processors that power these machines all speak radically different tongues. Your program would have to be recompiled for the target machine before it would work. It may even have to be rewritten.

There are no such restrictions on interpreted Perl code. All you need is some version of the Perl interpreter—called *perl*—on the target computer. Perl interpreters have been written for every popular computer platform, from Sun to Alpha to Apple to Intel and more, and with very few exceptions your Perl programs should transport unchanged into every environment.

This feature won't sound very important to novice programmers. However, porting C code even between the different flavors of Unix is an art that not many people have the patience or skill to do full time. It is tedious, difficult, and time-consuming. The capability to develop and test code on one computer and then simply drop it into another, as you can with Perl, is a boon cherished by all professional programmers.

Perl programs are not compiled, which is why we refer to them as *scripts*. Like shell scripts in Unix or batch and command files on MS-DOS and Windows NT, Perl programs are just text files that run through an application to process their commands.

However, make no mistake about it: Perl programs are just that—programs, with all the power and versatility the word implies. If you've never written a line of code in your life, Perl will forever spoil you against the more traditional programming languages. If you are a programmer but this is your introduction to Perl, you will find yourself using it more and more as your familiarity with it increases, because it makes things so *easy*.

For the nuts and bolts of Web site processing, administration, and maintenance; tedious system chores that should *always* be hidden from users; and the creation of truly dynamic Web pages, Perl can't be beat.

BUILDING A PERL SCRIPT

Now that you have a little background, you're going to write your first Perl program. It's a simple example that gives you the basic idea of how a Perl script is written and run. All of our subsequent examples will build on this one.

"Hello World" probably seems kind of dumb, but those of us who have been programming for a while have a soft spot for this snippet of code. It's the first programming example given in the monumental *C Programming Language*, by Brian Kernighan and Dennis Ritchie, which was published in 1976. Many programmers cut their teeth on this work; forgive us, please, if we remember it fondly.

USING EXISTING PERL SCRIPTS

Perl scripts are simply text files that you can create using your favorite text editor. Perl is the language of choice for Web developers these days because of its ease of use on Unix machines. Its popularity also has other benefits: for one thing, a huge body of existing code out there in the ether. Most of it is free, which means you can simply drop it into your Web server and run it, regardless of the operating system that powers your computer. Most of that code was written, tested, and debugged by Unix programmers who had their own Web sites to maintain. You can find lots of stuff in Usenet—go to comp.lang.perl. Or try one of the Web search engines such as Yahoo!.

CONTINUED ➡

So it makes sense for you to be running Perl on your Web site, if only from the standpoint of the effort you want to put into writing software. If you have a task to perform and someone else has already written the code to perform it—and has no compunction at all about you using it—then why shouldn't you avoid reinventing wheels?

First Things First: Perls before Code

You can't do anything without the Perl language interpreter. Make sure you have a copy of it before you go further or you'll get snotty error messages from whatever operating system you're using.

TIP

You can get Perl for Win32—Windows NT and Windows 95/98—by pointing your Web browser to http://www.ActiveState.com/. Unix sources for Perl are numerous and ever-changing; the best way to find them is in the Internet newsgroups at comp.sources.unix. MacPERL for the Macintosh is available at http://www.iis.ee.ethz.ch/~neeri/macintosh/perl.html.

I'll make very few assumptions about the computer you are using or the operating system that it runs. However, most of the really good Perls that can be obtained are intended to run on Windows NT and Windows 95/98 or Unix, and most of our examples will emphasize those two platforms.

Installing the Perl interpreter can be as simple as running a setup program or as complicated as extracting the source code and compiling it yourself.

Fortunately, Perl is included in many Unix distributions these days. If that's the case on your system, obviously you don't have to do anything. The Perl executable for NT and Windows 95/98 can be downloaded for free from Microsoft's Web site and several others. It performs flawlessly.

COMPILING YOUR OWN PERL INTERPRETER...

Compiling the Perl source code yourself is the method preferred by Unix system administrators, who usually have a rather macho attitude about such things. Because the most freely available C code for Perl was written primarily for Unix systems, it compiles easily most of the time.

Likewise, compiling the code for Windows NT and Windows 95/98 is possible, but only for the most daring of systems gurus; the process certainly is beyond the scope of this book. Both of the latest versions of the most popular C/C++ development packages available for Windows—Visual C++ from Microsoft and Borland C++ for Windows from Borland International—contain quirks that prevent a straightforward compilation of the Perl source code. Unless you want to change the functionality of Perl (which is an exercise of dubious logical value in itself) and devote hours to debugging someone else's code, you're much better off simply using whatever executable files you can find for the operating system you're using.

Loading the Interpreter

Regardless of your operating system, once you have the Perl interpreter, you're ready to go. On Unix, things will be a little easier if you put the Perl interpreter in a subdirectory that is included in your PATH environment string, which is a system variable that maps out where the operating system should look when you type the name of a program at the command line. In other words, if you have loaded PATH by typing **PATH=/usr/bin;/usr/me;/pub/local/etc** at the command line and you then enter **perl**, the operating system will look in each of those directories for Perl before it gives up and complains to you that the command couldn't be found. The same is true in Windows NT and Windows 95/98.

TIP

The setup program for the Win32 Perl at www.activeware.com will ask you if you want Perl to be added to your PATH. If you answer affirmatively, the change will take place the next time to restart your computer.

As we discussed earlier, Perl scripts are simple text files that you can create using your favorite text editor. To put together your first Perl program, start that text editor now and enter the following lines:

```
#!/usr/bin/perl


print "Hello World!", "\n";


#       End hello.pl
```

NOTE

The first line in the program begins with Perl's "comment" character (#), which will be ignored by the interpreter. However, it must contain the path to your Perl interpreter. If your system's Perl interpreter is not in /usr/bin, change the path to the correct subdirectory.

That's fairly easy, isn't it? We'll explain what's going on in the next section; for now, save the file as hello.pl ("hello.pl" in quotes if you're using Notepad on Windows 95/98 or NT) and close your text editor.

Running the "Hello" Example

The hello.pl is about as tiny as programs get, both in the writing and in the execution. It is intended to be run from the *command line*, which means the shell in Unix, the console command processor in Windows NT, or CMD.EXE or COMMAND.COM in Windows 95/98.

TIP

To avoid the confusion of having to refer to both operating system methods when the term *command line* is used, we'll henceforth refer to the Unix shell and the NT/95/98 console as the command line. Also, because Perl adheres to the Unix convention of specifying path names with the forward slash (/) rather than Microsoft's backslash (\), we will adhere to it, too, in the text of our examples. Remember the difference when you're typing commands in the NT console.

Open a command-line window (a shell in Unix, a command console or MS-DOS window in Windows 95/98 and NT). Because Perl is an interpreted language, you won't be running your first Perl program directly.

Part iii

You have to run `perl` with your Perl program as an argument to it. If, when you installed the Perl software on your system, you put it somewhere in your PATH, then you can simply type:

```
perl hello.pl
```

Otherwise you'll have to type in the full path to `perl` followed by the name of your program. For example, if you installed Perl in `/myprogs/perl`, and that subdirectory is not in your PATH environment variable, you would have to type:

```
/myprogs/perl hello.pl
```

In any event, when you run the program, the result should look something like Figure 10.5.

Notice that the program prints "Hello, World!" with a line-ender to the screen.

Congratulations! You are now a Perl programmer.

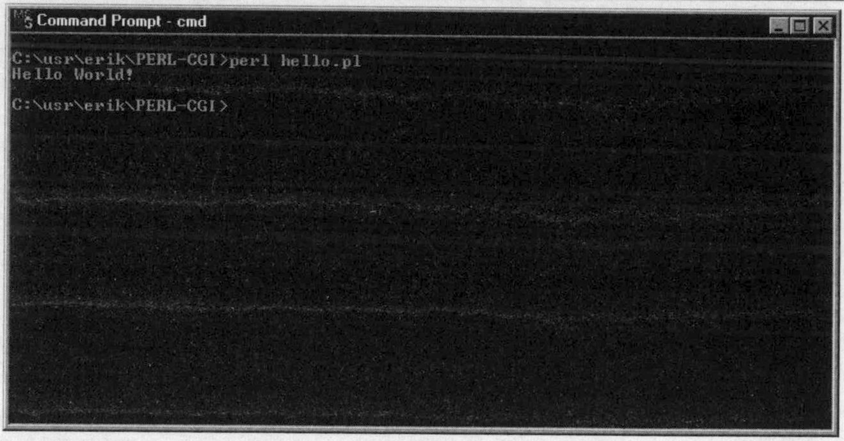

FIGURE 10.5: The results of running your first Perl program

How Perl Programs Run

In a technical sense, the Perl interpreter is a language compiler that doesn't write its translated output to a file on the disk. Its "output file" is the screen, which is called *standard output,* or *stdout,* in systems parlance.

If a program name is given on the command line, the interpreter first checks the validity of each line, dumping out error messages for incorrect code and stopping if it finds any. If your program passes muster, the interpreter executes each of its lines of code.

One of the convenient aspects of doing it this way is that you find out immediately if your program does something wrong—and programs inevitably do! Most developers work on "windowed" systems, and they run the text editor with their Perl program code in one window and keep the command-line screen in another (see Figure 10.6). It is then quite easy to pop from window to window, writing and fixing code in the text editor and testing the code from the command line. With Perl, you get all your errors at once, and that speeds up the coding process. With a compiled language such as C or C++, you have to write the code, compile it, fix any errors that have cropped up in the compilation, compile it again, link it to the external libraries it needs, then—*whew!*—run it and see what errors occur there. Then you get to start all over again. It's little wonder that Perl has become so popular!

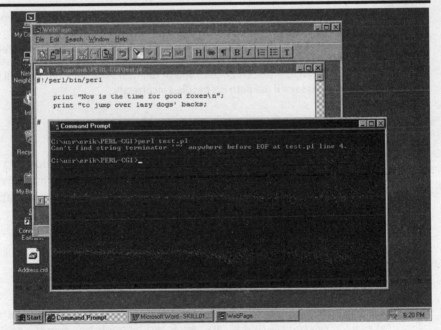

FIGURE 10.6: The two-window debugging process

Dissecting the "Hello" Example

We have briefly covered the first line in the program. We'll now take apart this line, `#!/usr/bin/perl`, piece by piece:

 # (pound sign)   This is Perl's "comment" character, which means that anything following it up to the end of the line is ignored by the interpreter. This is where you can document your program so that others (or *you* after you haven't touched the program in a few months!) can understand what is being accomplished in the code.

! (exclamation point)   This *first* comment line is a special case. Unix aficionados will read to the exclamation point (!) and recognize it as an instruction to the shell—a command for the command line. Strictly speaking, this tells the shell to run the Perl interpreter with the program code as its input.

NOTE

The first line is required, and it should always contain the full path to your Perl interpreter, which may or may not be in /usr/bin. I used /usr/bin as an example because it is a common place to put it. Oddly, though there is no direct way under Windows 95/98 or NT to run a command with the ! character, the Win32 Perl interpreter requires you to follow this convention. You will get an error message if the path is specified incorrectly.

The Heart of the Program: *print*

We have used only one real Perl function in this short program—`print`. This function is a real workhorse, especially in Web programming, where you will use Perl to construct HTML pages. `print` is a function that you very likely will use in every program you write.

How does `print` work? We'll go into a detailed description later, because `print` can do a lot. For now, let's look at what it does in `hello.pl`:

```
print "Hello, World!", "\n";
```

The unadorned `print`, as we have used it in the example program, takes a list of *strings*—that is, text enclosed by quotation marks—as its *arguments,* or *parameters.*

TIP

The terms *argument* and *parameter* will be used interchangeably in reference to the data you will use with Perl functions.

In this case, we are telling `print` that we want it to "print" the phrases "Hello World!" and "\n" to the screen. Notice that the two phrases, which are the `print` function's arguments, are separated by a comma. It is also important that the line ends with a semicolon. *All* code lines in Perl must end with the semicolon; the interpreter will complain bitterly if you forget to do this, and it's usually the first thing you will do wrong. Be forewarned!

WARNING

All code lines in Perl must end in a semicolon. Why? The interpreter can't decide for itself where a code statement ends, because it may extend for more than one line. The semicolon tells the interpreter, "This statement ends here."

The Strange \n

"Hello World!" is easy enough to figure out, but what is this \n? C-language programmers and others who are, by necessity, familiar with Unix conventions know this as the *newline* character. If you've never seen this before, remember carefully the backslash (\) that precedes the n. This is called an *escape* character because it gives a special meaning to the character that follows it. The \n specifically refers to the linefeed character, with a value of 10 in the ASCII character set.

The linefeed is the standard line-ender in Unix; the MS-DOS convention, which has been retained by Windows 95/98 and NT, is to end each line with a carriage return *and* a linefeed, which in a Perl `print` command would be set up as \r\n. However, the Perl interpreter knows what operating system it's running on and makes certain allowances for these differences. For now, whether you compose your code on Unix or Windows NT, you can use the simple \n as a line-ender.

Table 10.1 lists some other Perl "escaped" characters.

NOTE

Table 10.1 doesn't list all of the Perl special "escaped" characters. These are just the most common.

Part III

TABLE 10.1: Some of the Perl Special Characters

CHARACTER STRING	DOES THIS
\n	Newline or linefeed
\r	Carriage return
\t	Tab
\f	Formfeed
\b	Backspace
\033	ASCII 27 (Escape) in octal
\x1B	Same in hexadecimal
\cD	Control-D
\\	Backslash
\"	Double quote
\'	Single quote
\u	Uppercase next character
\U	Uppercase following characters
\l, \L	Same as above, but lowercase
\E	End \U or \L

The escaped double quote (\") can be somewhat confusing. It is used when you want to actually use the double-quote character in a string, rather than using it to *delimit* the string. For example, the Perl code

```
print "Hello World!", "\n";
```

would result in the following output to the screen:

```
Hello, World!
"Hello, World!"
```

Perl also allows a construct to keep you from loading up your strings with backslashes. You may use q/STRING/ and qq/STRING/ too, where *STRING* is the phrase enclosed between the slashes.

Goodbye to "Hello"

We have done just about all we can with this first version of "Hello World!" You should now be familiar with Perl comment lines, with emphasis on the important first line, which actually is an instruction. Additionally, you've gained a passing acquaintance with the workhorse `print` function and some of the things that you can do with it.

The results of running the new version of the script are illustrated in Figure 10.7.

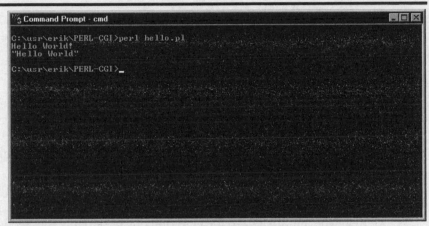

FIGURE 10.7: The new results of running `hello.pl`

Part iii

There's one more line in the program, however, and we shouldn't move on without explaining it:

```
#            End hello.pl
```

This is a comment line, as you have learned, but why? Obviously, it's the end of the program because there's no more program after it.

Yes, it *is* quite obvious in a tiny snippet of code such as we've typed into `hello.pl`. However, other programs will be much more complicated and much larger, and it won't be as clear where one subroutine starts or another ends.

It is simply good programming practice to document your code well, not just for others but for your own benefit. And good documentation starts with clearly marking the beginning and end of important sections of code.

VARIABLES, SCALARS, AND LISTS IN PERL

The code we've written so far is simple. Let's make it a bit more complicated—and therefore useful—by introducing three new concepts:

Variable   Data stored in specific memory location

Scalar   A single variable that defines either numeric or string (character) data

List   A number of scalars stored sequentially in one variable

Perl Variables: What's in a Name

The capability to store data in locations that have specific names lies at the heart of any useful programming language. Moving data to a specific spot in memory and being able to recall them by name (or location) at a later time is known as working with *variables*. Perl is no different in this respect.

If you have done any programming at all, you will be familiar with the concept of variables. However, the conventions used in Perl can be a little weird for the uninitiated, so if you're thinking of skipping this section, please don't!

Storing data in a variable is as straightforward as picking a name and setting it equal to a value. Complex programming languages, such as C, have lots of complex rules for what types of data can be stored where; in C, for example, integers have to go into `int` variables and strings of characters are stored as `char` arrays. Variables have to be declared and given types before they can be used.

Perl, despite all that it owes to C, plays very fast and loose with those rules. In Perl, you declare a variable merely by using it, which helps to make the Perl development process somewhat quicker and easier than programming in C.

WARNING

The rules of good, structured programming apply to Perl as they do to any other language: Make your Perl code readable by using lots of comments. Just because a language allows a fast and loose form of variable declaration is no excuse for writing "spaghetti code."

Introducing Scalars

The most fundamental data in Perl are called *scalars*. The word can be intimidating to beginners because its meaning is not immediately apparent. A scalar is nothing more than a single piece of data. Scalars differ from another fundamental Perl data type, the *list* (defined in the *Perl Lists* section below).

Perl regards numeric *and* string data as scalar values, and in most cases it's pretty good at telling the difference between the two and acting properly.

NOTE

In most programming languages, "strings" are simply strings of characters. "Now is the time for all good folks to come to the aid of their party" is a string. Notice that it is enclosed in quotes. This is important in Perl.

The important thing to remember about scalar variables is that they always begin with a dollar sign ($). You can call them anything you want—just never forget the dollar sign.

WARNING

Perl is a case-sensitive language, which means that it distinguishes between upper- and lowercase letters in names. Thus, it will regard $VariableName and $variablename as two different scalar variables.

We can create a second version of hello.pl to illustrate the concept of storing data in scalar variables. Type the following lines into your text editor and save the file as hello2.pl:

```
#!/usr/bin/perl


# hello2, a slightly more sophisticated "Hello World"


    $Hello = "Hello, World";   # String variable
    $TimeAround = 2;           # Numeric variable


    print $Hello, " for the ", $TimeAround, "nd time!", "\n";


#    End hello2.pl
```

Now run the program as we ran the one we created earlier. You'll see this on your screen (see Figure 10.8):

```
Hello, World for the 2nd time!
```

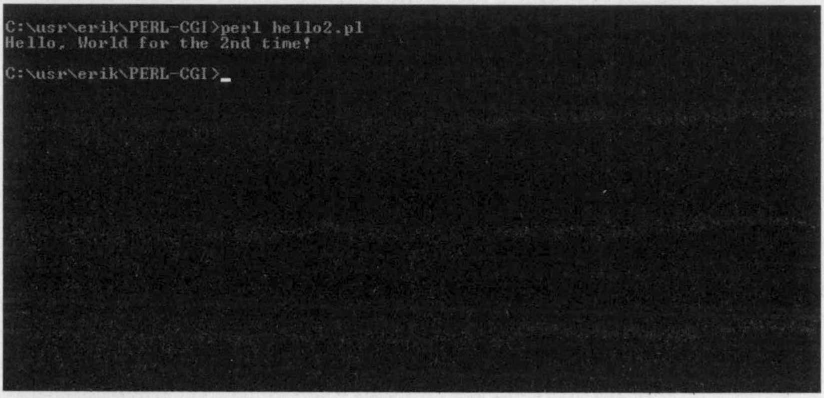

FIGURE 10.8:   Using variables in your Perl script

Notice that you were able to set the two variables, `$Hello` and `$TimeAround`, to two entirely unrelated types, yet the `print` function knew precisely what to do with them and assembled the resulting output string flawlessly. `print` is even smarter than we've made it appear here; the line could have been written to include the variables in one long string argument, such as the following:

```
print "$Hello for the ${TimeAround}nd time!";
```

The important thing to note here is that `TimeAround` was enclosed in curly braces to set it off from the `nd`. But you can see that `print` has no trouble culling the variables from the other parts of the string and behaving properly.

This "shorthand" capability is one of Perl's great strengths, as you will see when you begin working with more complicated programs. However, brevity in code is not necessarily an ideal to strive for, unless it directly leads to more efficient code. Writing a program that is clear and understandable is much more important.

Perl Lists

You have learned so far that scalar variables handle and store individual pieces of data. But what if you have a collection of related data? It would be convenient to store *all* of them in a variable, wouldn't it?

Perl lists are intended to do just that. Lists are similar to arrays in many other programming languages, where the variable name defines a starting point, index 0, and the members are stored consecutively. You just increase the index and add it to the starting point to arrive at the array member you want.

NOTE

A Perl *list* is the equivalent of an *array* in Visual Basic, C++, and many other languages. The terms will be used interchangeably.

The C language requires that all members of the array are of the same *type*, which really only means that they are all the same size. Perl doesn't care about type at all. Any old thing can go into a list—strings, numbers, characters, anything—and they all happily coexist.

What's in a List?

List notation in Perl is as specific as scalar notation. List names begin with the @ character; after that, you can call them anything you want.

Setting a list equal to something, or loading it with data, is a bit more complex, but we can make it understandable with a few examples.

An array of numbers would be set up like this:

```
@Numbers = (1, 2, 3, 4, 5, 6);
```

We now have an array of six consecutive numbers called @Numbers. In Perl, as in many other languages, arrays start at position 0, so if we were to set a scalar variable to the value of the first member of @Numbers,

```
$OneNumber = $Numbers[0];
```

$OneNumber would be equal to 1.

Notice that the notation changed a little in the last line: We referred to the first element of @Numbers with a dollar sign in front of it. But isn't that how we note a *scalar* value?

Yes, it is. And the notation is correct because just one member of a list *is* a scalar, so you must use the dollar sign in front of it. The *subscript,* which is the part of $Numbers[0] enclosed in brackets, is where you tell Perl which member of the array you want.

STREAMLINED PERL...

Here's a handy Perl shortcut. Because the members of the array are consecutive numbers, you could have initialized it like this:

```
@Numbers = (1..6);
```

It's the same as specifying each of the numbers from 1 to 6, as far as Perl is concerned.

Lists of Strings

When you load strings into an array, they need to be distinguished somehow. T\he Perl convention departs slightly from what we have learned so far, which is to enclose strings of characters in double quotes. This can be done with lists, but it is considered more correct to delimit lists of strings with single quotes ('').

Table 10.2 illustrates some of the things you can do with strings.

TABLE 10.2: Perl List Examples

INITIALIZATION	COMMENT
@list = (4..8);	same as @list = (4,5,6,7,8)
@list1 = ('red', 'green', 'blue');	array of colors
@list2 = (1, 'yellow', @list1);	same as @list2 = (1, 'yellow', 'red', 'green', 'blue');
@list3 = ();	null (empty) list
@list4 = (0,1, @list3, 3);	same as @list4 = (0,1,3);

Perl lists have numerous other features, which you'll see when you approach more complex programming topics. For now, you should know what a list is, how to initialize it, and how to access one of its members.

NOTE

Presumably, we're all fully qualified computer nerds here, so we are allowed to use "access" as a verb. Be advised, however, that the practice in common usage drives English-language purists to scowling fidgets.

PERL AND THE COMMON GATEWAY INTERFACE

You've learned a little about the Perl programming language. But how does it fit into the World Wide Web? The Common Gateway Interface (CGI) is the key. CGI has been used for many years as a facility for passing information from a Web page to a program that can process the information.

CGI, despite what many programmers put on their resumes, is not a programming language. It is, as the name states explicitly, an *interface*. It allows you to write a program that will take all of its input from an HTML document—a page on the World Wide Web—and *do something* with that input. You can regard CGI as a kind of pipeline between your Web page and a Perl program (see Figure 10.9): Whatever is entered on the page is available to your program through CGI.

HTML is quite good at describing how a Web page should look in a browser, but the language all by itself has virtually no facilities for processing information or making even rudimentary decisions.

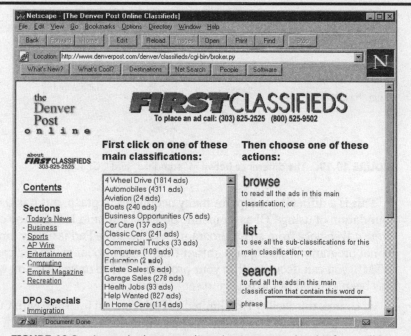

FIGURE 10.9: A search phrase or a list selection entered in this form will be processed by a Perl program through CGI.

WARNING

Some browsers include extensions to HTML that support all kinds of fancy interpretation. In the real world, however, you cannot depend on your Web site visitors possessing the latest and greatest browsers with all of their nonstandard HTML extensions.

When you run a Perl program from the command line, it takes its input, generally, from you, at your keyboard, and it sends its output, generally, back to you, on the screen. CGI reroutes those standard conventions. The Perl program's input comes from the Web page. Most importantly, CGI sends your program's output back to the Web server. If the output happens to be formatted correctly in HTML, the server will put it out as an HTML document to whatever browser is connected to it. In other words, a `print` statement from within your Perl program will be printing to the Web server, not to the screen (see Figure 10.10).

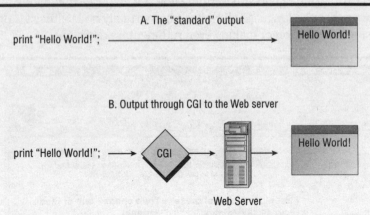

FIGURE 10.10:   The difference between "standard" and CGI output

This is a difficult concept for many neophytes to grasp, but it is the foundation of using CGI as a pipeline between Perl and HTML. You can *draw a Web page* from a Perl program. And, because Perl is a fully functional programming language, rather than a markup language such as HTML, you can decide within your program *what to draw* based on what has been entered in the page and sent to you.

Of course, this facility isn't limited to Perl. You can interface with CGI using *any* program written in *any* language (provided, of course, that it will run on your computer!). Indeed, there may be occasions when you need the brute force of C/C++ or some other high-level compiled language to tackle some process that would bring your Web server to its knees if the program were written in Perl. For example, a program that does a lot of heavy number crunching would be much more efficient in C or C++ than in Perl. Those occasions will be rare, however. Most of what you need to do can be accomplished more easily from a Perl script than from a compiled program. Additionally, your Perl program won't have to be rewritten and recompiled if you move to another operating system or computer platform.

What Is CGI, Anyway?

Does *Common Gateway Interface* mean much, if anything, to you? Probably not. Without CGI, however, there would be no reason to talk about Perl and Web pages because there would be no way to link the two.

CGI as a *concept* has been applied to many systems other than links between Web servers and application programs. For example, it would provide a clean and near-universal interface for database servers and their clients without the barriers introduced by proprietary systems. Software manufacturers sometimes seem to worry about making sure that you only do business with them, but a "common gateway" from one system to another provides a standard of sorts to which the manufacturers must adhere; if they can't deal with it, no one will buy their applications.

For now, anyone who actually knows what you're talking about when you bandy about terms such as *CGI* will assume that you're talking exclusively about World Wide Web applications. In that context, without the Web, there would be no CGI. And without the Internet, there would be no Web.

CGI: The Force Behind the Web

Whereas HTML gives the World Wide Web its *look*, CGI makes it *functional*. It is what its name implies: a "common gateway" between the Web server and applications that can be useful to the server, but that doesn't run as a part of it. CGI is the only way the server can communicate with these other applications, such as a database.

NOTE

Keep in mind that no support exists for CGI outside of HTTP servers. In other words, CGI only works with HTTP servers. Its uses outside that realm have been interesting, but strictly marginal.

A Common Gateway

In technical terms, a *gateway* is an interface or an application that allows two systems to pass information between them.

For example, Microsoft's old Mail program and its newer Exchange are limited to sending mail only to other Microsoft Mail users. A separate product provides a Simple Mail Transfer Protocol (SMTP) Gateway so that mail can be sent to and received from the Internet.

Likewise with your Web server. It doesn't know Perl from Adam, but through the mechanism of CGI it can handle requests from *clients*, or visitors to your site, and pass the results back.

Because the server is only following a set of rules for passing information, it does not know or care what you use in the background to process what it sends you. The functions are totally independent of one another. Thus, you can write CGI programs in *any* programming language. The only requirement is that the information you send back has to be formatted in a way that the server recognizes.

TIP

You can find a great deal of information on the formal CGI specification at http://hoohoo.ncsa.uiuc.edu/cgi/interface.html.

The CGI Environment

MS-DOS, Unix, and, to a limited extent, Windows users should be at least a little familiar with the concept of *environment variables*. For example, on both MS-DOS and Unix, an environment variable called PATH stores the list of directories through which the operating system will search when you type a program name on the command line.

To the operating system, whether it's Windows or Unix, the *environment* is a block of memory where variable names can be stored as string values, such as PATH=c:/bin;c:/usr/bin;c:/usr/local/bin. Taking this example further, whenever the user refers to %PATH% (on NT

and 95/98) or $PATH (on Unix), the operating system substitutes
c:/bin;c:/usr/bin;c:/usr/local/bin.

Programs can get into this block of memory, too. What makes this
facility especially useful is that the environment is in *global* memory,
which means that anything there is accessible by other programs running
at the same time.

The Web server fills in a standard list of environment variables when it
runs; it fills in others when requests are made of it. Because the Web
server runs all the time, anything it places in the environment can be
read by another program, such as your Perl script, if the other program
knows the names of the variables to read.

In the simplest sense, this is how CGI gets information between the
server and your program (see Figure 10.11). The details are a little more
complicated, however.

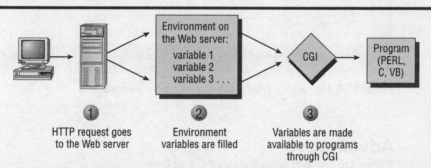

FIGURE 10.11:   The Web server, CGI, and the environment

CGI PROGRAMMING LANGUAGES

This chapter and the next deal with Perl as the preferred programming
vehicle for CGI applications. However, the HTTP-CGI gateway has no
requirements or preferences when it comes to the language in which a
CGI application is written. Let's examine briefly the advantages and disadvantages of some of the most widely used languages.

C, C++

C and, more recently, C++ are the most popular languages for application
and systems development. Figure 10.12 shows a snippet of code in C++.

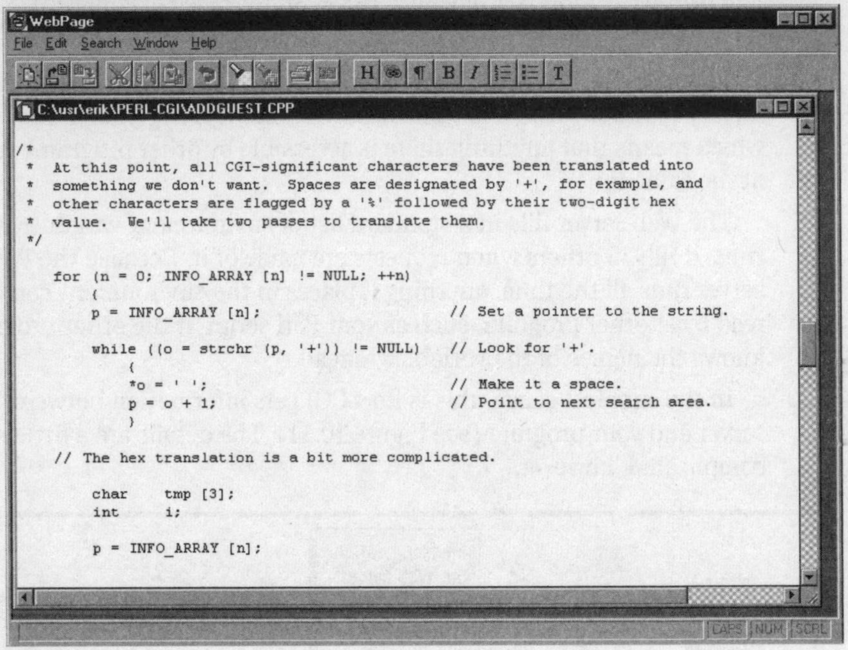

```
/*
 *  At this point, all CGI-significant characters have been translated into
 *  something we don't want.  Spaces are designated by '+', for example, and
 *  other characters are flagged by a '%' followed by their two-digit hex
 *  value.  We'll take two passes to translate them.
 */

    for (n = 0; INFO_ARRAY [n] != NULL; ++n)
        {
        p = INFO_ARRAY [n];                    // Set a pointer to the string.

        while ((o = strchr (p, '+')) != NULL)  // Look for '+'.
            {
            *o = ' ';                          // Make it a space.
            p = o + 1;                         // Point to next search area.
            }

    // The hex translation is a bit more complicated.

        char    tmp [3];
        int     i;

        p = INFO_ARRAY [n];
```

FIGURE 10.12: A C++ code snippet, which is very similar to C

Advantages

These are some of advantages of C and C++:

▶ When it comes to sheer, raw power, it is very difficult to beat these two compiled languages for either CGI or normal applications. For extremely large and complicated CGI projects, C or C++ probably is a better choice than Perl, especially on a busy Web site where processing speed will be a concern.

▶ Both languages are common on both Unix and Windows NT systems, so generally there are few problems porting code between the platforms.

▶ The popularity of C/C++ means that there is a large body of existing code that you can tap into.

Disadvantages

Some of the disadvantages of these two languages of shell languages are:

▶ As you learned earlier, there are so many nifty shortcuts built into Perl that you generally can accomplish a lot more in a lot less code than you can in C or C++. Perl's string-manipulation functions, especially, are so much stronger that it's almost ridiculous to try to do the same thing in C/C++.

▶ Here's something else to keep in mind: It would not be an exaggeration to say that upward of 90 percent of all CGI programs involve heavy string manipulation.

Visual Basic

Visual Basic is Microsoft's workhorse language for simple Windows application development. Figure 10.13 shows some VB code in a Word macro.

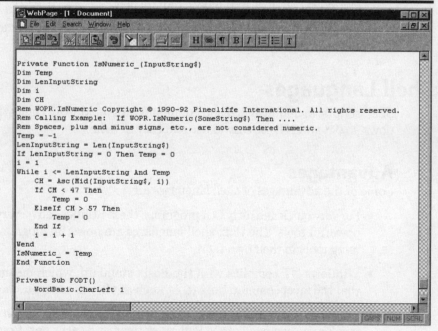

```
Private Function IsNumeric_(InputString$)
Dim Temp
Dim LenInputString
Dim i
Dim CH
Rem WOPR.IsNumeric Copyright © 1990-92 Pinecliffe International. All rights reserved.
Rem Calling Example:  If WOPR.IsNumeric(SomeString$) Then ....
Rem Spaces, plus and minus signs, etc., are not considered numeric.
Temp = -1
LenInputString = Len(InputString$)
If LenInputString = 0 Then Temp = 0
i = 1
While i <= LenInputString And Temp
    CH = Asc(Mid(InputString$, i))
    If CH < 47 Then
        Temp = 0
    ElseIf CH > 57 Then
        Temp = 0
    End If
    i = i + 1
Wend
IsNumeric_ = Temp
End Function

Private Sub FODT()
    WordBasic.CharLeft 1
```

FIGURE 10.13: A Visual Basic example in a Microsoft Word macro

Advantages

Some of the advantages of VB in a CGI context are:

- ▶ VB is Microsoft's version of the BASIC language, which has been around for decades and is familiar to just about anyone who's ever done any programming.

- ▶ It is easy to learn, easy to use, fast, and popular.

- ▶ In a totally Microsoft environment, it can work quickly and efficiently for CGI applications.

Disadvantages

Some of VB's disadvantages are:

- ▶ VB was developed primarily for doing Windows applications, so at least half of its power is wasted on CGI programs, which most often run in the background and depend on sending properly formatted HTML to a Web browser for display.

- ▶ VB would be extremely difficult, if not impossible, to port over to a Unix system.

Shell Languages

Shell scripts, including batch and command files on MS-DOS and Windows 95/98 and NT, are easy to use and easy to write.

Advantages

Some of the advantages of shell languages are:

- ▶ For very quick and dirty CGI programs, these utilities can be very powerful tools. The Unix shell languages are powerful programming tools in their own right.

- ▶ Windows NT complies with the Posix standard, which means that the most common Unix tools, such as sh, will run on it, too.

- ▶ Programs written in these languages are small and tight, don't involve the overhead of the Perl interpreter, and easily port from one system to another.

Disadvantages

Some of the disadvantages of shell languages are:

▶ Shell programs don't allow any of the flexibility and powerful control structures that "real" programming languages do.

▶ You constantly need to call other utilities such as grep or sed (or even Perl!).

WARNING

Anything of more than a minimum level of complexity should be avoided in the shell languages. They are slow, difficult to maintain, and generally not worth the trouble.

Proprietary CGI Methods

Some of the proprietary CGI methods, such as ActiveX from Microsoft and JavaScript from Netscape, are worth mentioning. These are very powerful tools, make no mistake about it. Because they take full and specific advantage of the hardware/software platforms on which they run, the proprietary packages are naturally much faster and much more efficient than more "traditional" CGI software.

After all, there's just no comparison between a program that runs according to a strictly imposed set of rules, basically on top of the operating system, and a program that is able to utilize even the most bare-metal of operating system functions.

However, it is not in the spirit of CGI to adhere to a particular hardware or software platform. Like the spirit of the Internet, it is to let as many people as possible, with as many varied machines as possible, become part of the community.

No restrictions—that's the way it's supposed to be.

WHAT'S NEXT?

Now you know enough about Perl to create and run a simple program, and you have an understanding of the CGI environment and how Perl and CGI work together on the Web. In the next chapter, you'll learn how to use Perl and CGI to build HTML forms that make your Web site interactive.

Part iii

Chapter 11

CREATING REAL-WORLD HTML FORMS WITH PERL AND CGI

F orms in HTML are what make the World Wide Web interactive; they make it something more than a collection of
good-looking graphics. Forms are what your Web site visitors will use to communicate with you, the Webmaster.

CGI—the Common Gateway Interface—is the heart of the
communication; Perl is the brain. With these two tools, introduced in Chapter 10, you will make your Web site *useful*—both
for your visitors and for you.

Adapted from *Perl CGI Programming: No experience
required.*, by Erik Strom

ISBN 0-7821-2157-8   448 pages $29.99

BUILDING AN HTML FORM

The concept of a form in the Hypertext Markup Language (HTML) is really quite simple. It gives the user the capability to *enter* information, rather than just *display* what you're presenting. This feature alone is what allows two-way communication over the World Wide Web (see Figure 11.1).

But HTML can't do anything with the information in a form all by itself. What it *can* do is send the information to something that knows how to deal with it.

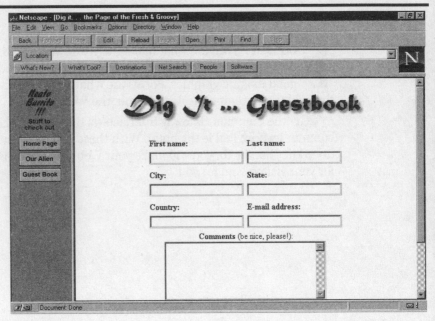

FIGURE 11.1: Two-way communication on the Web is accomplished with forms.

Through CGI, a Perl script can process the data a visitor deposits on your Web site and proceed according to your plan (see Figure 11.2).

This is important. Your intelligently written Perl script is capable of making decisions about how information should be digested and what to send back to the visitor as a result. Without the interaction that HTML forms allow, you would have no way of learning anything about your visitors.

You'd be working in the dark.

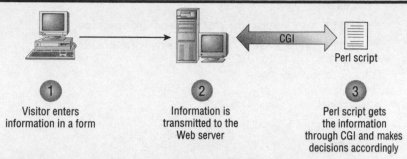

FIGURE 11.2: Processing visitor information through CGI and Perl

A Simple Form

Forms in HTML are used for two purposes: collecting information and creating interactivity between the visitor and the Web server. As an example of the former, you can create a small visitor information form with the following HTML code:

```
<HTML>
<HEAD>
<TITLE>Visitor Information Form</TITLE>
</HEAD>
<BODY>
<H1 ALIGN="LEFT">Visitor Information Form</H1>
<HR>
<FORM ACTION="perl.bat" METHOD="GET">
<B>
Last name: <INPUT TYPE="text" NAME="LastName" SIZE=16>
First Name: <INPUT TYPE="text" NAME="FirstName" SIZE=16>
<BR><BR>
Address: <INPUT TYPE="text" NAME="Address" SIZE=32>
City: <INPUT TYPE="text" NAME="City" SIZE=32>
<BR><BR>
State: <INPUT TYPE="text" NAME="State" SIZE=2>
<BR><BR>
```

Part iii

```
<CENTER>
<INPUT TYPE="submit" VALUE="Send Information">
<INPUT TYPE="reset" VALUE="Clear Form Fields">
</B>

</FORM>
</BODY>
</HTML>
```

NOTE

An "interactive" Web site is one that can tailor an individual response to a visitor's input.

If you save this as `form1.html`, you can run it in your Web browser by telling it to open the file in whatever location you've stored it. The result should look similar to Figure 11.3.

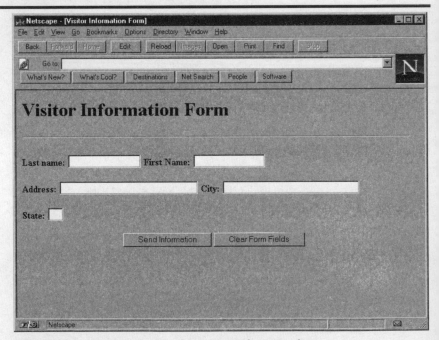

FIGURE 11.3:   The first version of the visitor information form

HTML FORMS REDUX

A form is kicked off in HTML with the <FORM> statement, of course, but there is a bit more to it than that. Here's a brief review of the form tools used in the example.

ACTION   The "action" the form should take when the user presses the button given an INPUT TYPE of submit. More often than not, this is a URL pointing to a CGI program.

INPUT TYPE   Indicates that some kind of interaction with the user, or some "input," is expected here. The type can be checkbox, hidden, image, password, radio, reset, submit, or text.

METHOD   Usually GET or POST, though the default is GET if no method is given. The method determines how the form data will be sent out to a CGI application. (You'll learn more about methods later in this chapter.)

NAME   Essentially a variable name; this string is sent to the CGI application along with the information in the field it names in the form *name = value*.

Table 11.1 lists the various input types, with details on what they do.

TABLE 11.1: HTML Input Types

TYPE	DESCRIPTION
checkbox	An on/off checked box that is used to indicate that a certain choice has been selected.
hidden	A field hidden from the user. It can be used to pass information between the browser and the Web server, and then to the CGI program.
image	An inline image (such as a GIF or JPEG file) with its URL indicated by SRC=. Clicking the image will submit the form data along with the *x-y* coordinates of where it was clicked (measured from the top-left corner of the image).
password	A one-line text field in which typed text is displayed as asterisks or some other character. Used for passwords, obviously.
radio	A radio button. Similar to a checkbox, but radio buttons usually are set up in groups with the same name given to each button. Only one button in the group can be "on"; clicking one turns off any others.

TABLE 11.1 continued: HTML Input Types

Type	Description
reset	A special button that resets (clears) the form. Its VALUE parameter determines what is displayed on the button.
submit	Another special button. This one submits the form data to the URL specified in the form's ACTION parameter. Its VALUE parameter determines what is displayed on the button.
text	A one-line field for entering text, with its width on the screen determined by the SIZE parameter.

Submitting the Form

form1.html uses very few of HTML's tricks, just a few text input types and the submit and reset buttons. Your purpose here is not to see how great-looking forms are put together, but to learn what happens when one of your visitors clicks that submit button.

There are two *methods* that can be used to send out the form's data—the information that has been entered in its fields—and these are specified in the METHOD parameter to the HTML FORM command. You have used GET in this example; the other choice is POST. The difference between them is in how they send the data. As you will see, your choice in methods will be determined by the amount of data in the form; *very* generally, GET is used for small amounts and POST for large amounts or when you want to hide the information from the user.

You used GET in the example for two reasons: First, you're only requesting a few pieces of information in this simple form. Second, without even loading it on a Web site, you can get a visual idea of how the data is sent when you submit the form.

Create something to fool the browser. On Windows NT or Windows 95/98, if Perl is in your path (and it should be, once you start writing programs in Perl!), you can create a little file called perl.bat that has nothing in it but the word perl. A shell script on Unix would accomplish the same thing.

Save it in the same directory in which you put form1.html; then crank up your Web browser of choice and open the file.

TIP

Netscape Navigator has an option on its File menu to Open File in Browser. Microsoft Internet Explorer brings up an Open File dialog box when you choose the Open option in its File menu.

Fill out the form with anything that fits. Figure 11.4 illustrates some suggested bogus data.

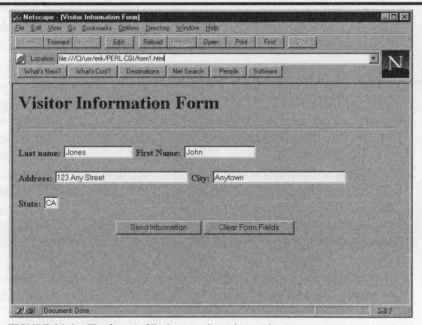

FIGURE 11.4:   The form is filled out and ready to submit.

Now submit the form by clicking the Send Information button.

Figure 11.5 illustrates what appears in Netscape Navigator's Location field when you ship this form. The "CGI" program you specified in the form's ACTION field doesn't do anything, of course, but you can see what would be shipped to it.

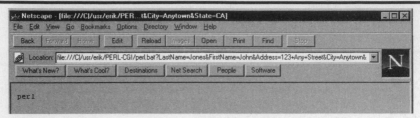

FIGURE 11.5: The URL sent by the form in Figure 11.4

This *query string* is set up by the browser as a URL. You don't have to worry about how it's done; any browser will do it automatically. However, you *do* have to interpret it in your CGI program, so you'd better know how it's put together.

URLs AND CGI

You have seen how an HTML form is built and the functions it uses to send information to the Web server. It's important to know exactly how the information should be presented, because your Perl program has to be able to interpret it.

URLs, or *Uniform Resource Locators*, were developed as a way to specify resources on the Internet with a single line of *printable* ASCII text. Notice the emphasis on "printable"—this will become important to you as you learn to decode the special characters sent in a URL. In its simplest and most familiar form, a URL simply gives the domain name of a Web site—for example, www.rcich.com.

URLs aren't limited to the World Wide Web. All of the major Internet protocols, such as FTP, Gopher, WAIS, and HTTP, can read and understand a URL. They are set up in a very specific way, containing:

- ▶ The protocol of the URL's server (Gopher, WAIS, HTTP, etc.)
- ▶ The server's domain name
- ▶ The server's TCP/IP port number, which if omitted will default to the well-known port for the service—again, Gopher, WAIS, HTTP, etc.
- ▶ The location of the resource on the server

The URL that was constructed by your browser in submitting form1 .html is set up in this fashion, with file:// as the protocol and the

domain name, port, and resource location all addressed in the path to
`perl.bat`. Figure 11.6 illustrates a full URL pointing over the Internet to
the same location.

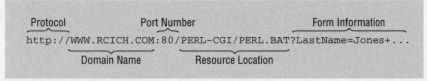

FIGURE 11.6:   The anatomy of a URL

"Printable" Characters

Like most other Internet protocols, URLs were originally designed to
ensure that they could be sent via e-mail. Most older mail systems were
capable of recognizing only 7-bit characters, so the characters used in a
URL must conform to that.

However, even some of these characters have a special meaning in a
URL. For example, the ampersand (&) is used to separate the parameters
in the query string. But you will encounter many occasions when you
have to send ampersands and plus signs and equal signs and even 8-bit,
non-ASCII characters in a URL. How can it be done?

The solution in the URL scheme of things is to *encode* these special
characters in the form

    %nn

where the percent sign (%) indicates that the next two characters are the
hexadecimal value of the actual, encoded character. A good example of
this is the question mark (?) that begins the query string in our example:

    perl.bat?LastName=Jones&FirstName=John&Address=123+Any+Street
    . . .

Again, this character has a special meaning in the URL because it indicates
that `perl.bat` should be run with the arguments that follow it. If a *literal*
question mark is included in any of the arguments, it is encoded as

    %26

because 26 is the hexadecimal code for a question mark in the ASCII table.

Table 11.2 shows the other printable ASCII characters that have a special meaning in a URL and therefore will be encoded by the browser.

TABLE 11.2: Printable Characters Encoded in URLs

CHARACTER	"HEX" VALUE
Tab	09
Space	20
"	22
<	3C
>	3E
[	5B
\	5C
]	5D
^	5E
`	60
{	7B
|	7C
}	7D
~	7E

Any control characters that wind up in a URL will be encoded, too.

Because you, as the CGI programmer, are sitting at the other end of this scheme, you don't have to deal with *encoding* characters. The rule for you will be simple: Any time you encounter a percent sign in a query string, you may assume that the next two characters are the hexadecimal code of the character that is really intended to be there.

TIP

If you're worried about getting literal percent signs in a URL, don't be. They will be encoded, too.

You don't have to be too concerned with the actual ASCII values of the characters, although every programmer usually has an ASCII table handy for reference. Perl has a number of handy tricks for turning hexadecimal values into characters, as you'll soon see.

What you'll have to do at your end is recognize an encoded character, strip off the percent sign, and send the remaining number to a Perl function that will translate it for you.

HEXADECIMAL NUMBERING: A LITTLE MATH LESSON

The *hexadecimal*, or base-16, number system is meat and potatoes to people who program for a living. This is primarily because it is a convenient way to represent the *binary*, or base-2, numbers that are meat and potatoes to computers.

Computers deal with data in *bits*, or ones and zeros that indicate an *on* or *off* state. So the binary numbering system is especially important, because binary numbers are the only kind that computers can process at the lowest level. However, this is a system in which there are only two allowable digits: 1 and 0. The *decimal* number 5 in this system would be 101 because it consists of 1 of 2^0 (1), 0 of 2^1 (0), and 1 of 2^2 (4): $1 + 0 + 4 = 5$.

In the hexadecimal numbering system, or "hex" for short, there are 16 allowable digits. In decimal, 0 through 9 are the numbers you would expect. The decimal numbers 10 through 15 are represented by the characters A through F. The hex number FF would be 255 in decimal because it consists of F of 16^0 (15) and F of 16^1 (16×15, or 240): $15 + 240 = 255$.

Because of its binary, on-off architecture, *everything* on a computer at some point boils down to a power of two. When you hear technicians talking about a 32-bit microprocessor, which is what powers most PCs these days, they are referring to a processor that handles data in chunks of 32 bits. That's a maximum number of one less than 2^{32}, or a binary number consisting of 32 ones:

    11111111111111111111111111111111

This number is not any less intimidating in decimal: 4,294,967,295.

CONTINUED →

The beauty of hex numbering is that each digit represents exactly four binary bits. You can't say that about decimal, where 32 bits comes out to that awful 4-billion-something. Broken down to 4 bits per digit, the hex value of $2^{32}-1$ is rather elegant:

```
1111 1111 1111 1111 1111 1111 1111 1111
 F    F    F    F    F    F    F    F
```

Plus, FFFFFFFF certainly is easier to keep track of than a number consisting of 32 ones.

URL Encoding with GET

The QUERY_STRING environment variable is the method of storage for the information passed from an HTML form to a CGI program through GET. When you use the GET method to pass the information, it is just tacked on to the end of the URL:

```
perl.bat?LastName=Jones&FirstName=John&Address=123+Any+Street
. . .
```

The arguments to the CGI application are separated from the application name by a question mark (?) and the URL is built in *name=value* pairs, with each pair separated from the others by an ampersand (&). Notice, too, that all of the spaces in the URL have been replaced with plus signs (+).

These three characters, plus the percent sign that will flag any encoded characters and the equal sign that separates the *name=value* pairs, are what you'll need to deal with in your Perl-CGI script.

To get a little practice with these concepts and to learn some new concepts in Perl, try writing a program to read the QUERY_STRING, decode it, and print all of its names and values in an HTML document.

Here's the program:

```
#!/perl/bin/perl


# geturl.pl
```

```perl
#
# A little Perl script to read, decode and print the names
# and values passed to it from an HTML form through CGI.


# Get HTML header, ender, define the page title.

   require "/pub/scripts/perl-cgi/html.pl"; # Full path.
   $Title = "Get Information From A URL";

# Get the query string.

   $QueryString = $ENV{'QUERY_STRING'};

# Use split to make an array of name-value pairs broken at
# the ampersand character.

   @NameValuePairs = split (/&/, $QueryString);

# Put up an HTML header, page title and a rule.

   &HTML_Header ($Title);
   print "<BODY>\n";
   print "<H1>$Title</H1>\n";
   print "<HR>\n";

# Split each of the name-value pairs and print them on the
page.

   foreach $NameValue (@NameValuePairs)
     {
     ($Name, $Value) = split (/=/, $NameValue);
     print "Name = $Name, value = $Value<BR>\n";
     }
```

```
# End the HTML document.

&HTML_Ender;


#              End geturl.pl
```

Store it as `geturl.pl` in a directory from which you can run Perl scripts over the Web server. Now, change the `ACTION=` string in `form1.html` to the correct path to `geturl.pl`. Also, move `form1.html` into a directory on your Web server. You'll be calling it up through your Web site this time, rather than as a simple file in the browser.

Start your browser and connect with the Web site with the correct URL to `form1.html`. Fill in the form with information similar to what has been entered in Figure 11.7. But this time use some characters that will be encoded by the browser when they're shipped through CGI.

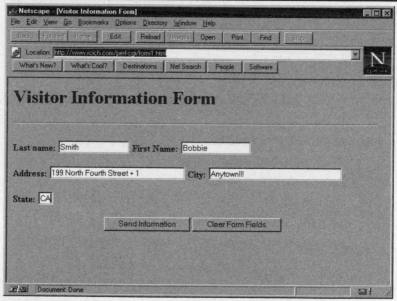

FIGURE 11.7: An information form with some special characters

When you click the Send Information button, the result should be similar to what is illustrated in Figure 11.8.

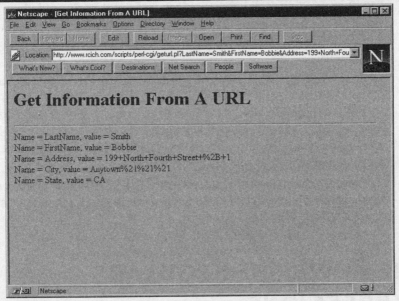

FIGURE 11.8: What the Perl script gets from the information form

Decoding a Query String

You no doubt noticed that the information displayed by `geturl.pl` is full of strange encodings and separators. You'll take care of those shortly. For now, let's examine how you broke a single URL into series of *name* and *value* pairs.

The hero in this program is `split`, another workhorse Perl function that you will use again and again in your applications. `split` is specified in this way:

```
split (/PATTERN/, STRING, LIMIT);
```

where the *PATTERN* argument is some delimiter or point of separation, *STRING* is the string to split, and the optional *LIMIT* tells `split` to do no more than the specified number of separations.

`split` returns an array of strings broken apart at the *PATTERN*, which is eliminated in the array. The *PATTERN* is *always* put between the forward slash (/) characters, but you can omit a specific value for it. This call to `split`,

```
@Array = split (//, $String);
```

would fill @Array with the contents of $String broken out at any instance of *white space*, which is spaces, tabs, and line-enders.

The PATTERN argument also can be a regular expression, which we'll cover shortly.

Other than split, there is very little in geturl.pl that you haven't seen before. You used the QUERY_STRING environment variable to obtain the URL submitted by form1.html; you broke the query string into individual *name=value* pairs by using split to separate it on the ampersand character; and you split up the pairs into their component parts by specifying the equal sign as the PATTERN.

However, the strings still have all of those URL-encoded characters in them, and it looks as if it will be a tedious job to take them out, doesn't it?

Well, let's see.

THE POWER OF REGULAR EXPRESSIONS

Change the foreach loop in geturl.pl to read this way:

```
# Split, decode each of the name-value pairs, and print them
on the page.

foreach $NameValue (@NameValuePairs)
{
($Name, $Value) = split (/=/, $NameValue);
$Value =~ tr/+/ /;
$Value =~ s/%([\dA-Fa-f][\dA-Fa-f])/ pack ("C", hex
($1))/eg;
print "Name = $Name, value = $Value<BR>\n";
}
```

If you've never worked with regular expressions, the two new lines in geturl.pl probably are among the weirdest things you've ever seen. However, install the new program, fill out form1.html in your Web browser, and submit it, using all the bizarre characters you want. Your result will be what you typed in, as illustrated in Figure 11.9.

Where did all the garbage go?

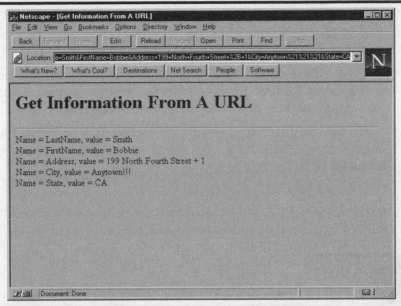

FIGURE 11.9:   All of the encoded characters are translated.

If you had any doubts about the power of Perl, this little trick should dispel them. If you have been intimidated by the perplexing and strange conventions of regular expressions, you now should feel inspired to learn them. You have accomplished *in two lines of code* what probably would have taken an entire program to do in C or C++. In Perl, you just have to learn the lingo.

They're easy to avoid, these Perl regular expressions. They generally look like something only Martians would understand. However, you now have seen what you can do with a simple, though cryptic-looking, regular expression. You simply have no choice but to learn more about them!

Let's begin by examining the two new lines in geturl.pl.

Translations, Substitutions

The first new line is fairly simple, though utterly meaningless to the untrained eye:

```
$Value =~ tr/+/ /;
```

A couple of new Perl concepts surface in this line:

▶ In the expression `"$String =~ /PATTERN/"`, the `=~` is the *match* operator, which is true if `$String` contains `/PATTERN/`.

▶ `tr` is the *translate* function, which turns all characters found between the first and second forward-slash characters following it into the characters between the second and third slashes.

You will use the `=~` operator frequently—always, in fact, when you want to change characters in a string into other characters. The specification for `tr` is

```
tr /SEARCH_LIST/REPLACE_LIST/
```

where SEARCH_LIST is the characters for which you want to search, and REPLACE_LIST is what their new values will be.

NOTE

There are three optional parameters to `tr` that go after the last slash: c, d, and s. We don't need them at this point, so we won't discuss them. (For the particular among you readers, they stand for complement, delete, and squeeze.)

The line from `geturl.pl` that utilizes `tr`,

```
$Value =~ tr/+/ /;
```

has the + character as its SEARCH_LIST and a space as its REPLACE_ LIST. Therefore, it will go through the `$Value` string and replace every occurrence of the plus character (+) with a space. This is handy in URLs, where all spaces are designated by plus signs.

The second new line in `geturl.pl` is trickier:

```
$Value =~ s/%([\dA-Fa-f][\dA-Fa-f])/ pack ("C", hex ($1))/eg;
```

It's a little easier to understand if it is explained in the sequence of events that it kicks off.

First of all, what does this code do? This is the program line that turns URL-encoded characters back into *printable* characters. Remember the %nn convention, in which special characters are encoded with a percent sign followed by their hexadecimal ASCII values? This is where the encoded values revert to real characters. Let's step through the program line:

▶ `s` is the Perl substitute function. Like `tr`, it takes everything it finds in `$Value` that matches the string between the first two forward slashes and replaces it with what is between the second two slashes.

▶ In this example, s has been told to look for % followed by two characters that are either digits, designated by \d, or the characters A through F (or a through f); in short, the valid hexadecimal numbers.

▶ The expression pack ("C", hex ($1)), which is specified as the REPLACE_LIST for s, is best understood if it is taken apart from the inside out. hex is a Perl function that expects its argument to be a hexadecimal number and returns a decimal number. $1 is the value found by the expression in the first set of parentheses in SEARCH_LIST, minus the percent sign. pack is a function that takes its second argument and "packs" it into a binary value or structure based on the template that is its first argument. In our example, the template is C, which tells pack to stuff the value in the second argument into a character.

▶ The e at the end of the line indicates to s that REPLACE_LIST is an expression rather than a string. Without it, every %nn string in $Value would be literally replaced with pack ("C", hex ($1)). e tells s to do the replacement with the result of the expression.

▶ The g following e tells s to do a global substitution; in other words, replace every instance of SEARCH_LIST in $Value with what is calculated in REPLACE_LIST. If you left this parameter off, s would do the operation on the first occurrence and then quit.

Here's a recap of the Perl regular-expression functions we've covered so far with their formal parameters:

▶ tr /SEARCH_LIST/REPLACE_LIST/   Translates a regular expression in SEARCH_LIST to the characters or expression in REPLACE_LIST.

▶ hex (EXPRESSION)   Interprets EXPRESSION as a hexadecimal number and returns the decimal value. For example, hex (10) would return 16.

▶ pack (TEMPLATE, EXPRESSION)   Packs EXPRESSION into a binary structure based on TEMPLATE.

YOU'RE RIGHT: REGULAR EXPRESSIONS *ARE* HARD

One of Perl's biggest strengths over bare-metal programming languages such as C and C++ comes from its ability to format text so easily. However, it uses regular expressions heavily to accomplish the formatting. Make no mistake about it, regular expressions are difficult.

But another of Perl's strengths is that you can write a workable, useful program in it without knowing *every detail* of the language, something you've already demonstrated in the examples we've built so far. As you gain more proficiency with Perl, your programs will utilize the knowledge you've gained, too.

You will learn about some hairy details of regular expressions in this chapter, but don't be too concerned if you don't get it right away. With practice, it'll come to you.

Meanwhile, it's helpful to think of regular expressions as nothing more than a search-and-replace function on steroids.

Regular Expressions in Detail

A regular expression is used to match a pattern in a string and, possibly, replace it with another pattern. The string can match any of the alternatives of the regular expression; alternatives are separated with a vertical bar (|), are evaluated from left to right, and always stop on the first match.

The building blocks of a regular expression are the characters used to represent events or other characters.

- ► ^ stands for the beginning of a string.
- ► $ stands for the end of the string.
- ► \B is a non-word boundary.
- ► \b is a single word boundary (see \w and \W).

Regular expressions may include *quantifiers,* which tell how many times an event or string must occur.

- ► {*bottom, top*} where bottom and top are numbers that mean the event must occur bottom times and no more than top times.

▶ {*number*,} means it has to happen at least number times.

▶ {*number*} indicates that it must happen *exactly* number times.

▶ * is the same as {0,}.

▶ + is the same as {1,}.

▶ ? is the same as {0,1}.

The period character, or *dot* (.), is an often-used tool because it matches *any* character except the newline. For specific characters, you may include them in lists enclosed by square brackets; ranges are indicated with a hyphen, as in A–Z.

The backslash (\) before a character gives it a special meaning. Table 11.3 illustrates the backslashed special characters.

TABLE 11.3: Special Characters In Regular Expressions

CHARACTER	MEANING
\n	Newline
\r	Carriage return
\t	Tab
\f	Formfeed
\d	A digit, or single number
\D	A non-digit
\s	White space, such as space, tab, or newline
\S	Non-white space
\w	An alphanumeric character
\W	Non-alphanumeric
\xnn	Where *nn* is a hex value, the character having that value
\0nn	Same as above, using octal (base-8) numbers

Part iii

Another convention you'll see often in regular expressions is the use of $1, $2, $3, etc. These scalar variables correspond, in left-to-right order, to the expressions in *parentheses* in SEARCH_LIST. What makes them especially valuable is that they maintain their value outside of the regular expression. For example, the string 19 May 1997 could be split into its parts with this code snippet:

```
$string =~ /(...) (..) (....)/;
$day = $1;
$month = $2;
$year = $3;
```

WARNING

$1, $2, $3, etc. are equivalent to \1, \2, \3, etc., in regular expressions. Keep this in mind if you mistakenly try to interpret a number literally by "escaping" it and the results aren't what you expect.

WHAT'S NEXT?

Learning how to create HTML forms has given you a glimpse of how powerful Perl, in conjunction with CGI, can be in building a Web site. Now we'll move on to another method for adding sophistication to your pages—Dynamic HTML (DHTML). The next chapter will introduce you to the advanced effects and functionality that are possible with DHTML.

Chapter 12

EXPLORING AND NAVIGATING DYNAMIC HTML

With the explosion of interest in the World Wide Web, *Hypertext Markup Language (HTML)* has assumed a prominent place in the computer world. HTML has evolved to meet the increasing demand for eye-catching—and mind-catching—Web sites. Until recently, however, the evolutionary process mostly involved new and improved tags and attributes. The end-products, static Web pages that often required repeated time-consuming round-trips between client and server machines, clearly showed that a new direction was in order.

Adapted from *Dynamic HTML: Master the Essentials*, by Joseph Schmuller

ISBN 0-7821-2277-9   608 pages $29.99

Dynamic HTML (DHTML) is that new direction. It combines HTML with Cascading Style Sheets (CSS) and scripting languages. What role does each member of this combination play?

▶ As you're undoubtedly aware, HTML specifies a Web page's elements, like a table, a heading, a paragraph, or a bulleted list.

▶ CSS enable you to decide how a Web browser renders those elements: You can use a CSS to determine (i.e., to *style*) an element's size, color, position, and a number of other features.

▶ Scripting languages enable you to manipulate the Web page's elements, so that the styles you assigned to them can change in response to an end user's input.

That last point is extremely important. Before DHTML, you often had to jump through complicated hoops to give end users the ability to change a Web page's features after it downloaded. One of those hoops, as I mentioned before, involved repeated communication with the server machine. This takes a lot of time, it and detracts from the Web-surfing experience. How many times have you clicked your browser's Stop button because everything was just taking too long? DHTML makes Web page events seemingly instantaneous: They occur within the browser after the page has downloaded. With DHTML, Web pages become very much like other software applications.

Microsoft and Netscape, the companies behind the two most popular Web browsers, each have a version of DHTML. Both are called "DHTML," and each vendor's version is compatible only with its own browser. Microsoft and Netscape have proposed separate versions of DHTML to the World Wide Web Consortium. Each, of course, hopes the Consortium adopts its proposal and stamps it the official version, but it's probably the case that a sort of hybrid will emerge.

SETTING UP

We'll jump into DHTML in the next section, but first we need to set up a template to use in the exercises later in this chapter. If you have a favorite text editor, feel free to use it throughout the exercises. If not, Windows 95/98 has provided one for you: Notepad.

You can set up Notepad to act as a convenient HTML editor:

1. Find Notepad in your system, open it, and select File ➢ New.

2. Next, select File ➢ Save As. Save the file as `Template`.

3. In this file, type these lines:

   ```
   <HTML>
   <HEAD>
   <TITLE>New Page</TITLE>
   </HEAD>
   <BODY>

   </BODY>
   </HTML>
   ```

4. Select File ➢ Save.

Whenever you have to create an HTML file, you can open `Template` and then save it under a new name with the extension `.htm`.

Your `Template` file should look like this:

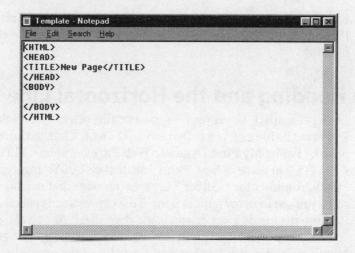

You now have a starting point for creating any HTML document.

Using DHTML in IE

Now, as promised, you're going to dive right into DHTML. You'll work with HTML, CSS, and scripting. You'll start with a page in IE and you'll endow it with a number of *dynamic effects*—effects that depend on user actions. Here are the dynamic effects you'll build into your first page:

▶ Moving your mouse through a heading on the top of the page will cause a hidden text display to appear and will change the color of the heading.

▶ Moving your mouse through the heading will also change the color and the content of a small box on the page.

▶ Clicking on the heading will cause a box in the center of the page to split into four boxes that move outward toward the corners of the page, revealing a short message in the center of the page.

▶ The centered message will appear to be layered above the text display.

▶ Moving the mouse out of the heading will return the page to its original appearance.

Figure 12.1 shows what the page will look like when you first open it in IE, and Figure 12.2 shows its appearance after a few mouse-clicks on the heading.

The Heading and the Horizontal Line

Let's get started. Open your Template file, select File ➤ Save As, and save the file as First Dynamic IE.htm. Change the title of the page by typing **My First Dynamic Web Page** between <TITLE> and </TITLE> in place of New Page. Inside the <BODY> tag, type **Style = "background-color : 'Silver'"** to give your page that macho silver-gray color you see in many applications. This expression is called a *style sheet*. Because it's inside a tag, it's an *inline* style sheet. As you can see, in this context, Style is an attribute and its value is a string. The string contains a style property, a colon, and the value of the property. A style sheet can hold more than one property-value pair, and when it does, a semicolon separates adjacent pairs. (You'll see an example of this in the next section, "The Hidden Message.") For much more about style sheets, see Chapter 8.

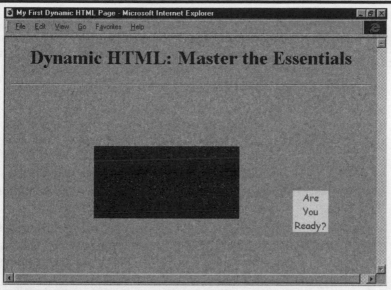

FIGURE 12.1:   Your first DHTML Web page, opened in IE

FIGURE 12.2:   The Web page after several mouse-clicks on the heading

458   **Chapter Twelve**

NOTE

If you've worked with HTML 3.*x*, you've probably used the attribute bgcolor to specify a Web page's background color. In HTML 4.0, this attribute is *deprecated*, meaning that (1) newer features of the language provide Web developers with greater capabilities, and (2) it may become obsolete in future versions of HTML.

Next, center an H1 heading by typing

```
<H1 Style = "text-align:center">Dynamic HTML: Master the
Essentials</H1>
```

after the <BODY> tag. To follow the heading with a horizontal line, type **<HR>**.

At this point, we're going to add an extremely important attribute to the <H1> tag. This attribute, ID, will give us a way of referring to the header when we have to work with it in a scripting language. Inside the <H1> tag, type **ID = h1Header**.

Your document should look like this:

```
<HTML>
<HEAD>
<TITLE>My First Dynamic HTML Page</TITLE>
</HEAD>
<BODY Style = "background-color:'silver'">
<H1 ID = h1Header Style = "text-align:center">Dynamic HTML:
Master the Essentials</H1>
<HR>
</BODY>
</HTML>
```

The page in IE looks like Figure 12.1, but without anything below the line under the heading.

WHAT'S IN A NAME?

When I assign an ID to an HTML element, I'll begin the ID with a lowercase prefix. That prefix will be the element tag (like h1, div, or p). The rest of the ID will be a descriptive term that tells you something about the element. It will begin with an uppercase letter, and all the rest will be lowercase (h1Header, for example).

This is similar to a naming convention that software developers use in other contexts. The prefix usually is an abbreviation, but every HTML element has a short name, so I'll use that name as the prefix.

If you're familiar with object-oriented programming, you've already seen this kind of notation. Is this naming convention subtly trying to tell you that DHTML turns HTML elements into objects? Exactly!

The Hidden Message

To create the remaining elements of the page, we'll divide the page into segments called DIVs. Each segment starts with <DIV> and ends with </DIV>. After we've created our segments, we'll script them to exhibit the desired effects.

Let's create a segment to hold the hidden message that you see in a large, bold, white font in Figure 12.2. Just after the <HR> tag, type

```
<DIV ID = divMessage>
</DIV>
```

Next, type the message between these two DIV tags. Put the message in a paragraph (that is, enclose it with a <P> and a </P>) and make it a bulleted list. Here's the HTML to type between the DIV tags:

```
<P> Topics in this book include
<UL>
<LI> Scripting
<LI> Cascading Style Sheets
<LI> Animation
<LI> ... And Many More!
</UL>
</P>
```

Part iii

We've typed the message, but so far its appearance in IE would be pretty nondescript. We haven't colored the text white, enlarged it, or made it bold. We also haven't positioned the message on the page.

To take care of the message's size, appearance, and position, we'll add information to the <DIV> tag. We add the information as a group of styling specifications in an inline style sheet. Within the <DIV> tag, type

```
Style = "Position:Absolute;Left:5%;Top:10%;
Visibility:Hidden;z-index:-1;font-style:normal;font-
weight:bold;
font-family:Normal;font-size:50;color:'White'"
```

The first property-value pair, `Position:Absolute`, tells the browser to position the DIV with respect to the top edge and left edge of the browser window.

NOTE

Another possible value for `Position` is `Relative`. In contrast to `Absolute`, `Relative` situates an element in relation to other elements on the page.

The next two property-value pairs show one way that style sheets let you specify position—via percentages of distance from the left edge and the top edge of the browser window. The first of the two pairs positions the DIV's left side 5% of the distance from the left edge to the right, and the second positions its top edge 10% of the distance from the top of the browser to the bottom. The fourth pair, `Visibility:Hidden`, keeps the message invisible when the page opens.

The next pair positions the DIV in the "third dimension." If you look closely at Figure 12.2, you'll see that the large, white-lettered message appears to be underneath the message in the center of the screen and underneath the page's heading. The `z-index` styling property determines this kind of layering: the lower the `z-index`, the deeper the apparent layer of its element.

NOTE

The word "layer" is important in Netscape's version of DHTML. For this reason, I'll try to avoid this word during our discussion of IE.

The remaining property-value pairs determine the message font's size, weight, appearance, and color. The font-size attribute's value, 50, specifies a font whose size is 50 pixels.

NOTE

In HTML 3.*x*, developers used the <FONT> tag to specify a font's aspects. In HTML 4.0, the <FONT> tag is *deprecated*. As I said in a previous note, this means that (1) newer features of the language provide Web developers with greater capabilities, and (2) this element may become obsolete in future versions of HTML. Font-size is a good example of "greater capabilities." Through its Size attribute, the <FONT> tag supports only seven possible font sizes. The newer font-size style property, on the other hand, can give you pixel-level precision when you specify the size of a font.

The Message at the Center of the Page

Now we'll create the message at the center of the page. Create a <DIV> called divLearn, and we'll position it by pixels, rather than percentages. We'll position it 180 pixels from the left edge of the page and 200 pixels from the top edge:

```
<DIV ID = divLearn Style
="Position:Absolute;Left:180;Top:200;">
```

It will be helpful to confine the message to a specific width—say, 210 pixels—so that we can make its text cover three lines. To overlay the message on top of the large white-font text display, we'll give it a z-index of 0. (Remember that the text display's z-index is –1.) Adding these specifications to the style sheet gives us

```
<DIV ID = divLearn Style
="Position:Absolute;Left:180;Top:200;Width:210;
z-index:0;">
```

The message will reside in a paragraph,

```
<P>
Learn how to create striking effects on your Web pages.
</P>
```

and we'll add some styling information to the <P> tag. In this tag, we can specify an appearance, size, and weight for the font. The entire <P> tag should look like this:

```
<P ID = pLearn Style = "font-family:cursive;font-
size:15pt;font-weight:bold">
```

Here's the HTML for the DIV:

```
<DIV ID = divLearn Style
="Position:Absolute;Left:180;Top:200;Width:210;
z-index:0;">

<P ID = pLearn Style = "font-family:cursive;font-
size:15pt;font-weight:bold">

Learn how to create striking effects on your Web pages.

</P>

</DIV>
```

The Moving Boxes

To create the effect of a box that splits into four boxes, we position four boxes in the center of the page and give them all the same background color. Each box will be a separate DIV. I used blue as the background color, but you can pick any color you like. I also specified a color property and a text-align property, because we'll use them in an exercise.

Here is one way to write the DIVs for the boxes:

```
<DIV ID = divBox1 Style="background-color:blue;color:blue;
text-align:center;Position:Absolute;Left:150;Top:180;
Width:120;Height:60;z-index:1 ">
</DIV>


<DIV ID = divBox2 Style="background-color:blue;color:blue;
text-align:center;Position:Absolute;Left:270;TOP:180;
Width:120;Height:60;z-index:1">
</DIV>


<DIV ID = divBox3 Style="background-color:blue;color:blue;
text-align:center;Position:Absolute;Left:150;Top:240;
Width:120;Height:60;z-index:1">
</DIV>
```

```
<DIV ID = divBox4 Style="background-color:blue;color:blue;
text-align:center;Position:Absolute;Left:270;Top:240;
Width:120;Height:60;z-index:1">
</DIV>
```

If you write the DIVs this way, you'll create the boxes in Figures 12.1 and 12.2, but the CSS syntax presents another possibility. Instead of writing the colors, text alignment, width, and height four times, we can put the style specifications for these properties at the beginning of the document, between <HEAD> and </HEAD>; give those specifications a name; and then use that name within each box's <DIV> tag.

Here's how to do it. After the <HEAD> tag in your document, type

```
<STYLE Type = "text/css">
</STYLE>
```

We'll put the style information between these two tags. To give a name ("bluebox") to the style specifications and specify the background color, color, text alignment, width, and height, for the boxes, type

```
.bluebox {background-color:blue;
        color:blue;
        text-align:center;
        width:120;
        height:60}
```

after your newly created <STYLE> tag. When you preface the name of a style with a dot, you create a style *class*. Note the consistent syntax for the style sheet. We still use a colon to separate a property from its value and a semicolon to separate adjacent property-value pairs.

TIP

In the Microsoft version of DHTML, you can omit Type = "text/css", as CSS is the only type of style sheet that Microsoft supports. In the Netscape version, you can't omit this expression, because Netscape supports another type of style sheet in addition to CSS.

With the style specified as a class in the head of your document, you insert the name of the class in each box's DIV. Here's the HTML for the movable boxes:

```
<DIV ID = divBox1 Class = "bluebox"
Style="Position:Absolute;Left:150;Top:180;z-index:1">
</DIV>
```

```
<DIV ID = divBox2 Class = "bluebox"
Style="Position:Absolute;Left:270;Top:180;z-index:1">
</DIV>


<DIV ID = divBox3 Class = "bluebox"
Style="Position:Absolute;Left:150;Top:240;z-index:1">
</DIV>


<DIV ID = divBox4 Class = "bluebox"
STYLE="Position:Absolute;Left:270;Top:240;z-index:1">
</DIV>
```

Save your work and open the page in IE; you'll see a display that looks like Figure 12.1, but without the little box in the lower-right corner.

Here's the exercise that uses the `color` and `text-align` properties you just set. It will show you how style sheets can combine to determine an HTML element's appearance. Follow these steps:

1. For the first movable box, between <DIV> and </DIV>, insert a paragraph that identifies the box:

    `<P>Box<BR>1</P>`

2. Do the same for the fourth movable box:

    `<P>Box<BR>4</P>`

3. In the first movable box's inline style sheet, add

    `color:white`

4. In the fourth movable box's inline style sheet, add

    `background-color:white`

In your document, the HTML for the movable boxes should now look like this:

```
<DIV ID = divBox1 Class = "bluebox"
Style="Position:Absolute;Left:150;Top:180;
z-index:1;color:white">
<P>Box<BR>1</P>
</DIV>
```

```
<DIV ID = divBox2 Class = "bluebox"
Style="Position:Absolute;Left:270;Top:180;z-index:1">
</DIV>

<DIV ID = divBox3 Class = "bluebox"
Style="Position:Absolute;Left:150;Top:240;z-index:1">
</DIV>

<DIV ID = divBox4 Class = "bluebox"
STYLE="Position:Absolute;Left:270;Top:240;z-index:1;
background-color:white">
<P>Box<BR>4</P>
</DIV>
```

Figure 12.3 shows the appearance of your page in IE with these changes in place.

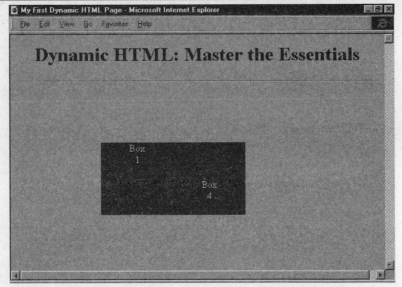

FIGURE 12.3:   Your page in IE, with modified styling specifications for two of the movable boxes

The effects of these changes show you that you can combine styles from the specification at the beginning of the document (between the <STYLE> and </STYLE> tags) and style from inline specifications. This combination is referred to as *cascading*—the "C" in CSS. As you saw in Chapter 8, cascading is just one of the benefits that style sheets provide.

Remove those changes from divBox1 and divBox4, and we'll move on to the next element.

The Changeable Box

We finish off the page design by creating the box in the lower-right corner. The box changes color and content when you pass the mouse through the heading at the top of the page. You can see this by comparing Figure 12.1 to Figure 12.2. By now, you've probably guessed that we'll implement the effect by writing two DIVs, assigning them different z-indices, and making one visible and one invisible. We'll write a script that switches the visibility of the DIVs when the mouse passes into the heading and returns to the original values when the mouse passes out of the heading.

Here's the HTML that sets up the two DIVs:

```
<DIV ID = divReady Style =
"Position:Absolute;Top:70%;Left:80%;Width:10%;
z-index:1;Visibility:Visible">

<P Align = Center Style = "font-family:cursive; Background-
Color:'Beige';Color:Chocolate">

Are<BR>You<BR>Ready?</P>

</DIV>


<DIV ID = divStarted Style =
"Position:Absolute;Top:70%;Left:80%;Width:10%;
z-index:0;Visibility:Hidden">

<P Align = Center Style = "font-family:cursive;
Background-Color:'BlanchedAlmond';Color:Blue">

Let's<BR>Get<BR>Started</P>

</DIV>
```

A Word about Color

We've used numerous color names in the HTML for our first page. What other color names can you use in your code? Table 12.1 presents some of the colors that IE and Navigator can render. For completeness, I've included their hexadecimal codes. It's important to test a color in both browsers. As our work with Netscape later in this chapter will show, the browsers react differently to different color names.

TABLE 12.1: Color Names and Their Hexadecimal Codes

COLOR NAME	CODE	COLOR NAME	CODE
ALICEBLUE	#F0F8FF	ANTIQUEWHITE	#FAEBD7
AQUA	#00FFFF	AQUAMARINE	#7FFFD4
AZURE	#F0FFFF	BEIGE	#F5F5DC
BISQUE	#FFE4C4	BLACK	#000000
BLANCHEDALMOND	#FFEBCD	BLUE	#0000FF
BLUEVIOLET	#8A2BE2	BROWN	#A52A2A
BURLYWOOD	#DEB887	CADETBLUE	#5F9EA0
CHARTREUSE	#7FFF00	CHOCOLATE	#D2691E
CORAL	#FF7F50	CORNFLOWER	#6495ED
CORNSILK	#FFF8DC	CRIMSON	#DC143C
CYAN	#00FFFF	DARKBLUE	#00008B
DARKCYAN	#008B8B	DARKGOLDENROD	#B8860B
DARKGRAY	#A9A9A9	DARKGREEN	#006400
DARKKHAKI	#BDB76B	DARKMAGENTA	#8B008B
DARKOLIVEGREEN	#556B2F	DARKORANGE	#FF8C00
DARKORCHID	#9932CC	DARKRED	#8B0000
DARKSALMON	#E9967A	DARKSEAGREEN	#8FBC8B
DARKSLATEBLUE	#483D8B	DARKSLATEGREY	#2F4F4F
DARKTURQUOISE	#00CED1	DARKVIOLET	#9400D3
DEEPPINK	#FF1493	DEEPSKYBLUE	#00BFFF
DIMGRAY	#696969	DODGERBLUE	#1E90FF
FIREBRICK	#B22222	FLORALWHITE	#FFFAF0
FORESTGREEN	#228B22	FUCHIA	#FF00FF
GAINSBORO	#DCDCDC	GHOSTWHITE	#F8F8FF
GOLD	#FFD700	GOLDENROD	#DAA520
GRAY	#808080	GREEN	#008000

Part iii

TABLE 12.1 continued: Color Names and Their Hexadecimal Codes

Color Name	Code	Color Name	Code
GREENYELLOW	#ADFF2F	HONEYDEW	#F0FFF0
HOTPINK	#FF69B4	INDIANRED	#CD5C5C
INDIGO	#4B0082	IVORY	#FFFFF0
KHAKI	#F0E68C	LAVENDER	#E6E6FA
LAVENDERBLUSH	#FFF0F5	LAWNGREEN	#7CFC00
LEMONCHIFFON	#FFFACD	LIGHTBLUE	#ADD8E6
LIGHTCORAL	#F08080	LIGHTCYAN	#E0FFFF
LIGHTGOLDENRODYELLOW	#FAFAD2	LIGHTGREEN	#90EE90
LIGHTGREY	#D3D3D3	LIGHTPINK	#FFB6C1
LIGHTSALMON	#FFA07A	LIGHTSEAGREEN	#20B2AA
LIGHTSKYBLUE	#87CEFA	LIGHTSLATEGRAY	#778899
LIGHTSTEELBLUE	#B0C4DE	LIGHTYELLOW	#FFFFE0
LIME	#00FF00	LIMEGREEN	#32CD32
LINEN	#FAF0E6	MAGENTA	#FF00FF
MAROON	#800000	MEDIUMAQUAMARINE	#66CDAA
MEDIUMBLUE	#0000CD	MEDIUMORCHID	#BA55D3
MEDIUMPURPLE	#9370DB	MEDIUMSEAGREEN	#3CB371
MEDIUMSLATEBLUE	#7B68EE	MEDIUMSPRINGGREEN	#00FA9A
MEDIUMTURQUOISE	#48D1CC	MEDIUMVIOLETRED	#C71585
MIDNIGHTBLUE	#191970	MINTCREAM	#F5FFFA
MISTYROSE	#FFE4E1	MOCCASIN	#FFE4B5
NAVAJOWHITE	#FFDEAD	NAVY	#000080
OLDLACE	#FDF5E6	OLIVE	#808000
OLIVEDRAB	#6B8E23	ORANGE	#FFA500
ORANGERED	#FF4500	ORCHID	#DA70D6
PALEGOLDENROD	#EEE8AA	PALEGREEN	#98FB98
PALETURQUOISE	#AFEEEE	PALEVIOLETRED	#DB7093

TABLE 12.1 continued: Color Names and Their Hexadecimal Codes

COLOR NAME	CODE	COLOR NAME	CODE
PAPAYAWHIP	#FFEFD5	PEACHPUFF	#FFDAB9
PERU	#CD853F	PINK	#FFC0CB
PLUM	#DDA0DD	POWDERBLUE	#B0E0E6
PURPLE	#800080	RED	#FF0000
ROSYBROWN	#BC8F8F	ROYALBLUE	#4169E1
SADDLEBROWN	#8B4513	SALMON	#FA8072
SANDYBROWN	#F4A460	SEAGREEN	#2E8B57
SEASHELL	#FFF5EE	SIENNA	#A0522D
SILVER	#C0C0C0	SKYBLUE	#87CEEB
SLATEBLUE	#6A5ACD	SLATEGRAY	#708090
SNOW	#FFFAFA	SPRINGGREEN	#00FF7F
STEELBLUE	#4682B4	TAN	#D2B48C
TEAL	#008080	THISTLE	#D8BFD8
TOMATO	#FF6347	TURQUOISE	#40E0D0
VIOLET	#EE82EE	WHEAT	#F5DEB3
WHITE	#FFFFFF	WHITESMOKE	#F5F5F5
YELLOW	#FFFF00	YELLOWGREEN	#9ACD32

Part iii

NOTE

See Chapter 5 for more information on using color in your Web pages.

Scripting the Dynamic Effects

We've set up a number of segments in our Web page, and if you open it in IE at this point, you'll see a display that looks like Figure 12.1. However, a user can't interact with this page in its present form to make it look like Figure 12.2. To enable interactivity, we have to add scripts.

Scripts make a Web page come alive. If we think of the elements on a page as actors on a stage, then a script tells them how to behave and interact with one another.

You write a script in a *scripting language*, a computer language designed to work inside a specific environment, such as an HTML document. Two scripting languages are prominent. One, VBScript, is a subset of Microsoft's popular Visual Basic. The other, JavaScript, has some of the syntax of Java, but is very different from Java. Both VBScript and JavaScript work with software structures called *objects*.

NOTE

You'll learn more about JavaScript and working with objects in Chapters 14 and 15.

Unlike programming languages that can create applications that run by themselves, a scripting language requires a piece of software called an *interpreter* to run its programs. IE has built-in interpreters for VBScript and JavaScript, and Navigator has a built-in interpreter for JavaScript. In this first IE-based exercise, we'll work with VBScript.

In an HTML document, one way to write scripts is to put them inside this set of tags:

```
<SCRIPT Language = "VBScript">
<!--
-->
</SCRIPT>
```

You place this code in your document somewhere between <HEAD> and </HEAD>.

You put the body of your script between <!-- and -->. These two structures represent the beginning and end of a comment. Since a browser ignores comments, it won't process your script if it doesn't have the interpreter specified by the Language attribute in the <SCRIPT> tag.

Our script will set up the behaviors for the Web page elements for these situations:

▶ The mouse passes into the heading

▶ Mouse-clicks occur with the cursor in the heading

▶ The mouse passes out of the heading

The Mouse Passes into the Heading

As I said earlier, when the mouse passes into the heading, we want the color of the heading to change, the large-font message to become visible, and the box in the lower-right corner to change its colors and its content.

Passing the cursor into the heading is an *onMouseOver* event. (Think of an *event* as a signal to the Web page from the outside world.) Remember that we've given the heading an ID so we can refer to it in our script. We'll write a *subroutine* for the heading's onMouseOver event.

We start the subroutine with this line:

```
Sub h1Header_onMouseOver
```

Sub lets the browser know that a subroutine definition follows, h1Header is the ID we gave the heading, and onMouseOver is the specific event that causes the subroutine to respond.

One of the behaviors that we want to happen as a result of this event is the change in the heading's color. We represent the heading's color as

```
h1Header.Style.Color
```

You can read this expression as "h1Header's Style's Color." In this context, a dot is like an apostrophe followed by *s*.

NOTE

A more detailed explanation is that h1Header is an object, Style is a property of the object, and Color is a property of Style.

To change the heading's color from the default black to something a bit livelier, like goldenrod, type

```
h1Header.Style.Color = "Goldenrod"
```

Next, we'll make the message with the large font visible. The ID for that message is divMessage, so the code to make it visible is

```
divMessage.Style.Visibility = "Visible"
```

Similarly, we switch the Visibility property for the two boxes in the lower-right corner of the page:

```
divReady.Style.Visibility = "Hidden"
divStarted.Style.Visibility = "Visible"
```

We must end every subroutine with

```
End Sub
```

The entire subroutine for the heading's `onMouseOver` event is:

```
Sub h1Header_onMouseOver
    h1Header.Style.Color = "Goldenrod"
    divMessage.Style.Visibility = "Visible"
    divReady.Style.Visibility = "Hidden"
    divStarted.Style.Visibility = "Visible"
End Sub
```

The script in this subroutine illustrates a fundamental principle of DHTML—it changes CSS information in response to a user event.

Mouse-Clicks Occur with the Cursor in the Heading

When the mouse passes into the heading and the user clicks the mouse, the message in the middle of the page becomes visible, and the box in the middle of the page splits into four boxes that move toward the corners of the page with each click. The effect is something like animation, as the boxes appear to move across the page.

You already know how to make an element visible:

```
pLearn.Style.Visibility = "Visible"
```

Now for the tricky part—moving the boxes. Let's say we want the first box, `divBox1`, to move 20 pixels to the left and 20 pixels toward the top each time we click the mouse. This composite movement will take `divBox1` toward the upper-left corner. The box to its immediate right, `divBox2`, should go 20 pixels to the right and 20 toward the top (i.e., toward the upper-right corner). `divBox3` should move 20 to the left and 20 toward the bottom, and `divBox4` should move 20 to the right and 20 toward the bottom. (You can use other numbers of pixels if you like.) In the coordinate system of browsers, the upper-left corner is at (0,0) so that movement toward the right is positive, movement toward the left is negative, movement toward the bottom is positive, and movement toward the top is negative.

With all these considerations in mind, we can set up the desired movement with:

```
Call MoveElementBy(divBox1,-20,-20)
Call MoveElementBy(divBox2,20,-20)
```

```
Call MoveElementBy(divBox3,-20,20)
Call MoveElementBy(divBox4,20,20)
```

Each line calls the subroutine MoveElementBy, which takes three *arguments* (items a subroutine needs in order to do its job)—the ID of the element to move, the number of pixels to move it in the horizontal direction, and the number of pixels to move it in the vertical direction.

This is all very straightforward, except for one problem: VBScript has no built-in subroutine called MoveElementBy. Where will this subroutine come from? We have to build it ourselves. The first line of the subroutine's definition should look like this:

```
Subroutine MoveElementBy(ElementID, LeftMovementAmount,
TopMovementAmount)
```

Setting this up is a little more challenging than it looks, because MoveElementBy has to move an element a specified number of pixels. The positional information of an element, however, is not in numerical form—it's in a string. For example, if divBox1 is 200 pixels from the left edge of the window, the value of divBox1.Style.Left isn't the number 200, it's the string "200px". We somehow have to turn "200px" into the number 200.

NOTE
There's a way around this, but I want to take the opportunity to show you some of the aspects of VBScript.

Fortunately, VBScript provides some help. We'll use two built-in *functions* to turn the string "200px" into the string "200", and another built-in function to convert the string "200" into the integer 200. (In VBScript, a function is like a subroutine except that it returns a value.)

The function InStr searches a string for the presence of a target string. If InStr finds the target, it returns the position in which the target begins. For example,

```
InStr("200px", "px")
```

returns 4. Our strategy, then, will be to set a variable equal to

```
InStr(ElementID.Style.Left,"px")
```

and another variable equal to

```
InStr(ElementID.Style.Top,"px")
```

where ElementID is the ID of the element we're moving:

```
intPxPositionLeft = InStr(ElementID.Style.Left,"px")
intPxPositionTop = InStr(ElementID.Style.Top,"px")
```

The int prefix indicates that the variables hold integer information. We then use these variables in another built-in function, called Left. This function starts from the leftmost character in a string and returns a specified number of characters. The expression

```
Left("200px",3)
```

returns the string "200". We'll take the value that Left returns and use it as the argument for the VBScript function CInt, which converts a string into an integer. The expression

```
CInt(Left(ElementID.Style.Left, intPxPositionLeft-1))
```

turns an element's Left edge location into an integer, and

```
CInt(Left(ElementID.Style.Top, intPxPositionTop-1))
```

turns the element's Top edge location into an integer.

Here's the VBScript for moving the boxes in response to a mouse-click:

```
Sub h1Header_onClick
  pLearn.Style.Visibility = "Visible"
  Call MoveElementBy(divBox1,-20,-20)
  Call MoveElementBy(divBox2,20,-20)
  Call MoveElementBy(divBox3,-20,20)
  Call MoveElementBy(divBox4,20,20)
End Sub
Sub MoveElementBy(ElementID,LeftMovementAmount,
TopMovementAmount)
  dim intPxPositionLeft
   dim intPxPositionTop
  intPxPositionLeft = InStr(ElementID.Style.Left,"px")
  intPxPositionTop = InStr(ElementID.Style.Top,"px")
  ElementID.Style.Left = _
   CInt(Left(ElementID.Style.Left,intPxPositionLeft-1)) + _
    LeftMovementAmount
```

```
ElementID.Style.Top = _
    CInt(Left(ElementID.Style.Top,intPxPositionTop-1)) +
    TopMovementAmount
End Sub
```

> **NOTE**
> The underscore is VBScript's line-continuation character.

In the second subroutine, the `dim` statement defines the variables we use to store the returned values of the `InStr` function. VBScript allows you to create variables on the fly, but it's a good idea to define them explicitly as we've done here.

The Mouse Passes Out of the Heading

After the scripting you've just created, the script for moving the mouse out of the heading is pretty tame:

```
Sub h1Header_onMouseOut
    h1Header.Style.Color = "Black"
    divBox1.Style.Top = 200
    divBox1.Style.Left = 150
    divBox2.Style.Top = 200
    divBox2.Style.Left = 270
    divBox3.Style.Top = 235
    divBox3.Style.Left = 150
    divBox4.Style.Top = 235
    divBox4.Style.Left = 270
    divMessage.Style.Visibility = "Hidden"
    divReady.Style.Visibility = "Visible"
    divStarted.Style.Visibility = "Hidden"
    pLearn.Style.Visibility = "Hidden"
End Sub
```

This Sub just returns all the elements to their original settings.

An Important Tip

If you save your work and open the page in IE, it will look like Figure 12.1 and your scripts will enable you to perform mouse actions that activate the dynamic effects. You'll encounter one problem, however. Moving the mouse into and out of the heading will result in flicker; because it's text, the heading sets off an irregularly shaped area—sometimes the cursor is in that area, sometimes it's not, and it's not always obvious which is which. The irregularity of the heading area's shape causes another problem—mouse-clicks on the heading might not work as you'd like them to.

You can easily solve these problems by wrapping the heading in a DIV and positioning the DIV at the top of the page. Here's what the HTML for the heading should look like:

```
<DIV Style = "Position:Absolute;Left:10;Top:0;Width:100%">
<H1 ID = h1Header Style = "text-align:center">Dynamic HTML:
Master the Essentials</H1>
<HR>
</DIV>
```

Including the <HR> tag in the DIV preserves the positional relationship between the heading and the horizontal line.

The Whole File

Here's the entire First Dynamic IE.htm file

First Dynamic IE.htm

```
<HTML>
<HEAD>
<STYLE Type = "text/css">
.bluebox {background-color:blue;
     color:blue;
     text-align:center;
     width:120;
     height:60}
</STYLE>


<SCRIPT LANGUAGE = "VBSCRIPT">
```

```
Sub h1Header_onMouseOver
     h1Header.Style.Color = "Goldenrod"
     divMessage.Style.Visibility = "Visible"
     divReady.Style.Visibility = "Hidden"
     divStarted.Style.Visibility = "Visible"
End Sub

Sub h1Header_onMouseOut
     h1Header.Style.Color = "Black"
     divBox1.Style.Top = 180
     divBox1.Style.Left = 150
     divBox2.Style.Top = 180
     divBox2.Style.Left = 270
     divBox3.Style.Top = 240
     divBox3.Style.Left = 150
     divBox4.Style.Top = 240
     divBox4.Style.Left = 270
     divMessage.Style.Visibility = "Hidden"
     divReady.Style.Visibility = "Visible"
     divStarted.Style.Visibility = "Hidden"
End Sub

Sub h1Header_onClick
     pLearn.Style.Visibility = "Visible"
     Call MoveElementBy(divBox1,-20,-20)
     Call MoveElementBy(divBox2,20,-20)
     Call MoveElementBy(divBox3,-20,20)
     Call MoveElementBy(divBox4,20,20)
End Sub

Sub MoveElementBy(ElementID,LeftMovementAmount,
TopMovementAmount)
     pPositionTop = InStr(ElementID.Style.Top,"px")
     pPositionLeft = InStr(ElementID.Style.Left,"px")
```

```
        ElementID.Style.Top = _
         CInt(Left(ElementID.Style.Top,pPositionTop-1)) + _
    TopMovementAmount
         ElementID.Style.Left = _
          CInt(Left(ElementID.Style.Left,pPositionLeft-1)) + _
    LeftMovementAmount
End Sub


</SCRIPT>
<TITLE>My First Dynamic HTML Page</TITLE>
</HEAD>
<BODY Style = "background-color:'Silver'">
<DIV Style = "Position:Absolute;Left:10;Top:0:Width:100%">
<H1 ID = h1Header Style = "text-align:center">Dynamic HTML:
Master the Essentials</H1>
<HR>
</DIV>
<DIV ID = divMessage Style =
"Position:Absolute;Left:5%;Top:10%;
Visibility:Hidden;z-index:-1;font-style:normal;
font-weight:bold;font-family:Normal;
font-size:50;color:'White'">
<P> Topics in this book include
<UL>
<LI> Scripting
<LI> Cascading Style Sheets
<LI> Animation
<LI> ... And Many More!
</UL>
</P>
</DIV>


<DIV ID = divLearn
Style="Position:Absolute;Left:180;Top:200;Width:210;
z-index:0;">
```

```
<P ID = pLearn Style = "font-family:cursive;font-size:15pt;
font-weight:bold">
Learn how to create striking effects on your Web pages.
</P>
</DIV>


<DIV ID = divBox1 Class = "bluebox"
Style="Position:Absolute;Left:150;Top:180;z-index:1">
</DIV>


<DIV ID = divBox2 Class = "bluebox"
Style="Position:Absolute;Left:270;Top:180;z-index:1">
</DIV>


<DIV ID = divBox3 Class = "bluebox"
Style="Position:Absolute;Left:150;Top:240;z-index:1">
</DIV>


<DIV ID = divBox4 Class = "bluebox"
STYLE="Position:Absolute;Left:270;Top:240;z-index:1">
</DIV>


<DIV ID = divReady Style =
"Position:Absolute;Top:70%;Left:80%;Width:10%;
z-index:1;Visibility:Visible">
<P Style = "text-align:center;font-family:cursive;Background-
Color:'Beige';Color:Chocolate">
Are<BR>You<BR>Ready?</P>
</DIV>


<DIV ID = divStarted Style =
"Position:Absolute;Top:70%;Left:80%;Width:10%;
z-index:0;Visibility:Hidden">
<P Style = "text-align:center;font-family:cursive;Background-
Color:'BlanchedAlmond';Color:Blue">
```

```
Let's<BR>Get<BR>Started</P>
</DIV>

</BODY>
</HTML>
```

Open this file in IE to see all the effects that turn Figure 12.1 into Figure 12.2.

USING DHTML IN NAVIGATOR

To round out your introduction to Dynamic HTML, let's put a similar page together for Netscape Navigator. We'll have to make a few changes, but most of the effects will remain:

- ▶ Moving the mouse into the heading will change the color of the heading and make a large-font message appear.

- ▶ Mouse-clicks will make boxes in the middle of the page move out toward the corners. In this version, the mouse-click will occur on an on-screen button, rather than on the heading.

- ▶ A mouse-click on another button will return all the elements to their original settings.

I've eliminated the small changeable box from this page, but you can put it in as an exercise. Figure 12.4 shows what this page looks like in Netscape with the dynamic effects visible.

To start things off, open your Template, save it as First Dynamic Nav.htm, and change the title to **My First Dynamic Web Page**. Next, change the background color to silver. In the IE version, you did this by putting the style sheet

```
Style = "background-color:'silver'"
```

into the <BODY> tag. If you do that in the Navigator version, you'll run into trouble. As you'll see again and again, Navigator is quirky when it comes to rendering colors specified in style sheets. (Future versions of Navigator will no doubt solve this problem.) To work around this, insert the deprecated attribute Bgcolor into the <BODY> tag:

```
Bgcolor = "Silver"
```

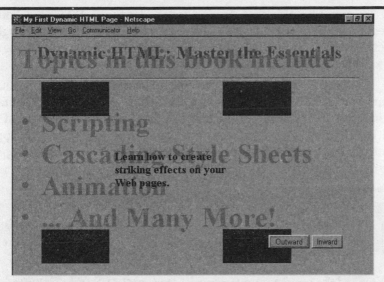

FIGURE 12.4: Your DHTML page in Netscape, with dynamic effects visible

The Heading and the Horizontal Line

We start out as before, by creating the heading and the horizontal line beneath it. The HTML is the same as before, so your file should look like this:

```
<HTML>
<HEAD>
</HEAD>
<TITLE>My First Dynamic HTML Page</TITLE>
<BODY Bgcolor = "Silver">
<Center>
<H1>Dynamic HTML: Master the Essentials</H1></Center>
<HR>
</BODY>
</HTML>
```

The *<LAYER>* Tag

In our IE version, we used <DIV> tags to divide our page into segments. We then used VBScript to apply dynamic effects to those divisions.

To segment a Web page, Navigator provides the <LAYER> tag. You begin a segment with <LAYER> and end it with </LAYER>. Although both <LAYER> and <DIV> segment a page and support the z-index, they differ in important ways.

Netscape designed the <LAYER> tag to behave like a piece of transparent paper laid on top of a Web page. Between <LAYER> and </LAYER>, you insert HTML elements. You provide the <LAYER> tag with an ID (via either ID or Name) and with attributes and values that specify its appearance and position. You use JavaScript to change those values in response to user events. Dynamic effects result from these scripted changes.

NOTE
As I write this, <LAYER> is a cornerstone of Netscape's Dynamic HTML. This may change, however, because the World Wide Web Consortium has rejected the <LAYER> tag.

One of the important differences between <DIV> and <LAYER> is that the <LAYER> tag doesn't work with inline style sheets. You can use inline style sheets to set styles for HTML elements that reside inside a layer, but you can't assign IDs to these elements and then script them. You can only script behaviors for the <LAYER> tag, and programmatically change only the attributes that the <LAYER> tag supports. This limits the type of scripting you can do, compared with the Microsoft version. To create similar effects from one browser to the other, you often have to exercise some ingenuity, as you'll see later in this chapter.

Default positioning presents another important difference. If you don't include values for TOP and LEFT, a <DIV> defaults to a position based on where it appears in the flow of the HTML document. A <LAYER>, on the other hand, defaults to a position seven pixels from the left edge of the browser window and seven pixels from the top. With multiple layers this can get messy, as they will all default to the same position.

Back to the Heading and the Horizontal Line

Now that you know about Netscape's <LAYER> tag, let's put the heading and the horizontal line into a layer. Remember, we start with <LAYER> and end with </LAYER>, and we have to provide positional information:

```
<LAYER Name = layerHeader Left = 10 Top = 10 z-index = 0
<Center>
<H1>Dynamic HTML: Master the Essentials</H1></Center>
```

```
<HR>
</LAYER>
```

Notice the Name attribute, and note also that we've provided a z-index value. This value, 0, puts the layer at the same level as the document. Higher numbers make the layer appear on top of the document; negative numbers make the layer appear below the document.

We added the z-index because we can't reference the heading and change its color with a script. Instead, we have to exercise the ingenuity I mentioned in the last section. To make the heading appear to change color, we'll create another heading, which resides in a layer just below this one; give the new heading a different color; make the layer invisible; and script a visibility swap. Here's the other heading and its enclosing layer:

```
<LAYER Name = layerUnderHeader Left = 10 Top = 10 z-index = -1
Visibility = "hide">

<Center>

<H1 Style = "color:'khaki'">Dynamic HTML: Master the
Essentials</H1></Center>

<HR>
</LAYER>
```

The z-index, -1, and the Visibility value, "hide", hint at the script that will appear to change the color of the page's heading.

NAVIGATOR, COLORS, AND CSS

I didn't use goldenrod for the new heading color this time, because Navigator renders it as a darkish green when you specify this color in a CSS. Of course, Navigator renders khaki as a darkish green in this context, too. As I pointed out before, Navigator—at least my release—is iffy when you specify colors in a CSS. If you use the code values instead of the names, you'll get the same result.

You can prove to yourself that Navigator understands the colors in Table 12.1, however. Within any of the <LAYER> tags that we create in this exercise, set the Bgcolor attribute equal to any of the color-names in Table 12.1. You'll find them rendered very nicely as background colors when you open the file in Navigator. In fact, we'll use one of those colors when we set up our movable boxes. (Remember that we used Bgcolor as a substitute for Style = "background-color: 'Silver'" when we set the background color for the body of the page.)

The Hidden Message

As in the IE version, we'll implement the large-font hidden message by putting it inside a paragraph, and we'll provide the styling specifications in an inline style sheet:

```
<P Style = "color:'green'; font-size:50px;
font-weight:bold">Topics in this book include

<UL Style = "color:'green'; font-size:50px;
font-weight:bold">

<LI> Scripting

<LI> Cascading Style Sheets

<LI> Animation

<LI> ... And Many More!

</UL>

</P>
```

You'll immediately see three differences between the IE version and this one:

▶ In the IE version, we didn't put a style sheet in the <UL> tag. In IE, the <UL> tag inherited the <P> tag's style. In Navigator, it doesn't, although the <LI> elements do inherit the <UL>'s style.

▶ In IE, we didn't put px after the font-size value. With no unit after the value, IE defaults to px; Navigator does not. If you omit the unit name after the value, Navigator defaults to normal-sized font.

▶ Although Figure 12.4 isn't in color, you probably noticed that the color of the large-font message isn't white. As you can see from the style sheets, we've set it to green. Why? In the context of a style sheet, Navigator doesn't render white as a text color—it defaults to black. (This is consistent with the situation I described in the sidebar "Navigator, Colors, and CSS.") Later releases of Navigator 4.x will probably clear this up. If you like, you can use the <FONT> tag to set the text color to white, but I'd prefer that you became accustomed to working with style sheets rather than with deprecated elements.

Now let's put this message in a layer and give the layer a name, a position, a visibility, and a z-index. Precede the <P> tag with

```
<LAYER ID = layerMessage Left=10 Top=10 Visibility = "hide"
z-index = -2 >
```

and follow the </P> tag with

```
</LAYER>
```

The Message at the Center of the Page

The paragraph that holds the centered message is the same as the one in the IE version, except that it has no ID. The <LAYER> tag that precedes it holds the position, width, and z-index specifications:

```
<LAYER NAME = layerLearn LEFT = 180 TOP = 200 Width = 210
z-index = 0>
<P Style="font-family:Cursive;font-weight:bold;
font-size:15pt">
Learn how to create striking effects on your Web pages.
</P>
</LAYER>
```

The Movable Boxes

The easiest way to implement the movable boxes is to create each one as a separate layer and position them appropriately. To make them appear as blue boxes, we set the (somewhat infamous) Bgcolor attribute to blue:

```
<LAYER NAME = layerBox1 Bgcolor = "blue" LEFT = 150 TOP = 180
Width = 120 Height = 60 z-index = 1>
</LAYER>


<LAYER NAME = layerBox2 Bgcolor = "blue" LEFT = 270 TOP = 180
Width = 120 Height = 60 z-index = 1>
</LAYER>


<LAYER NAME = layerBox3 Bgcolor = "blue" LEFT = 150 TOP = 240
Width = 120 Height = 60 z-index = 1>
</LAYER>
```

```
<LAYER NAME = layerBox4 Bgcolor = "blue" LEFT = 270 TOP = 240
Width = 120 Height = 60 z-index = 1>
</LAYER>
```

The Clickable Buttons

This version of our Web page has two buttons in the lower-right corner. One is labeled Outward, and the other is labeled Inward. Clicking on the Outward button will move the boxes toward the corners, and clicking on the Inward button will return them to their original positions.

I put these buttons on the page because they support the onClick event. The <LAYER> tag does not support this event, so clicking on the heading would have no effect. Since I wanted a mouse-click to move the boxes, I added these buttons.

The buttons are examples of *form controls*, so named because they reside between <FORM> and </FORM> tags. You specify a button inside an <INPUT> tag by assigning the value button to the attribute Type. You label the button by assigning a string to the attribute Value:

```
<FORM>
<INPUT Type = button Value = "Outward">
<INPUT Type = button Value = "Inward">
</FORM>
```

We wrap the form in a layer so that we can position it within the page. Precede the <FORM> tag with

```
<LAYER Left = 450 Top = 350>
```

and follow the </FORM> tag with </LAYER>.

Scripting the Dynamic Effects

Once again, we'll write scripts to make our Web page come alive. This time we'll write our scripts in JavaScript, the only scripting language Navigator supports.

In our IE version, we put VBScript between <SCRIPT> and </SCRIPT> tags. In this version, we'll write our JavaScript inline (i.e., inside HTML tags). It's not necessary to do it this way—I'm just illustrating another way to add script. Both ways, tagged and inline, work in both browsers.

The Mouse Passes Into and Out of the Heading

We begin our inline scripting with the events associated with the heading. The heading, you'll remember, resides in a LAYER called layerHeader. Since we're concerned with the mouse moving into and out of the heading, we'll write script for the onMouseOver and onMouseOut events inside the <LAYER> tag for layerHeader.

When the mouse moves into the heading, we want to make the large-font message appear and have the heading's color change. We're making the heading seem to change colors by making layerHeader invisible and layerUnderHeader visible. This means that we'll want these settings:

```
layerMessage.visibility = "show"
layerHeader.visibility = "hide"
layerUnderHeader.visibility = "show"
```

To put these settings into inline JavaScript code, you write them inside a quoted string and separate them with semicolons. (Make sure you change the double quotes around the attribute values to single quotes.) Then you set this string as the value of onMouseOver and put the whole thing inside the <LAYER> tag:

```
<LAYER Name = layerHeader Left = 10 Top = 10 z-index = 0
onMouseOver = "layerMessage.visibility = 'show';
        layerHeader.visibility = 'hide';
        layerUnderHeader.visibility = 'show'"
```

Don't add the closing angle bracket yet, because you still have to add the code for onMouseOut, which returns the settings to their starting values:

```
onMouseOut = "layerMessage.visibility = 'hide';
        layerUnderHeader.visibility = 'hide'
        layerHeader.visibility = 'show'" >
```

Note the closing angle bracket, indicating that we've finished scripting the behaviors for this layer.

Part iii

WARNING

JavaScript is case-sensitive, so don't even think about beginning visibility with an uppercase "V."

Mouse-Clicks Occur on the Response Buttons

We finish by scripting behaviors for the onClick event in the tags that define the on-screen response buttons. When we click the button labeled Outward, we want the boxes to move outward, and when we click the button labeled Inward, we want the boxes to move back into their starting positions.

Fortunately, JavaScript layers have built-in *methods* that will handle these effects for us. (Think of a method as a procedure that the layer knows how to follow.) The first method, offset, is something like the MoveElementBy subroutine we wrote. It takes two arguments—the distance to move the layer in the horizontal direction and the distance to move it in the vertical direction. Here's the code to write inside the first response button's <INPUT> tag:

```
<INPUT Type = button Value = "Outward"
  onClick = "layerBox1.offset(-20,-20);
        layerBox2.offset(20,-20);
        layerBox3.offset(-20,20);
        layerBox4.offset(20,20);">
```

The second built-in method is called moveTo. As its name suggests, moveTo moves a layer to a location specified by the method's two arguments:

```
<INPUT Type = button Value = "Inward"
  onClick = "layerBox1.moveTo(150,180);
        layerBox2.moveTo(270,180);
        layerBox3.moveTo(150,240);
        layerBox4.moveTo(270,240);">
```

The Whole File

Here's the entire First Dynamic Nav.htm listing:

First Dynamic Nav.htm

```
<HTML>
<HEAD>
</HEAD>
<TITLE>My First Dynamic HTML Page</TITLE>
<BODY Bgcolor = "Silver">
<LAYER Name = layerHeader Left = 10 Top = 10 z-index = 0
onMouseOver = "layerMessage.visibility = 'show';
               layerHeader.visibility = 'hide';
               layerUnderHeader.visibility = 'show'"

onMouseOut = "layerMessage.visibility = 'hide';
              layerUnderHeader.visibility = 'hide'
              layerHeader.visibility = 'show'" >
<Center>
<H1>Dynamic HTML: Master the Essentials</H1></Center>
<HR>
</LAYER>


<LAYER Name = layerUnderHeader Left = 10 Top = 10
z-index = -1 Visibility = "hide">
<Center>
<H1 Style = "color:'khaki'">Dynamic HTML: Master the
Essentials</H1></Center>
<HR>
</LAYER>
<Layer ID = layerMessage Left=10 Top=10
Visibility = "hide" z-index = -2 >
```

```
<P Style = "color:'green'; font-size:50px;
font-weight:bold">Topics in this book include

<UL Style = "color:'green'; font-size:50px;
font-weight:bold">

<LI> Scripting

<LI> Cascading Style Sheets

<LI> Animation

<LI> ... And Many More!

</UL>

</P>

</LAYER>


<LAYER NAME = layerLearn LEFT = 180 TOP = 200 Width = 210
z-index = 0>

<P Style="font-family:Cursive;font-weight:bold;
font-size:15pt">

Learn how to create striking effects on your Web pages.

</P>

</LAYER>


<LAYER NAME = layerBox1 Bgcolor = "blue" LEFT = 150 TOP = 180
Width = 120 Height = 60 z-index = 1>

</LAYER>


<LAYER NAME = layerBox2 Bgcolor = "blue" LEFT = 270 TOP = 180
Width = 120 Height = 60 z-index = 1>

</LAYER>


<LAYER NAME = layerBox3 Bgcolor = "blue" LEFT = 150 TOP = 240
Width = 120 Height = 60 z-index = 1>

</LAYER>


<LAYER NAME = layerBox4 Bgcolor = "blue" LEFT = 270 TOP = 240
Width = 120 Height = 60 z-index = 1>

</LAYER>
```

```
<LAYER Left = 450 Top = 350>
<FORM>
<INPUT Type = button Value = "Outward"
  onClick = "layerBox1.offset(-20,-20);
        layerBox2.offset(20,-20);
        layerBox3.offset(-20,20);
        layerBox4.offset(20,20);">


<INPUT Type = button Value = "Inward"
  onClick = "layerBox1.moveTo(150,180);
        layerBox2.moveTo(270,180);
        layerBox3.moveTo(150,240);
        layerBox4.moveTo(270,240);">


</FORM>
</LAYER>
</BODY>
</HTML>
```

Open this file in Navigator to see the scripted effects. Mousing over
the heading will make the heading's color appear to change and will display the hidden message. Moving the mouse out of the header will return
the heading color to its starting value. Clicking the Outward button will
make the box in the middle split apart, and the resulting four boxes will
move toward the four corners of the Web page. Clicking the Inward button will immediately move all the boxes back to the center.

WHAT'S NEXT?

You now have an idea of what you can achieve with DHTML and its combination of HTML, cascading style sheets, and scripting. You also have a
feel for the similarities and differences between the dueling DHTMLs
from Microsoft and Netscape. In the next chapter, you'll look at a feature
that's specific to the Internet Explorer version of DHTML—the ability to
change the content of downloaded Web page elements.

Chapter 13

WORKING WITH TEXT:
DYNAMICALLY CHANGING CONTENT

In the previous chapter, you got a glimpse of the power of
Dynamic HTML. You were introduced to techniques, such
as animation and drag-and-drop, that change the location
and appearance of objects on a page after the page has downloaded. The Internet Explorer version of DHTML doesn't end
there: In addition to changing a downloaded element's style,
you can change its content, as the exercises in this chapter
will show.

Adapted from *Dynamic HTML: Master the Essentials*, by
Joseph Schmuller
ISBN 0-7821-2277-9   608 pages $29.99

NOTE

The information in this chapter is specific to Microsoft Internet Explorer; the technology that is discussed will not work in any version of Netscape Navigator.

INTRODUCING *TEXTRANGES*

The `textRange` object is an IE structure that enables you to refer to a particular part of a document. You can create a `textRange` object that encompasses part of a page. The text within that part of the page is then a property of that object—a property you can manipulate via scripts and events to perform useful tasks, such as finding and replacing specific words and phrases.

Here's an exercise to acquaint you with this concept. Figure 13.1 shows the page you're about to build. Based on a file called `Buttons and Text.htm`, it includes two buttons, a text area, and a text input. The text in these elements will change as a result of event-handlers that you'll script.

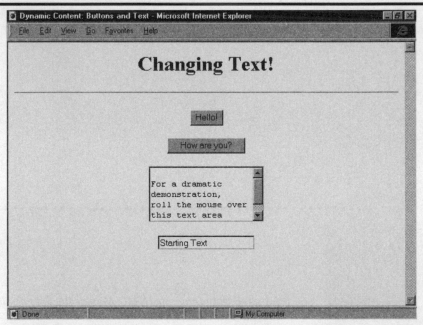

FIGURE 13.1: `Buttons and Text.htm`, a page that illustrates the `textRange` concept

Start by creating the file in your text editor, and save it as `Buttons and Text.htm`. Here's how the HTML should look:

```
<HTML>
<HEAD>
<TITLE>Dynamic Content: Buttons and Text</TITLE>

<BODY>
<H1 Style = "text-align:center">
Changing Text!
</H1>
<HR>
<CENTER>
<BR>

<BUTTON>
Hello!
</BUTTON>
<BR><BR>

<BUTTON>
How are you?
</BUTTON>
<BR><BR>
<TEXTAREA Rows = 5>
For a dramatic demonstration,
roll the mouse over this text area
</TEXTAREA>

<FORM>
<INPUT Type = Text Value = "Starting Text">
</FORM>

</CENTER>

</BODY>
</HTML>
```

We'll write `newText`, a JScript function that provides new text for each element. An element will call the function, with the new text as one of its arguments. The function will create a `textRange` on that element and then set the `textRange`'s text to that argument.

In the HEAD, create a SCRIPT element. Since we'll be writing a JScript function (every JavaScript procedure is a function), we can omit the `Language` attribute. As always, the first line of the function provides the name and the arguments, along with an opening curly bracket to start things off:

```
function newText(ScreenElement,NewCaption) {
```

The `ScreenElement` argument will refer to the on-screen element calling the function as a result of an event, and the `NewCaption` argument will contain the new text.

Now we'll create the `textRange` object. To do this, we invoke the `createTextRange` method, which is available only on BUTTON, TEXT input, TEXT AREA, and BODY elements. For our function, the code is

```
r = ScreenElement.createTextRange();
```

The final step is to set the `text` property of the newly created `textRange` object to the new caption we want to display. The function's second argument supplies the new caption:

```
r.text = NewCaption;
```

Close it with a right curly bracket, and you're done.

Now we have to call this function from an event associated with each element. For the buttons, we can call it as a result of a click or a double-click, and for the other two, we can call it as a result of a `mouseover` event. (Other combinations are possible, of course.) In the opening tag for the first button, add

```
onclick = "newText(this,'Clicked')"
```

The JavaScript keyword that `this` refers to the current object.

In the opening tag for the second button, add

```
onclick = "newText(this,'I am fine')"
ondblclick = "newText(this,'')"
```

In <TEXTAREA>, add

```
onmouseover = "newText(this,'I Have Changed!')"
```

and in the TEXT input,

```
onmouseover = "newText(this,'Finishing Text')"
```

The entire Buttons and Text.htm file should look like this:

Buttons and Text.htm

```
<HTML>
<HEAD>
<TITLE>Dynamic Content: Buttons and Text</TITLE>
<SCRIPT>
function newText(ScreenElement,NewCaption) {
r = ScreenElement.createTextRange();
r.text = NewCaption;

}
</SCRIPT>
<BODY>
<H1 Style = "text-align:center">
Changing Text!
</H1>
<HR>
<CENTER>
<BR>

<BUTTON onclick = "newText(this,'Clicked')">
Hello!
</BUTTON>
<BR><BR>
```

```
<BUTTON onclick = "newText(this,'I am fine')"
ondblclick = "newText(this,'')">
How are you?
</BUTTON>
<BR><BR>

<TEXTAREA Rows = 5 onmouseover = "newText(this,'I Have
Changed!')">
For a dramatic demonstration,
roll the mouse over this text area
</TEXTAREA>

<FORM>
<INPUT Type = Text Value = "Starting Text"
onmouseover = "newText(this,'Finishing Text')">
</FORM>

</CENTER>

</BODY>
</HTML>
```

After you open the page in IE, click the buttons, and move your mouse over the other two elements, it will look like Figure 13.2.

If you double-click on the second button, you'll see it shrink as a result of passing an empty string as the second argument to newText for the double-click event. Click again and I am fine returns.

Here's some behavior to note. After you've changed the text in all four controls, press F5 to refresh the page. You'll find that the original button captions return, but the original text lines in the other two elements do not. Select View ➤ Source and then select File ➤ Save in your text editor. Return to the page, press F5, and all the original values come back. Using the createTextRange method to alter text on buttons produces a different result than using it to alter text in text inputs and text areas.

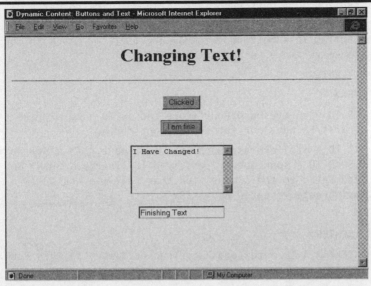

FIGURE 13.2:   Buttons and Text.htm after you click the buttons and move the mouse over the text area and the text input

MOVING THROUGH TEXT

Let's move on to another level of complexity. textRanges have a number of methods, and we'll use some of them in the next exercise to move through a document's BODY. As we do, we'll track the values of some textRange properties. Figure 13.3 shows the page we'll create.

Lay out the page according to this HTML code:

```
<HTML>
<HEAD>
<TITLE>Moving Through Text</TITLE>
</HEAD>
<BODY ID = bodyDocument>
<H1 style = "text-align:center">Moving Through Text</H1>
<HR>
<CENTER>
<BUTTON ID = buttonReset Title = "Click to reset the
textRange">Reset</BUTTON>
<BUTTON ID = buttonMove Title = "Click to move the textRange
forward">Forward</BUTTON>
```

Part iii

```
<BUTTON ID = buttonBookmark Title = "Click to set a
bookmark">Bookmark</BUTTON>

<BUTTON ID = buttonMoveToBookmark Title = "Click to move to a
bookmark">Move to Bookmark</BUTTON>

</CENTER>

<BR>

<P ID = pGettysburg>Four score and <B ID = boldPhrase>seven
years</B> ago, our fathers brought forth,

<I ID = italicPhrase>upon this continent,</I> a new nation,
<SPAN ID = spanLiberty>conceived in liberty,</SPAN> and
dedicated to the proposition that "all men are <B ID =
boldCreated>created equal</B>"</P>


<CENTER>

<TEXTAREA ID = textareaRangeTracker Rows = 10 Cols = 60>

</TEXTAREA>


</BODY>

</HTML>
```

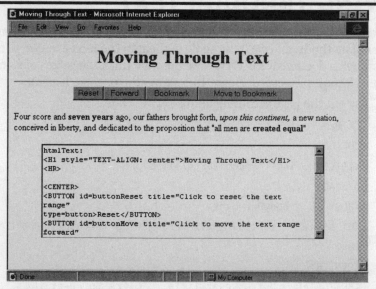

FIGURE 13.3: Moving through Text.htm, a page that uses textRange methods
and tracks textRange properties

We'll use a technique you've seen before, a continuously updated multiline text area, to track property values as we weave our way through the BODY. As the file and Figure 13.3 show, a famous sentence will serve as our test bed. Note the tags in that sentence:

```
<P ID = pGettysburg>Four score and <B ID = boldPhrase>seven
years</B> ago, our fathers brought forth,
```

```
<I ID = italicPhrase>upon this continent,</I> a new nation,
<SPAN ID = spanLiberty>conceived in liberty,</SPAN> and
dedicated to the proposition that "all men are <B ID =
boldCreated>created equal</B>"</P>
```

They'll help us test some features of textRanges. Specifically, we're going to track

► htmlText   The text and HTML in a textRange

► text   The plain text in a textRange

► parentElement   The HTML element that contains a textRange

► bookmark   A unique identifier for a position in an element

Starting the Script

Now we'll add some script. Create a SCRIPT element whose Language attribute is "VBScript". Some global variables will get things moving:

```
dim glblRange
dim glblMark
dim glblParentElement
dim glblResetFlag
```

The first refers to the textRange that we'll set and reset, the second to a bookmark that we'll set and move to, the third to the HTML element that contains the textRange, and the last to a variable whose value will change when we click the Reset button. We make these variables global so that we can update their values in the text area after we manipulate them in subroutines throughout the script.

Next, we initialize some values when the browser window opens:

```
sub window_onload
    set glblRange = document.body.createTextRange()
```

Part III

```
            textAreaRangeTracker.Value = ""
            glblResetFlag = 1
            updateRangeTracker
      end sub
```

The first line creates a `textRange` on the whole BODY of the document. The second blanks out the text area. The third line assigns a value to the reset flag because we want to know when we've set (or reset) the `textRange` to cover the entire BODY. Why? When we get into the script, we'll add functionality that highlights the `textRange` as we set it. Highlighting surrounds the `textRange` in a color (it's set to red on my computer). Rather than bathe everything in a color when the `textRange` covers the whole BODY, we set a flag to tell us when to avoid highlighting. The fourth line calls a function that updates the text area.

Adding Functionality

The next subroutine adds functionality to the buttons and takes advantage of the event model. Rather than write a separate event-handler for each button, we'll just write a function that captures a `click` event at the document level, examines the event's source element, and reacts appropriately for each source element. Then it updates the text area:

```
      sub document_onclick

          Select Case window.event.srcElement.id
            Case "buttonReset"
                call glblRange.expand("textedit")
                textAreaRangeTracker.Value = ""
                glblResetFlag = 1


            Case "buttonMove"
                call glblRange.move("word",1)


            Case "buttonBookmark"


                glblMark = glblRange.getbookmark
```

```
    Case "buttonMoveToBookmark"
        if glblMark <> empty then
                    call glblRange.moveToBookmark(glblMark)
        end if

    Case else
        exit sub
End Select


    updateRangeTracker


  end sub
```

Let's examine each `Case` in the `Select Case` structure. The first one,

```
    Case "buttonReset"
        call glblRange.expand("textedit")
        textAreaRangeTracker.Value = ""
        glblResetFlag = 1
```

goes into action when the Reset button is the source element of the `click` event. The first line calls the `textRange expand` method. As its name implies, this method expands a `textRange`. Its argument, a string, indicates the amount of expansion. When the argument is `"textedit"`, the expanded range includes the entire BODY. The next line blanks out the text area and the last one updates the reset flag.

The second case,

```
    Case "buttonMove"
        call glblRange.move("word",1)
```

invokes the `textRange move` method. This method collapses the `textRange` and moves the empty range by the amount indicated in the arguments. Our arguments tell it to move the range one word to the right. If we want it to move two words, we make the second argument 2, and so forth. If we want it to move to the left, we make the second argument negative. We can also move the range by sentences or characters rather than by words.

Part iii

The third case,

```
Case "buttonBookmark"
    glblMark = glblRange.getbookmark
```

uses the `textRange` bookmark method to mark a range that we can return to via the code in the fourth case:

```
Case "buttonMoveToBookmark"
    if glblMark <> empty then
            call glblRange.moveToBookmark(glblMark)
    else
            exit sub
    end if
```

The `if` statement prevents an error from occurring if we try to invoke this method without a bookmark set. The `else` prevents highlighting the entire page if you click this button when you open the page, or if you click it after clicking Reset.

NOTE

What gets "set" when you set a bookmark? The `getbookmark` method generates an *opaque string* that uniquely identifies the bookmark. An opaque string is one you can't examine or modify. When the Microsofters say "opaque," they're not kidding. As you'll see when you start experimenting with this page, a bookmark string can look like this: ☐☐B☐☐☐☐☐☐☐☐☐☐☐☐☐☐☐☐?! svp!-phb!gbuifst!csoJ☐☐☐☐☐☐☐☐☐☐☐☐☐☐☐?!tsfiubg! scspvhiu!gpÏ

`Case else` exits the subroutine if a click does not occur on a button.

Mousing through the Text

Now we'll code a subroutine that moves the `textRange` around as we move the mouse through the opening sentence of the Gettysburg Address. We'll write an event-handler for `onmousemove` for the P element that holds that sentence:

```
sub pGettysburg_onmousemove
    call glblRange.moveToPoint(window.event.x, window.event.y)
    updateRangeTracker
end sub
```

This subroutine invokes the textRange moveToPoint method, which collapses the textRange and moves it to the point specified by the coordinates in its arguments. The onmousemove event continually updates window.event.x and window.event.y to give the mouse cursor's current position.

The next line updates the text area.

Tracking the Property Values

The updateRangeTracker subroutine, referred to in each of the other subroutines, takes care of the text area after performing three other tasks:

```
sub updateRangeTracker
    call glblRange.expand("word")

    if glblResetFlag = 0 then
      glblRange.select
    end if

    set glblParentElement = glblRange.parentElement()

    textAreaRangeTracker.Value = "htmlText: " &
      glblRange.htmlText & chr(13) _
    & "text: " & glblRange.text & chr(13) _
    & "parent element: " & glblParentElement.id & chr(13) _
    & "bookmark: " & glblMark

    glblResetFlag = 0

    end sub
```

The first task is to expand the textRange to include a word. When you move a textRange, you collapse it and relocate it to a point within the document. The expand method arbitrarily includes one following word. (As an exercise, you might try to create a way to empower the user to set the amount of expansion.)

The next task visualizes the textRange for you. If the reset flag is 0 (meaning that the Reset button has not been clicked), the subroutine calls the text area `select` method. This method applies highlighting to the `textRange`. If the reset flag is 1, the entire BODY is the `textRange`, and highlighting is not applied. In that case, highlighting would obscure the text area's contents.

The third task calls the `parentElement` method to get the HTML element that contains the `textRange`.

Next, the subroutine updates the text area and sets the reset flag to 0.

The Whole File

Here's `Moving through Text.htm`.

Moving through Text.htm

```
<HTML>
<HEAD>
<SCRIPT Language = "VBScript">

dim glblRange
dim glblMark
dim glblParentElement
dim glblResetFlag

sub window_onload
    set glblRange = document.body.createTextRange()
    textAreaRangeTracker.Value = ""
    glblResetFlag = 1
    updateRangeTracker
end sub


sub document_onclick

    Select Case window.event.srcElement.id

        Case "buttonReset"
            call glblRange.expand("textedit")
```

```
        textAreaRangeTracker.Value = ""
        glblResetFlag = 1

    Case "buttonMove"
        call glblRange.move("word",1)

    Case "buttonBookmark"
        glblMark = glblRange.getbookmark

    Case "buttonMoveToBookmark"
        if glblMark <> empty then
          call glblRange.moveToBookmark(glblMark)
        else
          exit sub
        end if

    Case else
        exit sub
    End Select

    updateRangeTracker

end sub

sub pGettysburg_onmousemove
    call glblRange.moveToPoint(window.event.x, window.event.y)
    updateRangeTracker
end sub

sub updateRangeTracker
    call glblRange.expand("word")
```

```
        if glblResetFlag = 0 then
          glblRange.select
        end if

        set glblParentElement = glblRange.parentElement()

        textAreaRangeTracker.Value = "htmlText: " &
➡         glblRange.htmlText & chr(13) _
        & "text: " & glblRange.text & chr(13) _
        & "parent element: " & glblParentElement.id & chr(13) _
        & "bookmark: " & glblMark

        glblResetFlag = 0

      end sub

    </SCRIPT>
    <TITLE>Moving Through Text</TITLE>
    </HEAD>
    <BODY ID = bodyDocument>
    <H1 style = "text-align:center">Moving Through Text</H1>
    <HR>
    <CENTER>
    <BUTTON ID = buttonReset Title = "Click to reset the
    textRange">Reset</BUTTON>
    <BUTTON ID = buttonMove Title = "Click to move the textRange
    forward">Forward</BUTTON>
    <BUTTON ID = buttonBookmark Title = "Click to set a
    bookmark">Bookmark</BUTTON>
    <BUTTON ID = buttonMoveToBookmark Title = "Click to move to a
    bookmark">Move to Bookmark</BUTTON>
    </CENTER>
    <BR>
```

```
<P ID = pGettysburg>Four score and <B ID = boldPhrase>seven
years</B> ago, our fathers brought forth,
<I ID = italicPhrase>upon this continent,</I> a new nation,
<SPAN ID = spanLiberty>conceived in liberty,</SPAN> and
dedicated to the proposition that "all men are <B ID =
boldCreated>created equal</B>"</P> </P>


<CENTER>
<TEXTAREA ID = textareaRangeTracker Rows = 10 Cols = 60>
</TEXTAREA>


</BODY>
</HTML>
```

This page, like others in this chapter, is designed as a test bed for you to discover important aspects of textRanges and pick up some insights. When you open it in IE, note what happens to the parent element as you move through the Gettysburg Address sentence, either by clicking the Move button or by moving the mouse. You'll find that a textRange that seems, by virtue of its htmlText property, to be in one parent element is really in another. For example, in the phrase

```
<B ID = boldPhrase>seven years</B>
```

you would expect that both seven and years have boldPhrase as their parent element. When you move the textRange to years, however, and expand it to include the word, you'll find that the parent element is pGettysburg, the encompassing paragraph. Figure 13.4 shows this situation.

On the other hand, in

```
<B ID = boldCreated>created equal</B>
```

both created and equal have boldCreated as their parent element. The difference is that in the first case (the word "years" in the phrase "seven years") a blank space follows the second word. In the second, a punctuation mark (the close quote) follows the second word. Experiment with the document. In your text editor, replace the close quote with a letter or a word (with no space between equal and your substitution). What happens to the parent element of equal?

Note the opaque string when you set a bookmark. When you reset the textRange, it doesn't go away.

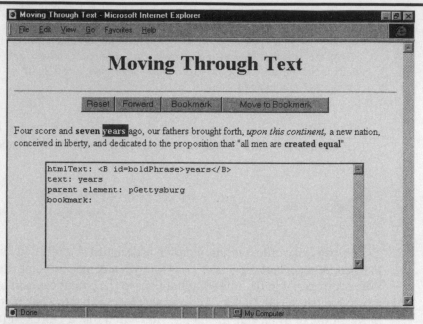

FIGURE 13.4: Moving through `text.htm` with the `textRange` on years

SEARCHING FOR TEXT

I mentioned earlier that `textRanges` are helpful because they enable you to perform useful tasks such as finding and replacing text. In this exercise, you'll learn how to implement a search capability, and in the next, you'll learn about replacement. In both exercises, we use modal dialog boxes.

We'll create the uncluttered page, `Find Text.htm`, that is shown in Figure 13.5. Pressing the Find... button will bring up a modal dialog box for entering text (see Figure 13.6). Clicking OK on the dialog box will close that window. In the event of a match, the matched text will appear highlighted in the main window. Otherwise, a message box will appear. It will display the searched-for text string and inform the user that no match was found.

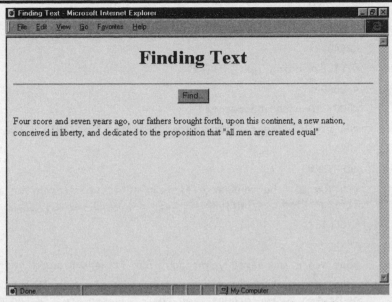

FIGURE 13.5:   Find Text.htm, a page with a text-search capability

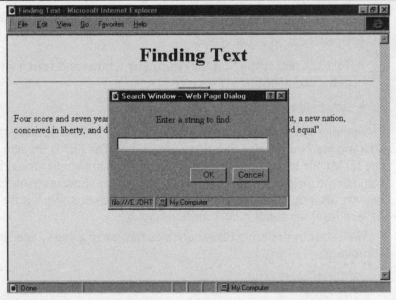

FIGURE 13.6:   The modal dialog box for entering the searched-for text

The HTML for laying out the page is straightforward:

```
<HTML>
<HEAD>
<TITLE>Finding Text</TITLE>
</HEAD>
<BODY ID = bodyDocument>
<H1 style = "text-align:center">Finding Text</H1>
<HR>
<CENTER>
<BUTTON ID = buttonSearch Title = "Click to search for a text
string">Find...</BUTTON>
</CENTER>
<BR>
Four score and seven years ago, our fathers brought forth,
upon this continent, a new nation, conceived in liberty, and
dedicated to the proposition that "all men are created equal"
</BODY>
</HTML>
```

Next, we have to script a `button-click` event to do three things for us:

- ▶ Open the modal dialog box.
- ▶ Take the text string that the dialog box returns and search for it in the document.
- ▶ React appropriately if no match is found.

Opening a modal dialog box is the job of the `window.openModal-Dialog` method, which takes three arguments. The first is the name of the HTML file to open, the second is an optional argument for sending a value to the dialog box, and the third specifies the appearance of the dialog box. We won't use the second argument in this exercise, but we'll have more to say about it later in this chapter.

We'll start by declaring three variables that we're going to need in this subroutine:

```
dim strDialogValue
dim range
dim match
```

We use this code to open the dialog box:

```
strDialogValue = window.showModalDialog("Search
Window.htm",null,"dialogWidth:300px;dialogHeight:200px")
```

The variable `strDialogValue` will hold the text string entered into the modal dialog box. If the return value is an empty string, we'll want to exit the subroutine:

```
if strDialogValue = "" then
    exit sub
  end if
```

If `strDialogValue` is not an empty string, we'll create a `textRange` that encompasses the BODY of the document and then use the `textRange`'s `findText` method to look for a match:

```
set range = document.body.createTextRange()
match = range.findText(strDialogValue)
```

If a match is found, we'll want to highlight the match. If not, we'll want to open a message box that tells the user that no match was found:

```
if match <> false then
    range.select()
  else
    MsgBox "Couldn't find " & strDialogValue,,"No Match"
  end if
```

Note the searched-for text in the message box, which adds to the usefulness of the message.

Here's the `Find Text.htm` file.

Find Text.htm

```
<HTML>
<HEAD>
<SCRIPT Language = "VBScript">

sub buttonSearch_onclick()
```

Part iii

```
dim strDialogValue
dim range
dim match

  strDialogValue = window.showModalDialog("Search
➤   Window.htm",null,"dialogWidth:300px;dialogHeight:200px")

  if strDialogValue = "" then
    exit sub
  end if

  set range = document.body.createTextRange()
  match = range.findText(strDialogValue)

  if match <> false then
    range.select()
  else
    MsgBox "Couldn't find " & strDialogValue,,"No Match"
  end if

end sub

</SCRIPT>
<TITLE>Finding Text</TITLE>
</HEAD>
<BODY ID = bodyDocument>
<H1 style = "text-align:center">Finding Text</H1>
<HR>
<CENTER>
<BUTTON ID = buttonSearch Title = "Click to search for a text
string">Find...</BUTTON>
</CENTER>
<BR>
```

Four score and seven years ago, our fathers brought forth,
upon this continent, a new nation, conceived in liberty, and
dedicated to the proposition that "all men are created equal"

```
</BODY>
</HTML>
```

Before we can use it, of course, we have to code Search Window.htm.

Search Window.htm

```
<HTML>
<HEAD>
<SCRIPT Language = "JScript">


function doOK() {
   if (textSearch.value == "") {
     alert("Enter a string or click Cancel");
     return
   }
   window.returnValue = textSearch.value;
   window.close();

}

function doCancel() {
   window.returnValue = "";
   window.close();
}
</SCRIPT>
<TITLE>Search Window</TITLE>
</HEAD>
<BODY style = "background-color:silver">
<BR>
```

```
<P style = "text-align:center">Enter a string to find:</P>
<CENTER>
<INPUT ID = textSearch Type = text Style = "width:90%">
</CENTER>
<Button style = "Position:absolute;top:70%;left:48%;width:60"
onclick = "doOK()">OK</Button>
<Button style = "Position:absolute;top:70%;left:73%;width:60"
onclick = "doCancel()">Cancel</Button>
</BODY>
</HTML>
```

When you have the two documents coded, open them in IE and experiment with the textRange's findText capability. You'll find that this is a quick and easy way to add a useful feature to your Web pages.

REPLACING TEXT

Text replacement, another useful textRange-related task, enables users to change the content on your Web page. We'll work on a page that superficially resembles the page in the previous exercise. Save Find Text.htm as Replace Text.htm. In the new page, change the heading and the title to Replacing Text. Put the Gettysburg Address's opening sentence into a P element, and assign pGettysburg as the P element's ID.

In this exercise, we use the textRange's createRange method in conjunction with the document's selection property. Highlighting an item in the on-screen sentence assigns a value to document.selection, which is an object as well as a property of the document. The createRange method is especially designed for creating a textRange from document .selection. The idea is to create the range and open a modal dialog box. In the modal box, the user will enter the text that replaces the selection. When the user clicks OK on the dialog box, the box closes and the text in the main window is changed.

To coordinate with the selection process, the script is an event-handler for the onmouseup event on the P element. It starts by setting a variable to the document.selection object, invoking the createRange method, and opening the dialog box:

```
set selected = document.selection
   set range = selected.createRange()
   strDialogValue = window.showModalDialog("Replace
➡  Window.htm", range.text,"dialogWidth:300px;
➡  dialogHeight:250px")
```

Take careful note of the second argument to showModalDialog. This argument sends the selection-based textRange to the dialog box. The box will display it in a read-only text box so that users can see the string they're replacing.

TIP

Microsoft documentation indicates that you can use a variable in this argument. This isn't precisely true. If you set a variable equal to a string and then put that variable in this argument, you'll get an error message when you try to open the dialog window. Apparently, the dialog box has to see a string as a property of an object, as in our example. A quoted string works in that argument, too.

If the dialog box returns an empty string because the user clicked Cancel, we'll exit the subroutine. If not, we'll assign the returned string as the new value of the range's text property. Here's Replace Text.htm.

Replace Text.htm

```
<HTML>
<HEAD>
<SCRIPT Language = "VBScript">

sub pGettysburg_onmouseup
   set selected = document.selection
   set range = selected.createRange()
   strDialogValue = window.showModalDialog("Replace
➡  Window.htm",range.text,"dialogWidth:300px;
➡  dialogHeight:250px")
```

```
      if strDialogValue = "" then
        exit sub
      end if

      range.text = strDialogValue
    end sub

</SCRIPT>
<TITLE>Replacing Text</TITLE>
</HEAD>
<BODY ID = bodyDocument>
<H1 style = "text-align:center">Replacing Text</H1>
<HR>
<P ID = pGettysburg> Four score and seven years ago, our
fathers brought forth, upon this continent, a new nation,
conceived in liberty, and dedicated to the proposition that
"all men are created equal" </P>
</BODY>
</HTML>
```

Here's Replace Window.htm.

Replace Window.htm

```
<HTML>
<HEAD>
<SCRIPT Language = "VBScript">
sub window_onload
    textOriginal.Value = window.dialogArguments
    textReplace.Focus
end sub
</SCRIPT>

<SCRIPT Language = "JScript">

function doOK() {
```

```
      if (textReplace.value == "") {
        alert("Enter a string or click Cancel");
        return
      }
      window.returnValue = textReplace.value;
      window.close();


    }


    function doCancel() {
      window.returnValue = "";
      window.close();
    }
    </SCRIPT>
    <TITLE>Replace Window</TITLE>
    </HEAD>
    <BODY style = "background-color:silver">
    <BR>
    <P style = "text-align:center"> Original: </P>
    <CENTER>
    <INPUT ID = textOriginal Type = text Readonly Style =
    "width:90%; background-color:silver">
    </CENTER>
    <P style = "text-align:center">Replace with:</P>
    <CENTER>
    <INPUT ID = textReplace Type = text Style = "width:90%">
    </CENTER>
    <Button style = "Position:absolute;top:85%;left:48%;width:60"
    onclick = "doOK()">OK</Button>
    <Button style = "Position:absolute;top:85%;left:73%;width:60"
    onclick = "doCancel()">Cancel</Button>
    </BODY>
    </HTML>
```

It's very similar to the dialog box in the preceding exercise, except for the extra text input that holds the original string in read-only fashion. Also, the script has an additional feature. We've added some VBScript for the window's `onload` event. As you can see, VBScript and JScript can peacefully coexist in a document, as long as they're in separate SCRIPT elements.

The information in the second argument of `window.showModal-Dialog` gets stored in `window.dialogArguments`. In the `onload` event-handler, the line

```
textOriginal.Value = window.dialogArguments
```

puts that information into one of the text inputs. The next line,

```
textReplace.Focus
```

puts the focus in the other text input so that the user can immediately start typing when the window opens.

Figure 13.7 shows the page with some selected text, along with the dialog box. The dialog box contains the original text and the replacement text.

With apologies to President Lincoln, Figure 13.8 shows the page after numerous replacements have updated the original message for life in the 1990s.

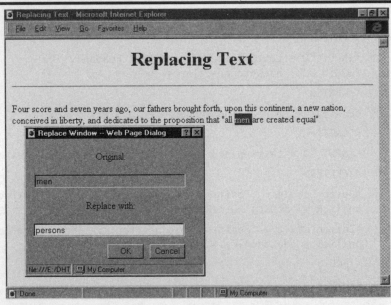

FIGURE 13.7: `Replace Text.htm` and `Replace Window.htm`, two pages designed for text replacement

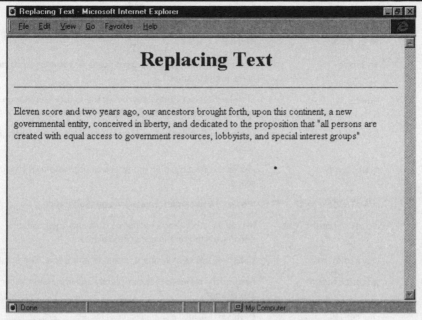

FIGURE 13.8: `Replace Text.htm` after numerous text replacements

SUMMARIZING THE *TEXTRANGE*

The `textRange` has a number of useful methods. Table 13.1 summarizes them for you.

TABLE 13.1: textRange Methods

METHOD	WHAT IT DOES
collapse	Shrinks a textRange and creates an insertion point at either the beginning or the end of the current range
compareEndPoints	Compares two textRanges
duplicate	Returns a duplicate of a textRange
expand	Expands a textRange by a character, word, or sentence
findText	Searches for text in the document; sets the start and end points of the range to encompass the search string
getBookmark	Provides an opaque string that uniquely identifies a location within the document

TABLE 13.1 continued: textRange Methods

METHOD	WHAT IT DOES
inRange	Determines whether a specified range is within or equal to the current textRange
move	Shrinks the textRange and moves the empty textRange by a specified number of characters, words, or sentences
moveEnd	Moves the end position of the textRange and thus changes its scope
moveStart	Moves the start position of the textRange and thus changes its scope
moveToBookmark	Moves to a bookmark created via getBookmark
moveToElementText	Moves the textRange so that its start and end positions encompass the text in a specified element
moveToPoint	Collapses the textRange and moves it to a specified point
parentElement	Returns the element that completely encompasses the current textRange
pasteHTML	Pastes HTML into a specified textRange
scrollIntoView	Scrolls the textRange into view in the browser
select	Highlights the current textRange
setEndPoint	Sets the end point of one textRange based on the end point of another

TRACKING CONTENT PROPERTIES

The textRange is just one way of working with text. IE supplies another. In the IE world, most elements in an HTML document support four content properties:

▶ innerText   A string that specifies all the text in the element and in any enclosed elements, excluding any HTML tags. Assigning a new string to this property replaces the contents but not the end tags. Any new tags are rendered as text.

▶ outerText   Identical to innerText, but assigning a new string replaces the start and end tags as well as the text. If you assign an empty string to this property, you completely remove an element from the document.

▶ innerHTML   A string that specifies all the text and HTML tags in an element, excluding start and end tags. New tags inserted into this property are interpreted as tags, not as text.

▶ outerHTML   The same as innerHTML, but includes start and end tags.

In the next exercise, you'll build a page that will serve as a test bed for learning about these properties. You'll create the page that appears in Figure 13.9, which is based on a file called Content Properties.htm.

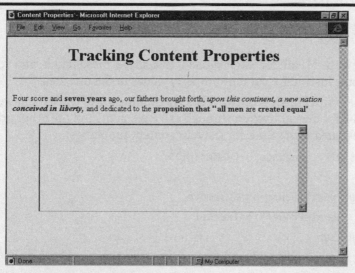

FIGURE 13.9: Content Properties.htm, a page for tracking innerText, outerText, innerHTML, and outerHTML

The HTML is similar to code you've seen before:

```
<HTML>
<HEAD>
<TITLE>Content Properties</TITLE>
</HEAD>
<BODY ID = bodyDocument>
<H1 style = "text-align:center">Tracking Content
Properties</H1>
```

```
<HR>

<P ID = pGettysburg><SPAN>Four score and <A><B ID =
boldPhrase>seven years</B></A></SPAN> ago, our fathers
brought forth,

<I ID = italicPhrase>upon this continent, a new nation <B
ID = boldLiberty>conceived in liberty,</B></I> and dedicated
to the <B>proposition <A>that "all men</A></B> are <B ID =
boldCreated>created equal</B>"</P>


<CENTER>

<TEXTAREA ID = textareaPropertiesTracker Rows = 10 Cols = 60>

</TEXTAREA>

</BODY>

</HTML>
```

Type the HTML for the P element just as I've presented it, and you'll see some instructive content property values in the text area.

The script consists of two VBScript subroutines. One is an event-handler for onmousemove through the P element, and the other updates the text area with values for the four content properties:

```
<SCRIPT Language = "VBScript">


sub pGettysburg_onmousemove
    updatePropertiesTracker
end sub


sub updatePropertiesTracker

    textAreaPropertiesTracker.Value = "innerText: " &
➥    window.event.srcElement.innerText & chr(13) _
    & "outerText: " & window.event.srcElement.outerText &
➥    chr(13) _
    & "innerHTML: " & window.event.srcElement.innerHTML &
➥    chr(13) _
    & "outerHTML: " & window.event.srcElement.outerHTML


end sub
```

Notice that we're taking advantage of the IE event model. When you move the mouse through an element, that element becomes the source element of the event, and we use the source element to update the values in the text area.

Moving the mouse through the sentence will continuously update the content properties. Take note of the values of the properties as you move the mouse. The interesting elements are the ones that contain other elements. For example, with the mouse on *Four*, you'll see the values in Figure 13.9:

```
innerText: Four score and seven years

outerText: Four score and seven years

innerHTML: Four score and <A><B id=boldPhrase>seven
years</B></A>

outerHTML: <SPAN>Four score and <A><B id=boldPhrase>seven
years</B></A></SPAN>
```

As you can see, the innerText and outerText values look the same, and they don't include tags. The innerHTML and outerHTML values have the tags; the start and end tags appear in outerHTML.

CHANGING CONTENT PROPERTIES

After you've experimented with the page in the preceding section, you'll be ready to change some of the content properties. This exercise gives you a test bed for doing just that. Save the file from the previous exercise as Changing Content Properties.htm. Change the title and the heading accordingly. You're going to develop the page that appears in Figure 13.10.

Take the subroutines out of the SCRIPT element, as you'll replace them with new ones. Immediately after the HTML code for the TEXT AREA, add this code to create the SELECT element (the drop-down list) and the button at the bottom of the page:

```
<SELECT ID = selectOptions style =
"position:absolute;top:340;left:350">

<OPTION Value = "InnerText">InnerText

<OPTION Value = "OuterText">OuterText

<OPTION Value = "InnerHTML">InnerHTML

<OPTION Value = "OuterHTML">OuterHTML

</SELECT>

<BUTTON ID = buttonChange style =
"position:absolute;top:340;left:450">Change...</BUTTON>
```

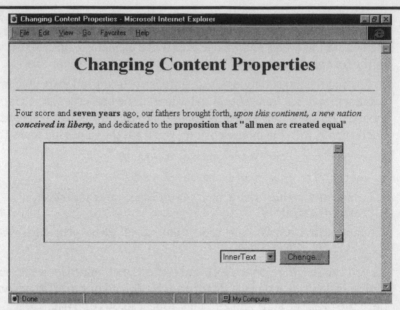

FIGURE 13.10: Changing Content Properties.htm, a test bed for changing innerText, outerText, innerHTML, and outerHTML

You'll click on the sentence to select an element, select a content property from the drop-down list, and click the Change button to open a dialog box so that you can make the change. The dialog box will present the string to be changed in a text box that you can start typing in as soon as the box opens.

Now we address the script. It will consist of three subroutines. One is an event-handler for the onclick event in the P element. We use onclick rather than onmousemove so that we don't have to worry about stray mouse movements when we select an area in pGettysburg. Another subroutine is an event-handler for the onclick event for the button, and the third updates the text area.

We begin by declaring glblObjElement, a global variable that will store the element selected in pGettysburg. The first subroutine is a short one:

```
sub pGettysburg_onclick
    updatePropertiesTracker
    set glblObjElement = window.event.srcElement
end sub
```

It calls the update subroutine and sets the global variable to the source element of the `click` event—the element clicked within `pGettysburg`. Sometimes the source element will be `pGettysburg`. In that case, we'll have to guard against user input that changes this element. Why? Changing the name of `pGettysburg` would cause this event-handler to stop functioning. We'll put the safeguard into the next subroutine.

The second subroutine is considerably longer. As the event-handler for the button's `onclick` event, it has to open the dialog box. The dialog box it opens will contain the string to be changed, which will differ as a result of the property we select from the drop-down list. Therefore, we begin with a `Select Case` structure whose test expression is the value of the SELECT element:

```
Select Case selectOptions.Value

  Case "InnerText"

    strDialogValue = window.showModalDialog("Content Edit
➥    Window.htm", glblObjElement.innerText,"
➥    dialogWidth:450px;dialogHeight:250px")

    if strDialogValue <> "" then

      glblObjElement.innerText = strDialogValue

    end if


  Case "OuterText"

    strDialogValue = window.showModalDialog("Content Edit
➥    Window.htm", glblObjElement.outerText,
➥    "dialogWidth:450px;dialogHeight:250px")

    if strDialogValue <> "" then

      glblObjElement.outerText = strDialogValue

    end if

  Case "InnerHTML"

    strDialogValue = window.showModalDialog("Content Edit
➥    Window.htm", glblObjElement.innerHTML,"
➥    dialogWidth:450px;dialogHeight:250px")

    if strDialogValue <> "" then

      glblObjElement.innerHTML = strDialogValue

    end if

  Case "OuterHTML"

    if glblObjElement.id = "pGettysburg" then
```

```
      MsgBox "Make another selection"
      exit sub
   end if
   strDialogValue = window.showModalDialog("Content Edit
➡   Window.htm", glblObjElement.outerHTML,"
➡   dialogWidth:450px;dialogHeight:250px")
   if strDialogValue <> "" then
      glblObjElement.outerHTML = strDialogValue
   end if
   Case Else
   MsgBox "Should never get here"
   end select
```

In each case, we open a dialog box. One difference among the cases is the second argument, the value we send to the dialog box. (Remember the Tip in the previous section: This argument should be an object and its property.) The other difference is the content property we change when the value comes back from the dialog box (if this value isn't an empty string). You'll notice that I've widened the dialog box from the previous versions. This will accommodate longer strings.

The "OuterHTML" case's first if statement guards against changing the pGettysburg element—the possibility I mentioned earlier. If the source element of the onclick is pGettysburg, the user never gets the opportunity to change its outerHTML and thus render sub pGettysburg_onclick inoperative. Instead, a message box opens advising the user to make another selection.

One eventuality that we have to anticipate is the entry of invalid HTML code into the dialog box. For example, a P element can't contain another P element. Entering a <P> tag as the start tag for an outerHTML will generate an error message. To keep the program from crashing in this case, we add on error resume next to the start of this subroutine. We also add some code at the end that generates an informative message box if an error occurs:

```
if err.number <> 0 then
   MsgBox "Error: " & err.description & " from: " &
➡      err.source,,"Attempt to Add Invalid HTML"
end if
```

First of all, the notation should tell you that a generated error is an object. Like any other object, it has properties, and we can examine those properties. If an error does occur, the err.number will not be 0, and the message box will display the indicated properties. (It's not the case that every error has a description.)

The third subroutine uses the source element of the pGettysburg onclick event to update the text area:

```
sub updatePropertiesTracker

    on error resume next

    textAreaPropertiesTracker.Value = "innerText: " &
➡    window.event.srcElement.innerText & chr(13) _

    & "outerText: " & window.event.srcElement.outerText &
➡    chr(13) _

    & "innerHTML: " & window.event.srcElement.innerHTML &
➡    chr(13) _

    & "outerHTML: " & window.event.srcElement.outerHTML


end sub
```

This one begins with on error resume next so that we don't generate an error when the window opens and no source element exists.

Here's the whole Changing Content Properties.htm file.

Changing Content Properties.htm

```
<HTML>
<HEAD>
<SCRIPT Language = "VBScript">
dim glblObjElement


sub pGettysburg_onclick
    updatePropertiesTracker
    set glblObjElement = window.event.srcElement
end sub


sub buttonChange_onclick
 on error resume next
 Select Case selectOptions.Value
```

```
      Case "InnerText"
      strDialogValue = window.showModalDialog("Content Edit
➥   .Window.htm", glblObjElement.innerText,"dialogWidth:
➥   .450px;dialogHeight:250px")
        if strDialogValue <> "" then
        glblObjElement.innerText = strDialogValue
        end if


      Case "OuterText"
      strDialogValue = window.showModalDialog("Content Edit
➥   Window.htm", glblObjElement.outerText,"dialogWidth:
➥   450px;dialogHeight:250px")
        if strDialogValue <> "" then
        glblObjElement.outerText = strDialogValue
        end if
      Case "InnerHTML"
      strDialogValue = window.showModalDialog("Content Edit
➥   Window.htm", glblObjElement.innerHTML,"
➥   dialogWidth:450px;dialogHeight:250px")
        if strDialogValue <> "" then
        glblObjElement.innerHTML = strDialogValue
        end if
      Case "OuterHTML"
        if glblObjElement.id = "pGettysburg" then
          MsgBox "Make another selection"
          exit sub
        end if
      strDialogValue = window.showModalDialog("Content Edit
➥   Window.htm", glblObjElement.outerHTML,"
➥   dialogWidth:450px;dialogHeight:250px")
        if strDialogValue <> "" then
          glblObjElement.outerHTML = strDialogValue
        end if
      Case Else
      MsgBox "Should never get here"
      end select
```

```
if err.number <> 0 then
    MsgBox "Error: " & err.description & " from: " &
err.source,,"Attempt to Add Invalid HTML"
end if


end sub


sub updatePropertiesTracker
    on error resume next
    textAreaPropertiesTracker.Value = "innerText: " &
➡   window.event.srcElement.innerText & chr(13) _
    & "outerText: " & window.event.srcElement.outerText &
➡   chr(13) _
    & "innerHTML: " & window.event.srcElement.innerHTML &
➡   chr(13) _
    & "outerHTML: " & window.event.srcElement.outerHTML


end sub

</SCRIPT>
<TITLE>Changing Content Properties</TITLE>
</HEAD>
<BODY ID = bodyDocument>
<H1 style = "text-align:center">Changing Content
Properties</H1>
<HR>
<P ID = pGettysburg><SPAN>Four score and <A><B ID =
boldPhrase>seven years</B></A></SPAN> ago, our fathers
brought forth,
<I ID = italicPhrase>upon this continent, a new nation <B ID
= boldLiberty>conceived in liberty,</B></I> and dedicated to
the <B>proposition <A>that "all men</A></B> are <B ID =
boldCreated>created equal</B>"</P>
<CENTER>
```

Part iii

```
<TEXTAREA ID = textareaPropertiesTracker Rows = 10 Cols = 60>
</TEXTAREA>
<SELECT ID = selectOptions style =
"position:absolute;top:340;left:350">
<OPTION Value = "InnerText">InnerText
<OPTION Value = "OuterText">OuterText
<OPTION Value = "InnerHTML">InnerHTML
<OPTION Value = "OuterHTML">OuterHTML
</SELECT>
<BUTTON ID = buttonChange style =
"position:absolute;top:340;left:450">Change...</BUTTON>
</BODY>
</HTML>
```

Here's the dialog box Content Edit Window.htm.

Content Edit Window.htm

```
<HTML>
<HEAD>
<SCRIPT Language = "VBScript">
sub window_onload
    textChange.Value = window.dialogArguments
    textChange.Focus
end sub
</SCRIPT>

<SCRIPT Language = "JScript">

function doOK() {
    if (textChange.value == "") {
      alert("Enter a string or click Cancel");
      return
    }
```

```
        window.returnValue = textChange.value;
        window.close();

    }

    function doCancel() {
        window.returnValue = "";
        window.close();
    }
    </SCRIPT>
    <TITLE>Content Change Window</TITLE>
    </HEAD>
    <BODY style = "background-color:silver">
    <BR>
    <P style = "text-align:center">Edit the Content Property:</P>
    <CENTER>
    <INPUT ID = textChange Type = text Style = "width:95%">
    </CENTER>
    <Button style = "Position:absolute;top:85%;left:48%;width:60"
    onclick = "doOK()">OK</Button>
    <Button style = "Position:absolute;top:85%;left:73%;width:60"
    onclick = "doCancel()">Cancel</Button>
    </BODY>
    </HTML>
```

As in the preceding exercise, in the VBScript onload event-handler, the window.dialogArguments property provides the value passed from the main window. The second line in that event-handler puts the focus on the text input.

Use this window and the dialog box to change aspects of the sentence, and note the effects. After each change, you have to click the element again to see the updated values in the text area. Figure 13.11 shows the page after a change to the outerHTML of the last two words in the sentence. The change in the figure was from <B> and </B> to <I> and </I> as the start and end tags (along with a change to the ID). As the figure shows, the two words went from bold (in Figure 13.10) to italic.

Part III

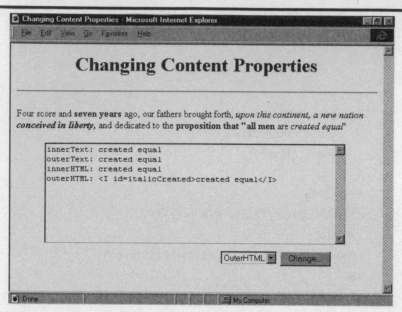

FIGURE 13.11:   The appearance of Changing Content Properties.htm after changing the outerHTML of the last two words

INSERTING CONTENT

IE provides two more methods for changing downloaded text: insert-AdjacentText and insertAdjacentHTML. As their names imply, the first inserts text into an element and the second inserts HTML and text into an element. Each method takes two arguments. The first specifies where in the element to insert the string, and the second is the string to insert. For the first argument, four choices are available:

- ▶ BeforeBegin   Immediately before the element
- ▶ AfterBegin   Immediately after the start of the element and before all other content in the element
- ▶ BeforeEnd   Immediately before the end of the element and after all other content in the element
- ▶ AfterEnd   Immediately after the element

Our test bed page for working with these methods appears in Figure 13.12.

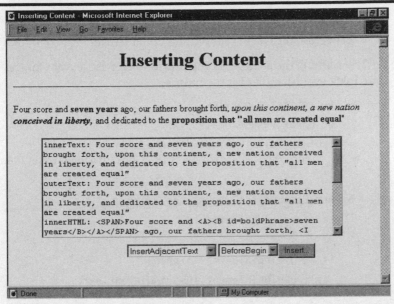

FIGURE 13.12: Inserting Content.htm, a test bed page for working with insertAdjacentText and insertAdjacentHTML

You can use the file from the preceding exercise as a template to set this one up. It's called Inserting Content.htm. The major difference in the HTML is the extra drop-down at the bottom of the page. One drop-down is for choosing the insertion method, the other is for choosing the location. That part of the HTML looks like this:

```
<SELECT ID = selectTypeOptions style =
"position:absolute;top:340;left:200">
<OPTION Value = "InsertAdjacentText">InsertAdjacentText
<OPTION Value = "InsertAdjacentHTML">InsertAdjacentHTML
</SELECT>

<SELECT ID = selectPositionOptions style =
"position:absolute;top:340;left:350">
<OPTION Value = "BeforeBegin">BeforeBegin
<OPTION Value = "AfterBegin">AfterBegin
<OPTION Value = "BeforeEnd">BeforeEnd
<OPTION Value = "AfterEnd">AfterEnd
</SELECT>
```

```
<BUTTON ID = buttonInsert style =
"position:absolute;top:340;left:450">Insert...</BUTTON>
```

The script is the same as in the previous exercise, except for the onclick event-handler for the button:

```
sub buttonInsert_onclick

  on error resume next

  strDialogValue = window.showModalDialog("Insert
➥   Window.htm",, "dialogWidth:450px;dialogHeight:250px")


 Select Case selectTypeOptions.Value
  Case "InsertAdjacentText"


    if strDialogValue <> "" then
     call glblObjElement.insertAdjacentText
➥     (selectPositionOptions.value,strDialogValue)
    end if


  Case "InsertAdjacentHTML"


    if strDialogValue <> "" then
     call glblObjElement.insertAdjacentHTML
➥     (selectPositionOptions.value,strDialogValue)
    end if


  Case Else
  MsgBox "Should never get here"
  end select


 if err.number <> 0 then
   MsgBox "Error: " & err.description & " from: " &
➥   err.source,, "Attempt to Add Invalid HTML"
 end if


 end sub
```

As you can see, this subroutine opens the dialog window before it gets to the `Select Case` structure. The `Select Case` determines what happens to the string when it comes back from the dialog. It bases the determination on the values selected in the drop-downs. The cases in the `Select Case` come from the drop-down that contains `insertAdjacentText` and `insertAdjacentHTML`. The location choice from the other drop-down is incorporated into the first argument of the calls to the insertion methods. Here's the whole `Inserting Content.htm` file.

Inserting Content.htm

```
<HTML>
<HEAD>
<SCRIPT Language = "VBScript">
dim glblObjElement

sub pGettysburg_onclick
   updatePropertiesTracker
   set glblObjElement = window.event.srcElement
end sub

sub buttonInsert_onclick
   on error resume next
   strDialogValue = window.showModalDialog("Insert
      Window.htm",, "dialogWidth:450px;dialogHeight:250px")

Select Case selectTypeOptions.Value
  Case "InsertAdjacentText"

    if strDialogValue <> "" then
      call glblObjElement.insertAdjacentText
         (selectPositionOptions.value,strDialogValue)
    end if


  Case "InsertAdjacentHTML"

    if strDialogValue <> "" then
```

```
          call glblObjElement.insertAdjacentHTML
➥           (selectPositionOptions.value,strDialogValue)
      end if

    Case Else
      MsgBox "Should never get here"
    end select


    if err.number <> 0 then
       MsgBox "Error: " & err.description & " from: " &
➥       err.source,, "Attempt to Add Invalid HTML"
    end if


    end sub



    sub updatePropertiesTracker
      on error resume next
      textAreaPropertiesTracker.Value = "innerText: " &
➥       window.event.srcElement.innerText & chr(13) _
      & "outerText: " & window.event.srcElement.outerText &
➥       chr(13) _
      & "innerHTML: " & window.event.srcElement.innerHTML &
➥       chr(13) _
      & "outerHTML: " & window.event.srcElement.outerHTML

    end sub


</SCRIPT>
<TITLE>Inserting Content</TITLE>
</HEAD>
<BODY ID = bodyDocument>
<H1 style = "text-align:center">Inserting Content</H1>
<HR>
```

```
<P ID = pGettysburg><SPAN>Four score and <A><B ID =
boldPhrase>seven years</B></A></SPAN> ago, our fathers
brought forth,

<I ID = italicPhrase>upon this continent, a new nation <B
ID = boldLiberty>conceived in liberty,</B></I> and dedicated
to the<B>proposition <A>that "all men</A></B> are <B ID =
boldCreated>created equal</B>"</P><CENTER>

<TEXTAREA ID = textareaPropertiesTracker Rows = 10 Cols = 60>
</TEXTAREA>


<SELECT ID = selectTypeOptions style =
"position:absolute;top:340;left:200">

<OPTION Value = "InsertAdjacentText">InsertAdjacentText

<OPTION Value = "InsertAdjacentHTML">InsertAdjacentHTML

</SELECT>


<SELECT ID = selectPositionOptions style =
"position:absolute;top:340;left:350">

<OPTION Value = "BeforeBegin">BeforeBegin

<OPTION Value = "AfterBegin">AfterBegin

<OPTION Value = "BeforeEnd">BeforeEnd

<OPTION Value = "AfterEnd">AfterEnd

</SELECT>


<BUTTON ID = buttonInsert style =
"position:absolute;top:340;left:450">Insert...</BUTTON>

</BODY>

</HTML>
```

Here's the dialog window `Insert Window.htm`.

Insert Window.htm

```
<HTML>
<HEAD>


<SCRIPT Language = "VBScript">
sub window_onload
```

```
         textInsert.Focus
      end sub
      </SCRIPT>


      <SCRIPT Language = "JScript">


      function doOK() {
         if (textInsert.value == "") {
           alert("Enter a string or click Cancel");
           return
         }
         window.returnValue = textInsert.value;
         window.close();


      }


      function doCancel() {
         window.returnValue = "";
         window.close();
      }
      </SCRIPT>
      <TITLE>Insert Window</TITLE>
      </HEAD>
      <BODY style = "background-color:silver">
      <BR>
      <P style = "text-align:center">Insert:</P>
      <CENTER>
      <INPUT ID = textInsert Type = text Style = "width:95%">
      </CENTER>
      <Button style = "Position:absolute;top:85%;left:48%;width:60"
      onclick = "doOK()">OK</Button>
      <Button style = "Position:absolute;top:85%;left:73%;width:60"
      onclick = "doCancel()">Cancel</Button>
      </BODY>
      </HTML>
```

Because we don't pass any values to this window, we don't work with `window.dialogArguments`.

Practice inserting text and HTML, and notice the effects on the page. As one of your exercises, try inserting tags with `insertAdjacentText`. You should see the tags rendered as text on the page.

WHAT'S NEXT?

As Web pages become more like standard software applications, users will expect to be able to do the same things on Web pages that they do in applications. As you have seen, dragging and dropping, text insertion and deletion, and text change are all capabilities that you can add to your Web pages today with Dynamic HTML. JavaScript and JScript, which you'll read about in the next chapter, open up more possibilities for creating dynamic Web pages that respond to a variety of user inputs and can access advanced browser capabilities, such as multimedia and style sheets.

Chapter 14

INTRODUCING JAVASCRIPT AND JSCRIPT

This chapter looks in detail at the JavaScript language, which you first encountered in Chapter 9. I'll show you how JavaScript works with both the Netscape and Microsoft browsers and Web servers, and how to embed JavaScript statements in HTML documents. I'll then cover JavaScript's use of *types* and *variables*, and show you how to use *arrays*. By the time you have finished this chapter, you'll be able to write simple scripts and include them in your Web pages.

Adapted from *Mastering JavaScript and JScript*, by James Jaworski

ISBN 0-7821-2492-5 $39.99   Available in March 1999

JavaScript and Browsers, JavaScript and Servers

JavaScript is a script-based programming language that supports the development of both client and server components of Web-based applications. On the client side, it can be used to write programs that are executed by a Web browser within the context of a Web page. On the server side, it can be used to write Web server programs that can process information submitted by a Web browser and then update the browser's display accordingly. Figure 14.1 provides an overview of how JavaScript supports both client and server Web programming.

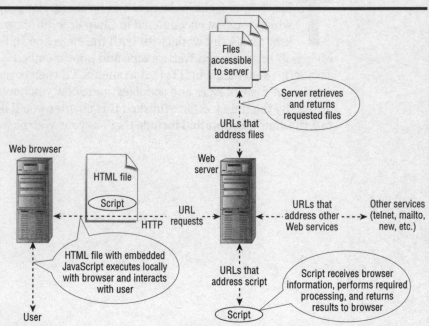

FIGURE 14.1: JavaScript supports both client and server Web applications.

NOTE

Microsoft's version of JavaScript is named JScript. In this chapter and the next, "JavaScript" is used to refer to both JavaScript and JScript unless the reference is to one but not the other. In those cases, the references are specified with "Netscape's JavaScript" and "Microsoft's JScript."

On the left side of the figure, a Web browser displays a Web page. As you probably know by now, this a result of the browser acting on the instructions contained in an HTML file. The browser reads the HTML file and displays elements of the file as they are encountered. In this case, the HTML file (which the browser has retrieved from a Web server, seen on the right) contains embedded JavaScript code. The process of reading the HTML file and identifying the elements contained in the file is referred to as parsing. When a script is encountered during parsing, the browser executes the script before continuing with further parsing.

The script can perform actions, such as generating HTML code that affects the display of the browser window. It can perform actions that affect the operation of plug-ins, Java applets, or ActiveX components. The script can also define JavaScript language elements that are used by other scripts. Figure 14.2 summarizes the parsing of HTML files that contain JavaScript scripts.

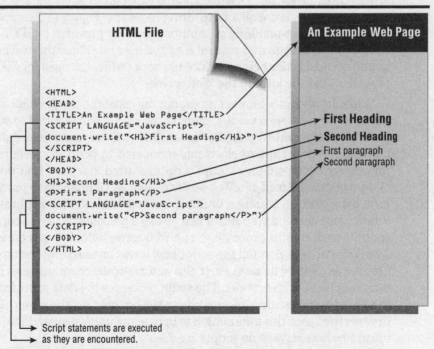

HTML File

An Example Web Page

```
<HTML>
<HEAD>
<TITLE>An Example Web Page</TITLE>
<SCRIPT LANGUAGE="JavaScript">
document.write("<H1>First Heading</H1>")
</SCRIPT>
</HEAD>
<BODY>
<H1>Second Heading</H1>
<P>First Paragraph</P>
<SCRIPT LANGUAGE="JavaScript">
document.write("<P>Second paragraph</P>")
</SCRIPT>
</BODY>
</HTML>
```

First Heading

Second Heading

First paragraph

Second paragraph

Part iii

Script statements are executed as they are encountered.

FIGURE 14.2: HIML files are parsed and displayed one element at a time.

Some scripts may define functions for handling *events* that are generated by user actions. For example, you might write a script to define a function for handling the event "submitting a form" or "clicking a link." The event handlers can then perform actions such as validating the form's data, generating a custom URL for the link, or loading a new Web page.

JavaScript's event-handling capabilities provide greater control over the user interface than HTML alone. For example, when a user submits an HTML form, a browser that isn't implementing JavaScript handles the "submit form" event by sending the form data to a CGI program for further processing. The CGI program processes the form data and returns the results to the Web browser, which displays the results to the user. By comparison, when a user submits an HTML form using a browser that *does* implement JavaScript, a JavaScript event-handling function may be called to process the form data. This processing may vary from validating the data (that is, checking to see that the data entered by the user is appropriate for the fields contained in the form) to performing all of the required form processing, eliminating the need for a CGI program. In other words, JavaScript's event-handling capabilities allow the *browser* to perform some, if not all, of the form processing. Figure 14.3 compares JavaScript's event-handling capabilities to those provided by HTML. Besides providing greater control over the user interface, these event-handling capabilities help to reduce network traffic, the need for CGI programs, and the load on the Web server.

While JavaScript's browser programming capabilities can eliminate the need for *some* server-side programs, others are still required to support more advanced Web applications, such as those that access database information, support electronic commerce, or perform specialized processing. Server-side JavaScript scripts are used to replace traditional CGI programs. Instead of a Web server calling a CGI program to process form data, perform searches, or implement customized Web applications, a JavaScript-enabled Web server can invoke a precompiled JavaScript script to perform this processing. The Web server automatically creates JavaScript objects that tell the script how it was invoked and the type of browser requesting its services; it also automatically communicates any data supplied by the browser. The script processes the data provided by the browser and returns information to the browser, via the server. The browser then uses this information to update the user's display. Figure 14.4 illustrates how server-side scripts are used.

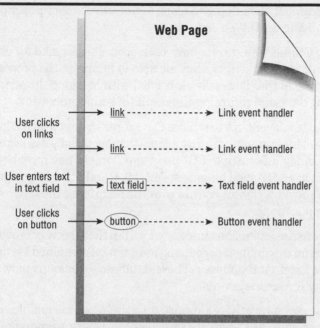

FIGURE 14.3:   Event-handling functions enable scripts to respond to user actions.

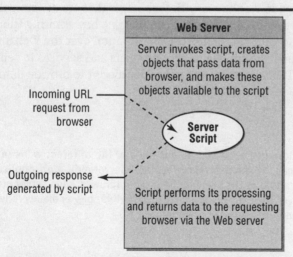

FIGURE 14.4:   Server-side scripts are used to replace CGI programs.

There are several advantages to using server-side JavaScript scripts on Netscape and Microsoft Web servers:

▶ Because these Web servers have been specially designed for executing JavaScript scripts, they are able to minimize the processing overhead that is usually associated with invoking the script, passing data, and returning the results of script processing.

▶ You can use JavaScript to replace CGI scripts written in other languages. This eliminates the problems that are usually associated with managing multiple CGI programs, which may have been written in an OS shell language, Perl, tcl, C and other languages. It also provides tighter control over the security of these server-side applications.

▶ The database extensions integrated within these servers provide a powerful capability for accessing information contained in compatible external databases. These database extensions may be used by server-side scripts.

The database connectivity supported by these servers enables even beginning programmers to create server-side JavaScript programs to update databases with information provided by browsers (usually through forms) and to provide Web users with Web pages that are dynamically generated from database queries. You can imagine how exciting this is for researchers gathering and reporting information over the Web and for entrepreneurs who have catalogs full of products and services to sell over the Web. Figure 14.5 illustrates the use of JavaScript to provide database connectivity to Web applications.

NOTE

In this section, I've provided an overview of the different ways in which JavaScript can be used for browser and server-side Web applications. JavaScript's syntax is the same for both client (browser) *and* server programming; however, the examples I will be using in this chapter mainly reflect how JavaScript relates to browser programming.

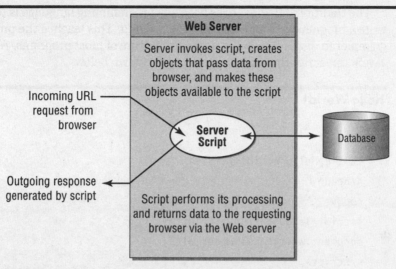

FIGURE 14.5:   Netscape and Microsoft Web servers provide database connectivity to server-side scripts.

EMBEDDING JAVASCRIPT IN HTML

JavaScript statements can be included in HTML documents by enclosing the statements between an opening `<script>` tag and a closing `</script>` tag. Within the opening tag, the LANGUAGE attribute is set to `"JavaScript"` to identify the script as being JavaScript as opposed to some other scripting language, such as Visual Basic Script (VBScript). The script tag is typically used as follows:

```
<script language="JavaScript">
 JavaScript statements
</script>
```

The script tag may be placed in either the *head* or the *body* of an HTML document. In many cases, it is better to place the script tag in the head of a document to ensure that all JavaScript definitions have been made before the body of the document is displayed. You'll learn more about this in the subsection, "Use of the Document Head," later in this section.

Part iii

The traditional first exercise with any programming language is to write a program to display the text *Hello World!* This teaches the programmer to display output, a necessary feature of most programs. A JavaScript script that displays this text is shown below.

Hello World!

```
<html>
<head>
<title>Hello World!</title>
</head>
<body>
<script language="JavaScript">
document.write("Hello World!")
</script>
</body>
</html>
```

The body of our example document (the lines between the `<body>` and the `</body>` tags) contains a single element: a script, identified by the `<script>` and `</script>` tags. The opening script tag has the attribute `language="JavaScript"` to identify the script as JavaScript. The script has a single statement, `document.write("Hello World!")`, that writes the text *Hello World!* to the body of the current `document` object. Figure 14.6 shows how the HTML document is displayed by a JavaScript-enabled browser—Netscape Navigator 4.5. The text written by the script becomes part of the HTML document displayed by the browser.

Other Language Attributes

All JavaScript-capable browsers will process JavaScript code if the LANGUAGE attribute is set to *"JavaScript"*. However, the LANGUAGE attribute can also be set to the following other values in order to limit the browsers that are able to process JavaScript code:

▶ *JavaScript1.1*   Used to limit execution of a script to browsers that support JavaScript 1.1. These browsers are Navigator 3 and later, Internet Explorer 4 and later, and Opera 3.5 and later.

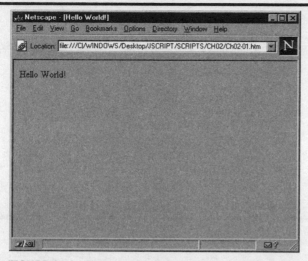

FIGURE 14.6: The very simple result of Listing 14.1, Hello World!, displayed by Netscape Navigator

- ▶ *JavaScript1.2*   Used to limit execution of a script to browsers that support JavaScript 1.2. These browsers are Navigator 4 and later and Internet Explorer 4 and later.

- ▶ *JavaScript1.3*   Used to limit execution of a script to browsers that support JavaScript 1.3. These browsers are limited to Navigator 4.06 and later.

- ▶ *JScript*   Used to limit execution of a script to browsers that support JScript. These browsers are limited to Internet Explorer 3.0 and later.

Table 14.1 identifies which of the above attributes are supported by popular browsers. If a browser does not support an attribute, it will simply ignore the <SCRIPT> tags.

TABLE 14.1: Browser Support of the LANGUAGE Attribute

BROWSER	JAVASCRIPT	JAVASCRIPT1.1	JAVASCRIPT1.2	JAVASCRIPT1.3	JSCRIPT
Navigator 2	X				
Navigator 3	X	X			
Navigator 4	X	X	X		

TABLE 14.1 continued: Browser Support of the LANGUAGE Attribute

BROWSER	JAVASCRIPT	JAVASCRIPT1.1	JAVASCRIPT1.2	JAVASCRIPT1.3	JSCRIPT
Navigator 4.06	X	X	X	X	
Navigator 4.5	X	X	X	X	
Internet Explorer 3	X				X
Internet Explorer 4	X	X	X		X
Internet Explorer 5	X	X	X		X
Opera 3.21	X	X	X	X	
Opera 3.5	X	X	X	X	

NOTE

The Opera browser reports that it supports the LANGUAGE attribute values JavaScript, JavaScript1.1, JavaScript1.2, and JavaScript1.3, but it only supports up to JavaScript version 1.1 as of Opera 3.5.

TIP

To ensure that more browsers are able to execute your scripts, set the LANGUAGE attribute to *"JavaScript"*. Your JavaScript code can then perform checks to detect which type and version of browser is currently executing a script. Chapter 15, "Working with Objects," covers browser-detection techniques.

NOTE

In addition the LANGUAGE attribute, Internet Explorer 4 and later support the use of conditional compilation directives. These directives are used to limit script execution to selected portions of scripts.

Telling Non-JavaScript Browsers to Ignore Your Code

Not all browsers support JavaScript. Older browsers, such as the Netscape Navigator 1, Internet Explorer 2, and the character-based Lynx browser, do not recognize the script tag and, as a consequence, display as text all the JavaScript statements that are enclosed between `<script>` and `</script>`. Figures 14.7 and 14.8 show how the preceding JavaScript script is displayed by Internet Explorer 2 and by DosLynx.

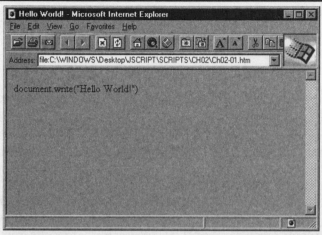

FIGURE 14.7:   Internet Explorer 2 displays the Hello World! script instead of executing it.

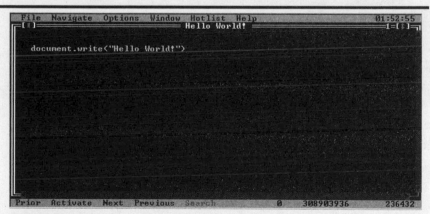

FIGURE 14.8:   DosLynx displays the Hello World! script instead of executing it.

Fortunately, HTML provides a method to conceal JavaScript statements from such JavaScript-challenged browsers. The trick is to use HTML *comment* tags to *surround* the JavaScript statements. Because HTML comments are displayed only within the code used to create a Web page, they do not show up as part of the browser's display. The use of HTML comment tags is as follows:

```
<!- Begin hiding JavaScript
JavaScript statements
// End hiding JavaScript ->
```

The <!– tag begins the HTML comment and the –> tag ends the comment. The // string identifies a JavaScript comment, as you'll learn later in this chapter in the section "JavaScript Comments."

The comment tags cause the JavaScript statements to be treated as comments by JavaScript-challenged browsers. JavaScript-enabled browsers, on the other hand, know to ignore the comment tags and process the enclosed statements as JavaScript. The script below shows how HTML comments are used to hide JavaScript statements. Figure 14.9 shows how Internet Explorer 2 displays the HTML document that results from this script.

Using HTML Comments to Hide JavaScript Code

```html
<html>
<head>
<title>Using HTML comments to hide JavaScript code</title>
</head>
<body>
<script language="JavaScript">
<!- Begin hiding JavaScript
document.write("Hello World!")
// End hiding JavaScript ->
</script>
</body>
</html>
```

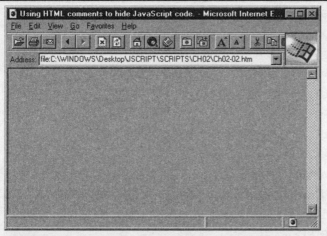

FIGURE 14.9:   Result of using HTML comments with Internet Explorer 2. Compare to Figures 14.7 and 14.8.

The Noscript Tag

Versions 2 and later of Netscape Navigator and versions 3 and later of Microsoft Internet Explorer support JavaScript. These browsers account for nearly 90 percent of browser use on the Web, and their percentage of use is increasing. This means that most browser requests come from JavaScript-capable browsers. However, there are still popular browsers, such as Lynx, that do not support JavaScript. In addition, both Navigator and Internet Explorer provide users with the option of *disabling* JavaScript. The `<noscript>` tag was created for those browsers that can't or won't process JavaScript. It is used to display markup that is an alternative to executing a script. The HTML instructions contained inside the tag are displayed by JavaScript-challenged browsers (as well as by JavaScript-capable browsers that have JavaScript disabled). The script shown below illustrates the use of the `<noscript>` tag. Figure 14.10 shows the Web page created by the following code as displayed by a JavaScript-capable browser. Compare that display to Figure 14.11, which shows how it is displayed by Internet Explorer 2, a non-JavaScript browser.

Part iii

Using the Noscript Tag

```html
<html>
<head>
<title>Using the noscript tag.</title>
</head>
<body>
<script language="JavaScript">
<!- Begin hiding JavaScript
document.write("Hello World!")
// End hiding Javascript ->
</script>
<NOSCRIPT>
[JavaScript]
</NOSCRIPT>
</body>
</html>
```

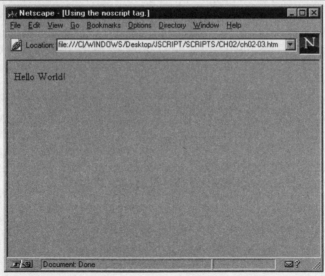

FIGURE 14.10:   Using the `<noscript>` tag with Navigator, a JavaScript-capable browser

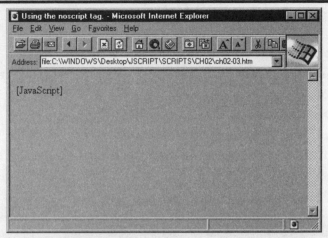

FIGURE 14.11: Using the <noscript> tag with Internet Explorer 2, a non-JavaScript browser

The Script Tag's SRC Attribute

The script tag itself provides an alternative way to include JavaScript code in an HTML document, via the tag's SRC attribute, which may be used to specify a *file* containing JavaScript statements. Here's an example of the use of the SRC attribute:

```
<script language="JavaScript" SRC="src.js">
</script>
```

In the above example, the file `src.js` is a file containing JavaScript statements. (The file could have been named anything, but it should end with the `.js` extension; I just chose `src.js` to help you remember the SRC attribute.) Note that the closing `</script>` tag is still required.

If the file `src.js` contains the code

```
<!- Begin hiding JavaScript
document.write("This text was generated by code in the
➡ src.js file.")
// End hiding JavaScript ->
```

then the HTML document shown below would produce the browser display shown in Figure 14.12.

Inserting Source JavaScript Files

```
<html>
<head>
<title>Using the SRC attribute of the script tag.</title>
</head>
<body>
<script language="JavaScript" SRC="src.js">
</script>
</body>
</html>
```

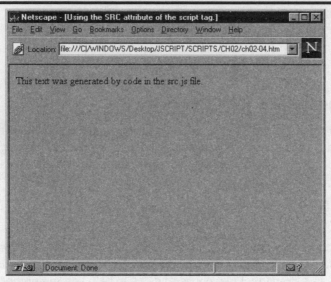

FIGURE 14.12: Using the SRC attribute of the <script> tag to include JavaScript code

NOTE

The SRC attribute may have a URL as its attribute value. Web servers that provide the source file, however, *must* report the file's MIME type as application/x-javascript; otherwise, browsers will not load the source file.

JavaScript Entities

JavaScript entities allow the value of an HTML attribute to be provided by a JavaScript *expression*. This allows attribute values to be dynamically calculated during the loading of a Web page.

A JavaScript entity begins with &{ and ends with };. The following example shows how the HREF attribute of a link may be specified by the JavaScript linkTo variable:

```
<A HREF="&{linkTo};">Click here.</A>
```

The value of linkTo, which must be calculated earlier in the script, must be a valid URL.

NOTE

You'll learn about variables in the section, "Variables—Value Storehouses," later in this chapter.

The following code shows how the above tag can be used to create a link to this book's Web page.

Using JavaScript Entities

```
<html>
<head>
<title>Using the JavaScript entities.</title>
<script language="JavaScript"><!-
linkTo="http://www.jaworski.com/javascript"
// ->
</script>
</head>
<body>
<A HREF="&{linkTo};">Click here.</A>
</body>
</html>
```

WARNING

Microsoft Internet Explorer does not support JavaScript entities. Use of entities with Internet Explorer may lead to scripting errors.

Part iii

JAVASCRIPT COMMENTS

The JavaScript language provides comments of its own. These comments are used to insert notes and processing descriptions into scripts. The comments are ignored (as intended) when the statements of a script are parsed by JavaScript-enabled browsers.

JavaScript comments use the syntax of C++ and Java. The // string identifies a comment that continues to the end of a line. An example of a single line comment follows:

```
// This JavaScript comment continues to the end of the line.
```

The /* and */ strings are used to identify comments that may span multiple lines. The comment begins with /* and continues up to */. An example of a multiple line comment follows:

```
/* This is
an example
of a multiple
line comment */
```

The script shown below illustrates the use of JavaScript comments. The script contains four statements that, if they weren't ignored, would write various capitalizations of the text *Hello World!* to the current document. However, since the first three of these statements are contained in comments, and since browsers ignore comments, these statements have no effect on the Web page generated by the script. Figure 14.13 shows how the JavaScript comments in shown below are handled by a JavaScript-capable browser.

Using JavaScript Comments

```
<html>
<head>
<title>Using JavaScript comments</title>
</head>
<body>
<script language="JavaScript">
<!- Begin hiding JavaScript
```

```
// document.write("hello world!")
/* document.write("Hello world!")
document.write("Hello World!") */
document.write("HELLO WORLD!")
// End hiding Javascript ->
</script>
</body>
</html>
```

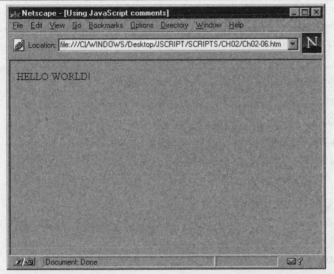

FIGURE 14.13:   How JavaScript comments are handled by a JavaScript-capable browser

NOTE

Throughout the rest of this chapter, all browser references will be to JavaScript-capable browsers, unless otherwise specified.

Part iii

Use of the Document Head

The head of an HTML document provides a great place to include Java-Script definitions. Since the head of a document is processed before its body, placing definitions in the head will cause them to be defined before they are used. This is important because any attempt to use a variable before it is defined results in an error. The code below shows how JavaScript definitions can be placed in the head of an HTML document. The script contained in the document head defines a variable named *greeting* and sets its value to the string *Hi Web surfers!* (You'll learn all about variables in the section, "Variables–Value Storehouses," later in this chapter.) The script contained in the document's body then writes the value of the `greeting` variable to the current document. Figure 14.14 shows how this document is displayed.

Using the Head for Definitions

```
<HTML>
<HEAD>
<TITLE>Using the HEAD for definitions</TITLE>
<SCRIPT language="JavaScript">
<!-
greeting = "Hi Web surfers!"
// ->
</SCRIPT>
</HEAD>
<BODY>
<SCRIPT language="JavaScript">
<!-
document.write(greeting)
// ->
</SCRIPT>
</BODY>
</HTML>
```

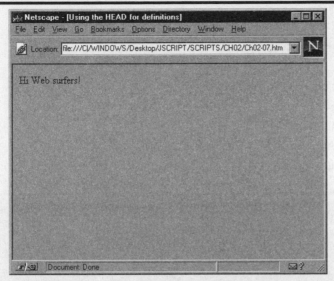

FIGURE 14.14: How the greeting variable is displayed

It is important to make sure that all definitions occur before they are used; otherwise an error will be displayed when your HTML document is loaded by a browser. Below is the code for an HTML document that will generate a "use before definition" error. In this listing, the head contains a JavaScript statement that writes the value of the `greeting` variable to the current document; however, the `greeting` variable is not defined until the body of the document. Figure 14.15 shows how this error is displayed by a browser.

Example of Use before Definition

```
<HTML>
<HEAD>
<TITLE>Use before definition</TITLE>
<SCRIPT language="JavaScript">
<!-
document.write(greeting)
// ->
</SCRIPT>
```

Part iii

```
</HEAD>
<BODY>
<SCRIPT language="JavaScript">
<!-
greeting = "Hi Web surfers!"
// ->
</SCRIPT>
</BODY>
</HTML>
```

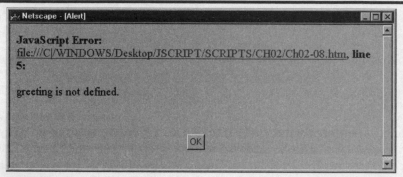

FIGURE 14.15:   JavaScript generates an error when a variable is used before it is defined.

GENERATING HTML

The examples presented so far have shown how you can use JavaScript to write simple text to the document object. By including HTML tags in your JavaScript script, you can also use JavaScript to generate HTML elements that will be displayed in the current document. The following example illustrates this concept. Figure 14.16 shows how the Web page generated by this script is displayed.

Using JavaScript to Create HTML Tags

```
<HTML>
<HEAD>
<TITLE>Using JavaScript to create HTML tags</TITLE>
```

```
<SCRIPT LANGUAGE="JavaScript">
<!-
greeting = "<H1>Hi Web surfers!</H1>"
welcome = "<P>Welcome to <CITE>Mastering JavaScript and
JScript </CITE>.</P>"
// ->
</SCRIPT>
</HEAD>
<BODY>
<SCRIPT LANGUAGE="JavaScript">
<!-
document.write(greeting)
document.write(welcome)
// ->
</SCRIPT>
</BODY>
</HTML>
```

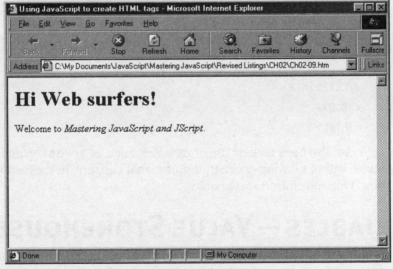

FIGURE 14.16: Generating HTML from JavaScript

In the script contained in the head of the HTML document, the variables greeting and welcome are assigned text strings containing embedded HTML tags. These text strings are displayed by the script contained in the body of the HTML document:

▶ The greeting variable contains the heading *Hi Web surfers!*, which is surrounded by the HTML heading tags <H1> and </H1>.

▶ The welcome variable is assigned the string *Welcome to Mastering JavaScript and JScript*.

　　▶ The citation tags, <CITE> and </CITE>, cause the welcome variable's string to be cited as a literary reference (which means it shows up in italic).

　　▶ The paragraph tags, <P> and </P>, that surround the welcome text are used to mark it as a separate paragraph.

The HTML document generated by the script is equivalent to the following:

```
<HTML>
<HEAD>
<TITLE>Using JavaScript to create HTML tags</TITLE>
</HEAD>
<BODY>
<H1>Hi Web surfers!</H1>
<P>Welcome to <CITE>Mastering JavaScript and JScript
</CITE>.</P>
</BODY>
</HTML>
```

So far, I've been making use of variables, such as greeting and welcome, without having explicitly defined what they are. In the next section, I formally introduce variables.

VARIABLES—VALUE STOREHOUSES

JavaScript, like other programming languages, uses variables to store values so they can be used in other parts of a program. Variables are names that are associated with these stored values. For example, the variable imageName may be used to refer to the name of an image file to be displayed and the variable `totalAmount` may be used to display the total amount of a user's purchase.

Variable names can begin with an uppercase letter (A through Z), a lowercase letter (a through z), an underscore character (_), or a dollar sign character ($). The remaining characters can consist of letters, the underscore character, the dollar sign character, or digits (0 through 9). Examples of variable names are as follows:

```
orderNumber2
_123
SUM
Image7
Previous_Document
```

Variable names are case-sensitive. This means that a variable named `sum` refers to a different value than one named `Sum`, `sUm`, or `SUM`.

WARNING

Since variable names are case-sensitive, it is important to make sure that you use the same capitalization each time you use a variable.

WARNING

The dollar sign ($) character is reserved for machine-generated code and should not be used in your scripts. In particular, it should not be used for scripts that will be run by earlier browsers that are not fully ECMAScript-compatible.

Part iii

Types and Variables

Unlike Java and some other programming languages, JavaScript does not require you to specify the *type* of data contained in a variable. (It doesn't even allow it.) In fact, the same variable may be used to contain a variety of different values, such as the text string *Hello World!*, the integer *13*, the floating-point value *3.14*, or the logical value *true*. The JavaScript interpreter keeps track of and converts the type of data contained in a variable.

JavaScript's automatic handling of different types of values is a double-edged sword. On one side, it frees you from having to explicitly specify the type of data contained in a variable and from having to convert from one data type to another. On the other side, since JavaScript automatically converts values of one type to another, it is important to keep track of what types of values should be contained in a variable and how they are converted in expressions involving variables of other types. The next section, "Types and Literal Values," identifies the types of values that JavaScript supports. The later section, "Conversion between Types," discusses important issues related to type conversion.

Types and Literal Values

JavaScript supports four primitive types of values along with complex types, such as arrays and objects. *Primitive types* are types that can be assigned a single literal value, such as a number, string, or Boolean value. Here are the primitive types that JavaScript supports:

- ▶ Number   Consists of integer and floating-point numbers and the special NaN (not a number) value. Numbers use a 64-bit IEEE 754 format.

- ▶ Boolean   Consists of the logical values true and false.

- ▶ String   Consists of string values that are enclosed in single or double quotes.

- ▶ The Null type   Consists of a single value, null, which identifies a null, empty, or nonexistent reference.

- ▶ The Undefined type   Consists of a single value, undefined, which is used to indicate that a variable has not been assigned a value.

WARNING
The undefined value was introduced with the ECMAScript specification and is not supported by browsers that are not fully ECMAScript-compatible. This includes Navigator 4.05 and earlier and Internet Explorer 3.

In JavaScript, you do not declare the type of a variable as you do in other languages, such as Java and C++. Instead, the type of a variable is implicitly defined based on the literal values that you assign to it. For example, if you assign the integer *123* to the variable total, then total will support number operations. If you assign the string value *The sum of all accounts* to total, then total will support string operations. Similarly, if you assign the logical value *true* to total, then total will support Boolean operations.

It is also possible for a variable to be assigned a value of one type and then later in the script's execution to be assigned a value of another type. For example, the variable total could be assigned *123*, then *The sum of all accounts*, and then *true*. The type of the variable would change with the type of value assigned to it. The different types of literal values that can be assigned to a variable are covered in the following subsections.

Number Types—Integers and Floating-Point Numbers

When working with numbers, JavaScript supports both integer and floating-point values. It transparently converts from one type to another as values of one type are combined with values of other types in numerical expressions. For example, integer values are converted to floating-point values when they are used in floating-point expressions.

Integer Literals

Integers can be represented in JavaScript in decimal, hexadecimal, or octal form:

▶ A decimal (base-10) integer is what nonprogrammers are used to seeing—the digits 0 through 9, with each new column representing a higher power of 10.

▶ A hexadecimal (base-16) integer in JavaScript must always begin with the characters 0x or 0X in the two leftmost columns. Hexadecimal uses the digits 0 through 9 to represent the values zero through nine and the letters A through F to represent the values normal people know as 10 through 15.

▶ An octal (base-8) integer in JavaScript must always begin with the character 0 in the leftmost column. Octal uses only the digits 0 through 7.

Examples of decimal, hexadecimal, and octal integers are provided in Table 14.2.

TABLE 14.2: Examples of Decimal, Hexadecimal, and Octal Integers for the Same Values

DECIMAL NUMBER	HEXADECIMAL EQUIVALENT	OCTAL EQUIVALENT
19	0x13	023
255	0xff	0377
513	0x201	01001
1024	0x400	02000
12345	0x3039	030071

The program shown below illustrates the use of JavaScript hexadecimal and octal integers. Figure 14.17 shows how the Web page generated by this program is displayed. Note that the hexadecimal and octal integers are converted to decimal before they are displayed.

Using JavaScript Integers

```
<HTML>
<HEAD>
<TITLE>Using JavaScript integers</TITLE>
</HEAD>
<BODY>
<SCRIPT LANGUAGE="JavaScript">
<!-
document.write("0xab00 + 0xcd = ")
document.write(0xab00 + 0xcd)
document.write("<BR>")
document.write("0xff - 0123 = ")
document.write(0xff - 0123)
document.write("<BR>")
document.write("-0x12 = ")
document.write(-0x12)
// ->
</SCRIPT>
</BODY>
</HTML>
```

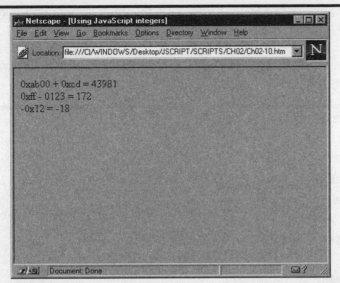

FIGURE 14.17:   Using hexadecimal and octal integers

Floating-Point Literals   Floating-point literals are used to represent numbers that require the use of a decimal point, or very large or small numbers that must be written using exponential notation.

A floating-point number must consist of either a number containing a decimal point or an integer followed by an exponent. The following are valid floating-point numbers:

```
-4.321
55.
12e2
1e-2
7e1
-4e-4
.5
```

As you can see in the examples above, floating-point literals may contain an initial integer, followed by an optional decimal point and fraction, followed by an optional exponent ("e" or "E") and its integer exponent value. For example, 4e6 equals 4 x 10 to the sixth power, which equals 4,000,000. Also, the initial integer and integer exponent value may be signed as positive or negative (+ or −). Up to 20 significant digits may be used to represent floating-point values.

The script shown below, which generates the page shown in Figure 14.18, illustrates how JavaScript displays these values. Notice that JavaScript simplifies the display of these numbers whenever possible.

Using Floating-Point Numbers

```
<HTML>
<HEAD>
<TITLE>Using floating-point numbers</TITLE>
</HEAD>
<BODY>
<SCRIPT LANGUAGE="JavaScript">
<!-
document.write(-4.321)
document.write("<BR>")
document.write(55.)
document.write("<BR>")
document.write(12e2)
document.write("<BR>")
document.write(1e-2)
document.write("<BR>")
document.write(7e1)
document.write("<BR>")
document.write(-4e-4)
document.write("<BR>")
document.write(.5)
// ->
</SCRIPT>
</BODY>
</HTML>
```

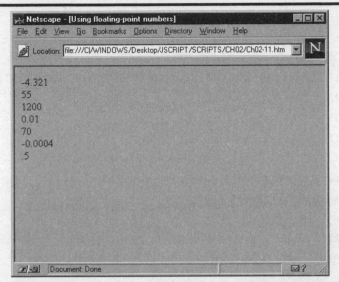

FIGURE 14.18:   How JavaScript displays floating-point numbers

Boolean Values

JavaScript, like Java and unlike C, supports a pure Boolean type that consists of the two values `true` and `false`. Several logical operators may be used in Boolean expressions. JavaScript automatically converts the Boolean values `true` and `false` into 1 and 0 when they are used in numerical expressions. The script shown below illustrates this automatic conversion. Figure 14.19 shows the results of this conversion as displayed by Navigator.

NOTE

A *Boolean value* is a value that is either true or false. The word *Boolean* is taken from the name of the mathematician George Boole, who developed much of the fundamental theory of mathematical logic.

Conversion of Logical Values to Numeric Values

```
<HTML>
<HEAD>
<TITLE>Conversion of logical values to numeric values</TITLE>
</HEAD>
<BODY>
<SCRIPT LANGUAGE="JavaScript">
<!-
document.write("true*5 + false*7 = ")
document.write(true*5 +false*7)
// ->
</SCRIPT>
</BODY>
</HTML>
```

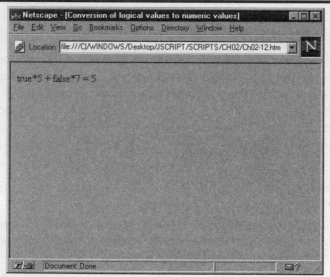

FIGURE 14.19: How logical values are converted to other types

String Values

JavaScript provides built-in support for strings of characters. A string is a sequence of zero or more characters that are enclosed by double (") or single quotes ('). If a string begins with a double quote, then it must end with a double quote. Likewise, if a string begins with a single quote, then it must end with a single quote.

To insert a quote character in a string, you must precede it with the backslash (\) escape character. The following are examples of the use of the escape character to insert quotes into strings:

```
"He asked, \"Who owns this book?\""
'It\'s Bill\'s book.'
```

The following script illustrates the use of quotes within strings. Figure 14.20 shows how the strings are displayed. Note that single quotes do not need to be coded with escape characters when they are used within double-quoted strings. Similarly, double quotes do not need to be coded when they are used within single-quoted strings.

Using Quotes within Strings

```
<HTML>
<HEAD>
<TITLE>Using quotes within strings</TITLE>
</HEAD>
<BODY>
<SCRIPT LANGUAGE="JavaScript">
<!-
document.write("He said, \"That's mine!\"<BR>")
document.write('She said, "No it\'s not."<BR>')
document.write('That\'s all folks!')
// ->
</SCRIPT>
</BODY>
</HTML>
```

Part iii

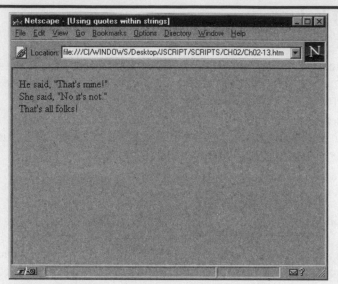

FIGURE 14.20:   How quotes are inserted into strings

JavaScript defines special formatting characters for use in strings. These characters are identified in Table 14.3.

TABLE 14.3: Special Formatting Characters

CHARACTER	MEANING
\'	single quote
\"	double quote
\\	backslash
\n	new line
\r	carriage return
\f	formfeed
\t	horizontal tab
\b	backspace

The script below shows how these formatting characters are used. Figure 14.21 displays the Web page generated by this script. The Web page

uses the HTML *preformatted text* tags to prevent the formatting characters from being treated as HTML whitespace characters. Notice that the
backspace character is incorrectly displayed, the formfeed character is
ignored, and the carriage return character is displayed in the same manner as the new line character. Even though these characters are not fully
supported in the display of Web pages, they may still be used to insert
formatting codes within data and files that JavaScript produces.

Using Special Formatting Characters

```
<HTML>
<HEAD>
<TITLE>Using special formatting characters</TITLE>
</HEAD>
<BODY>
<PRE>
<SCRIPT LANGUAGE="JavaScript">
<!-
document.write("This shows how the \bbackspace character
➡ works.\n")
document.write("This shows how the \ttab character works.\n")
document.write("This shows how the \rcarriage return
➡ character works.\n")
document.write("This shows how the \fform feed character
➡ works.\n")
document.write("This shows how the \nnew line character
➡ works.\n")
// ->
</SCRIPT>
</PRE>
</BODY>
</HTML>
```

Part iii

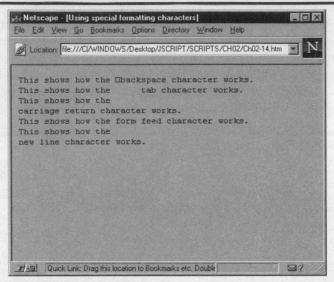

FIGURE 14.21: This is how formatting characters are handled. Note that your Web browser does not process all characters.

The *null* Value

The null value is common to all JavaScript types. It is used to set a variable to an initial value that is different from other valid values. Use of the null value prevents the sort of errors that result from using uninitialized variables. The null value is automatically converted to default values of other types when used in an expression, as you'll see in the following section, "Conversion between Types."

The *undefined* Value

The undefined value indicates that a variable has been created but not assigned a value. Like the null value, the undefined value is common to all JavaScript types and is automatically converted to default values of these types. The undefined value is converted to NaN for numeric types, false for Boolean, and "undefined" for strings.

Conversion between Types

JavaScript automatically converts values from one type to another when they are used in an expression. This means that you can combine different types in an expression and JavaScript will try to perform the type conversions that are necessary for the expression to make sense. For example, the expression, `"test"` + 5 will convert the numeric 5 to a string "5" and append it to the string *"test"*, producing *"test5"*. JavaScript's automatic type conversion also allows you to assign a value of one type to a variable and then later assign a value of a different type to the same variable.

How does JavaScript convert from one type to another? The process of determining when a conversion should occur and what type of conversion should be made is fairly complex. JavaScript converts values when it evaluates an expression or assigns a value to a variable. When JavaScript assigns a value to a variable, it changes the type associated with the variable to the type of the value that is assigns.

When JavaScript evaluates an expression, it parses the expression into its component unary and binary expressions based upon the order of precedence of the operators it contains. It then evaluates the component unary and binary expressions of the parse tree. Figure 14.22 illustrates this process. Each expression is evaluated according to the operators involved. If an operator takes a value of a type that is different than the type of an operand, then the operand is converted to a type that is valid for the operator.

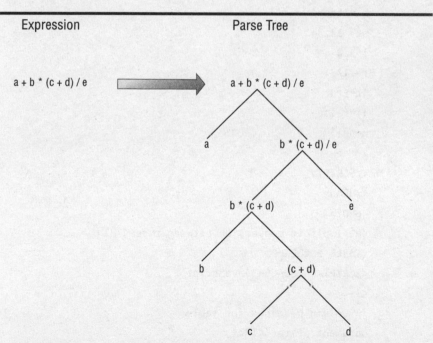

FIGURE 14.22: Expressions are evaluated based on the types of operators involved.

Part iii

Some operators, such as the + operator, may be used for more than one type. For example, `"a"+"b"` results in the string *"ab"* when the + operator is used with string values, but it assumes its typical arithmetic meaning when used with numeric operands. What happens when JavaScript attempts to evaluate `"a"+3`? JavaScript converts the integer 3 into the string *"3"* and yields *"a3"* for the expression. In general, JavaScript will favor string operators over all others, followed by floating-point, integer, and logical operators.

The script shown below illustrates JavaScript conversion between types when the + operator is used. Figure 14.23 shows how the Web page resulting from this script is displayed.

Automatic Conversion between Types

```
<HTML>
<HEAD>
<TITLE>Implicit conversion between types</TITLE>
<SCRIPT LANGUAGE="JavaScript">
<!-
s1="test"
s2="12.34"
i=123
r=.123
lt=true
lf=false
n=null
// ->
</SCRIPT>
</HEAD>
<BODY>
<H1>Implicit conversion between types</H1>
<TABLE BORDER=2>
<SCRIPT LANGUAGE="JavaScript">
<!-
// Column headings for table
document.write("<TR>")
document.write("<TH>row + column</TH>")
```

```
document.write("<TH>string \"12.34\"</TH>")
document.write("<TH>integer 123</TH>")
document.write("<TH>float .123</TH>")
document.write("<TH>logical true</TH>")
document.write("<TH>logical false</TH>")
document.write("<TH>null</TH>")
document.write("</TR>")
// First operand is a string
document.write("<TR>")
document.write("<TH>string \"test\"</TH>")
document.write("<TD>")
document.write(s1+s2)
document.write("</TD><TD>")
document.write(s1+i)
document.write("</TD><TD>")
document.write(s1+r)
document.write("</TD><TD>")
document.write(s1+lt)
document.write("</TD><TD>")
document.write(s1+lf)
document.write("</TD><TD>")
document.write(s1+n)
document.write("</TD>")
document.write("</TR>")
// First operand is an integer
document.write("<TR>")
document.write("<TH>integer 123</TH>")
document.write("<TD>")
document.write(i+s2)
document.write("</TD><TD>")
document.write(i+i)
document.write("</TD><TD>")
document.write(i+r)
document.write("</TD><TD>")
```

```
document.write(i+lt)
document.write("</TD><TD>")
document.write(i+lf)
document.write("</TD><TD>")
document.write(i+n)
document.write("</TD>")
document.write("</TR>")
// First operand is a float
document.write("<TR>")
document.write("<TH>float .123</TH>")
document.write("<TD>")
document.write(r+s2)
document.write("</TD><TD>")
document.write(r+i)
document.write("</TD><TD>")
document.write(r+r)
document.write("</TD><TD>")
document.write(r+lt)
document.write("</TD><TD>")
document.write(r+lf)
document.write("</TD><TD>")
document.write(r+n)
document.write("</TD>")
document.write("</TR>")
// First operand is a logical true
document.write("<TR>")
document.write("<TH>logical true</TH>")
document.write("<TD>")
document.write(lt+s2)
document.write("</TD><TD>")
document.write(lt+i)
document.write("</TD><TD>")
document.write(lt+r)
document.write("</TD><TD>")
```

```
document.write(lt+lt)
document.write("</TD><TD>")
document.write(lt+lf)
document.write("</TD><TD>")
document.write(lt+n)
document.write("</TD>")
document.write("</TR>")
// First operand is a logical false
document.write("<TR>")
document.write("<TH>logical false</TH>")
document.write("<TD>")
document.write(lf+s2)
document.write("</TD><TD>")
document.write(lf+i)
document.write("</TD><TD>")
document.write(lf+r)
document.write("</TD><TD>")
document.write(lf+lt)
document.write("</TD><TD>")
document.write(lf+lf)
document.write("</TD><TD>")
document.write(lf+n)
document.write("</TD>")
document.write("</TR>")
// First operand is null
document.write("<TR>")
document.write("<TH>null</TH>")
document.write("<TD>")
document.write(n+s2)
document.write("</TD><TD>")
document.write(n+i)
document.write("</TD><TD>")
document.write(n+r)
document.write("</TD><TD>")
```

```
document.write(n+1t)
document.write("</TD><TD>")
document.write(n+1f)
document.write("</TD><TD>")
document.write(n+n)
document.write("</TD>")
document.write("</TR>")
// ->
</SCRIPT>
</TABLE>
</BODY>
</HTML>
```

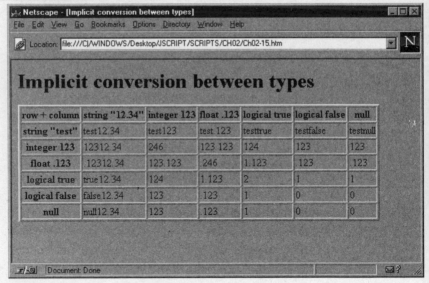

FIGURE 14.23: Conversion table for the + operator

Note that in all cases where string operands are used with a non-string operator, JavaScript converts the other operator into a string:

▶ Numeric values are converted to their appropriate string value.

▶ Boolean values are converted to *1* and *0* to support numerical operations.

▶ The null value is converted to *null* for string operations, *false* for logical operations, and *0* for numerical operations.

Let's take a look at the preceding code. The script in the document head defines the variables to be used in the table's operations. The s1 and s2 variables are assigned string values. The i and r variables are assigned integer and floating-point values. The lt and lf variables are assigned logical values. The n variable is assigned the null value.

The script in the document body is fairly long. However, most of the script is used to generate the HTML tags for the cells of the conversion table. The script is surrounded by the tags <TABLE BORDER=2> and </TABLE>. The script then generates the cells of the table one row at a time. The <TR> and </TR> tags mark a row of the table. The <TH> and </TH> tags mark header cells. The <TD> and </TD> tags identify normal non-header table cells.

First, the column header row is displayed. Then each row of the table shown in Figure 14.23 is generated by combining the operand at the row heading with the operand at the table heading using the + operator.

NOTE

Internet Explorer displays the page shown in Figure 14.23 slightly differently. If a decimal number has a magnitude less than 1, Internet Explorer adds a 0 before the decimal when displaying the number or converting it to a string value. For example, .123 is displayed as 0.123.

Conversion Functions

Functions are collections of JavaScript code that perform a particular task and often return a value. A function may take zero or more parameters. These parameters are used to specify the data to be processed by the function.

JavaScript provides three functions that are used to perform explicit type conversion. These are eval(), parseInt(), and parseFloat().

NOTE

Functions are referenced by their name with the empty parameter list "()" appended. This makes it easier to differentiate between functions and variables in the discussion of scripts.

The `eval()` function can be used to convert a string expression to a numeric value. For example, the statement `total = eval("432.1*10")`, results in the value *4321* being assigned to the `total` variable. The `eval()` function takes the string value *"432.1*10"* as a parameter and returns the numeric value *4321* as the result of the function call. If the string value passed as a parameter to the `eval()` function does not represent a numeric value, then use of `eval()` results in an error.

The `parseInt()` function is used to convert a string value into an integer. Unlike `eval()`, `parseInt()` returns the first integer contained in the string or *0* if the string does not begin with an integer. For example, `parseInt("123xyz")` returns *123* and `parseInt("xyz")` returns *0*. The `parseInt()` function also parses hexadecimal and decimal integers.

The `parseFloat()` function is similar to the `parseInt()` function. It returns the first floating-point number contained in a string or *0* if the string does not begin with a valid floating-point number. For example, `parseFloat("2.1e4xyz")` returns *21000* and `parseFloat("xyz")` returns *0*.

The script shown below illustrates the use of JavaScript's explicit conversion functions. Figure 14.24 shows how the Web page that this script generates is displayed.

Explicit Conversion Functions

```
<HTML>
<HEAD>
<TITLE>Using Explicit Conversion Functions</TITLE>
</HEAD>
<BODY>
<H1 ALIGN="CENTER">Using Explicit Conversion Functions</H1>
<SCRIPT LANGUAGE="JavaScript"><!-
document.write('eval("12.34*10") = ')
document.write(eval("12.34*10"))
document.write("<BR>")
document.write('parseInt("0x10") = ')
document.write(parseInt("0x10"))
document.write("<BR>")
document.write('parseFloat("5.4321e6") = ')
```

```
document.write(parseFloat("5.4321e6"))
// -></SCRIPT>
</BODY>
</HTML>
```

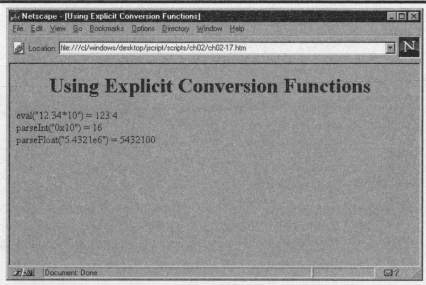

FIGURE 14.24: Using the JavaScript conversion functions

The Object Type and Arrays

In addition to the primitive types discussed in the previous sections, JavaScript supports the Object type. This type is referred to as a complex data type because it is built from the primitive types. The Object type, and objects in general, will be discussed in Chapter 15, "Working with Objects." In this chapter, I'll cover a special JavaScript object—the array.

NOTE

Arrays are a special type of JavaScript object.

Arrays—Accessing Indexed Values

Arrays are objects that are capable of storing a sequence of values. These values are stored in indexed locations within the array. For example, suppose you have a company with five employees and you want to display the names of your employees on a Web page. You could keep track of their names in an array variable named `employee`. You would declare the array using the statement

```
employee = new Array(5)
```

and store the names of your employees in the array using the following statements:

```
employee[0] = "Bill"
employee[1] = "Bob"
employee[2] = "Ted"
employee[3] = "Alice"
employee[4] = "Sue"
```

You could then access the names of the individual employees by referring to the individual elements of the array. For example, you could display the names of your employees using statements such as the following:

```
document.write(employee[0])
document.write(employee[1])
document.write(employee[2])
document.write(employee[3])
document.write(employee[4])
```

The script shown below illustrates the use of arrays. Figure 14.25 shows how the Web page generated by this script is displayed.

Using JavaScript Arrays

```
<HTML>
<HEAD>
<TITLE>Using Arrays</TITLE>
</HEAD>
<BODY>
<H1 ALIGN="CENTER">Using Arrays</H1>
```

```
<SCRIPT LANGUAGE="JavaScript"><!-
employee = new Array(5)
employee[0] = "Bill"
employee[1] = "Bob"
employee[2] = "Ted"
employee[3] = "Alice"
employee[4] = "Sue"
document.write(employee[0]+"<BR>")
document.write(employee[1]+"<BR>")
document.write(employee[2]+"<BR>")
document.write(employee[3]+"<BR>")
document.write(employee[4])
// -></SCRIPT>
</BODY>
</HTML>
```

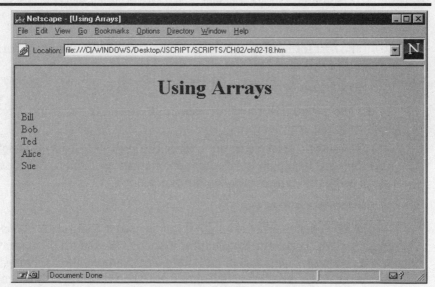

FIGURE 14.25: Arrays allow multiple values to be stored with a single variable

The *length* of an array is the number of elements that it contains. In the preceding example script, the length of the employee array is 5. The individual elements of an array are referenced using the name of the array followed by the index of the array element enclosed in brackets. Because the first index is 0, the last index is one less than the length of the array. For example, suppose that you have an array named day of length 7 that contains the names of the days of the week. The individual elements of this array would be accessed as day[0], day[1], ..., day[6].

Declaring Arrays

An array must be declared before it is used. An array may be declared using either of the following two statement forms:

▶ arrayName = new Array(*arrayLength*)

▶ arrayName = new Array()

NOTE

A third form of array declaration is discussed in the following subsection, "Constructing Dense Arrays."

In the first form, the length of the array is explicitly specified. An example of this form is:

```
days = new Array(7)
```

In the above example, days corresponds to the array name and 7 corresponds to the array length.

In the second array declaration form, the length of the array is not specified and results in the declaration of an array of length 0. An example of using this type of array declaration follows:

```
order = new Array()
```

This declares an array of length 0 that is used to keep track of customer orders. JavaScript automatically extends the length of an array when new array elements are initialized. For example, the following statements create an order array of length 0 and then subsequently extend the length of the array to 100 and then 1000.

```
order = new Array()
order[99] = "Widget #457"
order[999] = "Delux Widget Set #10"
```

When JavaScript encounters the reference to order[99] in the above example, it extends the length of the array to 100 and initializes order[99] to *"Widget #457"*. When JavaScript encounters the reference to order[999] in the third statement, it extends the length of order to 1000 and initializes order[999] to *"Delux Widget Set #10"*.

Even if an array is initially declared to be of fixed initial length, it still may be extended by referencing elements that are outside the current size of the array. This is accomplished in the same manner as with zero-length arrays. The script below shows how fixed-length arrays are expanded as new array elements are referenced. Figure 14.26 shows how the Web page that this script generates is displayed.

Extending the Length of an Array

```
<HTML>
<HEAD>
<TITLE>Extending Arrays</TITLE>
</HEAD>
<BODY>
<H1 ALIGN="CENTER">Extending Arrays</H1>
<SCRIPT LANGUAGE="JavaScript"><!-
order = new Array()
document.write("order.length = "+order.length+"<BR>")
order[99] = "Widget #457"
document.write("order.length = "+order.length+"<BR>")
order[999] = "Delux Widget Set #10"
document.write("order.length = "+order.length+"<BR>")
// -></SCRIPT>
</BODY>
</HTML>
```

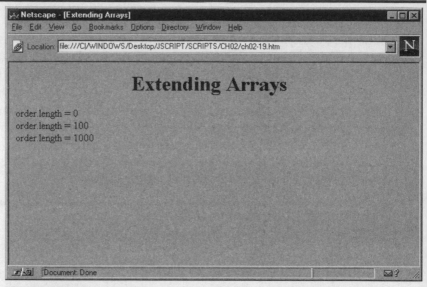

FIGURE 14.26: An array's length dynamically expands as new elements are referenced.

Constructing Dense Arrays

A *dense array* is an array that is initially declared with each element being assigned a specified value. Dense arrays are used in the same manner as other arrays; they are just declared and initialized in a more efficient manner. Dense arrays are declared by *listing* the values of the array elements in the array declaration, in place of the array length. Dense array declarations take the following form:

```
arrayName = new Array(value0, value1, ... , valuen)
```

In the above declaration, because we start counting at zero, the length of the array is n+1.

When creating short length arrays, the dense array declaration is very efficient. For example, an array containing the three-letter abbreviations for the days of the week may be declared using the following statement:

```
day = new Array('Sun','Mon','Tue','Wed','Thu','Fri','Sat')
```

The Elements of an Array

JavaScript does not place any restrictions on the values of the elements of an array. These values could be of different types or refer to other arrays or objects. For example, you could declare an array as follows:

```
junk = new Array("s1",'s2',4,3.5,true,false,null,new
Array(5,6,7))
```

The `junk` array has length 8, and its elements are as follows:

```
junk[0]="s1"
junk[1]='s2'
junk[2]=4
junk[3]=3.5
junk[4]=true
junk[5]=false
junk[6]=null
junk[7]=a new dense array consisting of the values 5, 6, & 7
```

The last element of the array, `junk[7]`, contains an array as its value. The three elements of `junk[7]` can be accessed using *a second set of subscripts*, as follows:

```
junk[7][0]=5
junk[7][1]=6
junk[7][2]=7
```

The script shown below illustrates the use of arrays within arrays. Figure 14.27 shows the Web page that results from execution of this script.

An Array within an Array

```
<HTML>
<HEAD>
<TITLE>Arrays within Arrays</TITLE>
</HEAD>
<BODY>
<H1 ALIGN="CENTER">Arrays within Arrays</H1>
<SCRIPT LANGUAGE="JavaScript"><!-
junk = new Array("s1",'s2',4,3.5,true,false,null,new
Array(5,6,7))
```

```
document.write("junk[0] = "+junk[0]+"<BR>")
document.write("junk[1] = "+junk[1]+"<BR>")
document.write("junk[2] = "+junk[2]+"<BR>")
document.write("junk[3] = "+junk[3]+"<BR>")
document.write("junk[4] = "+junk[4]+"<BR>")
document.write("junk[5] = "+junk[5]+"<BR>")
document.write("junk[6] = "+junk[6]+"<BR>")
document.write("junk[7][0] = "+junk[7][0]+"<BR>")
document.write("junk[7][1] = "+junk[7][1]+"<BR>")
document.write("junk[7][2] = "+junk[7][2])
// -></SCRIPT>
</BODY>
</HTML>
```

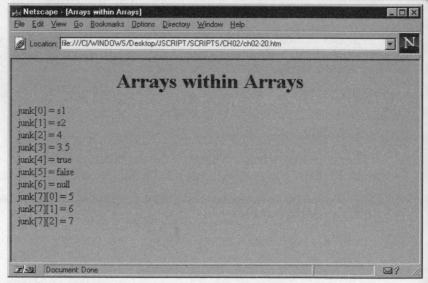

FIGURE 14.27: An array may contain another array as the value of one of its elements.

Objects and the *length* Property

JavaScript arrays are implemented as objects. *Objects* are named collections of data that have properties and may be accessed via methods. A *property* returns a value that identifies some aspect of the state of an object. *Methods* are used to read or modify the data contained in an object.

The length of an array is a property of an array. You can access the property of any object in JavaScript by appending a period (.) plus the name of the property to the name of the object, as shown here:

```
objectName.propertyName
```

For example, the length of an array is determined as follows:

```
arrayName.length
```

Now consider the following array:

```
a = new Array(2,4,6,8,10)
```

The value returned by `a.length` is *5*.

WHAT'S NEXT?

This chapter provided a solid introduction to JavaScript. You learned how JavaScript works and how JavaScript statements are embedded in HTML documents. You also learned about JavaScript's use of types and variables, and how JavaScript automatically converts values of one type to another. In the next chapter, you'll learn how to declare and use JavaScript objects in your Web pages.

Part iii

Chapter 15

WORKING WITH OBJECTS

One of the most important features of JavaScript is that it is an object-based language. This simplifies the design of JavaScript programs and enables them to be developed in a more intuitive, modular, and reusable manner.

This chapter describes JavaScript's support of objects and object-based programming. It introduces the JavaScript Object Model and summarizes the predefined JavaScript objects. It also shows how to create your own object types. When you finish this chapter, you'll be able to define and use objects in your Web pages.

Adapted from *Mastering JavaScript and JScript*, by James Jaworski

ISBN 0-7821-2492-5 $39.99   Available in March 1999

WHAT ARE OBJECTS?

Most people know that objects are entities that exist in the real world of people, places, and things. But they also exist in the cyber world of computers and networking. Examples of real-world objects include you, the book you are reading, and the lamp that provides you with light. Examples of cyber-world objects are the Web pages that you create and the individual HTML elements they contain. It is these types of objects that I will be discussing in relation to JavaScript.

An object consists of two things:

▶ A collection of *properties* that contain data

▶ *Methods* that enable operations on the data contained in those properties

When you view something as an object, you look at it in terms of its properties and methods. Table 15.1 identifies some of the properties and methods that could apply to the example objects mentioned in the previous paragraph.

TABLE 15.1: Examples of Objects, Properties, and Methods

OBJECT	PROPERTIES	METHODS
You (real-world object)	height weight hairColor	eat() exercise() grow()
This book (real-world object)	pages currentPage	turnPageForward() turnPageBackward() goToPage()
A lamp (real-world object)	onOffState	turnOn() turnOff()
A Web page (cyber-world object)	title bgColor links	open() close() write()
An HTML button (cyber-world object)	name value	setLabel()

WHAT IS OBJECT-ORIENTED PROGRAMMING?

The field of software engineering has evolved over the fifty or so years of the computer's existence. This evolution has brought about different approaches and strategies to the task of creating high-quality software while minimizing development time and costs. The most successful development approach currently in use is the object-oriented approach. This approach *models* the elements of a software application as objects—by modeling I mean object types are named, their properties are identified, and their methods are described. Once an object type is defined, it can then be used to create specific instances of other objects of that type and to construct other, more complex object types.

Object Types and Instances

An *object type* is a template from which specific objects of that type are created. It defines the properties and methods that are common to all objects of that type. For example, let's consider a person's mailing address as an object type. I'll name it `mailAddress` and give it the properties of `streetAddress`, `city`, `state`, and `postalCode`. In addition to these properties, I'll define `changeAddress()` as a method for changing one person's address and `findAddress()` as a method for finding another person's address. Don't worry about how I'm doing this—you'll learn that later. For this explanation, just focus on what's being done.

NOTE

An object type is referred to as a *class* in object-oriented languages such as Java and C++.

When I define the `mailAddress` object type, I haven't specified anyone's address. I've only developed a template for the creation of an address—kind of like a blank Rolodex card. The address type can be *instantiated*, which is the programming term for creating a specific *instance* of that type of object; in this case, it would mean creating a specific person's address record. This is similar to producing a Rolodex card, filling it in, and sticking it in the Rolodex.

The capability to define an object type from which specific object instances can then be created is a very basic but important feature of object-oriented software development.

Creating Object Types

While the definition and instantiation of object types is a basic feature of object-oriented languages, it is not the only feature these languages provide. The ability to use object types to define *other* object types is what really gives object-oriented programming its power. There are two major ways in which this is accomplished: through *object composition* and *inheritance*.

Object Composition

One approach to developing object types is to define primitive object types that serve as simple building blocks from which more complex types may be composed. This approach is referred to as *object composition*. Consider the process of building a house. At some point, somebody must construct the boards, nails, and glass panes that are used as the basic building blocks for constructing most homes. These building objects are assembled into more complex objects such as doors, windows, and pre-fabricated walls. These more complex objects are then, in turn, assembled into larger objects that eventually are integrated into a finished home. In the same way that boards, nails, glass panes, and other simple objects are used to construct a wide variety of different homes, simple object types are used in programming to create more complex object types that are eventually integrated into a final software application. For example, the `mailAddress` object may be used to create an employment application form, which is itself used to create a personnel database system.

Object composition is closely related to and depends on the capability to support *object reuse*. When an object type is defined, it is often very desirable that it be defined in such a way that it can be reused in other software applications. This simplifies the development of other applications, and naturally leads to cost and schedule savings. The reuse of software objects is just as important as the reuse of technology in other engineering disciplines. Imagine the state of the automotive industry if the wheel had to be reinvented for every new type of car that's been developed.

Encapsulation—Packaging Objects   Software objects are reusable when they follow certain design principles. One of the most important of these principles is *encapsulation*. Encapsulation is the packaging of the properties and methods of an object into a container with an appropriately defined interface. The object's interface must provide the methods and properties that enable the object to be used in the manner that is intended, and must do it without providing methods or properties that would allow the object to be misused. If this abstract description is difficult to fathom, consider the interface of an automobile. Auto designers provide standardized steering, braking, and throttling capabilities in all cars, since these capabilities are basic to driving. However, no automobile manufacturer provides drivers with the capability to manually control the firing of spark plugs from the dashboard. Even if drivers were provided with this capability, they more than likely could not use it to any advantage.

Modularity and Information Hiding   Encapsulation depends upon two important concepts for its success. The first concept, *modularity*, refers to an object's being complete in and of itself and not accessing other objects outside their defined interfaces. Modular objects are said to be "loosely coupled," which means that dependencies between objects are minimized, and internal changes to an object do not require changes in other objects that make use of the object. The second concept, *information hiding*, refers to the practice of limiting information about an object to that which is required to use the object's interface. It is accomplished by removing information about the internal operation of an object from the object's interface.

Inheritance—A Hierarchical Approach to Object Design

The second major way of constructing object types from other object types is through inheritance. In this approach, higher-level, more abstract object types are defined from which lower-level, more concrete object types are derived. When a lower-level object type is created, it identifies one or more higher-level object types as its parent types. The child type inherits all of the properties and methods of its parents. This eliminates the need to redefine these properties and methods. The child type is free to redefine any of the methods that it inherits or to add new properties and methods. This enables the child type to tailor its inherited characteristics to new situations.

As an example, consider the various types of objects that may be constructed to implement a scrolling marquee. At the highest level, a genericMarquee may be constructed that has the basic properties scrolledText and scrollRate. It may provide basic methods, such as startScrolling() and stopScrolling(). From this generic marquee, more complex marquees may be created. For example, horizontalMarquee and verticalMarquee object types may be constructed that add the property scrollDirection to those inherited from genericMarquee. These, in turn, may be further refined into marquees that use colored text and backgrounds. The properties textColor and backgroundColor and the methods randomTextColor() and randomBackgroundColor() could be added.

Using inheritance, more sophisticated, tailored object types can be created from those that are already defined. This is done by just adding the properties and methods needed to differentiate the new objects from their parents. Once a useful object type is created, it can then be reused many times to create several child objects and numerous generations of offspring.

Classification and Inheritance   Object-oriented programming languages, such as Java and C++ (but not JavaScript), refer to an object's type as its "class," and provide the capability to develop child classes from parent classes using inheritance. The resulting class structure is referred to as a *classification scheme*. The classification schemes that result from object-oriented development mimic those that are fundamental to the way we as human beings acquire and organize knowledge. For example, we develop general class names, such as "animal," that we use to refer to large groups of real-world objects. We then develop names of subclasses, such as "mammal, " "bird, " and "insect, " which we use to refine our concept of animal. We continue to develop more detailed classes that differentiate between objects of the same class. The same sort of classification process is carried out by developers of object-oriented programs.

Single and Multiple Inheritance   Part of the reason that inheritance is a successful approach to object development is that it mimics the way we acquire and organize knowledge—it is therefore intuitive to us. In addition to this, inheritance is efficient, because it only requires you to define the properties and methods that are unique for an object's type.

Some languages, notably Java, enforce a more restricted form of inheritance, known as single inheritance. Single inheritance requires that a child class have only one parent. However, a parent may have multiple children. Since a child class inherits its properties and methods from a single parent, it is an exact duplicate of its parent before it adds its own unique properties and methods.

Other languages, notably C++, support *multiple inheritance*. As you might expect, multiple inheritance allows child classes to inherit their properties and methods from more than one parent class. Multiple inheritance is much more powerful than single inheritance, because it allows independent, but complementary, branches of the class structure to be fused together into a single branch.

Multiple inheritance does, however, introduce some difficulties with respect to name resolution. Suppose that class C is the child of both class A and class B. Suppose also that both class A and B define different save() methods. Which of these two methods is inherited by class C? How does the compiler determine which method to use for objects of class C? Although it is certainly possible to develop naming schemes and compilers that resolve naming difficulties resulting from multiple inheritance, these solutions often require a significant amount of additional compilation and runtime processing.

Polymorphism—Many Methods with the Same Name   While at first it may appear to be undesirable to have many methods of the same name, the capability to do so is actually a feature of object-oriented programming. *Polymorphism* is the capability to take on different forms. It allows an object type to define several different implementations of a method. These methods are differentiated by the types and number of parameters they accept. For example, several different `print()` methods may be defined, each of which is used to print objects of different object types. Other `print()`methods may be defined which take a different number of parameters. The interpreter, compiler, or runtime system selects the particular `print()` method that is most appropriate for the object being printed. Polymorphism allows the programmer to use a standard method, such as `print()`, to perform a particular operation and to define different forms of the method to be used with different parameters. This promotes standardization and reusable software and eliminates the need to come up with many slightly different names to distinguish the same operation being performed with different parameters.

JavaScript's Object-Based Programming Features

In the previous section, you learned about the capabilities that are common to object-oriented programming languages. JavaScript does not support several of the capabilities described, though Java does. In this section, you'll learn which object-oriented programming capabilities JavaScript supports and how they are used to develop object-based JavaScript programs.

JavaScript is not a fully object-oriented programming language. It does not support the basic object-oriented programming capabilities of classification, inheritance, encapsulation, and information hiding. However, this is not as bad as it first appears. JavaScript is a scripting language, not a full programming language. The features that it does provide are geared toward providing a capability to quickly and easily generate scripts that execute in the context of a Web page or a server-side application.

JavaScript is referred to as an *object-based* language. It supports the development of object types and the instantiation of these types to create object instances. It provides great support for object composition, but only fair support for modularity and object reuse. Table 15.2 summarizes JavaScript's object-based programming capabilities.

TABLE 15.2: JavaScript's Object-Based Programming Capabilities

CAPABILITY	DESCRIPTION
Object types	JavaScript supports both predefined and user-defined object types. However, JavaScript does not provide capabilities for type enforcement. An object of any type may be assigned to any variable.
Object instantiation	Object types are instantiated using the new operator to create specific object instances.
Object composition	Object types may be defined in terms of other predefined or user-defined object types.
Modularity	JavaScript code may be defined in a modular fashion, but JavaScript does not provide any features that enforce modular software development.
Object reuse	JavaScript software may be reused via the SRC attribute of the script tag. Software may be made available for reuse via the Internet.
Information hiding	JavaScript does not provide any capabilities to support information hiding.
Encapsulation	Because JavaScript lacks information-hiding capabilities, it cannot be used to develop encapsulated object types. Any method or property that is defined for a type is always directly accessible.
Inheritance	JavaScript does not provide any language features that support inheritance between object types.
Classification	Because JavaScript does not support inheritance, it cannot be used to develop a hierarchy of object types.
Polymorphism	JavaScript supports polymorphism using the arguments array for function definitions.

Although JavaScript does not provide all of the features of full object-oriented programming languages such as Java, it does provide a suite of object-based features that are specially tailored to browser and server scripting. These features include a number of predefined browser and server objects and the capability to access related objects through the properties and methods of other objects. If this seems very abstract at this point, don't worry—you'll see several concrete examples of these features throughout this chapter.

THE JAVASCRIPT OBJECT MODEL

JavaScript supports a simple object model that is supported by a number of predefined objects. The *JavaScript Object Model* centers around the specification of object types that are used to create specific object instances. Object types under this model are defined in terms of properties and methods:

▶ Properties are used to access the data values contained in an object. Properties, by default, can be updated as well as read, although some properties of the predefined JavaScript objects are read-only.

▶ Methods are functions that are used to perform operations on an object. Methods may use the object's properties to perform these operations.

NOTE

This chapter describes the JavaScript Object Model as implemented by both Navigator and Internet Explorer. Keep in mind that each of these browsers provides additional browser-specific objects, methods, and properties.

Using Properties

An object's properties are accessed by combining the object's name and its property name as follows:

```
objectName.propertyName
```

For example, the background color of the current Web document is identified by the bgColor property of the predefined document object. If you wanted to change the background color to white, you could use the following JavaScript statement:

```
document.bgColor="white"
```

The above statement assigns the string "white" to the bgColor property of the predefined document object. The script below shows how this statement can be used in an example script. Figure 15.1 shows the Web page that it produces. Several buttons are displayed with the names of different colors. When a button is clicked, the button's onClick event handler changes the background of the document by setting the document.bgColor property.

Using JavaScript properties

```
<HTML>
<HEAD>
<TITLE>Using Properties</TITLE></HEAD>
<BODY>
<H1>Using Properties</H1>
<FORM>
<P><INPUT TYPE="BUTTON" NAME="red" VALUE="Red"
 ONCLICK='document.bgColor="red"'></P>
<P><INPUT TYPE="BUTTON" NAME="white" VALUE="White"
 ONCLICK='document.bgColor="white"'></P>
<P><INPUT TYPE="BUTTON" NAME="blue" VALUE="Blue"
 ONCLICK='document.bgColor="blue"'></P>
</FORM>
</BODY>
</HTML>
```

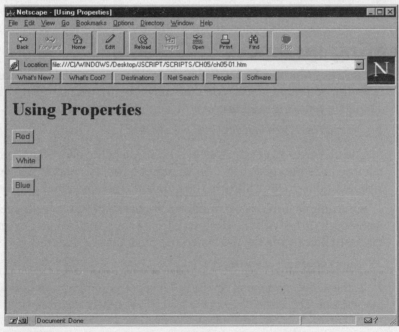

FIGURE 15.1: Using properties to change background colors

Using Methods

An object's methods are accessed in the same manner as its properties:

```
objectName.methodName(parameterList)
```

The parameters, if any, are separated by commas. The parentheses must be used even if no parameters are specified. An example of a method invocation is

```
r=Math.random()
```

The random() method of the predefined Math object is invoked. This method returns a random floating-point number between 0 and 1. The number is then assigned to the r variable.

You have been using the methods of predefined JavaScript objects since your first script in Chapter 14, "Introducing JavaScript and JScript." You've used the write() method of the document object to generate HTML entities that are written to the current document. You've also used the alert() method of the window object to display popup dialog boxes. In the next section, you'll be introduced to some of the objects that are automatically created by JavaScript-capable browsers. Later in this chapter, all of the predefined JavaScript objects will be introduced in summary form.

Creating Instances of Objects

Instances of objects of a particular object type are created using the new operator. You've previously used the new operator to create array objects. The same syntax is used to create objects of other types:

```
variable = new objectType(parameters)
```

The objectType(parameters) portion of the above statement is referred to as the *constructor*. Some object types have more than one constructor. Constructors differ in the number of parameters that they allow.

For example, Date is a predefined JavaScript object type. To create an instance of Date with the current date and time and assign it to the currentDate variable, you would use the following statement:

```
currentDate = new Date()
```

In the above statement, the Date() constructor does not take any parameters. The Date object type also allows object instances to be created for a specified date. For example, the following statement creates an instance of Date for January 1, 1999:

```
currentDate = new Date(99,1,1)
```

The constructor used in the above statement, Date(99,1,1), takes three parameters. The Date object type provides other constructors in addition to the ones described in this section. (The Date object type is formally introduced later in this chapter in the section, "The Date Object Type.")

BROWSER OBJECTS

When a Web page is loaded by a JavaScript-capable browser, the browser creates a number of JavaScript objects that provide access to the Web page and the HTML elements it contains. These objects are used to update and interact with the loaded Web page. Table 15.3 identifies these objects and summarizes their use.

TABLE 15.3: Browser Objects

OBJECT	USE
window	To access a browser window or a frame within a window. The window object is assumed to exist and does not require the "window." prefix when referring to its properties and methods.
document	To access the document that is currently loaded into a window. A document refers to an HTML document that provides content, that is, one that has HEAD and BODY tags.
location	To represent a URL. It can be used to create a URL object, access parts of a URL, or modify an existing URL.
history	To maintain a history of the URLs accessed within a window.
frame object frames array	To access an HTML frame. The frames array is used to access all frames within a window.
link object links array	To access a text- or image-based source anchor of a hypertext link. The links array is used to access all link objects within a document. Internet Explorer combines the link object with the anchor object.
anchor object anchors array	To access the target of a hypertext link. The anchors array is used to access all anchor objects within a document.
image object images array	To access an image that is embedded in an HTML document. The images array is used to access all image objects within a document.

TABLE 15.3 continued: Browser Objects

Object	Use
area	To access an area within a client-side imagemap.
applet object applets array	To access a Java applet. The applets array is used to access all applets in a document.
event Event	To access information about the occurrence of an event. The event object provides information about a specific event. The Event (capitalized) object provides constants that are used to identify events.
form object forms	To access an HTML form. The forms array is used to access all forms within a document.
elements	To access all form elements (fields or buttons) contained within a form.
text	To access a text field of a form.
textarea	To access a text area field of a form.
radio	To access a set of radio buttons of a form or to access an individual button within the set.
checkbox	To access a checkbox of a form.
button	To access a form button that is not a submit or reset button.
submit	To access a submit button of a form.
reset	To access a reset button of a form.
select option	To access a select list of a form. The option object is used to access the elements of a select list.
password	To access a password field of a form.
hidden	To access a hidden field of a form.
FileUpload	To access a file upload element of a form.
navigator	To access information about the browser that is executing a script.
screen	To access information about the size and color depth of a user's screen.
embed object embeds array	To access an embedded object. The embeds array provides access to all embedded objects in a document.
mimeType object mimeTypes array	To access information about a particular MIME type supported by a browser. The mimeTypes array is an array of all mimeType objects supported by a browser. Internet Explorer provides tacit support for mimeTypes, returning an empty array.
plugin object plugins array	To access information about a particular browser plug-in. The plugins array is an array of all plug-ins supported by a browser. Internet Explorer provides tacit support for plugins, returning an empty array.

Table 15.3 summarizes the predefined objects that are created by a JavaScript-capable browser when a Web page is loaded. JavaScript also supports object types that are independent of the Web page that is loaded. These objects are described in the section, "Other Predefined Object Types," later in this chapter.

The Browser Object Hierarchy

Your browser creates the objects presented in Table 15.3 as the results of Web pages that you design. For example, if you create a Web page with three forms, then the forms array will contain three form objects corresponding to the forms that you have defined. Similarly, if you define a document with seven links, then the links array will contain seven link objects that correspond to your links.

The browser objects are organized into a hierarchy that corresponds to the structure of loaded Web documents and the current state of the browser. This hierarchy is referred to as an *instance hierarchy*. The window and navigator objects are the highest-level objects in this hierarchy.

The *Window* Object   The window object represents a browser window, and it has properties that are used to identify the objects of the HTML elements that the window comprises. For example, the frames array is a property of a window object. If the window uses the frameset tag to define multiple frames, then the frames array contains the frame object associated with each frame. The window's location property refers to the location object that contains the URL associated with the window. The window's screen property may be used to obtain the user's screen dimensions and color depth.

If a window contains displayable content, as opposed to a frameset tag, then the window object's document property refers to the document object associated with the window. The document object contains properties that reference objects that are displayed in the window. These properties include the links, anchors, images, and forms arrays. The links array identifies all link objects contained in a document. The anchors array identifies all named anchors. Link objects refer to the source of a hyperlink, while anchor objects refer to the named destinations of a link. The images, applets, and forms arrays identify all image, applet, and form objects contained in a document. A document's area property refers to an area within a client-side imagemap that is defined in the document. A document's history property refers to a `history` object that contains a list of URLs that the user has visited within a particular window.

NOTE

Internet Explorer combines the `link` and anchor **objects. Both links and anchors can be accessed via the** `anchors` **array.**

A `document` object's `forms` array identifies all `form` objects that are defined in the document. Although a document may define any number of forms, usually only one form is defined. The `form` object provides access to the individual elements defined for a particular form via the `elements` array. The `elements` array refers to `text`, `textarea`, `radio`, `checkbox`, `button`, `submit`, `reset`, `select`, `password`, `hidden`, and `FileUpload` form fields. These fields may also be individually accessed by their names.

The *Navigator* Object   The `navigator` object, like the `window` object, is a top-level object in the browser hierarchy. The `navigator` object is used to describe the configuration of the browser being used to display a window. Two of its properties, `mimeTypes` and `plugins`, contain the list of all MIME types and plug-ins supported by the browser. Internet Explorer returns empty arrays for the `mimeTypes` and `plugins` properties.

Hierarchical Object Identifiers

Because your browser organizes the various objects of a Web page according to the instance hierarchy described in the previous section, a hierarchical naming scheme is used to identify these objects. For example, suppose an HTML document defines three forms, and the second form has seven elements. Also suppose the fifth element of the second form is a radio button. You can access the name of this radio button using the following identifier:

```
document.forms[1].element[4].name
```

The above identifier refers to the name of the fifth element of the second form of the current document. (Remember that array indices begin at 0.) You could display this name using the following statement:

```
document.write(document.forms[1].element[4].name)
```

NOTE

You do not have to identify the window object when you refer to the current window's properties and methods—your browser will assume the current window object by default. There is one exception, however: in event-handling code, it is the current document object that is assumed by default.

In most cases, you can refer to a property or method of a browser-created object by starting with document and using the property names of the objects that contain the object (such as links, anchors, images, and forms) to identify the object within the instance hierarchy. When you have named the object in this fashion, you can then use the object's property or method name to access the data and functions defined for that object.

The following script provides an example of using hierarchical names to access the elements defined within a Web document. The document defines a number of functions in the document head. It begins by invoking the open() method of the window object to open a second browser window. This second window is assigned to the outputWindow variable and is used to write the description of the objects defined for the HTML document shown below. The open() method takes two parameters—the URL of the document to be loaded in the window and a window name. Because you don't want to load a document at another URL, set the URL parameter to a blank string.

Using Hierarchical Object Identifiers

```
<HTML>
<HEAD>
<TITLE>Using Hierarchical Object Identifiers</TITLE>
<SCRIPT LANGUAGE="JavaScript"><!-
outputWindow = open("","output")
function setupWindow() {
 outputWindow.document.write("<HTML><HEAD><TITLE>Output
 Window</TITLE></HEAD><BODY>")
}
function describeBrowser() {
 outputWindow.document.write("<H2>Browser Properties</H2>")
 outputWindow.document.write(navigator.appCodeName+" ")
```

```
      outputWindow.document.write(navigator.appName+" ")
      outputWindow.document.write(navigator.appVersion+"<BR>")
      outputWindow.document.write(navigator.mimeTypes.length+"
        MIME types are defined. ")
      outputWindow.document.write(navigator.plugins.length+"
        plug-ins are installed.")
    }
    function describeWindow() {
     outputWindow.document.write("<H2>Window Properties</H2>")
     outputWindow.document.write("Frames: "+frames.length+"<BR>")
     outputWindow.document.write("URL: "+location.href+"<BR>")
    }
    function describeDocument() {
     outputWindow.document.write("<H2>Document Properties</H2>")
     describeLinks()
     describeForms()
    }
    function describeLinks(){
     outputWindow.document.write("<H3>Links</H3>")
     outputWindow.document.write("This document contains "
        +document.links.length+" links:<BR>")
     for(i=0;i<document.links.length;++i)
        outputWindow.document.write(document.links[i].href+"<BR>")
    }
    function describeForms() {
     outputWindow.document.write("<H3>Forms</H3>")
     for(i=0;i<document.forms.length;++i) describeForm(i)
    }
    function describeForm(n) {
     outputWindow.document.write("Form "+n+" has "
        +document.forms[n].elements.length+" elements:")
     for(j=0;j<document.forms[n].elements.length;++j)
        outputWindow.document.write(" "
```

```
        + document.forms[n].elements[j].name)
  outputWindow.document.write("<BR>")
}
function finishWindow() {
  outputWindow.document.write("<FORM><INPUT Type='button'
    Value='Close Window' onClick='window.close()'></FORM>")
  outputWindow.document.write("</BODY></HTML>")
}
// -></SCRIPT></HEAD>
<BODY>
<H1>Using Hierarchical Object Identifiers</H1>
<P><A HREF="http://www.jaworski.com/javascript">Link to
 Mastering JavaScript and JScript home page.</A></P>
<P><A HREF="http://home.netscape.com/">Link to Netscape's
 home page.</A></P>
<FORM>
<P><INPUT TYPE="TEXT" NAME="textField1"
 VALUE="Enter text here!"></P>
<P><INPUT TYPE="CHECKBOX" NAME="checkbox1"
 CHECKED="CHECKED">I'm checkbox1.</P>
<P><INPUT TYPE="CHECKBOX" NAME="checkbox2"> I'm
checkbox2.</P>
<INPUT TYPE="SUBMIT" NAME="submitButton" VALUE="Click here!">
</FORM>
<SCRIPT LANGUAGE="JavaScript"><!-
setupWindow()
describeBrowser()
describeWindow()
describeDocument()
finishWindow()
// -></SCRIPT>
</BODY>
</HTML>
```

The `setupWindow()` function is used to generate the head of the second document and its opening body tag. It uses the `outputWindow` variable to select the second window as the target for writing. This function and other functions in the script write their output using statements of the form:

```
outputWindow.document.write()
```

These statements tell JavaScript to write to the `document` object of the `window` object identified by the `outputWindow` variable.

The `describeBrowser()` function displays some of the `navigator` object's properties to the second window. It also uses the `outputWindow` variable to select this window. It displays the `appCodeName`, `appName`, and `appVersion`, and uses the `length` property of the `mimeTypes` and `plugins` arrays to determine the number of MIME types and plug-ins supported by the browser.

The `describeWindow()` function displays some properties of the original (first) window. It displays the number of frames defined by the window and the URL of the document loaded into the window. Since the window does not define any frames, the length of the `frames` array is 0. The `href` property of the window's `location` object is used to get the text string corresponding to the URL. The URL displayed when you execute the script will be different depending on the directory from which you run the files of this chapter.

The `describeDocument()` function displays some of the properties associated with the current document in the second window. It invokes the `describeLinks()` and `describeForms()` functions to perform this processing.

The `describeLinks()` function uses the `length` property of the `links` array to identify the number of links contained in the document. It then executes a `for` loop to display the URL associated with each of these links. The `href` attribute of the `link` object is used to get the text string corresponding to the URL.

The `describeForms()` function uses the `length` property of the `forms` array to iterate through the document's links and display each one. The `displayForm()` function is used to display each form.

The `displayForm()` function uses the `length` property of the `elements` array of each `form` object to identify the number of elements contained in a form. It takes a single parameter, identified by the `n` variable. This parameter identifies the index into the `forms` array of the form object being displayed. The name of each field element is displayed by referencing the name property of each object contained in the elements array of each form object identified in the forms array. This is a good example of using hierarchical object naming to access the low-level elements of an HTML document.

The finishWindow() function appends the following HTML to the body of the document displayed in the second window:

```
<FORM>
<INPUT Type='button' Value='Close Window'
onClick='window.close()'>
</FORM>
</BODY>
</HTML>
```

The form is used to create a button, labeled *Close Window*, that is used to close the second window. The onClick attribute of the INPUT tag is assigned the event-handling code, window.close(), which is used to close the window when the button is clicked. The window object should be explicitly referenced in event handlers to ensure that the current window is closed and not the current document. The </BODY> and </HTML> tags are used to end the displayed document.

The main body of the HTML document defines two links—one to the *Mastering JavaScript and JScript* home page and one to Netscape's home page. The document then defines a form with four elements—a text field, two checkboxes, and a submit button.

The script contained in the main body of the document invokes the setupWindow(), describeBrowser(), describeWindow(), describeDocument(), and finishWindow() functions to display the contents of the first window in the second window referenced by the outputWindow object. This script is placed at the end of the document so that the various HTML elements of the document are defined when the script is invoked.

A second window is created to display the various properties of the document. The Web browser displays this second window as shown in Figure 15.2. When the user clicks the Close Window button, the original document, shown in Figure 15.3, is displayed. You can also use your browser's Window pull-down menu to switch between the two windows.

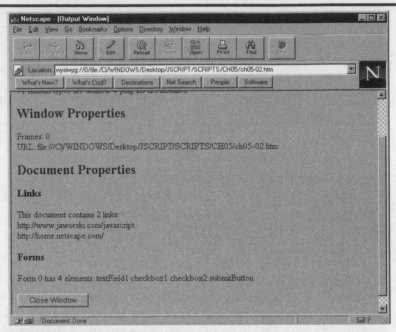

FIGURE 15.2: The output window

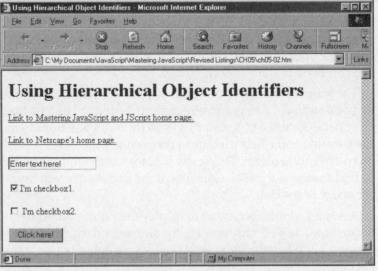

FIGURE 15.3: The original document window

OTHER PREDEFINED OBJECT TYPES

In addition to the predefined browser objects discussed in earlier sections, JavaScript also provides general-purpose object types that support common operations. These object types (except the RegExp object type) are defined by the ECMAScript 1 specification and are described in the following sections.

The *Array* Object

The Array object allows arrays to be accessed as objects. The ECMAScript 1 specification defines two properties for the Array object: length and prototype. The length property identifies the length of an array. The prototype property is a property that is supported by all object types. It allows additional properties and methods to be defined for an object type. It is covered in the section, "Adding Properties and Methods to an Object Type," later in this chapter.

ECMAScript 1 defines the following Array methods:

toString()   Returns a string version of an array. Array elements are separated by commas.

join(*separator*)   Returns a string version of an array. Array elements are separated by the *separator* string. If no separator is specified, a comma is used.

reverse()   Reverses the elements of an array—that is, the last element appears first and the first element appears last.

sort(*comparisonFunction*)   Sorts the elements of an array according to a comparison function. If no comparison function is specified, the array elements are sorted in dictionary order. If a comparison function is specified, it should take two parameters, p1 and p2, and return a negative integer if p1 is less than p2, zero if p1 equals p2, and a positive integer if p1 is greater than p2.

The following script illustrates the use of the above methods. It creates an array of integers 0 through 10 and applies the toString(), join(':'), reverse(), and sort() methods to it. Figure 15.4 shows the results it displays.

Using the Methods of the *Array* Object

```
<HTML>
<HEAD>
<TITLE>Using Arrays</TITLE>
<SCRIPT LANGUAGE="JavaScript"><!-
// -></SCRIPT></HEAD>
<BODY>
<H1>Using Arrays</H1>
<SCRIPT LANGUAGE="JavaScript"><!-
myArray = [0, 1, 2, 3, 4, 5, 6, 7, 8, 9, 10]
document.write("myArray: "+myArray+"<P>")
document.write("myArray.toString():
  "+myArray.toString()+"<P>")
document.write("myArray.join(':'): "+myArray.join(':')+"<P>")
document.write("myArray.reverse(): "+myArray.reverse()+"<P>")
document.write("myArray.sort: "+myArray.sort())
// -></SCRIPT>
</BODY>
</HTML>
```

NOTE
Internet Explorer and Navigator provide browser-specific Array methods in addition to those of the ECMAScript specification.

The *Boolean* Object

The Boolean object allows Boolean values to be accessed as objects. It supports the prototype property and the toString() and valueOf() methods. The toString() method returns the string-equivalent of a Boolean value. The valueOf() method returns *true* or *false* depending on the value of the underling object.

Boolean objects are created by identifying their value as an argument to the constructor:

```
myBoolean = new Boolean(false)
yourBoolean = new Boolean(true)
```

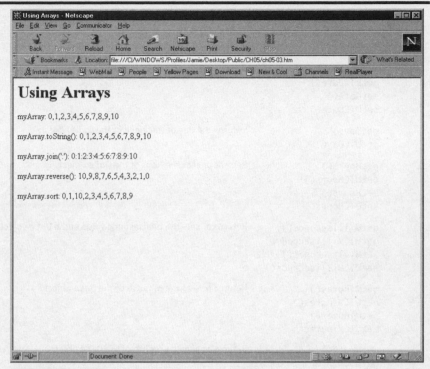

FIGURE 15.4:   The results of applying array methods

The *Date* Object

The Date object provides a common set of methods for working with dates and times. These methods are summarized in Table 15.4. The methods with UTC in their names refer to Universal Coordinated Time, which is the time set by the World Time Standard. The Date object type supports the prototype property. Instances of the Date object may be created with any of the constructors shown in Table 15.5. The script following Table 15.5 illustrates the use of the Date object.

TABLE 15.4: Methods of the Date Object

METHOD	DESCRIPTION
getDate() getUTCDate() setDate() setUTCDate()	Returns or sets the day of the month of the Date object.
getDay() getUTCDay()	Returns the day of the week of the Date object.
getHours() getUTCHours() setHours() setUTCHours()	Returns or sets the hour of the Date object.
getMilliseconds() getUTCMilliseconds() setMilliseconds() setUTCMilliseconds()	Returns or sets the milliseconds value of the Date object.
getMinutes() getUTCMinutes() setMinutes() setUTCMinutes()	Returns or sets the minutes of the Date object.
getMonth() getUTCMonth() setMonth() setUTCMonth()	Returns or sets the month of the Date object.
getSeconds() getUTCSeconds() setSeconds() setUTCSeconds()	Returns or sets the seconds of the Date object.
getTime() setTime()	Returns or sets the time of the Date object.
getTimeZoneOffset()	Returns the time zone offset (in minutes) of the Date object.
getYear() getFullYear() getUTCFullYear() setYear() setFullYear() setUTCFullYear()	Returns or sets the year of the Date object. The full-year methods use four-digit year values.
toGMTString()	Converts a date to a string in Internet GMT (Greenwich Mean Time) format.
toLocaleString()	Converts a date to a string in *locale* format, which means the format commonly used in the geographical region in which the user is located.

TABLE 15.4 continued: Methods of the Date Object

METHOD	DESCRIPTION
toString()	Returns a string value of a Date object.
valueOf()	Returns the number of milliseconds since midnight, January 1, 1970.
toUTCString()	Returns a string that represents the time in UTC.

TABLE 15.5: Date Constructors

CONSTRUCTOR	DESCRIPTION
Date()	Creates a Date instance with the current date and time.
Date(*dateString*)	Creates a Date instance with the date specified in the *date-String* parameter. The format of the *dateString* is "*month day, year hours:minutes:seconds*".
Date(*milliseconds*)	Creates a Date instance with the specified number of milliseconds since midnight, January 1, 1970.
Date(*year*, *month*, *day*, *hours*, *minutes*, *seconds*, *milliseconds*)	Creates a Date instance with the date specified by the year, month, day, hours, minutes, seconds, and milliseconds integers. The year and month parameters must be supplied. If other parameters are included, then all preceding parameters must be supplied.

Using the *Date* Object

```
<HTML>
<HEAD>
<TITLE>Using the Date Object Type</TITLE>
</HEAD>
<BODY>
<H1>Using the Date Object Type</H1>
<SCRIPT LANGUAGE="JavaScript"><!-
currentDate = new Date()
with (currentDate) {
 document.write("Date:
"+getMonth()+"/"+getDate()+"/"+getYear() +"<BR>")
```

```
    document.write("Time: "+getHours()+":"+getMinutes()+":
      " +getSeconds())
  }
  // -></SCRIPT>
  </BODY>
  </HTML>
```

The above document uses the methods of the `Date` object type to write the current date and time to the current `document` object. The `currentDate` variable is assigned a new `Date` object, which is created using the `new` operator and the `Date()` constructor. A `with` statement is used to make the object stored with `currentDate` the default object for object references. The two `write()` method invocations use the `getMonth()`, `getDate()`, `getYear()`, `getHours()`, `getMinutes()`, and `getSeconds()` methods to access the various components of a `Date` object. Figure 15.5 shows the Web page generated by the preceding script.

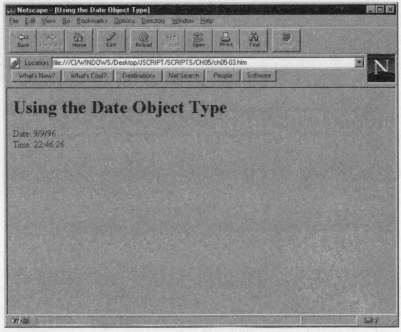

FIGURE 15.5: Using the Date object

The *Function* Object

The Function object allows functions to be accessed as objects. It can be used to dynamically create and invoke a function during a script's execution. The ECMAScript 1 specification identifies the length and prototype properties. The length property identifies the number of parameters defined for a function. Navigator and Internet Explorer define the arguments property and the caller property. The arguments property is an array that identifies the arguments that are passed to a function when it is invoked. The caller property identifies the function that invoked a particular function. Navigator also defines the arity property, which is identical to the length property.

The ECMAScript 1 specification defines the toString() and valueOf() methods. The toString() method returns a string representation of the function. The valueOf() method returns the function itself. Navigator also defines the call() and apply() methods, which can be used to invoke a Function object.

Function objects are created by supplying the function's parameters and body to the Function() constructor:

```
variable = new Function("p1", "p2", ..., "pn", "body")
```

The opening and closing brackets ({ and }) of the function body are not specified. The following function returns x-squared plus y-squared:

```
myFunction = new Function("x", "y", "return x*x + y*y")
```

The script below illustrates the use of the Function object. It creates a function that surrounds a string with braces ([and]). Figure 15.6 shows the results that are displayed by this script.

Using the *Function* Object

```
<HTML>
<HEAD>
<TITLE>Using the Function Object</TITLE>
<BODY><H1>
<SCRIPT LANGUAGE="JavaScript"><!-
addBraces = new Function("s","return '['+s+']'")
document.write(addBraces("This"))
document.write(addBraces("is"))
document.write(addBraces("a"))
```

```
document.write(addBraces("test."))
// -></SCRIPT>
</H1></BODY>
</HTML>
```

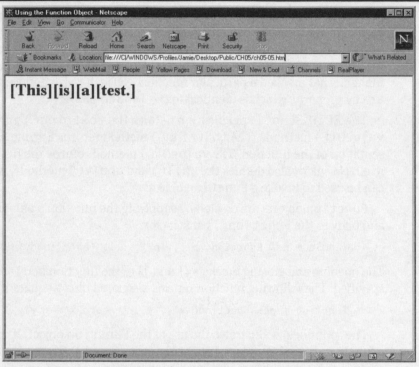

FIGURE 15.6:   The results of the dynamically created function

The *Global* Object

The ECMAScript specification defines the Global object to associate an object with the globally accessible variables and functions defined in earlier versions of JavaScript. Navigator and Internet Explorer implement the Global object but do not allow it to be explicitly created (via new Global()) or referenced (via "Global."). Instead, its properties and methods are referenced directly as global variables and functions.

The ECMAScript specification defines two constant properties: NaN and Infinity. The NaN constant means *not a number*. The Infinity property represents positive infinity. Methods defined for the `Global` object are as follows:

escape(*string*)   Converts the *string* into a new string where certain characters are converted into escape sequences in accordance with RFC 1738

eval(*x*)   Evaluates and returns the value of the expression *x*

isFinite(*number*)   Returns *true* if *number* is finite and *false* otherwise

isNaN(*number*)   Returns *true* if *number* is not a number and *false* otherwise

parseFloat(*string*)   Parses the *string* as a floating-point value

parseInt(*string, radix*)   Parses the *string* as an integer of base *radix*

unescape(*string*)   Converts strings encoded by `escape()` back to their original value

The above methods can be used to support numerical tests and URL encoding/decoding in accordance with RFC 1738.

The *Math* Object

The `Math` object provides a standard library of mathematical constants and functions. The constants are defined as properties of `Math` and are listed in Table 15.6. The functions are defined as methods of `Math` and are summarized in Table 15.7. Specific instances of `Math` are not created because `Math` is a built-in object and not an object type. The script following Table 15.7 illustrates the use of the `Math` object; Figure 15.7 shows the Web page it generates.

TABLE 15.6: Math Properties

PROPERTY	DESCRIPTION
E	Euler's constant
LN2	The natural logarithm of 2
LN10	The natural logarithm of 10

TABLE 15.6 continued: Math Properties

PROPERTY	DESCRIPTION
LOG2E	The base-2 logarithm of e
LOG10E	The base-10 logarithm of e
PI	The constant π
SQRT1_2	The square root of ½
SQRT2	The square root of 2

TABLE 15.7: Math Methods

METHOD	DESCRIPTION
abs(x)	Returns the absolute value of x
acos(x)	Returns the arc cosine of x in radians
asin(x)	Returns the arc sine of x in radians
atan(x)	Returns the arc tangent of x in radians
atan2(x,y)	Returns the angle of the polar coordinate corresponding to (x,y)
ceil(x)	Returns the least integer that is greater than or equal to x
cos(x)	Returns the cosine of x
exp(x)	Returns e^x
floor(x)	Returns the greatest integer that is less than or equal to x
log(x)	Returns the natural logarithm of x
max(x,y)	Returns the greater of x and y
min(x,y)	Returns the lesser of x and y
pow(x,y)	Returns x^y
random()	Returns a random number between 0 and 1
round(x)	Returns x rounded to the closest integer
sin(x)	Returns the sine of x
sqrt(x)	Returns the square root of x
tan(x)	Returns the tangent of x

Using the *Math* Object

```
<HTML>
<HEAD>
<TITLE>Using the Math Object</TITLE>
</HEAD>
<BODY>
<H1>Using the Math Object</H1>
<SCRIPT LANGUAGE="JavaScript"><!-
document.write(Math.PI+"<BR>")
document.write(Math.E+"<BR>")
document.write(Math.ceil(1.234)+"<BR>")
document.write(Math.random()+"<BR>")
document.write(Math.sin(Math.PI/2)+"<BR>")
document.write(Math.min(100,1000)+"<BR>")
// -></SCRIPT>
</BODY>
</HTML>
```

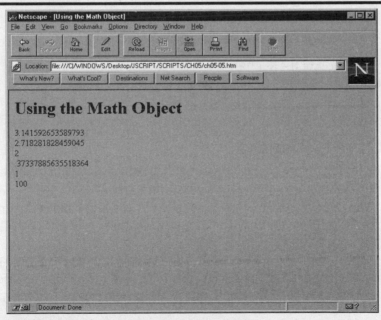

FIGURE 15.7: Example of using the Math object

The *Number* Object

The Number object type allows numbers to be treated as objects. The ECMAScript 1 specification defines the following Number properties:

MAX_VALUE   The number is the maximum possible numeric value

MIN_VALUE   The number is the minimum possible numeric value

NaN   The number is not a number

NEGATIVE_INFINITY   The number is negative infinity

POSITIVE_INFINITY   The number is positive infinity

prototype   The prototype property that is supported by all object types

The above properties are used to identify numbers as having special characteristics. They are not normally used in scripts. Instead, use the properties and methods of the Global object.

The ECMAScript 1 specification defines the following Number methods:

toString(*radix*)   Returns a string that represents the number in base *radix*

valueOf()   Returns the numeric value of the Number object

Instances of the Number object are created by supplying a numeric value to the Number() constructor:

```
myNumber = new Number(123.456)
```

The *Object* Object

The Object object is the base object from which all other objects are derived. Its properties and methods are available to other object types.

The Object object supports the prototype and constructor properties. The constructor property identifies the name of the object's constructor.

The Object object supports the toString() and valueOf() methods. The toString() method converts an object to a string representation. The valueOf() method returns the primitive value (number, string, or Boolean) of an object if one is associated with the object. Otherwise, it returns the object itself.

Object objects can be created by supplying a number, string, Boolean value, or function in the Object() constructor. However, this is rarely done. Instead, it is better to use the constructor of the specific object type (that is, Number(), String(), Boolean(), or Function()).

The *String* Object

The String object type allows strings to be accessed as objects. It supports the length and prototype properties. The length property identifies the string's length in characters.

The String object type provides a set of methods for manipulating strings. The methods defined in the ECMAScript 1 specification are summarized in Table 15.8. Any JavaScript string value or variable containing a string value is able to use these methods. Both Netscape and Internet Explorer define String methods in addition to those contained in Table 15.8.

TABLE 15.8: String Methods

METHOD	DESCRIPTION
charAt(*index*)	Returns a string that consists of the character at the specified index of the string to which the method is applied
charCodeAt(*index*)	Returns the Unicode encoding of the character at the specified index
fromCharCode(*codes*)	Creates a string from a comma-separated sequence of character codes
indexOf(*pattern*)	Returns the index of the first string specified by the *pattern* parameter that is contained in a string; returns -1 if the pattern is not contained in the string
indexOf(*pattern*, *startIndex*)	Same as the previous method except that searching starts at the position specified by *startIndex*
lastIndexOf(*pattern*)	Returns the index of the last string specified by the *pattern* parameter that is contained in a string; returns -1 if the pattern is not contained in the string.

TABLE 15.8 continued: String Methods

METHOD	DESCRIPTION
lastIndexOf(*pattern, startIndex*)	Same as the previous method except that searching starts at the position specified by *startIndex*
split(*separator*)	Separates a string into an array of substrings based upon the *separator*
substring(*startIndex*)	Returns the substring of a string beginning at *startIndex*
substring(*startIndex, endIndex*)	Returns the substring of a string beginning at *startIndex* and ending at *endIndex*
toLowerCase()	Returns a copy of the string converted to lowercase
toString()	Returns the string value of the object
toUpperCase()	Returns a copy of the string converted to uppercase
valueOf()	Returns the string value of the object

The script below illustrates the use of the `String` object type. The script in the document body begins by defining the function `displayLine()`, which displays text followed by the `<BR>` tag. The `displayLine()` function is used to display several text strings that are modified using sample string methods. Figure 15.8 shows the Web page generated by this script.

Using the *String* Object

```
<HTML>
<HEAD>
<TITLE>Using the String Object Type</TITLE>
</HEAD>
<BODY>
<SCRIPT LANGUAGE="JavaScript"><!-
function displayLine(text) {
 document.write(text+"<BR>")
}
```

```
s = new String("This is a test of the JavaScript String
  methods.")
displayLine('s = '+s)
displayLine('s.charAt(1) = '+s.charAt(1))
displayLine('s.charCodeAt(1) = '+s.charCodeAt(1))
displayLine('s.indexOf("is") = '+s.indexOf("is"))
displayLine('s.lastIndexOf("is") = '+s.lastIndexOf("is"))
displayLine('s.substring(22,32) = '+s.substring(22,32))
displayLine('s.toLowerCase() = '+s.toLowerCase())
displayLine('s.toUpperCase() = '+s.toUpperCase())
split = s.split(" ")
for(i=0; i<split.length; ++i)
 displayLine('split['+i+'] = '+split[i])
// -></SCRIPT>
</BODY>
</HTML>
```

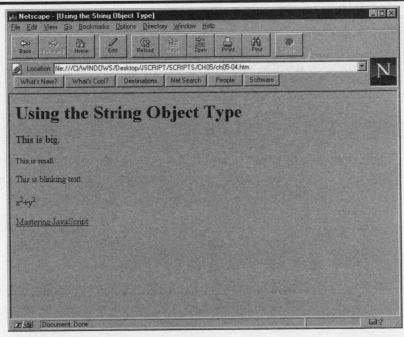

FIGURE 15.8: Using the String object

Creating *String* Objects

`String` objects may be created in the same manner as other JavaScript objects using the new operator. For example, the variable `text` may be assigned the string `"I am a string"` using the statement:

```
text = new String("I am a string")
```

The above statement is equivalent to:

```
text = "I am a string"
```

Regular Expressions and the *RegExp* Object

Support for *regular expressions* was introduced in JavaScript 1.2. Regular expressions are string expressions that describe a pattern of characters. They provide a powerful capability for finding patterns in text strings and performing search and replace operations on text. Regular expressions make use of a very compact, powerful, but somewhat arcane syntax. In JavaScript, regular expressions are implemented using the `RegExp` object.

NOTE

Although regular expressions were not included in the ECMAScript 1 specification, they will be included in ECMAScript 2.

COLOR CONSTANTS

JavaScript defines a number of color constants that can be used with methods and functions that take color parameters. Some of these color constants are `"red"`, `"orange"`, `"yellow"`, `"green"`, `"blue"`, `"white"`, `"black"`, and `"brown"`.

DEFINING OBJECT TYPES

JavaScript provides you the capability to define your own object types and create specific object instances. To create a new object type, you simply define a function that is used to construct specific instances of the object type. Essentially, this constructor function does two things:

- ▶ It assigns values to the object type's properties.
- ▶ It identifies other functions to be used as the object type's methods.

As an example of defining a new object type, we'll create the `table` object type. This object type will be used to create simple tables using JavaScript and write them to the current document.

NOTE

The function used as a constructor of an object type must have the same name as the object type.

Identifying and Assigning Properties   The first thing that we'll do is identify the properties of the `table` object type. The number of rows and columns of the table are obvious properties with which to start. Let's name these properties `table.rows` and `table.columns`. We'll also need to define a property to store the elements of the table. Let's call this property `table.data` and let it be an array of the following length:

```
table.rows * table.columns
```

Because HTML allows some table cells to be designated as header cells, let's also define the property table.header as an array of the same length as above, table.rows * table.columns, where each element is a Boolean value indicating whether a table cell is a header cell. Finally, let's define a property, table.border, that identifies the border width of the table. The following code shows how the table constructor would be defined using the items we just identified.

```
function table(rows,columns) {
  this.rows = rows
  this.columns = columns
  this.border = 0
  this.data = new Array(rows*columns)
  this.header = new Array(rows*columns)
}
```

As you can see, the `table()` constructor takes the parameters `rows` and `columns`, and assigns them to `this.rows` and `this.columns`. The `this` prefix is a special keyword that is used to refer to the current object. For example, the statement `this.rows = rows` assigns the value stored in the `rows` parameter to the `rows` property of the current object. Similarly, `this.columns = columns` assigns the `columns` parameter to the `columns` property of the current object. The parameters of the `table()` constructor do not have to be named rows and columns—they could have been named x and y. However, it is common to see parameters named after the object type properties to which they are assigned.

The `border` property of the current object is set to the default value of 0. This results in the creation of a borderless table. As mentioned earlier, the `data` and `header` properties are each assigned an array of size `rows * columns`.

In order to create an object that is an instance of the `table` object type, you use the `new` operator in conjunction with the `table` constructor. For example, the following statement creates a table of three rows by four columns and assigns it to the `t` variable:

```
t = new table(3,4)
```

Defining Methods   So far, we've defined the properties of the `table` object type. However, we'll need to define some methods to update the values of the `data`, `header`, and `border` properties and to write the `table` object to a `document` object.

Methods are defined by assigning the name of an already defined function to a method name in an object type constructor. For example, suppose the `table_setValue()` function is defined as follows. This function sets the value of the table cell at the specified `row` and `column` parameters to the `value` parameter.

```
function table_setValue(row,col,value) {
  this.data[row*this.columns+col]=value
}
```

We can use the above-defined `table_setValue()` function as the `setValue()` method of the `table` object type by including the following statement in the `table` constructor:

```
this.setValue = table_setValue
```

Note that trailing parentheses are not used in the above statement. The new table constructor is as follows:

```
function table(rows,columns) {
  this.rows = rows
  this.columns = columns
  this.border = 0
  this.data = new Array(rows*columns)
  this.header = new Array(rows*columns)
  this.setValue = table_setValue
}
```

An example of invoking the setValue() method for the table object stored in the t variable follows:

```
t.setValue(2,3,"Hello")
```

The above statement sets the table data value at row 2 and column 3 to "Hello".

Definition of the *table* Object

The following script provides a complete definition of the table object. Note that functions must be defined before they can be assigned to a method name.

Definition of the *table* object (table.js)

```
function table_getValue(row,col) {
  return this.data[row*this.columns+col]
}
function table_setValue(row,col,value) {
  this.data[row*this.columns+col]=value
}
function table_set(contents) {
  var n = contents.length
  for(var j=0;j<n;++j) this.data[j]=contents[j]
}
function table_isHeader(row,col) {
  return this.header[row*this.columns+col]
}
```

```
function table_makeHeader(row,col) {
 this.header[row*this.columns+col]=true
}
function table_makeNormal(row,col) {
 this.header[row*this.columns+col]=false
}
function table_makeHeaderRow(row) {
 for(var j=0;j<this.columns;++j)
 this.header[row*this.columns+j]=true
}
function table_makeHeaderColumn(col) {
 for(var i=0;i<this.rows;++i)
 this.header[i*this.columns+col]=true
}
function table_write(doc) {
 doc.write("<TABLE BORDER="+this.border+">")
 for(var i=0;i<this.rows;++i) {
  doc.write("<TR>")
  for(var j=0;j<this.columns;++j) {
    if(this.header[i*this.columns+j]) {
       doc.write("<TH>")
       doc.write(this.data[i*this.columns+j])
       doc.write("</TH>")
    }else{
       doc.write("<TD>")
       doc.write(this.data[i*this.columns+j])
       doc.write("</TD>")
    }
  }
  doc.writeln("</TR>")
 }
 doc.writeln("</TABLE>")
```

```
    }
    function table(rows,columns) {
     this.rows = rows
     this.columns = columns
     this.border = 0
     this.data = new Array(rows*columns)
     this.header = new Array(rows*columns)
     this.getValue = table_getValue
     this.setValue = table_setValue
     this.set = table_set
     this.isHeader = table_isHeader
     this.makeHeader = table_makeHeader
     this.makeNormal = table_makeNormal
     this.makeHeaderRow = table_makeHeaderRow
     this.makeHeaderColumn = table_makeHeaderColumn
     this.write = table_write
    }
```

The preceding script adds the getValue(), set(), isHeader(), makeHeader(), makeNormal(), makeHeaderRow(), makeHeader-Column(), and write() methods to the table definition introduced in the previous section.

The getValue() method returns the data value stored at a specified row and column. The set() method stores an array of values as the contents of a table. The makeHeader() and makeNormal() methods are used to identify whether a cell should or should not be a header cell. The makeHeaderRow() and makeHeaderColumn() methods are used to designate an entire row or column as consisting of header cells. The write() method is used to write a table to a document object.

Using the *table* Object

The following script provides an example of the use of the table object. The document's body contains a script that creates, initializes, and displays a three-row by four-column table object. Using the SRC attribute of the script tag, it includes the `table.js` file presented in the previous section. It begins by creating a `table` object and assigning it to the `t` variable. It then creates an array, named `contents`, that contains a list of values. The `set()` method is invoked to assign the contents array to the cells of the table stored at `t`. The table's `border` property is set to 4 pixels, and the cells of column 0 are designated as header cells. Finally, the `write()` method is used to write the table to the current `document` object. Figure 15.9 shows the Web page resulting from the script below.

Using the *table* Object

```
<HTML>
<HEAD>
<TITLE>Defining Object Types</TITLE>
<SCRIPT LANGUAGE="JavaScript" SRC="table.js"><!-
// -></SCRIPT>
</HEAD>
<BODY>
<H1>Defining Object Types</H1>
<SCRIPT LANGUAGE="JavaScript"><!-
t = new table(3,4)
contents = new
Array("This","is","a","test","of","the","table",
  "object.","Let's","see","it","work.")
t.set(contents)
t.border=4
t.makeHeaderColumn(0)
t.write(document)
// -></SCRIPT>
</BODY>
</HTML>
```

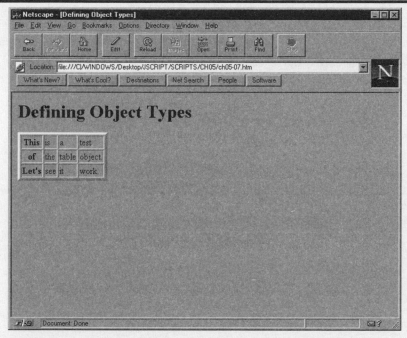

FIGURE 15.9: An example table

Adding Properties and Methods to an Object Type

Object types that can be instantiated with the new operator are referred to as *instantiable* object types. They include all user-defined object types and most of the predefined object types. Examples of object types that are not instantiable are Math and Global. JavaScript provides the capability to add properties and methods to already defined instantiable object types via the prototype property.

For example, suppose we wanted to add a background color attribute to the table object type defined in previous section. We could add the new attribute with the following statement:

```
table.prototype.bgColor = "cyan"
```

The above statement uses the prototype property of the table object type to create a new property called bgColor to represent the background color of the table.

Now that we've defined the bgColor property, we should create an additional method called colorWrite() that writes a table using the bgColor property. The following function performs this processing:

```
function table_colorWrite(doc) {
 doc.write("<TABLE BORDER="+this.border+"BGCOLOR="
  +this.bgColor+">")
 for(var i=0;i<this.rows;++i) {
 doc.write("<TR>")
 for(var j=0;j<this.columns;++j) {
   if(this.header[i*this.columns+j]) {
     doc.write("<TH>")
     doc.write(this.data[i*this.columns+j])
     doc.write("</TH>")
   }else{
     doc.write("<TD>")
     doc.write(this.data[i*this.columns+j])
     doc.write("</TD>")
   }
  }
 }
  doc.writeln("</TR>")
 }
 doc.writeln("</TABLE>")
}
```

We can use the table_colorWrite() function in the listing above as the colorWrite() method by including the following statement in our script:

```
table.prototype.colorWrite=table_colorWrite
```

The following script updates the script shown in the preceding section to make use of the new bgColor property and the colorWrite() method. Figure 15.10 shows the Web page that results from this script. Note that we did not have to modify the original table.js file that is included via the SRC attribute.

TIP

Always *create* an object of the object type being modified before using the object type's `prototype` property. This will ensure that any new properties and methods are correctly added.

Updating an Object Type Definition

```
<HTML>
<HEAD>
<TITLE>Updating Object Types</TITLE>
<SCRIPT LANGUAGE="JavaScript" SRC="table.js"><!-
// -></SCRIPT>
</HEAD>
<BODY>
<H1>Updating Object Types</H1>
<SCRIPT LANGUAGE="JavaScript"><!--
function table_colorWrite(doc) {
 doc.write("<TABLE BORDER="+this.border+"
➥ BGCOLOR="+this.bgColor+">")
 for(var i=0;i<this.rows;++i) {
  doc.write("<TR>")
  for(var j=0;j<this.columns;++j) {
   if(this.header[i*this.columns+j]) {
    doc.write("<TH>")
    doc.write(this.data[i*this.columns+j])
    doc.write("</TH>")
   }else{
    doc.write("<TD>")
    doc.write(this.data[i*this.columns+j])
    doc.write("</TD>")
   }
  }
  doc.writeln("</TR>")
 }
 doc.writeln("</TABLE>")
}
```

```
t = new table(3,4)
table.prototype.bgColor="cyan"
table.prototype.colorWrite=table_colorWrite
contents = new Array("This","is","a","test","of",
➡ "the","table","object.", "Let's","see","it","work.")
t.set(contents)
t.border=4
t.makeHeaderColumn(0)
t.colorWrite(document)
// -></SCRIPT>
</BODY>
</HTML>
```

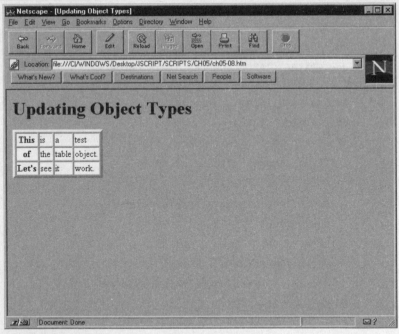

FIGURE 15.10: Tables with a background color

DELETING PROPERTIES AND METHODS

The `delete` operator can be used to delete an element of an array. It can also be used to delete a property or method of a user-defined object. Its syntax is as follows:

```
delete objectName.propertyName
delete objectName.methodName
```

For example, suppose the `myTable` variable refers to a `table` object. The following statement deletes the `header` property of the object referenced by `myTable`:

```
delete myTable.header
```

There are few occasions in which it is desirable to delete a property or method of an existing object. As such, the `delete` operator is rarely used.

THE *EVENT*, *EVENT*, AND *ERROR* OBJECTS

An instance of the `event` object is created whenever an event occurs during the execution of a script. Navigator and Internet Explorer each define a different set of properties for the `event` object. Both browsers use the `type` property to identify the type of event that occurred and the `screenX` and `screenY` properties to identify the screen location at which the event occurred. Navigator and Internet Explorer also implement some similar properties with different names, as summarized in Table 15.9.

TABLE 15.9: Similar Navigator and Internet Explorer Event Properties

NAVIGATOR PROPERTY	INTERNET EXPLORER PROPERTY	DESCRIPTION
pageX, pageY	clientX, clientY	The location of the event relative to the Web page
target	srcElement	The event source
which	button	The mouse button associated with the event

TABLE 15.9 continued: Similar Navigator and Internet Explorer
Event Properties

NAVIGATOR PROPERTY	INTERNET EXPLORER PROPERTY	DESCRIPTION
key	keyCode	The Unicode character code of the character corresponding to the key press
modifiers	altKey, ctrlKey, shiftKey	The state of the Alt, Control, or Shift keys

WHAT'S NEXT?

Now you have a sense of the advantages of objects, and you're well on your way toward using that valuable feature in the JavaScript programs you write for your Web pages. The next chapter will introduce you to Extensible Markup Language (XML) and the promise it holds as an emerging Web technology.

Chapter 16

LEARNING ABOUT XML

Extensible Markup Language (XML) bridges the gap between the complex world of SGML (Standard Generalized Markup Language) and the sometimes limited Web world of HTML (Hypertext Markup Language). This chapter answers some common XML questions and, in doing so, investigates what XML really is and the role it is going to play as a Web technology.

Adapted from *XML In Record Time*, by Natanya Pitts

ISBN 0-7821-2340-6   576 pages $29.99

ANSWERS TO SOME COMMON XML QUESTIONS

Welcome to the new and exciting world of XML. As the newest addition to the Web technology pantheon, XML has caused quite a stir. While the excitement surrounding XML has been quick to grow and is full of promises, it seems that the answer to "What is XML?" is quite often conspicuously absent. You may have already heard that XML will allow you to create your own tags and that it's going to be the next big Web "thang." Both of those statements are accurate, but there's much more to XML than just the ability to create your own tags. XML will pave the way for Web-based, customized document description and dissemination solutions. No longer will Web developers have to force all of their content into the HTML mold. Once XML takes off, it will change the way we design and deploy Web documents.

XML FAQS ONLINE

XML FAQs are just beginning to appear on the Internet, and most are focused on one particular implementation or another of XML. Two good XML FAQs are:

- ▶ The W3C's XML Working Group's XML FAQ maintained by Peter Flynn at http://www.ucc.ie/xml/

- ▶ The Microsoft XML FAQ maintained by Microsoft at http://www.microsoft.com/xml/xmlfaq.htm

Peter Flynn's XML FAQ is a bit on the technical side, but it is updated regularly and is a wonderful quick reference when you're wondering about some aspect of XML. This FAQ is maintained by Flynn on behalf of the World Wide Web Consortium's (W3C) XML Working Group—the powers that be in the XML world—and is the closest thing to an official FAQ as there will ever be. The Microsoft XML FAQ is less extensive than Flynn's, but it is easy to read and contains a lot of useful information. Granted, this FAQ is written from the Microsoft point of view and does contain some purely Microsoft-oriented material, but it is a solid resource that Microsoft updates on a regular basis.

Although all of this is well and good, many questions about XML have elusive or difficult-to-find answers, and without those answers, you won't know whether XML is the right technology for you. I've found that while even the best computer books explain many things very well and provide tutorials, sample code, and other things that a user might need to get started with the technology, they don't really address fundamental questions the user might have. The wide variety of FAQs—lists of frequently asked questions and their answers—available for most Internet- and Web-related subjects indicates that basic questions about a technology do need to be answered before one can jump into learning how to use it. The same is true for XML.

By way of introduction to XML and this book, I've put together my own XML FAQ that answers the most common and important XML questions. My FAQ is not exhaustive by any means, but it does highlight key XML issues, dispel any myths about XML from the beginning, and provide you with a strong foundation with which to begin learning about and working with XML.

THE WORLD WIDE WEB CONSORTIUM: THE ULTIMATE AUTHORITY

The Internet and World Wide Web are built on standards that are accepted worldwide. These standards make it possible for different kinds of computers, running different operating systems and software, to talk to each other. The W3C was created to ensure that the standards governing the Internet and Web do not favor one vendor or operating system over another. In addition, the W3C oversees the maintenance of existing standards to ensure they are kept up-to-date to meet the growing needs of the Internet and Web. The W3C is also responsible for organizing the teams of industry specialists who develop new standards.

The official standards for HTML, graphics, style sheets, Web servers, and a wide variety of other Web technologies have all been developed and are maintained by the W3C. The W3C can only recommend new standards and hope that individual companies create products that adhere to those standards. Generally, if a company wants its product to sell well and have a large user base, the company will design the product by the W3C's recommended

CONTINUED ➡

standard. All of the major Internet and Web software and hardware developers are members of the W3C and involve themselves directly in the development of the standards to which their products should adhere.

The W3C maintains a Web site at http://www.w3.org/ that includes full documentation for all the standards they are responsible for as well as information about those standards and initiatives still under development. If you're working with Internet or Web technologies and haven't visited the W3C's Web site, you should take some time to do so now. The resources available at the site are second to none.

What Is XML?

The W3C XML Activity page, located at http://www.w3.org/XML/Activity.html, provides this answer to the question:

> XML—the eXtensible Markup Language—is a simple and very flexible language based on SGML. Although originally envisaged to meet the challenges involved in large-scale publishing, XML is set to play an increasingly important role in the markup of a wide variety of data on the Web. Not only will XML help people find the information they want but the wealth of XML metadata on the Web—information *about* information—will help many Web-based applications.
>
> XML will make it easier for information consumers and producers to find each other; many tasks involving search or information exchange can be automated with XML, providing a common framework for representing information—everyone should benefit.

In nongeek speak, this means that XML is a language for creating markup languages—or a meta–markup language—specifically geared toward one type of content. A markup language uses tags embedded directly into the text to describe the various pieces and parts of the text.

In the following example, the <PARA> and <ITALICS> tags describe a paragraph and an italicized word:

```
<PARA>"XML - the eXtensible Markup Language - is a simple and
very flexible language based on SGML. Although originally
envisaged to meet the challenges involved in large-scale
publishing, XML is set to play an increasingly important
role in the markup of a wide variety of data on the Web. Not
only will XML help people find the information they want,
but the wealth of XML metadata on the Web - information
<ITALICS>about</ITALICS> information - will help many Web-
based applications.</PARA>
```

A markup language does not worry about how the content it describes is formatted but is, instead, concerned with accurately describing its content. HTML is a markup language, and the concept of a markup language is key to understanding and implementing XML.

In short, XML is a markup language that can run on any platform, operating system, or environment and is designed to provide developers with a mechanism to better describe their content. It was originally designed for publishing projects but has been developed to make the exchange of data on the Web easier and more efficient. XML does this by allowing developers to write their own *document-type definitions* (DTDs) that describe sets of tags and attributes that can be used to describe specific kinds of content. DTDs are markup language rule books that define what markup elements can be used to describe a document. If you want to create your own tags, you'll have to first define them in a DTD. The individual markup languages that XML defines are called *XML vocabularies,* or applications, and XML defines these through DTDs.

XML is being developed under the auspices of the W3C's XML Working Group to ensure that its mechanisms are standard and don't promote one vendor over another. While each XML vocabulary will have a specific purpose and type of content it is designed to describe, all must adhere strictly to the rules of XML, making all the vocabularies XML subsets. Two examples of XML vocabularies are the Genealogical Markup Language (GedML) and the Chemical Markup Language (CML). Both are XML vocabularies and have been developed according to the XML specification, but each has a very different purpose. GedML is designed to describe ancestral data, whereas CML was created specifically to describe chemical formulas and molecules. Both are defined by DTDs that specify the

Part iii

elements that can be used to describe genealogical and chemical information, respectively. In general, XML provides a standardized set of rules for describing DTDs and their documents for exchange over the Internet and Web. You can use XML to write the DTD that defines your own vocabulary and documents to go along with it or to create documents according to a DTD for a vocabulary that someone else has already written.

XML is sufficiently robust and extensive that it can be used to describe not only content but also *metadata*. Metadata is information that describes other information. An example of metadata we've all worked with is a card catalog in a library. Each card, or electronic entry in a computerized catalog, is an information resource that provides information about another information resource, usually a book, magazine, or bit of film. A consistent method for describing metadata, such as with XML, will eventually lead to more organized cataloging of Web resources, making it easier for denizens of the Web to conduct efficient searches of the millions of existing Web pages.

In a nutshell, XML provides both a more extensive means for describing document content and a mechanism for describing metadata, using a method that will work on all computers, regardless of platform or operating system. XML takes Web data to the next level, using vocabularies defined by DTDs tailored to specific kinds of content.

Why Was XML Developed?

XML was developed because document designers and content specialists realized that HTML was simply too narrow in scope to handle the many tasks it had been given. Not all content can be described as paragraphs, lists, tables, and forms. Because HTML was the only available mechanism for describing Web content, all Web content was squeezed into paragraph, list, table, and form molds. If you've ever tried to put a square peg into a round hole, you'll know why this paradigm simply wasn't working.

The members of the W3C's various working groups realized that HTML simply couldn't be expanded to accommodate every type of data because it would become too cumbersome. They could have opted to develop a series of markup languages, each with its own specific purpose, but they realized there was no way they could anticipate everyone's markup needs. Returning to the world of SGML wasn't an option either, because SGML was an overkill solution.

XML was developed to provide a structured environment for developers to create DTDs for content that doesn't fit into the HTML mold. By defining a *metalanguage* for creating Web-based markup languages, rather than a whole new group of markup languages, the W3C provided a mechanism for creating customizable solutions for the Web that work within the existing Web infrastructure.

What Is XML's Relationship to HTML?

In many ways, XML is a distant cousin of HTML and may in the future actually be its parent. Both XML and HTML are descendants of SGML, but while XML is a meta–markup language, HTML is a specialized markup language. SGML is the granddaddy of all markup languages and the basis for both XML and HTML. Eventually HTML will probably become an XML vocabulary, used to describe simple documents and to make Web sites backward-compatible with older Web browsers.

HTML paved the way for XML by giving developers a taste of what is possible when you combine a nonproprietary markup language and data exchanged over the Internet. The extensive use of HTML to describe documents of all kinds rooted out the many needs and issues for which developers would have to find solutions. HTML was created to meet a specific need at the European Laboratory for Particle Physics in Switzerland (CERN) and soon became the solution for a wider variety of needs. XML is being built expressly to serve the needs revealed by widespread use of HTML.

If you know something about HTML, you know something about XML. For the time being, the Web is still built with HTML, so you'll need to know HTML to implement your XML solutions. Many of the new tools being built to parse and display data described with XML vocabularies are programmed in Java for easy implementation in the Web environment. To include a Java applet in a Web page, you have to use HTML— and that probably won't change anytime soon. At least for the foreseeable future, HTML and XML are going to coexist in the Web world, and HTML will be a necessary part of implementing XML solutions on the Web.

Can I Use XML to Design Web Pages?

Unfortunately, this question can't be answered with a simple "Yes" or "No." Both Internet Explorer 4 and 5, as well as Netscape Navigator 5, have some support for XML—as described in the answer to the next question—but it is limited in scope and application. You can't simply create an XML document, stick it on your Web site, and expect your average Web browser to know what to do with it. At present, there's no easy way to include XML in a Web page. Determined developers have to program their Web pages with a scripting language, such as ECMAScript (a standardized version of JavaScript), to convert an XML document into HTML for viewing in a Web browser—not a very practical solution. For now, the most practical reason for learning XML is that many emerging Web technologies include XML as part of their solution, and future Web pages will almost certainly be built using XML.

Do Internet Explorer and Netscape Navigator Support XML?

The developers at both Microsoft and Netscape realize the importance of including XML support in their browser offerings; however, the status of XML as a developing technology currently has limited that support. Internet Explorer 4 for Windows 95/98/NT currently ships with a nonvalidating XML parser written in C++. You can also download a validating Java-based parser as an add-in.

NOTE

A *parser* is a software component that reads an XML document and creates output from which an application, such as a Web browser, can generate a display. The section "How Do I Process and Display XML Documents?" later in the chapter includes more detailed information about parsers.

Either parser can hand off the results of a parsed document to an XML viewer written in Java or ActiveX. In addition, Internet Explorer includes support for an XML Object Model (XOM). The XOM provides Web scripts created in JavaScript or Visual Basic access to all the elements in an XML document, as parsed by either the IE C++ or Java parser.

Internet Explorer also supports the Channel Definition Format (CDF) and the Open Software Description (OSD) vocabularies. CDF is the mechanism that makes Internet Explorer's channels possible and is the first full implementation of an XML vocabulary at work on the Web. OSD is designed to describe software packages as part of a system that allows for hands-off software installation over a network.

Netscape's release of the Mozilla source code—also known as Navigator 5—includes a version of the *expat* parser written by James Clark and includes support for the Resource Description Frameworks (RDF) vocabulary. RDF is intended to describe Web resources in a standard and consistent way, and it may soon change the way we all search for information on the Web.

As XML becomes less a developing technology and more an implemented technology, you can expect to see full support for XML in Web browsers. Still, because XML developers will be able to create their own DTDs and documents, we can't expect every browser to know how those documents should be displayed. Most likely, the browsers will support a handful of the key XML vocabularies and leave the creation of browsers for other vocabularies to the vocabulary developers themselves.

Can I Really Create and Use My Own XML Tags?

Yes, you can. Although the answer is simple, creating and implementing your own tags isn't as simple. Remember that tags are used to describe a document's content and that a DTD specifies which tags can be used in a document. To create your own tags, you'll have to create your own DTD, as discussed earlier in this chapter. To make things even more fun, you have to play by the rules of XML for your DTDs and documents to function correctly. The mechanisms that make up a DTD aren't that complicated to define and describe, but designing an efficient, effective, and extensible DTD is a whole other story.

Don't think I'm trying to scare you away from XML or from creating your own markup; rather, I'm pointing out that XML isn't the walk in the park that HTML is. The key to creating your own markup isn't in understanding how to define elements and attributes but in the quiet art of DTD design. Becoming a DTD design pro takes a bit of practice and the willingness to learn from others and from your own mistakes.

Finally, although you can create your own markup, it's important to know when to design your own DTD and when to use someone else's. Many XML vocabularies are already under development to meet an assortment of Web content needs, including describing mathematical and chemical content, identifying Web metadata, facilitating financial transactions over the Web, and more. Companies or groups of companies are building the majority of these vocabularies to meet their own needs. Inevitably, specialized tools and browsers will be developed for these vocabularies, making their implementation much easier. New vocabularies are being developed every day, as well; if a current one doesn't meet your needs, it's quite possible that one will be released in the not-so-distant future that will.

The whole motivation behind XML is to provide developers with a standard environment in which to develop specialized markup. However, for the standard environment to be extensible enough to meet a wide variety of needs, it has to be a bit sophisticated, so working within the environment requires some study.

How Do I Process and Display XML Documents?

XML documents are processed by applications called *parsers*. The parser reads the document and generates output based on the document's content and the markup used to describe that content. In some instances, the document must be compared to and abide by the rules specified in its DTD. When properly constructed, these documents are called *valid*. Parsers that have the ability to compare a document to its DTD and determine whether the document is valid are called *validating parsers*. Even if a document does not have to be validated, it must still conform to the general rules of document creation established in the XML specification. Documents that obey all the general rules are considered well-formed. All parsers check to make sure an XML document is well-formed, but only validating parsers also check to see if a document is valid. While all documents must be well formed, not all must be valid.

Specialized browsers are currently being developed that know how to interpret the output from a parser and render a display of the XML document using that output. XML is a new technology, so parsers and browsers are just beginning to appear. A parser can process any XML document and a validating parser can discern the validity of any XML document, but most browsers currently under development are designed to display documents written for one DTD or another. For example, the JUMBO browser was developed specifically to display documents described with the Chemical Markup Language (CML), an XML vocabulary. CML is used to describe chemical and molecular compounds, and JUMBO is designed to display those compounds based on the results of parsed CML documents. Although JUMBO can understand and might attempt to display the contents of other parsed non-CML documents, the end results might not be as effective as with CML documents.

Because XML is an Internet and Web technology and the developers of the various vocabularies realize that specialized browsers will be needed to properly view their documents, the majority of parsers and browsers are being written as Java applets. Because all the major browsers support Java, specialized XML browsers written in Java can be embedded easily in Web pages, and the display of XML documents can be quickly integrated into the current Web infrastructure.

Is XML Just a Passing Fad?

This question can be asked of almost every Web technology and probably of the Web itself. In my opinion, based on reading the opinions of the powers that be, XML is here to stay. XML provides an elegant and extensible solution to many needs that have arisen since HTML became the language of the Web. XML requires that document developers understand some new concepts and learn a few new skills. Web browsers will have to handle documents differently and support a wider variety of markup vocabularies. However, developers will be able to choose from a collection of languages rather than having to mangle a single language, and browser developers won't have to create proprietary solutions to a wide variety of user needs. Indeed, if XML works as it was intended, it will bring a long-awaited standardization to the Web that will propel the dissemination of information into a new era, probably just as we celebrate the new millennium.

Part iii

GETTING READY TO WORK WITH XML

As the answers to this chapter's XML FAQ have shown, XML is not just another version of HTML. There are many issues a budding XML developer must address, including how to read a DTD and write documents for it, how to process an XML document, and what kind of XML support is included in the different Web browsers. The status of XML as a developing technology means resources and information about it are scarce, and it takes effort to put your finger on how you can use XML as part of a workable, real-world solution.

WHAT'S NEXT?

Over the course of this book, our authors have given you a solid background in HTML and its implementation in site design. In addition, they've introduced you to other languages that you can use to augment HTML and enhance your pages even more. The next step is up to you. You should now feel free to experiment with what you've learned while building sites of your own—just be sure to keep this book nearby. In addition to the chapters you've just completed, the Appendix—a comprehensive guide to HTML tags and their attributes, the properties used in creating style sheets, the components of JavaScript, HTML special characters, and HTML color codes—will prove invaluable as you venture further into site design.

PART iV

APPENDIX

HTML MASTER'S REFERENCE

Adapted from *Mastering HTML 4.0*, by Deborah S. Ray and Eric J. Ray

ISBN 0-7821-2102-0   1,040 pages $49.99

HTML Tags and Attributes

This section is a comprehensive reference guide to all HTML tags, including standard tags and those introduced by Netscape Navigator and Microsoft Internet Explorer. For each tag, we've provided sample code and indicated the following:

▶ The version of HTML with which the tag is associated

▶ Whether browsers widely support the tag

▶ Whether to pair the tag with a closing tag

For each tag's attributes, we've provided sample code and indicated the following:

▶ The version of HTML with which the attribute is associated

▶ Whether browsers widely support the attribute

If tags and attributes appear in the HTML 4 standard, in the HTML 3.2 standard, or in the HTML 2 standard, the version number appears next to Standard. We indicate tags or attributes that are specific to a browser, such as Internet Explorer. In general, a variety of browsers recognize technology-specific tags, such as those for frames, and other browsers rarely recognize browser-specific tags. HTML 2 was the first official HTML standard. The number of tags that this standard defined is small compared with what is in use today. HTML 2 did not support tables, client-side imagemaps, or frames. You can safely use all HTML 2 tags and attributes.

HTML 3.2 remains backward-compatible with HTML 2, but provides many new tags. Included in HTML 3.2 is support for tables, client-side imagemaps, embedded applets, and many new attributes that help control alignment of objects within documents. You can assume that most browsers support or soon will support all HTML 3.2 tags and attributes.

HTML 4 remains backward-compatible with other versions of HTML and expands the capabilities to better address multiple languages and browser technologies such as speech or Braille. Additionally, most formatting tags and attributes are deprecated (strongly discouraged) in HTML 4 in favor of style sheets.

Specifying that a tag or an attribute is Common means that approximately 75 to 80 percent of browsers in common use accommodate the tag. All recent versions of both Internet Explorer and Netscape Navigator recognize Common tags and attributes.

We indicate variables as follows:

Variable	What You Substitute
n	A number (such as a size)
URL	Some form of address (as in a hyperlink)
#RRGGBB	A color value or a color name
...	Some other value, such as a title or a name

!

<!-- -->

Inserts comments into a document. Browsers do not display comments, although comments are visible in the document source.

> **Standard:** HTML 2
> **Common:** Yes
> **Paired:** Yes
> **Sample:**

```
<!-- Here is the picture of Fido
-->
<IMG SRC="fidopic.jpg">
```

<!DOCTYPE>

Appears at the beginning of the document and indicates the HTML version of the document.

The HTML 2 standard is:

```
<!DOCTYPE HTML PUBLIC
"-//IETF//DTD HTML 2 //EN">
```

The HTML 3.2 standard is:

```
<!DOCTYPE HTML PUBLIC
"-//W3C//DTD/ HTML 3.2 Final//EN">
```

The HTML 4 standard is:

```
<!DOCTYPE HTML PUBLIC
"-//W3C//DTD/ HTML 4 Final//EN">
```

> **Standard:** HTML 2
> **Common:** Yes
> **Paired:** No
> **Sample:**

```
<!DOCTYPE HTML PUBLIC
"-//W3C//DTD/ HTML 4 Final//EN">
```

A

<A>

Also called the *anchor* tag, identifies a link or a location within a document. You commonly use this tag to create a hyperlink, using the HREF= attribute. You can also use the <A> tag to identify sections within a document, using the NAME= attribute.

> **Standard:** HTML 2
> **Common:** Yes
> **Paired:** Yes
> **Sample:**

```
<A HREF="http://www.raycomm
.com/">Visit RayComm</a>
```

Attribute Information

ACCESSKEY="..."

Assigns a key sequence to the element.

> **Standard:** HTML 4
> **Common:** No
> **Sample:**

```
<A HREF="help.html"
ACCESSKEY="H">HELP</a>
```

CHARSET="..."

Specifies character encoding of the data designated by the link. Use the name of a character set defined in RFC2045. The default value for this attribute, appropriate for all Western languages, is "ISO-8859-1".

> **Standard:** HTML 4
> **Common:** No
> **Sample:**

```
<A HREF="help.html" CHARSET="ISO-
8859-1">HELP</a>
```

CLASS="..."

Indicates the style class to apply to the <A> element.

Standard: HTML 4

Common: No

Sample:

```
<A HREF="next.html"
CLASS="casual">Next</A>
```

COORDS="x1, y1, x2, y2"

Identifies the coordinates that define a clickable area. Measure coordinates, in pixels, from the top left corner of the image.

Standard: HTML 4

Common: No

Sample:

```
<A SHAPE="RECT"
COORDS="20,8,46,30"
HREF="food.html">
```

HREF="URL"

Specifies the relative or absolute location of a file to which you want to provide a hyperlink.

Standard: HTML 2

Common: Yes

Sample:

```
<A HREF="details.html">More
Info</a>
```

ID="..."

Assigns a unique ID selector to an instance of the <A> tag. When you then assign a style to that ID selector, it affects only that one instance of the <A> tag.

Standard: HTML 4

Common: No

Sample:

```
<A HREF="next.html"
ID="123">Next</A>
```

NAME="..."

Marks a location within the current document with a name. The browser can then quickly move to specific information within a document. You can link to existing named locations in a document by using a fragment URL, consisting of a pound sign (#) and the name (from within that document), or by using a more complete URL, including a pound sign and a name (from other documents or sites).

Standard: HTML 2

Common: Yes

Sample:

```
<A HREF="#ingredients"
>Ingredients</A><BR><A
NAME="ingredients"><h1>
Ingredients</H1>
```

REL="..."

Specifies relationship hyperlinks.

Standard: HTML 3.2

Common: No

Sample:

```
<A REV="made"
HREF="mailto:bob@company.com">
```

REV="..."

Specifies reverse relationship hyperlinks.

Standard: HTML 3.2

Common: No

Sample:

```
<A REV="Previous" HREF="http://
www.raycomm.com/firstdoc.htm">
```

SHAPE="{RECT, CIRCLE, POLY}"

Specifies the type of shape used to represent the clickable area. SHAPE=RECT indicates that the shape is rectangular. SHAPE=CIRCLE specifies that the shape is a circle. SHAPE=POLY indicates that the shape is a polygon represented by three or more points.

Standard: HTML 4

Common: No

Sample:

```
<A SHAPE="RECT"
COORDS="20,8,46,30"
HREF="food.html">
```

STYLE="..."

Specifies style sheet commands that apply to the contents within the <A> tags.

Standard: HTML 4

Common: No

Sample:

```
<A STYLE="background: red"
HREF="page2.html">Page 2</A>
```

TABINDEX="*n*"

Indicates where the element appears in the tabbing order of the document.

Standard: HTML 4

Common: No

Sample:

```
<A HREF="food.html"
TABINDEX="4">Food</A>
```

TARGET="..."

Indicates the name of a specific frame into which you load the linked document. You establish frame names within the <FRAME> tag. The value of this attribute can be any single word.

Standard: HTML 4

Common: Yes

Sample:

```
<A HREF="/frames/frame2.html"
TARGET="pages">Go to Page 2</a>
```

TITLE="..."

Specifies text assigned to the tag that you can use for context-sensitive help

within the document. Browsers may use this to show tool tips over the hyperlink.

Standard: HTML 4

Common: Yes

Sample:

```
<A HREF="page2.html" TITLE="Go to
the next page">
```

Other Attributes

This tag also accepts the lang, dir, onClick, onDblClick, onMouseDown, onMouseUp, onMouseOver, onMouse-Move, onMouseOut, onKeyPress, onKeyDown, and onKeyUp attributes. See the "Element-Independent Attributes" section of this reference for definitions and examples.

<ACRONYM>

Indicates an acronym in a document.

Standard: HTML 4

Common: No

Paired: Yes

Sample:

```
<P><ACRONYM>HTTP</ACRONYM> stands
for HyperText Transfer
Protocol</P>
```

Attribute Information

CLASS="..."

Indicates which style class applies to the <ACRONYM> element.

Standard: HTML 4

Common: No

Sample:

```
<P><ACRONYM
CLASS="casual">HTTP</ACRONYM>
stands for HyperText Transfer
Protocol</P>
```

ID="..."

Assigns a unique ID selector to an instance of the <ACRONYM> tag. When you then assign a style to that ID selector, it affects only that one instance of the <ACRONYM> tag.

Standard: HTML 4

Common: No

Sample:

```
<P><ACRONYM
ID="123">HTTP</ACRONYM> stands
for HyperText Transfer
Protocol</P>
```

STYLE="..."

Specifies style sheet commands that apply to the definition.

Standard: HTML 4

Common: No

Sample:

```
<P><ACRONYM STYLE="background:
blue; color: white">ESP</ACRONYM>
stands for extra-sensory
perception.</P>
```

TITLE="..."

Specifies text assigned to the tag. For the <ACRONYM> tag, use this to provide the expansion of the term. You might also use this attribute for context-sensitive help within the document. Browsers may use this to show tool tips over the text.

Standard: HTML 4

Common: No

Sample:

```
<P><ACRONYM TITLE="HyperText
Transfer Protocol">HTTP</ACRONYM>
stands for HyperText Transfer
Protocol</P>
```

Other Attributes

This tag also accepts the lang, dir, onClick, onDblClick, onMouseDown, onMouseUp, onMouseOver, onMouse-Move, onMouseOut, onKeyPress, onKeyDown, and onKeyUp attributes. See the Element-Independent Attributes section of this reference for definitions and examples.

<ADDRESS>

In a document, distinguishes an address from normal document text.

Standard: HTML 2

Common: Yes

Paired: Yes

Sample:

```
I live at:
```

```
<ADDRESS>123 Nowhere Ave<BR>City,
State 12345</ADDRESS>
```

Attribute Information

ALIGN={LEFT, RIGHT, CENTER}

Indicates how the address text is aligned within the document. ALIGN=LEFT positions the address text flush with the left side of the document. ALIGN=RIGHT positions the address text flush with the right side of the document. ALIGN= CENTER centers the address text between the left and right edges of the document.

Standard: HTML 3.2; deprecated in favor of style sheets

Common: Yes

Sample:

```
<ADDRESS ALIGN="CENTER">123
Anywhere St.</ADDRESS>
```

CLASS="..."

Indicates the style class to apply to the <ADDRESS> element.

Standard: HTML 4

Common: No

Sample:
```
<ADDRESS CLASS="casual">123 First
Ave.</ADDRESS>
```

ID="..."
Assigns a unique ID selector to an instance of the <ADDRESS> tag. When you then assign a style to that ID selector, it affects only that one instance of the <ADDRESS> tag.

Standard: HTML 4
Common: No
Sample:
```
<ADDRESS ID="123">1600
Pennsylvania</ADDRESS>
```

STYLE="..."
Specifies style sheet commands that apply to the contents within the <ADDRESS> tags.

Standard: HTML 4
Common: Yes
Sample:
```
<ADDRESS STYLE="background: red">
```

TITLE="..."
Specifies text assigned to the tag. You might use this attribute for context-sensitive help within the document. Browsers may use this to show tool tips over the address text.

Standard: HTML 4
Common: No
Sample:
```
<ADDRESS TITLE="Address">
```

Other Attributes
This tag also accepts the lang, dir, onClick, onDblClick, onMouseDown, onMouseUp, onMouseOver, onMouse-Move, onMouseOut, onKeyPress, onKeyDown, and onKeyUp attributes.

See the Element-Independent Attributes section of this reference for definitions and examples.

<APPLET>

Embeds a Java applet object into an HTML document. Typically, items that appear inside the <APPLET> tags allow browsers that do not support Java applets to view alternative text. Browsers that do support Java ignore all information between the <APPLET> tags.

Standard HTML 3.2; deprecated in HTML 4 in favor of <OBJECT>
Common: Yes
Paired: Yes
Sample:
```
<APPLET CODE="game.class">It
appears your browser does not
support Java. You're missing out
on a whole world of neat
things!</APPLET>
```

Attribute Information

ALIGN={LEFT, CENTER, RIGHT}
Specifies the horizontal alignment of the Java applet displayed. For example, a value of CENTER tells the browser to place the applet evenly spaced between the left and right edges of the browser window.

Standard: HTML 3.2; deprecated in HTML 4 in favor of style sheets.
Common: No
Sample:
```
<APPLET ALIGN=CENTER
CODE=""http://www.raycomm.com/
checkers.class">You lose. Would
you like to play again? Hit the
RELOAD button.<BR></APPLET>
```

ALT="..."

Displays a textual description of a Java applet, if necessary.

Standard: HTML 3.2

Common: No

Sample:

```
<APPLET CODE=""http://www
.raycomm.com/checkers.class">ALT=
"A Game of checkers">We could
have had a relaxing game of
checkers if your browser sup-
ported Java applets. I'll gladly
play with you if you enable Java
applets or upgrade to a browser
that supports Java.</APPLET>
```

CODE="*URL*"

Specifies the relative or absolute location of the Java bytecode file on the server.

Standard: HTML 3.2

Common: No

Sample:

```
<APPLET CODE="http://www
.raycomm.com/checkers.class">
```

Dang! Your browser does not support Java applets. You may want
to consider installing a newer
web browser.

```
</APPLET>
```

CODEBASE="*URL*"

Specifies the directory where you can find all necessary Java class files on the WWW server. If you set this attribute, you need not use explicit URLs in other references to the class files. For example, you would not need an explicit reference in the CODE= attribute.

Standard: HTML 3.2

Common: No

Sample:

```
<APPLET CODEBASE="http://www
.raycomm.com/checkers.class"
CODE="checkers.html">
```

If your browser supported inline
Java applets, you'd be looking at
a very attractive checkerboard
right now.

```
</APPLET>
```

HEIGHT="*n*"

Specifies the height (measured in pixels) of the Java applet object within the document.

Standard: HTML 3.2

Common: No

Sample:

```
<APPLET HEIGHT="200"
CODE="checkers.class">
```

Since your browser does not support inline Java applets, we
won't be playing checkers today.

```
</APPLET>
```

HSPACE="*n*"

Specifies an amount of blank space (measured in pixels) to the left and right of the Java applet within the document.

Standard: HTML 3.2

Common: No

Sample:

```
<APPLET HSPACE="10"
CODE="/checkers.class">
```

Sorry. Due to the fact your
browser does not support embedded
Java applets, you'll have to play
checkers the old way today.

```
</APPLET>
```

NAME="..."

Assigns the applet instance a name so that other applets can identify it within the document.

Standard: Internet Explorer

Common: No

Sample:

```
<APPLET SRC="/checkers.class"
NAME="Checkers">

</APPLET>
```

PARAM NAME="..."

Passes program parameters to the Java applet.

Standard: HTML 3.2

Common: No

Sample:

```
<APPLET CODE="/checkers.class"
PARAM COLOR="red">
```

Since your browser does not support inline Java applets, I win this game of checkers by forfeit.

```
</APPLET>
```

TITLE="..."

Specifies text assigned to the tag. You might use this attribute for context-sensitive help within the document. Browsers may use this to show tool tips over the embedded applet.

Standard: HTML 4

Common: No

Sample:

```
<APPLET SRC="/java/thing.class"
TITLE="Thing">
```

VSPACE="n"

Specifies the amount of vertical space (measured in pixels) above and below the Java applet.

Standard: HTML 3.2

Common: No

Sample:

```
<APPLET VSPACE="10"
CODE="/checkers.class">
```

If you had a Java-capable browser, you could be playing checkers!

```
</APPLET>
```

WIDTH="n"

Specifies the width (measured in pixels) of a Java applet within a document.

Standard: HTML 3.2

Common: No

Sample:

```
<APPLET WIDTH="350"
CODE="/checkers.class">
```

Checkers can be a lot of fun, but it's more fun if your browser supports Java. Sorry.

```
</APPLET>
```

Other Attributes

This tag also accepts the lang, dir, onClick, onDblClick, onMouseDown, onMouseUp, onMouseOver, onMouse-Move, onMouseOut, onKeyPress, onKeyDown, and onKeyUp attributes. See the Element-Independent Attributes section of this reference for definitions and examples.

‹AREA›

Defines an area within a client-side imagemap definition (see the ‹MAP› tag). It indicates an area where visitors can choose to link to another document.

Standard: HTML 3.2
Common: Yes
Paired: No
Sample:

```
<AREA SHAPE=RECT
COORDS="20,8,46,30"
HREF="food.html">
```

Attribute Information

ALT="..."
Provides a textual description for visitors who have text-only browsers.

Standard: HTML 4
Common: Yes
Sample:

```
<AREA ALT="This blue rectangle
links to blue.html"
HREF="blue.html">
```

CLASS="..."
Indicates the style class you want to apply to the ‹AREA› element.

Standard: HTML 4
Common: No
Sample:

```
<AREA CLASS="casual" SHAPE="RECT"
COORDS="20,8,46,30"
HREF="food.html">
```

COORDS="x1, y1, x2, y2"
Identifies the coordinates within an imagemap that define the imagemap area. Measure coordinates, in pixels, from the top left corner of the image.

Standard: HTML 3.2
Common: Yes
Sample:

```
<AREA SHAPE="RECT"
COORDS="20,8,46,30"
HREF="food.html">
```

HREF="URL"
Identifies the location of the document you want to load when the indicated imagemap area is selected.

Standard: HTML 3.2
Common: Yes
Sample:

```
<AREA SHAPE="RECT"
COORDS="20,8,46,30"
HREF="food.html">
```

ID="..."
Assigns a unique ID selector to an instance of the ‹AREA› tag. When you then assign a style to that ID selector, it affects this instance of the ‹AREA› tag.

Standard: HTML 4
Common: No
Sample:

```
<AREA ID="123">
```

NOHREF
Defines an imagemap area that does not link to another document.

Standard: HTML 3.2
Common: Yes
Sample:

```
<AREA SHAPE="RECT"
COORDS="20,8,46,30" NOHREF>
```

NOTAB
Excludes the imagemap area from the tab order.

Standard: Internet Explorer

Common: Yes

Sample:

```
<AREA SHAPE="RECT"
COORDS="20,8,46,30"
HREF="food.html" NOTAB>
```

SHAPE="{RECT, CIRCLE, POLY}"

Specifies the type of shape used to represent the imagemap area. SHAPE=RECT indicates that the shape of the imagemap area is rectangular. SHAPE=CIRCLE specifies that the shape of the imagemap area is a circle. SHAPE=POLY indicates that the shape of the imagemap area is a polygon represented by three or more points.

Standard: HTML 3.2

Common: Yes

Sample:

```
<AREA SHAPE="RECT"
COORDS="20,8,46,30"
HREF="food.html">
```

STYLE="..."

Specifies style sheet commands that apply to the imagemap area.

Standard: HTML 4

Common: No

Sample:

```
<AREA SHAPE="RECT"
COORDS="20,8,46,30"
HREF="food.html"
STYLE="background: red">
```

TABINDEX="n"

Indicates where the imagemap area appears in the tabbing order of the document.

Standard: HTML 4

Common: Yes

Sample:

```
<AREA SHAPE="RECT"
COORDS="20,8,46,30"
HREF="food.html" TABINDEX=4>
```

TARGET="..."

Identifies which named frame the linked document selected should load. For example, when visitors select an area within an imagemap, the linked document may load in the same frame or in a different frame, specified by TARGET="...".

Standard: HTML 4

Common: Yes

Sample:

```
<AREA SHAPE="RECT"
COORDS="20,8,46,30"
HREF="food.html"
TARGET="leftframe">
```

TITLE="..."

Specifies text assigned to the tag. You might use this attribute for context-sensitive help within the document. Browsers may use this to show tool tips over the imagemap area.

Standard: HTML 4

Common: No

Sample:

```
<AREA SHAPE="RECT"
COORDS="20,8,46,30"
HREF="food.html" NAME="Food!">
```

Other Attributes

This tag also accepts the lang and dir attributes. See the Element-Independent Attributes section of this reference for definitions and examples.

B

<B>

Indicates text that should appear in boldface.

Standard: HTML 2
Common: Yes
Paired: Yes
Sample:

The afternoon was <B>so</B> hot!

Attribute Information

CLASS="..."
Indicates which style class applies to the <B> element.

Standard: HTML 4
Common: No
Sample:

<B CLASS="casual">Boom!</B>

ID="..."
Assigns a unique ID selector to an instance of the <B> tag. When you assign a style to that ID selector, it affects only that one instance of the <B> tag.

Standard: HTML 4
Common: No
Sample:

I work for <B ID="123">Widgets Inc.</B>

STYLE="..."
Specifies style sheet commands that apply to the contents within the <B> tags.

Standard: HTML 4
Common: No

Sample:

<B STYLE="background: red">

TITLE="..."
Specifies text assigned to the tag. You might use this attribute for context-sensitive help within the document. Browsers may use this to show tool tips over the boldface

Standard: HTML 4
Common: No
Sample:

<B TITLE="Species">Dog Species</B>

Other Attributes
This tag also accepts the lang, dir, onClick, onDblClick, onMouseDown, onMouseUp, onMouseOver, onMouse-Move, onMouseOut, onKeyPress, onKeyDown, and onKeyUp attributes. See the Element-Independent Attributes section of this reference for definitions and examples.

<BASE>

Identifies the location where all relative URLs in your document originate.

Standard: HTML 2
Common: Yes
Paired: No
Sample:

<BASE HREF="http://www.raycomm.com/info/">

Attribute Information

HREF="*URL*"

Indicates the relative or absolute location of the base document.

Standard: HTML 2

Common: Yes

Sample:

```
<BASE HREF="http://www.raycomm
.com/">
```

TARGET="..."

Identifies in which named frame you load a document (see the HREF= attribute).

Standard: HTML 4

Common: Yes

Sample:

```
<BASE HREF="http://www.raycomm
.com/frames/" TARGET="main">
```

<BASEFONT>

Provides a font setting for normal text within a document. Font settings (see the <FONT> tag) within the document are relative to settings specified with this tag. Use this tag in the document header (between the <HEAD> tags).

Standard: HTML 3.2; deprecated in HTML 4 in favor of style sheets

Common: Yes

Paired: No

Sample:

```
<BASEFONT SIZE="5">
```

Attribute Information

COLOR="#RRGGBB" or "..."

Sets the font color of normal text within a document. Color names may substitute for the explicit RGB hexadecimal values.

Standard: HTML 3.2; deprecated in HTML 4 in favor of style sheets

Common: Yes

Sample:

```
<BASEFONT SIZE="2"
COLOR="#FF00CC">
```

FACE="...,..."

Specifies the font face of normal text within a document. You can set this attribute to a comma-separated list of font names. The browser selects the first name matching a font available.

Standard: HTML 3.2; deprecated in HTML 4 in favor of style sheets

Common: Yes

Sample:

```
<BASEFONT FACE="Avant Guard,
Helvetica, Arial">
```

SIZE="*n*"

Specifies the font size of normal text within a document. Valid values are integer numbers in the range 1 to 7 with 3 being the default setting.

Standard: HTML 3.2; deprecated in HTML 4 in favor of style sheets

Common: Yes

Sample:

```
<BASEFONT SIZE="5">
```

<BDO>

Indicates text that should appear with the direction (left to right or right to left) specified, overriding other language-specific settings.

Standard: HTML 4

Common: No

Paired: Yes

Sample:

```
<P LANG="IW" DIR="RTL">This
Hebrew text contains a number,
<BDO="LTR">29381</BDO>, that must
appear left to right.</P>
```

Attribute Information

This tag accepts the lang and dir attributes. See the Element-Independent Attributes section of this reference for definitions and examples.

<BGSOUND>

Embeds a background sound file within documents. Use in the document head of documents intended for visitors who use Internet Explorer.

Standard: Internet Explorer

Common: Yes

Paired: No

Sample:

```
<BGSOUND SRC="scream.wav">
```

Attribute Information

LOOP="{n, INFINITE}"

Specifies the number of times a background sound file repeats. The value INFINITE is the default.

Standard: Internet Explorer

Common: No

Sample:

```
<BGSOUND SRC="bugle.wav"
LOOP="2">
```

SRC="*URL*"

Indicates the explicit or relative location of the sound file.

Standard: Internet Explorer

Common: No

Sample:

```
<BGSOUND SRC="wah.wav">
```

<BIG>

Indicates that text display in a larger font.

Standard: HTML 3.2

Common: Yes

Paired: Yes

Sample:

```
<BIG>Lunch</BIG>
<p>Lunch will be served at 2 p.m.
```

Attribute Information

CLASS="..."

Indicates which style class applies to the <BIG> element.

Standard: HTML 4

Common: No

Sample:

```
<BIG CLASS="casual">
Instructions</BIG>
```

ID="..."

Assigns a unique ID selector to an instance of the <BIG> tag. When you then assign a style to that ID selector, it affects only that one instance of the <BIG> tag.

Standard: HTML 4

Common: No

Sample:

```
<BIG ID="123">REMINDER:</BIG>
Eat 5 servings of fruits and
vegetables every day!
```

STYLE="..."

Specifies style sheet commands that apply to the contents within the <BIG> tags.

Standard: HTML 4

Common: No

Sample:

```
<BIG STYLE="background: red">
```

TITLE="..."

Specifies text assigned to the tag. You might use this attribute for context-sensitive help within the document. Browsers may use this to show tool tips over the text inside the <BIG> tags.

Standard: HTML 4

Common: No

Sample:

```
<BIG TITLE="Bigger">
```

Other Attributes

This tag also accepts the lang, dir, onClick, onDblClick, onMouseDown, onMouseUp, onMouseOver, onMouse-Move, onMouseOut, onKeyPress, onKeyDown, and onKeyUp attributes. See the Element-Independent Attributes section of this reference for definitions and examples.

<BLINK>

A Netscape-specific tag that makes text blink on and off.

Standard: Netscape Navigator; style sheets offer the same functionality in a more widely recognized syntax.

Common: No

Paired: Yes

Sample:

```
<P><BLINK>NEW INFO</BLINK>:
We moved!
```

Attribute Information

CLASS="..."

Indicates which style class applies to the <BLINK> element.

Standard: HTML 4

Common: No

Sample:

```
<BLINK CLASS="casual">NEW
INFORMATION</BLINK>
```

ID="..."

Assigns a unique ID selector to an instance of the <BLINK> tag. When you then assign a style to that ID selector, it affects only that one instance of the <BLINK> tag.

Standard: HTML 4

Common: No

Sample:

```
<BLINK ID="123">12 Hour
Sale!</BLINK>
```

STYLE="..."

Specifies style sheet commands that apply to the contents within the <BLINK> tags.

Standard: HTML 4

Common: No

Sample:

```
<BLINK STYLE="background: red">
```

<BLOCKQUOTE>

Provides left and right indention of affected text and is useful for quoting a direct source within a document. Use for indention is deprecated. Use <BLOCK-QUOTE> to signify only a block quotation.

Standard: HTML 2

Common: Yes

Paired: Yes

Sample:

```
Dr. Henry's remarks are
below:<BLOCKQUOTE>I really like
the procedure.</BLOCKQUOTE>
```

Attribute Information

CITE="..."
Specifies a reference URL for the quotation.

Standard: HTML 4

Common: No

Sample:

```
<BLOCKQUOTE CITE="http://www
.clement.moore.com/xmas.html">
Twas the night...</BLOCKQUOTE>
```

CLASS="..."
Indicates which style class applies to the <BLOCKQUOTE> element.

Standard: HTML 4

Common: No

Sample:

```
<BLOCKQUOTE CLASS="casual">
Twas the night before
Christmas...</BLOCKQUOTE>
```

ID="..."
Assigns a unique ID selector to an instance of the <BLOCKQUOTE> tag. When you then assign a style to that ID selector, it affects only that one instance of the <BLOCKQUOTE> tag.

Standard: HTML 4

Common: No

Sample:

```
On July 12, John wrote a profound
sentence in his diary:
<BLOCKQUOTE ID="123">I woke up
this morning at nine and it was
raining.</BLOCKQUOTE>
```

STYLE="..."
Specifies style sheet commands that apply to the contents within the <BLOCKQUOTE> tags.

Standard: HTML 4

Common: No

Sample:

```
<BLOCKQUOTE STYLE="background:
red">
```

TITLE="..."
Specifies text assigned to the tag. You might use this attribute for context-sensitive help within the document. Browsers may use this to show tool tips over the quoted text.

Standard: HTML 4

Common: No

Sample:

```
<BLOCKQUOTE TITLE="Quotation">
```

Other Attributes
This tag also accepts the lang, dir, onClick, onDblClick, onMouseDown, onMouseUp, onMouseOver, onMouse-Move, onMouseOut, onKeyPress, onKeyDown, and onKeyUp attributes. See the Element-Independent Attributes section of this reference for definitions and examples.

<BODY>

Acts as a container for the body of the document. It appears after the <HEAD> tag and is followed by the </HTML> tag. In HTML 3.2, the <BODY> tag also sets various color settings and background characteristics of the document; however, in HTML 4, those formatting attributes are deprecated in favor of style sheets.

Standard: HTML 2

Common: Yes

Paired: Yes

Sample:

```
<BODY>
<H1>HELLO!</H1>
</BODY>
```

Attribute Information

ALINK="#RRGGBB" or "..."

Indicates the color of hyperlink text while the text is selected. Color names can substitute for the RGB hexadecimal values.

Standard: HTML 3.2; deprecated in HTML 4 in favor of style sheets

Common: Yes

Sample:

```
<BODY BGCOLOR="#000ABC"
TEXT="#000000" LINK="#FFFFFF"
VLINK="#999999" ALINK="#FF0000">
```

BACKGROUND="URL"

Specifies the relative or absolute location of an image file that tiles across the document's background.

Standard: HTML 3.2; deprecated in HTML 4 in favor of style sheets

Common: Yes

Sample:

```
<BODY BACKGROUND=
"images/slimey.gif">
```

BGCOLOR="#RRGGBB" or "..."

Indicates the color of a document's background. Color names can substitute for the RGB hexadecimal values.

Standard: HTML 3.2; deprecated in HTML 4 in favor of style sheets

Common: Yes

Sample:

```
<BODY BGCOLOR="#000ABC"
TEXT="#000000" LINK="#FFFFFF"
VLINK="#999999" ALINK="#FF0000">
```

BGPROPERTIES="FIXED"

Specifies the behavior of the background image (see the BACKGROUND attribute.) BGPROPERTIES=FIXED indicates that the background image remains in place as you scroll the document, creating a watermark effect.

Standard: Internet Explorer

Common: No

Sample:

```
<BODY BACKGROUND="waves.jpg"
BGPROPERTIES="FIXED">
```

CLASS="..."

Indicates which style class applies to the <BODY> element.

Standard: HTML 4

Common: No

Sample:

```
<BODY CLASS="casual">
```

ID="*n*"

Assigns a unique ID selector to the
<BODY> tag.

> **Standard**: HTML 4
> **Common**: No
> **Sample**:

```
<BODY ID="123">
```

LEFTMARGIN="*n*"

Specifies the width (in pixels) of a margin of white space along the left edge of the entire document.

> **Standard**: Internet Explorer
> **Common**: No
> **Sample**:

```
<BODY LEFTMARGIN="30">
```

LINK="*#RRGGBB*" or "..."

Indicates the color of hyperlink text within the document, which corresponds to documents not already visited by the browser. Color names can substitute for the RGB hexadecimal values.

> **Standard**: HTML 3.2; deprecated in HTML 4 in favor of style sheets
> **Common**: Yes
> **Sample**:

```
<BODY BGCOLOR="#000ABC"
TEXT="#000000" LINK="#FFFFFF"
VLINK="#999999" ALINK="#FF0000">
```

SCROLL="{YES, NO}"

Indicates whether scrolling is possible within the document body.

> **Standard**: Internet Explorer 4
> **Common**: No
> **Sample**:

```
<BODY BGCOLOR="silver"
SCROLL="NO">
```

STYLE="..."

Specifies style sheet commands that apply to the document body.

> **Standard**: HTML 4
> **Common**: No
> **Sample**:

```
<BODY STYLE="background: red">
```

TEXT="*#RRGGBB*" or "..."

Indicates the color of normal text within the document. Color names can substitute for the RGB hexadecimal values.

> **Standard**: HTML 3.2; deprecated in HTML 4 in favor of style sheets.
> **Common**: Yes
> **Sample**:

```
<BODY BGCOLOR="#000ABC"
TEXT="#000000" LINK="#FFFFFF"
VLINK="#999999" ALINK="#FF0000">
```

TITLE="..."

Specifies text assigned to the tag. You might use this attribute for context-sensitive help within the document. Browsers may use this to show tool tips.

> **Standard**: HTML 4
> **Common**: No
> **Sample**:

```
<BODY TITLE="Document body">
```

TOPMARGIN="*n*"

Specifies the size (in pixels) of a margin of white space along the top edge of the entire document.

> **Standard**: Internet Explorer
> **Common**: No
> **Sample**:

```
<BODY TOPMARGIN="10">
```

VLINK="#*RRGGBB*" or "..."
Indicates the color of hyperlink text within the document, which corresponds to documents already visited by the browser. Color names can substitute for the RGB hexadecimal values.

Standard: HTML 3.2; deprecated in HTML 4 in favor of style sheets

Common: Yes

Sample:

```
<BODY BGCOLOR="#000ABC"
TEXT="#000000" LINK="#FFFFFF"
VLINK="#999999" ALINK="#FF0000">
```

Other Attributes
This tag also accepts the lang, dir, onload, onunload, onClick, onDbl-Click, onMouseDown, onMouseUp, onMouseOver, onMouseMove, onMouseOut, onKeyPress, onKey-Down, and onKeyUp attributes. See the "Element-Independent Attributes" section of this reference for definitions and examples.

Breaks a line of continuous text and prevents text alignment around images.

Standard: HTML 2

Common: Yes

Paired: No

Sample:

```
I live at:<P>123 Nowhere
Ave<BR>New York, NY 12345
```

Attribute Information

CLASS="..."
Indicates which style class applies to the element.

Standard: HTML 4

Common: No

Sample:

```
<BR CLASS="casual">
```

CLEAR="{ALL, LEFT, RIGHT, NONE}"
Discontinues alignment of text to inline graphic images. The sample demonstrates how you can force the text to appear after the image and not alongside it.

Standard: HTML 3.2

Common: Yes

Sample:

```
<IMG SRC="portrait.jpg"
ALIGN="RIGHT"><BR CLEAR="ALL">
```
```
<P>The above photo was taken when
I was in Florida.
```

ID="..."
Assigns a unique ID selector to an instance of the <BR> tag. When you then assign a style to that ID selector, it affects only that one instance of the <BR> tag.

Standard: HTML 4

Common: No

Sample:

```
<BR ID="123">
```

STYLE="..."
Specifies style sheet commands that apply to the <BR> tag.

Standard: HTML 4

Common: No

Sample:

```
<BR STYLE="background: red">
```

TITLE="..."

Specifies text assigned to the tag. You might use this attribute for context-sensitive help within the document. Browsers may use this to show tool tips.

Standard: HTML 4

Common: No

Sample:

```
<BR CLEAR="ALL" TITLE="Stop
image wrap">
```

<BUTTON>

Sets up a button to submit or reset a form as well as to activate a script. Use the <IMG> tag between the opening and closing <BUTTON> tags to specify a graphical button.

Standard: HTML 4

Common: No

Paired: Yes

Sample:

```
<BUTTON TYPE="BUTTON" VALUE="Run
Program" onclick(doit)>Click
it</BUTTON>
```

Attribute Information

ACCESSKEY="..."

Associates a key sequence with the button.

Standard: HTML 4

Common: Yes

Sample:

```
<BUTTON ACCESSKEY="B">Click
Me!</BUTTON>
```

CLASS="..."

Indicates which style class applies to the <BUTTON> element.

Standard: HTML 4

Common: No

Sample:

```
<BUTTON CLASS="casual"
TYPE="SUBMIT" VALUE="Submit">
```

DISABLED

Denies access to the input method.

Standard: HTML 4

Common: No

Sample:

```
<BUTTON TYPE="SUBMIT" NAME="Pass"
DISABLED>
```

ID="*n*"

Assigns a unique ID selector to an instance of the <INPUT> tag. When you then assign a style to that ID selector, it affects only that one instance of the <INPUT> tag.

Standard: HTML 4

Common: No

Sample:

```
<BUTTON ID="123" TYPE="SUBMIT"
VALUE="Submit">
```

NAME="..."

Gives a name to the value you pass to the form processor.

Standard: HTML 4

Common: Yes

Sample:

```
<BUTTON TYPE="BUTTON" NAME="RUN-
PROG" VALUE="Click to Run">
```

STYLE="..."

Specifies style sheet commands that apply to the element.

Standard: HTML 4

Common: No

Sample:

```
<BUTTON STYLE="background: red"
TYPE="BUTTON" NAME="RUNPROG"
VALUE="Click to Run">
```

TABINDEX="*n*"

Specifies where the input method appears in the tab order. For example, TABINDEX=3 places the cursor at the button element after the visitor presses the Tab key three times.

Standard: HTML 4

Common: No

Sample:

```
<BUTTON TYPE="BUTTON" NAME=
"RUNPROG" VALUE="Click to Run"
TABINDEX="3">
```

TITLE="..."

Specifies text assigned to the tag. You might use this attribute for context-sensitive help within the document. Browsers may use this to show tool tips over the input method.

Standard: HTML 4

Common: No

Sample:

```
<BUTTON TYPE="SUBMIT" NAME="cc"
VALUE="visa" TITLE="Visa">
```

TYPE="..."

Indicates the kind of button to create. SUBMIT produces a button that, when selected, submits all the name-value pairs to the form processor. RESET sets all the input methods to their empty or default settings. BUTTON creates a button with no specific behavior that can interact with scripts.

Standard: HTML 4

Common: Yes

Sample:

```
<BUTTON TYPE="BUTTON" VALUE="Send
Data..." onclick(verify())>
</FORM>
```

VALUE="..."

Sets the default value for the button face.

Standard: HTML 4

Common: No

Sample:

```
<BUTTON TYPE="BUTTON" NAME="id"
VALUE="Press Me">
```

Other Attributes

This tag also accepts the lang, dir, onfocus, onblur, onClick, onDbl-Click, onMouseDown, onMouseUp, onMouseOver, onMouseMove, onMouseOut, onKeyPress, onKey-Down, and onKeyUp attributes. See the Element-Independent Attributes section of this reference for definitions and examples.

C

<CAPTION>

Used inside <TABLE> tags to specify a description for a table.

Standard: HTML 3.2

Common: Yes

Paired: Yes

Sample:

```
<TABLE>
  <CAPTION VALIGN="TOP"
  ALIGN="CENTER">  Test Grades
  For COOKING 101  </CAPTION>
  <TR>
```

```
<TH>Student</TH><TH>Grade</TH>
</TR>
<TR>
   <TD>B. Smith</TD><TD>88</TD>
</TR>
<TR>
   <TD>J. Doe</TD><TD>45</TD>
</TR>
</TABLE>
```

Attribute Information

ALIGN="{TOP, BOTTOM, LEFT, RIGHT}"

Indicates whether the caption appears at the top, bottom, left, or right of the table.

Standard: HTML 3.2; LEFT and RIGHT added in HTML 4

Common: Yes

Sample:

```
<CAPTION ALIGN="TOP">Seattle
Staff Directory</CAPTION>
```

CLASS="..."

Indicates which style class applies to the <CAPTION> element.

Standard: HTML 4

Common: No

Sample:

```
<CAPTION CLASS="casual">Hydrogen
vs Oxygen</CAPTION>
```

ID="..."

Assigns a unique ID selector to an instance of the <CAPTION> tag. When you then assign a style to that ID selector, it affects only that one instance of the <CAPTION> tag.

Standard: HTML 4

Common: No

Sample:

```
<TABLE>
   <CAPTION ID="123">Great
   Painters</CAPTION>
```

STYLE="..."

Specifies style sheet commands that apply to the contents of the <CAPTION> tags.

Standard: HTML 4

Common: No

Sample:

```
<CAPTION STYLE="background: red">
```

TITLE="..."

Specifies text assigned to the tag. You might use this attribute for context-sensitive help within the document. Browsers may use this to show tool tips over the caption.

Standard: HTML 4

Common: Yes

Sample:

```
<CAPTION TITLE="Table caption">
```

Other Attributes

This tag also accepts the `lang`, `dir`, `onClick`, `onDblClick`, `onMouseDown`, `onMouseUp`, `onMouseOver`, `onMouseMove`, `onMouseOut`, `onKeyPress`, `onKeyDown`, and `onKeyUp` attributes. See the Element-Independent Attributes section of this reference for definitions and cxamples.

<CENTER>

Positions text an equal distance between the left and right edges of the document. This tag, now officially replaced by the

<DIV ALIGN="CENTER"> attribute, was included in HTML 3.2 only because of its widespread use.

> **Standard:** HTML 3.2; deprecated in HTML 4
>
> **Common:** Yes
>
> **Paired:** Yes
>
> **Sample:**

<CENTER><BLINK><H1>ONE-DAY SALE!</H1></BLINK></CENTER>

<CITE>

Provides an in-text citation of a proper title such as the title of a book. Most browsers display the text inside the <CITE> tags in italics.

> **Standard:** HTML 2
>
> **Common:** Yes
>
> **Paired:** Yes
>
> **Sample:**

I just finished reading <CITE>Being Digital</CITE> by Nicholas Negroponte.

Attribute Information

CLASS="..."
Indicates which style class applies to the <CITE> element.

> **Standard:** HTML 4
>
> **Common:** No
>
> **Sample:**

This came from <CITE CLASS="casual">Thoreau's Walden Pond</CITE>

ID="..."
Assigns a unique ID selector to an instance of the <CITE> tag. When you then assign a style to that ID selector, it

affects only that one instance of the <CITE> tag.

> **Standard:** HTML 4
>
> **Common:** No
>
> **Sample:**

I read about this in <CITE ID="123"> World Weekly News</CITE>

STYLE="..."
Specifies style sheet commands that apply to the contents within the <CITE> tags.

> **Standard:** HTML 4
>
> **Common:** No
>
> **Sample:**

<CITE STYLE="background: red">

TITLE="..."
Specifies text assigned to the tag. You might use this attribute for context-sensitive help within the document. Browsers may use this to show tool tips over the cited text.

> **Standard:** HTML 4
>
> **Common:** No
>
> **Sample:**

<CITE TITLE="Citation">FDA Vegetable Pamphlet</CITE>

Other Attributes
This tag also accepts the lang, dir, onClick, onDblClick, onMouseDown, onMouseUp, onMouseOver, onMouse-Move, onMouseOut, onKeyPress, onKeyDown, and onKeyUp attributes. See the Element-Independent Attributes section of this reference for definitions and examples.

<CODE>

Embeds excerpts of program source code into your document text. This is useful if you want to show program source code inline within a paragraph of normal text. For showing formatted segments of source code longer than one line, use the <PRE> tag.

> **Standard**: HTML 2
> **Common**: Yes
> **Paired**: Yes
> **Sample**:

```
To display the value of the cost
variable use the
<CODE>printf("%0.2f\n", cost);
</CODE> function call.
```

Attribute Information

CLASS="..."

Indicates which style class applies to the <CODE> element.

> **Standard**: HTML 4
> **Common**: No
> **Sample**:

```
<CODE CLASS="casual>x++;</CODE>
```

ID="..."

Assigns a unique ID selector to an instance of the <CODE> tag. When you then assign a style to that ID selector, it affects only that one instance of the <CODE> tag.

> **Standard**: HTML 4
> **Common**: No
> **Sample**:

```
<CODE ID="123">while(x)
x-;</CODE>
```

STYLE="..."

Specifies style sheet commands that apply to the contents within the <CODE> tags.

> **Standard**: HTML 4
> **Common**: No
> **Sample**:

```
<BODY STYLE="background: red">
```

TITLE="..."

Specifies text assigned to the tag. You might use this attribute for context-sensitive help within the document. Browsers may use this to show tool tips over the code text.

> **Standard**: HTML 4
> **Common**: No
> **Sample**:

```
<CODE TITLE="C
Code">exit(1);</CODE>
```

Other Attributes

This tag also accepts the lang, dir, onClick, onDblClick, onMouseDown, onMouseUp, onMouseOver, onMouse-Move, onMouseOut, onKeyPress, onKeyDown, and onKeyUp attributes. See the Element-Independent Attributes section of this reference for definitions and examples.

<COL>

Specifies attributes for a table column.

> **Standard**: HTML 4
> **Common**: No
> **Paired**: No
> **Sample**:

```
<TABLE>
<COLGROUP>
    <COL ALIGN="RIGHT">
```

```
<COL ALIGN="CENTER">
<TR>  <TD>This cell is aligned
right</TD>
   <TD>This cell is centered</TD>
</TR>
</TABLE>
```

Attribute Information

ALIGN="{LEFT, RIGHT, CENTER, JUSTIFY, CHAR}"

Specifies how text within the table columns will line up with the edges of the table cells, or if ALIGN=CHAR, on a specific character (the decimal point).

Standard: HTML 4

Common: No

Sample:

```
<COL ALIGN="CENTER">
```

CHAR="..."

Specifies the character on which cell contents will align, if ALIGN="CHAR". If you omit CHAR=, the default value is the decimal point in the specified language.

Standard: HTML 4

Common: No

Sample:

```
<COL ALIGN="CHAR" CHAR=",">
```

CHAROFF="n"

Specifies the number of characters from the left at which the alignment character appears.

Standard: HTML 4

Common: No

Sample:

```
<COL ALIGN="CHAR" CHAR=","
CHAROFF="7">
```

ID="..."

Assigns a unique ID selector to an instance of the <COL> tag. When you assign a style to that ID selector, it affects only that one instance of the <COL> tag.

Standard: HTML 4

Common: No

Sample:

```
<COL ID="123">
```

SPAN="n"

Indicates the number of columns in the group.

Standard: HTML 4

Common: No

Sample:

```
<COLGROUP>
   <COL ALIGN="RIGHT" SPAN="2">
```

STYLE="..."

Specifies style sheet commands that apply to the contents of the <COL> tags.

Standard: HTML 4

Common: No

Sample:

```
<COL STYLE="background: black">
```

TITLE="..."

Specifies text assigned to the tag. You might use this attribute for context-sensitive help within the document. Browsers may use this to show tool tips over the table column.

Standard: HTML 4

Common: No

Sample:

```
<COL TITLE="Table column">
```

WIDTH="n"

Specifies the horizontal dimension of a column (in pixels or as a percentage). Special values of "0*" force the column to the minimum required width, and "2*" requires that the column receive proportionately twice as much space as it otherwise would.

Standard: HTML 4

Common: No

Sample:

`<COL WIDTH="100">`

VALIGN="{TOP, BOTTOM, BASE-LINE, MIDDLE}"

Vertically positions the contents of the table column. VALIGN="TOP" positions the contents flush with the top of the column. VALIGN="BUTTON" positions the contents flush with the bottom. VALIGN="CENTER" positions the contents at the center of the column. VALIGN="BASELINE" aligns the contents with the baseline of the current text font.

Standard: HTML 4

Common: No

Sample:

`<COL VALIGN="TOP">`

Other Attributes

This tag also accepts the lang, dir, onClick, onDblClick, onMouseDown, onMouseUp, onMouseOver, onMouse-Move, onMouseOut, onKeyPress, onKeyDown, and onKeyUp attributes. See the Element-Independent Attributes section of this reference for definitions and examples.

<COLGROUP>

Specifies characteristics for a group of table columns.

Standard: HTML 4

Common: No

Paired: Yes

Sample:

```
<TABLE>
<COLGROUP VALIGN="TOP">
  <COL ALIGN="RIGHT">
  <COL ALIGN="CENTER">
<TR>
  <TD>This cell is aligned top
  and right</TD>
  <TD>This cell is aligned top
  and centered</TD>
</TR>
</TABLE>
```

Attribute Information

ALIGN="{LEFT, RIGHT, CENTER, JUSTIFY, CHAR}"

Specifies how text within the table columns lines up with the edges of the table cells, or if ALIGN=CHAR, on a specific character (the decimal point).

Standard: HTML 4

Common: No

Sample:

`<COLGROUP ALIGN="CENTER">`

CHAR="..."

Specifies the character on which cell contents align, if ALIGN="CHAR". If you omit CHAR=, the default value is the decimal point in the specified language.

Standard: HTML 4

Common: No

Sample:

```
<COLGROUP ALIGN="CHAR" CHAR=",">
```

CHAROFF="*n*"

Specifies the number of characters from the left at which the alignment character appears.

Standard: HTML 4

Common: No

Sample:

```
<COLGROUP ALIGN="CHAR" CHAR=","
CHAROFF="7">
```

ID="..."

Assigns a unique ID selector to an instance of the tag. When you then assign a style to that ID selector, it affects only that one instance of the tag.

Standard: HTML 4

Common: No

Sample:

```
<COLGROUP ID="123">
```

SPAN="*n*"

Indicates how many consecutive columns exist in the column group and to which columns the specified attributes apply.

Standard: HTML 4

Common: No

Sample:

```
<COLGROUP>
  <COL ALIGN="RIGHT" SPAN="2">
```

STYLE="..."

Specifies style sheet commands that apply to the contents of the `<COLGROUP>` tags.

Standard: HTML 4

Common: No

Sample:

```
<COLGROUP STYLE="color: red">
```

TITLE="..."

Specifies text assigned to the tag. You might use this attribute for context-sensitive help within the document. Browsers may use this to show tool tips over the column group.

Standard: HTML 4

Common: No

Sample:

```
<COLGROUP TITLE="Column Group">
```

WIDTH="*n*"

Specifies the horizontal dimension of columns within the column group (in pixels or as a percentage). Special values of "0*" force the column to minimum required width, and "2*" requires that the column receive proportionately twice as much space as it otherwise would.

Standard: HTML 4

Common: No

Sample:

```
<COLGROUP WIDTH=100>
  <COL ALIGN="RIGHT">
```

VALIGN="{TOP, BOTTOM, BASELINE, MIDDLE}"

Vertically positions the contents of the table column. VALIGN="TOP" positions the contents flush with the top of the column. VALIGN="BOTTOM" positions the contents flush with the bottom. VALIGN="CENTER" positions the contents at the vertical center of the column. VALIGN="BASELINE" aligns the contents with the baseline of the current text font.

Standard: HTML 4

Common: No

Sample:

```
<COLGROUP VALIGN="TOP">
```

Other Attributes

This tag also accepts the lang, dir, onClick, onDblClick, onMouseDown, onMouseUp, onMouseOver, onMouse-Move, onMouseOut, onKeyPress, onKeyDown, and onKeyUp attributes. See the Element-Independent Attributes section of this reference for definitions and examples.

<COMMENT>

Indicates an author comment. Because these tags are Netscape-specific, we encourage you to use the <!--...--> tags instead.

Standard: Netscape Navigator

Common: Yes

Paired: Yes

Sample:

```
<COMMENT>This document was cre-
ated September 19, 1997
</COMMENT>
```

D

<DD>

Contains a definition in a definition list. Use this tag inside <DL> tags. This tag can contain block-level elements.

Standard: HTML 2

Common: Yes

Paired: Yes, optional

Sample:

```
<DL><DT>Butter
<DD>Butter is a dairy product.
</DL>
```

Attribute Information

CLASS="..."

Indicates which style class applies to the <DD> element.

Standard: HTML 4

Common: No

Sample:

```
<DL>
  <DT>HTML
  <DD CLASS="casual">Hypertext
  Markup Language
</DD>
```

ID="..."

Assigns a unique ID selector to an instance of the <DD> tag. When you then assign a style to that ID selector, it affects only that one instance of the <DD> tag.

Standard: HTML 4

Common: No

Sample:

```
<DL>
  <DT>RS-232C
  <DD ID="123">A standard for
  serial communication between
  computers.
</DL>
```

STYLE="..."

Specifies style sheet commands that apply to the definition.

Standard: HTML 4

Common: No

Sample:

```
<DD STYLE="background: blue;
color: white">
```

TITLE="..."

Specifies text assigned to the tag. You might use this attribute for context-sensitive help within the document. Browsers may use this to show tool tips over the definition.

Standard: HTML 4

Common: No

Sample:

```
<DD TITLE="Definition">
```

Other Attributes

This tag also accepts the lang, dir, onClick, onDblClick, onMouseDown, onMouseUp, onMouseOver, onMouse-Move, onMouseOut, onKeyPress, onKeyDown, and onKeyUp attributes. See the Element-Independent Attributes section of this reference for definitions and examples.

<DEL>

Indicates text marked for deletion in the document. May be either block-level or inline, as necessary.

Standard: HTML 4

Common: No

Paired: Yes

Sample:

```
<P>HTTP stands for HyperText
Transfer <DEL>Transport</DEL>
Protocol</P>
```

Attribute Information

CITE="url"

Indicates address of reference (definitive source, for example) for deletion.

Standard: HTML 4

Common: No

Sample:

```
<DEL CITE="http://www.w3.org/">
HTML 3.0 was used for 10
years.</DEL>
```

CLASS="..."

Indicates which style class applies to the <DEL> element.

Standard: HTML 4

Common: No

Sample:

```
<DEL CLASS="casual">POP stands
for Post Office Protocol</DEL>
```

DATETIME="..."

Indicates the date and time in precisely this format: YYYY-MM-DDThh:mm:ssTZD. For example, 1997-07-14T08:30:00-07:00 indicates July 14, 1997, at 8:30 AM, in U.S. Mountain Time (7 hours from Greenwich time). This time could also be presented as 1997-07-14T08:30:00Z.

Standard: HTML 4

Common: No

Sample:

```
<DEL DATETIME="1997-07-
14T08:30:00Z">POP stands for Post
Office Protocol</DEL>
```

ID="..."

Assigns a unique ID selector to an instance of the tag. When you then assign a style to that ID selector, it

affects only that one instance of the
<DEL> tag.

Standard: HTML 4

Common: No

Sample:

```
<DEL ID="123">WWW stands for
World Wide Web</DEL>
```

STYLE="..."

Specifies style sheet commands that
apply to the deleted text.

Standard: HTML 4

Common: No

Sample:

```
<DEL STYLE="background: blue;
color: white">ESP stands for
extra-sensory perception.</DEL>
```

TITLE="..."

Specifies text assigned to the tag. You
might use this attribute for context-
sensitive help within the document.
Browsers may use this to show tool tips
over the text.

Standard: HTML 4

Common: No

Sample:

```
<DEL TITLE="Definition">More
deleted text.</DEL>
```

Other Attributes

This tag also accepts the lang, dir,
onClick, onDblClick, onMouseDown,
onMouseUp, onMouseOver, onMouse-
Move, onMouseOut, onKeyPress,
onKeyDown, and onKeyUp attributes.
See the Element-Independent Attributes
section of this reference for definitions
and examples.

<DFN>

Indicates the definition of a term in the
document.

Standard: HTML 3.2

Common: No

Paired: Yes

Sample:

```
<DFN>HTTP stands for HyperText
Transfer Protocol</DFN>
```

Attribute Information

CLASS="..."

Indicates which style class applies to the
<DFN> element.

Standard: HTML 4

Common: No

Sample:

```
<DFN CLASS="casual">POP stands
for Post Office Protocol</DFN>
```

ID="..."

Assigns a unique ID selector to an
instance of the <DFN> tag. When you
then assign a style to that ID selector, it
affects only that one instance of the
<DFN> tag.

Standard: HTML 4

Common: No

Sample:

```
<DFN ID="123">WWW stands for
World Wide Web</DFN>
```

STYLE="..."

Specifies style sheet commands that
apply to the definition.

Standard: HTML 4

Common: No

Sample:

```
<DFN STYLE="background: blue;
color: white">ESP stands for
extra-sensory perception.</DFN>
```

TITLE="..."

Specifies text assigned to the tag. You might use this attribute for context-sensitive help within the document. Browsers may use this to show tool tips over the definition text.

> **Standard:** HTML 4
> **Common:** No
> **Sample:**

```
<DFN TITLE="Definition">
```

Other Attributes

This tag also accepts the lang, dir, onClick, onDblClick, onMouseDown, onMouseUp, onMouseOver, onMouse-Move, onMouseOut, onKeyPress, onKeyDown, and onKeyUp attributes. See the Element-Independent Attributes section of this reference for definitions and examples.

<DIR>

Contains a directory list. Use the <LI> tag to indicate list items within the list. Use <UL>, rather than this deprecated tag.

> **Standard:** HTML 2; deprecated in HTML 4. Use <UL> instead.
> **Common:** Yes
> **Paired:** Yes
> **Sample:**

```
Choose a music genre:<DIR>
  <LI><A HREF="rock/">Rock</A>
  <LI><A HREF="country/
  ">Country</A>
```

```
  <LI><A HREF="na/">New Age</A>
</DIR>
```

Attribute Information

CLASS="..."

Indicates which style class applies to the <dir> element.

> **Standard:** HTML 4
> **Common:** No
> **Sample:**

```
<DIR CLASS="casual">
  <LI>Apples
  <LI>Kiwis
  <LI>Mangos
  <LI>Oranges
</DIR>
```

COMPACT

Causes the list to appear in a compact format. This attribute probably will not affect the appearance of the list as most browsers do not present lists in more than one format.

> **Standard:** HTML 2; deprecated in HTML 4
> **Common:** No
> **Sample:**

```
<DIR COMPACT>...
</DIR>
```

ID="..."

Assigns a unique ID selector to an instance of the <dir> tag. When you then assign a style to that ID selector, it affects only that one instance of the <dir> tag.

> **Standard:** HTML 4
> **Common:** No

Sample:

```
<DIR ID="123">
  <LI>Thingie 1
  <LI>Thingie 2
</DIR>
```

STYLE="..."

Specifies style sheet commands that apply to the <DIR> element.

Standard: HTML 4

Common: No

Sample:

```
<DIR STYLE="background: blue;
color: white">
  <LI>Thingie 1
  <LI>Thingie 2
</DIR>
```

TITLE="..."

Specifies text assigned to the tag. You might use this attribute for context-sensitive help within the document. Browsers may use this to show tool tips over the directory list.

Standard: HTML 4

Common: No

Sample:

```
<DIR TITLE="Directory List">
```

Other Attributes

This tag also accepts the lang, dir, onClick, onDblClick, onMouseDown, onMouseUp, onMouseOver, onMouse-Move, onMouseOut, onKeyPress, onKeyDown, and onKeyUp attributes. See the Element-Independent Attributes section of this reference for definitions and examples.

<DIV>

Indicates logical divisions within a document. You can use these to apply alignment, line-wrapping, and particularly style sheet attributes to a section of your document. <DIV ALIGN=CENTER> is the official replacement for the <CENTER> tag.

Standard: HTML 3.2

Common: No

Paired: Yes

Sample:

```
<DIV ALIGN="CENTER"
STYLE="background: blue">

<FONT SIZE=+2>All About Formic
Acid</FONT>

</DIV>
```

Attribute Information

ALIGN="{LEFT, CENTER, RIGHT, JUSTIFY}"

Specifies whether the contents of the section align with the left or right margins (LEFT, RIGHT), are evenly spaced between them (CENTER), or if the text stretches between the left and right margins (JUSTIFY).

Standard: HTML 3.2; deprecated in HTML 4 in favor of style sheets

Common: No

Sample:

```
<DIV ALIGN="RIGHT">
Look over here!</DIV>
<DIV ALIGN="LEFT">
Now, look over here!</DIV>
```

CLASS="..."

Indicates which style class applies to the
<DIV> element.

Standard: HTML 4

Common: No

Sample:

```
<DIV CLASS="casual">
```

DATAFLD="..."

Selects a column from a previously identified source of tabulated data (see the
DATASRC= attribute).

Standard: Internet Explorer 4

Common: No

Sample:

```
<DIV DATASRC="#data_table">
<DIV DATAFLD="name"></DIV>
</DIV>
```

DATAFORMATAS="{TEXT, HTML, NONE}"

Indicates how tabulated data formats
within the <DIV> element.

Standard: Internet Explorer 4

Common: No

Sample:

```
<DIV DATAFORMATAS="HTML"
DATASRC="#data_table">
```

DATASRC="..."

Specifies the source of data for data
binding.

Standard: Internet Explorer 4

Common: No

Sample:

```
<DIV DATASRC="#data_table">
```

ID="..."

Assigns a unique ID selector to an
instance of the <DIV> tag. When you
then assign a style to that ID selector, it
affects only that one instance of the
<DIV> tag.

Standard: HTML 4

Common: No

Sample:

```
<DIV ID="123">
```

NOWRAP

Disables line-wrapping for the section.

Standard: Netscape Navigator

Common: No

Sample:

```
<HR>
<DIV ALIGN="LEFT" NOWRAP>
The contents of this section will
not automatically wrap as you
size the window.
</DIV><HR>
```

STYLE="..."

Specifies style sheet commands that
apply to the contents within the
<DIV> tags.

Standard: HTML 4

Common: No

Sample:

```
<DIV STYLE="background: red">
```

TITLE="..."

Specifies text assigned to the tag. You
might use this attribute for context-
sensitive help within the document.
Browsers may use this to show tool tips
over the contents of the <DIV> tags.

Standard: HTML 4

Common: No

Sample:

```
<DIV TITLE="Title"
CLASS="casual">
```

Other Attributes

This tag also accepts the lang, dir, onClick, onDblClick, onMouseDown, onMouseUp, onMouseOver, onMouse-Move, onMouseOut, onKeyPress, onKeyDown, and onKeyUp attributes. See the Element-Independent Attributes section of this reference for definitions and examples.

<DL>

Contains the <DT> and <DD> tags that form the term and definition portions of a definition list.

    Standard: HTML 2
    Common: Yes
    Paired: Yes
    Sample:

<DL><DT>Hygiene

<DD>Always wash your hands before preparing meat.</DL>

Attribute Information

CLASS="..."

Indicates which style class applies to the <DL> element.

    Standard: HTML 4
    Common: No
    Sample:

<DL CLASS="casual">

  <DT>RAM

  <DD>Random Access Memory

</DL>

COMPACT

Causes the definition list to appear in a compact format. This attribute probably will not affect the appearance of the list as most browsers do not present lists in more than one format.

    Standard: HTML 2; deprecated
                      in HTML 4
    Common: No
    Sample:

<DL COMPACT>...

</DL>

ID="..."

Assigns a unique ID selector to an instance of the <DD> tag. When you then assign a style to that ID selector, it affects only that one instance of the <DD> tag.

    Standard: HTML 4
    Common: No
    Sample:

<DL ID="123">

  <DT>Food

  <DD>We will be eating 3 meals/day.

</DL>

STYLE="..."

Specifies style sheet commands that apply to contents within the <DL> tags.

    Standard: HTML 4
    Common: No
    Sample:

<DL STYLE="background: red">

TITLE="..."

Specifies text assigned to the tag. You might use this attribute for context-sensitive help within the document. Browsers may use this to show tool tips over the definition list.

    Standard: HTML 4
    Common: No

Sample:

```
<DL TITLE="Definition List">
```

Other Attributes

This tag also accepts the `lang`, `dir`, `onClick`, `onDblClick`, `onMouseDown`, `onMouseUp`, `onMouseOver`, `onMouse-Move`, `onMouseOut`, `onKeyPress`, `onKeyDown`, and `onKeyUp` attributes. See the Element-Independent Attributes section of this reference for definitions and examples.

<DT>

Contains the terms inside a definition list. Place the <DT> tags inside <DL> tags.

Standard: HTML 2
Common: Yes
Paired: Yes, optional
Sample:

```
<DL><DT>Hygiene
```

```
<DD>Always wash your hands before preparing meat.</DL>
```

Attribute Information

CLASS="..."

Indicates which style class applies to the <DT> element.

Standard: HTML 4
Common: No
Sample:

```
<DL>
```

```
<DT CLASS="casual">CUL8R
```

```
<DD>See You Later
```

```
</DL>
```

ID="..."

Assigns a unique ID selector to an instance of the <DT> tag. When you then assign a style to that ID selector, it affects only that one instance of the <DT> tag.

Standard: HTML 4
Common: No
Sample:

```
<DL>
```

```
<DT ID="123">Caffeine
```

```
<DD>Avoid caffeine during the stress management course.
```

```
</DL>
```

STYLE="..."

Specifies style sheet commands that apply to the contents within the <DT> tags.

Standard: HTML 4
Common: No
Sample:

```
<DT STYLE="background: red">
```

TITLE="..."

Specifies text assigned to the tag. You might use this attribute for context-sensitive help within the document. Browsers may use this to show tool tips over the definition term.

Standard: HTML 4
Common: No
Sample:

```
<DT TITLE="Term">Programmer</DT>
```

```
<DD>A method for converting cof-fee into applications.
```

Other Attributes

This tag also accepts the lang, dir, onClick, onDblClick, onMouseDown, onMouseUp, onMouseOver, onMouse-Move, onMouseOut, onKeyPress, onKeyDown, and onKeyUp attributes. See the Element-Independent Attributes section of this reference for definitions and examples.

E

<EM>

Makes the text stand out. Browsers usually do this with italic or boldface.

Standard: HTML 2
Common: Yes
Paired: Yes
Sample:

```
It is <EM>very</EM> important to
read the instructions before
beginning.
```

Attribute Information

CLASS="..."

Indicates which style class applies to the <EM> element.

Standard: HTML 4
Common: No
Sample:

```
Did you say my house was on<EM
CLASS="casual">FIRE?!</EM>
```

ID="..."

Assigns a unique ID selector to an instance of the <EM> tag. When you then assign a style to that ID selector, it affects only that one instance of the <EM> tag.

Standard: HTML 4
Common: No
Sample:

```
I have complained <EM
ID="123">ten</EM>times about the
leaking faucet.
```

STYLE="..."

Specifies style sheet commands that apply to the contents within the <EM> tags.

Standard: HTML 4
Common: No
Sample:

```
<EM STYLE="background: red">
```

TITLE="..."

Specifies text assigned to the tag. You might use this attribute for context-sensitive help within the document. Browsers may use this to show tool tips over the emphasized text.

Standard: HTML 4
Common: No
Sample:

```
<EM TITLE="Emphasis">
```

Other Attributes

This tag also accepts the lang, dir, onClick, onDblClick, onMouseDown, onMouseUp, onMouseOver, onMouse-Move, onMouseOut, onKeyPress, onKeyDown, and onKeyUp attributes. See the Element-Independent Attributes section of this reference for definitions and examples.

<EMBED>

Places an embedded object into a document. Examples of embedded objects include MIDI files and digital video files. Because the <EMBED> tag is not standard, we suggest you use the <OBJECT> tag instead. If the browser does not have built-in support for an object, visitors will need a plug-in to use the object within the document.

> **Standard**: Netscape Navigator, supported by Internet Explorer
>
> **Common**: No
>
> **Paired**: No
>
> **Sample**:

```
<EMBED SRC="fur_elise.midi">
```

Attribute Information

ACCESSKEY="..."
Specifies a key sequence that binds to the embedded object.

> **Standard**: Internet Explorer 4
>
> **Common**: No
>
> **Sample**:

```
<EMBED SRC="st.ocx"
ACCESSKEY="E">
```

ALIGN="{LEFT, RIGHT, CENTER, ABSBOTTOM, ABSMIDDLE, BASE-LINE, BOTTOM, TEXTTOP, TOP}"
Indicates how an embedded object is positioned relative to the document borders and surrounding contents. ALIGN="LEFT", ALIGN="RIGHT", or ALIGN="CENTER" makes the embedded object float between the edges of the frame either to the left, right, or evenly between. The behavior is similar to that of the ALIGN= attribute of the <IMG> tag.

ALIGN="TEXTTOP" or ALIGN="TOP" lines up the top of the embedded object with the top of the current text font. ALIGN="ABSMIDDLE" lines up the middle of the embedded object with the

middle of the current text font. ALIGN="ABSBOTTOM" lines up the bottom of the embedded object with the bottom of the current text font. ALIGN="BASE-LINE" or ALIGN="BOTTOM" lines up the bottom of the embedded object with the baseline of the current text font.

> **Standard**: Internet Explorer 4
>
> **Common**: No
>
> **Sample**:

```
<EMBED SRC="song.mid" ALIGN="CEN-
TER">
```

HEIGHT="*n*"
Specifies the vertical dimension of the embedded object. (See the UNITS= attribute for how to measure dimensions.)

> **Standard**: Netscape Navigator
>
> **Common**: No
>
> **Sample**:

```
<EMBED SRC="rocket.avi"
WIDTH="50" HEIGHT="40">
```

HIDDEN
Indicates that the embedded object should not be visible.

> **Standard**: Internet Explorer 4
>
> **Common**: No
>
> **Sample**:

```
<EMBED SRC="song.mid" HIDDEN>
```

NAME="..."
Gives the object a name by which other objects can refer to it.

> **Standard**: Netscape Navigator
>
> **Common**: No
>
> **Sample**:

```
<EMBED SRC="running.avi"
NAME="movie1">
```

OPTIONAL PARAM="..."

Indicates additional parameters. For example, AVI movies accept the AUTOSTART attribute.

> **Standard**: Netscape Navigator
> **Common**: No
> **Sample**:

```
<EMBED SRC="explode.avi"
AUTOSTART="true">
```

PALETTE="*#RRGGBB*|*#RRGGBB*"

Indicates the foreground and background colors for the embedded object. You can specify colors with hexadecimal RGB values or with color names.

> **Standard**: Netscape Navigator
> **Common**: No
> **Sample**:

```
<EMBED SRC="flying.avi"
PALETTE="Red|Black">
```

SRC="*URL*"

Indicates the relative or absolute location of the file containing the object you want to embed.

> **Standard**: Netscape Navigator
> **Common**: No
> **Sample**:

```
<EMBED SRC="beethoven_9.midi">
```

TITLE="..."

Specifies text assigned to the tag. You might use this attribute for context-sensitive help within the document. Browsers may use this to show tool tips over the embedded object.

> **Standard**: Internet Explorer 4
> **Common**: No
> **Sample**:

```
<EMBED SRC="explode.avi"
TITLE="movie">
```

UNITS="{PIXELS, EN}"

Modifies the behavior of the HEIGHT= and WIDTH= attributes. UNITS=PIXELS measures attributes in pixels. UNITS=EN measures dimensions in EN spaces.

> **Standard**: Netscape Navigator
> **Common**: No
> **Sample**:

```
<EMBED SRC="rocket.avi"
WIDTH="50" HEIGHT="40">
```

WIDTH="*n*"

Indicates the horizontal dimension of the embedded object. (See the UNITS= attribute for how to measure dimensions.)

> **Standard**: Netscape Navigator
> **Common**: No
> **Sample**:

```
<EMBED SRC="cartoon.avi"
WIDTH="50">
```

Other Attributes

This tag also accepts the lang, dir, onClick, onDblClick, onMouseDown, onMouseUp, onMouseOver, onMouse-Move, onMouseOut, onKeyPress, onKeyDown, and onKeyUp attributes. See the Element-Independent Attributes section of this reference for definitions and examples.

F

<FIELDSET>

Groups related form elements.

> **Standard**: HTML 4
> **Common**: No
> **Paired**: Yes

Sample:

```
<FORM ...>
<FIELDSET>
...logically related field
elements...
</FIELDSET>
</FORM>
```

Attribute Information

CLASS="..."
Indicates which style class applies to the <FIELDSET> element.

Standard: HTML 4
Common: No
Sample:

```
<FIELDSET CLASS="casual">Group
Rates</FIELDSET>
```

ID="..."
Assigns a unique ID selector to an instance of the <FIELDSET> tag. When you then assign a style to that ID selector, it affects only that one instance of the <FIELDSET> tag.

Standard: HTML 4
Common: No
Sample:

```
<FIELDSET ID="123">now!</FIELD-
SET>
```

STYLE="..."
Specifies style sheet commands that apply to the contents within the <FIELDSET> tags.

Standard: HTML 4
Common: No
Sample:

```
<FIELDSET STYLE="background:
red">
```

TITLE="..."
Specifies text assigned to the tag. You might use this attribute for context-sensitive help within the document. Browsers may use this to show tool tips over the font text.

Standard: HTML 4
Common: No
Sample:

```
<FIELDSET TITLE="Personal data
fields">
```

Other Attributes
This tag also accepts the lang, dir, onClick, onDblClick, onMouseDown, onMouseUp, onMouseOver, onMouse-Move, onMouseOut, onKeyPress, onKeyDown, and onKeyUp attributes. See the Element-Independent Attributes section of this reference for definitions and examples.

<FONT>

Alters or sets font characteristics of the font the browser uses to display text.

Standard: HTML 3.2; deprecated in HTML 4 in favor of style sheets
Common: Yes
Paired: Yes
Sample:

```
The cat was really <FONT
SIZE="+3">BIG!</FONT>
```

Attribute Information

COLOR="#RRGGBB" or "..."
Indicates the color the browser uses to display text. Color names can substitute for the RGB hexadecimal values.

Standard: HTML 3.2; deprecated
                 in HTML 4 in favor of
                 style sheets.

Common: Yes

Sample:

```
<FONT COLOR=#FF0000><H2>Win A
Trip!</H2></FONT> <FONT
COLOR="lightblue"><p>That's
right! A trip to Hawaii can be
yours if you scratch off the
right number!</FONT>
```

FACE="...,..."

Specifies a comma-separated list of font
names the browser uses to render text. If
the browser does not have access to the
first named font, it tries the second, then
the third, and so forth.

Standard: Netscape Navigator and
                 Internet Explorer, not
                 introduced in standard
                 HTML in favor of style
                 sheets.

Common: Yes

Sample:

```
<FONT SIZE=+1 FACE="Avant Guard,
Helvetica, Lucida Sans, Arial">
```

SIZE=n

Specifies the size of the text affected by
the FONT tag. You can specify the size relative to the base font size (see the
<BASEFONT> tag) which is normally 3.
You can also specify the size as a digit in
the range 1 through 7.

Standard: HTML 3.2; deprecated
                 in HTML 4 in favor of
                 style sheets.

Common: Yes

Sample:

```
<BASEFONT SIZE=4>
```

```
<FONT SIZE=+2>This is a font of
size 6</FONT> <FONT SIZE=1>This
is a font of size 1</FONT>
```

<FORM>

Sets up a container for a form tag.
Within the <FORM> tags, you can place
form input tags such as <FIELDSET>,
<INPUT>, <SELECT>, and <TEXTAREA>.

Standard: HTML 2

Common: Yes

Paired: Yes

Sample:

```
<FORM METHOD=POST
ACTION="/cgi-bin/search.pl">
```

```
Search : <INPUT TYPE=TEXT
NAME="name" SIZE=20><BR>
```

```
<INPUT TYPE=SUBMIT VALUE="Start
Search"> </FORM>
```

Attribute Information

ACCEPT-CHARSET="..."

Specifies the character encodings for
input data that the server processing the
form must accept. The value is a list of
character sets as defined in RFC2045,
separated by commas.

Standard: HTML 4

Common: No

Sample:

```
<FORM METHOD=POST
ACCEPT-CHARSET="ISO-8859-1"
ACTION="/stat-collector.cgi">
```

ACCEPT="..."

Specifies a list of MIME types, separated
by commas, that the server processing
the form will handle correctly.

Standard: HTML 4

Common: No

Sample:

```
<FORM METHOD=POST
ACCEPT="image/gif, image/jpeg
"ACTION="/image-collector.cgi">
```

ACTION="*URL*"

Specifies the explicit or relative location of the form processing CGI application.

> **Standard**: HTML 2
>
> **Common**: Yes
>
> **Sample:**

```
<FORM METHOD=POST
ACTION="/stat-collector.cgi">
```

CLASS="..."

Indicates which style class applies to the <FORM>.

> **Standard**: HTML 4
>
> **Common**: No
>
> **Sample:**

```
<FORM METHOD=POST CLASS="casual
"ACTION="/stat-collector.cgi">
```

ENCTYPE="..."

Specifies the MIME type used to submit (post) the form to the server. The default value is "application/x-www-form-urlencoded". Use the value "multipart/form-data" when the returned document includes files.

> **Standard**: HTML 4
>
> **Common**: No
>
> **Sample:**

```
<FORM METHOD=POST ENCTYPE=
"application/x-www-
form-urlencoded"ACTION=
"/stat-collector.cgi">
```

ID="..."

Assigns a unique ID selector to an instance of the <FORM> tag. When you then assign a style to that ID selector, it affects only that one instance of the <FORM> tag.

> **Standard**: HTML 4
>
> **Common**: No
>
> **Sample:**

```
<FORM ACTION="/cgi-bin/ttt.pl"
METHOD=GET ID="123">
```

METHOD={POST,GET}

Changes how form data is transmitted to the form processor. When you use METHOD=GET, the form data is given to the form processor in the form of an environment variable (*QUERY_STRING*). When you use METHOD=POST, the form data is given to the form processor as the standard input to the program.

> **Standard**: HTML 2
>
> **Common**: Yes
>
> **Sample:**

```
<FORM METHOD=POST
ACTION="/cgi-bin/www-search">

Enter search keywords:
<INPUT TYPE=TEXT NAME="query"
SIZE=20>

<INPUT TYPE=SUBMIT
VALUE="Search">

</FORM>
```

NAME="..."

Assigns the form a name accessible by bookmark, script, and applet resources.

> **Standard**: Internet Explorer
>
> **Common**: No
>
> **Sample:**

```
<FORM METHOD=POST
ACTION="/cgi-bin/ff.pl"NAME="ff">
```

STYLE="..."

Specifies style sheet commands that apply to the contents within the <FORM> tags.

Standard: HTML 4

Common: No

Sample:

```
<FORM  STYLE="background: red">
```

TARGET="..."

Identifies in which previously named frame the output from the form processor should appear.

Standard: HTML 4

Common: Yes

Sample:

```
<FORM TARGET="output" METHOD=GET
ACTION="/cgi-bin/thingie.sh">
```

TITLE="..."

Specifies text assigned to the tag. You might use this attribute for context-sensitive help within the document. Browsers may use this to show tool tips over the fill-out form.

Standard: HTML 4

Common: No

Sample:

```
<FORM METHOD=POST ACTION="/cgi-
bin/ff.pl"TITLE="Fill-out form">
```

Other Attributes

This tag also accepts the lang, dir, onsubmit, onreset, onClick, onDbl-Click, onMouseDown, onMouseUp, onMouseOver, onMouseMove, onMouseOut, onKeyPress, onKey-Down, and onKeyUp attributes. See the Element-Independent Attributes section of this reference for definitions and examples.

<FRAME>

Defines a frame within a frameset (see the <FRAMESET> tag). The <FRAME> tag specifies the source file and visual characteristics of a frame.

Standard: HTML 4

Common: Yes

Paired: No

Sample:

```
<FRAMESET ROWS="*,70">

  <FRAME SRC="frames/body.html"
  NAME="body">

  <FRAME SRC="frames/buttons
  .html" NAME="buttons" SCROLLING
  =NO NORESIZE>

</FRAMESET>
```

Attribute Information

BORDER="n"

Specifies the thickness of the border (in pixels) around a frame. Use BORDER=0 to specify a frame with no border.

Standard: Netscape Navigator

Common: Yes

Sample:

```
<FRAME SRC="hits.html"
BORDER="2">
```

BORDERCOLOR="#RRGGBB" or "..."

Specifies the color of the border around the frame. Use the color's hexadecimal RGB values or the color name.

Standard: Internet Explorer,
         Netscape Navigator

Common: Yes

Sample:

```
<FRAME SRC="hits.html"
BORDERCOLOR="red">
```

FRAMEBORDER={1,0}

Indicates whether the frame's border is visible. A value of 1 indicates that the border is visible, and a value of 0 indicates that it is not visible.

>   **Standard**: HTML 4
>
>   **Common**: No
>
>   **Sample**:

```
<FRAME SRC="weather.html"
FRAMEBORDER=0>
```

MARGINHEIGHT="n"

Specifies the vertical dimension (in number of pixels) of the top and bottom margins in a frame.

>   **Standard**: HTML 4
>
>   **Common**: No
>
>   **Sample**:

```
<FRAME SRC="cats.html"
MARGINHEIGHT=10>
```

MARGINWIDTH="n"

Specifies the horizontal dimension (in pixels) of the left and right margins in a frame.

>   **Standard**: HTML 4
>
>   **Common**: No
>
>   **Sample**:

```
<FRAME SRC="dogs.html"
MARGINWIDTH=10>
```

NAME="..."

Gives the frame you are defining a name. You can use this name later to load new documents into the frame (see the TARGET= attribute) and within scripts to control attributes of the frame. Reserved names with special meaning include _blank, _parent, _self, and _top.

>   **Standard**: HTML 4

>   **Common**: Yes
>
>   **Sample**:

```
<FRAME SRC="/cgi-bin/weather.cgi"
NAME="weather">
```

NORESIZE

Makes a frame's dimensions unchangeable. Otherwise, if a frame's borders are visible, visitors can resize the frame by selecting a border and moving it with the mouse.

>   **Standard**: HTML 4
>
>   **Common**: Yes
>
>   **Sample**:

```
<FRAME SRC="bottom.html"
NAME="bottom" NORESIZE
SCROLLING=NO>
```

SCROLLING={YES, NO, AUTO}

Indicates whether a scrollbar is present within a frame when text dimensions exceed the dimensions of the frame. Set SCROLLING=NO when using a frame to display only an image.

>   **Standard**: HTML 4
>
>   **Common**: Yes
>
>   **Sample**:

```
<FRAME NAME="titleimg"
SRC="title.html" SCROLLING=NO>
```

SRC="URL"

Specifies the relative or absolute location of a document that you want to load within the defined frame.

>   **Standard**: HTML 4
>
>   **Common**: Yes
>
>   **Sample**:

```
<FRAME NAME="main"
SRC="intro.html">
```

<FRAMESET>

Contains frame definitions and specifies frame spacing, dimensions, and attributes. Place <FRAME> tags inside <FRAMESET> tags.

Standard: HTML 4
Common: Yes
Paired: Yes
Sample:

```
<FRAMESET COLS="*,70">
    <FRAME SRC="frames/body.html"
    NAME="body">
    <FRAME SRC="frames/side.html"
    NAME="side">
</FRAMESET>
```

Attribute Information

BORDER="*n*"

Specifies the thickness of borders (in pixels) around frames defined within the frameset. You can also control border thickness with the <FRAME> tag.

Standard: Netscape Navigator
Common: No
Sample:

```
<FRAMESET COLS="*,150" BORDER=5>
    <FRAME SRC="left.html"
    NAME="main">
    <FRAME SRC="side.html"
    NAME="side">
</FRAMESET>
```

BORDERCOLOR="*#RRGGBB*" or "..."

Sets the color of the frame borders. Color names can substitute for the hexadecimal RGB color values.

Standard: Netscape Navigator,
Internet Explorer
Common: Yes
Sample:

```
<FRAMESET BORDERCOLOR="Red"
ROWS="100,*">
    <FRAME SRC="top.html"
    NAME="title">
    <FRAME SRC="story.html"
    NAME="Story">
</FRAMESET>
```

COLS="..."

Specifies the number and dimensions of the vertical frames within the current frameset.

Set COLS= to a comma-separated list of numbers or percentages to indicate the width of each frame. Use the asterisk (*) to represent a variable width. A frame of variable width fills the space left over after the browser formats space for the other frames (<FRAMESET COLS="100, 400,10% *">).

Setting COLS= with percentage values controls the ratio of frame horizontal space relative to the amount of space available within the browser (<FRAMESET COLS="10%,*">).

You cannot use COLS= and ROWS= in the same tag.

Standard: HTML 4
Common: Yes
Sample:

```
<FRAMESET COLS="*,100,*">
    <FRAME SRC="left.html"
    NAME="left">
    <FRAME SRC="middle.html"
    NAME="middle">
    <FRAMESET ROWS=2>
```

```
<FRAME SRC="top.html"
NAME="top">
<FRAME SRC="bottom.html"
NAME="bottom">
</FRAMESET>
```
```
</FRAMESET>
```

FRAMESPACING="n"

Specifies the space (in pixels) between frames within the browser window.

Standard: Internet Explorer

Common: No

Sample:

```
<FRAMESET ROWS="*,100"
FRAMESPACING=10>
<FRAME SRC="top.html"
NAME="top">
<FRAME SRC="middle.html"
NAME="middle">
</FRAMESET>
```

ROWS="..."

Specifies the number and dimensions of the horizontal frames within the current frameset.

Set ROWS= to a comma-separated list of numbers or percentages to indicate the height of each frame. Use the asterisk (*) to represent a variable height. A frame of variable height fills the space remaining after the browser formats space for the other frames (<FRAMESET ROWS="100,400,*">).

Setting ROWS= to a comma-separated list of percentages allows you to control the ratio of frame vertical space relative to the space available within the browser (<FRAMESET ROWS="10%,*">).

You cannot use ROWS= and COLS= in the same tag.

Standard: HTML 4

Common: Yes

Sample:

```
<FRAMESET ROWS="*,100,*">
<FRAME SRC="top.html"
NAME="top">
<FRAME SRC="middle.html"
NAME="middle">
<FRAMESET COLS=2>
<FRAME SRC="bottom1.html"
NAME="left">
<FRAME SRC="bottom2.html"
NAME="right">
</FRAMESET>
</FRAMESET>
```

Other Attributes

This tag also accepts the onload and onunload attributes. See the Element-Independent Attributes section of this reference for definitions and examples.

H

<Hn>

Specifies headings in a document. Headings are numbered 1–6, with <H1> representing the heading for the main heading in the document and <H3> representing a heading for a nested subtopic. Generally, text inside heading tags appears in boldface and may be larger than normal document text.

Standard: HTML 2

Common: Yes

Paired: Yes

Sample:

```
<H1>Caring For Your Canary</H1>
```

This document explains how you should take care of a canary. With proper care, you and your new bird will have a lasting, happy relationship.

`<H2>Feeding</H2>`

Attribute Information

ALIGN={LEFT, CENTER, RIGHT}

Positions the heading in the left, right, or center of a document.

Standard: HTML 3.2; deprecated in HTML 4 in favor of style sheets

Common: Yes

Sample:

`<H3 ALIGN=RIGHT>History Of The Platypus</H3>`

CLASS="..."

Indicates which style class applies to the `<Hn>` element.

Standard: HTML 4

Common: No

Sample:

`<H1 CLASS="casual" ALIGN=LEFT>River Tours</H1>`

ID="..."

Assigns a unique ID selector to an instance of the `<Hn>` tag. When you then assign a style to that ID selector, it affects only that one instance of the `<Hn>` tag.

Standard: HTML 4

Common: No

Sample:

`<H2 ID="123">Paper Products</H2>`

STYLE="..."

Specifies style sheet commands that apply to the heading.

Standard: HTML 4

Common: No

Sample:

`<H1 STYLE="background: red">`

TITLE="..."

Specifies text assigned to the tag. You might use this attribute for context-sensitive help within the document. Browsers may use this to show tool tips over the heading.

Standard: HTML 4

Common: No

Sample:

`<H1 TITLE="Headline">`

Other Attributes

This tag also accepts the `lang`, `dir`, `onClick`, `onDblClick`, `onMouseDown`, `onMouseUp`, `onMouseOver`, `onMouse-Move`, `onMouseOut`, `onKeyPress`, `onKeyDown`, and `onKeyUp` attributes. See the Element-Independent Attributes section of this reference for definitions and examples.

<HEAD>

Contains document head information. You can place any of the following tags within the document head: `<LINK>`, `<META>`, `<TITLE>`, `<SCRIPT>`, `<BASE>`, and `<STYLE>`.

Standard: HTML 2

Common: Yes

Paired: Yes

Sample:

`<HTML>`

```
<HEAD>
<TITLE>Making a Peanut-Butter and
Jelly Sandwich</TITLE>
<LINK REL=Parent
HREF="sandwiches.html">
</HEAD>
```

Attribute Information

PROFILE="URL"

Specifies the address of data profiles.
You might use this attribute to specify
the location of, for example, <META> tag
information.

    Standard: HTML 4

    Common: No

    Sample:

```
<HEAD PROFILE="http://www
.raycomm.com/general.html">
</HEAD<
```

Other Attributes

This tag also accepts the lang and dir
attributes. See the Element-Independent
Attributes section of this reference for
definitions and examples.

<HR>

Draws horizontal lines (rules) in your
document. This is useful for visually separating document sections.

    Standard: HTML 2

    Common: Yes

    Paired: No

    Sample:

```
<H2>Birthday Colors</H2>
<HR ALIGN=LEFT WIDTH="60%">
<P>Birthdays are usually joyous
celebrations so we recommend
bright colors.
```

Attribute Information

ALIGN={LEFT, CENTER, RIGHT}

Positions the line flush left, flush right,
or in the center of the document. These
settings are irrelevant unless you use the
WIDTH= attribute to make the line
shorter than the width of the document.

    Standard: HTML 3.2; deprecated
                 in HTML 4 in favor of
                 style sheets

    Common: Yes

    Sample:

```
<H2 ALIGN=LEFT>Shopping List</H2>
<HR WIDTH="40%" ALIGN=LEFT>
<UL TYPE=SQUARE>
<LI>Eggs
<LI>Butter
<LI>Bread
<LI>Milk
</UL>
```

CLASS="..."

Indicates which style class applies to the
<HR> element.

    Standard: HTML 4

    Common: No

    Sample:

```
<HR CLASS="casual" WIDTH="50%">
```

COLOR="#*RRGGBB*" or "..."

Specifies the color of the line. The color
name can substitute for the hexadecimal
RGB values.

    Standard: Internet Explorer. style
                 sheets provide equivalent
                 functionality.

    Common: No

    Sample:

```
<HR COLOR=#09334C>
```

ID="n"

Assigns a unique ID selector to an instance of the <HR> tag. When you then assign a style to that ID selector, it affects only that one instance of the <HR> tag.

Standard: HTML 4

Common: No

Sample:

```
<HR ID="123">
```

NOSHADE

Specifies that the browser not shade the line.

Standard: HTML 3.2

Common: Yes

Sample:

```
<HR NOSHADE ALIGN=CENTER
WIDTH="50%">

<IMG SRC="Bobby.jpg" ALIGN=CENTER
BORDER=0 ALT="Bobby">

<BR CLEAR=ALL>

<HR NOSHADE ALIGN=CENTER
WIDTH="50%">
```

SIZE="n"

Specifies the thickness of the line (in pixels).

Standard: HTML 3.2; deprecated in HTML 4 in favor of style sheets

Common: Yes

Sample:

```
<HR SIZE=10>
```

STYLE="..."

Specifies style sheet commands that apply to the horizontal rule.

Standard: HTML 4

Common: No

Sample:

```
<HR WIDTH="50%" STYLE="color:
red">
```

TITLE="..."

Specifies text assigned to the tag. You might use this attribute for context-sensitive help within the document. Browsers may use this to show tool tips over the horizontal rule.

Standard: HTML 4

Common: No

Sample:

```
<HR TITLE="A line">
```

WIDTH="n"

Specifies the length of the line. You can specify the value with an absolute number of pixels or as a percentage to indicate how much of the total width available is used.

Standard: HTML 3.2; deprecated in HTML 4 in favor of style sheets

Common: Yes

Sample:

```
<H2 ALIGN=CENTER>The End!</H2>

<HR WIDTH="85%">

<P ALIGN=CENTER>

<A HREF="/index.html">Home</A> |

<A HREF="Story3.html">Next
Story</A> |

<A HREF="Story1.html">Prev
Story</A>
```

Other Attributes

This tag also accepts the onClick, onDblClick, onMouseDown, onMouseUp, onMouseOver, onMouse-Move, onMouseOut, onKeyPress, onKeyDown, and onKeyUp attributes.

See the Element-Independent Attributes section of this reference for definitions and examples.

<HTML>

Contains the entire document. Place these tags at the top and bottom of your HTML file.

Standard: HTML 2
Common: Yes
Paired: Yes
Sample:

```
<HTML>
<HEAD><TITLE>Test Page</TITLE></HEAD>
<BODY>
  <H1>Is this working?</H1>
</BODY>
</HTML>
```

Attribute Information

This tag accepts the `lang` and `dir` attributes. See the Element-Independent Attributes section of this reference for definitions and examples.

I

<I>

Italicizes text.

Standard: HTML 2
Common: Yes
Paired: Yes
Sample:

```
After this, Tom told me to read<I>Mastering HTML</I>. I had no choice but to do so.
```

Attribute Information

CLASS="..."
Indicates which style class applies to the <I> element.

Standard: HTML 4
Common: No
Sample:

```
This mouse is
<I CLASS="casual">enhanced</I>
```

ID="..."
Assigns a unique ID selector to an instance of the <I> tag. When you then assign a style to that ID selector, it affects only that one instance of the <I> tag.

Standard: HTML 4
Common: No
Sample:

```
He called it a <I ID="123">Doo-Dad</I>!
```

STYLE="..."
Specifies style sheet commands that apply to italicized text.

Standard: HTML 4
Common: No
Sample:

```
<I STYLE="color: green">
```

TITLE="..."
Specifies text assigned to the tag. You might use this attribute for context-sensitive help within the document. Browsers may use this to show tool tips over the italicized text.

Standard: HTML 4
Common: No
Sample:

```
<I TITLE="Italicized">
```

Other Attributes

This tag also accepts the `lang`, `dir`, `onClick`, `onDblClick`, `onMouseDown`, `onMouseUp`, `onMouseOver`, `onMouse-Move`, `onMouseOut`, `onKeyPress`, `onKeyDown`, and `onKeyUp` attributes. See the Element-Independent Attributes section of this reference for definitions and examples.

<IFRAME>

Creates floating frames within a document. Floating frames differ from normal frames because they are independently manipulable elements within another HTML document.

Standard: HTML 4

Common: No

Paired: Yes

Sample:

```
<IFRAME NAME="new_win"
    SRC="http://www.raycomm.com">
</IFRAME>
```

Attribute Information

ALIGN={LEFT, CENTER, RIGHT}

Specifies how the floating frame lines up with respect to the left and right sides of the browser window.

Standard: HTML 4; deprecated usage. Use style sheets instead.

Common: No

Sample:

```
<IFRAME ALIGN=LEFT
SRC="goats.html"NAME="g1">
```

BORDER="n"

Indicates the thickness of a border around a floating frame (in pixels).

Standard: Internet Explorer 4

Common: No

Sample:

```
<IFRAME SRC="joe.html"
NAME="Joe"BORDER=5>
```

BORDERCOLOR="#RRGGBB" or "..."

Specifies (in hexadecimal RGB values or the color name) the color of the border around a floating frame.

Standard: Internet Explorer 4

Common: No

Sample:

```
<IFRAME SRC="joe.html"
NAME="Joe"BORDERCOLOR=#5A3F2E>
```

FRAMEBORDER={0,1}

Indicates whether the floating frame has visible borders. A value of 0 indicates no border, and a value of 1 indicates a visible border.

Standard: HTML 4

Common: No

Sample:

```
<IFRAME SRC="main.html"
NAME="main"FRAMEBORDER=0>
```

FRAMESPACING="n"

Indicates the space (in pixels) between adjacent floating frames.

Standard: Internet Explorer 4

Common: No

Sample:

```
<IFRAME SRC="joe.html" NAME="Joe"
FRAMESPACING=10>
```

HEIGHT="*n*"

Specifies the vertical dimension (in pixels) of the floating frame.

Standard: HTML 4

Common: No

Sample:

```
<IFRAME SRC="joe.html"
NAME="Joe"WIDTH=500 HEIGHT=200>
```

HSPACE="*n*"

Indicates the size (in pixels) of left and right margins within the floating frame.

Standard: Internet Explorer 4

Common: No

Sample:

```
<IFRAME SRC="joe.html"
NAME="Joe"HSPACE=10 VSPACE=10>
```

ID="..."

Assigns a unique ID selector to an instance of the <IFRAME> tag. When you then assign a style to that ID selector, it affects only that one instance of the <IFRAME> tag.

Standard: HTML 4

Common: No

Sample:

```
<IFRAME SRC="Joe.html" NAME="Joe"
ID="123">
```

MARGINHEIGHT="*n*"

Specifies the size of the top and bottom margins (in pixels) within the floating frame.

Standard: HTML 4

Common: No

Sample:

```
<IFRAME SRC="top.html"
NAME="topbar" MARGINHEIGHT=50>
```

MARGINWIDTH="*n*"

Specifies the size of the left and right margins (in pixels) within the floating frame.

Standard: HTML 4

Common: No

Sample:

```
<IFRAME SRC="body.html"
NAME="body"MARGINWIDTH=50>
```

NAME="..."

Assigns the frame a unique name. You can use this name within other frames to load new documents in the frame and to manipulate the attributes of the frame.

Standard: HTML 4

Common: No

Sample:

```
<IFRAME SRC="joe.html" NAME="Joe"
WIDTH=500 HEIGHT=200>
```

NORESIZE

Specifies that the floating frame cannot resize. Because the HTML 4 specification forbids resizable inline frames, this attribute is only relevant to Internet Explorer.

Standard: Internet Explorer

Common: No

Sample:

```
<IFRAME SRC="joe.html"
NAME="Joe"NORESIZE>
```

SCROLLING={YES, NO}

Indicates whether the floating frame has scrollbars.

Standard: HTML 4

Common: No

Sample:

```
<IFRAME SRC="top.html"
SCROLLING=NO>
```

SRC="*URL*"

Specifies the relative or absolute location of the document file to load in the floating frame.

Standard: HTML 4

Common: No

Sample:

```
<IFRAME NAME="pics" SRC="pics/">
```

STYLE="..."

Specifies style sheet commands that apply to the floating frame.

Standard: HTML 4

Common: No

Sample:

```
<IFRAME SRC="dots.html"
NAME="dots" STYLE="background:
red">
```

WIDTH="*n*"

Specifies the horizontal dimension (in pixels) of the floating frame.

Standard: HTML 4

Common: No

Sample:

```
<IFRAME SRC="joe.html" NAME="Joe"
WIDTH=500 HEIGHT=200>
```

VSPACE="*n*"

Indicates the size (in pixels) of top and bottom margins within the floating frame.

Standard: Internet Explorer 4

Common: No

Sample:

```
<IFRAME SRC="joe.html" NAME="Joe"
HSPACE=10 VSPACE=10>
```

Other Attributes

This tag also accepts the `lang`, `dir`, `onClick`, `onDblClick`, `onMouseDown`, `onMouseUp`, `onMouseOver`, `onMouse-Move`, `onMouseOut`, `onKeyPress`, `onKeyDown`, and `onKeyUp` attributes. See the Element-Independent Attributes section of this reference for definitions and examples.

<IMG>

Places an inline image in a document. You can use the attributes `ISMAP=` and `USEMAP=` with the `<IMG>` tag to implement imagemaps.

Standard: HTML 2

Common: Yes

Paired: No

Sample:

```
<IMG SRC="images/left_arrow.gif"
ALT="<-">
```

Attribute Information

ALIGN={LEFT, RIGHT, TOP, MIDDLE, BOTTOM}

Specifies the appearance of text that is near an inline graphic image. For example, if you use RIGHT, the image appears flush to the right edge of the document, and the text appears to its left. Using LEFT produces the opposite effect.

HTML 2 mentions only attribute values of TOP, MIDDLE, and BOTTOM. TOP aligns the top of the first line of text after the

<IMG> tag to the top of the image. BOT-TOM (the default) aligns the bottom of the image to the baseline of the text. MIDDLE aligns the baseline of the first line of text with the middle of the image.

HTML 3.2 added LEFT and RIGHT to the list of attribute values.

You can use the <BR> tag to control specific points where text stops wrapping around an image and continues below the instance of the image.

Standard: HTML 2; deprecated in HTML 4 in favor of style sheets

Common: Yes

Sample:

```
<IMG SRC="red_icon.gif"
ALIGN=LEFT>
```

It's about time for volunteers to pitch in.<BR CLEAR=ALL>

ALT="..."

Provides a textual description of images, which is useful for visitors who have text-only browsers. Some browsers may also display the ALT= text as a floating message when the visitor places the mouse pointer over the image.

Standard: HTML 2

Common: Yes

Sample:

```
<IMG SRC="smiley.gif" ALT=":-)">
```

BORDER="*n*"

Specifies the width (in pixels) of a border around an image. The default value is usually 0 (no border). The border color is the color of normal text within your document.

Standard: HTML 3.2

Common: Yes

Sample:

```
<IMG SRC="portrait.jpg" BORDER=2>
```

CLASS="..."

Indicates which style class applies to the <IMG> element.

Standard: HTML 4

Common: No

Sample:

```
<IMG CLASS="casual"
SRC="dots.gif">
```

CONTROLS

If the image is a video file, indicates the playback controls that appear below the image.

Standard: Internet Explorer 2

Common: No

Sample:

```
<IMG DYNSRC="foo.avi" CONTROLS>
```

DATAFLD="..."

Indicates a column in previously identified tabular data.

Standard: Internet Explorer 4

Common: No

Sample:

```
<IMG SRC="thing.gif"
DATAFLD="color">
```

DATASRC="..."

Specifies the location of tabular data to be bound.

Standard: Internet Explorer 4

Common: No

Sample:

```
<IMG SRC="thing.gif"
DATASRC="#data_table">
```

DYNSRC=*"URL"*

Specifies the relative or absolute location of a dynamic image (VRML, video file, and so on).

Standard: Internet Explorer 2

Common: No

Sample:

```
<IMG DYNSRC="foo.avi">
```

HEIGHT=*"n"*

Specifies the vertical dimension of the image (in pixels). If you don't use this attribute, the image appears in the default height. Use this attribute, along with the WIDTH= attribute, to fit an image within a space. You can fit a large image into a smaller space, and you can spread a smaller image. Some Web designers use the WIDTH= and HEIGHT= attributes to spread a single pixel image over a large space to produce the effect of a larger solid-color image.

Standard: HTML 3.2

Common: Yes

Sample:

```
<IMG SRC="images/smiley.jpg"
WIDTH=50 HEIGHT=50>
```

HSPACE=*"n"*

Establishes a margin of white space (in pixels) to the left and right of a graphic image. (See the VSPACE= attribute for how to control the top and bottom margins around an image.)

Standard: HTML 3.2

Common: Yes

Sample:

```
<IMG SRC="pics/pinetree.jpg"
HSPACE=20 VSPACE=15>
```

ID=*n*

Assigns a unique ID selector to an instance of the <IMG> tag. When you then assign a style to that ID selector, it affects only that one instance of the <IMG> tag.

Standard: HTML 4

Common: No

Sample:

```
<IMG SRC="grapes.jpg" ID="123">
```

ISMAP

Indicates that the graphic image functions as a clickable imagemap. The ISMAP= attribute instructs the browser to send the pixel coordinates to the server imagemap CGI application when a visitor selects the image with the mouse pointer. When HTML 2 established the ISMAP= attribute, imagemaps were implemented in a server-side fashion only. Now, client-side imagemaps are more popular (see the USEMAP= attribute).

Standard: HTML 2

Common: Yes

Sample:

```
<A HREF="/cgi-bin/
imagemap/mymap">
```

```
<IMG ISMAP
SRC="images/main.gif"></A>
```

LOWSRC=*"URL"*

Indicates the absolute or relative location of a lower resolution version of an image.

Standard: Netscape Navigator

Common: No

Sample:

```
<IMG SRC="bigpic.jpg"
LOWSRC="lilpic.jpg">
```

LOOP={*n*, INFINITE}

Indicates the number of times a video file plays back.

Standard: Internet Explorer 2

Common: No

Sample:

```
<IMG DYNSRC="bar.avi"
LOOP=INFINITE>
```

NAME="..."

Specifies a name by which bookmarks, scripts, and applets can reference the image.

Standard: Internet Explorer 4

Common: No

Sample:

```
<IMG SRC="tweakie.jpg"
NAME="img_1">
```

SRC="*URL*"

Specifies the relative or absolute location of a file that contains the graphic image you want to embed in a document.

Standard: HTML 2

Common: Yes

Sample:

```
<IMG SRC="images/left_arrow.gif"
ALT="<-">
```

START={FILEOPEN, MOUSEOVER}

Specifies the event that triggers the playback of a dynamic image. START=FILEOPEN starts playback when the browser has completely downloaded the file. START=MOUSEOVER starts playback when a visitor places the mouse pointer over the image.

Standard: Internet Explorer 2

Common: No

Sample:

```
<IMG DYNSRC="ship.vrm"
START=MOUSOVER>
```

STYLE="..."

Specifies style sheet commands that apply to the inline image.

Standard: HTML 4

Common: No

Sample:

```
<IMG SRC="dots.gif"
STYLE="background: red">
```

TITLE="..."

Specifies text assigned to the tag. You might use this attribute for context-sensitive help within the document. Browsers may use this to show tool tips over the image.

Standard: HTML 4

Common: No

Sample:

```
<IMG SRC="pics/jill.jpg"
TITLE="Image">
```

USEMAP="*URL*"

Specifies the location of the client-side imagemap data (see the <MAP> tag). Because the <MAP> tag gives the map data an anchor name, be sure to include the name with the URL of the document that contains the map data.

Standard: HTML 3.2

Common: Yes

Sample:

```
<IMG ISMAP SRC="map1.gif"
USEMAP="maps.html#map1">
```

VRML="..."

Specifies the absolute or relative location of a VRML world to embed in a document.

Standard: Internet Explorer 4

Common: No

Sample:

```
<IMG VRML="vr/myroom.vrml">
```

VSPACE=*"n"*

Establishes a margin of white space (in pixels) above and below a graphic image. (See the HSPACE= attribute for how to control the left and right margins of an image.)

Standard: HTML 3.2

Common: Yes

Sample:

```
<IMG SRC="pics/pinetree.jpg"
HSPACE=20 VSPACE=15>
```

WIDTH=*"n"*

Specifies the horizontal dimension of the image (in pixels). If you don't use this attribute, the image appears in the default width. Use this attribute, along with the HEIGHT= attribute, to fit an image within a space. You can fit a large image into a smaller space, and you can spread a smaller image. Some Web designers use WIDTH= and HEIGHT= to spread a single pixel image over a large space to produce the effect of a larger solid-color image.

Standard: HTML 3.2

Common: Yes

Sample:

```
<IMG SRC="images/smiley.jpg"
WIDTH=50 HEIGHT=50>
```

Other Attributes

This tag also accepts the lang, dir, onClick, onDblClick, onMouseDown, onMouseUp, onMouseOver, onMouse-Move, onMouseOut, onKeyPress, onKeyDown, and onKeyUp attributes. See the Element-Independent Attributes section of this reference for definitions and examples.

<INPUT>

Identifies several input methods for forms. This tag must appear between the opening and closing <FORM> tags.

Standard: HTML 2

Common: Yes

Paired: No

Sample:

```
<FORM ACTION="/cgi-bin/order/"
METHOD=POST>

<INPUT NAME="qty" TYPE="TEXT"
SIZE=5>

<INPUT TYPE="submit"
VALUE="Order">

</FORM>
```

Attribute Information

ACCEPT="..."

Specifies a list of acceptable MIME types for submitted files.

Standard: HTML 4

Common: No

Sample:

```
<INPUT TYPE=FILE
ACCEPT="image/gif">
Please submit a GIF image.
```

ALIGN={LEFT, CENTER, RIGHT}

Lines up a graphical submit button (TYPE=IMAGE). The behavior of this tag is identical to that of the ALIGN= attribute of the <IMG> tag.

Standard: HTML 3.2; deprecated in HTML 4 in favor of style sheets

Common: Yes

Sample:

```
<INPUT TYPE=IMAGE
SRC="picture.gif" ALIGN=RIGHT>
```

CHECKED
Use with TYPE=RADIO or TYPE=CHECKBOX to set the default state of those input methods to True.

Standard: HTML 2

Common: Yes

Sample:

```
<INPUT TYPE=CHECKBOX CHECKED
NAME="foo" VALUE="1"><BR>

2 <INPUT TYPE=CHECKBOX NAME="foo"
VALUE="2"><BR>
```

CLASS="..."
Indicates which style class applies to the <INPUT> element.

Standard: HTML 4

Common: No

Sample:

```
<INPUT CLASS="casual" TYPE=TEXT
NAME="age">
```

DATAFLD="..."
Selects a column from previously identified tabular data.

Standard: Internet Explorer 4

Common: No

Sample:

```
<DIV DATASRC="#data_table">

<INPUT TYPE=TEXT NAME="color"
DATAFLD="colorvals">
```

DATASRC="..."
Specifies the location of tabular data to be bound.

Standard: Internet Explorer 4

Common: No

Sample:

```
<INPUT TYPE=TEXT
DATASRC="#data_table"
DATAFLD="dataval1">
```

DISABLED="..."
Disables an instance of the input method so that data cannot be accepted or submitted.

Standard: HTML 4

Common: No

Sample:

```
<INPUT TYPE=PASSWORD NAME="Pass"
DISABLED>
```

ID="n"
Assigns a unique ID selector to an instance of the <INPUT> tag. When you then assign a style to that ID selector, it affects only that one instance of the <INPUT> tag.

Standard: HTML 4

Common: No

Sample:

```
Age:
<INPUT TYPE=TEXT NAME="age"
ID="123">
```

MAXLENGTH="n"
Indicates the number of characters you can enter into a text input field and is only useful to input methods of type TEXT or PASSWORD. Contrary to the SIZE= attribute, MAXLENGTH= does not affect the size of the input field shown on the screen.

Standard: HTML 2

Common: Yes

Sample:

```
Phone: <INPUT TYPE=TEXT
NAME="phone" MAXLENGTH=11>
```

NAME="..."
Gives a name to the value you pass to the form processor. For example, if you collect a person's last name with an input

method of type TEXT, you assign the NAME= attribute something like "last-name." This establishes a *name-value pair* for the form processor.

Standard: HTML 2

Common: Yes

Sample:

```
Enter your phone number: <INPUT
TYPE="text" NAME="phone" SIZE=10>
```

NOTAB

Removes the input element from the tab order.

Standard: Internet Explorer

Common: No

Sample:

```
Hair color:

<INPUT TYPE=TEXT NAME="hcolor"
NOTAB>
```

READONLY

Indicates that changes to the input method data cannot occur.

Standard: HTML 4

Common: No

Sample:

```
<INPUT TYPE=TEXT NAME="desc"
VALUE="1/4 inch flange assy"
READONLY>
```

SIZE="*n*"

Specifies the width of the input method (in characters). This applies only to input methods of type TEXT or PASSWORD. HTML 4 specifies size measurements in pixels for all other input methods, but pixel size specification is little supported.

Standard: HTML 2

Common: Yes

Sample:

```
Your Age: <INPUT TYPE="text"
NAME="Age" SIZE=5><BR>
```

SRC="*URL*"

Implements a graphic image for a submit button. For this to work, indicate TYPE=IMAGE.

Standard: HTML 3.2

Common: Yes

Sample:

```
<INPUT TYPE=IMAGE
SRC="/images/push-button.gif">
```

STYLE="..."

Specifies style sheet commands that apply to the input element.

Standard: HTML 4

Common: No

Sample:

```
<INPUT TYPE=RADIO NAME="food"
VALUE="1" STYLE="background:
red">
```

TABINDEX="*n*"

Specifies where the input method appears in the tab order. For example, TABINDEX=3 places the cursor at the input element after the visitor presses the Tab key three times.

Standard: Internet Explorer

Common: No

Sample:

```
Credit card number:

<INPUT TYPE=TEXT
NAME="ccard"TABINDEX=5>
```

TITLE="..."

Specifies text assigned to the tag. You might use this attribute for context-sensitive help within the document. Browsers may use this to show tool tips over the input method.

Standard: HTML 4

Common: No

Sample:

```
<INPUT TYPE=RADIO NAME="cc"
VALUE="visa" TITLE="Visa">
```

TYPE="..."

Indicates the kind of input method to use. Valid values are TEXT, PASSWORD, RADIO, CHECKBOX, SUBMIT, RESET, IMAGE, FILE, HIDDEN, and BUTTON.

TEXT produces a simple one-line text input field that is useful for obtaining simple data such as a person's name, a person's age, a dollar amount, and so on. To collect multiple lines of text, use the <TEXTAREA> tag.

PASSWORD gives the visitor a simple one-line text input field similar to the TEXT type. When visitors enter data into the field, however, they do not see what they type.

TYPE=RADIO produces a small radio button that can be turned on and off. Use radio buttons when you want a visitor to select only one of several items. For multiple-value selections, see the CHECKBOX type or the <SELECT> tag.

SUBMIT produces a button that, when selected, submits all the name-value pairs to the form processor.

RESET sets all the input methods to their empty or default settings.

TYPE=IMAGE replaces the submit button with an image. The behavior of this value is identical to that of the submit button, except that the x,y coordinates of the mouse position over the image when selected are also sent to the form processor.

BUTTON creates a button with no specific behavior that can interact with scripts.

> **Standard**: HTML 2

Common: Yes

Sample:

```
<FORM METHOD=POST ACTION="/cgi-
bin/thingie">
```

```
Name: <INPUT TYPE=TEXT
NAME="name"><BR>
```

```
Password: <INPUT TYPE=PASSWORD
NAME="pass"><BR>
```

```
Ice Cream:  Vanilla<INPUT
TYPE=RADIO VALUE="1" CHECKED
NAME="ice_cream"> Chocolate<INPUT
TYPE=RADIO VALUE="2"
NAME="ice_cream"><br>
```

```
<INPUT TYPE=SUBMIT VALUE="Send
Data...">
```

```
</FORM>
```

USEMAP="*URL*"

Indicates the relative or absolute location of a client-side imagemap to use with the form.

> **Standard**: HTML 4
>
> **Common**: No
>
> **Sample:**

```
<INPUT SRC="mapimage.gif"
USEMAP="maps.html#map1">
```

VALUE="..."

Sets the default input value method. Required when <INPUT> is set to TYPE=RADIO or CHECKBOX.

> **Standard**: HTML 2
>
> **Common**: Yes
>
> **Sample:**

```
<INPUT TYPE=HIDDEN NAME="id"
VALUE="123">
```

Other Attributes

This tag also accepts the lang, dir, onfocus, onblur, onselect, onchange, onClick, onDblClick, onMouseDown, onMouseUp, onMouseOver, onMouseMove, onMouseOut, onKeyPress, onKeyDown, and onKeyUp attributes. See the Element-Independent Attributes section of this reference for definitions and examples.

<INS>

Indicates text to be inserted in the document. May be either block-level or inline, as necessary.

> **Standard**: HTML 4
> **Common**: No
> **Paired**: Yes
> **Sample**:

```
<P>HTTP stands for HyperText
<INS>Transfer</INS>Protocol</P>
```

Attribute Information

CITE="*URL*"
Indicates address of reference (definitive source, for example) for insertion.

> **Standard**: HTML 4
> **Common**: No
> **Sample**:

```
<INS CITE="http://www.w3.org/">
HTML 2 was used for 2 years.
</INS>
```

CLASS="..."
Indicates which style class applies to the <INS> element.

> **Standard**: HTML 4
> **Common**: No
> **Sample**:

```
<INS CLASS="joeadd">POP stands
for Post Office Protocol</INS>
```

DATETIME="..."
Indicates the date and time in precisely this format: YYYY-MM-DDThh:mm:ssTZD. For example, 1997-07-14T08:30:00-07:00 indicates July 14, 1997, at 8:30 AM, in U.S. Mountain Time (7 hours from Greenwich time). This time could also be presented as 1997-07-14T08:30:00Z.

> **Standard**: HTML 4
> **Common**: No
> **Sample**:

```
<INS DATETIME="1997-07-
14T08:30:00Z">POP stands for Post
Office Protocol</INS>
```

ID="..."
Assigns a unique ID selector to an instance of the <INS> tag. When you then assign a style to that ID selector, it affects only that one instance of the <INS> tag.

> **Standard**: HTML 4
> **Common**: No
> **Sample**:

```
<INS ID="123">WWW stands for
World Wide Web</INS>
```

STYLE="..."
Specifies style sheet commands that apply to the inserted text.

> **Standard**: HTML 4
> **Common**: No
> **Sample**:

```
<INS STYLE="background: blue;
color: white">ESP stands for
extra-sensory perception.</INS>
```

TITLE="..."
Specifies text assigned to the tag. You might use this attribute for context-sensitive help within the document.

Browsers may use this to show tool tips over the inserted text.

> **Standard**: HTML 4
>
> **Common**: No
>
> **Sample**:

```
<INS TITLE="Definition">More
deleted text.</INS>
```

Other Attributes

This tag also accepts the lang, dir, onClick, onDblClick, onMouseDown, onMouseUp, onMouseOver, onMouse-Move, onMouseOut, onKeyPress, onKeyDown, and onKeyUp attributes. See the Element-Independent Attributes section of this reference for definitions and examples.

<ISINDEX>

Inserts an input field into the document so that visitors can enter search queries. The queries then go to a CGI application indicated by the ACTION= attribute.

> **Standard**: HTML 2; deprecated in HTML 4 in favor of <FORM>
>
> **Common**: Yes
>
> **Paired**: No
>
> **Sample**:

```
<ISINDEX PROMPT="Keyword Search"
ACTION="/cgi-bin/search.cgi">
```

Attribute Information

ACTION="*URL*"

Specifies the URL of the application that processes the search query. If you don't include ACTION=, the query goes to a URL formed from the document base (see the <BASE> tag).

> **Standard**: HTML 2

> **Common**: Yes
>
> **Sample**:

```
<ISINDEX ACTION="/cgi-bin/index-
search">
```

PROMPT="..."

Changes the input prompt for keyword index searches. If you don't specify PROMPT=, the browser displays a default prompt.

> **Standard**: HTML 3.2
>
> **Common**: Yes
>
> **Sample**:

```
<ISINDEX PROMPT="Search for
something">
```

K

<KBD>

Specifies keyboard input within a document.

> **Standard**: HTML 2
>
> **Common**: Yes
>
> **Paired**: Yes
>
> **Sample**:

```
Press <KBD>CTRL+S</KBD> to save
your document.
```

Attribute Information

CLASS="..."

Indicates which style class applies to the <KBD> element.

> **Standard**: HTML 4
>
> **Common**: No
>
> **Sample**:

```
Now press the <KBD
CLASS="casual">F4</KBD> key!
```

ID="..."

Assigns a unique ID selector to an instance of the <KBD> tag. When you then assign a style to that ID selector, it affects only that one instance of the <KBD> tag.

Standard: HTML 4

Common: No

Sample:

```
Press <KBD ID="123">F1</KBD> for
help.
```

STYLE="..."

Specifies style sheet commands that apply to the text within the <KBD> tags.

Standard: HTML 4

Common: No

Sample:

```
<KBD STYLE="background:
red">F10</KBD>
```

TITLE="..."

Specifies text assigned to the tag. You might use this attribute for context-sensitive help within the document. Browsers may use this to show tool tips over the keyboard text.

Standard: HTML 4

Common: No

Sample:

```
Now press the <KBD
TITLE="Keyboard stuff">F4</KBD>
key.
```

Other Attributes

This tag also accepts the lang, dir, onClick, onDblClick, onMouseDown, onMouseUp, onMouseOver, onMouse-Move, onMouseOut, onKeyPress, onKeyDown, and onKeyUp attributes. See the Element-Independent Attributes section of this reference for definitions and examples.

L

<LABEL>

Provides identifying text for a form widget.

Standard: HTML 4

Common: No

Paired: Yes

Sample:

```
<LABEL FOR="idname">First
Name</LABEL>
<INPUT TYPE="TEXT" ID="idname">
```

Attribute Information

ACCESSKEY="..."

Assigns a keystroke to the element.

Standard: HTML 4

Common: No

Sample:

```
<LABEL FOR="idname" ACCESSKEY=H>
```

CLASS="..."

Indicates which style class applies to the <INPUT> element.

Standard: HTML 4

Common: No

Sample:

```
<LABEL FOR="idname"
CLASS="short">First Name</LABEL>
<INPUT TYPE="TEXT" ID="idname">
```

FOR="..."
Specifies the ID of the widget associated with the label.

Standard: HTML 4

Common: No

Sample:

```
<LABEL FOR="idname">First
Name</LABEL>
<INPUT TYPE="TEXT" ID="idname">
```

ID="n"
Assigns a unique ID selector to an instance of the <INPUT> tag. When you then assign a style to that ID selector, it affects only that one instance of the <INPUT> tag.

Standard: HTML 4

Common: No

Sample:

```
<LABEL FOR="idname"
ID="234">First Name</LABEL>
<INPUT TYPE="TEXT" ID="idname">
```

STYLE="..."
Specifies style sheet commands that apply to the input element.

Standard: HTML 4

Common: No

Sample:

```
<LABEL FOR="idname"
STYLE="background : red">
First Name</LABEL>
<INPUT TYPE="TEXT" ID="idname">
```

TABINDEX="n"
Specifies where the input method appears in the tab order. For example, TABINDEX=3 places the cursor at the input element after the visitor presses the Tab key three times.

Standard: HTML 4

Common: No

Sample:

```
Credit card number:
<INPUT TYPE=TEXT
NAME="ccard"TABINDEX=5>
```

TITLE="..."
Specifies text assigned to the tag. You might use this attribute for context-sensitive help within the document. Browsers may use this to show tool tips over the input method.

Standard: HTML 4

Common: No

Sample:

```
<INPUT TYPE=RADIO NAME="cc"
VALUE="visa" TITLE="Visa">
```

Other Attributes
This tag also accepts the lang, dir, onfocus, onblur, onselect, onchange, onClick, onDblClick, onMouseDown, onMouseUp, onMouseOver, onMouseMove, onMouseOut, onKeyPress, onKeyDown, and onKeyUp attributes. See the Element-Independent Attributes section of this reference for definitions and examples.

<LAYER>

Defines a layer within a document, which you can than manipulate with Java-Script. Specify the layer's contents by placing HTML between the <LAYER> tags or by using the SRC= attribute.

Standard: Netscape Navigator 4

Common: No

Paired: Yes

Sample:

```
<LAYER SRC="top.html" HEIGHT=100
WIDTH=100 Z-INDEX=4 NAME="top"
VISIBILITY=SHOW>
</LAYER>
```

Attribute Information

ABOVE="..."

Specifies the name of a layer above which the current layer should appear.

Standard: Netscape Navigator 4

Common: No

Sample:

```
<LAYER SRC="grass.gif" Z-INDEX=1
NAME="Grass" VISIBILITY=SHOW>
<LAYER SRC="dog.gif"
ABOVE="Grass"NAME="Dog">
```

BACKGROUND="*URL*"

Specifies the relative or absolute location of an image file that the browser tiles as the background of the layer.

Standard: Netscape Navigator 4

Common: No

Sample:

```
<LAYER Z-INDEX=5 NAME="info"
BACKGROUND="goo.gif">
<H1>Hi there</H1></LAYER>
```

BELOW="..."

Specifies the name of a layer below which the current layer should appear.

Standard: Netscape Navigator 4

Common: No

Sample:

```
<LAYER BACKGROUND="road.jpg"
NAME="Road" UNDER="Car">
</LAYER>
```

BGCOLOR="*#RRGGBB*" or "..."

Specifies the background color of the layer. Use either the hexadecimal RGB values or the color name.

Standard: Netscape Navigator 4

Common: No

Sample:

```
<LAYER BGCOLOR=#FF0011><DIV
ALIGN=CENTER>
    <H1><BLINK>EAT AT
    JOES!</BLINK></H1>
</DIV>
</LAYER>
```

CLIP="*x1, y1, x2, y2*"

Indicates the dimensions of a clipping rectangle that specifies which areas of the layer are visible. Areas outside this rectangle become transparent.

You can give the x and y coordinates in pixels or as percentages to indicate relative portions of the layer. You can omit *x1* and *y1* if you want to clip from the top left corner of the layer.

Standard: Netscape Navigator 4

Common: No

Sample:

```
<LAYER SRC="hawk.jpg"
CLIP="20%,20%">
</LAYER>
```

HEIGHT="*n*"

Specifies the vertical dimension of the layer (in pixels or as a percentage of the browser window height).

Standard: Netscape Navigator 4

Common: No

Sample:

```
<LAYER SRC="frame.gif"
ABOVE="bg"NAME="frame"
WIDTH=200 HEIGHT=200>
```

LEFT="n"

Specifies the layer's horizontal position (in pixels) relative to the left edge of the parent layer. Use the TOP= attribute for vertical positioning.

Standard: Netscape Navigator 4

Common: No

Sample:

```
<LAYER LEFT=100 TOP=150>This
layer is at {100,150}</LAYER>
```

NAME="..."

Gives the layer a name by which other layer definitions and JavaScript code can reference it.

Standard: Netscape Navigator 4

Common: No

Sample:

```
<LAYER SRC="car.gif"
NAME="CarPic"ABOVE="Road">

</LAYER>
```

SRC="URL"

Specifies the relative or absolute location of the file containing the contents of the layer.

Standard: Netscape Navigator 4

Common: No

Sample:

```
<LAYER SRC="ocean.jpg"></LAYER>
```

TOP="n"

Specifies the layer's vertical position (in pixels) relative to the top edge of the parent layer. Use the LEFT= attribute for horizontal positioning.

Standard: Netscape Navigator 4

Common: No

Sample:

```
<LAYER LEFT=100 TOP=150>This
layer is at {100,150}</LAYER>
```

VISIBILITY={SHOW, HIDE, INHERIT}

Indicates whether the layer is initially visible. VISIBILITY=SHOW indicates the layer is initially visible. VISIBILITY =HIDE indicates the layer is not initially visible. VISIBILITY=INHERIT indicates the layer has the same initial visibility attribute as its parent layer.

Standard: Netscape Navigator 4

Common: No

Sample:

```
<LAYER SRC="grass.gif" Z-INDEX=1
NAME="Grass" VISIBILITY=SHOW>
```

WIDTH="n"

Specifies the horizontal dimension of the layer (in pixels or as a percentage of the browser window width).

Standard: Netscape Navigator 4

Common: No

Sample:

```
<LAYER SRC="frame.gif"
ABOVE="bg"NAME="frame"
WIDTH=200 HEIGHT=200>
```

Z-INDEX="n"

Specifies where the layer appears in the stack of layers. Higher values indicate a position closer to the top of the stack.

Standard: Netscape Navigator 4

Common: No

Sample:

```
<LAYER Z-INDEX=0 NAME="Bottom">

You may never see this text
ifother layers are above it.

</LAYER>
```

<LEGEND>

Specifies a description for a fieldset. Use inside <FIELDSET> tags.

Standard: HTML 4

Common: No

Paired: Yes

Sample:

```
<FORM><FIELDSET>
  <LEGEND VALIGN=TOP
  ALIGN=CENTER>
  Test Grades For COOKING 101
  </LEGEND>...
</FORM>
```

Attribute Information

ALIGN={TOP, BOTTOM, LEFT, RIGHT}

Indicates whether the legend appears at the top, bottom, left, or right of the fieldset.

Standard: HTML 4

Common: No

Sample:

```
<LEGEND ALIGN=TOP>
Seattle Staff Directory
</LEGEND>
```

CLASS="..."

Indicates which style class applies to the <LEGEND> element.

Standard: HTML 4

Common: No

Sample:

```
<LEGEND CLASS="casual">Hydrogen
vs Oxygen</LEGEND>
```

ID="..."

Assigns a unique ID selector to an instance of the <LEGEND> tag. When you then assign a style to that ID selector, it affects only that one instance of the <LEGEND> tag.

Standard: HTML 4

Common: No

Sample:

```
<LEGEND ID="123">Great
Painters</LEGEND>
```

STYLE="..."

Specifies style sheet commands that apply to the contents of the <LEGEND> tags.

Standard: HTML 4

Common: No

Sample:

```
<LEGEND STYLE="background: red">
```

TITLE="..."

Specifies text assigned to the tag. You might use this attribute for context-sensitive help within the document. Browsers may use this to show tool tips over the legend.

Standard: HTML 4

Common: Yes

Sample:

```
<LEGEND TITLE="of Sleepy Hollow">
```

Other Attributes

This tag also accepts the lang, dir, onClick, onDblClick, onMouseDown, onMouseUp, onMouseOver, onMouse-Move, onMouseOut, onKeyPress, onKeyDown, and onKeyUp attributes. See the Element-Independent Attributes section of this reference for definitions and examples.

<LI>

Places items into ordered (see the <OL> tag), menu (see the <MENU> tag), directory (see the <dir> tag), and unordered (see the <UL> tag) lists.

Standard: HTML 2

Common: Yes

Paired: Yes, optional

Sample:

```
My favorite foods are:<UL>
  <LI>Pepperoni Pizza
  <LI>Lasagna
  <LI>Taco Salad
  <LI>Bananas
</UL>
```

Attribute Information

CLASS="..."

Indicates which style class applies to the <LI> element.

Standard: HTML 4

Common: No

Sample:

```
<LI CLASS="casual">Dogs
```

ID=*n*

Assigns a unique ID selector to an instance of the <LI> tag. When you then assign a style to that ID selector, it affects only that one instance of the <LI> tag.

Standard: HTML 4

Common: No

Sample:

```
<LI ID="123">Bees</LI>
```

STYLE="..."

Specifies style sheet commands that apply to the list item.

Standard: HTML 4

Common: No

Sample:

```
<LI STYLE="background: red">
```

TITLE="..."

Specifies text assigned to the tag. You might use this attribute for context-sensitive help within the document. Browsers may use this to show tool tips over the list item.

Standard: HTML 4

Common: No

Sample:

```
<LI TITLE="List Item">Thingie
```

TYPE="..."

Specifies the bullets for each unordered list item (see the <UL> tag) or the numbering for each ordered list item (see the <OL> tag). If you omit the TYPE= attribute, the browser chooses a default type.

Valid TYPE values for unordered lists are DISC, SQUARE, and CIRCLE.

Valid TYPE values for ordered lists are 1 for Arabic numbers, a for lowercase letters, A for uppercase letters, i for lowercase Roman numerals, and I for uppercase Roman numerals.

Standard: HTML 3.2

Common: Yes

Sample:

```
<UL>
 <LI TYPE=SQUARE>Food
 <OL>
   <LI TYPE=1>Spaghetti
   <LI TYPE=1>Tossed Salad
 </OL>
</UL>
```

VALUE="..."

Sets a number in an ordered list. Use this attribute to continue a list after interrupting it with something else in your document. You can also set a number in an ordered list with the START= attribute of the <OL> tag.

Because unordered lists do not increment, the VALUE= attribute is meaningless when used with them.

> **Standard**:   HTML 3.2
>
> **Common**:   Yes
>
> **Sample**:

```
<OL TYPE=1>
    <LI VALUE=5>Watch
    <LI>Compass
</OL>
```

Other Attributes

This tag also accepts the lang, dir, onClick, onDblClick, onMouseDown, onMouseUp, onMouseOver, onMouse-Move, onMouseOut, onKeyPress, onKeyDown, and onKeyUp attributes. See the Element-Independent Attributes section of this reference for definitions and examples.

<LINK>

Establishes relationships between the current document and other documents. Use this tag within the <HEAD> section. For example, if you access the current document by choosing a hyperlink from the site's home page, you can establish a relationship between the current document and the site's home page (see the REL= attribute). At this time, however, most browsers don't use most of these relationships. You can place several <LINK> tags within the <HEAD> section of your document to define multiple relationships.

With newer implementations of HTML, you can also use the <LINK> tag to establish information about Cascading Style Sheets. Some other relationships that the <LINK> tag defines include the following:

CONTENTS: A table of contents.

INDEX: An index.

GLOSSARY: A glossary of terms.

COPYRIGHT: A copyright notice.

NEXT: The next document in a series (use with REL=).

PREVIOUS: The previous document in a series (use with REV=).

START: The first document in a series.

HELP: A document offering help or more information.

BOOKMARK: A bookmark links to a important entry point within a longer document.

STYLESHEET: An external style sheet.

ALTERNATE: Different versions of the same document. When used with lang, ALTERNATE implies a translated document; when used with MEDIA, it implies a version for a different medium.

> **Standard**:   HTML 2
>
> **Common**:   Yes
>
> **Paired**:   No

Sample:

```
<HEAD>
<TITLE>Prices</TITLE>
<LINK REL=Top
HREF="http://www.raycomm.com/">
<LINK REL=Search
HREF="http://www.raycomm.com/
search.html">
</HEAD>
```

Attribute Information

HREF="*URL*"

Indicates the relative or absolute location of the resource you are establishing a relationship to/from.

> **Standard:** HTML 2
> **Common:** Yes
> **Sample:**

```
<LINK REL=Prev HREF="page1.html">
```

MEDIA="..."

Specifies the destination medium for style information. It may be a single type or a comma-separated list. Media types include the following:

> Screen—for online viewing (default setting)
>
> Print—for traditional printed material and for documents on-screen viewed in print preview mode
>
> Projection—for projectors
>
> Braille—for Braille tactile feedback devices
>
> Speech—for a speech synthesizer
>
> All—applies to all devices

> **Standard:** HTML 4
> **Common:** No
> **Sample:**

```
<LINK MEDIA=SCREEN
REL="STYLESHEET"
HREF="/global.css">
```

NAME="..."

Specifies a name by which bookmarks, scripts, and applets can reference the relationship.

> **Standard:** Internet Explorer 4
> **Common:** No
> **Sample:**

```
<LINK REL="Search"
HREF="/search.html"NAME="Search">
```

REL="..."

Defines the relationship you are establishing between the current document and another resource. The HTML 3.2 specification includes several standard values for the REL= attribute. REL=Top defines the site home page or the top of the site hierarchy. REL=Contents usually defines the location of a resource that lists the contents of the site. REL=Index provides a link to an index of the site. REL=Glossary indicates the location of a glossary resource. REL=Copyright indicates the location of a copyright statement. REL=Next and REL=Previous establish relationships between documents or resources in a series. REL=Help indicates the location of a help resource. REL=Search specifies the location of a search resource. REL=style sheet specifies information about style sheets.

> **Standard:** HTML 2
> **Common:** Yes

Sample:

```
<LINK REL=Help
HREF="/Help/index.html">

<LINK REL=style sheet
HREF="sitehead.css">

</HEAD>
```

REV="..."

Establishes reverse relationships between the current document and other resources. One common use is REV="made", after which you can set the HREF= attribute to a mailto: URL to contact the author of the document.

> **Standard:** HTML 2
> **Common:** Yes
> **Sample:**

```
<LINK REV=made
HREF="mailto:jdoe@somewhere.com">
```

TARGET="..."

Specifies the name of a frame in which the referenced link appears.

> **Standard:** Internet Explorer 4
> **Common:** No
> **Sample:**

```
<LINK TARGET="_blank" REL="Home"
HREF="http://www.mememe.com/">
```

TITLE="..."

Specifies text assigned to the tag that can be used for context-sensitive help within the document. Browsers may use this to show tool tips.

> **Standard:** HTML 4
> **Common:** Yes
> **Sample:**

```
<LINK REL=Top HREF="/index.html"
TITLE="Home Page">
```

TYPE="..."

Specifies the MIME type of a style sheet to import with the <LINK> tag.

> **Standard:** HTML 4
> **Common:** No
> **Sample:**

```
<LINK REL=STYLESHEET
TYPE="text/css"HREF="/style/main
.css">
```

Other Attributes

This tag also accepts the lang, dir, onfocus, onblur, onchange, onselect, onClick, onDblClick, onMouseDown, onMouseUp, onMouseOver, onMouseMove, onMouseOut, onKeyPress, onKeyDown, and onKeyUp attributes. See the Element-Independent Attributes section of this reference for definitions and examples.

<LISTING>

Specifies preformatted text to include within a document. Unlike the <PRE> tags, the browser does not interpret HTML tags within the <LISTING>tags. HTML 3.2 declared this tag obsolete, so use <PRE> instead.

> **Standard:** Obsolete
> **Common:** Yes
> **Paired:** Yes
> **Sample:**

```
The output from these reports is
shown below.
<LISTING>
Company     Q1     Q2      Q3     Q4
---------   ---    ---     ---    ----
Widget Inc. 4.5m   4.6m    6.2m   4.5m
Acme Widget 5.9m   10.2m   7.3m   6.6m
West Widget 2.2m   1.3m    3.1m   6.1m
</LISTING>
```

M

<MAP>

Specifies a container for client-side imagemap data. Inside the <MAP> container, you place instances of the <AREA> tag.

>   **Standard**:   HTML 3.2
>   **Common**:   Yes
>   **Paired**:   Yes
>   **Sample**:

```
<MAP NAME="mainmap"> <AREA
NOHREF ALT="Home" SHAPE=RECT
COORDS="0,0,100,100">

  <AREA HREF="yellow.html"
  ALT="Yellow" SHAPE=RECT
  COORDS="100,0,200,100">

  <AREA HREF="blue.html"
  ALT="Blue" SHAPE=RECT
  COORDS="0,100,100,200">

  <AREA HREF="red.html" ALT="Red"
  SHAPE=RECT
  COORDS="100,100,200,200">

</MAP>
```

Attribute Information

CLASS="..."
Indicates which style class applies to the element.

>   **Standard**:   HTML 4
>   **Common**:   No
>   **Sample**:

```
<MAP CLASS="casual" NAME="simba">
```

ID="..."
Indicates an identifier to associate with the map. You can also use this to apply styles to the object.

>   **Standard**:   HTML 4
>   **Common**:   No
>   **Sample**:

```
<MAP ID="123" NAME="simba">
```

NAME="..."
Establishes a name for the map information you can later reference by the USEMAP= attribute of the <IMG> tag.

>   **Standard**:   HTML 3.2
>   **Common**:   Yes
>   **Sample**:

```
<MAP NAME="housemap">

. . .

<IMG SRC="house.gif"
USEMAP="#housemap" BORDER=0
ALT="Map of House">
```

STYLE="..."
Specifies style sheet commands that apply to the contents within the <MAP> tags.

>   **Standard**:   HTML 4
>   **Common**:   No
>   **Sample**:

```
<MAP STYLE="background: black">
```

TITLE="..."
Specifies text assigned to the tag. You might use this attribute for context-sensitive help within the document. Browsers may use this to show tool tips.

>   **Standard**:   HTML 4
>   **Common**:   No
>   **Sample**:

```
<MAP TITLE="imagemap spec">
```

<MARQUEE>

Displays a scrolling text message within a document. Only Internet Explorer recognizes this tag.

Standard: Internet Explorer
Common: No
Paired: Yes
Sample:

```
<MARQUEE DIRECTION=LEFT
BEHAVIOR=SCROLL SCROLLDELAY=250
SCROLLAMOUNT=10>Big sale today on
fuzzy wuzzy widgets!</MARQUEE>
```

Attribute Information

ALIGN={LEFT, CENTER, RIGHT, TOP, BOTTOM}

Specifies the alignment of text outside the marquee.

Standard: Internet Explorer
Common: No
Sample:

```
<MARQUEE WIDTH=200 HEIGHT=50
ALIGN=LEFT DIRECTION=LEFT>
```

How To Groom Your Dog</MARQUEE>

BEHAVIOR={SLIDE, SCROLL, ALTERNATE}

Indicates the type of scrolling. BEHAVIOR=SCROLL scrolls text from one side of the marquee, across, and off the opposite side. BEHAVIOR= SLIDE scrolls text from one side of the marquee, across, and stops when the text reaches the opposite side. BEHAVIOR=ALTERNATE bounces the marquee text from one side to the other.

Standard: Internet Explorer
Common: No

Sample:

```
<MARQUEE DIRECTION=LEFT
BEHAVIOR=ALTERNATE>GO BEARS! WIN
WIN WIN!</MARQUEE>
```

BGCOLOR="#RRGGBB" or "..."

Specifies the background color of the marquee. Use a hexadecimal RGB color value or a color name.

Standard: Internet Explorer
Common: No
Sample:

```
<MARQUEE BGCOLOR="red"
DIRECTION=LEFT>Order opera
tickets here!</MARQUEE>
```

DATAFLD="..."

Selects a column from a block of tabular data.

Standard: Internet Explorer 4
Common: No
Sample:

```
<MARQUEE DATASRC="#data_table"
DATAFLD="nitems">
```

DATAFORMATAS={TEXT, HTML, NONE}

Specifies how items selected from tabular data format within the document.

Standard: Internet Explorer 4
Common: No
Sample:

```
<MARQUEE DATASRC="#data_table"
DATAFLD="nitems"
DATAFORMATAS=HTML>
```

DATASRC="..."

Specifies the location of tabular data to be bound within the document.

Standard: Internet Explorer 4
Common: No

Sample:

```
<MARQUEE DATASRC="#data_table"
DATAFLD="nitems">
```

DIRECTION={LEFT, RIGHT}

Indicates the direction in which the marquee text scrolls.

Standard: Internet Explorer

Common: No

Sample:

```
<MARQUEE DIRECTION=LEFT>Order
opera tickets here!</MARQUEE>
```

HEIGHT="n"

Specifies the vertical dimension of the marquee (in pixels).

Standard: Internet Explorer

Common: No

Sample:

```
<MARQUEE WIDTH=300 HEIGHT=50>
GO BEARS!</MARQUEE>
```

HSPACE="n"

Specifies the size of the margins (in pixels) to the left and right of the marquee.

Standard: Internet Explorer

Common: No

Sample:

```
<MARQUEE DIRECTION=LEFT
HSPACE=25>Check out our detailed
product descriptions!</MARQUEE>
```

ID="..."

Assigns a unique ID selector to an instance of the <MARQUEE> tag. When you then assign a style to that ID selector, it affects only that one instance of the <MARQUEE> tag.

Standard: Internet Explorer 4

Common: No

Sample:

```
<MARQUEE ID="3d4">
```

LOOP={n, INFINITE}

Controls the appearance of the marquee text.

Standard: Internet Explorer

Common: No

Sample:

```
<MARQUEE LOOP=5>December 12 is
our big, all-day sale!</MARQUEE>
```

SCROLLAMOUNT="n"

Indicates how far (in pixels) the marquee text shifts between redraws. Decrease this value for a smoother (but slower) scroll; increase it for a faster (but bumpier) scroll.

Standard: Internet Explorer

Common: No

Sample:

```
<MARQUEE SCROLLAMOUNT=10
SCROLLDELAY=40>Plant a tree for
Arbor Day!
</MARQUEE>
```

SCROLLDELAY="n"

Indicates how often (in milliseconds) the marquee text redraws. Increase this value to slow the scrolling action; decrease it to speed the scrolling action.

Standard: Internet Explorer

Common: No

Sample:

```
<MARQUEE DIRECTION=RIGHT
SCROLLDELAY=30>Eat at
Joe's!</MARQUEE>
```

STYLE="..."

Specifies style sheet commands that apply to the text within the <MARQUEE> tags.

> **Standard:** Internet Explorer 4
>
> **Common:** No
>
> **Sample:**

<MARQUEE STYLE="background: red">

TITLE="..."

Specifies text assigned to the tag. You might use this attribute for context-sensitive help within the document. Browsers may use this to show tool tips over the marquee.

> **Standard:** Internet Explorer 4
>
> **Common:** No
>
> **Sample:**

<MARQUEE TITLE="Scrolling Marquee">

VSPACE="n"

Specifies the size of the margins (in pixels) at the top and bottom of the marquee.

> **Standard:** Internet Explorer
>
> **Common:** No
>
> **Sample:**

<MARQUEE DIRECTION=LEFT VSPACE=25>Check out our detailed product descriptions!</MARQUEE>

WIDTH="n"

Specifies the horizontal dimension (in pixels) of the marquee.

> **Standard:** Internet Explorer
>
> **Common:** No
>
> **Sample:**

<MARQUEE WIDTH=300>

Go Bears!</MARQUEE>

<MENU>

Defines a menu list. Use the <LI> tag to indicate list items. Use <UL> instead of this deprecated element.

> **Standard:** HTML 2; deprecated in HTML 4
>
> **Common:** No
>
> **Paired:** Yes
>
> **Sample:**

Now you can:<MENU>

<LI>Eat the sandwich

<LI>Place the sandwich in the fridge

<LI>Feed the sandwich to the dog

</MENU>

Attribute Information

CLASS="..."

Indicates which style class applies to the <MENU> element.

> **Standard:** HTML 4
>
> **Common:** No
>
> **Sample:**

<MENU CLASS="casual">

<LI>Information

<LI>Members

<LI>Guests

</MENU>

COMPACT

Specifies that the menu list appear in a space-saving form.

> **Standard:** HTML 2; deprecated in HTML 4
>
> **Common:** Yes

Sample:

```
<H2>Drinks Available</H2>
<MENU COMPACT>
   <LI>Cola</LI>
   <LI>Fruit Drink</LI>
   <LI>Orange Juice</LI>
   <LI>Water</LI>
</MENU>
```

ID="..."

Assigns a unique ID selector to an instance of the <MENU> tag. When you then assign a style to that ID selector, it affects only that one instance of the <MENU> tag.

Standard: HTML 4

Common: No

Sample:

```
You'll need the following:
<MENU ID="123">
   <LI>Extra socks
   <LI>Snack crackers
   <LI>Towel
</MENU>
```

STYLE="..."

Specifies style sheet commands that apply to the menu list.

Standard: HTML 4

Common: Yes

Sample:

```
<MENU STYLE="background: black;
color: white">
```

TITLE="..."

Specifies text assigned to the tag. You might use this attribute for context-sensitive help within the document. Browsers may use this to show tool tips over the menu list.

Standard: HTML 4

Common: No

Sample:

```
<MENU TITLE="Menu List">
```

Other Attributes

This tag also accepts the lang, dir, onClick, onDblClick, onMouseDown, onMouseUp, onMouseOver, onMouse-Move, onMouseOut, onKeyPress, onKeyDown, and onKeyUp attributes. See the Element-Independent Attributes section of this reference for definitions and examples.

<META>

Specifies information about the document to browsers, applications, and search engines. Place the <META> tag within the document head. For example, you can use the <META> tag to instruct the browser to load a new document after 10 seconds (client-pull), or you can specify keywords for search engines to associate with your document.

Standard: HTML 2

Common: Yes

Paired: No

Sample:

```
<HEAD>
<TITLE>Igneous Rocks In North
America</TITLE>
<META HTTP-EQUIV="Keywords"
CONTENT="Geology, Igneous,
Volcanos">
</HEAD>
```

Attribute Information

CONTENT="..."

Assigns values to the HTTP header field. When using the REFRESH HTTP header, assign a number along with a URL to the CONTENT= attribute; the browser then loads the specified URL after the specified number of seconds.

Standard: HTML 2

Common: Yes

Sample:

```
<META HTTP-EQUIV="Refresh" CON-
TENT="2; URL=nextpage.html">
```

HTTP-EQUIV="..."

Indicates the HTTP header value you want to define, such as Refresh, Expires, or Content-Language. Other header values are listed in RFC2068.

Standard: HTML 2

Common: Yes

Sample:

```
<META HTTP-EQUIV="Expires"
CONTENT="Tue, 04 Aug 1997
22:39:22 GMT">
```

NAME="..."

Specifies the name of the association you are defining, such as Keywords or Description.

Standard: HTML 2

Common: Yes

Sample:

```
<META NAME="Keywords"
CONTENT="travel,automobile">

<META NAME="Description"
CONTENT="The Nash Metro moves
fast and goes beep beep.">
```

Other Attributes

This tag also accepts the lang and dir attributes. See the Element-Independent Attributes section of this reference for definitions and examples.

<MULTICOL>

Formats text into newspaper-style columns.

Standard: Netscape Navigator 4

Common: No

Paired: Yes

Sample:

```
<MULTICOL COLS=2 GUTTER=10>
. . .
</MULTICOL>
```

Attribute Information

COLS="n"

Indicates the number of columns.

Standard: Netscape Navigator 4

Common: No

Sample:

```
<MULTICOL COLS=4>
```

GUTTER="n"

Indicates the width of the space (in pixels) between multiple columns.

Standard: Netscape Navigator 4

Common: No

Sample:

```
<MULTICOL COLS=3 GUTTER=15>
```

WIDTH="n"

Indicates the horizontal dimension (in pixels or as a percentage of the total width available) of each column.

Standard: Netscape Navigator 4

Common: No

Sample:

```
<MULTICOL COLS=2 WIDTH="30%">
```

N

<NOBR>

Disables line-wrapping for a section of text. To force a word break within a <NOBR> clause, use the <WBR> tag.

Standard: Netscape Navigator
Common: Yes
Paired: Yes
Sample:

```
<NOBR>This entire line of text
will remain on one single line in
the browser window until the
closing tag appears. That doesn't
happen until right now.</NOBR>
```

Attribute Information

CLASS="..."

Indicate which style class applies to the element.

Standard: Netscape Navigator
Common: No
Sample:

```
<NOBR CLASS="casual">
```

ID="..."

Assigns a unique ID selector to an instance of the <NOBR> tag. When you then assign a style to that ID selector, it affects only that one instance of the <NOBR> tag.

Standard: Netscape Navigator
Common: No
Sample:

```
You'll need the following:
<NOBR ID="123">
```

STYLE="..."

Specifies style sheet commands that apply to the nonbreaking text.

Standard: Netscape Navigator
Common: Yes
Sample:

```
<NOBR STYLE="background: black">
```

<NOFRAMES>

Provides HTML content for browsers that do not support frames or are configured not to present frames. You can include a <BODY> tag within the <NOFRAMES> section to provide additional formatting and style sheet features.

Standard: HTML 4
Common: Yes
Paired: Yes
Sample:

```
<FRAMESET COLS="*,70">
    <FRAME SRC="frames/body.html"
    NAME="body">
    <FRAME SRC="frames/side.html"
    NAME="side">
</FRAMESET>
<NOFRAMES>
    <p>Your browser doesn't support
    frames. Please follow the links
    below for the rest of the story.
    <p><a href="Prices.html">
    Prices</a> | <a href="About.
    html">About Us</a> | <a href
    ="Contact.html">Contact Us</a>
</NOFRAMES>
```

Attribute Information

TITLE="..."

Specifies text assigned to the tag. You might use this attribute for context-sensitive help within the document. Browsers may use this to show tool tips.

Standard: HTML 4

Common: No

Sample:

```
<NOFRAMES TITLE="HTML for non-
framed browsers">
```

<NOSCRIPT>

Provides HTML content for browsers that do not support scripts. Use the <NOSCRIPT> tags inside a script definition.

Standard: HTML 4

Common: No

Paired: Yes

Sample:

```
<NOSCRIPT>

Because you can see this, you can
tell that your browser will not
run (or is set not to run)
scripts. </NOSCRIPT>
```

O

<OBJECT>

Embeds a software object into a document. The object can be an ActiveX object, a QuickTime movie, or any other objects or data that a browser supports.

Use the <PARAM> tag to supply parameters to the embedded object. You can place messages and other tags between the <OBJECT> tags for browsers that do not support embedded objects.

Standard: HTML 4

Common: No

Paired: Yes

Sample:

```
<OBJECT CLASSID="/thingie.py">

<PARAM NAME="thing" VALUE=1>

Sorry. Your browser does not
support embedded objects. If it
supported these objects you
would not see this message.

</OBJECT>
```

Attribute Information

ALIGN={LEFT, CENTER, RIGHT, TEXTTOP, MIDDLE, TEXTMIDDLE, BASELINE, TEXTBOTTOM, BASELINE}

Indicates how the embedded object lines up relative to the edges of the browser windows and/or other elements within the browser window.

Using ALIGN=LEFT, ALIGN=RIGHT, or ALIGN=CENTER will cause the embedded object to *float* between the edges of the window either to the left, right, or evenly between. The behavior is similar to that of the ALIGN= attribute of the <IMG> tag.

ALIGN=TEXTTOP aligns the top of the embedded object with the top of the surrounding text.

ALIGN=TEXTMIDDLE aligns the middle of the embedded object with the middle of the surrounding text.

ALIGN=TEXTBOTTOM aligns the bottom of the embedded object with the bottom of the surrounding text.

ALIGN=BASELINE aligns the bottom of the embedded object with the baseline of the surrounding text.

ALIGN=MIDDLE aligns the middle of the embedded object with the baseline of the surrounding text.

Standard: HTML 4; deprecated in favor of style sheets

Common: No

Sample:

```
<OBJECT DATA="shocknew.dcr"
TYPE="application/director"
WIDTH=288 HEIGHT=200 ALIGN=RIGHT>
```

BORDER="*n*"

Indicates the width (in pixels) of a border around the embedded object. BORDER=0 indicates no border.

Standard: HTML 4

Common: No

Sample:

```
<OBJECT DATA="shocknew.dcr"
TYPE="application/director"
WIDTH=288 HEIGHT=200 BORDER=10>
```

CODEBASE="..."

Specifies the absolute or relative location of the base directory in which the browser will look for data and other implementation files.

Standard: HTML 4

Common: No

Sample:

```
<OBJECT CODEBASE="/~fgm/code/">
</OBJECT>
```

CODETYPE="..."

Specifies the MIME type for the embedded object's code.

Standard: HTML 4

Common: No

Sample:

```
<OBJECT CODETYPE="application/
x-msword">
</OBJECT>
```

CLASS="..."

Indicates which style class applies to the element.

Standard: HTML 4

Common: No

Sample:

```
<OBJECT CLASS="casual"
CODETYPE="application/x-msword">
</OBJECT>
```

CLASSID="..."

Specifies the URL of an object resource.

Standard: HTML 4

Common: No

Sample:

```
<OBJECT CLASSID="http://www
.raycomm.com/bogus.class">
```

DATA="*URL*"

Specifies the absolute or relative location of the embedded object's data.

Standard: HTML 4

Common: No

Sample:

```
<OBJECT DATA="/~fgm/goo.AVI">
</OBJECT>
```

DATAFLD="..."

Selects a column from a block of tabular data.

Standard: Internet Explorer 4

Common: No

Sample:

```
<OBJECT DATA="dataview.ocx"
DATASRC="#data_table"
DATAFLD="datafld1">
```

DATASRC="..."

Specifies the location of tabular data to be bound within the document.

Standard: Internet Explorer 4

Common: No

Sample:

```
<OBJECT DATA="dataview.ocx"
DATASRC="#data_table">
```

DECLARE

Defines the embedded object without actually loading it into the document.

Standard: HTML 4

Common: No

Sample:

```
<OBJECT CLASSID="clsid:99B42120-
6EC7-11CF-A6C7-00AA00A47DD3"
DECLARE>
</OBJECT>
```

HEIGHT="n"

Specifies the vertical dimension (in pixels) of the embedded object.

Standard: HTML 4

Common: No

Sample:

```
<OBJECT DATA="shocknew.dcr"
TYPE="application/director"
WIDTH=288 HEIGHT=200 VSPACE=10
HSPACE=10>
```

HSPACE="n"

Specifies the size of the margins (in pixels) to the left and right of the embedded object.

Standard: HTML 4

Common: No

Sample:

```
<OBJECT DATA="shocknew.dcr"
TYPE="application/director"
WIDTH=288 HEIGHT=200 VSPACE=10
HSPACE=10>
```

ID="..."

Indicates an identifier to associate with the embedded object. You can also use this to apply styles to the object.

Standard: HTML 4

Common: No

Sample:

```
<OBJECT DATA="shocknew.dcr"
TYPE="application/director"
WIDTH=288 HEIGHT=200 VSPACE=10
HSPACE=10 ID="swave2">
```

NAME="..."

Specifies the name of the embedded object.

Standard: HTML 4

Common: No

Sample:

```
<OBJECT CLASSID="clsid:99B42120-
6EC7-11CF-A6C7-00AA00A47DD3"
NAME="Very Cool Thingie">
</OBJECT>
```

SHAPES

Indicates that the embedded object has shaped hyperlinks (that is, imagemaps).

Standard: HTML 4

Common: No

Sample:

```
<OBJECT DATA="navbar.gif" SHAPES>
```

STANDBY="..."

Specifies a message that the browser displays while the object is loading.

Standard: HTML 4

Common: No

Sample:

```
<OBJECT STANDBY="Please wait.
Movie loading." WIDTH=100
HEIGHT=250>

<PARAM NAME=SRC
VALUE="TheEarth.AVI">

<PARAM NAME=AUTOSTART VALUE=TRUE>

<PARAM NAME=PLAYBACK VALUE=FALSE>

</OBJECT>
```

TABINDEX="*n*"

Indicates the place of the embedded object in the tabbing order.

Standard: HTML 4

Common: No

Sample:

```
<OBJECT CLASSID="clsid:99B42120-
6EC7-11CF-A6C7-00AA00A47DD3"
TABINDEX=3>

</OBJECT>
```

TITLE="..."

Specifies text assigned to the tag. You might use this attribute for context-sensitive help within the document. Browsers may use this to show tool tips over the embedded object.

Standard: HTML 4

Common: No

Sample:

```
<OBJECT TITLE="Earth Movie"
WIDTH=100 HEIGHT=250>
 <PARAM NAME=SRC
 VALUE="TheEarth.AVI">
 <PARAM NAME=AUTOSTART
 VALUE=TRUE>
 <PARAM NAME=PLAYBACK
 VALUE=FALSE>
</OBJECT>
```

TYPE="..."

Indicates the MIME type of the embedded object.

Standard: HTML 4

Common: No

Sample:

```
<OBJECT DATA="shocknew.dcr"
TYPE="application/x-director"
WIDTH=288 HEIGHT=200
VSPACE=10 HSPACE=10>
```

USEMAP="*URL*"

Indicates the relative or absolute location of a client-side imagemap to use with the embedded object.

Standard: HTML 4

Common: No

Sample:

```
<OBJECT USEMAP="maps.html#map1">
```

VSPACE="*n*"

Specifies the size of the margin (in pixels) at the top and bottom of the embedded object.

Standard: HTML 4

Common: No

Sample:

```
<OBJECT DATA="shocknew.dcr"
TYPE="application/director"
WIDTH=288 HEIGHT=200 VSPACE=10
HSPACE=10>

</OBJECT>
```

WIDTH="*n*"

Indicates the horizontal dimension (in pixels) of the embedded object.

Standard: HTML 4

Common: No

Sample:

```
<OBJECT DATA="shocknew.dcr"
TYPE="application/director"
WIDTH=288 HEIGHT=200 VSPACE=10
HSPACE=10>
```

Other Attributes

This tag also accepts the lang, dir, onClick, onDblClick, onMouseDown, onMouseUp, onMouseOver, onMouse-Move, onMouseOut, onKeyPress, onKeyDown, and onKeyUp attributes. See the Element-Independent Attributes section of this reference for definitions and examples.

<OL>

Contains a numbered (ordered) list.

> **Standard:** HTML 2
> **Common:** Yes
> **Paired:** Yes
> **Sample:**

```
<OL TYPE=i>
  <LI>Introduction
  <LI>Part One
  <OL TYPE=A>
    <LI>Chapter 1
    <LI>Chapter 2
  </OL>
</OL>
```

Attribute Information

CLASS="..."

Indicates which style class applies to the <OL> element.

> **Standard:** HTML 4
> **Common:** No

Sample:

```
<OL CLASS="casual">
  <LI>Check engine oil
  <LI>Check tire pressures
  <LI>Fill with gasoline
<OL>
```

COMPACT

Indicates that the ordered list appears in a compact format. This attribute may not affect the appearance of the list as most browsers do not present lists in more than one format.

> **Standard:** HTML 2, deprecated in HTML 4
> **Common:** No
> **Sample:**

```
<OL COMPACT>
```

ID="*n*"

Assigns a unique ID selector to an instance of the <OL> tag. When you then assign a style to that ID selector, it affects only that one instance of the <OL> tag.

> **Standard:** HTML 4
> **Common:** No
> **Sample:**

```
Recommended bicycle accessories:
<OL ID="123">
  <LI>Water bottle
  <LI>Helmet
  <LI>Tire pump
</OL>
```

START="..."

Specifies the value at which the ordered list should start.

> **Standard:** HTML 2
> **Common:** Yes

Sample:

`<OL TYPE=A START=F>`

STYLE="..."

Specifies style sheet commands that apply to the ordered list.

   Standard: HTML 4

   Common: Yes

   Sample:

`<OL STYLE="background: black; color: white">`

TITLE="..."

Specifies text assigned to the tag. You might use this attribute for context-sensitive help within the document. Browsers may use this to show tool tips over the ordered list.

   Standard: HTML 4

   Common: No

   Sample:

`<OL TITLE="Ordered list">`

TYPE="..."

Specifies the numbering style of the ordered list. Possible values are 1 for Arabic numbers, i for lower case Roman numerals, I for uppercase Roman numerals, a for lowercase letters, and A for uppercase letters.

   Standard: HTML 2

   Common: Yes

   Sample:

`<OL TYPE=a>`

  `<LI>Breakfast`

  `<LI>Mrs. Johnson will speak`

  `<LI>Demonstration`

  `<LI>Lunch`

`</OL>`

Other Attributes

This tag also accepts the lang, dir, onClick, onDblClick, onMouseDown, onMouseUp, onMouseOver, onMouse-Move, onMouseOut, onKeyPress, onKeyDown, and onKeyUp attributes. See the Element-Independent Attributes section of this reference for definitions and examples.

<OPTION>

Indicates items in a fill-out form selection list (see the <SELECT> tag).

   Standard: HTML 2

   Common: Yes

   Paired: No

   Sample:

`Select an artist from the 1970s:<SELECT NAME="artists">`

  `<OPTION>Boston`

  `<OPTION SELECTED>Pink Floyd`

  `<OPTION>Reo Speedwagon`

`</SELECT>`

Attribute Information

CLASS="..."

Indicate which style class applies to the element.

   Standard: HTML 4

   Common: No

   Sample:

`<OPTION NAME="color" CLASS="casual">`

DISABLED="..."

Denies access to the input method.

   Standard: HTML 4

   Common: No

Sample:

```
<OPTION VALUE="Bogus"
DISABLED>Nothing here
```

ID="*n*"

Assigns a unique ID selector to an instance of the `<OPTION>` tag. When you then assign a style to that ID selector, it affects only that one instance of the `<OPTION>` tag.

> **Standard**: HTML 4
> **Common**: No
> **Sample:**

```
<OPTION ID="123">Mastercard
```

SELECTED

Marks a selection list item as preselected.

> **Standard**: HTML 2
> **Common**: Yes
> **Sample:**

```
<OPTION SELECTED VALUE=1>Ice
Cream</OPTION>
```

TITLE="..."

Specifies text assigned to the tag. You might use this attribute for context-sensitive help within the document. Browsers may use this to show tool tips over the selection list option.

> **Standard**: HTML 4
> **Common**: No
> **Sample:**

```
<OPTION TITLE="Option">Thingie
```

VALUE="..."

Indicates which data is sent to the form processor if you choose the selection list item. If the VALUE= attribute is not present within the `<OPTION>` tag, the text between the `<OPTION>` tags is sent instead.

> **Standard**: HTML 2
> **Common**: Yes
> **Sample:**

```
<OPTION
VALUE=2>Sandwiches</OPTION>
```

Other Attributes

This tag also accepts the `lang`, `dir`, `onfocus`, `onblur`, `onchange`, `onselect`, `onClick`, `onDblClick`, `onMouseDown`, `onMouseUp`, `onMouseOver`, `onMouseMove`, `onMouseOut`, `onKeyPress`, `onKeyDown`, and `onKeyUp` attributes. See the Element-Independent Attributes section of this reference for definitions and examples.

P

`<P>`

Indicates a paragraph in a document.

> **Standard**: HTML 2
> **Common**: Yes
> **Paired**: Yes, optional
> **Sample:**

```
<P >As soon as she left, the
phone began ringing. "Hello," I
said after lifting the
receiver.</P>

<P>"Is she gone yet?" said the
voice on the other end.</P>
```

Attribute Information

ALIGN={LEFT, CENTER, RIGHT}

Aligns paragraph text flush left, flush right, or in the center of the document.

> **Standard**: HTML 3.2; deprecated in HTML 4 in favor of style sheets
> **Common**: Yes

Sample:

```
<P ALIGN=CENTER>There will be fun
and games for everyone!
```

CLASS="..."

Indicates which style class applies to the <P> element.

Standard: HTML 4

Common: No

Sample:

```
<P CLASS="casual">Tom turned at
the next street and stopped.
```

ID="n"

Assigns a unique ID selector to an instance of the <P> tag. When you then assign a style to that ID selector, it affects only that one instance of the <P> tag.

Standard: HTML 4

Common: No

Sample:

```
<P ID="123">This paragraph is
yellow on black!
```

STYLE="..."

Specifies style sheet commands that apply to the contents of the paragraph.

Standard: HTML 4

Common: No

Sample:

```
<P STYLE="background: red; color:
white">
```

TITLE="..."

Specifies text assigned to the tag. You might use this attribute for context-sensitive help within the document. Browsers may use this to show tool tips over the paragraph.

Standard: HTML 4

Common: No

Sample:

```
<P TITLE="Paragraph">
```

WIDTH="n"

Specifies the horizontal dimension of the paragraph (in pixels).

Standard: Internet Explorer 4

Common: No

Sample:

```
<P WIDTH=250>
```

Other Attributes

This tag also accepts the lang, dir, onClick, onDblClick, onMouseDown, onMouseUp, onMouseOver, onMouse-Move, onMouseOut, onKeyPress, onKeyDown, and onKeyUp attributes. See the Element-Independent Attributes section of this reference for definitions and examples.

<PARAM>

Specifies parameters passed to an embedded object. Use the <PARAM> tag within the <OBJECT> or <APPLET> tags.

Standard: HTML 4

Common: No

Paired: No

Sample:

```
<OBJECT CLASSID="/thingie.py">
 <PARAM NAME="thing" VALUE=1>
 Sorry. Your browser does not
 support embedded objects.
</OBJECT>
```

Attribute Information

DATAFLD="..."

Selects a column from a block of tabular data.

Standard: Internet Explorer 4

Common: No

Sample:

```
<PARAM DATA="dataview.ocx"
DATASRC="#data_table"
DATAFLD="datafld1">
```

DATASRC="..."

Specifies the location of tabular data to be bound within the document.

Standard: Internet Explorer 4

Common: No

Sample:

```
<PARAM DATA="dataview.ocx"
DATASRC="#data_table">
```

NAME="..."

Indicates the name of the parameter passed to the embedded object.

Standard: HTML 4

Common: No

Sample:

```
<PARAM NAME="startyear"
VALUE="1920">
```

TITLE="..."

Specifies text assigned to the tag. You might use this attribute for context-sensitive help within the document. Browsers may use this to show tool tips.

Standard: HTML 4

Common: No

Sample:

```
<PARAM TITLE="Object parameter
"NAME="size" VALUE="0">
```

TYPE="..."

Specifies the MIME type of the data found at the specified URL. Use this attribute with the VALUETYPE=REF attribute.

Standard: HTML 4

Common: No

Sample:

```
<PARAM NAME="data"
VALUE="/data/sim1.zip"
VALUETYPE=REF
TYPE="application/
x-zip-compressed">
```

VALUE="..."

Specifies the value associated with the parameter passed to the embedded object.

Standard: HTML 4

Common: No

Sample:

```
<PARAM NAME="startyear"
VALUE="1920">
```

VALUETYPE={REF, OBJECT, DATA}

Indicates the kind of value passed to the embedded object. VALUETYPE=REF indicates a URL passed to the embedded object. VALUETYPE=OBJECT indicates that the VALUE attribute specifies the location of object data. VALUETYPE= DATA indicates that the VALUE= attribute is set to a plain text string. Use this for passing alphanumeric data to the embedded object.

Standard: Internet Explorer 3, HTML 4

Common: No

Sample:

```
<PARAM NAME="length" VALUE="9"
VALUETYPE=DATA>
```

<PLAINTEXT>

Specifies that text appears as preformatted. This tag is obsolete; the <PRE> tag has replaced it.

Standard: Obsolete

Common: No

Paired: Yes

Sample:

```
<PLAINTEXT>Now go to the store
and buy:
Wrapping paper
Tape
Markers
</PLAINTEXT>
```

<PRE>

Contains preformatted plain text. This is useful for including computer program output or source code within your document.

Standard: HTML 2

Common: Yes

Paired: Yes

Sample:

```
Here's the source code:
<PRE>
#include <stdio.h>
void main()
{
  printf("Hello World!\n");
}
</PRE>
```

Attribute Information

CLASS="..."

Indicates which style class applies to the <PRE> element.

Standard: HTML 4

Common: No

Sample:

```
<PRE CLASS="casual">BBQ
INFO</PRE>
```

ID="..."

Assigns a unique ID selector to an instance of the <PRE> tag. When you then assign a style to that ID selector, it affects only that one instance of the <PRE> tag.

Standard: HTML 4

Common: No

Sample:

```
An example of an emotion:
<PRE ID="123">

  :-)

</PRE>
```

STYLE="..."

Specifies style sheet commands that apply to the contents within the <PRE> tags.

Standard: HTML 4

Common: Yes

Sample:

```
<PRE STYLE="background : red">
```

TITLE="..."

Specifies text assigned to the tag. You might use this attribute for context-sensitive help within the document. Browsers may use this to show tool tips over the preformatted text.

Standard: HTML 4

Common: No

Sample:

```
<PRE TITLE="preformatted text">
```

WIDTH="*n*"

Specifies the horizontal dimension of the preformatted text (in pixels).

Standard: HTML 4

Common: No

Sample:

```
<PRE WIDTH=80>
```

Other Attributes

This tag also accepts the `lang`, `dir`, `onClick`, `onDblClick`, `onMouseDown`, `onMouseUp`, `onMouseOver`, `onMouse-Move`, `onMouseOut`, `onKeyPress`, `onKeyDown`, and `onKeyUp` attributes. See the Element-Independent Attributes section of this reference for definitions and examples.

Q

<Q>

Quotes a direct source within a paragraph. Use <BLOCKQUOTE> to signify only a longer or block quotation.

> **Standard**: HTML 4
> **Common**: No
> **Paired**: Yes
> **Sample**:

```
Dr. Henry remarked <Q>I really
like the procedure.</Q>
```

Attribute Information

CITE="..."
Specifies a reference URL for a quotation.

> **Standard**: HTML 4
> **Common**: No
> **Sample**:

```
<BLOCKQUOTE
CITE="http://www.clement.moore
.com/xmas.html">

Twas the night..."

</BLOCKQUOTE>
```

CLASS="..."
Indicates which style class applies to the <BLOCKQUOTE> element.

> **Standard**: HTML 4
> **Common**: No
> **Sample**:

```
<BLOCKQUOTE CLASS="casual">

Twas the night before
Christmas...</BLOCKQUOTE>
```

ID="..."
Assigns a unique ID selector to an instance of the <BLOCKQUOTE> tag. When you then assign a style to that ID selector, it affects only that one instance of the <BLOCKQUOTE> tag.

> **Standard**: HTML 4
> **Common**: No
> **Sample**:

```
On July 12, John wrote a profound
sentence in his diary:

<BLOCKQUOTE ID="123">I woke up
this morning at nine and it was
raining.</BLOCKQUOTE>
```

STYLE="..."
Specifies style sheet commands that apply to the contents within the <BLOCKQUOTE> tags.

> **Standard**: HTML 4
> **Common**: No
> **Sample**:

```
<BLOCKQUOTE STYLE="background:
red">
```

TITLE="..."
Specifies text assigned to the tag. You might use this attribute for context-sensitive help within the document. Browsers may use this to show tool tips over the quoted text.

> **Standard**: HTML 4
> **Common**: No
> **Sample**:

```
<BLOCKQUOTE TITLE="Quotation">
```

Other Attributes

This tag also accepts the `lang`, `dir`, `onClick`, `onDblClick`, `onMouseDown`, `onMouseUp`, `onMouseOver`, `onMouse-Move`, `onMouseOut`, `onKeyPress`, `onKeyDown`, and `onKeyUp` attributes. See the Element-Independent Attributes section of this reference for definitions and examples.

S

<SAMP>

Indicates a sequence of literal characters.

    Standard: HTML 2
    Common: Yes
    Paired: Yes
    Sample:

```
An example of a palindrome is the
word <SAMP>TOOT</SAMP>.
```

Attribute Information

CLASS="..."

Indicates which style class applies to the <SAMP> element.

    Standard: HTML 4
    Common: No
    Sample:

```
The PC screen read:

<SAMP CLASS="casual">Command Not
Found</SAMP>
```

ID="..."

Assigns a unique ID selector to an instance of the <SAMP> tag. When you then assign a style to that ID selector, it affects only that one instance of the <SAMP> tag.

    Standard: HTML 4
    Common: No

    Sample:

```
Just for fun, think of how many
words end with the letters
<SAMP ID="123">ing</SAMP>.
```

STYLE="..."

Specifies style sheet commands that apply to the contents within the <SAMP> tags.

    Standard: HTML 4
    Common: Yes
    Sample:

```
<SAMP STYLE="background: red">
```

TITLE="..."

Specifies text assigned to the tag. You might use this attribute for context-sensitive help within the document. Browsers may use this to show tool tips.

    Standard: HTML 4
    Common: No
    Sample:

```
<SAMP TITLE="Sample">
```

Other Attributes

This tag also accepts the `lang`, `dir`, `onClick`, `onDblClick`, `onMouseDown`, `onMouseUp`, `onMouseOver`, `onMouse-Move`, `onMouseOut`, `onKeyPress`, `onKeyDown`, and `onKeyUp` attributes. See the Element-Independent Attributes section of this reference for definitions and examples.

<SCRIPT>

Contains browser script code. Examples include JavaScript and VBScript. It is a good idea to place the actual script code within the comment tags so that browsers that don't support the <SCRIPT> tag code can ignore it.

    Standard: HTML 3.2
    Common: Yes

Paired: Yes

Sample:

```
<SCRIPT LANGUAGE="JavaScript">
<!- . . . ->
</SCRIPT>
```

Attribute Information

LANGUAGE="..."
Indicates the type of script.

Standard: HTML 4,
           Internet Explorer

Common: Yes

Sample:

```
<SCRIPT LANGUAGE="JavaScript">
```

SRC="*URL*"
Specifies the relative or absolute location of a script to include in the document.

Standard: HTML 4,
           Internet Explorer

Common: Yes

Sample:

```
<SCRIPT type="text/javascript"
SRC="http://www.some.com/sc/
script.js">
</SCRIPT>
```

TYPE="..."
Indicates the MIME type of the script. This is an alternative to the LANGUAGE attribute for declaring the type of scripting.

Standard: HTML 3.2

Common: Yes

Sample:

```
<SCRIPT type="text/javascript">
 document.write
 ("<EM>Great!<\/EM>")
</SCRIPT>
```

<SELECT>

Specifies a selection list within a form. Use the <OPTION> tags to specify items in the selection list.

Standard: HTML 2

Common: Yes

Paired: Yes

Sample:

```
What do you use our product
for?<BR>
<SELECT MULTIPLE NAME="use">
  <OPTION VALUE=1>Pest control
  <OPTION VALUE=2>Automotive
  lubricant
  <OPTION VALUE=3>Preparing
  pastries
  <OPTION SELECTED VALUE=4>
  Personal hygiene
  <OPTION VALUE=5>Other
</SELECT>
```

Attribute Information

ACCESSKEY="..."
Indicates a keystroke sequence associated with the selection list.

Standard: HTML 4

Common: No

Sample:

```
<SELECT NAME="size" ACCESSKEY=S>
```

CLASS="..."
Indicates which style class applies to the element.

Standard: HTML 4

Common: No

Sample:

```
<SELECT NAME="color"
CLASS="casual">
```

DATAFLD="..."

Indicates a column from previously identified tabular data.

Standard: Internet Explorer 4

Common: No

Sample:

```
<SELECT NAME="color"
DATASRC="#data_table"
DATAFLD="clr">
```

DISABLED

Denies access to the selection list.

Standard: HTML 4

Common: No

Sample:

```
<SELECT NAME="color" DISABLED>
```

ID="..."

Assigns a unique ID selector to an instance of the <SELECT> tag. When you then assign a style to that ID selector, it affects only that one instance of the <SELECT> tag.

Standard: Internet Explorer 4

Common: No

Sample:

```
<SELECT ID="123" NAME="salary">
```

MULTIPLE

Indicates that a visitor can select more than one selection list item at the same time.

Standard: HTML 2

Common: Yes

Sample:

```
<SELECT MULTIPLE>
```

NAME="..."

Gives a name to the value you are passing to the form processor. This establishes a *name-value pair* with which the form processor application can work.

Standard: HTML 2

Common: Yes

Sample:

```
What is your shoe size?
<SELECT SIZE=4 NAME="size">
   <OPTION>
   <OPTION>
   <OPTION>
   <OPTION>
   <OPTION>
   <OPTION>
</SELECT>
```

READONLY

Indicates that your visitor cannot modify values within the selection list.

Standard: Internet Explorer 4

Common: No

Sample:

```
<SELECT NAME="color" READONLY>
```

SIZE="*n*"

Specifies the number of visible items in the selection list. If there are more items in the selection list than are visible, a scrollbar provides access to the other items.

Standard: HTML 2

Common: Yes

Sample:

```
<SELECT SIZE=3>
```

STYLE="..."

Specifies style sheet commands that apply to the contents within the <SELECT> tags.

Standard: HTML 4

Common: Yes

Sample:

```
<SELECT STYLE="background: red"
NAME="color">
```

TABINDEX="*n*"

Indicates where in the tabbing order the selection list is placed.

Standard: HTML 4

Common: No

Sample:

`<SELECT NAME="salary TABINDEX=3>`

TITLE="..."

Specifies text assigned to the tag. You might use this attribute for context-sensitive help within the document. Browsers may use this to show tool tips over the selection list.

Standard: HTML 4

Common: No

Sample:

`<SELECT TITLE="Select List" NAME="Car">`

Other Attributes

This tag also accepts the `lang`, `dir`, `onfocus`, `onblur`, `onchange`, `onselect`, `onClick`, `onDblClick`, `onMouseDown`, `onMouseUp`, `onMouseOver`, `onMouseMove`, `onMouseOut`, `onKeyPress`, `onKeyDown`, and `onKeyUp` attributes. See the Element-Independent Attributes section of this reference for definitions and examples.

<SMALL>

Specifies text that should appear in a small font.

Standard: HTML 3.2

Common: Yes

Paired: Yes

Sample:

`<P>Our lawyers said we need to include some small print:`

`<P><SMALL>By reading this document, you are breaking the rules and will be assessed a $2000 fine.</SMALL>`

Attribute Information

CLASS="..."

Indicates which style class applies to the <SMALL> element.

Standard: HTML 4

Common: No

Sample:

`<SMALL CLASS="casual">Void where prohibited</SMALL>`

ID="..."

Assigns a unique ID selector to an instance of the <SMALL> tag. When you then assign a style to that ID selector, it affects only that one instance of the <SMALL> tag.

Standard: HTML 4

Common: No

Sample:

`Most insects are <SMALL ID="123">small</SMALL>.`

STYLE="..."

Specifies style sheet commands that apply to the contents within the <SMALL> tags.

Standard: HTML 4

Common: Yes

Sample:

`<SMALL STYLE="background: red">`

TITLE="..."

Specifies text assigned to the tag. You might use this attribute for context-sensitive help within the document. Browsers may use this to show tool tips over the text inside the <SMALL> tags.

Standard: HTML 4

Common: No

Sample:

```
<SMALL TITLE="Legalese">Actually
doing any of this will subject
you to risk of criminal prosecu-
tion.</SMALL>
```

Other Attributes

This tag also accepts the `lang`, `dir`, `onClick`, `onDblClick`, `onMouseDown`, `onMouseUp`, `onMouseOver`, `onMouse-Move`, `onMouseOut`, `onKeyPress`, `onKeyDown`, and `onKeyUp` attributes. See the Element-Independent Attributes section of this reference for definitions and examples.

<SPACER>

A Netscape-specific tag that specifies a blank space within the document. We recommend using style sheets or other formatting techniques unless you're developing documents exclusively for visitors using Netscape Navigator.

Standard: Netscape Navigator 4

Common: No

Paired: No

Sample:

```
<SPACER TYPE=HORIZONTAL SIZE=150>
Doctors Prefer MediWidget 4 to 1
```

Attribute Information

SIZE="*n*"

Specifies the dimension of the spacer (in pixels).

Standard: Netscape Navigator 3

Common: No

Sample:

```
<SPACER TYPE=HORIZONTAL SIZE=50>
<IMG SRC="rosebush.jpg">
```

TYPE={HORIZONTAL, VERTICAL}

Indicates whether the spacer measures from left to right or from top to bottom.

Standard: Netscape Navigator 3

Common: No

Sample:

```
<P>After you've done this, take a
moment to review your work.
<SPACER TYPE=VERTICAL SIZE=400>
<P>Now, isn't that better?
```

<SPAN>

Defines an inline section of a document affected by style sheet attributes. Use <DIV> to apply styles at the block-element level.

Standard: HTML 4

Common: No

Paired: Yes

Sample:

```
<SPAN STYLE="background:
red">...</SPAN>
```

Attribute Information

CLASS="..."

Indicates which style class applies to the <SPAN> element.

Standard: HTML 4

Common: No

Sample:

```
<SPAN CLASS="casual">
```

DATAFLD="..."

Selects a column from a previously identified source of tabular data (see the DATASRC= attribute).

Standard: Internet Explorer 4

Common: No

Sample:

```
<SPAN DATASRC="#data_table">
  <SPAN DATAFLD="name"></SPAN>
</SPAN>
```

DATAFORMATAS={TEXT, HTML, NONE}

Indicates the format of tabular data within the <SPAN> element.

Standard: Internet Explorer 4

Common: No

Sample:

```
<SPAN DATAFORMATAS=HTML
DATASRC="#data_table">
```

DATASRC="..."

Specifies the source of data for data binding.

Standard: Internet Explorer 4

Common: No

Sample:

```
<SPAN DATASRC="#data_table">
```

ID="..."

Assigns a unique ID selector to an instance of the <SPAN> tag. When you then assign a style to that ID selector, it affects only that one instance of the <SPAN> tag.

Standard: HTML 4

Common: No

Sample:

```
<SPAN ID="123">
```

STYLE="..."

Specifies style sheet commands that apply to the contents within the <SPAN> tags.

Standard: HTML 4

Common: No

Sample:

```
<SPAN STYLE="background: red">
```

TITLE="..."

Specifies text assigned to the tag. You might use this attribute for context-sensitive help within the document. Browsers may use this to show tool tips.

Standard: HTML 4

Common: No

Sample:

```
<SPAN TITLE="Section"
STYLE="background: red">
```

Other Attributes

This tag also accepts the lang, dir, onClick, onDblClick, onMouseDown, onMouseUp, onMouseOver, onMouse-Move, onMouseOut, onKeyPress, onKeyDown, and onKeyUp attributes. See the Element-Independent Attributes section of this reference for definitions and examples.

<STRIKE>, <S>

Indicate a strikethrough text style.

Standard: HTML 3.2; deprecated in HTML 4 in favor of style sheets

Common: Yes

Paired: Yes

Sample:

```
My junior high biology teacher
was <STRIKE>sorta</STRIKE> really
smart.
```

Attribute Information

CLASS="..."
Indicates which style class applies to the <STRIKE> element.

>Standard: HTML 4
>
>Common: No
>
>Sample:

```
<STRIKE CLASS="casual">Truman
</STRIKE> lost.
```

ID="..."
Assigns a unique ID selector to an instance of the <STRIKE> tag. When you then assign a style to that ID selector, it affects only that one instance of the <STRIKE> tag.

>Standard: HTML 4
>
>Common: No
>
>Sample:

```
Don <STRIKE ID="123">ain't
</STRIKE>isn't coming tonight.
```

STYLE="..."
Specifies style sheet commands that apply to the contents within the <STRIKE> tags.

>Standard: HTML 4
>
>Common: No
>
>Sample:

```
<STRIKE STYLE="background: red">
```

TITLE="..."
Specifies text assigned to the tag. You might use this attribute for context-sensitive help within the document. Browsers may use this to show tool tips over the text.

>Standard: HTML 4
>
>Common: No
>
>Sample:

```
He was <STRIKE TITLE="omit">
Ambitious</STRIKE>
<B>Enthusiastic</B>.
```

Other Attributes
This tag also accepts the lang, dir, onClick, onDblClick, onMouseDown, onMouseUp, onMouseOver, onMouse-Move, onMouseOut, onKeyPress, onKeyDown, and onKeyUp attributes. See the Element-Independent Attributes section of this reference for definitions and examples.

<STRONG>

Indicates strong emphasis. The browser will probably display the text in a bold-face font.

>Standard: HTML 2
>
>Common: Yes
>
>Paired: Yes
>
>Sample:

```
If you see a poisonous spider in
the room then <STRONG>Get out of
there!</STRONG>
```

Attribute Information

CLASS="..."
Indicates which style class applies to the <STRONG> element.

>Standard: HTML 4
>
>Common: No
>
>Sample:

```
Did you say my dog is
<STRONG CLASS="casual">DEAD?!
</STRONG>
```

ID="..."

Assigns a unique ID selector to an instance of the <STRONG> tag. When you then assign a style to that ID selector, it affects only that one instance of the <STRONG> tag.

> **Standard:**   HTML 4
>
> **Common:**   No
>
> **Sample:**

```
Sure, you can win at gambling.
But it's more likely you will
<STRONG ID="123">lose</STRONG>.
```

STYLE="..."

Specifies style sheet commands that apply to the contents within the <STRONG> tags.

> **Standard:**   HTML 4
>
> **Common:**   No
>
> **Sample:**

```
<STRONG STYLE="background: red">
```

TITLE="..."

Specifies text assigned to the tag. You might use this attribute for context-sensitive help within the document. Browsers may use this to show tool tips over the emphasized text.

> **Standard:**   HTML 4
>
> **Common:**   No
>
> **Sample:**

```
I mean it was <STRONG
TITLE="emphasis">HOT!</STRONG>
```

Other Attributes

This tag also accepts the `lang`, `dir`, `onClick`, `onDblClick`, `onMouseDown`, `onMouseUp`, `onMouseOver`, `onMouseMove`, `onMouseOut`, `onKeyPress`, `onKeyDown`, and `onKeyUp` attributes. See the Element-Independent Attributes section of this reference for definitions and examples.

<STYLE>

Contains style sheet definitions and appears in the document head (see the <HEAD> tag). Place style sheet data within the comment tags (<!--... -->) to accommodate browsers that do not support the <STYLE> tag.

> **Standard:**   HTML 3.2
>
> **Common:**   No
>
> **Paired:**   Yes
>
> **Sample:**

```
<HTML>
<HEAD>
<TITLE>Edible Socks: Good or
Bad?</TITLE>
<STYLE TYPE="text/css">
<!--
  @import url(http://www.raycomm
  .com/mhtml/styles.css)
  H1 { background: black; color:
yellow }
  LI DD { background: silver;
color: black }
-->
</STYLE>
</HEAD>
```

Attribute Information

MEDIA="..."

Specifies the destination medium for style information. It may be a single type or a comma-separated list. Media types include the following:

Screen—for online viewing (default setting)

Print—for traditional printed material and for documents on screen viewed in print preview mode

Projection—for projectors

Braille—for Braille tactile feedback device

Speech—for a speech synthesizer

All—applies to all devices

Standard: HTML 4
Common: No
Sample:

```
<HEAD>
<TITLE>Washington DC
Taverns</TITLE>
<STYLE TYPE="text/css"
MEDIA="all">
<!--
  @import url(Error! Bookmark not
defined.
  H1 { background: black; color:
white}
  LI DD { background: silver;
color: darkgreen }
-->
</STYLE>
</HEAD>
```

TITLE="..."
Specifies text assigned to the tag. You might use this attribute for context-sensitive help within the document. Browsers may use this to show tool tips.

Standard: HTML 4
Common: No
Sample:

```
<STYLE TITLE="Stylesheet 1"
TYPE="text/css">
<!-- H1 { background: black;
color: yellow }
  LI DD { background: silver;
color: black }
-->
</SCRIPT>
```

TYPE="..."
Specifies the MIME type of the style sheet specification standard used.

Standard: HTML 4
Common: No
Sample:

```
<HEAD>
<TITLE>Washington DC
Taverns</TITLE>
<STYLE TYPE="text/css">
<!--
  @import url(Error! Bookmark not
defined.
  H1 { background: black; color:
white}
  LI DD { background: silver;
color: darkgreen }
-->
</STYLE>
</HEAD>
```

Other Attributes
This tag also accepts the `lang` and `dir` attributes. See the Element-Independent Attributes section of this reference for definitions and examples.

<SUB>

Indicates subscript text.

Standard: HTML 3.2
Common: Yes
Paired: Yes
Sample:

```
<P>Chemists refer to water as
H<SUB>2</SUB>O.
```

Attribute Information

CLASS="..."
Indicates which style class applies to the <SUB> element.

Standard: HTML 4

Common: No

Sample:

```
<SUB CLASS="casual">2</SUB>
```

ID="..."

Assigns a unique ID selector to an instance of the <SUB> tag. When you then assign a style to that ID selector, it affects only that one instance of the <SUB> tag.

Standard: HTML 4

Common: No

Sample:

```
. . . At the dentist I ask for lots of
NO<SUB ID="123">2</SUB>.
```

STYLE="..."

Specifies style sheet commands that apply to the contents within the <SUB> tags.

Standard: HTML 4

Common: No

Sample:

```
<SUB STYLE="background: red">
```

TITLE="..."

Specifies text assigned to the tag. You might use this attribute for context-sensitive help within the document. Browsers may use this to show tool tips over the subscripted text.

Standard: HTML 4

Common: No

Sample:

```
Before he died, he uttered,
"Groovy."<SUB
TITLE="Footnote">2</SUB>
```

Other Attributes

This tag also accepts the lang, dir, onClick, onDblClick, onMouseDown, onMouseUp, onMouseOver, onMouse-Move, onMouseOut, onKeyPress, onKeyDown, and onKeyUp attributes. See the Element-Independent Attributes section of this reference for definitions and examples.

<SUP>

Indicates superscript text.

Standard: HTML 3.2

Common: Yes

Paired: Yes

Sample:

```
<P>Einstein's most famous equa-
tion is probably E=mc<SUP>2</SUP>.
```

Attribute Information

CLASS="..."

Indicates which style class applies to the <SUP> element.

Standard: HTML 4

Common: No

Sample:

```
<STYLE>
<!--
  SUP.casual {background: black;
    color: yellow}
-->
</STYLE>

. . .

z<SUP CLASS="casual">2</SUP> =
x<SUP CLASS="casual">2</SUP> +
y<SUP CLASS="casual">2</SUP>
```

ID="..."

Assigns a unique ID selector to an instance of the <PRE> tag. When you then assign a style to that ID selector, it affects only that one instance of the <SUP> tag.

> **Standard:** HTML 4
> **Common:** No
> **Sample:**

```
<STYLE>
<!--
  #123 {background: black;
    color: yellow}
-->
</STYLE>
. . . Pythagorean theorem says
z<SUP ID="123">2</SUP>=4+16.
```

STYLE="..."

Specifies style sheet commands that apply to the contents within the <SUP> tags.

> **Standard:** HTML 4
> **Common:** No
> **Sample:**

```
<SUP STYLE="background: red">
```

TITLE="..."

Specifies text assigned to the tag. You might use this attribute for context-sensitive help within the document. Browsers may use this to show tool tips over the superscripted text.

> **Standard:** HTML 4
> **Common:** No
> **Sample:**

```
x<SUP TITLE="Exponent">2</SUP>
```

Other Attributes

This tag also accepts the lang, dir, onClick, onDblClick, onMouseDown, onMouseUp, onMouseOver, onMouse-Move, onMouseOut, onKeyPress, onKeyDown, and onKeyUp attributes. See the Element-Independent Attributes section of this reference for definitions and examples.

T

<TABLE>

Specifies a container for a table within your document. Inside these tags you can place <TR>, <TD>, <TH>, <CAPTION>, and other <TABLE> tags.

> **Standard:** HTML 3.2
> **Common:** Yes
> **Paired:** Yes
> **Sample:**

```
<TABLE BORDER=0>  <TR>
    <TD><IMG SRC="Pine.jpg"
BORDER=0 ALT="Pine"></TD>
    <TD VALIGN=MIDDLE><P>Pine
trees naturally grow at higher
elevations.
    They require less water and
do not shed leaves in the
fall.</TD>  </TR>
</TABLE>
```

Attribute Information

ALIGN={LEFT, CENTER, RIGHT}

Positions the table flush left, flush right, or in the center of the window.

> **Standard:** HTML 3.2
> **Common:** Yes
> **Sample:**

```
<TABLE ALIGN=CENTER>
```

BACKGROUND="*URL*"

Specifies the relative or absolute location of a graphic image file loaded as a background image for the entire table.

Standard: Internet Explorer 3, Netscape Navigator 4

Common: No

Sample:

`<TABLE BACKGROUND="paper.jpg">`

BGCOLOR="*#RRGGBB*" or "*...*"

Specifies the background color within all table cells in the table. You can substitute color names for the hexadecimal RGB values.

Standard: Deprecated in HTML 4 in favor of style sheets

Common: No

Sample:

`<TABLE BGCOLOR="Peach">`

BORDER="*n*"

Specifies the thickness (in pixels) of borders around each table cell. Use a value of 0 to produce a table with no visible borders.

Standard: HTML 3.2

Common: Yes

Sample:

`<TABLE BORDER=0>`

BORDERCOLOR="*#RRGGBB*" or "*...*"

Specifies the color of the borders of all the table cells in the table. You can substitute color names for the hexadecimal RGB values.

Standard: Internet Explorer 3.0

Common: No

Sample:

`<TABLE BORDERCOLOR=#3F9A11>`

BORDERCOLORDARK="*#RRGGBB*" or "*...*"

Specifies the darker color used to draw 3-D borders around the table cells. You can substitute color names for the hexadecimal RGB values.

Standard: Internet Explorer 4

Common: No

Sample:

`<TABLE BORDERCOLORDARK="silver">`

BORDERCOLORLIGHT="*#RRGGBB*" or "*...*"

Specifies the lighter color used to draw 3-D borders around the table cells. You can substitute color names for the hexadecimal RGB values.

Standard: Internet Explorer 4

Common: No

Sample:

`<TABLE BORDERCOLORLIGHT="white">`

CELLPADDING="*n*"

Specifies the space (in pixels) between the edges of table cells and their contents.

Standard: HTML 3.2

Common: Yes

Sample:

`<TABLE CELLPADDING=5>`

CELLSPACING="*n*"

Specifies the space (in pixels) between the borders of table cells and the borders of adjacent cells.

Standard: HTML 3.2

Common: Yes

Sample:

`<TABLE BORDER=2 CELLSPACING=5>`

CLASS="..."
Indicates which style class applies to the
<TABLE> element.

   Standard: HTML 4

   Common: No

   Sample:

<TABLE CLASS="casual" BORDER=2>

COLS="n"
Specifies the number of columns in the
table.

   Standard: HTML 4

   Common: No

   Sample:

<TABLE BORDER=2 COLS=5>

FRAME={VOID, BORDER, ABOVE, BELOW, HSIDES, LHS, RHS, VSIDES, BOX}
Specifies the external border lines
around the table. For the FRAME=
attribute to work, set the BORDER=
attribute with a non-zero value.

FRAME=VOID indicates no border lines.

FRAME=BOX or FRAME=BORDER indicates border lines around the entire
table. This is the default.

FRAME=ABOVE specifies a border line
along the top edge.

FRAME=BELOW draws a border line along
the bottom edge.

FRAME=HSIDES draws border lines along
the top and bottom edges.

FRAME=LHS indicates a border line along
the left side.

FRAME=RHS draws a border line along
the right edge.

FRAME=VSIDES draws border lines along
the left and right edges.

   Standard: HTML 4

   Common: No

   Sample:

<TABLE BORDER=2 RULES=ALL
FRAME=VSIDES>

ID="n"
Assigns a unique ID selector to an
instance of the <TABLE> tag. When you
then assign a style to that ID selector, it
affects only that one instance of the
<TABLE> tag.

   Standard: HTML 4

   Common: No

   Sample:

<TABLE ID="123">

RULES={NONE, ROWS, COLS, GROUPS, ALL}
Specifies where rule lines appear inside
the table. For the RULES= attribute to
work, set the BORDER= attribute.

RULES=NONE indicates no rule lines.

RULES=ROWS indicates rule lines
between rows.

RULES=COLS draws rule lines between
columns.

RULES=ALL draws all possible rule lines.

RULES=GROUPS specifies rule lines
between the groups defined by the
<TFOOT>, <THEAD>, <TBODY>, and
<COLGROUP> tags.

   Standard: HTML 4

   Common: No

   Sample:

<TABLE BORDER=2 RULES=BASIC>

STYLE="..."
Specifies style sheet commands that
apply to the contents of cells in the table.

Standard: HTML 4

Common: No

Sample:

```
<TABLE STYLE="background: red">
```

TITLE="..."

Specifies text assigned to the tag. You might use this attribute for context-sensitive help within the document. Browsers may use this to show tool tips over the table.

Standard: HTML 4

Common: No

Sample:

```
<TABLE TITLE="Table">
```

WIDTH="*n*"

Specifies the width of the table. You can set this value to an absolute number of pixels or to a percentage amount so that the table is proportionally as wide as the available space.

Standard: HTML 3.2

Common: Yes

Sample:

```
<TABLE ALIGN=CENTER WIDTH="60%">
```

Other Attributes

This tag also accepts the lang, dir, onClick, onDblClick, onMouseDown, onMouseUp, onMouseOver, onMouse-Move, onMouseOut, onKeyPress, onKeyDown, and onKeyUp attributes. See the Element-Independent Attributes section of this reference for definitions and examples.

<TBODY>

Defines the table body within a table. This tag must *follow* the <TFOOT> tag.

Standard: HTML 4

Common: No

Paired: Yes

Sample:

```
<TABLE>
<THEAD>...
</THEAD>
<TFOOT>...
</TFOOT>
<TBODY>...
</TBODY>
```

Attribute Information

ALIGN="{LEFT, RIGHT, CENTER, JUSTIFY, CHAR}"

Specifies how text within the table footer will line up with the edges of the table cells, or if ALIGN=CHAR, on a specific character (the decimal point).

Standard: HTML 4

Common: Yes

Sample:

```
<TR>
<THEAD>
<TH><B>Television</B></TH>
<TH> <IMG SRC="tv.gif" ALT="TV"
BORDER="0">  </TH>
</THEAD>
</TR>
```

CHAR="..."

Specifies the character on which cell contents will align, if ALIGN="CHAR". If you omit CHAR=, the default value is the decimal point in the specified language.

Standard: HTML 4

Common: No

Sample:

```
<THEAD ALIGN="CHAR" CHAR=",">
```

CHAROFF="*n*"
Specifies the number of characters from the left at which the alignment character appears.

> **Standard**: HTML 4
> **Common**: No
> **Sample**:

```
<THEAD ALIGN="CHAR" CHAR=","
CHAROFF="7">
```

CLASS="..."
Indicates which style class applies to the <TBODY> element.

> **Standard**: HTML 4
> **Common**: No
> **Sample**:

```
<TBODY CLASS="casual">
```

ID="*n*"
Assigns a unique ID selector to an instance of the <TBODY> tag. When you then assign a style to that ID selector, it affects only that one instance of the <TBODY> tag.

> **Standard**: HTML 4
> **Common**: No
> **Sample**:

```
<TBODY ID="123">
```

STYLE="..."
Specifies style sheet commands that apply to the contents between the <TBODY> tags.

> **Standard**: HTML 4
> **Common**: No
> **Sample**:

```
<TBODY STYLE="background: red">
```

TITLE="..."
Specifies text assigned to the tag. You might use this attribute for context-sensitive help within the document. Browsers may use this to show tool tips over the table body.

> **Standard**: HTML 4
> **Common**: No
> **Sample**:

```
<TBODY TITLE="Table Body">
```

VALIGN={TOP, BOTTOM, MIDDLE, BASELINE}
Specifies the vertical alignment of the contents of the table body.

> **Standard**: Internet Explorer 4
> **Common**: No
> **Sample**:

```
<TBODY VALIGN=MIDDLE>
```

Other Attributes
This tag also accepts the lang, dir, onClick, onDblClick, onMouseDown, onMouseUp, onMouseOver, onMouse-Move, onMouseOut, onKeyPress, onKeyDown, and onKeyUp attributes. See the Element-Independent Attributes section of this reference for definitions and examples.

<TD>

Contains a table cell. These tags go inside the <TR> tags.

> **Standard**: HTML 3.2
> **Common**: Yes
> **Paired**: Yes
> **Sample**:

```
<TR>
  <TD>Bob Jones</TD>
  <TD>555-1212</TD>
  <TD>Democrat</TD>
</TR>
```

Attribute Information

ALIGN={LEFT, RIGHT, CENTER, JUSTIFY, CHAR}

Specifies how text within the table header will line up with the edges of the table cells, or if ALIGN=CHAR, on a specific character (the decimal point).

Standard: HTML 4

Common: Yes

Sample:

```
<TR>
   <TD><B>Television</B></TD>
   <TD> <IMG SRC="tv.gif" ALT="TV"
   BORDER=0> </TD>
</TR>
```

AXIS="..."

Specifies an abbreviated cell name.

Standard: HTML 4

Common: No

Sample:

```
<TD AXIS="TV"><B>Television</B>
</TD>
```

AXES="..."

Lists AXIS values that pertain to the cell.

Standard: HTML 4

Common: No

Sample:

```
<TD AXES="TV,
Programs"><B>Television</B></TD>
```

BACKGROUND="URL"

Specifies the relative or absolute location of a graphic image file for the browser to load as a background graphic for the table cell.

Standard: Internet Explorer, Netscape Navigator

Common: No

Sample:

```
<TD BACKGROUND="waves.gif">
```

BGCOLOR="#RRGGBB" or "..."

Specifies the background color inside a table cell. You can substitute the hexadecimal RGB values for the appropriate color names.

Standard: Deprecated in HTML 4 in favor of style sheets

Common: No

Sample:

```
<TR><TD BGCOLOR="Pink">Course
Number</TD>
<TD BGCOLOR="Blue">Time
taught</TD></TR>
```

BORDERCOLOR="#RRGGBB" or "..."

Indicates the color of the border of the table cell. You can specify the color with hexadecimal RGB values or by the color name.

Standard: Internet Explorer 2

Common: No

Sample:

```
<TR><TD BORDERCOLOR="Blue">
```

BORDERCOLORDARK="#RRGGBB" or "..."

Indicates the darker color used to form 3-D borders around the table cell. You can specify the color with its hexadecimal RGB values or with its color name.

Standard: Internet Explorer 4

Common: No

Sample:

```
<TD BORDERCOLORLIGHT=#FFFFFF
BORDERCOLORDARK=#88AA2C>
```

BORDERCOLORLIGHT="#*RRGGBB*" or "..."

Indicates the lighter color used to form 3-D borders around the table cell. You can specify the color with its hexadecimal RGB values or with its color name.

Standard: Internet Explorer 4

Common: No

Sample:

```
<TD BORDERCOLORLIGHT=#FFFFFF
BORDERCOLORDARK=#88AA2C>
```

CHAR="..."

Specifies the character on which cell contents will align, if ALIGN="CHAR". If you omit CHAR=, the default value is the decimal point in the specified language.

Standard: HTML 4

Common: No

Sample:

```
<TD ALIGN="CHAR" CHAR=",">
```

CHAROFF="*n*"

Specifies the number of characters from the left at which the alignment character appears.

Standard: HTML 4

Common: No

Sample:

```
<TD ALIGN="CHAR" CHAR=","
CHAROFF="7">
```

CLASS="..."

Indicates which style class applies to the <TD> element.

Standard: HTML 4

Common: No

Sample:

```
<TD CLASS="casual">Jobs
Produced</TD>
```

COLSPAN="*n*"

Specifies that a table cell occupy one column more than the default of one. This is useful when you have a category name that applies to more than one column of data.

Standard: HTML 3.2

Common: Yes

Sample:

```
<TR><TD COLSPAN=2>Students</TD>
</TR>

<TR><TD>Bob Smith</TDH><TD>John
Doe</TD></TR>
```

ID="*n*"

Assigns a unique ID selector to an instance of the <TD> tag. When you then assign a style to that ID selector, it affects only that one instance of the <TD> tag.

Standard: HTML 4

Common: No

Sample:

```
<TD ID="123">
```

NOWRAP

Disables the default word-wrapping within a table cell, thus maximizing the amount of the cell's horizontal space.

Standard: Deprecated in HTML 4 in favor of style sheets

Common: No

Sample:

```
<TD NOWRAP>The contents of this
cell will not wrap at all</TD>
```

ROWSPAN="*n*"

Specifies that a table cell occupy more rows than the default of 1. This is useful when several rows of information are related to one category.

Standard: HTML 3.2

Common: Yes

Sample:

```
<TR><TD VALIGN=MIDDLE ALIGN=RIGHT
ROWSPAN=3>Pie Entries</TD>

<TD>Banana Cream</TD>
<TD>Mrs. Robinson</TD></TR>

<TR><TD>Strawberry
Cheesecake</TD>
<TD>Mrs. Barton</TD></TR>

<TR><TD>German Chocolate</TD>
<TD>Mrs. Larson</TD></TR>
```

STYLE="..."

Specifies style sheet commands that apply to the contents of the table cell.

> **Standard:** HTML 4
>
> **Common:** No
>
> **Sample:**

```
<TD STYLE="background: red">
```

TITLE="..."

Specifies text assigned to the tag. You might use this attribute for context-sensitive help within the document. Browsers may use this to show tool tips over the table header.

> **Standard:** HTML 4
>
> **Common:** No
>
> **Sample:**

```
<TD TITLE="Table Cell Heading">
```

VALIGN={TOP, MIDDLE, BOTTOM, BASELINE}

Aligns the contents of a cell with the top, bottom, baseline, or middle of the cell.

> **Standard:** HTML 3.2
>
> **Common:** Yes
>
> **Sample:**

```
<TD VALIGN=TOP>
<IMG SRC="images/bud.gif
BORDER=0></TD>
```

WIDTH="*n*"

Specifies the horizontal dimension of the cell in pixels or as a percentage of the table width.

> **Standard:** HTML 3.2; not listed
>   in HTML 4
>
> **Common:** Yes
>
> **Sample:**

```
<TD WIDTH=200
ALIGN=LEFT><H2>African
Species</H2></TD>
```

Other Attributes

This tag also accepts the lang, dir, onClick, onDblClick, onMouseDown, onMouseUp, onMouseOver, onMouse-Move, onMouseOut, onKeyPress, onKeyDown, and onKeyUp attributes. See the Element-Independent Attributes section of this reference for definitions and examples.

<TEXTAREA>

Defines a multiple-line text input field within a form. Place the <TEXTAREA> tags inside the <FORM> tags. To specify a default value in a <TEXTAREA> field, place the text between the <TEXTAREA> tags.

> **Standard:** HTML 2
>
> **Common:** Yes
>
> **Paired:** Yes
>
> **Sample:**

```
Enter any comments here:

<TEXTAREA NAME="comments" COLS=40
ROWS=5>

No Comments.

</TEXTAREA>
```

Attribute Information

ACCESSKEY="..."
Assigns a keystroke sequence to the <TEXTAREA> element.

Standard: HTML 4

Common: No

Sample:

```
<TEXTAREA COLS=40 ROWS=10
NAME="Story"ACCESSKEY=S>
```

CLASS="..."
Indicates which style class applies to the <TEXTAREA> element.

Standard: HTML 4

Common: No

Sample:

```
<TEXTAREA CLASS="casual">
```

COLS="*n*"
Indicates the width (in character widths) of the text input field.

Standard: HTML 2

Common: Yes

Sample:

```
<TEXTAREA NAME="desc" COLS=50
ROWS=3></TEXTAREA>
```

DATAFLD="..."
Selects a column from a previously identified source of tabular data (see the DATASRC= attribute).

Standard: Internet Explorer 4

Common: No

Sample:

```
<TEXTAREA DATASRC="#data_table"
DATAFLD="name" NAME="st1">
```

DATASRC="..."
Specifies the source of data for data binding.

Standard: Internet Explorer 4

Common: No

Sample:

```
<TEXTAREA DATASRC="#data_table"
DATAFLD="name" NAME="st1">
```

DISABLED
Denies access to the text input field.

Standard: HTML 4

Common: No

Sample:

```
<TEXTAREA ROWS=10 COLS=10
NAME="Comments" DISABLED>
```

ID="*n*"
Assigns a unique ID selector to an instance of the <TEXTAREA> tag. When you then assign a style to that ID selector, it affects only that one instance of the <TEXTAREA> tag.

Standard: HTML 4

Common: No

Sample:

```
<TEXTAREA ID="123">
```

NAME="..."
Names the value you pass to the form processor. For example, if you collect personal feedback, assign the NAME= attribute something like "comments". This establishes a *name-value pair* with which the form processor can work.

Standard: HTML 2

Common: Yes

Sample:

```
<TEXTAREA COLS=30 ROWS=10
NAME="recipe"></TEXTAREA>
```

READONLY
Specifies that the visitor cannot change the contents of the text input field.

Standard: HTML 4

Common: No

Sample:

```
<TEXTAREA ROWS=10
COLS=10NAME="Notes" READONLY>
```

ROWS="*n*"

Indicates the height (in lines of text) of the text input field.

Standard: HTML 2

Common: Yes

Sample:

```
<TEXTAREA NAME="desc" COLS=50
ROWS=3></TEXTAREA>
```

STYLE="..."

Specifies style sheet commands that apply to the <TEXTAREA> tag.

Standard: HTML 4

Common: No

Sample:

```
<TEXTAREA STYLE="background:
red">
```

TABINDEX=*n*

Indicates where <TEXTAREA> appears in the tabbing order.

Standard: HTML 4

Common: No

Sample:

```
<TEXTAREA ROWS=5 COLS=40
NAME="story"TABINDEX=2>
```

TITLE="..."

Specifies text assigned to the tag. You might use this attribute for context-sensitive help within the document. Browsers may use this to show tool tips over the text entry input method.

Standard: HTML 4

Common: No

Sample:

```
<TEXTAREA COLS=10 ROWS=2
NAME="tt"TITLE="Text Entry Box">
```

Other Attributes

This tag also accepts the lang, dir, onfocus, onblur, onchange, onselect, onClick, onDblClick, onMouseDown, onMouseUp, onMouseOver, onMouseMove, onMouseOut, onKeyPress, onKeyDown, and onKeyUp attributes. See the Element-Independent Attributes section of this reference for definitions and examples.

<TFOOT>

Defines a table footer within a table. It must *precede* the <TBODY> tag.

Standard: HTML 4

Common: No

Paired: Yes

Sample:

```
<TFOOT>
<TR>
<TD>Totals</TD><TD>$100.25</TD>
</TR>
</TFOOT>
</TABLE>
```

Attribute Information

ALIGN={LEFT, RIGHT, CENTER, JUSTIFY, CHAR}

Specifies how text within the table footer will line up with the edges of the table cells, or if ALIGN=CHAR, on a specific character (the decimal point).

Standard: HTML 4

Common: Yes

Sample:
```
<TR>
 <THEAD>
  <TH><B>Television</B></TH>
  <TH> <IMG SRC="tv.gif"
  ALT="TV" BORDER=0>  </TH>
 </THEAD>
</TR>
```

CHAR="..."
Specifies the character on which cell contents will align, if ALIGN="CHAR". If you omit CHAR=, the default value is the decimal point in the specified language.

> **Standard**: HTML 4
> **Common**: No
> **Sample:**

`<THEAD ALIGN="CHAR" CHAR=",">`

CHAROFF="n"
Specifies the number of characters from the left at which the alignment character appears.

> **Standard**: HTML 4
> **Common**: No
> **Sample:**

```
<THEAD ALIGN="CHAR" CHAR=","
CHAROFF="7">
```

CLASS="..."
Indicates which style class applies to the <TFOOT> element.

> **Standard**: HTML 4
> **Common**: No
> **Sample:**

`<TFOOT CLASS="casual">`

ID="n"
Assigns a unique ID selector to an instance of the <TFOOT> tag. When you

then assign a style to that ID selector, it affects only that one instance of the <TFOOT> tag.

> **Standard**: HTML 4
> **Common**: No
> **Sample:**

`<TFOOT ID="123">`

STYLE="..."
Specifies style sheet commands that apply to the contents between the <TFOOT> tags.

> **Standard**: HTML 4
> **Common**: No
> **Sample:**

`<TFOOT STYLE="background: red">`

TITLE="..."
Specifies text assigned to the tag. You might use this attribute for context-sensitive help within the document. Browsers may use this to show tool tips over the table footer.

> **Standard**: HTML 4
> **Common**: No
> **Sample:**

`<TFOOT TITLE="Table Footer">`

VALIGN={TOP, BOTTOM, MIDDLE, BASELINE}
Aligns the contents of the table footer with the top, bottom, or middle of the footer container.

> **Standard**: Internet Explorer 4
> **Common**: No
> **Sample:**

`<TFOOT ALIGN=CENTER VALIGN=TOP>`

Other Attributes
This tag also accepts the lang, dir, onClick, onDblClick, onMouseDown,

onMouseUp, onMouseOver, onMouse-
Move, onMouseOut, onKeyPress,
onKeyDown, and onKeyUp attributes.
See the Element-Independent Attributes
section of this reference for definitions
and examples.

<TH>

Contains table cell headings. The <TH>
tags are identical to the <TD> tags except
that text inside <TH> is usually emphasized with boldface font and centered
within the cell.

> **Standard:** HTML 3.2
> **Common:** Yes
> **Paired:** Yes, optional
> **Sample:**

```
<TABLE>
<TH>Name</TH><TH>Phone No</TH>
<TD>John Doe</TD>
<TD>555-1212</TD>
<TD>Bob Smith</TD>
<TD>555-2121</TD>
</TABLE>
```

Attribute Information

ALIGN={LEFT, RIGHT, CENTER, JUSTIFY, CHAR}

Specifies how text within the table
header will line up with the edges of the
table cells, or if ALIGN=CHAR, on a specific character (the decimal point).

> **Standard:** HTML 4
> **Common:** Yes
> **Sample:**

```
<TR>
  <TH><B>Television</B></TH>
  <TH> <IMG SRC="tv.gif"
  ALT="TV" BORDER=0> </TH>
</TR>
```

AXIS="..."

Specifies an abbreviated cell name.

> **Standard:** HTML 4
> **Common:** No
> **Sample:**

```
<TH AXIS="TV">
<B>Television</B></TH>
```

AXES="..."

Lists AXIS values that pertain to the cell.

> **Standard:** HTML 4
> **Common:** No
> **Sample:**

```
<TH AXES="TV,
Programs"><B>Television</B></TH>
```

BACKGROUND="*URL*"

Specifies the relative or absolute location
of a graphic image file for the browser to
load as a background graphic for the
table cell.

> **Standard:** Internet Explorer,
>   Netscape Navigator
> **Common:** No
> **Sample:**

```
<TH BACKGROUND="waves.gif">
```

BGCOLOR="*#RRGGBB*" or "..."

Specifies the background color inside a
table cell. You can substitute the hexadecimal RGB values for the appropriate
color names.

> **Standard:** Deprecated in HTML 4 in
>   favor of style sheets
> **Common:** No
> **Sample:**

```
<TR><TH BGCOLOR="Pink">Course
Number</TH>
<TH BGCOLOR="Blue">Time
taught</TH></TR>
```

BORDERCOLOR="#*RRGGBB*" or "..."
Indicates the color of the border of the table cell. You can specify the color with hexadecimal RGB values or by the color name.

> **Standard:** Internet Explorer 2
> **Common:** No
> **Sample:**

```
<TR><TH BORDERCOLOR="Blue">
```

BORDERCOLORDARK="#*RRGGBB*" or "..."
Indicates the darker color used to form 3-D borders around the table cell. You can specify the color with its hexadecimal RGB values or with its color name.

> **Standard:** Internet Explorer 4
> **Common:** No
> **Sample:**

```
<TH BORDERCOLORLIGHT=#FFFFFF-
BORDERCOLORDARK=#88AA2C>
```

BORDERCOLORLIGHT="#*RRGGBB*" or "..."
Indicates the lighter color used to form 3-D borders around the table cell. You can specify the color with its hexadecimal RGB values or with its color name.

> **Standard:** Internet Explorer 4
> **Common:** No
> **Sample:**

```
<TH BORDERCOLORLIGHT=#FFFFFF
BORDERCOLORDARK=#88AA2C>
```

CHAR="..."
Specifies the character on which cell contents align, if ALIGN="CHAR". If you omit CHAR=, the default value is the decimal point in the specified language.

> **Standard:** HTML 4
> **Common:** No

> **Sample:**

```
<TH ALIGN="CHAR" CHAR=",">
```

CHAROFF="*n*"
Specifies the number of characters from the left at which the alignment character appears.

> **Standard:** HTML 4
> **Common:** No
> **Sample:**

```
<TH ALIGN="CHAR" CHAR=","
CHAROFF="7">
```

CLASS="..."
Indicates which style class applies to the <TH> element.

> **Standard:** HTML 4
> **Common:** No
> **Sample:**

```
<TH CLASS="casual">Jobs
Produced</TH>
```

COLSPAN="*n*"
Specifies that a table cell occupy more columns than the default of one. This is useful if a category name applies to more than one column of data.

> **Standard:** HTML 3.2
> **Common:** Yes
> **Sample:**

```
<TR><TH COLSPAN=2>
Students</TH></TR>
<TR><TD>Bob Smith</TDH>
<TD>John Doe</TD></TR>
```

ID="*n*"
Assigns a unique ID selector to an instance of the <TH> tag. When you then assign a style to that ID selector, it affects only that one instance of the <TH> tag.

> **Standard:** HTML 4

Common: No

Sample:

```
<TH ID="123">
```

NOWRAP

Disables default word-wrapping within a table cell, maximizing the the cell's horizontal space.

Standard: Deprecated in HTML 4 in favor of style sheets

Common: No

Sample:

```
<TH NOWRAP>The contents of this
cell will not wrap at all</TH>
```

ROWSPAN="*n*"

Specifies that a table cell occupy more rows than the default of 1. This is useful if several rows of information relate to one category.

Standard: HTML 3.2

Common: Yes

Sample:

```
<TR><TH VALIGN=MIDDLE ALIGN=RIGHT
ROWSPAN=3>Pie Entries</TH>

<TD>Banana Cream</TD>
<TD>Mrs. Robinson</TD></TR>

<TR><TD>Strawberry
Cheesecake</TD>
<TD>Mrs. Barton</TD></TR>

<TR><TD>German Chocolate</TD>
<TD>Mrs. Larson</TD></TR>
```

STYLE="..."

Specifies style sheet commands that apply to the contents of the table cell.

Standard: HTML 4

Common: No

Sample:

```
<TH STYLE="background: red">
```

TITLE="..."

Specifies text assigned to the tag. You might use this attribute for context-sensitive help within the document. Browsers may use this to show tool tips over the table header.

Standard: HTML 4

Common: No

Sample:

```
<TH TITLE="Table Cell Heading">
```

VALIGN={TOP, MIDDLE, BOTTOM, BASELINE}

Aligns the contents of a cell with the top, bottom, baseline, or middle of the cell.

Standard: HTML 3.2

Common: Yes

Sample:

```
<TH VALIGN=TOP><IMG
SRC="images/bud.gif
BORDER=0></TH>
```

WIDTH="*n*"

Specifies the horizontal dimension of the cell in pixels or as a percentage of the table width.

Standard: HTML 3.2; not listed in HTML 4

Common: Yes

Sample:

```
<TH WIDTH=200 ALIGN=LEFT>
<H2>African Species</H2></TH>
```

Other Attributes

This tag also accepts the lang, dir, onClick, onDblClick, onMouseDown, onMouseUp, onMouseOver, onMouse-Move, onMouseOut, onKeyPress, onKeyDown, and onKeyUp attributes. See the Element-Independent Attributes section of this reference for definitions and examples.

<THEAD>

Defines a table header section. At least one table row must go within <THEAD>.

Standard: HTML 4
Common: No
Paired: Yes
Sample:

```
<TABLE RULES=ROWS>
 <THEAD>
 <TR><TD>Column 1
<TD>Column 2
 </THEAD>
```

Attribute Information

ALIGN={LEFT, RIGHT, CENTER, JUSTIFY, CHAR}

Specifies how text within the table header will line up with the edges of the table cells, or if ALIGN=CHAR, on a specific character (the decimal point).

Standard: HTML 4
Common: Yes
Sample:

```
<TR>
 <THEAD>
 <TH><B>Television</B></TH>
 <TH> <IMG SRC="tv.gif"
ALT="TV" BORDER=0> </TH>
 </THEAD>
 </TR>
```

CHAR="..."

Specifies the character on which cell contents align, if ALIGN="CHAR". If you omit CHAR=, the default value is the decimal point in the specified language.

Standard: HTML 4
Common: No
Sample:

```
<THEAD ALIGN="CHAR" CHAR=",">
```

CHAROFF="n"

Specifies the number of characters from the left at which the alignment character appears.

Standard: HTML 4
Common: No
Sample:

```
<THEAD ALIGN="CHAR" CHAR=","
CHAROFF="7">
```

CLASS="..."

Indicates which style class applies to the <THEAD> element.

Standard: HTML 4
Common: No
Sample:

```
<THEAD CLASS="casual">
```

ID="n"

Assigns a unique ID selector to an instance of the <THEAD> tag. When you then assign a style to that ID selector, it affects only that one instance of the <THEAD> tag.

Standard: HTML 4
Common: No
Sample:

```
<THEAD ID="123">
```

STYLE="..."

Specifies style sheet commands that apply to the contents between the <THEAD> tags.

Standard: HTML 4

Common: No

Sample:

```
<THEAD STYLE="background: red">
```

TITLE="..."

Specifies text assigned to the tag. You might use this attribute for context-sensitive help within the document. Browsers may use this to show tool tips over the table head.

Standard: HTML 4

Common: No

Sample:

```
<THEAD TITLE="Table Heading">
```

VALIGN={TOP, MIDDLE, BOTTOM, BASELINE}

Aligns the contents of the table header with respect to the top and bottom edges of the header container.

Standard: HTML 4

Common: No

Sample:

```
<THEAD ALIGN=LEFT VALIGN=TOP>
```

Other Attributes

This tag also accepts the lang, dir, onClick, onDblClick, onMouseDown, onMouseUp, onMouseOver, onMouse-Move, onMouseOut, onKeyPress, onKeyDown, and onKeyUp attributes. See the Element-Independent Attributes section of this reference for definitions and examples.

<TITLE>

Gives the document an official title. The <TITLE> tags appear inside the document header inside the <HEAD> tags.

Standard: HTML 2

Common: Yes

Paired: Yes

Sample:

```
<HTML>
<HEAD>
<TITLE>How To Build A
Go-Cart</TITLE>
</HEAD>
```

Attribute Information

This tag also accepts the lang and dir attributes. See the Element-Independent Attributes section of this reference for definitions and examples.

<TR>

Contains a row of cells in a table. You must place the <TR> tags inside the <TABLE> container, which can contain <TH> and <TD> tags.

Standard: HTML 3.2

Common: Yes

Paired: Yes, optional

Sample:

```
<TABLE>
<TR><TH COLSPAN=3>Test
Scores</TH></TR>
<TR>
   <TD>Bob Smith</TD>
   <TD>78</TD>
   <TD>85</TD>
</TR>
<TR>
```

```
<TD>John Doe</TD>
<TD>87</TD>
<TD>85</TD>
</TR>
</TABLE>
```

Attribute Information

ALIGN={LEFT, RIGHT, CENTER, JUSTIFY, CHAR}

Specifies how text within the table row will line up with the edges of the table cells, or if ALIGN=CHAR, on a specific character (the decimal point).

Standard: HTML 4

Common: Yes

Sample:

```
<TR ALIGN=CENTER >
   <TD><B>Television</B></TD>
   <TD> <IMG SRC="tv.gif"
   ALT="TV" BORDER=0> </TD>
</TR>
```

BGCOLOR="#*RRGGBB*" or "..."

Specifies the background color of table cells in the row. You can substitute the color names for the hexadecimal RGB values.

Standard: Deprecated in HTML 4 in favor of style sheets

Common: No

Sample:

```
<TR BGCOLOR="Yellow">
   <TD><IMG SRC="Bob.jpg"
   ALT="Bob"    BORDER=0></TD>
   <TD ALIGN=LEFT VALIGN=MIDDLE>
   Bob Smith sitting at his desk
   on a July afternoon.</TD>
</TR>
```

BORDERCOLOR="#*RRGGBB*" or "..."

Specifies the color of cell borders within the row. Currently, only Internet Explorer accepts this attribute. You can substitute color names for the hexadecimal RGB values.

Standard: Internet Explorer 2

Common: No

Sample:

```
<TR BORDERCOLOR="#3F2A55">
   <TD ALIGN=RIGHT VALIGN=MIDDLE>
   Computers</TD>
   <TD><IMG SRC="Computers.jpg">
   </TD>
</TR>
```

BORDERCOLORDARK="#*RRGGBB*" or "..."

Indicates the darker color for the 3-D borders around the table row. You can specify the color with its hexadecimal RGB values or with its color name.

Standard: Internet Explorer 4

Common: No

Sample:

```
<TR BORDERCOLORLIGHT="silver"
BORDERCOLORDARK="black">
```

BORDERCOLORLIGHT="#*RRGGBB*" or "..."

Indicates the lighter color for 3-D borders around the table row. You can specify the color with its hexadecimal RGB values or with its color name.

Standard: Internet Explorer 4

Common: No

Sample:

```
<TR BORDERCOLORLIGHT="silver"
BORDERCOLORDARK="black">
```

CHAR="..."

Specifies the character on which cell contents align, if ALIGN="CHAR". If you omit CHAR=, the default value is the decimal point in the specified language.

Standard: HTML 4

Common: No

Sample:

```
<TR ALIGN="CHAR" CHAR=",">
```

CHAROFF="n"

Specifies the number of characters from the left at which the alignment character appears.

Standard: HTML 4

Common: No

Sample:

```
<TR ALIGN="CHAR" CHAR=","
CHAROFF="7">
```

CLASS="..."

Indicates which style class applies to the <TR> element.

Standard: HTML 4

Common: No

Sample:

```
<TR CLASS="casual">
  <TD>Uranium</TD>
  <TD>Plutonium</TD>
  <TD>Radon</TD>
</TR>
```

ID="n"

Assigns a unique ID selector to an instance of the <TR> tag. When you then assign a style to that ID selector, it affects only that one instance of the <TR> tag.

Standard: HTML 4

Common: No

Sample:

```
<TR ID="123">
```

NOWRAP

Indicates that text within table cells in the row not wrap. This may cause the table to expand beyond the horizontal dimensions of the current document.

Standard: Internet Explorer 3; deprecated in HTML 4 in favor of style sheets

Common: No

Sample:

```
<TR NOWRAP>
  <TD>In this table cell I'm
  going to type a lot of
  stuff.</TD>
  <TD>In this table cell I'm
  going to  continue to type a
  lot of stuff.</TD>
</TR>
```

STYLE="..."

Specifies style sheet commands that apply to all cells in the table row.

Standard: HTML 4

Common: No

Sample:

```
<TR STYLE="background: red">
```

TITLE="..."

Specifies text assigned to the tag. You might use this attribute for context-sensitive help within the document. Browsers may use this to show tool tips.

Standard: HTML 4

Common: No

Sample:

```
<TR TITLE="Table Row">
```

VALIGN={TOP, MIDDLE, BOTTOM, BASELINE}

Specifies the vertical alignment of the contents of all cells within the row.

Standard: HTML 3.2

Common: Yes

Sample:

```
<TR VALIGN=TOP>
  <TD ALIGN=CENTER>John
  Smith</TD>
  <TD ALIGN=CENTER>Bob Doe</TD>
</TR>
```

Other Attributes

This tag also accepts the lang, dir, onClick, onDblClick, onMouseDown, onMouseUp, onMouseOver, onMouse-Move, onMouseOut, onKeyPress, onKeyDown, and onKeyUp attributes. See the Element-Independent Attributes section of this reference for definitions and examples.

<TT>

Displays text in a monospace font.

Standard: HTML 2

Common: Yes

Paired: Yes

Sample:

```
After I typed in help, the words
<TT>help: not found</TT> appeared
on my screen.
```

Attribute Information

CLASS="..."

Indicates which style class applies to the <TT> element.

Standard: HTML 4

Common: No

Sample:

```
I sat down and began to type.
<P><TT CLASS="casual">It was a
dark and stormy night.</TT>
```

ID="n"

Assigns a unique ID selector to an instance of the <TT> tag. When you then assign a style to that ID selector, it affects only that one instance of the <TT> tag.

Standard: HTML 4

Common: No

Sample:

```
<TT ID="123">
```

STYLE="..."

Specifies style sheet commands that apply to the contents within the <TT> tags.

Standard: HTML 4

Common: No

Sample:

```
<TT STYLE="background: red">
```

TITLE="..."

Specifies text assigned to the tag. You might use this attribute for context-sensitive help within the document. Browsers may use this to show tool tips over the text within the <TT> tags.

Standard: HTML 4

Common: No

Sample:

```
Now, type <TT TITLE="User
Typing">MAIL</TT> and hit the
<KBD>ENTER</KBD> key.
```

Other Attributes

This tag also accepts the lang, dir, onClick, onDblClick, onMouseDown, onMouseUp, onMouseOver, onMouse-Move, onMouseOut, onKeyPress, onKeyDown, and onKeyUp attributes. See the Element-Independent Attributes section of this reference for definitions and examples.

U

<U>

Underlines text in a document. Use this tag with moderation since underlined text can confuse visitors accustomed to seeing hyperlinks as underlined text.

Standard: HTML 2; deprecated in HTML 4 in favor of style sheets

Common: Yes

Paired: Yes

Sample:

After waterskiing, I was
<U>really</U> tired.

Attribute Information

CLASS="..."

Indicates which style class applies to the <U> element.

Standard: HTML 4

Common: No

Sample:

Have you seen <U CLASS="casual">
True Lies</U> yet?

ID="*n*"

Assigns a unique ID selector to an instance of the <U> tag. When you then assign a style to that ID selector, it affects only that one instance of the <U> tag.

Standard: HTML 4

Common: No

Sample:

<U ID="123">

STYLE="..."

Specifies style sheet commands that apply to the contents within the <U> tags.

Standard: HTML 4

Common: No

Sample:

<U STYLE="background: red">

TITLE="..."

Specifies text assigned to the tag. You might use this attribute for context-sensitive help within the document. Browsers may use this to show tool tips over the underlined text.

Standard: HTML 4

Common: No

Sample:

Read the book <U
TITLE="BookTitle">Walden</U> and
you'll be enlightened.

Other Attributes

This tag also accepts the lang, dir, onClick, onDblClick, onMouseDown, onMouseUp, onMouseOver, onMouse-Move, onMouseOut, onKeyPress, onKeyDown, and onKeyUp attributes. See the Element-Independent Attributes section of this reference for definitions and examples.

\<UL\>

Contains a bulleted (unordered) list. You can then use the \<LI\> (List Item) tag to add bulleted items to the list.

Standard: HTML 2
Common: Yes
Paired: Yes
Sample:
```
Before you can begin, you
need:<UL>
  <LI>Circular saw
  <LI>Drill with Phillips bit
  <LI>Wood screws
</UL>
```

Attribute Information

CLASS="..."
Indicates which style class applies to the \<UL\> element.

Standard: HTML 4
Common: No
Sample:
```
<UL CLASS="casual">
  <LI>Hexagon</LI>
  <LI>Pentagon</LI>
  <LI>Octagon</LI>
</UL>
```

COMPACT
Indicates that the unordered list appears in a compact format. This attribute may not affect the appearance of the list as most browsers do not present lists in more than one format.

Standard: HTML 2; deprecated in HTML 4
Common: No

Sample:
```
<UL COMPACT>
  <LI>Flour
  <LI>Sugar
  <LI>Wheat
  <LI>Raisins
</UL>
```

ID="*n*"
Assigns a unique ID selector to an instance of the \<UL\> tag. When you then assign a style to that ID selector, it affects only that one instance of the \<UL\> tag.

Standard: HTML 4
Common: No
Sample:
```
<UL ID="123">
```

SRC="*URL*"
Specifies the relative or absolute location of an image file to use for the bullets in the unordered list. Style sheets provide a browser-independent method that is equivalent to this attribute.

Standard: Internet Explorer 4
Common: No
Sample:
```
<UL SRC="blueball.gif">
```

STYLE="..."
Specifies style sheet commands that apply to the contents of the unordered list.

Standard: HTML 4
Common: No
Sample:
```
<UL STYLE="background: red">
```

TITLE="..."

Specifies text assigned to the tag. You might use this attribute for context-sensitive help within the document. Browsers may use this to show tool tips over the unordered list.

Standard: HTML 4

Common: No

Sample:

```
<UL TITLE="Food List">
 <LI>Spaghetti
 <LI>Pizza
 <LI>Fettuccini Alfredo
</UL>
```

TYPE={SQUARE, CIRCLE, DISC}

Specifies the bullet type for each unordered list item. If you omit the TYPE= attribute, the browser chooses a default type.

Standard: HTML 2

Common: Yes

Sample:

```
<UL TYPE=DISC>
  <LI>Spaghetti
  <UL TYPE=SQUARE>
    <LI>Noodles
    <LI>Sauce
    <LI>Cheese
  </UL>
</UL>
```

Other Attributes

This tag also accepts the lang, dir, onClick, onDblClick, onMouseDown, onMouseUp, onMouseOver, onMouse-Move, onMouseOut, onKeyPress, onKeyDown, and onKeyUp attributes.

See the Element-Independent Attributes section of this reference for definitions and examples.

V

<VAR>

Indicates a placeholder variable in document text. This is useful when describing commands for which the visitor must supply a parameter.

Standard: HTML 2

Common: Yes

Paired: Yes

Sample:

```
To copy a file in DOS type
<SAMP>COPY <VAR>file1</VAR>
<VAR>file2</VAR></SAMP> and press
the ENTER key.
```

Attribute Information

CLASS="..."

Indicates which style class applies to the <VAR> element.

Standard: HTML 4

Common: No

Sample:

```
I, <VAR CLASS="casual">your
name</VAR>, solemnly swear to
tell the truth.
```

ID="n"

Assigns a unique ID selector to an instance of the <VAR> tag. When you then assign a style to that ID selector, it affects only that one instance of the <VAR> tag.

Standard: HTML 4

Common: No

Sample:

```
<VAR ID="123">
```

STYLE="..."

Specifies style sheet commands that apply to the contents within the <VAR> tags.

Standard: HTML 4
Common: No
Sample:

```
<VAR STYLE="background: red">
```

TITLE="..."

Specifies text assigned to the tag. You might use this attribute for context-sensitive help within the document. Browsers may use this to show tool tips over the text within the <VAR> tags.

Standard: HTML 4
Common: No
Sample:

```
Use a H<VAR TITLE="Heading Level
Number">n</VAR> tag.
```

Other Attributes

This tag also accepts the lang, dir, onClick, onDblClick, onMouseDown, onMouseUp, onMouseOver, onMouse-Move, onMouseOut, onKeyPress, onKeyDown, and onKeyUp attributes. See the Element-Independent Attributes section of this reference for definitions and examples.

W

<WBR>

Forces a word break. This is useful in combination with the <NOBR> tag to permit line breaks where they could otherwise not occur.

Standard: Netscape Navigator
Common: No
Paired: No
Sample:

```
<NOBR>
This line would go on forever,
except that I have this neat tag
called WBR that does <WBR>this!
</NOBR>
```

X

<XMP>

Includes preformatted text within a document. Unlike the <PRE> tag, the browser does not interpret HTML tags within the <XMP> tags. HTML 3.2 declared this tag obsolete; so use <PRE> instead.

Standard: Obsolete
Common: No
Paired: Yes
Sample:

```
The output from these reports is
shown below.
<XMP>
Company      Q1    Q2     Q3    Q4
----------   ---   ---    ---   ---
Widget Inc   4.5m  4.6m   6.2m  4.5m
Acme Widget  5.9m  10.2m  7.3m  6.6m
West Widget  2.2m  1.3m   3.1m  6.1m
</XMP>
```

Element-Independent Attributes and Event Handlers

Many HTML elements accept the attributes and event handlers described in this section. See the cross-references from individual elements for specific support information.

Attributes

dir="{LTR, RTL}"

Specifies the direction (left to right or right to left) for the text used within the section. This attribute is used most often within documents to override site-wide language direction specifications.

> **Standard:**   HTML 4
>
> **Common:**   No
>
> **Sample:**

```
<P>The following quote is in
Hebrew, therefore written right
to left, not left to right.
<Q LANG="IW" DIR="RTL">Hebrew
text goes here and is presented
right to left, not left to right.
</Q></P>
```

lang="..."

Specifies the language used within the section. This attribute is used most often within documents to override site-wide language specifications. Use standard codes for languages, such as DE for German, FR for French, IT for Italian, and IW for Hebrew. See ISO Specification 639 at www.sil.org/sgml/iso639a.html for more information about language codes.

Standard: HTML 4

Common: No

Sample:

```
<P>The following quote is in
German. <Q LANG="DE">Guten
Tag!</Q></P>
```

Event Handlers

Each of the following event handlers helps link visitor actions to scripts. See the JavaScript reference for a fuller explanation of their use.

onLoad="..."

Occurs when the browser finishes loading a window or all frames within a `<FRAMESET>`. This handler works with `<BODY>` and `<FRAMESET>` elements.

onUnload="..."

Occurs when the browser removes a document from a window or frame. This handler works with `<BODY>` and `<FRAMESET>` elements.

onClick="..."

Occurs when a visitor clicks the mouse over an element. This handler works with most elements.

onDblClick="..."

Occurs when a visitor double-clicks the mouse over an element. This handler works with most elements.

onMouseDown="..."

Occurs when a visitor presses the mouse button over an element. This handler works with most elements.

onMouseUp="..."

Occurs when a visitor releases the mouse button over an element. This handler works with most elements.

onMouseOver="..."

Occurs when a visitor moves the mouse over an element. This handler works with most elements.

onMouseMove="..."

Occurs when a visitor moves the mouse while still over an element. This handler works with most elements.

onMouseOut="..."

Occurs when a visitor moves the mouse away from an element. This handler works with most elements.

onFocus="..."

Occurs when a visitor moves the focus to an element either with the mouse or the tab key. This handler works with <LABEL>, <INPUT>, <SELECT>, <TEXTAREA>, and <BUTTON>.

onBlur="..."

Occurs when a visitor moves focus from an element either with the mouse or the tab key. This handler works with <LABEL>, <INPUT>, <SELECT>, <TEXTAREA>, and <BUTTON>.

onKeyPress="..."

Occurs when a visitor presses and releases a key over an element. This handler works with most elements.

onKeyDown="..."

Occurs when a visitor presses a key over an element. This handler works with most elements.

onKeyUp="..."

Occurs when a visitor releases a key over an element. This handler works with most elements.

onSubmit="..."

Occurs when a visitor submits a form. This handler works only with <FORM>.

onReset="..."

Occurs when a visitor resets a form. This handler works only with <FORM>.

onSelect="..."

Occurs when a visitor selects text in a text field. This handler works with the <INPUT> and <TEXTAREA> elements.

onChange="..."

Occurs when a visitor modifies a field and moves the input focus to a different control. This handler works with <INPUT>, <SELECT>, and <TEXTAREA>.

Cascading Style Sheets

This section lists all the properties that you can use to set up a style sheet or to introduce styles into a document. For a complete introduction to style sheets and their capabilities, including an introduction to some of the specialized terminology used in this reference section, see Chapter 8.

The properties are organized into the following categories:

- ▶ Font properties, which affect the style of the typeface
- ▶ Text properties, which control paragraph and line-spacing values
- ▶ Box padding, border, margin, and position properties, which place and format elements within boundaries on a page
- ▶ Color and background properties, which specify background colors and background images, not just for the whole page, but for each element individually
- ▶ Classification properties, which control the presentation (or lack thereof) of standard elements, including lists

Each entry in this reference includes a description of the property, a list of the property's values, notes about the use of the property, and examples of the properties used in statements.

NOTE

At the time of writing, the newest versions of Internet Explorer and Netscape Navigator supported most of these style sheet features, but not all. Be sure to test extensively in a variety of browsers before relying on the properties listed here.

Font Properties

The font properties control the display of text elements, such as headings and paragraphs. This is the most common type of formatting you'll use in style sheets. These properties—particularly the `font-family` property—are also the most problematic, because no standard exists for fonts. Therefore, what works on one system or one platform may not work on another. Fortunately, you can specify alternate font families, as well as a generic font family.

The six font properties cover the font family (typeface), weight, and effects such as small caps or italics. The first property, font, is a *shorthand* property, as explained below.

font

Use this property as a shortcut to incorporate any or all of the other font properties. If you use the font shorthand property, you can also set the line spacing, using the line-height property (listed in the "Text Properties" section of this reference). You can include one, many, or all of the font properties in this one property.

If you do not set font-style, font-variant, font-weight, or font-family, you accept the document default values for these properties. Shorthand properties do not have default settings; refer to entries for the individual properties for their default values.

If you set the font properties for an element, these settings are used by inline elements (such as EM) and by all elements of that type unless a class definition overwrites the settings.

Values

The possible values for the font property are the set of all possible values listed in the individual property entries:

font-style	Sets the font to an oblique or italic face (optional)
font-variant	Sets the font to small caps (optional)
font-weight	Sets the font to lighter or bolder (optional)
font-size	Sets the size of the font (required)
line-height	Sets the line spacing for the font (optional)
font-family	Sets the font face or type used (required)

See the entries for the individual properties for more details about these values.

Notes

If you do not include a setting for a particular property (such as font-variant), the browser uses the parent value of that property.

The order of the properties in a statement is not important.

Examples

```
H1 {font: Arial, Helvetica, sans-serif bold 14pt/18pt}
```

This statement uses values for the font-family, font-style, font-size, and line-height (in that order). For the font-family, three values are listed, telling the browser to use Arial, and if Arial is not available, to use Helvetica, and if Helvetica is not available, to use a generic sans-serif font. The `font-style` is bold. The `font-size` is 14 points, and the `line-height` is 18 points.

```
H3 {font: 12pt/120% serif}
```

This statement sets the `font-size`, `line-height`, and `font-family` using a 12-point font, a line height of 120% (14.4 points), and a generic serif font family.

```
BODY {font: italic Helvetica 100%/130%}
```

This statement sets the base class for the document; all other tags will default to these values. It sets the `font-style` to italic, the `font-family` to Helvetica, the `font-size` to normal (100% of the browser default), and the `line-height` to 130%.

font-family

Use this property to change only the font family for an HTML tag or element. You can set a list of font families and include a generic family at the end of the list. The browser works through the list until it finds a matching font family available on the visitor's system.

The `font-family` property defaults to the browser settings. These may be the browser preferences, the browser default style sheet, or the visitor's default style sheet. If the default is the browser preferences or style sheet, your settings take precedence, but if it is the visitor's style sheet, your settings are overridden by the visitor's style sheet.

Inline elements (such as EM) use this property, as do child elements and all elements of that type unless the settings are overwritten by a class definition.

NOTE

A paragraph or heading tag is the child of the body tag; list items are the children of a list tag. Class definitions allow you to have more than one type or version of a tag for formatting. For example, a warning note could have its own class of paragraph tag.

Values

    `family` *name*   Sets a specific font family. Use any font name for the family name. For font names, check the list of fonts on your system.

    generic family   Sets a generic font family. Use one of the following for generic family names: `serif` for fonts such as Times or Palatino, `sans-serif` for fonts such as Helvetica, `cursive` for fonts such as Zapf-Chancery, `fantasy` for fonts such as Western or Circus, or `monospace` for fonts such as System or Courier.

You can list several choices for the font family and one choice for a generic family. Separate the list members with a comma.

Notes

With this property, you can list a series of alternatives separated by commas. End each list with a generic family name; the browser can then substitute an available font of the correct generic type when none of your specific family types are available. The browser works through the list from left to right until it finds a match on the visitor's system.

If a font name contains spaces, place that font name in quotation marks.

Examples

```
H1 {font-family: "Comic Sans MS", Architecture, sans-serif}
```

In this statement, the font choices for heading 1 tags (H1) are Comic Sans MS, Architecture, and a generic sans-serif. If the visitor's system has Comic Sans MS, it will use that font. Notice that Comic Sans MS is enclosed in quotation marks, because it includes a space. If Comic Sans MS is not available, the browser looks for Architecture. If neither font family is available, the browser uses a generic sans-serif font.

```
BODY {font-family: Arial, Helvetica, sans-serif}
```

This statement sets BODY, the base class for all text elements in your page, to Arial or Helvetica (in order of preference). If neither of these families is available, the browser uses a generic sans-serif font. Apply the properties you want as defaults for the page to the BODY tag.

font-size

Use this property to control the size of text using a variety of measurements. It is more flexible than the font tag in the HTML specification, which scales text only by reference to the default size.

Values

absolute size   Defines the font-size by using a table of computed font sizes. These values can be one of the following: xx-small, x-small, small, medium (the default), large, x-large, or xx-large. Different font families may have different table values; thus, a small in one family might not be exactly the same size as a small in another family.

relative size   Defines the font-size by using another table of values. For this type of sizing, you can use either larger or smaller. This is similar to the absolute size, but the resulting size is relative to the parent container font size rather than to the base browser font size.

length   Uses millimeter, centimeter, inch, point, pixel, pica, x-height (the height of the font's lowercase letter *x*), or em (the height of the font) units as measurements. This type of sizing forces a particular measurement to be used for the element, ignoring any browser settings. Specify the measurement after the number as follows: mm for millimeters, cm for centimeters, in for inches, pt for points, px for pixels, pc for picas, ex for x-height settings, or em for em settings. The em and ex settings generate a font size relative to the parent font.

percentage   Sets the font-size as a percentage of the parent element's font-size. Specify this value by including a % symbol after the number.

You can assign a single value for this property. If you use a keyword, such as x-large or larger, the browser recognizes the keyword and acts accordingly. If you use a numeric value, be sure to follow it with the appropriate measurement indicator, such as pt to indicate a point size or % to indicate a percentage.

Notes

When you use the absolute size value, the browser adjusts the font size according to the visitor's preferences. For example, if the default font size for the browser is 10 points, this corresponds to the medium value. The adjustment from medium is 1.5 for each increment in the list. So, if medium is 10 points, small is 6.7 points, and large is 15 points. Absolute size is the best choice for sizing fonts, because if the visitor changes the base font from 10 points to 14 points, your document scales with the change.

In terms of absolute size and relative size, the default is expressed as medium.

Length and percentage values do not use the absolute or relative tables of values. The font sizes are interpreted, and so they may appear different in different situations.

For length values, the default is taken from the browser or visitor settings. The em and ex values are interpreted as references to the parent font size. For example, 1.5em is equivalent to large, larger, and 150% for absolute, relative, and percentage font sizes.

Relative units set up the property in relation to the font and size properties. Use relative units wherever you can, because they scale more easily from situation to situation (for example, in different browsers and displays, or in the transition from display to printer). Relative units include em (1 em is equal to the font size), ex (the height of the lowercase letter *x* in a font), and px (screen pixels).

Absolute lengths are useful when the properties of the browser are well-known or when you want to set a particular font size to conform to a specification. Absolute units include inches, millimeters and centimeters, points (1 point = 1/72 inch), and picas (1 pica = 12 points). You cannot have a negative font size.

If the size is expressed as a percentage, the default is 100%. Any value less than 100% is smaller than the parent, and any value more than 100% is larger than the parent. For example, if the parent font is 12 points, and this property is set to 110%, the font size for this element is 13.2 points. If the font size is set to 80% of the 12-point parent, the element appears as 9.6 points.

Examples

```
BODY {font-size: 14pt}
```

This statement sets the base `font-size` to 14 points. This is useful when you want the presentation of text to be large, such as at a site for the visually impaired or for children.

```
P {font-size: 90%}
```

This statement uses a percentage value to make the `font-size` depend on the settings in the <BODY> tag. So, if this statement and the preceding one appear in the same style sheet, the font in the paragraph (P) will be 12.6 points.

```
ADDRESS {font-size: x-small}
```

This statement sets the `font-size` for the ADDRESS element using an absolute value. If this statement appears in the same style sheet as the first example, the `font-size` for the ADDRESS element will be 4 points.

font-style

Use this property to add emphasis with an oblique or italic version of the font. If the default setting inherited for a particular element is an italic style font, you can use the `font-style` property to set the current element to `normal`, sometimes called roman (or upright).

When you set the `font-style` for an element, inline elements (such as EM) and included block elements use this style. Also, if you set the `font-style` for a body or list container, all the elements within it use the setting.

Values

normal style   If you have set the default style to an oblique or italic style, the keyword `normal` sets the `font-style` to a roman or upright style.

italic style   If you want an italic `font-style`, the keyword depends on the font. Fonts with Italic, Cursive, or Kursiv in their names are usually listed as Italic in the browser's database.

oblique style   As with the italic style, the keyword for an oblique `font-style` depends on the font. Fonts with Oblique, Slanted, or Incline in their names are usually listed in the browser's database as Oblique fonts. The browser may also generate an oblique font from a family that does not have an oblique or italic style.

You can use one of the three values.

Notes

The browser maintains a list of the fonts available on the system, with the font name, font family, and values of the font such as oblique or italic.

Examples

```
BODY {font-style: oblique}
H1, H2, H3 {font-style: normal}
```

The first statement sets the base body (BODY) to an oblique version of the font. Because the heading levels 1, 2, and 3 (H1, H2, H3) inherit this from the BODY class, the second statement sets them to normal. If the base font is not oblique or italic, you do not need to set the font-style to normal.

```
BODY EM {font-style: italic}
```

This statement sets up the emphasis tag (EM) to be an italic font-style. This means that when you emphasize some inline text, it will be italicized automatically.

font-variant

Use this property to switch between normal and small-caps fonts. If you assign this property to an element, all included blocks and inline elements use the setting.

Values

normal variant   If the tag has inherited a small-caps setting from its parent, the keyword normal sets the font-variant to a regular font. This is the default.

small-caps variant   Sets the lowercase letters to display as uppercase letters in a smaller font size. Use the keyword small-caps.

Notes

In some cases, when a small-caps version of the font is not available to the browser, the browser creates small caps by using scaled uppercase letters.

Examples

```
H1 {font-variant: small-caps}
```

This statement sets the level-1 headings (H1) to a small-cap version of the default font.

```
ADDRESS {font-variant: small-caps}
```

This statement sets the contents of any <ADDRESS> tag to appear in small caps, using the default BODY font.

```
BODY EM {font-variant: small-caps}
```

This statement sets text in the inline element EM to use the small-caps version of the default font.

font-weight

Use this property to set the weight of a font, creating darker and lighter versions of the normal font. You can set the `font-weight` property as a relative weight or as a specific numeric value that represents a degree of darkness or heaviness for the font.

Values

normal weight   The keyword `normal` resets the font to its normal weight. This is the default.

relative weight   Sets the `font-weight` relative to the normal weight inherited by the element. These values can be one of the following: `bold`, `bolder`, `light`, or `lighter`.

gradient weight   Sets the `font-weight` as a degree of heaviness. These values can be one of the following: 100, 200, 300, 400 (same as `normal`), 500, 600, 700 (same as `bold`), 800, or 900.

You can use one value from the list.

Notes

When you set a `font-weight` value for an element, the child elements for that element inherit the weight of the font. This weight becomes their normal weight, and you can increase or decrease the weight based on the inherited weight. When you then set a child element's weight using a relative weight (for example, `bolder` or `lighter`), it is relative to the weight of the parent font.

The gradient weight value gives you greater control over the weight of the font. The numeric weight values must be stated exactly; partial numbers (such as 250) are not accepted.

There are no guarantees that the font family will include the full range of weight values. The browser will map the values you assign to those available for the font it uses. Fonts that have a weight lighter than normal are usually listed in the browser's database as Thinner, Light, or Extra-light.

Examples

```
P {font-weight: bold}
```

This statement makes the weight of the paragraph (P) font bold. Use this when your layout requires a heavier text presentation.

```
BODY {font-weight: 500}
```

This statement uses the numeric representation to set the base font weight to slightly heavier than normal. This will make the text for all the elements appear darker. All included and inline elements use this as their normal weight. If you then use the relative keywords, as in the next statement, the text is bolder (or lighter) than the 500 weight set in BODY.

```
H1 {font-weight: bolder}
```

This statement makes the H1 elements darker than the base font, regardless of what setting the base font has for its weight. If your base font were 900 in the <BODY> tag, however, there is no value that is bolder, and the browser would not be able to make the H1 text bolder.

```
BODY EM {font-weight: 400}
```

This statement controls the weight of emphasized text in the document. If the BODY weight is 500 or if you include emphasized text in a paragraph set to bold, as in the first statement in this section, the emphasized text would appear lighter.

Text Properties

Text properties control the layout or display of lines and words on a page and within a text element. These properties include the familiar values for spacing and aligning text within an area, as well as values for controlling text capitalization and effects (such as underlining and blinking). Combined with the font properties, the text properties give you control over the appearance of the text on your page. The font properties control the typeface; the text properties control the paragraph settings.

letter-spacing

Use this property to control the spacing between characters in words in a text element. The distance you set applies across the elements; you cannot insert larger and smaller spaces between characters. This property is useful if you want to add space between characters for an open-looking presentation.

This property defaults to the spacing set in the parent element or to the browser if no style is set. Inline and included block elements use the value set with the letter-spacing property.

Values

normal spacing   Resets the distance between characters to whatever is normal for the font and font size in use. Use the keyword normal. This is the default.

length   Sets a standard spacing length between characters. The value adds to the normal length inherited by the element from its parent, or reduces the normal length if you use a negative value.

Specify the measurement after the number as follows: mm for millimeters, cm for centimeters, in for inches, pt for points, px for pixels, pc for picas, ex for x-height settings, or em for em settings. The em and ex settings generate a font size relative to the parent font.

Notes

When you specify a length, relative units set up the property in relation to the font and size properties. Use relative units wherever you can, because they scale more easily from situation to situation (for example, in different browsers and displays, or in the transition from display to printer). Relative units include em (1 em is equal to the width of a capital *M* in a font), ex (the height of the lowercase letter *x* in a font), and px (screen pixels).

Absolute lengths are useful when the properties of the browser are well-known or when you want to set a particular letter spacing to conform to a specification. Absolute units include inches, millimeters and centimeters, points (1 point = 1/72 inch), and picas (1 pica = 12 points).

When you use a length unit, you can use a positive or a negative number or a decimal number (for example, 0.4em or 1.2em). If you use a negative value, be sure that you don't make your text illegible with too small spacing between characters.

Examples

```
H1 {letter-spacing: 2em}
```

This statement increases the character spacing in words found in the level-1 headings (H1) to twice the font size.

```
P {letter-spacing: -0.5em}
```

This statement decreases the character spacing for paragraphs in the document to one-half the font size.

line-height

Use this property to set the distance (leading or spacing) between lines of text within an element. Elements inherit the settings for this property; if you change the settings in the child element, you change the inherited results. For example, if you set unordered lists (UL) to 2 (for double-spaced) and then set list items (LI) to 1.5, you have effectively triple-spaced list items (2 × 1.5). In other words, the inheritance is cumulative, rather than a setting for a later element replacing the previous setting.

Values

normal height   Sets the spacing value to default to the browser-specific setting, which is usually 1 to 1.2 times the font size. Use the keyword normal. This is the default.

number   Sets the distance between the baselines of each line of text in the element to the font size multiplied by the specified number. For example, if the font size is 10 points and you set line-height to 2, the spacing will be 20 points.

length   Sets the spacing using one of the standard measurements. Some measurements are relative, and some are absolute. See the description of the length value for the letter-spacing property for valid measurements.

percentage   Sets the spacing to a percentage of the line's font size.

Notes

See the "Notes" section for the letter-spacing property for information about relative and absolute length settings.

When you use a length unit, you can use a positive or a negative number. If you use a negative number, you'll create overlapping text, which may make it illegible.

Using a percentage for the line-height property is a flexible way to set line spacing, because it adapts to the font and display of the browser. Child elements will inherit the result of this setting.

Examples

```
P {line-height: 1.2;
     font-size: 10pt}
P {line-height: 1.2em;
     font-size: 10pt}
P {line-height: 120%;
     font-size: 10pt}
```

These three statements produce the same result: The text will have 12 points between each line.

text-align

Use this property to arrange the text horizontally within the element box. This is useful for centering headings or creating effects with justification. You can set the alignment on any block-level element, such as P, H1, UL, and so on. The browser sets the property default (either from the browser properties, browser style sheet, or visitor style sheet). Inline and included block elements use the settings. For example, if you justify an unordered list (UL), the list items (which are included block elements) are justified.

Values

left alignment   Aligns text along the left margin, for a ragged-right layout. Use the keyword `left`.

right alignment   Aligns text along the right margin, for a ragged-left layout. Use the keyword `right`.

centered   Places the text a uniform distance from the left and right margins. Use the keyword `center`.

justified   Creates uniform line lengths. The browser will use word spacing to create lines of text that abut both the left and right margins of the element box. Use the keyword `justify`.

Examples

```
H1, H2 {text-align: center}
```

This statement centers both level 1 (H1) and level 2 (H2) headings across the width of the page (however wide or narrow the display is).

```
P.EMERG {text-align: right;
       Background: url(exclaim.gif) no-repeat}
```

This statement aligns paragraphs of class EMERG (P.EMERG) with the right margin of the element box. P.EMERG also has an icon that appears once at the left margin of the element box.

text-decoration

Use this property to control the effects used on text elements. This property is particularly useful for drawing attention to text elements, such as notes and warnings.

The default is not to use any text decoration, and the property is not inherited, although some properties do continue throughout sections. For example, a P with underlining will be underlined throughout, even through sections with other formatting, such as boldface. The decoration uses the settings from the `color` property (listed in the "Background and Color Properties" section).

Values

no text decoration   Leaves the text plain (unadorned). Use the keyword `none`. This is the default.

underlined   Draws a single, thin line under the text. Use the keyword `underline`.

overlined   Draws a single, thin line above the text. Use the keyword `overline`.

lined through   Draws a single, thin line through the text, like strikeout. Use the keyword `line-through`.

blinking   Makes the text blink. Use the keyword `blink`.

You can combine `underline`, `overline`, `line-through`, and `blink` in a single statement.

Notes

If you apply the `text-decoration` property to an element that has no text or is an empty element (such as BR), the property has no effect.

Examples

```
H1 {color: blue;
        text-decoration: underline}
```

This statement sets the level-1 headings (H1) to use the color blue and have an underline (it, too, will be blue).

```
P EM {text-decoration: blink}
```

This statement sets the emphasis in paragraphs (P EM) to blink. Because nothing else is set, the emphasis will use all the other paragraph (P) properties that you have set.

```
H1 EM {text-decoration: overline}
```

This statement sets the emphasized text in level-1 headings to have a line above it. If this statement appears in the same style sheet as the first statement in this section, this emphasized text will have a line above and a line below.

text-indent

Use this property to indent the first line of paragraphs. Traditionally, indented first lines compensated for a lack of space between paragraphs and acted as a visual cue for the reader. You can set the indent as an absolute or a relative measurement.

Elements use whatever setting the parent has, so if you set `text-indent` for BODY, all block elements, such as H1 and P, default to first-line indention. The default value is 0, for no indention.

Values

length   Sets the size of the first-line indent to the specified measurement. Some measurements are relative, and some are absolute. See the description of the length value for the `letter-spacing` property for valid measurements.

percentage   Sets the first-line indent to a percentage of the line length.

Notes

For most browsers, you can use negative values to create a hanging-indent format.

An indent is not added to the first line of the second text stream if the text within the element is separated by an inline element that breaks the line (such as BR).

See the "Notes" section for the `letter-spacing` property for information about relative and absolute length settings.

Examples

```
BODY {text-indent: 1%}
```

This statement creates a base class BODY with a first-line indent of 1% of the line length. Because a percentage is used, the ratio of indent to line length stays the same whether the browser window or font is sized larger or smaller.

```
H1 {text-indent: 3em}
```

In this statement, the indention for level-1 headings (H1) is also relative to the font size (em measurements are based on the font size). If this line appears in the same style sheet as the first statement, the indention is the base 1% plus an additional 3 ems.

```
P.WARN {text-indent: 2cm}
```

This statement specifies a 2-centimeter first-line indent. Since this is an absolute measurement, this setting can produce unexpected results on different machines.

text-transform

Use this property to set the capitalization standard for one or more elements. For example, if you want all uppercase letters for a warning or title case for all headings, you can set this property in one place and allow the browser to adjust the text. Child elements, including both block and inline elements, use the parent's setting for this property. The default is no transformation.

Values

no transformation   Does not change the case for any of the text. Use the keyword none. This is the default.

capitalized   Creates a title case element, capitalizing the first letter of each word in the element. Use the keyword `capitalize`.

uppercased   Sets all the text to uppercase. Use the keyword `uppercase`.

lowercased   Sets all the text to lowercase, eliminating any uppercase letters from the element. Use the keyword `lowercase`.

Examples

```
H1 {text-transform: capitalize}
```

This statement forces all the text in level-1 headings (H1) to use uppercase for the first letter of each word. This is a form of the title case.

```
P.HEADLINE {text-transform: uppercase}
```

In this statement, the paragraph class `P.HEADLINE` forces all the text into uppercase. This is not the same as setting a small-caps font (`font-variant: small-caps`), because no adjustment is made to the size of the lowercase letters.

vertical-align

Use this property to set inline text elements within a parent element to have different vertical alignment from the parent. The `vertical-align` property is an important layout tool for document designers. You could, for example, define a class for superscript or subscript text and apply it where required. This property is typically used to set the alignment between inline graphics (such as keycaps or toolbar icons) and the surrounding text. The default value is for alignment along the baselines of the elements. These settings are not used by any other elements.

Values

baseline alignment   Aligns the bottom of lowercase letters in the two elements. Use the keyword `baseline`. This is the default setting.

subscript alignment   Moves the inline element down below the baseline of the parent element. Use the keyword `sub`.

superscript alignment   Moves the inline element up from the baseline of the parent element. Use the keyword `super`.

top alignment   Similar to superscript, aligns the inline element with the highest part of the parent element. Use the keyword `top`. This works line by line. For example, if the line has no ascenders, `top` moves the inline text to the top of the x-height for the parent element.

text-top alignment   Aligns the inline element with the top of the ascender in the parent element. Use the keyword `text-top`.

middle alignment   Centers the inline text and the parent element text, aligning the mid-points of the two elements. Use the keyword `middle`. This may be required when you are using a large and small size for the two elements or when the inline element is an image.

bottom alignment   Aligns the inline element with the lowest part of the parent element on the same line. Use the keyword `bottom`. Use this with caution, because it may produce unexpected results.

text-bottom alignment   Aligns the bottom of the inline element with the bottom of the parent font's descender. Use the keyword `text-bottom`. This is the preferable method for aligning inline elements with the bottom of a textual parent element.

percentage   Raises or lowers (with negative values) the baseline of the inline element the given percentage above or below the baseline of the parent element. Use this in combination with the `line-height` property of the element.

Notes

If you use subscript (`sub`) or superscript (`super`) alignment, decrease the font size in relation to the parent element.

If you want to include inline images that replace words or letters in your text (such as toolbar buttons or keycaps), use a percentage value with the `vertical-align` property. This allows you to obtain precision in the placement of inline elements, such as images, that do not have a true baseline.

Examples

```
IMG.KEYCAP {vertical-align: -20%}
```

This statement creates an image class (`IMG`) called `KEYCAP`. Elements that you apply this class to will drop below the baseline of the parent text element; 20% of the image will be below the baseline of the parent element's text.

```
P.LOGRYTHM {vertical-align: super}
```

This statement creates a paragraph class called `LOGRYTHM` for superscripting. You could, for example, use this for the exponents in equations.

```
.REGMARK {vertical-align: text-top}
```

In this statement, a generic class, called `REGMARK`, aligns the inline element to the top of the parent font.

word-spacing

Use this property to control the spacing between words in a text element. As with the `letter-spacing` property, the distance you set applies across the elements; you cannot insert larger and smaller spaces between words, as in typesetting. This property is useful if you want to add space between words for an open-looking presentation.

This property assumes the settings for its parent element or the browser, and inline or included block elements use any changes you make in the `word-spacing` property.

Values

normal spacing   Resets the distance between words to whatever is normal for the font and font size in use. Use the keyword `normal`. This is the default.

length   Sets a standard spacing length between words. The value adds to the normal length inherited by the element from its parent, or reduces the normal length if you use a negative value. For example, if BODY sets the font size to 10pt and the word spacing to 1em, the child elements will use 10-point word spacing (1em = the point size). If you then add 0.4em to the word spacing, the child element has a wider word spacing than the parent. See the description of the length value for the letter-spacing property for valid measurements.

Notes

See the "Notes" section of the letter-spacing property for information about relative and absolute length settings.

When you use a length unit, you can use a positive or a negative number, as well as a decimal number (such as 0.4em). If you use a negative number, be careful that you do not eliminate the spaces between words, making your text unreadable.

Examples

```
H1 {word-spacing: 1em}
P {word-spacing: 0.4em}
```

In both these statements, the space between words in the elements will increase; the spacing in heading level 1 (H1) elements increases by 1 em, and paragraph (P) elements increase by 0.4 (4/10 of the font size).

Box Padding Properties

In the element box, the padding provides the distance between the element contents and the border. You can use the padding shorthand property to set the padding on all sides of the element or use the individual properties to set the padding on each side separately.

NOTE

With box properties, you can manipulate the layers around the element. These layers, from the element out, are padding, border, margin, and position. Each of these layers has its own set of properties, which are included in this reference in the order listed, beginning with box padding.

padding

Use this shorthand property to set the distance for all four padding directions (top, right, bottom, and left). This area uses the element's settings for background (such as color and image).

Padding is not inherited, so included and inline elements use the default of zero (0) rather than the settings from the parent element.

Values

length   Sets an absolute or a relative distance between the element contents and the inside of the box border. Specify the measurement after the number as follows: mm for millimeters, cm for centimeters, in for inches, pt for points, px for pixels, pc for picas, ex for x-height settings, or em for em settings. The em and ex settings generate a font size relative to the parent font.

percentage   Sets the distance between the element contents and the inside of the box border as a percentage of the parent element.

Use a single value to make the padding on each side equidistant. If you use two values, the browser uses the first one for the top and bottom padding, and the second one for the left and right padding. If you provide three values, the browser assigns them to the top padding, the left and right padding, and the bottom padding. If you provide all four values, the browser assigns them, in order, to the top, right, bottom, and left padding. You can mix value types—specifying padding in percentages for some and absolute measurements for other values.

Notes

You cannot have a negative padding value. You can use a decimal number, such as 0.4 or 1.2.

For length settings, relative units set up the property in relation to the font and size properties. Use relative units wherever you can because they scale more easily from situation to situation (for example, in different browsers and displays, or in the transition from display to printer). Relative units include em (1 em is equal to the width of a capital *M* in a font), ex (the height of the lowercase letter *x* in a font), and px (screen pixels).

Absolute lengths are useful when the properties of the browser are well-known or when you want to set a particular size to conform to a specification. Absolute units include inches, millimeters and centimeters, points (1 point = 1/72 inch), and picas (1 pica = 12 points).

Examples

```
H1 {font-size: 20pt;
      padding: 1em 0.5em}
H2 {font-size: 15pt;
      padding: 1em 0.5em}
```

If you include these two statements in a style sheet, the headings at levels 1 and 2 will have 20 and 15 points, respectively, between the content and the top and bottom borders. Heading 1 (H1) will have a left and right padding of 10 points; heading 2 (H2) will have a left and right padding of 7.5 points.

padding-bottom

Use this property to add space between the bottom of the contents and the border below. Padding is not inherited, so included and inline elements use the default of zero (0) rather than the settings from the parent element.

Values

> *length*   Sets an absolute or relative distance between the bottom of the contents and the border below. See the description of the length value for the padding property for valid measurements.

> *percentage*   Sets the bottom padding size to a percentage of the parent element.

Notes

See the "Notes" section for the padding property.

Examples

```
BODY {padding-bottom: 3em}
```

This statement sets the padding distance between the bottom of the page to 3 ems, which allows it to vary with the font size.

```
H1 {padding-bottom: 2pt}
```

This statement sets the distance for the bottom padding to 2 points for level-1 headings (H1). It will add a distance of 2 points to the space between the text of the heading and the location of the border, regardless of the font size of the heading.

```
P.CAP {padding-bottom: 0.5cm}
```

This statement sets up a paragraph class called CAP (P CLASS=CAP) in which the distance between the bottom of the element contents and the border location is an absolute value of ½ centimeter.

padding-left

Use this property to add space between the left edge of the contents and the border location. Padding is not inherited, so included and inline elements use the default of zero (0) rather than the settings from the parent element.

Values

> *length*   Sets an absolute or relative distance between the left edge of the contents and the border. See the description of the length value for the padding property for valid measurements.

> *percentage*   Sets the left padding size to a percentage of the parent element.

Notes

See the "Notes" section for the padding property.

Examples

```
ADDRESS {padding-left: 10%}
```

This statement adds space to the left of the ADDRESS elements. Unlike the left margin space, this padding space shows the element background. This space is a relative space; the amount of the space depends on the size of the element.

padding-right

Use this property to add space between the right edge of the contents and the border location. Padding is not inherited, so included and inline elements use the default of zero (0) rather than the settings from the parent element.

Values

> *length*   Sets an absolute or relative distance between the right edge of the contents and the border. See the description of the length value for the padding property for valid measurements.

> *percentage*   Sets the right padding size to a percentage of the parent element.

Notes

See the "Notes" section for the padding property.

Examples

```
P {padding-left: 8px;
    padding-right: 8px}
P {padding: 0 8px}
```

These two statements produce the same result. The first uses the individual properties to set the left and right padding to 8 pixels. The second uses the shorthand padding property to set the top and bottom padding to zero and the left and right padding to 8 pixels.

padding-top

Use this property to add space between the top of the contents and the border location. Padding is not inherited, so included and inline elements use the default of zero (0) rather than the settings from the parent element.

Values

length   Sets an absolute or a relative distance between the top of the contents and the border. See the description of the length value for the `padding` property for valid measurements.

percentage   Sets the top padding size to a percentage of the parent element.

Notes

See the "Notes" section for the `padding` property.

Examples

```
ADDRESS {padding-top: 1cm}
```

This statement adds a centimeter above the element contents before placing the border. Using an absolute measurement like this is less browser-sensitive than the relative values.

Box Border Properties

Every container has a border. Element borders reside between the padding and margin in the element container. By default, borders have no style set (they are not visible), regardless of color or width.

The default for the border is a medium-width line with no pattern that inherits the color (foreground) setting for the parent element.

You can use the `border` shorthand property to set all the border properties, or use the individual properties.

border

Use this shorthand property to set some or all of the border properties. You can set a single value for all four sides of the border.

Values

The possible values for the `border` property are the set of all possible values listed in the individual property entries:

`border-width`   Sets the border width for the border using a single value. This value can be one of the following: `value` `thin`, `medium`, `thick`, or a length measurement.

`border-style`   Sets the pattern used to fill the border. You can set the style to any of the following: `none`, `dotted`, `dashed`, `solid`, `double`, `groove`, `ridge`, `inset`, or `outset`.

`border-color`   Sets the color for all sides of the border. This value can be one of the color names or RGB values.

See the entries for the individual properties for details about these values.

Notes

Unlike other shorthand properties, you can use only a single setting for each value you include. The property is applied evenly to all sides of the box border.

See the "Notes" section for the `border-color`, `border-style`, and `border-color` properties.

Examples

`P.WARN {border: 2em double red}`

This statement generates a border around the paragraph class element WARN (P CLASS=WARN). The border is a red, double-line border that is 2 ems wide.

`P.NOTE {border: 2px ridge blue}`

This statement generates borders around the paragraph class element NOTE (P CLASS=NOTE). The border is a ridged, blue border that is 2 pixels wide.

border-bottom

Use this shorthand property to set some or all of the border properties for the bottom border of the element container.

Values

`border-width`   Sets the width for the bottom border. This value can be one of the following: `thin`, `medium`, `thick`, or a length measurement.

`border-style`   Sets the pattern used to fill the bottom border. You can set the style to any of the following: `none`, `dotted`, `dashed`, `solid`, `double`, `groove`, `ridge`, `inset`, or `outset`.

`border-color`   Sets the color for the bottom border. This value can be one of the color names or RGB values.

You can use one setting for each of the values of `border-bottom` property. See the entries for the individual properties for more details about these values.

Notes

See the "Notes" section for the `border-color`, `border-style`, and `border-color` properties.

Examples

```
P.SECTEND {color: blue;
      border-bottom: 0.5em dashed #8A2BE2}
      /* #8A2BE2 is a blueviolet color */
```

This statement overrides the foreground color for the SECTEND class of paragraphs (P CLASS=SECTEND) and replaces it with an RGB value (`blueviolet`). If you use an RGB value, it is helpful to include a comment that indicates what color you expect. See the entry for the `border-color` property for more information about specifying border colors. SECTEND paragraph text will appear blue and concludes with a dashed, violet-blue line that is 0.5 em thick. The em thickness associates the width of the border with the font size for the paragraph.

```
P.NOTE {color: green;
      border-bottom: 5em groove}
```

This statement specifies that NOTE class paragraphs (P CLASS=NOTE) will use the color green for foreground objects (such as text and the border) and have a grooved, 5-em terminating line.

border-bottom-width

Use this property to set the thickness of the bottom border for an element. The border width is, by default, a medium thickness and is unaffected by any border settings for the parent element.

Values

thin width   Sets a thin line for the bottom border. Use the keyword `thin`.

medium width   Sets a medium line for the bottom border. Use the keyword `medium`. This is the default.

thick width   Sets a relatively thick line for the bottom border. Use the keyword `thick`.

length   Sets the bottom border width using an absolute or a relative measurement. See the description of the length value for the `border-width` property for valid measurements.

You can use one of the values listed above to set the width of the bottom border.

Notes
See the "Notes" section for the `border-width` property.

Examples
```
P.UNDER {border-style: solid;
     border-bottom-width: 0.5cm;
     border-color: gray}
```

This creates a class of paragraph called UNDER (P CLASS=UNDER) in which the bottom border is ½ centimeter. This is an absolute setting, unaffected by the browser, page size, or element properties such as font.

```
H1 {border-style: solid;
     border-bottom-width: thin
     border-color: #F0F8FF}
```

This statement specifies the border as a standard, thin line.

border-color

Use this property to create a border using colors that are different from the foreground color for the element. The border color uses the foreground color of the element as a default setting. This shorthand property sets the visible border to the selected color(s).

Values

> *color* Sets the color for the border. This value can be one of the color names or RGB values. See the "Notes" section for valid values.

If you specify a single color, all four borders will appear as that color. If you include two colors, the top and bottom borders use the first color, and the left and right borders use the second color. If you include three colors, the top border uses the first color, the left and right borders use the second color, and the bottom border uses the third color. To give each border a unique color, list four colors; the borders use them in the following order: top, right, bottom, left.

Notes
You can either use color keywords or RGB values to specify border colors. If you name a color, the keyword must be one that the browser will recognize; the RGB colors are recognized by more browsers.

Color keywords include the following:

aqua	gray	navy	silver
black	green	olive	teal
blue	lime	purple	white
fuchsia	maroon	red	yellow

These colors are taken from the Windows VGA palette.

For an RGB specification, use any one of the three variants listed in Table A.1 to specify the color.

TABLE A.1: The RGB Values

Color	RGB Hex	RGB Integer	RGB Percent
Aqua	#00FFFF	rgb(0,255,255)	rgb(0%,100%,100%)
Black	#000000	rgb(0,0,0)	rgb(0%,0%,0%)
Blue	#0000FF	rgb(0,0,255)	rgb(0%,0%,100%)
Fuchsia	#FF00FF	rgb(255,0,255)	rgb(100%,0%,100%)
Gray	#808080	rgb(128,128,128)	rgb(50%,50%,50%)
Green	#008000	rgb(0,128,0)	rgb(0%,50%,0%)
Lime	#00FF00	rgb(0,255,0)	rgb(0%,100%,0%)
Maroon	#800000	rgb(128,0,0)	rgb(50%,0%,0%)
Navy	#000080	rgb(0,0,128)	rgb(0%,0%,50%)
Olive	#808000	rgb(128,128,0)	rgb(50%,50%,0%)
Purple	#800080	rgb(128,0,128)	rgb(50%,0%,50%)
Red	#FF0000	rgb(255,0,0)	rgb(100%,0%,0%)
Silver	#C0C0C0	rgb(192,192,192)	rgb(75%,75%,75%)
Teal	#008080	rgb(0,128,128)	rgb(0%,50%,50%)
White	#FFFFFF	rgb(255,255,255)	rgb(100%,100%,100%)
Yellow	#FFFF00	rgb(255,255,0)	rgb(100%,100%,0%)

For more information about choosing colors, refer to the list of 216 safe HTML colors in the HTML Color Codes section of this Appendix.

Examples

```
P.WARN {border-color: #8B0000} /* dark red border */
```

This statement specifies that the paragraphs of class WARN (P CLASS=WARN) are outlined with a dark red border.

```
P.DANCING {border-color: #F0F8FF #F0FFFF blue #5F9EA0}
```

This statement sets the border on each side of the element to a different color. This creates a multi-hued line around paragraphs of class DANCING (P CLASS=DANCING). The top is aliceblue, the right is azure, the bottom is blue, and the left is cadetblue.

border-left

Use this shorthand property to set some or all of the border properties for the border on the left side of the element container.

Values

`border-width`   Sets the width for the left border. This value can be one of the following: `thin`, `medium`, `thick`, or a length measurement.

`border-style`   Sets the pattern used to fill the left border. You can set the style to any of the following: `none`, `dotted`, `dashed`, `solid`, `double`, `groove`, `ridge`, `inset`, or `outset`.

`border-color`   Sets the color for the left border. This value can be one of the color names or RGB values.

You can use one value for each of the values of the `border-left` property. See the entries for the individual properties for more details about these values.

Notes

See the "Notes" section for the `border-color`, `border-style`, and `border-color` properties.

Examples

```
P.INSERT {border-left: thin solid red}
```

This statement places a thin, red line next to the INSERT class paragraphs (P CLASS= INSERT). This is a useful way to create a class for all your elements that insert "change bars" (lines that show that changes have been made in the text) in the left border.

border-left-width

Use this property to set the thickness of the border on the left side of an element. The border width is, by default, a medium thickness and is unaffected by any border settings for the parent element.

Values

thin width   Sets a thin line for the left border. Use the keyword `thin`.

medium width   Sets a medium line for the left border. Use the keyword `medium`. This is the default.

thick width   Sets a relatively thick line for the left border. Use the keyword `thick`.

length   Sets the left border width using an absolute or a relative measurement. See the description of the length value for the `border-width` property for valid measurements.

You can use one of the values listed above to set the width of the left border.

Notes

See the "Notes" section for the `border-width` property.

Examples

```
P.INSERT {border-style: dashed;
     border-left-width: 5em;
     border-color: red}
```

This statement creates a paragraph class called INSERT that uses a dashed, red line on the left border. The thickness of the line depends on the size of the paragraph font.

border-right

Use this shorthand property to set some or all of the border properties for the border to the right of the element contents.

Values

`border-width`   Sets the width for the right border. This value can be one of the following: `thin`, `medium`, `thick`, or a length measurement.

`border-style`   Sets the pattern used to fill the right border. You can set the style to any of the following: `none`, `dotted`, `dashed`, `solid`, `double`, `groove`, `ridge`, `inset`, or `outset`.

`border-color`   Sets the color for the right border. This value can be one of the color names or RGB values.

You can use one value for each of the values of the `border-left` property. See the entries for the individual properties for more details about these values.

Notes

See the "Notes" section for the `border-color`, `border-style`, and `border-color` properties.

Examples

```
P.NEWS {padding-right: 15em;

    border-right: thick dotted navy}
```

This creates a thick, dotted line that appears to the right of paragraphs of the class NEWS (P CLASS=NEWS). The line is navy blue and is 15 ems from the element contents.

```
H3.STRIKE {border-right: thick groove black}
```

This adds a thick, grooved, black line to the right of level-3 headings of the class STRIKE (H3 CLASS=STRIKE). This is a useful way to create a class that inserts an indicator that the information is out-of-date and about to be removed.

border-right-width

Use this property to set the thickness of the border on the right side of an element. The border width is, by default, a medium thickness and is unaffected by any border settings for the parent element.

Values

thin width   Sets a thin line for the right border. Use the keyword `thin`.

medium width   Sets a medium line for the right border. Use the keyword `medium`. This is the default.

thick width   Sets a relatively thick line for the right border. Use the keyword `thick`.

length   Sets the right border width using an absolute or a relative measurement. See the description of the length value for the `border-width` property for valid measurements.

You can use one of the values listed above to set the width of the right border.

Notes

See the "Notes" section for the `border-width` property.

Examples

```
P.STRIKE {border-style: dashed;

    border-right-width: 5px;

    border-color: blue}
```

This statement creates a paragraph class called STRIKE that uses a dashed, blue line on the right border of the element. The line is 5 pixels wide.

border-style

Use this property to display a border and specify a border style. You can create different effects by combining line styles with color and width. This property uses none as the default, not displaying the border at all, regardless of the color or width settings.

Values

no style   Prevents the display of one or more borders. Use the keyword none. This is the default.

dotted line   Sets the border as a dotted line, with spaces where the element background shows through. Use the keyword dotted.

dashed line   Sets the border as a series of dashes, alternating the element background and the border color. Use the keyword dashed.

solid line   Sets the border as a single, solid line in the border color or element foreground color. Use the keyword solid.

double lines   Sets the border as two solid lines in the border color or element foreground color. Use the keyword double.

grooved line   Sets the border as a 3-D rendering of a grooved line drawn in the border color. Use the keyword groove.

ridged line   Sets the border as a raised 3-D rendering peaking in the middle of the line, drawn in the border color. Use the keyword ridge.

inset border   Sets the border as a 3-D rendering creating the illusion that the inside of the element is sunken into the page. Use the keyword inset.

outset border   Sets the border as a 3-D rendering creating the illusion that the inside of the element is raised above the page. Use the keyword outset.

Use as many as four values from the list above to stylize the borders around an element. Since the initial setting for the border-style property is none, no borders are visible unless you set them up with a style plus a width.

Notes

Not all browsers can display the more esoteric styles, such as ridge, inset, and outset. If the browser cannot interpret the style, it will substitute a solid line. Some browsers may simply render all borders as solid lines.

Examples

```
P.LOOKNEW {border-style: outset;
      border-width: 0.5cm;
      border-color: gray}
```

This statement creates the illusion that the LOOKNEW class paragraph elements (P CLASS=LOOKNEW) are set above the page in a raised box.

```
P.DANCING {border-style: groove ridge inset outset;
      border-color: #F0F8FF #F0FFFF blue #5F9EA0}
```

With these properties, each side of the paragraphs in the class DANCING (P CLASS= DANCING) are a different shade of blue and a different style.

border-top

Use this shorthand property to set some or all of the border properties for the top border of the element container.

Values

    `border-width`   Sets the width for the top border. This value can be one of the following: `thin`, `medium`, `thick`, or a length measurement.

    `border-style`   Sets the pattern used to fill the top border. You can set the style to any of the following: `none`, `dotted`, `dashed`, `solid`, `double`, `groove`, `ridge`, `inset`, or `outset`.

    `border-color`   Sets the color for the top border. This value can be one of the color names or RGB values.

You can use one setting for each of the values of the `border-top` property. See the entries for the individual properties for more details about these values.

Notes

See the "Notes" section for the `border-color`, `border-style`, and `border-color` properties.

Examples

```
H1 {margin-top: 0.5in;
      color: red;
      background: white;
      padding: 9em;
      border-top: thin solid blue}
```

This statement creates level-1 headings (H1) that have red text on a white background and a thin, solid, blue line positioned 9 ems above the text. There is another line ½ inch above the heading. The 9-em padding is a relative value that depends on the font size and is equivalent to 9 blank lines above the heading.

border-top-width

Use this property to set the thickness of the border along the top of an element. The border width is, by default, a medium thickness and is unaffected by any border settings for the parent element.

Values

>*thin width*   Sets a thin line for the top border. Use the keyword `thin`.
>
>*medium width*   Sets a medium line for the top border. Use the keyword `medium`. This is the default.
>
>*thick width*   Sets a relatively thick line for the top border. Use the keyword `thick`.
>
>*length*   Sets the top border width using an absolute or a relative measurement. See the description of the length value for the `border-width` property for valid measurements.

You can use one of the values listed above to set the width of the top border.

Notes

See the "Notes" section for the `border-width` property.

Examples

```
H1, H2, H3 {font-size: 15pt;
     font-style: Futura, sans serif;
     border-style: solid;
     border-left-width: 1.5em}
```

This statement applies to the three levels of headings, giving each heading a solid line that is 1.5 ems. Since this is relative to the font, the line will be 22.5 points. The border color is not set, so the border uses the foreground color of the element.

border-width

Use this shorthand property to set the thickness of all the borders for an element. You can give the borders unique widths or use a single width for all the borders.

Values

thin width   Sets a thin line for the border. Use the keyword `thin`.

medium width   Sets a medium line for the border. Use the keyword `medium`. This is the default.

thick width   Sets a relatively thick line for the border. Use the keyword `thick`.

length   Sets the border width using an absolute or a relative measurement. Uses inch, millimeter, centimeter, point, pixel (the size according to the screen display), pica, x-height (the height of the font's lowercase letter *x*), or em (the width of a capital *M* in the font) units as measurements. This type of sizing forces a particular measurement to be used for the element, ignoring any browser's settings. Specify the measurement after the number as follows: `in` for inches, `mm` for millimeters, `cm` for centimeters, `pt` for points, `px` for pixels, `pc` for picas, `ex` for x-height settings, or `em` for em settings. With this property, the em and `ex` settings generate a border size relative to the parent font.

If you use one of the values above, it applies evenly to the borders on the four sides of the element. If you use two values, the browser applies the first to the top and bottom borders of the element, and the second to the left and right borders. If you include three values, the browser uses the first for the top border, the second for the left and right borders, and the last for the bottom border. If you use four values, the browser applies them in the following order: top, right, bottom, left.

Notes

The `thin` setting will always be less than or equal to the `medium` setting, which will always be less than or equal to the `thick` setting. The border widths do not depend on the element font or other settings. The `thick` setting, for example, is rendered in the same size wherever it occurs in a document. You can use the relative length values to produce variable (font-dependent) widths.

With a length setting, you cannot have a border with a negative width. You can use a decimal number, for example, 0.4 or 1.2.

Relative units set up the property in relation to the font and size properties. Use relative units wherever you can, because they scale more easily from situation to situation (for example, in different browsers and displays, or in the transition from display to printer). Relative units include em (1 em is equal to the width of a capital *M* in the font), `ex` (the height of the lowercase letter *x* in a font), and `px` (screen pixels).

Absolute lengths are useful when the properties of the browser are well-known or when you want to set a particular border size to conform to a specification. Absolute units include inches, millimeters and centimeters, points (1 point = 1/72 inch), and picas (1 pica = 12 points).

Examples

```
P.LOOKNEW {border-style: outset;
    border-width: 0.5cm;
    border-color: gray}
```

This statement sets all the borders for the paragraphs of class LOOKNEW (P CLASS=LOOKNEW) at ½ centimeter.

```
P.DANCING {border-style: groove ridge inset outset;
    border-width: thin thick medium 1cm;
    border-color: #F0F8FF #F0FFFF blue #5F9EA0}
```

This statement sets each border in the paragraphs of class DANCING (P CLASS=DANCING) at different widths. The top border is thin, the right border is thick, the bottom is medium, and the left border is 1 centimeter.

Box Margin Properties

Margins set the size of the box around an element. You measure margins from the border area to the edge of the box.

margin

Use this property as a shorthand to set up all the margins for an element's box. This measurement gives the browser the distance between the element border and the edge of the box. This area is always transparent, so you can view the underlying page background.

Values

length   Sets an absolute or a relative distance between the border and the box edge. See the `border-width` property in the "Box Border Properties" section for valid measurements.

percentage   Sets the margin size as a percentage of the parent element's width.

automatic   Use this optional value to set the margin to the browser's default. Use the keyword `auto`.

Use one of the values above. For length and percentage, you can use one, two, three, or four numbers. If you use one number, the browser applies it to all four margins (top, right, bottom, and left). If you use two numbers, the first number sets the top and bottom margin, and the second number sets the left and right margin. If you use three numbers, you are setting the top margin with the first, the right and left margins with the second, and the bottom margin with the third. You can mix length and percentage values.

Notes

You can use negative values for margins, but not all browsers will handle the settings correctly, and some may ignore the setting and substitute the default of zero (0) or use their own algorithm.

See the "Notes" section for the `border-width` property in the "Box Border Properties" section for information about relative and absolute length settings.

Examples

```
P.1 {margin: 5%}
```

This statement establishes paragraph margins, for paragraphs of class 1, to 5% each of the total width of the box.

```
P {margin: 2em 3pt}
```

This statement sets the paragraph elements' top and bottom margins to 2 ems (relative to the size of the font) and the left and right margins to 3 points.

```
P.NOTE {margin: 1em 3em 4em}
```

This statement sets the margins for paragraphs of class NOTE (P CLASS=NOTE). The top margin is 1 em (relative to the font size), the left and right margins are 3 ems, and the bottom margin is 4 ems. If the font size is 10 points, the top margin will be 10 points, the left and right margins will be 30 points, and the bottom margin will be 40 points.

margin-bottom

Use this property to set only the bottom margin of an element's box. The bottom margin is the distance between the bottom border and the bottom edge of the box. This generally defaults to zero (0) and is not used by included block or inline elements.

Values

length   Sets an absolute or relative distance between the border and the box's bottom edge. See the `border-width` property in the "Box Border Properties" section for valid measurements.

percentage   Sets the bottom margin size as a percentage of the parent element's width.

automatic   Use this optional value to set the bottom margin to the browser's default. Use the keyword `auto`.

You can use one of the values above to set the bottom margin.

Notes

See the "Notes" section for the `margin` property

Examples

```
P {margin-bottom: 4em}
```

This statement sets the bottom margin of all paragraphs to 4 ems. This is a relative measure, so the actual distance depends on the font. For example, if the font size is 10 points, the bottom margin will be the equivalent of 4 blank lines, or 40 points. This establishes a distance of 4 ems between the border and the box bottom.

```
H1 {margin-top:5em;
    margin-bottom: 1em}
```

This statement positions level-1 headings (H1) with the equivalent of five lines above and one line below. This creates a separation between the preceding topic and the heading and strengthens the association between the heading and its topic contents below.

margin-left

Use this property to set only the left margin of an element's box. The left margin is the distance between the border and the left edge of the box. You can use this to create indented text or other element placements. The default for the left margin is zero (0), or no space. The settings in one element are not used by its included or inline elements.

Values

length   Sets an absolute or a relative distance between the border and the box's left edge. See the `border-width` property in the "Box Border Properties" section for valid measurements.

percentage   Sets the left margin size as a percentage of the parent element's width.

automatic   Use this optional value to set the left margin to the browser's default. Use the keyword `auto`.

You can use one of the values above to set the left margin.

Notes

See the "Notes" section for the `margin` property.

Examples

```
BODY {margin-left: 3%}
```

This statement sets up a basic left margin for the page using the <BODY> tag. The browser should display this margin as 3% of the width of the page. No element within the page will appear outside this margin. If the browser shows 640 × 480 pixels, the body margin (left) uses 18 pixels.

```
P {margin-left: 1cm}
```

This statement sets a left margin for paragraphs at the absolute value of 1 centimeter. With this, you can add a left gutter to your page.

```
P {margin-left: 4em}
```

This statement creates a variable gutter for the paragraphs on a page. The actual size of the 4-em margin depends on the font size used for the paragraphs.

margin-right

Use this property to set just the right margin of an element's box. The right margin is the distance between the border and the right edge of the box. You can use this to force the element away from the right edge of the page. This generally defaults to zero (0) and is not used by included block or inline elements.

Values

length   Sets an absolute or a relative distance between the border and the box's right edge. See the `border-width` property in the "Box Border Properties" section for valid measurements.

percentage   Sets the right margin size as a percentage of the parent element's width.

automatic   Use this optional value to set the right margin to the browser's default. Use the keyword `auto`.

You can use one of the values above to set the right margin.

Notes

See the "Notes" section for the `margin` property.

Examples

```
BODY {margin-right: 0.5in}
```

This statement creates a margin on your page that is a ½-inch wide. Nothing will appear in this margin area.

```
P {margin-right: 10%}
```

This statement establishes an outside gutter that is 10% of the paragraph width. The actual distance depends on the paragraph width.

```
H1 {margin-right: 15em}
```

This statement creates an outside gutter whose size depends on the heading font size. This inserts a distance equal to 1.5 times the heading font size. This means that if the level-1 heading uses a 15-point font, for example, the distance between the border and box edge is less than it would be with a 20-point font. If you want all headings to wrap before the edge of the box, but at the same place in the page, use percentage or absolute measurements.

margin-top

Use this property to set only the top margin of an element's box. The top margin is the distance between the border and the top of the box. You can use this to insert space above an element, perhaps to visually reinforce its relationship with the elements around it. This generally defaults to zero (0) and is not used by included block or inline elements.

Values

length   Sets an absolute or a relative distance between the border and the box's top edge. See the `border-width` property in the "Box Border Properties" section for valid measurements.

percentage   Sets the top margin size as a percentage of the parent element's width.

automatic   Use this optional value to set the top margin to the browser's default. Use the keyword `auto`.

You can use one of the values above to set the top margin.

Notes
See the "Notes" section for the `margin` property.

Examples

```
H1 {margin-top:5em;
       margin-bottom: 1em}
```

This statement positions level-1 headings (H1) with the equivalent of five lines above and one line below. This creates a separation between the preceding topic and the heading and strengthens the association between the heading and its topic contents below.

```
BODY {margin-top: 1em}
```

This statement adds the equivalent of one line to the margin of any element inside the body of the document. The actual distance depends on the font size for the element.

```
P {margin-top: 5%}
```

This statement adds a variable distance (5% of the height) to paragraph elements.

```
H1 {margin-top: 1cm}
```

This statement adds an absolute distance of 1 centimeter to the space between the box edge and the border of level-1 headings (H1). Whatever the environment, the browser tacks a centimeter of transparent margin to the element's box.

Box Position Properties

The box position properties control the arrangement of elements in relation to one another and the page, rather than within themselves. The `float` and `clear` properties control which elements can sit next to each other. The `width` and `height` properties set dimensions for elements, giving you more control of the page layout.

clear

Use this property to allow or disallow other elements, usually inline images, to float beside the element specified. You can allow floating elements on either side, both sides, or neither side. The default is to allow floating elements on both sides of the element (the none setting). This property is not used by inline and included elements.

Values

no restrictions   Allows floating elements on either side of this element. Use the keyword none. This is the default.

not on left   Moves the element below any floating elements on the left. Use the keyword `left`.

not on right   Moves the element below any floating elements on the right. Use the keyword `right`.

not on both   Does not allow floating elements on either side of this element. Use the keyword both.

Use one of these values to designate the position for floating elements in relation to a particular element.

Notes

This property indicates where floating elements are not allowed.

Examples

```
P.PRODNAME {clear: none}
```

This statement creates a paragraph class, called PRODNAME (P CLASS=PRODNAME), that allows floating elements to appear on either side of it.

```
P {clear: right}
```

In this statement, the paragraph element allows floating elements on its left side, but not the right.

```
H1, H2, H3 {clear: both}
```

This statement prevents elements from appearing next to the headings in the document. All floating elements, usually images, are pushed up or down and appear above or below the headings.

float

Use this property to set an element in a position outside the rules of placement for the normal flow of elements. For example, the float property can raise an element from an inline element to a block element. This is usually used to place an image. The default, which is not an inherited value, is to display the element where it appears in the flow of the document (the none setting).

Values

no changes   Displays the element where it appears in the flow of the parent element. Use the keyword none. This is the default.

left float   Wraps other element contents to the right of the floating element. Use the keyword left.

right float   Wraps other element contents to the left of the floating element. Use the keyword right.

Notes

A floating element cannot overlap the margin in the parent element used for positioning. For example, an illustration that is a left-floating element (pushes other contents to the right of itself) cannot overlap the left margin of its parent container.

Examples

```
P {clear: none}
IMG.KEYCAP {float: none}
IMG.PRODLOGO {float: left}
```

These statements specify that if an image of class KEYCAP (IMG CLASS=KEYCAP) is inserted in the course of a paragraph, it appears within the flow of the text. If an image of class PRODLOGO (IMG CLASS=PRODLOGO) is inserted, it appears against the left margin of the parent element, and the text wraps on its right.

height

Use this property to set the height of an element on a page. Browsers will enforce the height, scaling the image to fit. This property will be familiar to anyone who has used the height and width values of an image on a Web page.

Values

length   Sets an absolute or a relative height for images in a particular element or class. Uses inch, centimeter, millimeter, point, pixel (the size according to the screen display values), pica, x-height (the height of the font's lowercase letter *x*), or em (the width of a capital *M* in the font) units as measurements. This type of sizing forces a particular measurement to be used for the element, ignoring any browser's settings. Specify the measurement after the number as follows: in for inches, cm for centimeters, mm for millimeters, pt for points, px for pixels, pc for picas, ex for x-height settings, or em for em settings. The em and ex settings generate a size relative to the parent font.

automatic   Allows the browser to either set the height to the actual image height or, if the width is set, preserve the aspect ratio of images. Use the keyword auto.

You can use one of these values for the height of elements.

Notes

Some browsers may not handle the height (or width) property if the element is not a replaced element (one that uses a pointer in the HTML source to indicate the file with the actual content).

Generally, replaced elements have their own intrinsic measurements. If you want to replace these dimensions with a height (and/or width) property setting, the browser tries to resize the replaced element to fit. To maintain the aspect ratio, you need to set one of the properties, height or width, to auto. To preserve the aspect ratio of images positioned with height, include the width property in the statement and set the width to auto. If you position an image with the width property, include the height property in the statement and set the height to auto.

If you need to set the size of an image, it's usually best to set it in proportion to the container element (using a relative setting); otherwise, leave these settings at auto, which allows the browser to use the image's original size.

You cannot use a negative value for the height or width of an element.

With a length setting, relative units set up the property in relation to the font and size properties. Use relative units wherever you can, because they scale more easily from situation to situation (for example, in different browsers and displays, or in the transition from display to printer). Relative units include em (1 em is equal to the width of a capital *M* in the font), ex (the height of the lowercase letter *x* in a font), and px (screen pixels).

Absolute units are useful when the properties of the browser are well-known or when you want to set a particular size to conform to a specification. Absolute units include inches, millimeters and centimeters, points (1 point = 1/72 inch), and picas (1 pica = 12 points).

Examples

```
IMG.KEYCAP {float: none;
    width: auto
    height: 1.2em;
    vertical-align: middle}
```

This statement creates an IMG class (IMG CLASS=KEYCAP) where the images appear in the text stream. These images have a controlled width and a height that is 1.2 ems. For example, in a stream of text with a font size of 12 points, the image will be 14.4 points. The statement also adjusts the vertical position of the image in relation to the line.

```
IMG.PRODLOGO {float: left;
    width: 2cm;
    height: auto}
```

In this statement, images of class, PRODLOGO (IMG CLASS=PRODLOGO), which have the text wrap on the right around them, have a controlled width of 2 centimeters. However, it is better to avoid absolute measurements and use relative values or the image's own values (by setting width and height to auto).

width

Use this property to set the width of an element on a page. Browsers will enforce the width, scaling the image to fit.

Values

length   Sets an absolute or relative width for images in a particular element or class. See the height property for valid measurements.

percentage   Sets the image size as a percentage of the parent element's width.

automatic   Allows the browser to either set the width to the actual image width or, if height is set, preserve the aspect ratio of images. Use the keyword auto.

You can use one of these values for the width of elements.

Notes

See the "Notes" section for the `height` property.

Examples

```
IMG.KEYCAP {float: none;
     width: auto
     height: 1.2em;
     vertical-align: middle}
```

In this statement, images of class KEYCAP (IMG CLASS=KEYCAP) will appear in the text stream aligned to the middle of the line of text where it appears. Its height is set to 1.2 ems and the width to `auto`, which allows the browser to position it properly (the height does not disturb the paragraph formatting around it, and the width is adjusted to fit).

```
IMG.PRODLOGO {float: left;
     width: 2cm;
     height: auto}
```

This statement creates an image class, PRODLOGO (IMG CLASS=PRODLOGO), that forces the text to wrap on the right of it, is 2 centimeters wide, and has whatever height is proportionate to the 2-centimeter width.

Background and Color Properties

Color affects the foreground elements, such as text and borders, and background properties affect the surface on which the document elements appear. You can set these globally and locally for individual elements. When you paint the background for an element, you are layering on top of the document's background. If you do not set a background for an element, it defaults to transparent, allowing the document background to show. The `color` property inherits from the document body.

You can control a wide variety of properties for backgrounds, including the position, repetition, and scrolling. You can use the `background` shorthand property to set all the background properties, or use the individual properties. The background is set relative to the element's box properties.

background

Use this property as a shorthand to include the full collection of background values. The `background` property will be familiar to anyone who has changed the page color of a Web page or added a graphic as wallpaper. This property now extends to individual elements, allowing you to have a variety of backgrounds. It also allows more functionality in the background, including scrolling and repetitions.

Values

The possible values for background are the set of all possible values listed in the individual property entries:

> `background-attachment`   Sets up a background that scrolls with the element.

> `background-color`   Sets a background color for the page or elements on the page.

> `background-image`   Sets an image behind the element.

> `background-position`   Positions the background within the element's box.

> `background-repeat`   Sets the number of times and direction that a background repeats.

See the entries for the individual properties for details about these values.

Notes

If you do not include a property (such as `background-repeat`), the browser uses the default. The order of the properties in a statement is not important.

Examples

```
BODY {background: url(sunshine.gif) blue repeat-y}
```

This statement sets up a background for the page using the <BODY> tag. If the browser cannot find the image, it uses a blue background. If needed, the background image repeats down the page (but not across the page).

```
HI {background: white}
```

This statement changes the background for level-1 headings (H1) to white using the color keyword. If this statement appears in the same style sheet as the first statement, the sunshine background is overlaid with a white box where the level-1 headings appear.

```
P EM {background: url(swirl.gif) yellow top left}
```

In this statement, paragraph emphasis (EM) is changed to a swirl GIF file that starts at the top-left corner of the element's box. If the GIF file cannot be found, the browser uses a yellow background.

background-attachment

Use this property to specify whether the background image of an element will scroll with the element or remain at a fixed location on the page. If the image is larger than the element box, visitors scrolling down the screen either see different parts of the background image (a fixed attachment) or a single part of the image (a scrolling attachment) that moves with the display of the element down the page.

The default, `scroll`, applies only to the element in the statement. Inline and included block elements do not inherit this property.

Values

scrolling   Moves the image with the element on the page so that the same part is visible when visitors scroll down the screen. Use the keyword `scroll`. This is the default.

fixed   Keeps the image fixed in relation to the page, so different parts are visible when visitors scroll down the screen. Use the keyword `fixed`.

Notes

Use this property in conjunction with the `background-image` property.

Examples

```
P { background-image: url(logo.gif);
     background-attachment: fixed}
```

This statement uses the image `logo.gif` as the background for the paragraphs in the document. The image is fixed to the page, not the contents of the paragraph.

background-color

Use this property to set the background color for the page or elements on the page. If you set the background for the base class BODY, your other tags will appear to inherit that color unless you change their background colors from transparent.

Values

color   Sets the color for the background. This value can be one of the color names or RGB values. See the `border-color` property in the "Box Border Properties" for color keywords and values.

transparent   Makes the page background the default for viewing. Use the keyword `transparent`.

Notes

This value sets the background color only. To set the background as an image, you need to use either the `background` property or the `background-image` property.

This property affects the box area owned by the element. This is set using the `margins` and `padding` properties, listed in the "Box Margin Properties" and "Box Padding Properties" sections.

When you set an element's background to transparent or don't set it at all, the page's background color or image appears in its place.

See the "Notes" section for the border-color property in the "Box Border Properties" section for information about color settings.

Examples

HI {background-color: blue}

In this statement, the background color for level-1 headings (H1) is set to blue using the color keyword.

P.NOTE {background-color: #800000}

This statement creates a paragraph class called NOTE (P CLASS=NOTE) that has a background color of maroon using the RGB hexadecimal value for the color.

background-image

Use this property to define an image for the background. The browser will look for additional information about the image's position, repetition, and attachment (or association). If you accept the defaults for these properties, your background image will not repeat, will be attached to the page (not the element), and will have a starting position at the upper-left corner of the element's box.

Values

no image   Does not use an image for the background. Use the keyword **none** if you need to override a previous statement. This is the default.

image url   Cues the browser that you are going to provide a filename. Use the keyword url.

Notes

The images you use must be GIF or JPG image files to ensure that all graphical browsers can read them.

You may also want to include a background-color property in case the image you have selected is not available.

Examples

```
P {
     background-image: url(litelogo.jpg);
     background-repeat: no-repeat;
     background-attachment: fixed; }
```

This statement sets up the document paragraphs to have a background image (called litelogo.jpg) that does not repeat and is fixed to the document canvas rather than to the element.

background-position

Use this property to position the element background within its space, using the initial position as a mark. Every element has a box that describes the area it controls. The background-position property is useful when your image is not the same size as the element for which it provides a background. With this property, you can indicate the position of the image relative to the element box.

Values

length   Sets the starting point on the element's box edge, in an absolute or a relative measurement, and also gives the coordinates as measurements. Uses inch, centimeter, millimeter, point, pixel (the size according to the screen display values), pica, x-height (the height of the font's lowercase letter *x*), or em (the height of the font) units as measurements. Specify the measurement after the number as follows: in for inches, cm for centimeters, mm for millimeters, pt for points, px for pixels, pc for picas, ex for x-height settings, or em for em settings. The em and ex settings generate a size relative to the parent font.

percentage   Indicates as a percentage where on the box edge the browser begins placing the image. You can repeat this value to give a vertical and horizontal starting point.

vertical position   Sets the vertical starting position. Use the keyword top, center, or bottom. The browser determines the size of the element box and works from there.

horizontal position   Sets the horizontal starting position. Use the keyword left, center, or right. The browser determines the width of the element box and works from there.

With the length and percentage settings, you can use two numbers to indicate the vertical and horizontal starting point. Unlike percentage, however, the length measurement does not apply to both the image and the element box in the same way. The length measurement indicates the coordinates inside the element box where the top-left corner of the image appears.

Notes

Using 0% 0% is synonymous with using top left. In the first case, the initial position of the image is determined this way; the upper-left corner of the image is considered 0% horizontal and 0% vertical, and the same is done with the element box. You could position an image using 50% 50%, and the browser would then begin at the middle of the element and the image. If the image is larger than the element box, you lose the edges that extend beyond the element box. Similarly, if your image is smaller than the element box, you will have an edge, inside your element box, with no image.

You can combine the percentage and length measures. It would be legal to set the property using 25% 2cm. This would start rendering the image at ¼ the way into the image at a ¼ the distance across the element box. The image would begin to appear 2 centimeters below the top of the element box.

The length measurements indicate the distance from the box border where the browser starts to render the image.

When you use a length unit, you can use a positive or a negative number. You can, in some cases, use a decimal number. Whichever system of measurement you choose to use must be communicated with the short form for the system (for example, cm or in).

Relative units set up the property in relation to the font and size properties. Use relative units wherever you can, because they scale more easily from situation to situation (for example, in different browsers and displays, or in the transition from display to printer). Relative units include em (1 em is equal to the width of a capital *M* in the font), ex (the height of the lowercase letter *x* in a font), and px (screen pixels).

Absolute lengths are useful when the properties of the browser are well-known or when you want to set a particular size to conform to a specification. Absolute units include the inches, millimeters and centimeters, points (1 point = 1/72 inch), and picas (1 pica = 12 points).

You can also use keywords to position the image within the element's box. Table A.2 gives you some corresponding values to work with.

TABLE A.2: Keywords and Their Values

Keyword	Percentage	Description
top left, left top	0% 0%	The top-left corner of the image starts at the top-left corner of the element box.
top, top center, center top	50% 0%	The horizontal middle of the image appears in the horizontal middle of the element box. The top of the image begins at the top of the element box.
right top, top right	100% 0%	The top-right corner of the image starts at the top-right corner of the element box.
left, left center, center left	0% 50%	The vertical middle of the image appears in the vertical middle of the element box. The left side of the image is flush against the left side of the element box.

TABLE A.2 continued: Keywords and Their Values

KEYWORD	PERCENTAGE	DESCRIPTION
center, center center	50% 50%	The absolute middle of the image positions over the absolute middle of the element box.
Right, right center, center right	100% 50%	The vertical middle of the image positions over the vertical middle of the element rightbox. The right edge of the image is flush against the right side of the element box.
bottom left, left bottom	0% 100%	The bottom-left corner of the image is positioned at the bottom-left corner of the element box.
bottom center, center bottom	50% 100%	The horizontal centers of the image and element box appear together, and the bottom edges of each remain together.
bottom right, right bottom	100% 100%	The lower-right corner of the image positions in the lower-right corner of the element box.

Examples

```
BODY {background-image: url(litelogo.gif);
        background-position: 50% 50%}
```

This sets the base class, BODY, to position a background image centered on the page.

```
H1 {background-image: url(exclaim.gif);
      background-position: top left}
```

In this statement, an image has been assigned to the background of heading level-1 (H1) tags that starts rendering at the upper-left corner of the element box.

background-repeat

Use this property to control whether an image repeats horizontally, vertically, both, or neither. Images normally repeat both horizontally and vertically, filling in the area within the element's margins. By default, backgrounds repeat both horizontally and vertically.

Values

horizontal and vertical repeat   Sets horizontal and vertical repetitions of the image. Use the keyword `repeat`. This is the default.

horizontal repeat   Sets horizontal repetitions only. Use the keyword `repeat-x`.

vertical repeat   Sets vertical repetitions only. Use the keyword `repeat-y`.

no repeat   Prevents repeated copies of the image from displaying. Use the keyword `no-repeat`.

Notes

This property works in conjunction with the `background-image` and `background-position` properties. Combining these properties into a single statement enables you to create a pattern of background images that enhance the presentation of information.

Examples

```
P {background-image: url(logo1.gif);
    background-color: blue;
    background-position: top left;
    background-repeat: repeat-y}
```

This statement adds a background to your document paragraphs. The first copy of the image appears in the upper-left corner of the page and repeats down the page. If the image is not found, the browser uses a blue background.

color

Use this property to set the foreground, or element, color. If the element is text, you can set the color of the text with this property. Both inline (such as images) and included block elements (such as EM) use this property.

Values

color   Sets the color for the background. This value can be one of the color names or RGB values. See the `border-color` property in the "Box Border Properties" for color keywords and values.

Notes

You can set this property using one of the three systems of RGB or by using a color keyword. Although most browsers should recognize the color keyword, individual browser/system configurations may display the same color differently.

Choose the system that makes the most sense to you and stick with that. See the HTML Color Codes section of this reference for color values and resources.

If you use RGB values, put a comment next to the line to help you remember what the color was supposed to be. Comments start with /* and end with */.

See the "Notes" section for the border-color property in the "Box Border Properties" section for more information about color settings.

Examples

```
BODY {color: black}
```

This statement uses the keyword black to set the default foreground color in the document to black.

```
P {color: #0000FF}
```

This statement changes the paragraph (P) foreground color to blue using the RGB hexadecimal value.

```
EM {color: rgb(75%,0%,0%)}
```

In this statement, emphasis (EM) is set to maroon using the RGB percentage value.

Classification Properties

This group of properties controls the presentation of some standard elements, such as the display and lists. The properties can change the type of an element from an inline to a block, from a list-item to an inline element, and so on. These properties also include controls for lists and list-items, giving you more control over the presentation of the bulleted lists on your page.

display

Use this property to change the display values of an element. You can change an element's type between inline, block, and list-item:

- ▶ An inline element does not start and stop on its own line, but is included in the flow of another element. A standard inline element is EM, for emphasis; you can also include images in the stream of text as an inline element.

- ▶ A block element starts on its own line and ends with another line break.

- ▶ A list-item is a subset of block elements, but is contained within a larger block element.

Every element has its own default value for display.

Values

> *no display*   Prevents the display of the element. Use the keyword `none`.
>
> *block display*   Sets the element with a line break before and after. Use the keyword `block`.
>
> *inline display*   Removes the line breaks from an element and forces it into the flow of another element. Use the keyword `inline`.
>
> *list-item display*   Sets the element as a line in a list. Use the keyword `list-item`.

Notes

You can use the `display` property values to create special elements such as run-in headings and running lists, as well as to force images into inline presentations.

Examples

```
H1 {display: inline}
```

This statement sets the browser not to force the level-1 headings (H1) onto a separate line. You could combine this with a line break (BR) before the heading, to start a new line, but let the contents of the section start right after the heading. You may want to extend the right margin of the heading to add some space between the heading and the content.

```
LI.INTEXT {display: inline}
```

Use this if you want to reformat your lists of the class INTEXT (LI CLASS=INTEXT) as a integral part of a paragraph. For example, you could list:

- ► `block`
- ► `inline`
- ► `list-item`
- ► `none`

Or you could list `block, inline, list-item, none.`

list-style

Use this shorthand property to set all the list properties in a single statement. If you set this property for a list element (as opposed to the list-item elements), the list-items use the settings you establish. You can override the list settings with individual list-item settings.

Values

The possible settings values for `list-style` are the set of all possible values listed in the individual property entries:

> `list-style-type` Sets the type of bullet used in the list. You can set the style type to any of the following: `disc`, `circle`, `square`, `decimal`, `lower-roman`, `upper-roman`, `lower-alpha`, `upper-alpha`, or `none`.

> `list-style-position` Sets a hanging outdent (`outside`), so that the bullet is not flush with the text of the list-item, or an indented bullet (`inside`), so that it is flush with the text of the list-items.

> `list-style-image` Sets an image to use for a bullet. Use the keyword `url`.

See the entries for the individual properties for details about these values.

Notes

These values apply only to elements with a display characteristic of `list-item`. If you use the `url` keyword to specify an image, you don't need to set the type, because the bullet position will be occupied by the image.

Examples

```
OL.OUTLINE {list-style: lower-roman inside}
```

This creates a list class called `OUTLINE` (`OL CLASS=OUTLINE`), which numbers the list-items.

```
LI.COMMENT {list-style: none}
```

If you use this statement in the same style sheet as the first statement, you can insert list-items that have no numbering.

list-style-image

Use this property to replace the standard bullet characters with an image of your choice. If you set this property for a list element (as opposed to the list-item elements), the list-items use the settings you establish. You can override the list settings with individual list-item settings.

Values

> *no image* Suppresses the image bullets that the element may have inherited.

> *image url* Identifies a specific image that you want to use for a bullet. Use the keyword `url`.

Notes

If you use an image, be sure it is a small image. Resize the image before assigning it as a bullet character.

If the browser cannot find the image identified in the `url`, it will default to `list-style-type` setting.

List-items use the settings from the lists. You can insert list-items with different settings, creating a series of effects (such as comments or highlights by using a different bullet or position).

Examples

```
LI.PRODICON {url (logo.gif)}
```

This replaces the bullet character for list-items of type PRODICON (LI CLASS= PRODICON) with an image called `logo.gif`.

list-style-position

Use this property to set an indent or outdent for the bullet. This property allows the bullet to stand out from the list contents (`outside`) or lays it flush with the list-items (`inside`). If you set this property for a list element (as opposed to the list-item elements), the list-items use the settings you establish. You can override the list settings with individual list-item settings

Values

indent   Aligns the bullet character with the left margin of the list-item contents. Use the keyword `inside`.

outdent   Creates a hanging-indent effect, with the bullet standing out from the left margin of the list-item contents. Use the keyword `outside`.

Notes

List-items use the settings from the lists. You can insert list-items with different settings, creating a series of effects (such as comments or highlights by using a different bullet or position).

Examples

```
UL {list-style-position: outside;
    list-style-type: circle}
LI.LEVEL2 {list-style-position: inside}
LI.PRODSTART {list-style-image: url (logolitl.gif)}
```

If you combine these three statements in a style sheet, your basic list-items in an unordered list will have a hollow circle that hangs outside the left margin of the list contents. You can add level-2 class list-items (LI CLASS=LEVEL2) that use the circle bullet but lay it flush to the list-item contents. This creates a visual effect where these list-items appear to be secondary. The third statement creates the effect of list headings by replacing the circle with a logo, and these list-items use the parent's list-style-position setting.

list-style-type

Use this property to indicate a style of bullet or numbering you want for your lists. You can create several list classes and list-item classes and then combine them to give your information navigational structure. If you set this property for a list element (as opposed to the list-item elements), the list-items use the settings you establish. You can override the list settings with individual list-item settings.

Values

no bullet   Suppresses the display of bullet characters. Use the keyword none.

disc bullet   Places a filled circle as the bullet. Use the keyword disc.

circle bullet   Places a hollow circle as the bullet. Use the keyword circle.

square bullet   Places a filled square as the bullet. Use the keyword square.

decimal bullet   Numbers the list-items using Arabic numerals (1, 2, 3, ...). Use the keyword decimal.

lowercase-roman bullet   Numbers the list-items using lowercase Roman numerals (i, ii, iii, ...). Use the keyword lower-roman.

uppercase-roman bullet   Numbers the list-items using uppercase Roman numerals (I, II, III, ...). Use the keyword upper-roman.

lowercase-alpha bullet   Letters the list-items using lowercase letters (a, b, c, ...). Use the keyword lower-alpha.

uppercase-alpha bullet   Letters the list-items using uppercase letters (A, B, C, ...). Use the keyword upper-alpha.

Notes

If you use numbering or lettering, and you insert list-items with an alternate type, the numbering includes the unnumbered list-items in its counts. For example:

```
A    full-featured
     WYSIWIG
     compliant
D    backward compatible
```

Examples

```
OL {list-style-type: lower-roman}
```

This statement sets up a numbering system for the ordered lists in the document (OL). These lists will use i, ii, iii, and so on as a "bullet" for each list-item.

```
LI.COMMENT {list-style-type: none}
```

You can override the list settings with a list-item setting. If you apply the list-item class COMMENT (LI CLASS=COMMENT) to an item in a numbered list, the browser includes it in the numbering, but does not display the number for the list-item.

white-space

Use this property to control the white space within an element. This setting controls the wrapping of text within the element. You can use the default, which produces results similar to what you see in Web pages already, or you can use the pre keyword to indicate that the content is already formatted correctly and should be displayed "as is." This property introduces a new value, nowrap, which relies on you to provide the information about when to wrap a line using line breaks (BR).

Values

no changes   Keeps the default of wrapping lines at the browser page size. Use the keyword normal. This is the default.

previous formatting   Assigns the formatting in the document source to the document display. Use the keyword pre.

no wrapping   Prevents the visitor from wrapping lines within an element. Use the keyword nowrap.

Notes

When you want to control the line wrap in paragraphs or headings, you can do it with this property. If you select normal, it overrides the settings of a parent element since browsers default to this setting. If your element is a preformatted entity (such as sample code), you may want to use the pre keyword to force the browser to display it exactly as it occurs in the source text. Use the nowrap keyword to prevent the browser from ending the line without an explicit instruction, such as BR, in the source.

Some browsers may ignore this setting and retain their own defaults. Even though the default value for white-space is listed as normal, some browsers will have a default setting for all HTML elements.

Examples

```
PRE {white-space: pre}
```

This statement indicates that the text in the element is preformatted. The spacing between characters, words, and lines is set in the source, as are the line breaks.

```
P {white-space: normal}
```

This statement sets the spacing in the paragraph elements (P) to normal, which is how text is currently displayed.

```
H1 {white-space: nowrap}
```

This statement prevents the browser from wrapping the level-1 headings (H1). For these headings to break across more than one line, you will need to explicitly add BR tags at the break spots.

JavaScript

This section covers the JavaScript statement keywords, objects, method and functions, and properties. These are all the pieces that you need to build a JavaScript for your page. We've included some examples here, but look in Chapter 14 and 15 to find the details of how to write JavaScript. In our explanations of the examples, we have used the term *entry* (rather than parameter or operator) to refer to the various parts of the syntax.

This reference sorts entries by general purpose; the sections cover the constructs, operators, escape character, reserved words, objects, methods and functions, and properties. Constructs are statement types that you can use to control the flow of a script. Operators are the algebraic, logical, and bitwise symbols for working with values in your statements. Escape character allows you to insert a special character into your text. Reserved words are terms that JavaScript either currently uses or plans to use in the future. The objects are the containers in which properties reside and which affect methods and functions.

Constructs

Constructs are the structures that you use in a JavaScript to control the flow of the script. If the course of the script depends on input or circumstance, you use a construct to direct the processing of the script. For example, to display the answer to a test question after a visitor has tried unsuccessfully to respond correctly, you can use a construct called an `if` statement.

This section contains an alphabetic list of JavaScript constructs. Each entry describes a single construct and provides its syntax and an example.

break

A `break` statement ends a series of `while` or `for` statements. Sometimes you want a condition that ignores everything else and jumps out of the loop to carry on with the rest of the script. You do this with a `break` statement. The syntax for the `break` statement is:

```
break
```

Example:

```
function alphacount (x)
    {
    var count = 0
    while (var < 1000)
        {
        if (var >= 990)
            break
```

```
        var += (getUserNumber())
        }
    }
```

This example is a function, `alphacount`, that adds user input until at least 990, but it could conceivably go as high as 1000. If the value is between 990 and 1000, the `break` statement is triggered, and the `while` statement ends.

comment

You place comments within your scripts to help you recall what variables represent or which conditions that change over time may affect loops or other calls. A comment does not perform a function; it is simply a note to yourself or to future users of the script. The syntax of the `comment` statement is:

```
// comment text
```

Example:

```
readMe="" //set the readMe variable to null
bigNews=1 //set the bigNews variable to 1
if (readMe < bigNews)
    {
    bigNews += song
    // add song to bigNews, increments bigNews by a user variable
    getStory(readMe) // this function retrieves the user's guess
    }
```

In this example, the variable declarations and the `if` statement are documented with comments.

continue

Like the `break` statement, `continue` breaks out of a `for` or a `while` loop. Instead of going to the next set of instructions past the loop, the `continue` statement sends the script back to the condition in the `while` statement or to the `update` expression in a `for` loop. The syntax of the `continue` statement is:

```
continue
```

Example:

```
while (cows!="home") {
    it (barnDoor = "open") {
        cows = "home"
        continue }
    callCows() }
```

In this `while` loop, the condition checks the value of the variable *cows*. As long as the value is not equal to "home", the loop continues. Within the loop is an `if` statement that checks the state of the *barnDoor*; when the variable *barnDoor* is "open", the statement sets the value of *cows* to "home" and sends the script back up to the condition statement. Otherwise, the loop continues to run the function `callCows`.

for

The `for` statement repeats an action for a counted number of times. You give the script the starting conditions, ending conditions, and iteration information. A starting condition could be `month=1`, indicating the repetitions begin at January. The ending condition, in this case, could be `month=12`, indicating the repetitions continue through the months of the year. Inside this repetition, you include a series of statements that perform a function (such as display a result: In January our sales were $1500K). The increment would likely be `month++`, indicating that the value of `month` is increased by 1 as each repetition is completed. The syntax of the `for` statement is:

```
for ([initial expression]; [condition];[update expression]) {
      statements
}
```

The `initial expression` entry is the statement or variable declaration, `condition` is the Boolean or comparison statement, and `update expression` is the incrementation scheme tied in with a variable in the condition.

Example:

```
horse = 100
for (cows=0, cows <= horse, horse++)
      { getCowCount(cows) }
```

This example simply repeats the function `getCowCount` until the number of cows is more than the number of horses. Each time the results of `getCowCount` is less than or equal to the number of horses (in the variable *horse*), the number of horses is incremented by 1. This loop could go on for a long time.

for in

The `for in` statement doesn't need counters to complete its repetitions. If, for example, you have a list of commands in objects that use the menu name (the File object contains all the menu items found under the File menu), you can iterate through the list, presenting them as part of a list of options. The benefit is that you can store the information in an object and update it once to use many times. When the list of menu items is complete, the script moves on to the next set of instructions. The syntax of the `for in` statement is:

```
for (variable in object) {
      statements }
```

The `variable` entry represents a value, and `object` is an array of object properties.

Example:

```
function house (rooms, location, floors, residents) {
     this.rooms = rooms
     this.location = location
     this.floors = floors
     this.residents = residents }
while (newHome != "no") {
     description = ""
     for (info in house) {
          description += house + "." + info + " = " + house[info]
          + "<BR>" }
     description += "<HR>"
     return description
     getNewHouse (newHome)
     }
```

In this example, the function `house` fills the information about the object `house`. The object `house` contains the properties: rooms, location, floors, and residents. The statement inside the `for in` loop generates a series of statements that fill the object. For example, if the user provided the following information, 10, London, 5, and 9, the variable description would end up being this series:

house.rooms = 10

house.location = London

house.floors = 5

house.residents = 9

function

This construct sets up a JavaScript function. The function makes some kind of calculation using information provided—words, numbers, or objects. With a function command you can fill an object with the selected information. For example, if you collect information from a visitor in several boxes, you can put this together into a single variable that you then use to address the visitor throughout the session. Define functions in the <HEAD> section of the Web page, because functions must be declared before they can be used. The syntax of the `function` statement is:

```
function name ([parameter} {,parameter] [..., parameter]) {
     statements }
```

Example:

```
// this function works out the grade for the test
function calc_pass_fail (ans_right, ans_wrong, ans_blank) {
        return ans_right / (ans_right + ans_wrong + ans_blank) }
```

In this example, the function `calc_pass_fail` reads in the variables *ans_right*, *ans_wrong*, and *ans_blank* to produce the person's percentage grade for the most recent test. Subsequent JavaScript scripts might control which page visitors see, depending on their grade.

if

The `if` statement works just like the spoken equivalent: *If this is true, do this.* Use this construct when you want the script to perform a task when the right conditions arise. For example, to include some information in a result page, use the `if` construct—if the user selects examples, include examples in the results page. The syntax of the `if` statement is:

```
if (condition) {
        statements }
```

Example:

```
if (tests = 0) {
        document.write("Take tests.")
        }
```

In this example, the `if` statement determines if the visitor has taken any tests. If the visitor has not taken any tests (tests = 0), `"Take tests."` appears on the screen.

if else

Like the `if` statement, this construct allows you to apply decision-making to the script: *If this is true, do this; otherwise, do this.* Use this construct when you have two alternatives that depend on the conditions. For example, suppose you want to display correct or incorrect notes next to the visitor's response in a test. If the visitor answers correctly, include a congratulations message; otherwise, show the correct answer. The syntax of the `if else` statement is:

```
if (condition) {
        statements }
else {
        statements }
```

Example:

```
if (tests != 0) {
     if (tests = 1) { document.write("lesson 2") }
     else {
          if (tests = 2) { document.write("lesson 3") }
          else {
               if (tests = 3) { document.write("lesson 4") }
          }
     }
else { document.write("lesson 1") }
```

In this example, the if statements check which test the visitor has completed and print the name of the next lesson. The first if statement simply tests whether the visitor has taken any tests; the test counter is incremented at the end of each test (not in this function or loop).

new

Use this construct to create a user-defined object. Creating an object is a process with two steps:

1. Define the object with a function.

2. Create an instance of the object with new.

The syntax of the new statement is:

```
objectName = new objectType ( parameter1 [, parameter2]
[…, parameterN])
```

The objectName entry is the name of the new object; this is how you refer to it in later code. The objectType entry is the object type, a function call that defines the object. The parameter1 … parameterN entries are the properties for the object.

Example:

```
function house (rooms, location, floors, residents) {
     this.rooms = rooms
     this.location = location
     this.floors = floors
     this.residents = residents }
newHouse new house (8, Praireville, 3, 4)
```

This example creates an object type called house and populates newHouse, which is of type house, with 8 rooms, a Praireville location, 3 floors, and 4 residents.

return

The return statement works in conjunction with the function statement. To display a calculated value, you include a return statement to bring the value back to the script. The syntax of the return statement is:

```
return
```

Example:

```
function square (x) {return x * x }
```

This simple example uses the return statement with the expression that generates the value that should be returned (the square of the number *x* passed to the function).

switch

The switch statement is similar to the if else statement in that it presents the script with a series of alternate routes that depend on conditions found. The switch statement is cleaner than nesting a series of if else statements. The syntax of the switch statement is:

```
switch (expression) {
        case1: statement;
        break;
        case2: statement;
        break;
        default statement; }
```

Example:

```
switch (infoType) {
        case ("reference") : destination = "refchapt.html";
        break;
        case ("how-to") : destination = "instruct.html";
        break;
        case ("overview") : destination = "intro.html";
        default : destination = "toc.html"; }
```

This example takes the value in the variable *infoType* and compares it to a list of known values. If the value in *infoType* matches any of the stated cases (reference, how-to, or overview), the script stores a page name in the destination variable. If no match is found, the script sets the destination to the table of contents (toc.html).

this

The construct this refers to the object in focus. For example, when filling an object's array (list of properties), you would have a series of this statements (one for each property). The syntax of the this statement is:

```
this[.propertyName]
```

Example:

```
function house (rooms, location, floors, residents) {
        this.rooms = rooms
        this.location = location
        this.floors = floors
        this.residents = residents }
newHouse new house (8, Praireville, 3, 4)
```

This example creates an object type called house and populates newHouse, which is of type house, with 8 rooms, a Praireville location, 3 floors, and 4 residents.

var

This is a keyword that indicates the statement is performing an assignment to a variable. You use this to set the initial value of the variables (always a good idea!) outside the function. The syntax of the var keyword is:

```
var varName [= value] [..., varName [= value]}
```

The *varName* entry is the name of the variable, and value becomes the contents of the variable.

Example:

```
var cust_id = 0, reading = 0
```

In this simple statement, *customer id* (cust_id) and *usage* (reading) variables are set to zero. This is in preparation for a function in which a customer number is assigned and a variable that tracks session activities is launched.

while

The while statement is similar to the if statement. It also is like its spoken equivalent: *While I'm gone, clean the house.* The while statement is also like the for and for in statements; it creates a loop that repeats a set of statements as long as a condition is true. The syntax of the while statement is:

```
while (condition) {
        statement; }
```

Example:

```
copies = 0
original = 0
while (copies <5) {
      copies++
      while (original < 10) {
            original++ }
      }
```

In this example, the two values, copies and original, are set to zero before entering the while loop. The outside loop checks that the number of copies made is less than 5. If that condition is true, the number of copies is incremented by 1, and then a second while loop iterates through the pages in the original.

with

To use a series of statements from the same object, such as the Math object, place them inside a with statement. You then need not identify each function, method, or property as belonging to the Math object. Usually when you write a statement that uses a function from an object, you have to include the object in the statement. The with construct lets you group a series of statements and identifies the parent object for the functions, methods, and properties. The syntax of the with statement is:

```
with (object) {
      statements; }
```

Example:

```
with (Math) {
      a = PI * r * r
      x = r * cos(theta)
      y = r * sin(theta) }
```

In this example, the object Math is used to assign values to the properties a, x, and y.

Operators

An operator is a symbol that represents an action; the most familiar operators are the mathematic symbols for addition, subtraction, multiplication, and division. JavaScript includes these basic actions and some more complex operations, each with a special symbol. As is the case with those familiar mathematic symbols, an order of operation defines the precedence of each operator in an expression.

Table A.3 defines the operators and presents them in their order of operation. You use parentheses to control the order or precedence in a statement. In the table, operrs of equal precedence are grouped together. For example, (), [], and . (period) have same precedence in the order of operation.

Some of these operators work on the bits in your values. To work on the bits, JavaScript verts your values to bits, performs the operation, and converts the value back to its ginal type. This can lead to some interesting results, particularly if you are unfamiliar h the bit values or if you miscalculate. Table A.4 lists the assignment operators.

ABLE A.3: JavaScript Operators

PERATOR	DESCRIPTION	WHAT IT DOES
	Function call or statement organizer	Organizes functions and forces a different order on the equations: x+2*y is the same asx+(2*y) because multiplication takes precedence over addition.
	Subscript	Use when you have a pointer and an element. For example, if you have an associative list (a variable that contains a set of values), you can use this to identify individual members in the list. These lists are called arrays.
	Members	Use when you are using the methods and properties for an object. For example, Math.abs calls the absolute function from the Math object.
	NOT	The Boolean negation symbol. Use it when your expression is designed to include everything except the item marked with this NOT symbol. For example, for names in phone book, if name ! BOB, call. This calls everyone except Bob.
	Ones complement	The bitwise equivalent of the NOT operator. Using this changes a 0 (zero) to a 1 (one) and vice versa.
+	Increment	Use in front of or behind a variable to add one to its value. For example, RIGHT++ is the same as RIGHT+1.
-	Decrement	Use in front of or behind a variable to subtract one from its value. For example, SUBMIT— is the same as SUBMITS-1.
	Multiply	Use to multiply two numeric values. These must be numbers.
	Divide	Use to divide two numeric values. If you use integers on both sides of the division expression, you won't get any decimal values. For example, if IN and OUT are declared as integers, and IN is 12 and OUT is 7, IN/OUT=1.

TABLE A.3 continued: JavaScript Operators

OPERATOR	DESCRIPTION	WHAT IT DOES
%	Modulo	Modulo division returns the remainder from a division operation. For example, 7/2 as an integer division gives you a result of 3. 7%2 gives you 1.
+	Addition	Combines two values (numbers or words).
-	Subtraction	Takes one value (number or word) out of another.
<<	Bitwise left shift	Moves the contents of an object or element left. This works on the bits in the object, moving them left and filling in the right with spaces. This converts the object into bits and then shifts them. For example, 7<<2 becomes 111 (the binary representation of 7) shifted left 2 places (11100) which, when converted back to integer values, is 28.
>>	Bitwise right shift	Like the left shift above, this moves the bits to the right; unlike the left shift, the bits shifted right drop out of the value. So, using the same example above, 7>>2 becomes 1.
>>>	Zero-fill right shift operator	This bitwise shift operator moves bits to the right and pads the left with zeros.
<	Less than	Compares two values. If the value on the right is larger than the value on the left, this operation returns True.
>	Greater than	Compares two values. If the value on the left is larger than the value on the right, this operation returns True.
<=	Less than or equal to	Compares two values. If the value on the right is equal to or larger than the value on the left, this operation returns True.
>=	Greater than or equal to	Compares two values. If the value on the left is equal to or larger than the value on the right, this operation returns True.
==	Equality	Compares two values. If they are equal, the operation returns True.
!=	Inequality	Compares two values. If they are not equal, the operation returns True.
&	Bitwise AND	Checks the bits of two values and determines where they are both the same. If the value is a multi-bit value, the operation checks each position. If the two values do not have a matching number of bits, the smaller value is left padded until the number of positions match. If they match, a 1 is returned. For example, 10&7 returns 2 because 1010 & 0111 only match in the second to last position, giving you 0010, which is 2.

TABLE A.3 continued: JavaScript Operators

OPERATOR	DESCRIPTION	WHAT IT DOES
^	Bitwise EOR (exclusive OR)	Returns True if one or the other of the values is 1. When the values match, it returns a 0. So, using the example above, 10^7 returns 1101 which is 13.
|	Bitwise OR	Returns true (1) if one value is 1. Unlike EOR, this operator returns True if both values are 1. So, the 10|7 expression returns 1111, which is 15.
&&	Logical AND	Unlike bitwise operators, logical operators compare expression results. Use the logical operators to link Boolean comparisons into a test for a branching statement. For example, if Bob is older than Ray, *and* Ray is not working today, send the package to Ray. The package is sent to Ray only if the two conditions are met.
||	Logical OR	Results in True if either expression is true. So, using the same example above, Ray would receive the package if *either* he was younger than Bob or was not working that day.
?:	If-else	This is the symbol for the if else construct, which is described in the Constructs section.
,	Comma	Separates values in a sequence, such as assignments to an object that contains an array.
operator=	Assignment	Creates assignments. Table A.4 shows the range of possibilities.

TABLE A.4: The Assignment Operators

OPERATOR	WHAT IT DOES
=	Puts the value on the right into the variable on the left; any contents are replaced.
+=	Adds the value on the right to the variable on the left; the contents are augmented.
*=	Multiplies the variable on the left by the value on the right and places the result in the variable.
/+	Divides the variable on the left by the value on the right and places the result in the variable.
%=	Divides the variable on the left by the value on the right and places the difference in the variable.
<<=	Performs a bitwise shift on the variable on the left equal to the value on the right; the result is placed in the variable.

TABLE A.4 continued: The Assignment Operators

Operator	What It Does
>>=	Performs a bitwise shift on the variable on the left equal to the value on the right; the result is placed in the variable.
>>>=	Performs a bitwise shift on the variable on the left equal to the value on the right; the result is placed in the variable.
&=	Performs a bitwise AND on the variable and value; the result is placed in the variable.
^=	Performs a bitwise EOR on the variable and the value; the result is placed in the variable.
|=	Performs a bitwise OR on the variable and the value; the result is placed in the variable.

Escape Character

The backslash (\) is the escape character in JavaScript. An escape character tells the system that the next character in the sequence is either a special instruction or is a reserved character being used in quoted text. Table A.5 lists the escape sequences that JavaScript uses.

TABLE A.5: The JavaScript Escape Sequences

Character	Function
\b	Backspace
\n	New line
\t	Tab
\r	Carriage return
\f	Formfeed
\\	Backslash (in text)
\'	Single quote (in text)
\"	Double quote (in text)
\ooo	Octal number
\hh	Hexadecimal number

Reserved Words

JavaScript has a number of reserved words—words that you cannot use for variables in your script. These words are either in use (for example, as functions) or are reserved for future use:

abstract	else	instanceof	super
Boolean	extends	int	switch
break	false	interface	synchronized
byte	final	long	this
cse	finally	native	throw
catch	float	new	throws
char	for	null	transient
class	function	package	true
const	goto	private	try
continue	if	protected	var
default	implements	public	void
do	import	return	while
double	in	static	with

Objects

Objects are a simple way of referring to parts of a Web page. Using objects gives structure to your Web pages and JavaScript scripts. In general, you apply methods, functions, and properties to objects to achieve a result.

This section contains an alphabetic listing of the available JavaScript objects. Each entry describes the object, gives its format, and shows an example. Each entry also contains a list of the associated properties, methods, and event handlers.

Anchor

The anchor object is text on a page that represents a destination for a link. The anchor object can also be a link object. The browser creates an anchor array when it opens the page. This array contains information about each anchor object. You can access the anchors or their length from this array.

The anchor object has the following format:

```
<A [HREF=URL] NAME="anchorname" [TARGET="windowName"]> anchorText </A>
```

To access the anchors array:

```
document.anchors.length
document.anchors.[index]
```

The `index` entry is an integer representing an anchor in the document.

The `anchor` object has no properties or methods. The `anchor` array has the property `length`, which you can use to get the number of anchors on the page from the array.

There are no event handlers for the `anchor` object, which is a property of `document`.

Example:

```
<A NAME="reference_library"><H1>Books on JavaScripting<H1></A>
```

This statement establishes a target in a document. If, for example, that document is called `JSIntro.html`, you can use the following statement in an `anchor` object or a `link` object to jump to the location of the line above:

```
<A HREF="JSIntro.html#reference_library">Reference Books for
Scripting</A>
```

button

This object is a push button on a form. The browser sets the appearance of the button, but you control the text prompt on the button and the action it performs. The `button` object has the following format:

```
<INPUT
TYPE="button"
NAME="buttonName"
VALUE="buttonText"
[onClick="handlerText"]>
```

The `buttonName` entry is the name for the button, which is how you identify the button. Each button on the page needs a unique `buttonName`. The `buttonText` entry is the label that appears on the button.

The `name` property reflects the NAME= attribute. The `value` reflects the VALUE= attribute. The button uses the `onClick` method and the `onClick` event handler. It is the property of `form`.

Example:

```
<INPUT
        TYPE="button"
        NAME="goNow"
        VALUE="Let's GO!"
        onClick="buttonClick(this.form)" >
```

In this example, a Let's Go button appears on the form. When the visitor clicks the button, the event handler onClick runs the function that processes the form.

checkbox

A checkbox appears on a form to let visitors make selections (none, one, or more) from a list. The checkbox object has the following format:

```
<INPUT
TYPE="checkbox"
NAME="checkboxName"
VALUE="checkboxValue"
[CHECKED]
[onClick="handlerText"]>
textToDisplay
```

The checkboxName entry is the name property for the checkbox object; you identify the checkbox with this name if you reference it in your script. The checkbox-Value entry is the return value when the checkbox is selected; this defaults to On. The CHECKED entry specifies that the checkbox appear as checked when the browser first displays it. The textToDisplay entry is the label, the option text next to the checkbox.

You can set the checkbox checked property, changing the state (on or off) of the checkbox. The defaultChecked property reflects the CHECKED attribute. The name property reflects the NAME= attribute, and the value property reflects the VALUE= attribute. The checkbox object uses the click method and the onClick event handler. It is the property of form.

Example:

```
<H3>Pick the modules that you want to study:</H3>
<BR><INPUT TYPE="checkbox" NAME="studymodul_newdocs" CHECKED>
Creating a new document
<BR><INPUT TYPE="checkbox" NAME="studymodul_trackdocs" CHECKED>
Tracking documents in the system
<BR><INPUT TYPE="checkbox" NMAE="studymodul_routedocs" CHECKED>
Route documents through the system
```

and so on...

In this example, you have a list of options; each option appears with its checkbox selected.

date

The date object lets you work with dates. It includes a large number of methods for getting date information, such as the calendar date or the time of day. Dates prior to 1970 are not allowed. The date object has the following format:

```
dateObjectName = new Date()
dateObjectName = new Date("month day, year hours: minutes: seconds")
dateObjectName = new Date(year, month, day)
dateObjectName = new Date(year, month, day, hours, minutes, seconds)
```

The new keyword generates a new object using the Date object. In the second statement, the properties month, day, year, hours, minutes, and seconds are string values. In the third and fourth statements, they are integers.

The date method has the following format:

```
dateObjectName.methodName(parameters)
```

The date object has no properties and uses the following methods:

getDate	getSeconds	setDate	setTime
getDay	getTime	setHours	setYear
getHours	getTimeZoneoffset	setMinutes	toGMTString
getMinutes	getYear	setMonth	toLocaleString
getMonth	parse	setSeconds	UTC

The date object has no event handlers because built-in objects have no event handlers. The date object is the property of no other object.

Example:

```
var logofftime= new Date();
logofftime=logofftime.getHours()+":"+logofftime.getMinutes()+":
"+logofftime.getSeconds();
```

In this example, the script creates a new date variable called *logofftime* and then populates that variable with the current time.

document

The document object is the container for the information on the current page. This object controls the display of HTML information for the visitor. The document object includes only the <BODY> sections of an HTML document and has the following format:

```
<BODY
        BACKGROUND="backgroundImage"
        BGCOLOR="backgroundColor"
        TEXT="foregroundColor"
```

```
        LINK="unusedLinkColor"
        ALINK="activeLinkColor"
        VLINK="followedLinkColor"
        [onLoad="handlerText"]
        [onUnload="handlerText"]>
    </BODY>
```

Although onLoad and onUnload are included in the <BODY> tag, they are not document event handlers—they are window event handlers.

The **document** object has the properties shown in Table A.6.

TABLE A.6: The Properties of the Document Object

PROPERTY	WHAT IT DOES/IS
alinkColor	Reflects the active link color
anchors	An array containing a list of the anchors on the document
bgColor	Reflects the background color
cookie	Specifies a cookie (information about the user/session)
fgColor	Reflects the foreground color for text and other foreground elements such as borders or lines
forms	An array containing a list of the forms in the document
lastModified	Reflects the date the document was last changed
linkColor	Reflects the basic link color
links	Reflects the link attributes
location	Reflects the location (URL) of the document
referrer	Reflects the location (URL) of the parent or calling document
title	Reflects the contents of the <TITLE> tag
vlinkColor	Reflects the color of past links activity

The **document** object also uses five methods—clear, close, open, write, and writeln—but uses no event handlers. Although the onLoad and onUnload event handlers are included in the <BODY> tag, they are window events. The document object is the property of window.

Example:
```
    function setMeUp() {
        document.alinkColor="darkcyan"
```

```
        document.linkColor="yellow"
        document.vlinkColor="white" }
    ...
<BODY onLoad="setMeUp()">
```

In this example, the settings for the link colors use the document properties. This is equivalent to the following <BODY> declaration:

```
<BODY
        ALINK="darkcyan"
        LINK="yellow"
        VLINK="white">
```

elements

The elements object is an array of the form objects in the order in which they occur in the source. This gives you an alternate access path to the individual form objects. You can also determine the number of form objects by using the length property. This is similar to the anchor array in that you can read from it, but not write to it. The elements object has the following format:

```
formName.elements[index]
formName.elements.length
```

The formName entry is either the name of the form or an element in the form's array. The index entry is an integer representing an object on a form.

The elements object uses the length property, which reflects the number of elements on a form. There are no methods and no event handlers for the elements object. It is the property of form.

Example:

```
userInfo.username.value
userInfo.elements[0].value
```

Both statements return the same value if the element username is the first item in the elements array.

form

This object defines the form with which users interact. It includes checkboxes, textareas, radio buttons, and so on. You use the form object to post data to a server. It has the following format:

```
<FORM
        NAME="formName"
        TARGET="windowName"
```

```
      ACTION="serverURL"
      METHOD=GET | POST
      ENCTYPE="encodingType"
      [onSubmit="handlerText"] >
</FORM>
```

The `windowName` entry is where form responses go. If you use this, the server responses are sent to a different window—another window, a frame, or a frame literal (such as _top). The `serverURL` is the location where the information from the form goes when it is posted. The `GET | POST` (GET or POST) commands specify how the information is sent to the server. With GET, which is the default, the information is appended to the receiving URL. With POST, the form sends the information in a data body that the server handles. The `encodingType` entry is the MIME encoding of the data sent. This defaults to `application/x-www-form-urlencoded`; you can also use `multipart/form-data`.

Here is the format for using the object's properties and methods:

```
formName.propertyName
formName.methodName(parameters)
forms[index].propertyName
forms[index].methodName(parameters)
```

The `formName` entry is the NAME= attribute of the form. The `propertyName` and `methodName` entries are one of the properties listed in Table A.7. The `index` entry is an integer representing the `form` object within the array. Statements one and three are equivalent, as are statements two and four.

TABLE A.7: The Properties of the Form Object

PROPERTY	WHAT IT DOES/IS
action	Reflects the server URL
elements	A list of the elements in the form
encoding	Reflects the ENCTYPE= attribute
length	The number of elements on the form
method	Indicates how the information is processed (GET or POST)
target	Reflects the window where forms go

The `form` object uses the `submit` method and the `onSubmit` event handler. It is the property of `document`.

Example:

```
function setCase (caseSpec){
if (caseSpec == "upper") {
     document.f1.userName.value=document.f1.userName.value
     .toUpperCase()
     document.f1.userPass.value=document.f1.userPass.value
     .toUpperCase()}
     else {
     document.f1.userName.value=document.f1.userName.value
     .toLowerCase()
     document.f1.userPass.value=document.f1.userPass.value
     .toLowerCase()}
}
</SCRIPT>
<BODY>
<FORM NAME="f1">
<P>Enter a name and password for the test page</P>
<B>Your name:</B>
<INPUT TYPE="text" NAME="userName" SIZE=20>
<BR><B>Your Password:</B>
<INPUT TYPE="text" NAME="userPass" SIZE=20>
<P>The system is case-sensitive, please choose an option below for
how we should save your name and password.</P>
<INPUT TYPE="radio" VALUE="off" NAME="upperRadio"
       onClick="setCase('upper')"
     "Set my info into uppercase letters.">
<INPUT TYPE="button" VALUE="on" NAME="lowerRadio"
       onClick="setCase('lower')"
     "Set my info to lowercase letters.">
</FORM>
```

In this example, the visitor enters his or her name and then can choose all uppercase or all lowercase for the information that gets saved.

frame

The frame object is a window within a window and has its own URL. A page can contain a series of frames. There is also a frames array that lists all the frames in your code. The frame object has the following format:

```
<FRAMESET
        ROWS="rowHeightList"
        COLS="columnWidthList"
        [onLoad="handlerText"]
        [onUnload="handlerText"] >
        [<FRAME SRC="locationOrURL" NAME="frameName">]
                [<NOFRAMES>
                [HTML tags and so on…
                for browsers that do not support frames]
                </NOFRAMES>
        </FRAMESET>
```

The rowHeightList entry is a comma-separated list of values that set the row height of the frame. The default unit of measure is pixels. The columnWidthList is a comma-separated list of values that set the column width of the frame. The default unit of measure is pixels.

The locationOrURL entry is the location of the document to be displayed in the frame. This URL cannot include an anchor name. The location object describes the URL components. The frameName entry is the target for links.

To use the object's properties, follow this format:

```
[windowReference.]frameName.propertyName
[windowReference.]frames[index].propertyName
window.propertyName
self.propertyName
parent.propertyName
```

The *windowReference* entry is a variable from the window object definition or one of the synonyms: top or parent. The frameName entry is the value of the NAME= attribute in the <FRAME> tag. The index entry is an integer representing a frame object in the array, and the PropertyName entry is one of the properties listed in Table A.8.

To use the object's array, follow this format:

```
[frameReference.]frames[index]
[frameReference.]frames.length
[windowReference.]frames[index]
[windowReference.]frames.length
```

TABLE A.8: The Properties of the Frame Object

PROPERTY	WHAT IT DOES/IS
frames	The array, or list, of frames in the document
name	Reflects the NAMES= attribute (as assigned in <FRAMESET>)
length	An integer that reflects the number of child frames within this frame
parent	The window or frame that contains this frame
self	The current frame
window	The current frame

The frames array has a length property that reflects the number of child frames within a frame. The frame object uses the clearTimeout and setTimeout methods.

The frame object does not use event handlers. Although the onLoad and onUnload event handlers appear within <FRAMESET>, they are event handlers for the window object. The frame object is a property of window. The frames array is a property of both frame and window.

Example:

This is a multipart example. The first piece of code sets up framed windows, which are structured the same (4 frames). The frameset comes after the <HEAD> tag and replaces the <BODY> tag.

```
<HTML>
<HEAD>
     <TITLE>Central Zoo: Front Entrance</TITLE>
</HEAD>
<FRAMESET COLS="40%, 60%" onLoad="alert('We\'re in like Flynn')">
<FRAME NAME="frame1" SRC="mainframe.html">
<FRAME NAME="frame2" SRC="littleframe.html">
</FRAMESET>
</HTML>
```

In this example, the form gives the visitor background color options that are controlled by push buttons. When a visitor selects a color, it is assigned to the background of the document in another frame. A visitor can also change the contents of the secondary frame. The calls in the first document (SRC=) populate the frames with the files.

hidden

The `hidden` object contains a text object that is suppressed, not displayed, on an HTML form. This object is used to pass information when the form is submitted. Although the visitor cannot change the value directly, the developer (you) can control the contents, changing it programmatically. The `hidden` object has the following format:

```
<INPUT
        TYPE="hidden"
        NAME="hiddenName"
        [VALUE="textValue"] >
```

The `hiddenName` entry is the name of the object, which allows you to access the object using the NAME= property. The `TextValue` entry is the initial value for the object.

The `hidden` object uses two properties—name and value. These reflect the object name and contents. The `hidden` object does not use any methods or event handlers. It is the property of `form`.

Example:

```
<FORM NAME="form1">
<INPUT   TYPE="hidden" NAME="hiddenPass">
<INPUT   TYPE="text" NAME="password" VALUE="" SIZE=5>
<INPUT   TYPE="button" NAME="test" VALUE="Test"
onClick="document.form1.hiddenPass.value=document.form1.password.val
ue; alert(document.form1.hiddenPass.value)">
</FORM>
```

This example reads in a password from a `text` object and stores it in the `hidden` object. As a test of the form, we've included a line that displays the `hidden` object in an alert, which is not something you would normally do.

history

The `history` object contains the list of visited URLs; this information is available in the history list of the browser. The `history` object has the following format:

```
history.length
```

```
history.methodName(parameters)
```

The `length` entry is an integer representing a position in the history list. The `methodName` entry is one of the methods listed below.

The `history` object uses the `length` property. There are three methods for the history object: back, forward, and go. Each of these navigate through the history list. The history object does not use event handlers. It is the property of `document`.

Example:

```
if (score < 65) { history.go(-2) }
```

The `if` statement checks the score against a satisfactory performance measure of 65. If the student scores less than 65 on the test, the browser goes back to the beginning of the lesson, two pages earlier.

```
<INPUT TYPE="button" NAME="reviewButton" VALUE="Look Again!"
       onClick=history.back() >
```

The `reviewButton` button performs the same function as the browser's back button.

link

A `link` object includes the text and images that contain the information for a hypertext jump. A `link` object is also an `anchor` object. When the jump is complete, the starting page location is stored in the destination document's `referrer` property. The `link` object has the following format:

```
<A HREF=locationOrURL
       [NAME="anchorName"]
       [TARGET="windowName"]
       [onClick="handlerText"]
       [onMouseOver="handlerText"] >
       linkText

</A>
```

The `locationOrURL` entry is the destination address. The `anchorName` entry is the current location within the jump-from page. The `windowName` is the window that the link is loaded into, if different from the current window. This can be an existing window, a frame, or a synonym such as `_top` or `_self`.

You can also define a link using the `link` method.

To use a link's properties, follow this format:

```
document.links[index].propertyName
```

The `index` entry is an integer representing the `link` object in the links array.

To use the links array, follow this format:

```
document.links[index]
document.links.length
```

You can read the links array, but you cannot write values to it.

Table A.9 list the properties of the link object.

TABLE A.9: The Properties of the Link Object

PROPERTY	WHAT IT DOES/IS
hash	Contains the anchor name in the URL
host	Contains the hostname:port portion of the URL
hostname	Contains the host and domain name or IP address of the network host
href	Includes the entire URL
pathname	Contains the URL-pathname (directory structure/location) part of the URL
port	Specifies the communication port on the server
protocol	Specifies the type of URL (for example, http or ftp)
search	Contains the page name (for example, index.html)
target	Reflects the TARGET= attribute

The links array uses the length property. The link object does not use any methods. The link object uses the onClick and onMouseOver event handlers. It is the property of document.

Example:

```
<SCRIPT>
      var there="http://www.raycomm.com/"
</SCRIPT>
</HEAD>
<BODY>
<FORM NAME="form1">
      <B>Choose a document, then click "Take me there" below.</B>
      <BR><INPUT TYPE="radio" NAME="destination" VALUE="Overview"
          onClick="there =
          'http://www.raycomm.com/intro.html'">
          Overview of JavaScripting
      <BR><INPUT TYPE="radio" NAME="destination" VALUE="HowTo"
          onClick="there =
          'http://www.raycomm.com/makeScript.html'">
          Learn to Make a Script
```

```
      <BR><INPUT TYPE="radio" NAME="destination" VALUE="Reference"
          onClick="there =
          'http://www.raycomm.com/refchapt.html'">
          JavaScript Reference Information
      <BR>
      <P><A HREF="" onClick="this.href=there"
          onMouseOver="self.status=there; return true;">
          <B>Take me there!</B>
      </A>
</FORM>
```

In this example, a form gives visitors access to the set of chapters. They can select a chapter/destination or go to the default destination.

location

The location object contains information about the current URL. It contains a series of properties that describe each part of the URL. A URL has the following structure:

```
protocol//hostname:port pathname search hash
```

The protocol specifies the type of URL (for example, http or ftp). The hostname contains the host and domain name or IP address of the network host. The port specifies the communication port on the server (not all addresses use this). The pathname is the directory structure/location on the server. The search value is the page name (for example, index.html). The hash value is preceded by the hash mark (#) and indicates a target anchor on the page.

Here are some common protocol types:

```
javascript    ftp         http        news
about         mailto      file        gopher
```

The location object has the following format:

```
[windowReference.]location.propertyName
```

The location object uses the same properties as the link object, as shown in Table A.9 earlier. The location object does not use any methods or event handlers. It is a property of document.

Example:

```
window.location.href="http://javatutorial.writelivelihood.com/"
```

In this example, the URL of the current page is set to the JavaTutorial home page.

```
parent.frame3.location.href="http://javatutorial.writelivelihood.com/"
```

This example opens the JavaTutorial home page in frame3.

```
<SCRIPT>
var there="http://www.raycomm.com/"
var takeLesson=""
document.write ("Welcome to " + document.location + ". Not ever
done!")
</SCRIPT>
```

This example displays a message at the top of the page that welcomes visitors to the current location.

Math

This is a built-in object that includes a large set of methods and properties for mathematic constants and operations. An example of a constant is *pi*, which is referenced as `Math.PI`. If you are using a series of expressions, you can use the `with` construct. In general, the math object has the following format:

```
varName = Math.propertyName [expression]
varName = Math.method()
```

The actual format will vary with the property in use. Check the property entries for the exact syntax.

The math object uses the following properties, each of which is described in the Properties section:

E	LN10	LOG2E	SQRT1_2
LN2	LOG10E	PI	SQRT2

The math object uses the following methods, each of which is described in the Methods and Functions section:

abs	atan	exp	max	sin
acos	ceil	floor	pow	sqrt
asin	cos	log	random	tan

The math object uses no event handlers since it is a built-in object. It is not a property of anything. See the entries for individual properties and methods for examples.

navigator

Use this object to determine a visitor's version of Netscape Navigator. It has the following format:

```
navigator.propertyName
```

Properties and Methods

The `navigator` object does not use any methods, and it contains the properties shown in Table A.10. It does not use any event handlers, and it is not the property of anything.

TABLE A.10: The Properties of the Navigator Object

PROPERTY	WHAT IT DOES
appCodeName	Contains the internal code name of the browser
appName	Contains the external name of the browser
appVersion	Contains the version number of the browser
userAgent	Contains the user-agent header

Example:

```
var userBrowser = navigator.appName + " " + navigator.appVersion
```

The values for the `navigator` properties `appName` and `appVersion` are in a variable called `userBrowser`. You can use this later to test the browser's suitability for the functionality available on your page.

password

The `password` object is a text field that conceals its value and displays asterisks in place of typed characters. A `password` object is part of a form and must be defined within a <FORM> tag. This object has the following format:

```
<INPUT
        TYPE="password"
        NAME="passwordName"
        [VALUE="textValue"]
        SIZE=integer >
```

The `passwordName` entry is the name of the object. The `textValue` entry is a default value for the password, and `size` is the length of the password field.

To use the `password` properties and methods, follow this format:

```
passwordName.propertyName
passwordName.methodName(parameters)
formName.elements[index].propertyName
formName.elements[index].methodName(parameters)
```

The passwordName entry is the value of the NAME= attribute in the password object. The formName entry is the form container or an element in the forms array. The propertyName is one of the properties listed below, and methodName is one of the methods listed below. The first and third statements are equivalents, as are the second and fourth statements.

The password object uses the properties listed in Table A.11 and uses the focus, blur, and select methods.

TABLE A.11: The Properties of the Password Object

PROPERTY	WHAT IT DOES
defaultValue	Reflects the VALUE= attribute
name	Reflects the NAME= attribute
value	Reflects the current contents of the password object's field

The password object does not use event handlers. It is a property of form.

Example:

```
<INPUT TYPE="password" NAME="password" VALUE="password.defaultValue"
SIZE=8>
```

This is useful if the visitor has already visited the site and created a password or if you have assigned passwords to visitors.

radio

A radio button forces a single selection from a set of options. Similar to the checkbox, it is a part of a form; unlike the checkbox, only one radio button can be selected from the set. The radio object has the following format:

```
<INPUT
        TYPE="radio"
        NAME="radioName"
        VALUE="buttonValue"
        [CHECKED]
        [onClick="handlerText"] >
        textToDisplay
```

The radioName entry is the name of the object. This offers you one method for addressing the radio object in your script. The buttonValue entry is the value that is returned to the server when the button is selected. The default is On. You can access this value using the `radio.value` property. The CHECKED attribute sets the button to selected, and `textToDisplay` is the label displayed next to the radio button.

The radio button uses the `click` method and the properties shown in Table A.12.

TABLE A.12: The Properties of the Radio Object

PROPERTY	WHAT IT DOES/IS
checked	Lets you set the selection through your script (rather than visitor interaction); good for situations in which one choice automatically determines several others
defaultChecked	Reflects the settings for the CHECKED attribute
length	The number of radio buttons in the object
name	Reflects the NAME= attribute (radioName above)
value	Reflects the VALUE= attribute (buttonValue above)

The `radio` object uses the `onClick` event handler, and it is the property of `form`.

Example:

```
<SCRIPT>
var there="http://www.raycomm.com/"
function checkThis(){
      confirm("Thanks for registering")}
</SCRIPT>
</HEAD>
<BODY onLoad="window.alert('Welcome! You can register through this
page. For future reference, this page is ' + '<P>' + document
.location)">
      <FORM NAME="form1" onSubmit="checkThis()">
      <B>Choose a document, then click "Take me there" below.</B>
      <BR><INPUT TYPE="radio" NAME="destination" VALUE="Overview"
            onClick="there = 'http://www.raycomm.com/intro.html'">
            Overview of JavaScripting
      <BR><INPUT TYPE="radio" NAME="destination" VALUE="HowTo"
            onClick="there =
            'http://www.raycomm.com/makeScript.html'">
            Learn to Make a Script
```

```
<BR><INPUT TYPE="radio" NAME="destination" VALUE="Reference"
        onClick="there =
        'http://www.raycomm.com/refchapt.html'">
        JavaScript Reference Information
<BR>
<P><A HREF="" onClick="this.href=there"
        onMouseOver="self.status=there; return true;">
        <B>Take me there!</B>
</A>
<P><INPUT TYPE="text" NAME="whoIs" VALUE="user" SIZE=15>
<P><INPUT TYPE="radio" NAME="lesson" VALUE="Lesson 1" CHECKED
        onClick="takeLesson='lesson1.htm'"> Lesson 1: Getting
        Started
<P><INPUT TYPE="radio" NAME="lesson" VALUE="Lesson 2"
        onClick="takeLesson='lesson2.htm'"> Lesson 2: Concepts
        and Operations
<P><INPUT TYPE="radio" NAME="lesson" VALUE="Lesson 3"
        onClick="takeLesson='lesson3.htm'"> Lesson 3: Projects
<P><INPUT TYPE="reset" VALUE="Defaults" NAME="resetToBasic">
<INPUT TYPE="submit" VALUE="Send it in!" NAME="submit_form1">
<HR>
</FORM>
</BODY>
```

This example creates two groups of radio buttons that set up the destination for the link/jump for the visitor or the course selections.

reset

This object is a reset button on a form. It clears the form fields of any visitor interaction/ entries and resets their values to the default. This is a form element and must be defined in the <FORM> tag. The onClick event handler cannot be canceled. Once the reset object is clicked, the form is reset, and all visitor entries are lost. The reset object has the following format:

```
<INPUT
        TYPE="reset"
        NAME="resetName"
        VALUE="buttonText"
        [onClick="handlerText"] >
```

The `resetName` entry is the name of the object. It allows you to access the object within your script. The `buttonText` entry is the label for the button.

To use the `reset` properties and methods, follow this format:

`resetName.propertyName`

`resetName.methodName(parameters)`

`formName.elements[index].propertyName`

`formName.elements[index].methodName(parameters)`

Statements one and three are equivalent, as are statements two and four.

The `reset` object has two properties. It uses the `click` method and the `onClick` event handler. It is a property of `form`.

Example:

```
<INPUT TYPE="reset" NAME="clearForm" VALUE="Start Over">
```

This statement places a reset button (this one says Start Over) that clears the current form when it is clicked.

```
<SCRIPT>
        var takeLesson=""
</SCRIPT>
</HEAD>
<BODY>
<FORM NAME="form1">
        <P><INPUT TYPE="text" NAME="whoIs" VALUE="user" SIZE=15>
        <P><INPUT TYPE="radio" NAME="lesson" VALUE="Lesson 1" CHECKED
onClick="takeLesson='lesson1.htm'"> Lesson 1: Getting Started
        <P><INPUT TYPE="radio" NAME="lesson" VALUE="Lesson 2"
onClick="takeLesson='lesson2.htm'"> Lesson 2: Concepts and
Operations
        <P><INPUT TYPE="radio" NAME="lesson" VALUE="Lesson 3"
onClick="takeLesson='lesson3.htm'"> Lesson 3: Projects
        <P><INPUT TYPE="reset" VALUE="Defaults" NAME="resetToBasic">
        <P><INPUT TYPE="submit" NAME="launch_lessons" VALUE="Start the
Learning!">
</FORM>
```

This example has a form on which visitors identify the kind of information they want (as in `Getting Started`, `Concepts and Operations`, `Projects`, and so on) and the lesson they want (selected from the list of radio buttons.) The `reset` statement clears any changes the visitor may have made and resets the form to `Getting`

`Started`. The `submit` statement sends the selections to be processed according to the instructions (not seen) for the form.

select

The `select` object presents the visitor with a drop-down list of preset choices. It contains an options array. This is a form element and must be defined within a `<FORM>` tag. The `select` object has the following format:

```
<SELECT>
      NAME="selectName"
      [SIZE="integer"]
      [MULTIPLE]
      [onBlur="handlerText"]
      [onChange="handerText"]
      [onFocus="handlerText"]
      <OPTION VALUE="optionValue" [SELECTED]> textToDisplay
[... <OPTION> textToDisplay
</SELECT>
```

The `selectName` entry is the name of the object; the `select` object contains the list. The `MULTIPLE` entry indicates that the object accepts multiple selections—such as checkboxes. If the list is not set to multiple, it is like a `radio` object, and only one choice, is available. The `OPTION` entry is a selection element in the list, and `optionValue` is the value returned to the system when the option is selected. The `SELECTED` entry indicates that the option is the default value for the list, and `textToDisplay` is the text shown in the list.

To select the object's properties and methods, follow this format:

```
selectName.propertyName
```

```
selectName.methodName(parameters)
```

```
formName.elements[index].propertyName
```

```
formName.elements[index].methodName(parameters)
```

To use an option's properties, follow this format:

```
selectName.options[index1].propertyName
```

```
formName.elements[index2].options[index1].propertyName
```

The `index1` entry is an integer representing the sequence of options in the list (the first option in the sequence is zero [0]), and `index2` is an integer representing the element in the form.

To use the options array, follow this format:

```
selectName.options
```

```
selectName.options[index]
selectName.options.length
```

The `selectName` entry is the value of the NAME= attribute in the `select` object. The `index` entry is an integer representing an option in the `select` object, and `length` is the number of options in the `select` object.

The elements in the options array are read-only. You can get the number of options from the list, but you cannot change the values in the list.

The `select` object uses the properties shown in Table A.13.

TABLE A.13: The Properties of the `Select` Object

PROPERTY	WHAT IT DOES
length	Reflects the number of options
name	Reflects the NAME= attribute
options	Reflects the <OPTION> tags
selectedIndex	Reflects the position of the selected option in the list (or the first of multiple options)

The options array uses the properties listed in Table A.14.

TABLE A.14: The Properties of the Options Array

PROPERTY	WHAT IT DOES
defaultSelected	Reflects the SELECTED= attribute indicating which option is the default selection for the list
index	Reflects the position of the option in the list (the list begins at zero)
length	Reflects the number of options
name	Reflects the NAME= attribute
selected	Lets you select an option from your script, rather than from visitor input
selectedIndex	Reflects the position of the selected option in the list
text	Reflects the textToDisplay for the option list item
value	Reflects the VALUE= attribute

The `select` object uses the `blur` and `focus` methods and the `onBlur`, `onChange`, and `onFocus` event handlers. The `select` object is a property of `form`. The options array is a property of `select`.

Example:

```
<SELECT NAME="lesson_list">

      <OPTION SELECTED> Introduction

      <OPTION>Installation

      <OPTION>Setting up an account

      <OPTION>Creating a document

      <OPTION>Filing a document

      <OPTION>Recovering a filed document

      <OPTION>Sending a document to the printer

</SELECT>
```

The form contains a list of chapters in a book, from which the visitor can select a single item.

string

A `string` object is a series of characters, such as a name, a phrase, or other information. It has the following format:

```
stringName.propertyName

stringName.methodName(parameters)
```

The `stringName` entry is the variable name (that owns the string). The `length` entry is the size of the string. This is a character count and includes spaces and special characters. The `methodName` entry is one of the methods listed below.

The `string` object has a single property, `length`, which is the number of characters in the string. The `string` object uses the following methods:

anchor	charAt	index	small	sup
big	fixed	italics	strike	toLowerCase
blink	fontcolor	lastIndexOf	sub	toUpperCase
bold	fontsize	link	substring	

Some of these methods will look familiar, as they deal with the format of the text in the `string` object.

Because it is a built-in object, the `string` object does not use event handlers. It is not a property of anything.

Example:

```
var user_id new string()
user_id = getUserText.value
user_id.toUpperCase()
```

This simple example takes the contents of the text field `getUserText` and assigns it to a newly created string variable called `user_id`. The last statement shifts the contents of the variable to uppercase.

submit

This object is a button on a form that starts the processing of the form. The submission is controlled by the form's `action` property. The `submit` object has the following format:

```
<INPUT>
        TYPE="submit"
        NAME="submitName"
        VALUE="buttonText"
        [onClick="handlerText"] >
```

To use the `submit` object's properties and methods, follow this format:

```
submitName.propertyName
submitName.methodName(parameters)
formName.elements[index].propertyName
formName.elements[index].methodName(parameters)
```

The `submit` object uses two properties—`name` and `value`. It uses a single method, `click`, and the `onClick` event handler. It is a property of `form`.

Example:

```
<FORM NAME="form1">
        <B>Choose a document, then click "Take me there" below.</B>
        <BR><INPUT TYPE="radio" NAME="destination" VALUE="Overview"
            onClick="there =
            'http://www.raycomm.com/intro.html'">
            Overview of JavaScripting
        <BR><INPUT TYPE="radio" NAME="destination" VALUE="HowTo"
             onClick="there =
            'http://www.raycomm.com/makeScript.html'">
            Learn to Make a Script
```

```
        <BR><INPUT TYPE="radio" NAME="destination" VALUE="Reference"
             onClick="there =
             'http://www.raycomm.com/refchapt.html'">
             JavaScript Reference Information
        <BR>
        <P><INPUT TYPE="submit" NAME="goThere" VALUE="Take Me!"
             onClick="window.open(there)">
   </FORM>
```

This example has a form on which a visitor identifies a lesson (selected from the list of radio buttons.) The submit statement opens the selected document in a new window.

text

The text object is a field on the form used to collect information from the visitor. The visitor can type short string sequences, such as a word, a phrase, or numbers, into the text object. Because the text object is a form element, it must be defined within a <FORM> tag. The text object has the following format:

```
<INPUT
        TYPE="text"
        NAME="textName"
        VALUE="textValue"
        SIZE=integer
        [onBlur="handlerText"]
        [onChange="handlerText"]
        [onFocus="handlerText"]
        [onSelect="handlerText"] >
```

The textName entry is the variable name for the object. The textValue entry is the initial value for the text object, and SIZE is the length of the box on the page.

To use the text object's properties and methods, follow this format:

```
textName.propertyName
textName.methodName(parameters)
formName.elements[index].propertyName
formName.elements[index].methodName(properties)
```

The text object has these three properties, shown in Table A.15.

TABLE A.15: The Properties of the Text Object

PROPERTY	WHAT IT DOES
defaultValue	Gets the default value setting
name	Reflects the variable's name
value	Contains the current contents of the text object

The text object uses these three methods: focus, blur, and select, and it uses the onBlur, onChange, onFocus, and onSelect event handlers. It is a property of form.

Example:

```
var userProfile="user"
<INPUT TYPE="text" NAME="userType" VALUE="user" SIZE="15" onChange=
"userProfile=this.value">
<INPUT TYPE="text" NAME="userGroup" VALUE="" SIZE="32" onChange=
"userProfile+=this.value">
```

These statements create a user profile by getting the text entries the visitor makes in the text objects' fields. The first statement sets the default for the variable *userProfile*. The next two statements change this variable only if the visitor changes the contents of the fields.

textarea

Like the text object, the textarea object offers a way for visitors to enter textual data. The textarea object is a multiline field, whereas the text object is a single line. The textarea object must also be defined within a <FORM> tag.

You can dynamically update the textarea object by setting the value property. The textarea object has the following format:

```
<TEXTAREA
    NAME="textareaName"
    ROWS="integer"
    COLS="integer"
    [onBlur="handlerText"]
    [onChange="handlerText"]
    [onFocus="handlerText"]
    [onSelect="handlerText"] >
    textToDisplay
</TEXTAREA>
```

The `textareaName` entry is the name of the object.

To use the properties and methods of the `textarea` object, follow this format:

```
textareaName.propertyName
```

```
textareaName.methodName(parameters)
```

```
formName.elements[index].propertyName
```

```
formName.elements[index].methodName(parameters)
```

The `textarea` object uses three properties—`defaultValue`, `name`, and `value`—and three methods: `focus`, `blur`, and `select`. It uses the `onBlur`, `onChange`, `onFocus`, and `onSelect` event handlers. It is a property of `form`.

Example:

```
<P>Decribe the FOLD function and give three examples of what you can
do with the FOLD function:</P>
```

```
<TEXTAREA NAME="foldEssay" ROWS=5 COLS=65
onChange="question3Essay=this.value">
```

```
</TEXTAREA>
```

This example gives the visitor a field in which to answer an essay question; the answer is stored in the variable *question3Essay*.

window

The `window` object is the topmost object for JavaScript's `document`, `location`, and `history` objects. The `self` and `window` properties are synonymous and refer to the current window. The keyword `top` refers to the uppermost window in the hierarchy, and `parent` refers to a window that contains one or more framesets. Because of its unique position, you do not have to address the properties of `window` in the same fashion as other objects: `close()` is the same as `window.close()` and `self.close()`.

The `window` object uses event handlers, but the calls to these handlers are put in the <BODY> and <FRAMESET> tags. It has the following format:

```
windowVar = window.open("URL", windowName" [,windowFeatures"])
```

The `windowVar` entry is the name of a new window, and `windowName` is the TARGET= attribute of the <FORM> and <A> tags.

To use a window's properties and methods, follow this format:

```
window.propertyName
```

```
window.methodName(parameters)
```

```
self.propertyName
```

```
self.methodName(parameters)
```

```
top.propertyName
```

```
top.methodName(parameters)
```

```
parent.propertyName
parent.methodName(parameters)
windowVar.propertyName
windowVar.methodName(parameters)
propertyName
methodName(parameters)
```

To define the onLoad or onUnload event handlers, include the statement in the <BODY> or <FRAMESET> tags.

```
<BODY
        [onLoad="handlerText"]
        [onUnload="handlerText"]
</BODY>
<FRAMESET
        [onLoad="handlerText"]
        [onUnload="handlerText"]  >
</FRAMESET>
```

The window object contains the properties shown in Table A.16.

TABLE A.16: The Properties of the Window Object

PROPERTY	WHAT IT DOES/IS
defaultStatus	The default message for the window's status bar
frames	A list (array) of the window's child frames
length	The number of frames in a parent window
name	Reflects the *windowName* variable
parent	A synonym for *windowName* where the window contains a frameset
self	A synonym for the current *windowName*
status	Contains a priority or transient message for the status bar
top	A synonym for the topmost browser window
window	A synonym for the current *windowName*

The window object also uses these methods:

alert	confirm	prompt	clearTimeout
close	open	setTimeout	

The window object uses two event handlers—onLoad and onUnload. It is not a property of anything.

Example:

```
<SCRIPT>
function checkThis(){
      windowReply=window.open("reginfo.html", "answerWindow",
      "scrollbars=yes, width=100, height=200")
      document.form1.submit();
      confirm("Thanks for registering");
      self.close()}
</SCRIPT>
```

This example opens a window with the registration information.

Methods and Functions

You use methods and functions to manipulate containers, which are objects. If you think of the browser as a stage, the actors and the sets are objects; the lines spoken and the actions taken (according to the script) are the methods and functions applied to the objects.

This section is an alphabetic listing of the JavaScript methods and functions. Each entry describes a single method or function and includes syntax information and examples and identifies the object to which the method or function belongs or affects.

abs

The abs method belongs to the math object and returns the value as an unsigned number. It has the following syntax:

```
Math.abs(number)
```

The number entry is any numeric expression or a property of an object.

Example:

```
<SCRIPT>
function tryMe(baseVal){
var baseVal=Math.random()
showMe = window.open("")
```

```
        with (Math) {
                showMe.document.write("<P>" + round(baseVal*random()))
                showMe.document.write("<P>" +
                    abs(round(baseVal*random())))
                //rounds number to the nearest integer
                showMe.document.write("<P>" + abs(baseVal/5))
                // return the absolute value
                showMe.alert("Close 'er up now, skip?")
                showMe.close()
    } }
```

acos

The acos method belongs to the math object and returns the arc cosine of a number in radians. It has the following syntax:

```
Math.acos(number)
```

The number entry is any numeric expression or a property of an object.

Example:

```
        with (Math) {
                msgWindow.document.write(acos(random()))
                // find the arc cosine
```

alert

The alert method belongs to the window object and displays a small dialog box with a message string and an OK button. It has the following syntax:

```
alert("message")
```

The message is any string expression or a property of an object.

Example:

```
<BODY onLoad="window.alert('Welcome! You can register through this
    page. For future reference, this page is ' + '<P>' +
    document.location)">
```

```
// this loads a message that includes the page address through
```

```
// the document.location
```

This example uses the alert dialog box at the beginning of the page display.

anchor

The anchor method belongs to the `string` object and generates an HTML anchor for a hypertext target in a document. Use the anchor method with the `write` or `writeln` method. It has the following syntax:

```
text.anchor(nameAttribute)
```

The `text` and `nameAttribute` entries are any string or property of an object.

Example:

```
var intro="Welcome the JavaScripting Tutorial!"
tocWindow=window.open("","displayWindow")
tocWindow.document.write(intro.anchor("contents_anchor")
for (x=0; x < 5; x++) {
     switch(x){
     case[1]: if (c1 != "true") {
          tocWindow.document.write (c1 + c1.anchor("overviewtoC")
               break;
          case[2]: if (c2 != "true") {
               tocWindow.document.write (c2 +
               ➥ c2.anchor("ObjectstoC")
               break;
          case[3]: if (c3 != "true") {
               tocWindow.document.write (c3 +
               ➥ c3.anchor("structuretoC")
               break;
          case[4]: if (c4 != "true") {
               tocWindow.document.write (c4 +
               ➥ c4.anchor("f_m_ptoC")
               break;
          case[5]: if (c5 != "true") {
               tocWindow.document.write (c5 +
               ➥ c5.anchor("formstoC")
               break;
          case[6]: if (c6 != "true") {
               tocWindow.document.write (c6 +
               ➥ c6.anchor("openwintoC")
               break;
```

```
case[7]: if (c7 != "true") {
        tocWindow.document.write (c7 +
        ➥ c7.anchor("cookietoC")
        break;
```

asin

The asin method belongs to the math object and returns the arc sine of a number in radians. It has the following syntax:

```
Math.asin(number)
```

The number entry is any numeric expression or a property of an object.

Example:

```
with (Math) {
        msgWindow.document.write(asin(random()))
        // find the arc sine
```

atan

The atan method belongs to the math object and returns the arc tangent of the number in radians. It has the following syntax:

```
Math.atan(number)
```

The number entry is any numeric expression or a property of an object.

Example:

```
with (Math) {
                msgWindow.document.write(atan(random()))
        // find the arc tangent
```

back

The back method belongs to the history object and uses the history list to return to the previous document. You can use this method to give visitors an alternative to the browser's back button. It has the following syntax:

```
history.back()
```

Example:

```
<P><INPUT TYPE="button" VALUE="Take Me Back!"
onClick="history.back()">
<INPUT TYPE="button" VALUE="Let's Keep Going!"
onClick="history.forward()">
```

This code puts two buttons beside each other on a line. The first button goes back to the last document; the second button is useful if the visitor has already moved back in the history list and is ready to go forward again.

big

The big method belongs to the string object and displays the associated string as a large font (as if the text were tagged with a <BIG> tag). It has the following syntax:

```
stringName.big()
```

The stringName entry is any string expression or a property of an object.

Example:

```
<SCRIPT>
var welcome="Welcome to our flashy new digs!"
document.write("<P>" + welcome.big())
alert("That's All Folks!")
</SCRIPT>
```

blink

The blink method belongs to the string object and displays the associated string as blinking, as if the text were tagged with a <BLINK> tag. It has the following syntax:

```
stringName.blink()
```

The stringName entry is any string expression or a property of an object.

Example:

```
<SCRIPT>
var welcome="Welcome to our flashy new digs!"
document.write("<P>" + welcome.blink())
alert("That's All Folks!")
</SCRIPT>
```

blur

The blur method belongs to the password, select, text, and textarea objects and is the programmatic way to move the focus off a form object such as a text object. It has the following syntax:

```
password.blur()
selectName.blur()
textName.blur()
textareaName.blur()
```

The password entry is either the NAME of a password object or an element in the elements array. The selectName entry is either the NAME of a select object or an element in the elements array. The textName entry is either the NAME of a text object or an element in the elements array. The textareaName entry is either the NAME of a textarea object or an element in the elements array.

Example:

```
<script>
var userPass=""
var userName=""
var formulate= new window()
    // set up the variables to be used later
    formulate.window.open()
    // open a window for the form
    document.formulate.userPass.focus()
    var timer=setTimeout("document.formulate.userPass.blur()",
    ➡ 8000)
    // put the focus onto the the password box for 8 secs
    clearTimeout(timer)
    document.formulate.userName.focus()
    timer=setTimeout("document.formulate.userName.blur()", 30000)
    // clear the timeout, put the focus on the username box for
    ➡ 30 secs
    document.formulate.userAuth.click()
    //force a selection in the userAuth checkbox
    clearTimeout(timer)
    msgWindow.window.close()
    // clear the timeout variable and close the window
</script>
...
    <form NAME="formulate">
    <input type="password" NAME="userPass" SIZE=5>tell us your
    ➡ secret
    <input type="text" name="userName" value="Name" size=15>
    <input type="checkbox" name="userAuth" value="Validate Me">
    authorize us to check this stuff out!
    </form>
```

bold

The `bold` method belongs to the `string` object and displays the associated string as bold, as if the text were tagged with a <BOLD> tag. It has the following syntax:

```
stringName.bold()
```

The `stringName` entry is any string expression or a property of an object.

Example:

```
<SCRIPT>
var welcome="Welcome to our flashy new digs!"
document.write("<P>" + welcome.bold())
alert("That's All Folks!")
</SCRIPT>
```

ceil

The `ceil` method belongs to the `math` object and returns the nearest integer that is equal to or greater than the given number. It has the following syntax:

```
Math.ceil(number)
```

The `number` entry is any numeric expression or a property of an object.

Example:

```
with (Math) {
        msgWindow.document.write(ceil(random()*baseVal))
        // return the integer nearest the number (greater or
        ➡ equal)
```

charAt

The `charAt` method belongs to the `string` object and returns the character found at the given `index` in the string. It has the following syntax:

```
stringName.charAt(index)
```

The `stringName` entry is any numeric expression or a property of an object.

Example:

```
<SCRIPT>
var welcome="Welcome to our flashy new digs!"
confirm(welcome)
for (var place=0; place < welcome.length; place++) {
```

```
document.write("<P>" + welcome.charAt(place));}
    // this for loop actually puts out each letter on its own line
</SCRIPT>
```

clear

The clear method belongs to the document object and empties the contents of the document window. It has the following syntax:

```
document.clear()
```

Example:

```
alert("That's All Folks!")
self.clear()
```

clearTimeout

The clearTimeout method belongs to the frame and window objects and resets the variable for the setTimeout method. It has the following syntax:

```
clearTimeout(timeoutID)
```

The timeoutID entry is the name of the value returned by a previous call to setTimeout.

Example:

```
<script>
var userPass=""
var userName=""
var formulate= new window()
    // set up the variables to be used later
    formulate.window.open()
    // open a window for the form
    document.formulate.userPass.focus()
    var timer=setTimeout("document.formulate.userPass.blur()",
    ➥ 8000)
    // put the focus onto the the password box for 8 secs
    clearTimeout(timer)
    document.formulate.userName.focus()
    timer=setTimeout("document.formulate.userName.blur()", 30000)
    // clear the timeout, put the focus on the username box for
    ➥ 30 secs
    document.formulate.userAuth.click()
    //force a selection in the userAuth checkbox
```

```
        clearTimeout(timer)
        msgWindow.window.close()
        // clear the timeout variable and close the window
    </script>
...
        <form NAME="formulate">
        <input type="password" NAME="userPass" SIZE=5>tell us your
        ➡ secret
        <input type="text" name="userName" value="Bobs your uncle"
        ➡ size=15>
        <input type="checkbox" name="userAuth" value="Validate Me">
        authorize us to check this stuff out!
        </form>
```

click

The click method belongs to the button, checkbox, radio, reset, and submit objects and simulates, programmatically, the visitor's click on a form object. It has the following syntax:

```
password.click()
selectName.click()
textName.click()
textareaName.click()
```

The password entry is either the NAME of a password object or an element in the elements array. The selectName entry is either the NAME of a select object or an element in the elements array. The textName entry is either the NAME of a text object or an element in the elements array. The textareaName is either the NAME of a textarea object or an element in the elements array.

Example:

```
<script>
var userPass=""
var userName=""
var formulate= new window()
        // set up the variables to be used later
        document.formulate.userAuth.click()
        //force a selection in the userAuth checkbox
        clearTimeout(timer)
```

```
    msgWindow.window.close()
    // clear the timeout variable and close the window
</script>
```

...

```
    <form NAME="formulate">
    <input type="password" NAME="userPass" SIZE=5>tell us your
    ➡ secret
    <input type="text" name="userName" value="Bobs your uncle"
    ➡ size=15>
    <input type="checkbox" name="userAuth" value="Validate Me">
    authorize us to check this stuff out!
    </form>
```

close (document object)

The close method that belongs to the document object and closes the stream to an object and forces the layout. It has the following syntax:

```
document.close()
```

Example:

```
<script>
var userPass=""
var userName=""
var formulate= new window()
    // set up the variables to be used later
    clearTimeout(timer)
    msgWindow.window.close()
    // clear the timeout variable and close the window
</script>
```

...

```
    <form NAME="formulate">
    <input type="password" NAME="userPass" SIZE=5>tell us your
    ➡ secret
    <input type="text" name="userName" value="Name" size=15>
    <input type="checkbox" name="userAuth" value="Validate Me">
    authorize us to check this stuff out!
    </form>
```

close (window object)

The close method that belongs to the window object and closes the given window. It has the following syntax:

```
windowReference.close()
```

The windowReference entry is any valid means of identifying a window object.

Example:

```
<SCRIPT>
alert("That's All Folks!")
self.close()
</SCRIPT>
```

confirm

The confirm method belongs to the window object and displays a small dialog box with the message string and two buttons, OK and Cancel. It has the following syntax:

```
confirm("message")
```

The message entry is a string expression or a property of an object.

Example:

```
<SCRIPT>
function checkThis(){
        windowReply=window.open("reginfo.html", "answerWindow",
        "scrollbars=yes, width=100, height=200")
        document.form1.submit();
        confirm("Thanks for registering");
        self.close()}
</SCRIPT>
```

This example displays the confirmation message when the visitor clicks the submit button.

cos

The cos method belongs to the math object and returns the cosine of the number. It has the following syntax:

```
Math.cos(number)
```

The number entry is any numeric expression or a property of an object.

Example:

```
<SCRIPT>
function tryMe(baseVal){
var baseVal=Math.random()
showMe = window.open("")
     with (Math) {
             showMe.document.write("<P>" + cos(baseVal))
             showMe.document.write("<P>" + abs(cos(baseVal)))
             // return the cosine of the number
} }
```

escape

The escape function returns the ASCII encoded value for the given string. It has the following syntax:

```
escape("string")
```

The string entry is a nonalphanumeric string that represents a reserved or unprintable character from the ISO Latin-1 character set. For example, escape(%26) returns &.

eval

The eval function runs a JavaScript expression, statement, function, or sequence of statements. The expression can include variables and object properties. It has the following syntax:

```
eval("string")
```

The string entry is a JavaScript expression, statement, function, or sequence of statements.

exp

The exp method belongs to the math object and returns the value equal to Euler's constant (e) raised to the power of the given number. It has the following syntax:

```
Math.exp(number)
```

The number entry is any numeric expression or a property of an object.

Example:

```
<SCRIPT>
function tryMe(baseVal){
```

```
var baseVal=Math.random()
showMe = window.open("")
    with (Math) {
            showMe.document.write("<P>" + exp(baseVal))
            showMe.document.write("<P>" + abs(exp(baseVal)))
            // return Euler's constant (e) to the power of the
            ➥ number given
} }
```

fixed

The `fixed` method belongs to the `string` object and displays the associated string as fixed width (monospaced), as if the text were tagged with a `<TT>` tag. It has the following syntax:

```
stringName.fixed()
```

The `stringName` entry is any string expression or a property of an object.

Example:

```
<SCRIPT>
var welcome="Welcome to our flashy new digs!"
document.write("<P>" + welcome.fixed())
</SCRIPT>
```

floor

The `floor` method belongs to the `math` object and returns the nearest integer that is equal to or less than the given number. It has the following syntax:

```
Math.floor(number)
```

The `number` entry is any numeric expression or a property of an object.

Example:

```
    with (Math) {
            msgWindow.document.write(random())
            // generate a random number
            msgWindow.document.write(floor(random()*baseVal))
            // return the integer nearest the number (less or equal)
```

focus

The focus method belongs to the password, select, text, and textarea objects and allows you to progammatically move the focus to a form object. This simulates the visitor's moving the cursor to the object. It has the following syntax:

```
password.focus()
selectName.focus()
textName.focus()
textareaName.focus()
```

The password entry is either the NAME of a password object or an element in the elements array. The selectName entry is either the NAME of a select object or an element in the elements array. The textName is either the NAME of a text object or an element in the elements array. The textareaName is either the NAME of a textarea object or an element in the elements array.

Example:

```
<script>
var userPass=""
var userName=""
var formulate= new window()
    // set up the variables to be used later
    formulate.window.open()
    // open a window for the form
    document.formulate.userPass.focus()
    var timer=setTimeout("document.formulate.userPass.blur()",
    ➥ 8000)
    // put the focus onto the the password box for 8 secs
    clearTimeout(timer)
    document.formulate.userName.focus()
    timer=setTimeout("document.formulate.userName.blur()", 30000)
    // clear the timeout, put the focus on the username box for
    ➥ 30 secs
    document.formulate.userAuth.click()
    //force a selection in the userAuth checkbox
    clearTimeout(timer)
    msgWindow.window.close()
    // clear the timeout variable and close the window
```

```
</script>
...
        <form NAME="formulate">
        <input type="password" NAME="userPass" SIZE=5>tell us your
        ➥ secret
        <input type="text" name="userName" value="Name" size=15>
        <input type="checkbox" name="userAuth" value="Validate Me">
        authorize us to check this stuff out!
        </form>
```

fontcolor

The fontcolor method belongs to the string object and displays the associated string in the given color, as if the text were tagged with a <FONT COLOR=" "> tag. It has the following syntax:

```
stringName.fontcolor(colorKeyword)
```

The stringName entry is any string expression or a property of an object.

Example:

```
<SCRIPT>
var welcome="Welcome to our flashy new digs!"
document.write("<P>" + welcome.fontcolor("crimson"))
</SCRIPT>
```

fontsize

The fontsize method belongs to the string object and displays the associated string at the given size, as if the text were tagged with a <FONT SIZE=" "> tag. It has the following syntax:

```
stringName.fontsize(size)
```

The stringName entry is any string expression or a property of an object.

Example:

```
<SCRIPT>
var welcome="Welcome to our flashy new digs!"
document.write("<P>" + welcome.fontsize(8))
</SCRIPT>
```

forward

The forward method belongs to the history object and uses the history list to recall a previously viewed document that the visitor has used the Back button or the back method to leave. You can use this method to give visitors an alternative to the browser's Forward button. You can also use the `history.go(1)` method to perform this action. It has the following syntax:

```
history.forward()
```

Example:

```
<P><INPUT TYPE="button" VALUE="Take Me Back!"
onClick="history.back()">
```

```
<INPUT TYPE="button" VALUE="Let's Keep Going!"
onClick="history.forward()">
```

This code puts two buttons beside each other on a line. The first button goes back to the last document. The second button is useful if the visitor has already moved back in the history list and is ready to go forward again.

getDate

The `getDate` method belongs to the `date` object and returns the day of the month (0–31) for the given date. It has the following syntax:

```
dateObjectName.getDate()
```

The `datObjectName` entry is any `date` object or a property of an object.

Example:

```
<SCRIPT>
function callMe(){
Xmas95 = new Date("December 25, 1995 23:15:00");
weekday = Xmas95.getDate();
confirm(weekday);
var who=1;
var docMod=document.lastModified
  switch (who) { // this switch has two streams
      case(1) :
              alert(docMod);
              chrono=new Date()
              alert(chrono.getDate());
              alert(chrono + " already?!");
              who++;
              break;
```

```
    case(2) :         docMod="";
            docMod.setDay(1);
            docMod.setMonth(6);
            docMod.setDate(30);
            docMod.setYear(1997);
            docMod.setTime(11, 59, 59);
            document.write("<P>" + chrono.fontcolor("darkmagenta"));
            who++;
            break;
    }
</SCRIPT>
```

getDay

The getDay method belongs to the date object and returns the day of the week (0–6) for the given date. It has the following syntax:

```
dateObjectName.getDay()
```

The getObjectName entry is any date object or a property of an object.

Example:

```
<SCRIPT>
function callMe(){
Xmas95 = new Date("December 25, 1995 23:15:00");
weekday = Xmas95.getDate();
confirm(weekday);
var who=1;
var docMod=document.lastModified
 switch (who) { // this switch has two streams
    case(1) :
            alert(docMod);
            chrono=new Date()
            alert(chrono.getDay());
            alert(chrono + " already?!");
            who++;
            break;
    case(2) :         docMod="";
            docMod.setDay(1);
```

```
            docMod.setMonth(6);
            docMod.setDate(30);
            docMod.setYear(1997);
            docMod.setTime(11, 59, 59);
            document.write("<P>" + chrono.fontcolor("darkmagenta"));
            who++;
            break;
    }
</SCRIPT>
```

getHours

The getHours method belongs to the date object and returns the hour (0–23) of the given date. It has the following syntax:

```
dateObjectName.getHours()
```

The datObjectName entry is any date object or a property of an object.

Example:

```
<SCRIPT>
function callMe(){
Xmas95 = new Date("December 25, 1995 23:15:00");
weekday = Xmas95.getDate();
confirm(weekday);
var docMod=document.lastModified
alert(docMod);
chrono=new Date()
alert(chrono.getHours());
alert(chrono + " already?!");
</SCRIPT>
```

getMinutes

The getMinutes method belongs to the date object and returns the minutes (0–59) for the given date. It has the following syntax:

```
dateObjectName.getMinutes()
```

The dateObjectName entry is any date object or a property of an object.

Example:

```
<SCRIPT>
function callMe(){
```

```
Xmas95 = new Date("December 25, 1995 23:15:00");
weekday = Xmas95.getDate();
confirm(weekday);
var docMod=document.lastModified
alert(docMod);
chrono=new Date()
alert(chrono.getMinutes());
alert(chrono + " already?!");
</SCRIPT>
```

getMonth

The getMonth method belongs to the date object and returns the month (0–11) of the given date. It has the following syntax:

```
dateObjectName.getMonth()
```

The dateObjectName entry is any date object or a property of an object.

Example:

```
<SCRIPT>
function callMe(){
Xmas95 = new Date("December 25, 1995 23:15:00");
weekday = Xmas95.getDate();
confirm(weekday);
var docMod=document.lastModified
alert(docMod);
chrono=new Date()
alert(chrono.getMonths());
alert(chrono + " already?!");
</SCRIPT>
```

getSeconds

The getSeconds method belongs to the date object and returns the seconds (0–59) of the given date. It has the following syntax:

```
dateObjectName.getSeconds()
```

The datObjectLName entry is any date object or a property of an object.

Example:

```
<SCRIPT>
function callMe(){
Xmas95 = new Date("December 25, 1995 23:15:00");
weekday = Xmas95.getDate();
confirm(weekday);
var docMod=document.lastModified
alert(docMod);
chrono=new Date()
alert(chrono.getSeconds());
alert(chrono + " already?!");
</SCRIPT>
```

getTime

The getTime method belongs to the date object and returns the time (number of milli-seconds since January 1, 1970 00:00:00) for the given date. It has the following syntax:

```
dateObjectName.getTime()
```

The dateObjectName entry is any date object or a property of an object.

Example:

```
<SCRIPT>
function callMe(){
Xmas95 = new Date("December 25, 1995 23:15:00");
weekday = Xmas95.getTime();
confirm(weekday);
var docMod=document.lastModified
alert(docMod);
chrono=new Date()
alert(chrono.getHours());
alert(chrono + " already?!");
</SCRIPT>
```

getTimezoneOffset

The getTimezoneOffset method belongs to the date object and returns the differ-ence between local time and GMT in minutes. It has the following syntax:

```
dateObjectName.getTimezoneOffset()
```

The `dateObjectName` entry is any `date` object or a property of an object.

Example:

```
<SCRIPT>
function callMe(){
Xmas95 = new Date("December 25, 1995 23:15:00");
weekday = Xmas95.getDate();
confirm(weekday);
var docMod=document.lastModified
alert(docMod);
chrono=new Date()
alert(chrono.get.timezoneOffset());
alert(chrono);
</SCRIPT>
```

getYear

The `getYear` method belongs to the `date` object and returns the last two digits of the year of the given date. It has the following syntax:

```
dateObjectName.getYear()
```

The `dateObjectName` entry is any `date` object or a property of an object.

Example:

```
<SCRIPT>
function callMe(){
Xmas95 = new Date("December 25, 1995 23:15:00");
weekday = Xmas95.getDate();
confirm(weekday);
var docMod=document.lastModified
alert(docMod);
chrono=new Date()
alert(chrono.getYear());
alert(chrono + " already?!");
</SCRIPT>
```

go

The go method belongs to the `history` object and uses the history list to recall a previously viewed document. You can use this method to give visitors an alternative to the browser's Back and Forward buttons. You can also use the back and forward methods. The go method has the following syntax:

```
history.go(number)
```

The number entry is a positive or negative integer. A positive integer moves the visitor forward, and a negative integer moves the visitor back.

Example:

```
<P><INPUT TYPE="button" VALUE="Take Me Back!"
onClick="history.back()">
```

```
<INPUT TYPE="button" VALUE="Let's Keep Going!"
onClick="history.forward()">
```

This code places two buttons beside each other on a line. The first button goes back to the last document. The second button is useful if the visitor has already moved back in the history list and is ready to go forward again.

Using the go method, these lines would appear like this:

```
<P><INPUT TYPE="button" VALUE="Take Me Back!"
onClick="history.go(-1)">
```

```
<INPUT TYPE="button" VALUE="Let's Keep Going!"
onClick="history.go(1)">
```

indexOf

The indexOf method belongs to the string object and returns the position of the first occurrence of the search value starting from the position given. It has the following syntax:

```
stringName.indexOf("searchValue", [fromIndex])
```

The stringName entry is any string or object property. The searchValue is a string from within stringName. The fromIndex entry is the starting position for the search; the default is zero (first position).

Example:

```
var champion="We are the champions! We are the champions!"
```

```
champion.indexOf("are")
```

```
chamption.lastIndexOf("are)
```

This example returns the number 3 for the indexOf statement and 25 for the lastIndexOf statement.

isNaN

The isNaN function is Unix-based; it determines whether the value given is a number. It has the following syntax:

```
isNaN(testValue)
```

Example:

```
floatValue=parseFloat(toFloat)
if isNaN (floatValue) {
      not Float()
}else {
      isFloat()
}
```

This example generates the value and then evaluates it.

italics

The `italics` method belongs to the `string` object and displays the associated string as italics or oblique, as if the text were tagged with a `<FONT STYLE=" ">` tag. It has the following syntax:

```
stringName.italics()
```

The `stringName` entry is any string expression or a property of an object.

Example:

```
<SCRIPT>
var welcome="Welcome to our flashy new digs!"
document.write("<P>" + welcome.italics())
</SCRIPT>
```

lastIndexOf

The `lastIndexOf` method belongs to the `string` object and returns the position of the last occurrence of the search value starting from the position given. It has the following syntax:

```
stringName.lastIndexOf("searchValue", [fromIndex])
```

The `stringName` entry is any string or object property. The `searchValue` entry is a string from within `stringName`. The `fromIndex` entry is the starting position for the search; the default is zero (first position).

Example:

```
var champion="We are the champions! We are the champions!"
champion.indexOf("are")
chamption.lastIndexOf("are)
```

This example returns the number 3 for the `indexOf` statement and 25 for the `lastIndexOf` statement.

link

The link method belongs to the anchor object and creates a jump to a URL. It has the following syntax:

```
linkText.link(hrefAttribute)
```

The linkText entry is a string or property that is used as the label for the link. The hrefAttribute entry is a valid URL for the destination.

Example:

```
var c1="JavaScripting Overview"

var c2="JavaScript Objects"

var c3="JavaScript Constructs"

…

document.write(c1.link("http://www.writelivelihood.com/JS/Courses/

js_overview.html")document.write(c2.link("http://www
.writelivelihood.com/JS/Courses/js_objects.html")

document.write(c3.link("http://www.writelivelihood.com/JS/

Courses/js_constructs.html")
```

You can use this example to build the table of contents for a dynamically selected course by including a selection form and a switch statement.

log

The log method belongs to the math object and returns the natural logarithm (base e) of the given number. It has the following syntax:

```
Math.log(number)
```

The number entry is any numeric expression or a property of an object.

Example:

```
with (Math) {
        msgWindow.document.write(log(baseVal))
        // return the natural logarithm (base of e) of the
        ➥ number
```

max

The max method belongs to the math object and returns the higher of two given numbers. It has the following syntax:

```
Math.max(number1, number2)
```

The number1 and number2 entries are any numeric expression or a property of an object.

Example

```
with (Math) {
        msgWindow.document.write(random())
        // generate a random number
        msgWindow.document.write(max(baseVal, (random()*3)))
        // return the highest value
```

min

The min method belongs to the math object and returns the lower of two given numbers. It has the following syntax:

```
Math.min(number1, number2)
```

The number1 and number2 entries are any numeric expression or a property of an object.

Example:

```
with (Math) {
        msgWindow.document.write(random())
        // generate a random number
        msgWindow.document.write(min(baseVal, (random()*3)))
        // return the lowest value
```

open (document object)

The open method for documents belongs to the window object and opens an output destination for the write and writeln statements. It has the following syntax:

```
document.open(["mimeType"])
```

The mimeType entry is any one of the following:

text/html	image/jpeg	image/gif
text/plain	image/x-bitmap	plugIn

Example:

```
<script>
var userPass=""
var userName=""
var formulate= new window()
        // set up the variables to be used later
        formulate.window.open()
</script>
```

open (window object)

The open method for window objects belongs to the window object and allows you to set up and open an instance of the browser for displaying information. It has the following syntax:

```
windowVar=window.open("URL", "windowName" [,"windowsFeatures"])
```

The windowVar entry is the name of the new window, and URL is the location of the document to be loaded into the new window. The windowName entry is used in the TARGET= attribute of the <FORM> and <A> tags. The windowsFeatures entry is a comma-separated list that can contain one or more of the following:

```
toolbar[=yes|no] | [=1|0]
location[=yes|no] | [=1|0]
directories[=yes|no] | [=1|0]
status[=yes|no] | [=1|0]
menubar[=yes|no] | [=1|0]
scrollbars[=yes|no] | [=1|0]
resizable[=yes|no] | [=1|0]
width=pixels
height=pixels
```

Example:

```
<script>
var userPass=""
var userName=""
var formulate= new window()
    // set up the variables to be used later
    formulate.window.open('http://www.raycomm.com'
            'titlebar=no,menubar=no,scrollbars=no')
```

parse

The parse method belongs to the date object and returns the number of milliseconds between a given date string and January 1, 1970 00:00:00 local time. It has the following syntax:

```
Date.parse(dateString)
```

The dateString entry is a date or an object property.

Example:

```
checkValue=Date.parse("1, 1, 99")
```

```
if isNaN (checkValue) {
      notGood()
}else {
      isGood()
}
```

This example generates the value and then evaluates it.

parseFloat

The parseFloat function determines if a value is a number and returns a floating point number for a string. It has the following syntax:

```
parseFloat(string)
```

The string entry is a string or object property.

Example:

```
toFloat="3.14"
floatValue=parseFloat(toFloat)
if isNaN (floatValue) {
      not Float()
}else {
      isFloat()
}
```

This example generates the value and then evaluates it.

parseInt

The parseInt function determines if a value is a number and returns an integer value of the given radix or base. It has the following syntax:

```
parseInt(string [,radix])
```

The string entry is a string or an object property, and the radix is an integer.

Example:

```
document.write(parseInt("F", 16))
      // the 16 indicates that the F is a hexidecimal number
      ➥ (base 16)
document.write(parseInt("1111", 2))
document.write(parseInt ("0xF"))
```

These examples return the same value, 15.

pow

The pow method belongs to the math object and returns the first number raised to the power of the second number. It has the following syntax:

```
Math.pow(base, exponent)
```

The base and exponent entries are any numeric expression or a property of an object.

Example:

```
with (Math) {
        msgWindow.document.write(random())
        // generate a random number

        msgWindow.document.write(pow(baseVal, random()))
        // raise the first number to the power of the second
        ➡ number
```

prompt

The prompt method belongs to the window object and displays a dialog box with a message and an input field. Even though prompt is a window method, you do not have to include the windowReference in the statement. The prompt method has the following syntax:

```
prompt(message, [inputDefault])
```

The message entry is a text string or an object property, and inputDefault is a string, an integer, or an object property.

Example:

```
<script>
var userPass=""
var userName=""
var formulate= new window()
        prompt ("Are you done yet?" 1)
</script>
...
        <form NAME="formulate">
        <input type="password" NAME="userPass" SIZE=5>tell us your
        ➡ secret
        <input type="text" name="userName" value="Name" size=15>
        <input type="checkbox" name="userAuth" value="Validate Me">
        authorize us to check this stuff out!
```

```
    </input>
    </form>
```

random

The random method belongs to the math object and generates a random number between 0 and 1. It has the following syntax:

```
Math.random()
```

Example:

```
<SCRIPT>
function tryMe(baseVal){
var baseVal=Math.random()
showMe = window.open("")
    with (Math) {
            var firstOne=(random())
            var secondOne=(abs(random()))
            showMe.document.write("<P>" + firstOne)
            showMe.document.write("<P>" + secondOne)
            // generate a random number
    } }
```

round

The round method belongs to the math object and returns the value of the number given to the nearest integer. It has the following syntax:

```
Math.round(number)
```

The number entry is any numeric expression or a property of an object.

Example:

```
<SCRIPT>
function tryMe(baseVal){
var baseVal=Math.random()
showMe = window.open("")
    with (Math) {
            var firstOne=(random())
            var secondOne=(abs(random()))
            showMe.document.write("<P>" + firstOne)
            showMe.document.write("<P>" + secondOne)
            // generate a random number
```

```
                 showMe.document.write("<P>" + round(baseVal*random()))
                 showMe.document.write("<P>"
              ➥ + abs(round(baseVal*random())))
                 //rounds number to the nearest integer
                 showMe.alert("Close 'er up now, skip?")
                 showMe.close()
     } }
```

select

Like the focus and blur methods, the select method performs an action programmatically. It belongs to the password, text, and textarea objects. The select
method selects the input area of a given password, text, or textarea form object. It has
the following syntax:

```
passwordName.select()

textName.select()

textareaName.select()
```

The passwordName entry is the NAME= attribute of the password object. The textName
entry is the NAME= attribute of the text object, and textareaName is the NAME=
attribute of the textarea object.

Example:

```
<script>
var userPass=""
var userName=""
var formulate= new window()
      // set up the variables to be used later
      document.formulate.userPass.select()
</script>
...
      <form NAME="formulate">
      <input type="password" NAME="userPass" SIZE=5>tell us your
secret
      <input type="text" name="userName" value="Name" size=15>
      <input type="checkbox" name="userAuth" value="Validate Me">
      authorize us to check this stuff out!
      </form>
```

setDate

The setDate method belongs to the date object and sets the day of the month for a given date. It has the following syntax:

```
dateObjectName.setDate(dayValue)
```

The dateObjectName entry is any date object or a property of an object. The day-Value is an integer between 1 and 31 or a property of an object representing the month.

Example:

```
<SCRIPT>
function callMe(){
Xmas95 = new Date("December 25, 1995 23:15:00");
weekday = Xmas95.getDate();
confirm(weekday);
var docMod=""
docMod.setDay(1);
docMod.setMonth(6);
docMod.setDate(30);
docMod.setYear(1997);
docMod.setTime(11, 59, 59);
alert(docMod);
</SCRIPT>
```

setHours

The setHours method belongs to the date object and sets the hour of the day for a given date. It has the following syntax:

```
dateObjectName.setHours(hoursValue)
```

The dateObjectName entry is any date object or a property of an object. The hours-Value entry is an integer between 0 and 23 or a property of an object representing the hour.

Example:

```
<SCRIPT>
function callMe(){
Xmas95 = new Date("December 25, 1995 23:15:00");
weekday = Xmas95.getDate();
confirm(weekday);
var docMod=""
```

```
docMod.setDay(1);
docMod.setMonth(6);
docMod.setDate(30);
docMod.setYear(1997);
docMod.setHours(11);
docMod.setMinutes(59);
docMod.setSeconds(59);
alert(docMod);
</SCRIPT>
```

setMinutes

The setMinutes method belongs to the date object and sets the minutes of the hour for a given date. It has the following syntax:

```
dateObjectName.setMinutes(minuteValue)
```

The dateObjectName entry is any date object or a property of an object. The minuteValue entry is an integer between 0 and 59 or a property of an object representing the minute.

Example:

```
<SCRIPT>
function callMe(){
Xmas95 = new Date("December 25, 1995 23:15:00");
weekday = Xmas95.getDate();
confirm(weekday);
var docMod=""
docMod.setDay(1);
docMod.setMonth(6);
docMod.setDate(30);
docMod.setYear(1997);
docMod.setHours(11);
docMod.setMinutes(59);
docMod.setSeconds(59);
alert(docMod);
</SCRIPT>
```

setMonth

The `setMonth` method belongs to the `date` object and sets the month of the year for a given date. It has the following syntax:

```
dateObjectName.setMonth(monthValue)
```

The `dateObjectName` entry is any `date` object or a property of an object. The `month-Value` is an integer between 0 and 11 or a property of an object representing the month. It has the following syntax:

Example:

```
<SCRIPT>
function callMe(){
Xmas95 = new Date("December 25, 1995 23:15:00");
weekday = Xmas95.getDate();
confirm(weekday);
var docMod=""
docMod.setDay(1);
docMod.setMonth(6);
docMod.setDate(30);
docMod.setYear(1997);
docMod.setHours(11);
docMod.setMinutes(59);
docMod.setSeconds(59);
alert(docMod);
</SCRIPT>
```

setSeconds

The `setSeconds` method belongs to the `date` object and sets the seconds of the minute for a given date. It has the following syntax:

```
dateObjectName.setSeconds(secondsValue)
```

The `dateObjectName` entry is any `date` object or a property of an object. The `second-Value` entry is an integer between 0 and 59 or a property of an object representing the seconds.

Example:

```
<SCRIPT>
function callMe(){
Xmas95 = new Date("December 25, 1995 23:15:00");
```

```
weekday = Xmas95.getDate();
confirm(weekday);
var docMod=""
docMod.setDay(1);
docMod.setMonth(6);
docMod.setDate(30);
docMod.setYear(1997);
docMod.setHours(11);
docMod.setMinutes(59);
docMod.setSeconds(59);
alert(docMod);
</SCRIPT>
```

setTime

The setTime method belongs to the date object and sets the number of milliseconds since January 1, 1970 00:00:00. It has the following syntax:

```
dateObjectName.setTime(timeValue)
```

The dateObjectName entry is any date object or a property of an object. The time-Value entry is an integer or a property of an object representing the number of milliseconds since the epoch.

Example:

```
<SCRIPT>
function callMe(){
Xmas95 = new Date("December 25, 1995 23:15:00");
weekday = Xmas95.getDate();
confirm(weekday);
var docMod=""
docMod.setDay(1);
docMod.setMonth(6);
docMod.setDate(30);
docMod.setYear(1997);
docMod.setTime(11, 59, 59);
alert(docMod);
</SCRIPT>
```

setTimeout

The setTimeout method belongs to the frame and window objects and evaluates an expression after the set number of milliseconds have past. It has the following syntax:

```
timeoutID=setTimeout(expression, msec)
```

The timeoutID entry is the identifer for the timeout variable; it is used later by the clearTimeout method. The expression entry is a string or a property of an object. The msec entry is a numeric value, a numeric string, or an object property representing the number of millisecond units for the timeout.

Example:

```
<script>
var userPass=""
var userName=""
var formulate= new window()
        // set up the variables to be used later
        formulate.window.open()
        // open a window for the form
        document.formulate.userPass.focus()
        var timer=setTimeout("document.formulate.userPass.blur()",
        ➡ 8000)
        // put the focus onto the the password box for 8 secs
        clearTimeout(timer)
        document.formulate.userName.focus()
        timer=setTimeout("document.formulate.userName.blur()", 30000)
        // clear the timeout, put the focus on the username box for
        ➡ 30 secs
        document.formulate.userAuth.click()
        //force a selection in the userAuth checkbox
        clearTimeout(timer)
        msgWindow.window.close()
        // clear the timeout variable and close the window
</script>
        <form NAME="formulate">
        <input type="password" NAME="userPass" SIZE=5>tell us your
        ➡ secret
        <input type="text" name="userName" value="Name" size=15>
```

```
<input type="checkbox" name="userAuth" value="Validate Me">
authorize us to check this stuff out!
</form>
```

setYear

The `setYear` method belongs to the `date` object and sets the year for a given date. It has the following syntax:

```
dateObjectName.setYear(yearValue)
```

The `dateObjectName` entry is any `date` object or a property of an object. The `yearValue` entry is a two-digit integer or a property of an object representing the year (you can use only the years between 1900 and 2000).

Example:

```
<SCRIPT>
function callMe(){
Xmas95 = new Date("December 25, 1995 23:15:00");
weekday = Xmas95.getDate();
confirm(weekday);
var docMod=""
docMod.setDay(1);
docMod.setMonth(6);
docMod.setDate(30);
docMod.setYear(1997);
docMod.setTime(11, 59, 59);
alert(docMod);
</SCRIPT>
```

sin

The `sin` method belongs to the `math` object and returns the sine of the given number. It has the following syntax:

```
Math.sin(number)
```

The `number` entry is any numeric expression or a property of an object.

Example:

```
<SCRIPT>
function tryMe(baseVal){
var baseVal=Math.random()
```

```
    showMe = window.open("")
        with (Math) {
                showMe.document.write("<P>" + sin(random()))
} }
```

small

The small method belongs to the **string** object and displays the associated string using a smaller font, as if the text were tagged with a <SMALL> tag. It has the following syntax:

```
stringName.small()
```

The **stringName** entry is any string expression or a property of an object.

Example:

```
<SCRIPT>
var welcome="Welcome to our flashy new digs!"
confirm(welcome)
        // this opens a small box with the text and an ok button
document.write("<P>" + welcome.small())
</SCRIPT>
```

sqrt

The sqrt method belongs to the **math** object and returns the square root of the given number. It has the following syntax:

```
Math.sqrt(number)
```

The **number** is any nonnegative numeric expression or a property of an object.

Example:

```
<SCRIPT>
function tryMe(baseVal){
var baseVal=Math.random()
showMe = window.open("")
        with (Math) {
                showMe.document.write("<P>" + sqrt(baseVal))
                showMe.document.write("<P>" + abs(sqrt(baseVal)))
                // return the square root of the number
} }
```

strike

The strike method belongs to the string object and displays the associated string with strikethrough. It has the following syntax:

```
stringName.strike()
```

The stringName entry is any string expression or a property of an object.

Example:

```
<SCRIPT>
var welcome="Welcome to our flashy new digs!"
confirm(welcome)
        // this opens a small box with the text and an ok button
document.write("<P>" + welcome.strike())
</SCRIPT>
```

sub

The sub method belongs to the string object and displays the associated string subscripted to the rest of the text. It has the following syntax:

```
stringName.sub()
```

The stringName entry is any string expression or a property of an object.

Example:

```
<SCRIPT>
var welcome="Welcome to our flashy new digs!"
confirm(welcome)
        // this opens a small box with the text and an ok button
document.write("<P>" + welcome.sub())
</SCRIPT>
```

submit

The submit method belongs to the form object and submits a form. It has the following syntax:

```
formName.submit()
```

The formName entry is the name of a form or an element in the forms array.

Example:

```
<SCRIPT>
function checkThis(){
        document.form1.submit();
```

```
        confirm("Thanks for registering");
        self.close()}

</SCRIPT>
</HEAD>


<BODY onLoad="window.alert('Welcome! You can register through this
page. For future reference, this page is ' + '<P>' +document.loca-
tion)">
<FORM NAME="form1">

        <P><INPUT TYPE="text" NAME="whoIs" VALUE="user" SIZE=15>

        <P><INPUT TYPE="radio" NAME="lesson" VALUE="Lesson 1" CHECKED
onClick="takeLesson='lesson1.htm'"> Lesson 1: Getting Started

        <P><INPUT TYPE="radio" NAME="lesson" VALUE="Lesson 2"
onClick="takeLesson='lesson2.htm'"> Lesson 2: Concepts and
Operations

        <P><INPUT TYPE="radio" NAME="lesson" VALUE="Lesson 3"
onClick="takeLesson='lesson3.htm'"> Lesson 3: Projects

        <P><INPUT TYPE="reset" VALUE="Defaults" NAME="resetToBasic">

        <INPUT TYPE="submit" VALUE="Send it in!" NAME="submit_form1"
onClick="checkThis()">

        <HR>


</FORM>
</BODY>
```

substring

The substring method belongs to the string object and returns a portion of a given string. It has the following syntax:

```
stringName.substring(index1, index2)
```

The stringName entry is the string or an object property. The index 1 entry is an integer representing the starting position of the substring within the string; this can be any integer from zero to stringName.length-1. The index 2 entry is an integer representing the ending position of the substring within the string; this can be any integer larger than index1 from zero to stringName.length-1.

Example:

```
var champion="We are the champions! We are the champions!"
document.write(champion.substring(11,19)
document.write(champion.substring(13,15)
```

This example returns "champions" and "amp".

sup

The sup method belongs to the string object and displays the associated string as a superscript to the surrounding text. It has the following syntax:

```
stringName.sup()
```

The stringName entry is any string expression or a property of an object.

Example:

```
<SCRIPT>
var welcome="Welcome to our flashy new digs!"
confirm(welcome)
        // this opens a small box with the text and an ok button
document.write("<P>" + welcome.sup())
alert("That's All Folks!")
self.close()
        // at the end, a box appears, with the message
        // That's All Folks! and an ok button
        // the next line closes the browser
</SCRIPT>
```

tan

The tan method belongs to the math object and returns the tangent of the given number. It has the following syntax:

```
Math.tan(number)
```

The number entry is any numeric expression or a property of an object that represents the size of an angle in radians.

Example:

```
with (Math) {
        msgWindow.document.write(tan(random()))
        //find the are tangent
```

toGMTString

The toGMTString method belongs to the date object and converts a date to a string, using the internet GMT conventions. The exact format varies according to the visitor's platform. It is generally more reliable to use the getMonth, getDay, and other such date methods to get the information if you plan to manipulate it at all. The toGMT-String method has the following syntax:

```
dataGMT.toLocalString()
```

The dateObjectName is any date object or a property of an object.

Example:

```
function (showDate) {
    var docMod="";
    docMod.setDay(1);
    docMod.setMonth(6);
    docMod.setDate(30);
    docMod.setYear(1997);
    docMod.setTime(11, 59, 59);
    docMod.toLocaleString();
    document.write("<P>" + docMod.fontcolor("darkmagenta"));
    docMod.toGMTString();
    document.write("<P>" + docMod.fontcolor("darkmagenta")) }
```

This converts the contents of the date variable *docMod* first to local time and then to GMT time before displaying each value.

toLocaleString

The toLocalString method belongs to the date object and converts a date to a string, using the local conventions. It is generally more reliable to use the getMonth, getDay, and other such date methods to get the information if you plan to manipulate it at all. The toLocalString method has the following syntax:

```
dataObjectName.toLocalString()
```

The dateObjectName entry is any date object or a property of an object.

Example:

```
function (showDate) {
    var docMod="";
    docMod.setDay(1);
    docMod.setMonth(6);
```

```
docMod.setDate(30);
docMod.setYear(1997);
docMod.setTime(11, 59, 59);
docMod.toLocaleString();
document.write("<P>" + docMod.fontcolor("darkmagenta"));
docMod.toGMTString();
document.write("<P>" + docMod.fontcolor("darkmagenta")) }
```

This converts the contents of the date variable docMod first to local time and then to GMT time before printing out each value.

toLowerCase

The toLowerCase method belongs to the string object and converts the contents of a text string to all lowercase letters. It has the following syntax:

```
stringName.toLowerCase()
```

The stringName entry is any string expression or a property of an object.

Example:

```
<SCRIPT>
    function upAndDown() {
        confirm(document.WhoAreYou.nameInfo.value.toUpperCase());
        confirm(document.WhoAreYou.FavFoodGroup.value.
        ➡ toLowerCase()); }
</SCRIPT>
</HEAD>
<BODY>
<form NAME="WhoAreYou">
    <input type="text" name="nameInfo" value="" size=30
maxlength=30>
    <input type="text" name="FavFoodGroup" size=15>
    <input type="submit" name="getGoing" value="Yumm!"
        onClick="upAndDown()">
</form>
```

toUpperCase

The toUpperCase method belongs to the string object and converts the contents of a text string to all uppercase letters. It has the following syntax:

```
stringName.toUpperCase()
```

The `stringName` is any string expression or a property of an object.

Example:

```
<SCRIPT>
        function upAndDown() {
                confirm(document.WhoAreYou.nameInfo.value.toUpperCase());
                confirm(document.WhoAreYou.FavFoodGroup.value
                ➥ .toLowerCase()); }
</SCRIPT>
</HEAD>

<BODY>
<form NAME="WhoAreYou">
        <input type="text" name="nameInfo" value="" size=30
maxlength=30>
        <input type="text" name="FavFoodGroup" size=15>
        <input type="submit" name="getGoing" value="Yumm!"
                onClick="upAndDown()">
</form>
```

unescape

Like the `escape` function, the `unescape` function converts an ASCII value. The `unescape` function takes the integer or hexadecimal value of the character and returns the ASCII character. It has the following syntax:

```
unescape("string")
```

The `string` entry is either an integer ("%integer") or a hexadecimal value ("hex").

UTC

The UTC method belongs to the `date` object and returns the number of milliseconds between the contents of a date object and the epoch (January 1, 1970 00:00:00, Universal Coordinated Time [GMT]). It has the following syntax:

```
Date.UTC(year, month, day [,hrs] [,min] [,sec])
```

The `year` entry is a two-digit representation of a year between 1900 and 2000. The `month` entry is a number between zero and 12 representing the month of the year. The `day` entry is a number between zero and 31 representing the day of the month. The `hrs` entry is a two-digit number between 00 and 23 representing the hour of the day. The `min` entry is a two-digit number between 00 and 59 representing the minute of the hour, and `sec` is a two-digit number between 00 and 59 representing the second of the minute.

Example:

```
<SCRIPT>
var welcome="Welcome to our flashy new digs!"
confirm(welcome)
      // this opens a small box with the text and an ok button
 var chrono=new Date()
var docMod=document.lastModified
var fakeBD=new Date("July 1, 1977 00:00:00")
var otherDisp= Date.UTC(fake BD)
      // create some new Date variables
</SCRIPT>
```

write

The write method belongs to the document object and sends expressions to the document as encoded HTML strings. It has the following syntax:

```
write(expression1 [,expression2] […, expression N])
```

The expression1 through expressionN entries are any JavaScript expression or a property of an object.

Example:

```
<SCRIPT>
var welcome="Welcome to our flashy new digs!"
confirm(welcome)
      // this opens a small box with the text and an ok button
document.write("<P>" + welcome.small())
document.write("<P>" + welcome.big())
document.write("<P>" + welcome.blink())
document.write("<P>" + welcome.bold())
document.write("<P>")
document.write("<P>" + welcome.fixed())
      // these write out the contents of welcome using a number of
      // text attributes
 </SCRIPT>
```

writeln

Like the `write` method, the `writeln` method belongs to the `document` object and sends expressions to the document as encoded HTML strings. The `writeln` method generates a newline character (hard return). HTML ignores the newline character excecpt within tags such as <PRE>. The `writeln` method has the following syntax:

```
writeln(expression1 [,expression2] [..., expression N])
```

The `expression1` through `expressionN` entries are any JavaScript expression or a property of an object.

Example:

```
<SCRIPT>
var welcome="Welcome to our flashy new digs!"
confirm(welcome)
      // this opens a small box with the text and an ok button
document.writeln(welcome.small())
document.writeln(welcome.big())
document.writeln(welcome.blink())
document.writeln(welcome.bold())
document.writeln("<P>" + welcome.fixed())
</SCRIPT>
```

Event Handlers

When users interact with your Web page through JavaScript scripts, you need event handlers to recognize the event and communicate back to your script. These event handlers help manage the interaction between your visitors and your JavaScript objects by providing the information in the visitor response to the JavaScript for later use.

This section is an alphabetic listing of the JavaScript event handlers. Each entry describes a single event handler, includes examples, and identifies the objects for which the event handler works. The syntax for these event handlers can be seen in the corresponding object listings.

onBlur

A blur occurs when the focus moves from one object to another on the page. The object that was in focus loses focus and is blurred.

Example:

```
onBlur="document.login.submit()"
```

When the visitor leaves the field, the system submits the information for logging into the next page.

The onBlur event handler works for the select, text, and textarea objects.

onChange

A change occurs when the visitor alters the contents of an object and then moves the focus from the object. The object is changed. Use the onChange event handler to validate the information submitted by visitors.

Example:

```
onChange="testName(this.value)"
```

This example sends the contents of the field to the testName function when the visitor changes information and leaves the field.

The onChange event handler works for the select, text, and textarea objects.

onClick

A click occurs when the visitor clicks an object on the page with the mouse. This event could lead to a selection or a change or could launch a piece of JavaScript code.

Example:

```
onClick="compute(this.form)"
```

When the visitor clicks the object, the script runs the compute function and sends the form contents.

This event handler has been updated to not act if the event handler returns false when it is employed by a checkbox, radio, submit, or reset object.

The onClick event handler works for the document, button, checkbox, radio, link, reset, and submit objects.

onDblClick

A double-click occurs when the visitor clicks twice quickly on an object on the page.

Example:

```
<a href="seeMyFamily.html" onDblClick="this.href='theFastTour'">
```

This example loads a different page if the visitor double-clicks a link.

This event is new in JavaScript 1.2, so it will not work with versions of Netscape Navigator 3 or earlier or with Internet Explorer 3 or earlier. The onDblClick event handler is not implemented in the Macintosh versions of the Netscape Navigator browser.

The onDblClick event handler works for the document, area (in an image map), and link objects.

onDragDrop

A drag-and-drop occurs when the visitor drops an object, such as a file, onto the browser window.

Example:

```
onDragDrop="send(newInfo)"
```

This passes the dropped object to a function called send. This could be preformatted data that the visitor can mail to you by dropping the file onto the Web page.

This event is new in JavaScript 1.2, so it will not work with versions of Netscape Navigator 3 or earlier or with Internet Explorer 3 or earlier.

The onDragDrop event handler works for the window object.

onFocus

The focus on a page is selected when the visitor either tabs or clicks a field or an object on the page. Selecting within a field does not create a focus event; rather, it generates a select event.

Example:

```
onFocus="msgWindow.document.write('tell me what you want!')"
```

When the visitor clicks in the field object, the script writes out the phrase "tell me what you want!"

The onFocus event handler works for the select, text, and textarea objects.

onKeyDown

A key down occurs as the visitor presses a keyboard key. This event precedes the keyPress event.

Example:

```
onKeyDown="msgWindow.document.write('tell me what you want!')"
```

When the visitor presses the key, the script writes out the phrase "tell me what you want!"

This event is new in JavaScript 1.2, so it will not work with versions of Netscape Navigator 3 or earlier or with Internet Explorer 3 or earlier.

The onKeyDown event handler works for the document, image, link, and textarea objects.

onKeyPress

A key press occurs when the visitor presses or holds a keyboard key. You can use this in combination with `fromCharCode` and `charCodeAt` methods to determine which key was pressed. This is useful when you prompt the visitor to type **y** for yes and any other key for no.

Example:

```
onKeyPress="msgWindow.document.write('tell me what you want!')"
```

When the visitor presses the key, the script writes out the phrase "tell me what you want!"

The `onKeyPress` event handler works for the `document`, `image`, `link`, and `textarea` objects.

This event is new in JavaScript 1.2, so it will not work with versions of Netscape Navigator 3 or earlier or with Internet Explorer 3 or earlier.

onKeyUp

A key up occurs when the visitor releases the keyboard key. You can use this to clear the results of the `onKeyPress` or `onKeyDown` event handlers.

Example:

```
onKeyUp="msgWindow.document.write('tell me what you want!')"
```

When the visitor releases the key, the script writes out the phrase "tell me what you want!"

The `onKeyUp` event handler works for the `document`, `image`, `link`, and `textarea` objects.

This event is new in JavaScript 1.2, so it will not work with versions of Netscape Navigator 3 or earlier or with Internet Explorer 3 or earlier.

onLoad

A load event occurs when the browser receives all the page information, including framesets, and displays it. Locate the `onLoad` event handler inside the `<BODY>` or `<FRAMESET>` tags.

Example:

```
<BODY onLoad="window.alert("Current as of " + document.lastModified
+ "!")">
```

This example opens an alert window after the page is loaded and displays a message that includes the `lastModified` property. This gives the visitor the document's modification date.

The `onLoad` event handler works for the `window` object.

onMouseDown

A mouse button down occurs when the visitor presses one of the mouse buttons. You can use the event properties to determine which button was pressed.

Example:

```
onMouseDown="msgWindow.document.write('tell me what you want!')"
```

When the visitor moves the mouse button down, the script writes out the phrase "tell me what you want!"

The onMouseDown event handler works for the button, document, and link objects.

This event is new in JavaScript 1.2, so will not work with versions of Netscape Navigator 3 or earlier or with Internet Explorer 3 or earlier.

onMouseMove

A mouse movement occurs when the visitor moves the mouse over any point on the page. This is not an event handler that works for any particular object, but can be evoked if an object requests the event.

Example:

```
onMouseMove="msgWindow.document.write('tell me what you want!')"
```

When the visitor moves the mouse, the script writes out the phrase, "tell me what you want!"

This event is new in JavaScript 1.2, so it will not work with versions of Netscape Navigator 3 or earlier or with Internet Explorer 3 or earlier.

onMouseOut

An onMouseOut event occurs when the visitor moves the mouse point off an object on the page. This event handler defines what should happen when the visitor removes the mouse from an object such as a link.

Example:

```
<a href="myFamily.html" onMouseOut="alert('Hey, we've got great pics
down this way, come back!')">Meet my Family</a>
```

When the visitor's mouse passes off the link (Meet my Family), an alert box appears with this message:

```
Hey, we've got great pics down this way, come back!
```

This event is new in JavaScript 1.2, so it will not work with versions of Netscape Navigator 3 or earlier or with Internet Explorer 3 or earlier.

The onMouseOut event handler works for the area, layer, and link objects.

onMouseOver

An onMouseOver event occurs when the visitor passes the mouse pointer over an object on the page. You must return True within the event handler if you want to set the status or defaultStatus properties.

Example:

```
onMouseOver="window.status="Come on in!"; return true"
```

The onMouseOver event handler works for the area, layer, and link objects.

onMouseUp

A mouse button up event occurs when the visitor releases the mouse button.

```
<a href="myFamily.html" onMouseUp="alert('Hey, we've got great pics
down this way, come back!')">Meet my Family</a>
```

When the visitor's mouse button moves back up while over the link (Meet my Family), an alert box appears with this message:

```
Hey, we've got great pics down this way, come back!
```

This event is new in JavaScript 1.2, so will not work with versions of Netscape Navigator 3 or earlier or with Internet Explorer 3 or earlier.

The onMouseUp event handler works for the button, document, and link objects.

onMove

A move occurs when a visitor or a browser-driven script moves a window or a frame.

```
onMove="window.status='Come on in!' "
```

When the window moves, the message "Come on in!" appears in the status line.

This event is new in JavaScript 1.2, so it will not work with versions of Netscape Navigator 3 or earlier or with Internet Explorer 3 or earlier.

The onMove event handler works for the window and frame objects.

OnReset

Use the onReset event handler to act when the form is reset.

Example:

```
<BODY>
<form onReset="alert('Please try again!) … >
<INPUT TYPE="text" NAME="newInTown" VALUE="" SIZE=100 MAXLENGTH=25>
<INPUT TYPE="Reset" NAME="Reset" VALUE="Reset">
</form>
```

This example prints a "Please try again!" alert box when the visitor resets the form.

The onReset event handler works for the form object.

onResize

A resize occurs when a visitor or a browser-driven script changes the size of the window or frame.

```
onMove="window.status='Stop that!'"
```

When the window is resized, the message "Stop that!" appears in the status line.

This event is new in JavaScript 1.2, so will not work with versions of Netscape Navigator 3 or earlier or with Internet Explorer 3 or earlier.

The onResize event handler works for the window and frame objects.

onSelect

A select event occurs when the visitor highlights text inside a text or textarea field.

Example:

```
onSelect="document.bgColor=blue"
```

The background color of the document changes to blue when the visitor selects text from the field.

The onSelect event handler works for the text and textarea objects.

onSubmit

When the document is one or more forms, use the onSubmit event handler to validate the contents of the form.

Example:

```
<SCRIPT>
        function hotelGuys (checksOut) {
                if (checksOut == "false") {
                        alert("Please fill in all fields.")}
                else {
                        document.forms[0].submit();
                        alert("We came here Jasper");}}
</SCRIPT>
…

<BODY>
<form onSubmit="hotelGuys(checksOut='true')">
<INPUT TYPE="text" NAME="newInTown" VALUE="" SIZE=100 MAXLENGTH=25>
<INPUT TYPE="submit" NAME="register" VALUE="">
</form>
```

This example uses an `if else` statement either to request more information from the visitor or to submit the form. Normally, you wouldn't set the state in the call. You would call another function that would test the entries, and that function would then call `hotelGuys`.

The `onSubmit` event handler works for the `form` object.

onUnload

The `unload` event occurs when the browser leaves a page. One good use for the `onUnload` event handler is to clear any function variables you may have set into motion with the `onLoad` or other event handlers.

Example:

```
<BODY onLoad="CountOn(4)" onUnload="ClearCount()">
```

A counter starts when the page begins loading. You can use this to display a splash-screen for a limited time. When the visitor leaves the page, the counter is reset to zero by the `ClearCount` function.

The `onUnload` event handler works for the `window` object.

Properties

Properties affect objects; unlike methods and functions, which do something within an object, properties assign attributes, such as appearance or size.

This section is an alphabetic listing of the JavaScript properties. Each entry describes a single property, includes syntax information and examples, and identifies which object the property affects.

action

The `action` property is part of the `form` object and contains the URL to which the `<FORM>` is submitted. You can set this property at any time. It has the following syntax:

```
formName.action=formActionText
```

The `formName` entry is either the form or an element from the forms array.

Example:

```
document.lesson3.action=http://www.raycomm.con/lesson3results.htm
```

This example loads the URL `http://www.raycomm.com/lesson3results.htm` into the `action` property for the form `lesson3`.

alinkColor

The `alinkColor` property is part of the `document` object and sets the color for an active link. Once the layout of the HTML code is complete, this becomes a read-only property of the **document** object, so you cannot change the **alinkColor** property. The color is expressed in hexadecimal (three sets of double hex digits) or as one of the color keywords. Place the code that sets this property before any <BODY> tags, and do not use the <BODY ALINK="..."> attribute. The **alinkColor** property has the following syntax:

```
document.alinkColor="colorLiteral"
document.alinkColor="colorRGB"
```

Example:

```
document.alinkColor="green"
document.alinkColor="008000"
```

The two statements are equivalent. The first statement sets the **alinkColor** using the keyword **green**, which is 008000 in hex.

anchors

The **anchors** property is part of the **anchor** object and is the array of objects listing the named anchors in the source. The array lists the anchors in the order in which they appear in the document. The **anchors** property has the following syntax:

```
document.anchors[index]
document.anchors.length
```

The **index** entry is an integer that represents the anchor's position in the list; **length** returns the number of items in the array.

Example:

```
var visitor=document.anchors.length
document.write("there are " + visitor + " links to other pages... can
you visit them all?")
```

The script stores the number of anchors in the variable *visitor* and uses that in a statement written out for the visitor.

appCodeName

The **appCodeName** property is a read-only part of the **navigator** object. It has the following syntax:

```
navigator.appCodeName
```

Example:

```
var whoAreYou=navigator.appCodeName
if (whoAreYou !="Mozilla") {
        document.write("Good job, carry on!")
```

This example gets the code name of the browser and, if it's not Mozilla, writes a note to the visitor.

appName

The appName property is a read-only part of the navigator object. It has the following syntax:

```
navigator.appName
```

Example:

```
var whoAreYou=navigator.appName

document.write("Hey! Good thing you're using " + whoAreYou + "!")
```

This example puts the application name into the variable *whoAreYou* and includes it in a statement displayed for the visitor.

appVersion

The appVersion property is a read-only part of the navigator object. It has the following syntax:

```
navigator.appVersion
```

The version is in the following format:

```
releaseNumber (platform; country)
```

Example:

```
document.write("You're checking us out with " +
navigator.appVersion)
```

This statement displays a result similar to this:

```
You're checking us out with 2.0 (Win95, I)
```

bgColor

The bgColor property is part of the document object and reflects the BGCOLOR= attribute of the <BODY> tag, but can be changed at any time. The default for bgColor is in the visitor's browser preferences. The bgColor property has the following syntax:

```
document.bgColor="colorLiteral"
document.bgColor="colorRGB"
```

Example:

```
document.bgColor="darkblue"
document.bgColor="00008B"
```

These statements are equivalent. Both set the background color to dark blue; one through the keyword, and the other through the hex value for the color.

checked

The `checked` property is a Boolean value representing the state of a `radio` or `checkbox` object. True or 1 is checked; false or 0 is cleared. The `checked` property has the following syntax:

```
checkboxName.checked
radioName[index].checked
```

The `checkboxName` entry is the NAME= attribute of a `checkbox` object. The `radioName` entry is the NAME= attribute of a `radio` object. The `index` entry represents the radio button with the `radio` object.

Example:

```
<INPUT TYPE="radio" NAME="=courseOption1" VALUE="courseOption"
onClick="techComm.checked='1'" >
```

This example sets the checkbox for the `techComm` value of `courseOption1` to checked when the visitor selects the `courseOption1` radio button.

cookie

A cookie is information stored by the browser. The `cookie` property is part of a document object that you can read using the `substring`, `charAt`, `indexOf`, and `lastIndexOf` methods. You can also write information to a cookie. The `cookie` property has the following syntax:

```
document.cookie
```

Example:

```
document.cookie="expires in " + counter + " days"
```

This example assigns the string that reads "`expires in n days`"; *n* is the number of days remaining and is set with `counter`.

defaultChecked

The `defaultChecked` property is part of the `checkbox` and `radio` objects. It indicates the default state (checked or not checked) of a checkbox or a radio button. You can read or set the property at any time. The `defaultChecked` property has the following syntax:

```
checkboxName.defaultChecked
radioName.[index].defaultChecked
```

Example:

```
document.chartForm.dataFocus[i].defaultChecked=true
```

The statement sets the radio button at position `i` in the array to the default for the `dataFocus` group of buttons.

defaultSelected

This property is similar to the `defaultChecked` property; it indicates whether the option in a `select` object is the default selection. Only `MULTIPLE` `select` objects can have more than a single item selected. The `defaultSelected` property is part of the `options` array and has the following syntax:

```
selectName.options[index].defaultSelected
```

The `selectName` entry refers to the `select` object either by the `NAME=` attribute or as an element within an array. The `index` entry is an integer representing an option in a `select` object.

Example:

```
<SCRIPT>

    function backAgain () {

            alert(document.javajive.lessonList.length);

            for (var a = 0; a < document.javajive.lessonList.length;
            ➥ a++) {

    if (document.javajive.lessonList.options[a].defaultSelected ==
    ➥ true) {

            document.javajive.lessonList.options[a].selected=true }
            }

    }

</SCRIPT>

</HEAD>

<BODY>

<FORM NAME="javajive" onSubmit="backAgain ()">

<SELECT NAME="lessonList">

    <OPTION SELECTED> Introduction

    <OPTION>Installation

    <OPTION>Setting up an account

    <OPTION>Creating a document

    <OPTION>Filing a document

    <OPTION>Recovering a filed document

    <OPTION>Sending a document to the printer

</SELECT>

<INPUT TYPE="submit" NAME="getchathere" VALUE="Submit">

</form>
```

In this example, the form contains a list of chapters in a book, from which the visitor can select a single item. The `backAgain` function cycles through the list of options to find which one(s) should be selected by default and resets the default.

defaultStatus

This property is part of the `window` object and contains the default message displayed in the status bar. You can set the `defaultStatus` property at any time. If you plan to use the status bar for an `onMouseOver` event handler statement, you must return True. The `defaultStatus` property has the following syntax:

```
windowReference.defaultStatus
```

The `windowReference` entry is one of the available window identifiers (such as `self`).

Example:

```
window.defaultStatus = "Finish the modules in less than a week!"
```

The default contents for the status bar display are set to a phrase that complements the purpose of the site.

defaultValue

This property is part of the `hidden`, `password`, `text`, and `textarea` objects. It contains the default information for a `password`, `text`, or `textarea` object. If the object is a `password`, the initial value is null, regardless of the `defaultValue`. For a `text` object, the `defaultValue` reflects the VALUE= attribute. For `textarea` objects, it is the contents of the object found between the <TEXTAREA> tags. If you set `default-Value` through a script, it overrides the initial value. The immediate display value of the object is not changed when you change the `defaultValue` through your script; if you later run a function that resets the defaults, your change appears.

The `defaultValue` property has the following syntax:

```
passwordName.defaultValue
```

```
textName.defaultValue
```

```
textareaName.defaultValue
```

Example:

```
document.javajive.lessonLeader.defaultValue="ee cummings"
```

```
...
```

```
<INPUT TYPE="reset" NAME="resetScoreCard" VALUE="Reset the Scores" >
```

A line in your script changes the default value of the `lessonLeader` text object, and later in the script, the default values are reset. When this second line is executed, the contents of the `lessonLeader` text object is updated with `ee cummings`.

E

This read-only math property is approximately 2.718, which is Euler's constant, the base of natural logarithms. It is part of the math object and has the following syntax:

```
Math.E
```

Example:

```
document.write("The base of natural logarithms is Euler's contant
which is: " + Math.E)
```

This statement displays the phrase followed by the value stored in the E property.

elements

The elements property is an array of the items in a form such as checkbox, radio, and text objects. These items are listed in the array, in the order in which they occur.

encoding

The encoding property is part of the form object and contains the MIME-encoding format information for the form. You can set the encoding property at any time; the initial value is the ENCTYPE= attribute of the <FORM> tag. The various encoding types may require specific values; check the specifications for the encoding type. The encoding property has the following syntax:

```
formName.encoding
```

Example:

```
function formEncode() (
        return document.javajive.encoding }
```

The formEncode function gets the MIME-encoding information from the form.

fgColor

This property is part of the document object and specifies the foreground color of the text. You can express the color using one of the color keywords or the hexadecimal RGB value. This property uses the browser preference settings as its initial value. You can change this value either by setting the COLOR= attribute of the <FONT> tag or by using the fontcolor method. The fgColor property has the following syntax:

```
document.fgColor
```

Example:

```
document.fgColor="darkred"
```
```
document.fgColor="8B0000"
```

These two statements are equivalent. The first uses the color keyword, and the second uses the hexadecimal RGB value for the same color.

forms

The `forms` property is an array that lists the objects in a form, in the order in which they occur in the code.

frames

The `frames` property is an array that lists the child frames within a frame.

hash

The `hash` property is part of the URL, and it identifies an anchor on the destination page. It is part of the `link` and `location` objects and has the following syntax:

```
location.hash
```

(See the examples for the `anchor` object and the `href` property.)

host

The `host` property is part of the URL, and it identifies the `hostname:port` for the page. This property is a concatenation of the `hostname` and `port` properties. You can set the `host` property; it is better to set the `href` property, however, if you want to change a location. The `host` property is part of the `link` and `location` objects and has the following syntax:

```
links[index].host
location.host
```

(See the examples for the `link` and `location` objects.)

hostname

The `hostname` property is part of the URL and identifies the host server by its DNS or IP address. If the `port` property is null, the `hostname` and `host` properties are the same. The `hostname` property is part of the `link` and `location` objects and has the following syntax:

```
links[index].hostname
location.hostname
```

(See the examples for the `link` and `location` objects.)

href

The `href` property is part of the `link` and `location` objects and contains the full URL. The `protocol`, `host`, `port`, `pathname`, `search`, and `hash` properties are substrings within the `href` property, which has the following syntax:

```
links[index].href
location.href
```

Example:

```
<script>
var question1="false"
var question2="false"
var question3="false"

function roundTheClock() {
     for (var x=0; x<6; x++) {
     switch(x){
          case(1): if (question1 != "true") {
               win1= new window.open (answer1.location.href) }
               break;
          case(2): if (question2 != "true") {
               win2= new window.open (answer2.location.href) }
               break;
          case(3): if (question3 != "true") {
               win3=new window.open (answer3.location.href) }
               break;
} } }


     </script>
```

In this example, the loop opens a series of windows with the answers to questions that the visitor anwered incorrectly.

index

The index property is part of the options array. It is an integer value that gives the position of an object within the options array of a select object. The index property has the following syntax:

```
selectName.options[indexValue].index
```

The selectName entry is the name of the select object or element in the elements array. The indexValue entry is an integer representing the option in a select object.

Example:

```
for (var x=0; x < document.jivejingle.courseSelect.length; x++) {
```

```
        document.write
(document.jivejingle.courseSelect.options[x].index) }
```

This example displays the contents of the list of `courseSelect`.

lastModified

The `lastModified` property is part of the `document` object. It is a read-only date string indicating when the document was last changed or updated and has the following syntax:

```
document.lastModified
```

Example:

```
<SCRIPT>
        document.write ("Welcome, this course description is current
as of " + document.lastModified)
</SCRIPT>
```

This script keeps the date current without manual intervention.

length

The `length` property works with objects and arrays; you can use it to get the number of elements within the object or array. It has the following syntax:

`formName.length`

> Returns the number of elements on a form.

`frameReference.length`

> Returns the number of frames within a frame.

`history.length`

> Returns the number of entries in the `history` object.

`radioName.length`

> Returns the number of buttons within a `radio` object.

`select.Name.length`

> Returns the number of objects in a `select` list object.

`stringName.length`

> Returns the number of character spaces in a `string`.

`windowReference.length`

> Returns the number of frames in a parent window.

```
anchors.length
elements.length
forms.length
frameReference.frames.length
windowReference.frames.length
links.length
selectName.options.length
```

Returns the number of entries in the array.

Example:

```
var visitor=document.anchors.length
document.write("there are " + visitor + " links to other pages… can
you visit them all?")
```

In this example, the script stores the number of anchors in the variable *visitor* and uses that in a statement displayed to the visitor.

The length property is found in the following objects:

frame	select
history	string
radio	window

And within the following arrays:

anchors	frames
elements	links
forms	options

linkColor

The `linkColor` property is part of the **document** object. It contains the setting for the inactive and unused links in a document. This property reflects the setting in the <BODY> tag of a document. After the layout, this is a read-only property. To set this property in a script, place the code before any <BODY> tags, and do not use the <BODY> LINK="…"> attribute. The `linkColor` property has the following syntax:

```
document.linkColor
```

Example:

```
document.write ("The " + document.linkColor + " jumps are places
you've never been!")
```

This statement displays the link color for the visitor.

links

The links property is an array of document links listed in source order.

LN2

The LN2 property is part of the built-in math object. It is a read-only constant that represents the natural logarithm of two (approximately 0.693) and has the following syntax:

```
Math.LN2
```

Example:

```
document.write ("Bob says your chances of winning are: " + longShot
+ " in " + longShot/Math.LN2)
```

This example computes a value and displays the results in a statement for the visitor.

LN10

The LN10 property is part of the built-in math object. It is a read-only constant that represents the natural logarithm of 10 (approximately 2.302) and has the following syntax:

```
Math.LN10
```

Example:

```
document.write ("Bob says your chances of winning are: " + longShot
+ " in " + longShot*Math.LN10)
```

This example computes a value and displays the results in a statement for the visitor.

location

The location property is part of the document object. It contains the complete URL of the document. Unlike the location object, you cannot change the document's location property. The location property has the following syntax:

```
document.location
```

Example:

```
<SCRIPT>
        var there="http://www.raycomm.com/"
        var takeLesson=""
        function weAre() {
                self.status='Welcome, this is ' + document.location + '
                our site is NEVER done!'}
        function checkThis(){
                alert("Thanks for registering")}
</SCRIPT>
```

```
</HEAD>
<BODY onLoad="window.alert('Welcome!'); weAre()">
```

This displays a notice to the visitor, including the document's location, in in the status line of the window.

LOG2E

The LOG2E property is part of the built-in math object. It is a read-only constant that represents the base-2 logarithm of E (approximately 1.442). It has the following syntax:

```
Math.LOG2E
```

Example:

```
document.write ("Bob says your chances of winning are: " + longShot
+ " in " + longShot*Math.LOG2E)
```

This example computes a value and displays the results in a statement for the visitor.

LOG10E

The LOG10E property is part of the built-in math object. It is a read-only constant that represents the base-10 logarithm of E (approximately 0.434). It has the following syntax:

```
Math.LOG10E
```

Example:

```
document.write ("Bob says your chances of winning are: " + longShot
+ " in " + longShot/Math.LOG2E)
```

This example computes a value and displays the results in a statement for the visitor.

method

The method property is part of the form object. It indicates how a form is sent to the server when it is submitted. This reflects the contents of the METHOD= attribute of the <FORM> tag. This property contains either GET or POST. You can set this property at any time. The method property has the following syntax:

```
formName.method
```

Example:

```
if (document.javajive.method == "GET") {
     document.write("The server will get your answers now.")
else { document.write("Your answers will be posted to the server
now.") } }
```

This example displays different text depending on the method.

name

This property is used to identify the objects and elements contained by a number of objects and arrays. For window objects, this is a read-only property; you can set the name of other objects.

In a window object, the name reflects the windowName attribute. In other objects, it reflects the NAME= attribute. The name property is the same for all radio buttons in a radio object.

The name property differs from the label used for the button, reset, and submit objects. The name property is not displayed; it is an internal, programmatic reference.

If a frame object contains several elements or objects with the same name, the browser creates an array using the name and listing the objects as they occur in the frame source.

The name property has the following syntax for window objects:

```
windowReference.name
window.Reference.frames.name
```

The name property has the following syntax for other objects:

```
objectName.name
frameReference.name
frameReference.frames.name
radioName[index].name
selectName.options.name
```

For a select object, objectName.name and selectName.options.name produce the same result.

For a frame object, objectName.name, frameReference.name, and frameReference.frames.name produce the same result.

Example:

```
newWindow=window.open("http://www.webwonders.net/testone.htm")
function whatYouBuilt () {
        for (var counter=0, counter<document.elements.length,
    ➡ counter++) {
                msgWindow.document.write(document.sample
                ➡.elements[counter].name + "<BR>") } }
```

In this example, the function loops through the loaded document and displays a list of the elements.

The name property is found in the following objects and arrays:

button	hidden	reset	text	options array
checkbox	password	select	textarea	
frame	radio	submit	window	

options

The options property is an array that contains a list of the options in a select object.

parent

The parent property is one of the synonyms available for referencing a window that contains the current frame. This is a read-only property for the window and frame objects. You can use this property when referencing one frame from another within a window or parent frame. It has the following syntax:

```
parent.propertyName
parent.methodName
top.frameName
top.frames[index]
```

The propertyName entry is the defaultStatus, status, length, name, or parent property. This could also be the length, name, or parent property when the reference is from a parent to a frame. The methodName entry is any method associated with the window object. (See the window object entry for more information about the available methods.) The frameName and frames[index] entries reference individual frames by either their NAME value or their position in an array of frames.

Example:

```
<INPUT TYPE="button" NAME="doItButton" VALUE="Make it so!"
      onClick="parent.frames[2].document.bgColor=colorChoice">
```

This example is part of the frame object example. In this statement, the background color of the sibling (index value2) of the current frame is set to the user's color choice.

pathname

The pathname property is part of the link and location objects. It is the part of the URL that indicates the directory location for the page on the server. You can set the pathname at any time, but if you need to change the document pathname, it is safer to use the href property. The pathname property has the following syntax:

```
location.pathname
```

(See the examples for the location object.)

PI

The PI property is part of the built-in `math` object. It is a read-only constant that represents the ratio of circle circumference to diameter (approximately 3.14159). The PI property has the following syntax:

```
Math.PI
```

Example:

```
document.write ("Bob says your chances of winning are: " + longShot
+ " in " + longShot*Math.PI)
```

This example computes a value and displays the results in a statement for the visitor.

port

The `port` property is part of the `link` and `location` objects. It is the `port` element in the URL and identifies the port, if any, used on the server. If this property is null, the `host` and `hostname` properties are the same. The `port` property has the following syntax:

```
location.port
```

(See the example for the `location` object.)

protocol

The `protocol` property is part of the `link` and `location` objects. It is part of the URL and uses the following protocols:

        `file`: accesses a local file system

        `ftp`: uses the FTP protocol (File Transfer Protocol)

        `gopher`: uses the Gopher protocol

        `http`: uses the HTTP protocol (HyperText Transfer Protocol)

        `mailto`: uses the SMTP protocol (Standard Mail Transfer Protocol)

        `news`: uses the NNTP protocol (Network News Transfer Protocol)

        `snews`: uses the secure NNTP protocol

        `https`: uses the secure HTTP protocol

        `telnet`: uses the Telnet protocol

        `tn3270`: uses the 3270 Telenet protocol

The `port` property has the following syntax:

```
location.protocol
```

(See the examples for the `link` and `location` objects.)

referrer

The `referrer` property is part of the `document` object. It is a read-only property of the `document` object that contains the originating document URL when a visitor jumps from an originating document to a destination document. The `referrer` property has the following syntax:

```
document.referrer
```

Example:

```
document.write("welcome, I see you joined us from " +
document.referrer + ". How's the weather back there?")
```

This statement displays a message for the visitor that includes the location URL of the original document.

search

The `search` property is found in the `link` and `location` objects. It is part of the URL; although you can change this property at any time, it is best to use the `href` property to change `location` attributes. The `search` property has the following syntax:

```
location.search
```

Example:

```
newWindow=window.open

        ("http://www.raycomm.com/Look/scripts?qt=property=elements")

with (document) {

        write("the href property is " + newWindow.location.href +
        ➡."<P>")

        write("the protocol property is " + newWindow.location
        ➡.protocol + "<P>")

        write("the host property is " + newWindow.location.host +
        ➡."<P>")

        write("the host name is " + newWindow.location.hostName +
        ➡."<P>")

        write("the port property is " + newWindow.location.port +
        ➡."<P>")

        write("the pathname property is" + newWindow.location.pathname
        ➡. + "<P>")

        write("the search property is " + newWindow.location.search +
        ➡. "<P>")

        write("the hash property is " + newWindow.location.hash +
        ➡."<P>")

        close() }
```

Which displays the following:

```
the href property is http://www.raycomm.com/Look/scripts?qt=
property=elements
the protocol property is http:
the host property is www.raycomm.com
the host name is www.raycomm.com
the port property is
the pathname property is /Look/scripts
the search property is ?qt=property=elements
the hash property is
```

selected

The `selected` property is part of the `options` array. It contains a Boolean value that indicates whether the `option` in a `select` object is currently selected. For selected options, this property is True. You can set this property programmatically. It has the following syntax:

```
selectName.options[index].selected
```

Example:

```
for (x=document.saleForm.buyTheseThings.length, x > 0, x-) {
    if (document.saleForm.buyTheseThings.options[x].selected =
    ➡."true") {
            document.saleForm.buyTheseThings.options[x].selected =
            ➡. "false"
    else {
            document.saleForm.buyTheseThings.options[x].selected =
            ➡."true" }

    } }
```

In this example, the `for` loop traverses the list of options altering the selections. The result is an inversion of the visitor's selections.

selectedIndex

The `selectedIndex` property is part of the `select` object and the `options` array. It contains information about the order in which a `select` object was defined. You can set the `selectedIndex` property at any time, and the displayed information is updated. The `selectedIndex` property works well with `select` objects that are not MULTIPLE select objects. It has the following syntax:

```
selectName.selectedIndex
selectName.options.selectedIndex
```

Example:

```
function (whatSelection) () {
        return document.saleForm.giveAwayOptions.selectedIndex }
```

This simple function brings back the selection from the list of options.

self

The self property is part of the window object. This property is a synonym for the current window or frame object. Use this read-only property to help keep your code clear. It has the following syntax:

```
self.propertyName
self.methodName
```

Example:

```
self.javatest.whichIsFunction.index[x]
document.javatest.whichIsFunction.index[x]
```

These two statements are equivalent.

SQRT1_2

The SQRT1_2 property is part of the built-in math object. It is a read-only constant that represents the square root of $1/2$ (approximately 0.707). It has the following syntax:

```
Math.SQRT1_2
```

Example:

```
document.write ("Bob says your chances of winning are: " + longShot
+ " in " + longShot/Math.SQRT1_2)
```

This example computes a value and displays the results in a statement for the visitor.

SQRT2

The SQRT2 property is part of the built-in math object. It is a read-only constant that represents the square root of 2 (approximately 1.414). It has the following syntax:

```
Math.SQRT2
```

Example:

```
document.write ("Bob says your chances of winning are: " + longShot
+ " in " + longShot*Math.SQRT2)
```

This example computes a value and displays the results in a statement for the visitor.

status

The `status` property is part of the `window` object. It contains a priority or transient message that is displayed in the status bar of the window. It has the following syntax:

```
windowReference.status
```

Example:

```
self.status="Welcome to our little home away from home!"
```

This example puts the message onto the window's status line.

target

The `target` property is part of the `form`, `link`, and `location` objects. It works for the `link` and `location` and the `form` objects slightly differently. For the `link` and `location` objects, the `target` property contains the window name for a jump. For the `form` object, it contains the destination for form submissions. Although you can set the `target` property at any time, it cannot assume the value of an expression or a variable (meaning you can't build those fancy statements such as `document.write`). The `target` property has the following syntax:

```
formName.target
linkName.target
```

Example:

```
self.status("When you submit your request, the information will
appear in " + self.buyTheseThings.target + ".")
```

This statement displays a message in the window status bar telling visitors where their selections will appear. This is useful if you want to confirm the request before displaying the information.

text

The `text` property is part of the `options` array. It is the displayed value in an options list. If you change the `text` property for an option list, the display character, initially set in the `<OPTION>` tag, does not change, but the internal information does change. The `text` property has the following syntax:

```
selectName.options[index].text
```

Example:

```
for (x=0, x < self.javajive.pickMe.length, x++) {
        if (self.javajive.pickMe.option[x].select == true) {
                document.write(self.javajive.pickMe.option[x].text) }

        }
```

This example tests to see if the option has been selected; if it has, it displays the option text. If you change the `text` property programmatically, the resulting list is different from the list of options the visitor sees and selects from.

title

The `title` property is part of the `document` object. It reflects the value between the `<TITLE>`, and you cannot change this value. The `title` property has the following syntax:

```
document.title
```

Example:

```
self.status(self.title)
```

top

The `top` property is part of the `window` object. It is a read-only synonym for the topmost window and has the following syntax:

```
top.propertyName
top.methodName
top.frameName
top.frames[index]
```

The `propertyName` entry is `defaultStatus`, `status`, or `length`. The `methodName` entry is any `window` method. The `frameName` and `frames[index]` entries are frame references for frames within the window.

Example:

```
top.close()
```

This closes the topmost window.

```
for (x=0, x<top.length, x++) {
        top.frame[x].close() }
```

This closes the frames on a page.

userAgent

The `userAgent` property is part of the `navigator` object. It is part of the HTTP protocol information. Servers use this property to identify the client browser. The `userAgent` property has the following syntax:

```
navigator.userAgent
```

Example:

```
document.write("You're using " + navigator.userAgent)
```

This displays the browser information, as in:

```
You're using Mozilla/2.0 (win16; I)
```

value

The `value` property differs for the various objects. In all cases, it reflects the VALUE= attribute of the object.

For `hidden`, `password`, `text`, and `textarea` objects or for an item in the options array, you can programmatically change the property. If you change it for the `text` and `textarea` objects, the display updates immediately. If you change it for the `password` object, security could give you some pause. If you evaluate your changes, you'll get the current value back; if a visitor changes it, security will not pass the changes. For the options array, the VALUE= attribute is not displayed, but is an internal representation.

For the `button`, `reset`, and `submit` objects, the `value` property is a read-only reflection of the text on the face of the button.

For `checkbox` and `radio` objects, the `value` property is returned to the server when the checkbox or radio button is selected. It is not the value of the selection; it is simply On or Off.

The `value` property has the following syntax:

```
objectName.value
radioName[index].value
selectName.options.[index].value
```

(For examples of the `value` property, see the appropriate object entry.)

The `value` property is part of the following objects and arrays:

button	password	submit	options (array)
checkbox	radio	text	
hidden	reset	textarea	

vLinkColor

The `vLinkColor` is a part of the `document` object. It contains the color settings for the links on the page that have been visited. To set this value programmatically, place your script ahead of the `<BODY>` tag; once the layout has been done, this becomes a read-only property. If you do set the property in a script, do not use the `<BODY VLINK="..."` attribute. To set the color, use either the color keyword or a hexadecimal RGB number (three double digits). The `vLinkColor` has the following syntax:

```
document.vLinkColor="colorLiteral"
document.vLinkColor="colorRGB"
```

Example:

```
document.write("To determine where you've been,

check the color of your inks!

<BR>If the link is " + document.linkColor + ", you haven't gone
there.

<BR>Could be a whole new world waiting for you!<BR>If the link is "

 + document.vLinkColor +

", you've followed that lead… where did it take you?")
```

In a document that contains linkColor=blue and document.vLinkColor=red, the result of this write statement is:

```
To determine where you've been, check the color of your links!

If the link is blue, you haven't gone there.

Could be a whole new world waiting for you!

If the link is red, you've followed that lead… Where did it take
you?
```

window

The window property is part of the frame and window objects. It is a synonym for the current window. Although you can use the window property to refer to the current frame, it is better to use the self property in that situation. This property is read-only and has the following syntax:

```
window.propertyName
```
```
window.methodName(parameters)
```

Example:

```
window.status="Welcome to our humble home away from home!"
```

This example displays the message in the status bar.

HTML Special Characters

Standard HTML Characters

The characters in Table A.17 were included in HTML 2 and HTML 3.2 and are also included in the current HTML 4 specification. Most browsers should display these characters, based on the mnemonic or numeric representation.

TABLE A.17: Standard HTML Characters

Symbol	Mnemonic Representation	Numeric Representation	Description
			Nonbreaking space
¡	&iexcl;	&#161;	Inverted exclamation mark
¢	&cent;	&#162;	Cent
£	&pound;	&#163;	Pound sterling
¤	&curren;	&#164;	General currency
¥	&yen;	&#165;	Yen
¦	&brvbar;	&#166;	Broken (vertical) bar
§	&sect;	&#167;	Section
¨	&uml;	&#168;	Umlaut (diaeresis)
©	&copy;	&#169;	Copyright sign
ª	&ordf;	&#170;	Ordinal indicator, feminine
«	&laquo;	&#171;	Angle quotation mark, left
¬	&not;	&#172;	Not
	&shy;	&#173;	Soft hyphen
®	&reg;	&#174;	Registered
¯	&macr;	&#175;	Macron
°	&deg;	&#176;	Degree
±	&plusmn;	&#177;	Plus-or-minus
²	&sup2;	&#178;	Superscript two
³	&sup3;	&#179;	Superscript three
´	&acute;	&#180;	Acute accent

TABLE A.17 continued: Standard HTML Characters

Symbol	Mnemonic Representation	Numeric Representation	Description
µ	&micro;	&#181;	Micro
¶	&para;	&#182;	Pilcrow (paragraph)
·	&middot;	&#183;	Middle dot
¸	&cedil;	&#184;	Cedilla
¹	&sup1;	&#185;	Superscript one
º	&ordm;	&#186;	Ordinal indicator, masculine
»	&raquo;	&#187;	Angle quotation mark, right
¼	&frac14;	&#188;	Fraction one-quarter
½	&frac12;	&#189;	Fraction one-half
¾	&frac34;	&#190;	Fraction three-quarters
¿	&iquest;	&#191;	Inverted question mark
À	&Agrave;	&#192;	Uppercase A, grave accent
Á	&Aacute;	&#193;	Uppercase A, acute accent
Â	&Acirc;	&#194;	Uppercase A, circumflex
Ã	&Atilde;	&#195;	Uppercase A, tilde
Ä	&Auml;	&#196;	Uppercase A, diaeresis or umlaut mark
Å	&Aring;	&#197;	Uppercase A, angstrom
Æ	&AElig;	&#198;	Uppercase AE diphthong (ligature)
Ç	&Ccedil;	&#199;	Uppercase C, cedilla
È	&Egrave;	&#200;	Uppercase E, grave accent
É	&Eacute;	&#201;	Uppercase E, acute accent
Ê	&Ecirc;	&#202;	Uppercase E, circumflex
Ë	&Euml;	&#203;	Uppercase E, umlaut (diaeresis)
Ì	&Igrave;	&#204;	Uppercase I, grave accent
Í	&Iacute;	&#205;	Uppercase I, acute accent
Î	&Icirc;	&#206;	Uppercase I, circumflex
Ï	&Iuml;	&#207;	Uppercase I, umlaut (diaresis)

TABLE A.17 continued: Standard HTML Characters

SYMBOL	MNEMONIC REPRESENTATION	NUMERIC REPRESENTATION	DESCRIPTION
Đ	&ETH;	&#208;	Uppercase Eth, Icelandic
Ñ	&Ntilde;	&#209;	Uppercase N, tilde
Ò	&Ograve;	&#210;	Uppercase O, grave accent
Ó	&Oacute;	&#211;	Uppercase O, acute accent
Ô	&Ocirc;	&#212;	Uppercase O, circumflex
Õ	&Otilde;	&#213;	Uppercase O, tilde
Ö	&Ouml;	&#214;	Uppercase O, umlaut (diaresis)
×	&times;	&#215;	Multiplication
Ø	&Oslash;	&#216;	Uppercase O, slash
Ù	&Ugrave;	&#217;	Uppercase U, grave accent
Ú	&Uacute;	&#218;	Uppercase U, acute accent
Û	&Ucirc;	&#219;	Uppercase U, circumflex
Ü	&Uuml;	&#220;	Uppercase U, umlaut (diaresis)
Ý	&Yacute;	&#221;	Uppercase Y, acute accent
þ	&THORN;	&#222;	Uppercase THORN, Icelandic
ß	&szlig;	&#223;	small sharp s, German
à	&agrave;	&#224;	Lowercase a, grave accent
á	&aacute;	&#225;	Lowercase a, acute accent
â	&acirc;	&#226;	Lowercase a, circumflex
ã	&atilde;	&#227;	Lowercase a, tilde
ä	&auml;	&#228;	Lowercase a, umlaut (diaresis)
å	&aring;	&#229;	Lowercase a, angstrom
æ	&aelig;	&#230;	Lowercase ae diphthong (ligature)
ç	&ccedil;	&#231;	Lowercase c, cedilla
è	&egrave;	&#232;	Lowercase e, grave accent
é	&eacute;	&#233;	Lowercase e, acute accent
ê	&ecirc;	&#234;	Lowercase e, circumflex

TABLE A.17 continued: Standard HTML Characters

Symbol	Mnemonic Representation	Numeric Representation	Description
ë	ë	ë	Lowercase e, umlaut (diaresis)
ì	ì	ì	Lowercase i, grave accent
í	í	í	Lowercase i, acute accent
î	î	î	Lowercase i, circumflex
ï	ï	ï	Lowercase i, umlaut (diaresis)
ð	ð	ð	Lowercase eth, Icelandic
ñ	ñ	ñ	Lowercase n, tilde
ò	ò	ò	Lowercase o, grave accent
ó	ó	ó	Lowercase o, acute accent
ô	ô	ô	Lowercase o, circumflex
õ	õ	õ	Lowercase o, tilde
ö	ö	ö	Lowercase o, umlaut (diaresis)
÷	÷	÷	Division
ø	ø	ø	Lowercase o, slash
ù	ù	ù	Lowercase u, grave accent
ú	ú	ú	Lowercase u, acute accent
û	û	û	Lowercase u, circumflex
ü	ü	ü	Lowercase u, umlaut (diaresis)
ý	ý	ý	Lowercase y, acute accent
þ	þ	þ	Lowrcase thorn, Icelandic
ÿ	ÿ	ÿ	Lowercase y, umlaut (diaresis)

Extended HTML Characters

Most of the extended HTML characters (see Table A.18) are new in HTML 4, and at the time of writing, relatively few browsers supported them. New browser versions are expected to support them.

TABLE A.18: Extended HTML Characters

SYMBOL	MNEMONIC REPRESENTATION	NUMERIC REPRESENTATION	DESCRIPTION
Œ	Œ	Œ	Latin uppercase ligature Œ
œ	œ	œ	Latin lowercase ligature œ
Š	Š	Š	Latin uppercase S with caron
š	š	š	Latin lowercase s with caron
Ÿ	Ÿ	Ÿ	Latin uppercase Y with umlaut
ƒ	ƒ	ƒ	Latin lowercase f with hook
ˆ	ˆ	ˆ	Modifier letter circumflex
~	˜	˜	Small tilde
Α	Α	Α	Greek uppercase alpha
Β	Β	Β	Greek uppercase beta
Γ	Γ	Γ	Greek uppercase gamma
Δ	Δ	Δ	Greek uppercase delta
Ε	Ε	Ε	Greek uppercase epsilon
Z	Ζ	Ζ	Greek uppercase zeta
Η	Η	Η	Greek uppercase eta
Θ	Θ	Θ	Greek uppercase theta
I	Ι	Ι	Greek uppercase iota
Κ	Κ	Κ	Greek uppercase kappa
Λ	Λ	Λ	Greek uppercase lambda
Μ	Μ	Μ	Greek uppercase mu
Ν	Ν	Ν	Greek uppercase nu
Ξ	Ξ	Ξ	Greek uppercase xi
O	Ο	Ο	Greek uppercase omicron
Π	Π	Π	Greek uppercase pi
Ρ	Ρ	Ρ	Greek uppercase rho
Σ	Σ	Σ	Greek uppercase sigma
Τ	Τ	Τ	Greek uppercase tau

TABLE A.18 continued: Extended HTML Characters

Symbol	Mnemonic Representation	Numeric Representation	Description
Υ	&Upsilon;	&#933;	Greek uppercase upsilon
Φ	&Phi;	&#934;	Greek uppercase phi
Χ	&Chi;	&#935;	Greek uppercase chi
Ψ	&Psi;	&#936;	Greek uppercase psi
Ω	&Omega;	&#937;	Greek uppercase omega
α	&alpha;	&#945;	Greek lowercase alpha
β	&beta;	&#946;	Greek lowercase beta
λ	&gamma;	&#947;	Greek lowercase gamma
δ	&delta;	&#948;	Greek lowercase delta
ε	&epsilon;	&#949;	Greek lowercase epsilon
ζ	&zeta;	&#950;	Greek lowercase zeta
η	&eta;	&#951;	Greek lowercase eta
ϑ	&theta;	&#952;	Greek lowercase theta
ι	&iota;	&#953;	Greek lowercase iota
κ	&kappa;	&#954;	Greek lowercase kappa
λ	&lambda;	&#955;	Greek lowercase lambda
μ	&mu;	&#956;	Greek lowercase mu
ν	&nu;	&#957;	Greek lowercase nu
ξ	&xi;	&#958;	Greek lowercase xi
o	&omicron;	&#959;	Greek lowercase omicron
π	&pi;	&#960;	Greek lowercase pi
ρ	&rho;	&#961;	Greek lowercase rho
ς	&sigmaf;	&#962;	Greek lowercase final sigma
σ	&sigma;	&#963;	Greek lowercase sigma
τ	&tau;	&#964;	Greek lowercase tau
φ	&phi;	&#966;	Greek lowercase phi
χ	&chi;	&#967;	Greek lowercase chi
ψ	&psi;	&#968;	Greek lowercase psi
ω	&omega;	&#969;	Greek lowercase omega
θ	&thetasym;	&#977;	Greek lowercase theta symbol
υ	&upsilon;	&#965;	Greek lowercase upsilon
ϒ	&upsih;	&#978;	Greek upsilon with hook symbol

TABLE A.18 continued: Extended HTML Characters

SYMBOL	MNEMONIC REPRESENTATION	NUMERIC REPRESENTATION	DESCRIPTION
π	&piv;	&#982;	Greek pi
			En space
			Em space
			Thin space
–	&ndash;	&#8211;	En dash
—	&mdash;	&#8212;	Em dash
`	&lsquo;	&#8216;	Left single quotation mark
'	&rsquo;	&#8217;	Right single quotation mark
‚	&sbquo;	&#8218;	Single low-9 quotation mark
"	&ldquo;	&#8220;	Left double quotation mark
"	&rdquo;	&#8221;	Right double quotation mark
„	&bdquo;	&#8222;	Double low-9 quotation mark
†	&dagger;	&#8224;	Dagger
‡	&Dagger;	&#8225;	Double dagger
•	&bull;	&#8226;	Bullet (small black circle)
…	&hellip;	&#8230;	Horizontal ellipsis (three-dot leader)
‰	&permil;	&#8240;	Per mille sign
′	&prime;	&#8242;	Prime (minutes or feet)
″	&Prime;	&#8243;	Double prime (seconds or inches)
‹	&lsaquo;	&#8249;	Single left-pointing angle quotation mark
›	&rsaquo;	&#8250;	Single right-pointing angle quotation mark
—	&oline;	&#8254;	Overline (spacing overscore)
/	&frasl;	&#8260;	Fraction slash
ℐ	&image;	&#8465;	Blackletter Uppercase I (imaginary part)
℘	&weierp;	&#8472;	Script Uppercase P (power set or Weierstrass p)
ℜ	&real;	&#8476;	Blackletter Uppercase R (real part symbol)
™	&trade;	&#8482;	Trademark
ℵ	&alefsym;	&#8501;	Alef (first transfinite cardinal)

TABLE A.18 continued: Extended HTML Characters

Symbol	Mnemonic Representation	Numeric Representation	Description
←	&larr;	&#8592;	Left arrow
↑	&uarr;	&#8593;	Up arrow
→	&rarr;	&#8594;	Right arrow
↓	&darr;	&#8595;	Down arrow
↔	&harr;	&#8596;	Left-right arrow
↵	&crarr;	&#8629;	Down arrow with corner Left (carriage return)
⇐	&lArr;	&#8656;	Left double arrow
⇑	&uArr;	&#8657;	Up double arrow
⇒	&rArr;	&#8658;	Right double arrow
⇓	&dArr;	&#8659;	Down double arrow
⇔	&hArr;	&#8660;	Left-right double arrow
∀	&forall;	&#8704;	For all
∂	&part;	&#8706;	Partial differential
∃	&exist;	&#8707;	There exists
∅	&empty;	&#8709;	Empty set (null set or diameter)
∇	&nabla;	&#8711;	Nabla (backward difference)
∈	&isin;	&#8712;	Element of
∉	&notin;	&#8713;	Not an element of
∋	&ni;	&#8715;	Contains as member
∏	&prod;	&#8719;	n-ary product (product sign)
∑	&sum;	&#8721;	N-ary sumation
−	&minus;	&#8722;	Minus
∗	&lowast;	&#8727;	Asterisk operator
√	&radic;	&#8730;	Square root (radical)
∝	&prop;	&#8733;	Proportional to
∞	&infin;	&#8734;	Infinity
∠	&ang;	&#8736;	Angle
∩	&cap;	&#8745;	Intersection (cap)
∪	&cup;	&#8746;	Union (cup)
∫	&int;	&#8747;	Integral
∴	&there4;	&#8756;	Therefore

TABLE A.18 continued: Extended HTML Characters

Symbol	Mnemonic Representation	Numeric Representation	Description
~	&sim;	&#8764;	Tilde operator (varies with or similar to)
≈	&cong;	&#8773;	Approximately equal to
≅	&asymp;	&#8776;	Almost equal to (asymptotic to)
≠	&ne;	&#8800;	Not equal to
	&equiv;	&#8801;	Identical to
≤	&le;	&#8804;	Less than or equal to
≥	&ge;	&#8805;	Greater than or equal to
⊂	&sub;	&#8834;	Subset of
⊃	&sup;	&#8835;	Superset of
⊄	&nsub;	&#8836;	Not a subset of
⊅	&sube;	&#8838;	Subset of or equal to
⊇	&supe;	&#8839;	Superset of or equal to
⊕	&oplus;	&#8853;	Circled plus (direct sum)
⊗	&otimes;	&#8855;	Circled times (vector product)
∧	&and;	&#8869;	Logical and (wedge)
⊥	&perp;	&#8869;	Up tack (orthogonal to or perpendicular)
∨	&or;	&#8870;	Logical or (vee)
·	&sdot;	&#8901;	Dot operator
	&lceil;	&#8968;	Left ceiling (apl upstile)
⌉	&rceil;	&#8969;	Right ceiling
⌊	&lfloor;	&#8970;	Left floor (apl downstile)
⌋	&rfloor;	&#8971;	Right floor
⟨	&lang;	&#9001;	Left-pointing angle bracket
⟩	&rang;	&#9002;	Right-pointing angle bracket
◊	&loz;	&#9674;	Lozenge
♠	&spades;	&#9824;	Spade
♣	&clubs;	&#9827;	Club (shamrock)
♥	&hearts;	&#9829;	Heart (valentine)
♦	&diams;	&#9830;	Diamond

HTML Color Codes

As we mentioned throughout the book, certain colors provide more uniform results than others. These listings present a variety of color codes for use in HTML documents, including the 216 safe colors. See Chapter 5 for more information about selecting colors for HTML documents.

In this section, you'll find the 216 safe colors, 16 basic (standard) color names, Netscape's color names, and finally a chart combining both the safe and the named colors, for ease of reference.

Safe Colors

Below is a list of all 216 "safe" colors that look consistently good in most situations, including backgrounds and broad expanses of color. Color names are not listed because the best colors (depicted here as a list of RRGGBB codes) do not necessarily correspond directly to named colors.

#000000	#0099FF	#3333CC	#33FF99	#669966
#000033	#00CC00	#3333FF	#33FFCC	#669999
#000066	#00CC33	#336600	#33FFFF	#6699CC
#000099	#00CC66	#336633	#660000	#6699FF
#0000CC	#00CC99	#336666	#660033	#66CC00
#0000FF	#00CCCC	#336699	#660066	#66CC33
#003300	#00CCFF	#3366CC	#660099	#66CC66
#003333	#00FF00	#3366FF	#6600CC	#66CC99
#003366	#00FF33	#339900	#6600FF	#66CCCC
#003399	#00FF66	#339933	#663300	#66CCFF
#0033CC	#00FF99	#339966	#663333	#66FF00
#0033FF	#00FFCC	#339999	#663366	#66FF33
#006600	#00FFFF	#3399CC	#663399	#66FF66
#006633	#330000	#3399FF	#6633CC	#66FF99
#006666	#330033	#33CC00	#6633FF	#66FFCC
#006699	#330066	#33CC33	#666600	#66FFFF
#0066CC	#330099	#33CC66	#666633	#990000
#0066FF	#3300CC	#33CC99	#666666	#990033
#009900	#3300FF	#33CCCC	#666699	#990066
#009933	#333300	#33CCFF	#6666CC	#990099
#009966	#333333	#33FF00	#6666FF	#9900CC
#009999	#333366	#33FF33	#669900	#9900FF
#0099CC	#333399	#33FF66	#669933	#993300

#993333	#99CCCC	#CC6633	#CCFFCC	#FF9933
#993366	#99CCFF	#CC6666	#CCFFFF	#FF9966
#993399	#99FF00	#CC6699	#FF0000	#FF9999
#9933CC	#99FF33	#CC66CC	#FF0033	#FF99CC
#9933FF	#99FF66	#CC66FF	#FF0066	#FF99FF
#996600	#99FF99	#CC9900	#FF0099	#FFCC00
#996633	#99FFCC	#CC9933	#FF00CC	#FFCC33
#996666	#99FFFF	#CC9966	#FF00FF	#FFCC66
#996699	#CC0000	#CC9999	#FF3300	#FFCC99
#9966CC	#CC0033	#CC99CC	#FF3333	#FFCCCC
#9966FF	#CC0066	#CC99FF	#FF3366	#FFCCFF
#999900	#CC0099	#CCCC00	#FF3399	#FFFF00
#999933	#CC00CC	#CCCC33	#FF33CC	#FFFF33
#999966	#CC00FF	#CCCC66	#FF33FF	#FFFF66
#999999	#CC3300	#CCCC99	#FF6600	#FFFF99
#9999CC	#CC3333	#CCCCCC	#FF6633	#FFFFCC
#9999FF	#CC3366	#CCCCFF	#FF6666	#FFFFFF
#99CC00	#CC3399	#CCFF00	#FF6699	
#99CC33	#CC33CC	#CCFF33	#FF66CC	
#99CC66	#CC33FF	#CCFF66	#FF66FF	
#99CC99	#CC6600	#CCFF99	#FF9900	

The color names and RGB values in Table A.19 are the 16 colors from the basic Windows VGA color palette. These color names are standard within the HTML 4 specification, and most browsers recognize their names. These colors look consistently clear—if often garish—on Windows computers.

TABLE A.19: Basic Colors and Names

COLOR NAME	RRGGBB VALUE
Aqua	#00FFFF
Black	#000000
Blue	#0000FF
Fuchsia	#FF00FF
Gray	#808080
Green	#008000
Lime	#00FF00
Maroon	#800000

TABLE A.19 continued: Basic Colors and Names

COLOR NAME	RRGGBB VALUE
Navy	#000080
Olive	#808000
Purple	#800080
Red	#FF0000
Silver	#C0C0C0
Teal	#008080
White	#FFFFFF
Yellow	#FFFF00

Named Colors

Table A.20 presents color names supported by Netscape Navigator (version 3 and later). These colors are not necessarily recommended for backgrounds, because they may not look their best in all visitors' browsers at all resolutions, but they are easy to remember and use. To accommodate all browsers that support colors, however, you must use the color code given in the second column rather than the name.

TABLE A.20: Color Names Supported by Netscape Navigator

NAME	CODE	NAME	CODE	NAME	CODE
Aliceblue	#F0F8FF	Antiquewhite	#FAEBD7	Aqua	#00FFFF
Aquamarine	#7FFFD4	Azure	#F0FFFF	Beige	#F5F5DC
Bisque	#FFE4C4	Black	#000000	Blanched-almond	#FFEBCD
Blue	#0000FF	Blueviolet	#8A2BE2	Brown	#A52A2A
Burlywood	#DEB887	Cadetblue	#5F9EA0	Chartreuse	#7FFF00
Chocolate	#D2691E	Coral	#FF7F50	Cornflower-blue	#6495ED
Cornsilk	#FFF8DC	Crimson	#DC143C	Cyan	#00FFFF
Darkblue	#00008B	Darkcyan	#008B8B	Dark-goldenrod	#B8860B
Darkgray	#A9A9A9	Darkgreen	#006400	Darkkhaki	#BDB76B
Darkmagenta	#8B008B	Darkolive-green	#556B2F		

TABLE A.20 continued: Color Names Supported by Netscape Navigator

NAME	CODE	NAME	CODE	NAME	CODE
Darkorange	#FF8C00	Darkorchid	#9932CC	Darkred	#8B0000
Darksalmon	#E9967A	Darkseagreen	#8FBC8F	Darkslateblue	#483D8B
Darkslategray	#2F4F4F	Darkturquoise	#00CED1	Darkviolet	#9400D3
Deeppink	#FF1493	Deepskyblue	#00BFFF	Dimgray	#696969
Dodgerblue	#1E90FF	Firebrick	#B22222	Floralwhite	#FFFAF0
Forestgreen	#228B22	Fuchsia	#FF00FF	Gainsboro	#DCDCDC
Ghostwhite	#F8F8FF	Gold	#FFD700	Goldenrod	#DAA520
Gray	#808080	Green	#008000	Greenyellow	#ADFF2F
Honeydew	#F0FFF0	Hotpink	#FF69B4	Indianred	#CD5C5C
Indigo	#4B0082	Ivory	#FFFFF0	Khaki	#F0E68C
Lavender	#E6E6FA	Lavender-blush	#FFF0F5	Lawngreen	#7CFC00
Lemonchiffon	#FFFACD	Lightblue	#ADD8E6	Lightcoral	#F08080
Lightcyan	#E0FFFF	Light-goldenrodyellow	#FAFAD2	Lightgreen	#90EE90
Lightgrey	#D3D3D3	Lightpink	#FFB6C1	Lightsalmon	#FFA07A
Lightseagreen	#20B2AA	Lightskyblue	#87CEFA	Lightslategray	#778899
Lightsteelblue	#B0C4DE	Lightyellow	#FFFFE0	Lime	#00FF00
Limegreen	#32CD32	Linen	#FAF0E6	Magenta	#FF00FF
Maroon	#800000	Medium-aquamarine	#66CDAA	Mediumblue	#0000CD
Medium-orchid	#BA55D3	Medium-purple	#9370DB	Medium-seagreen	#3CB371
Medium-slateblue	#7B68EE	Medium-springgreen	#00FA9A	Medium-turquoise	#48D1CC
Medium-violetred	#C71585	Midnightblue	#191970	Mintcream	#F5FFFA
Mistyrose	#FFE4E1	Moccasin	#FFE4B5	Navajowhite	#FFDEAD
Navy	#000080	Oldlace	#FDF5E6	Olive	#808000
Olivedrab	#6B8E23	Orange	#FFA500	Orangered	#FF4500

TABLE A.20 continued: Color Names Supported by Netscape Navigator

NAME	CODE	NAME	CODE	NAME	CODE
Orchid	#DA70D6	Pale-goldenrod	#EEE8AA	Palegreen	#98FB98
Paleturquoise	#AFEEEE	Palevioletred	#DB7093	Papayawhip	#FFEFD5
Peachpuff	#FFDAB9	Peru	#CD853F	Pink	#FFC0CB
Plum	#DDA0DD	Powderblue	#B0E0E6	Purple	#800080
Red	#FF0000	Rosybrown	#BC8F8F	Royalblue	#4169E1
Saddlebrown	#8B4513	Salmon	#FA8072	Sandybrown	#F4A460
Seagreen	#2E8B57	Seashell	#FFF5EE	Sienna	#A0522D
Silver	#C0C0C0	Skyblue	#87CEEB	Slateblue	#6A5ACD
Slategray	#708090	Snow	#FFFAFA	Springgreen	#00FF7F
Steelblue	#4682B4	Tan	#D2B48C	Teal	#008080
Thistle	#D8BFD8	Tomato	#FF6347	Turquoise	#40E0D0
Violet	#EE82EE	Wheat	#F5DEB3	White	#FFFFFF
Whitesmoke	#F5F5F5	Yellow	#FFFF00	Yellowgreen	#9ACD32

Table A.21 presents the named colors and "safe" colors together in a list. The numbered safe colors between named colors represent colors in the spectrum between those two points. For example, if you want to use a safe dark blue color, choose from the two "safe" colors—#000099 and #0000CC—that are between dark blue and medium blue in the table.

TABLE A.21: The Named Colors and the Safe Colors

NAME	CODE	NAME	CODE	NAME	CODE
Black	#000000	Darkblue	#0000CC	Blue	#003366
	#000033	Mediumblue	#0000CD		#003399
	#000066	Blue	#0000FF		#0033CC
Navy	#000080		#0000FF		#0033FF
Darkblue	#00008B		#003300	Darkgreen	#006400
	#000099		#003333		#006600

TABLE A.21 continued: The Named Colors and the Safe Colors

NAME	CODE	NAME	CODE	NAME	CODE
Darkgreen	#006633	Springgreen	#00FFCC	Limegreen	#339933
	#006666	Aqua	#00FFFF		#339966
	#006699	Cyan	#00FFFF		#339999
	#0066CC		#00FFFF		#3399CC
	#0066FF	Midnightblue	#191970		#3399FF
Green	#008000	Dodgerblue	#1E90FF		#33CC00
Teal	#008080	Lightseagreen	#20B2AA		#33CC33
Darkcyan	#008B8B	Forestgreen	#228B22		#33CC66
	#009900	Seagreen	#2E8B57		#33CC99
	#009933	Darkslategray	#2F4F4F		#33CCCC
	#009966	Limegreen	#32CD32		#33CCFF
	#009999		#330000		#33FF00
	#0099CC		#330033		#33FF33
	#0099FF		#330066		#33FF66
Deepskyblue	#00BFFF		#330099		#33FF99
	#00CC00		#3300CC		#33FFCC
	#00CC33		#3300FF		#33FFFF
	#00CC66		#333300	Medium-Seagreen	#3CB371
	#00CC99		#333333	Turquoise seagreen	#40E0D0
	#00CCCC		#333366		
	#00CCFF		#333399	Royalblue	#4169E1
Darkturquoise	#00CED1		#3333CC	Steelblue	#4682B4
Medium-springgreen	#00FA9A		#3333FF	Darkslateblue	#483D8B
			#336600	Medium-turquoise	#48D1CC
Lime	#00FF00		#336633		
	#00FF00		#336666	Indigo	#4B0082
	#00FF33		#336699	Darkolivegreen	#556B2F
	#00FF66		#3366CC	Cadetblue	#5F9EA0
Springgreen	#00FF7F		#3366FF	Cornflower-blue	#6495ED
	#00FF99		#339900		#660000

TABLE A.21 continued: The Named Colors and the Safe Colors

NAME	CODE	NAME	CODE	NAME	CODE
Cornflower-blue	#660033	Medium-aquamarine	#66CDAA	Darkseagreen	#8FBC8F
				Lightgreen	#90EE90
	#660066		#66FF00	Medium purple	#9370DB
	#660099		#66FF33		
	#6600CC		#6666FF	Darkviolet	#9400D3
	#6600FF		#66FF66	Palegreen	#98FB98
	#663300		#66FF99		#990000
	#663333		#66FFCC		#990033
	#663366		#66FFFF		#990066
	#663399	Dimgray	#696969		#990099
	#6633CC	Slateblue	#6A5ACD		#9900CC
	#6633FF	Olivedrab	#6B8E23		#9900FF
	#666600	Slategray	#708090	Darkorchid	#9932CC
	#666633	Lightslategray	#778899		#993300
	#666666	Medium-slateblue	#7B68EE		#993333
	#666699				#993366
	#6666CC	Lawngreen	#7CFC00		#993399
	#669900	Chartreuse	#7FFF00		#9933CC
	#669933	Aquamarine	#7FFFD4		#9933FF
	#669966	Maroon	#800000		#996600
	#669999	Purple	#800080		#996633
	#6699CC	Olive	#808000		#996666
	#6699FF	Gray	#808080		#996699
	#66CC00	Skyblue	#87CEEB		#9966CC
	#66CC33	Lightskyblue	#87CEFA		#9966FF
	#66CC66	Blueviolet	#8A2BE2		#999900
	#66CC99	Darkred	#8B0000		#999933
	#66CCCC	Darkmagenta	#8B008B		#999966
	#66CCFF	Saddlebrown	#8B4513		#999999

TABLE A.21 continued: The Named Colors and the Safe Colors

Name	Code	Name	Code	Name	Code
Darkorchid	#9999CC	Darkkhaki	#BDB76B	Medium-violetred	#CCCC33
	#9999FF	Silver	#C0C0C0		
	#99CC00	Medium-violetred	#C71585		#CCCC66
	#99CC33				#CCCC99
	#99CC66		#CC0000		#CCCCCC
	#99CC99		#CC0033		#CCCCFF
	#99CCCC		#CC0066		#CCFF00
	#99CCFF		#CC0099		#CCFF33
	#99FF00		#CC00CC		#CCFF66
	#99FF33		#CC00FF		#CCFF99
	#99FF66		#CC3300		#CCFFCC
	#99FF99		#CC3333		#CCFFFF
	#99FFCC		#CC3366	Indianred	#CD5C5C
	#99FFFF		#CC3399	Peru	#CD853F
Yellowgreen	#9ACD32		#CC33CC	Chocolate	#D2691E
Sienna	#A0522D		#CC33FF	Tan	#D2B48C
Brown	#A52A2A		#CC6600	Lightgrey	#D3D3D3
Darkgray	#A9A9A9		#CC6633	Thistle	#D8BFD8
Lightblue	#ADD8E6		#CC6666	Orchid	#DA70D6
Greenyellow	#ADFF2F		#CC6699	Goldenrod	#DAA520
Paleturquoise	#AFEEEE		#CC66CC	Palevioletred	#DB7093
Lightsteelblue	#B0C4DE		#CC66FF	Crimson	#DC143C
Powderblue	#B0E0E6		#CC9900	Gainsboro	#DCDCDC
Firebrick	#B22222		#CC9933	Plum	#DDA0DD
Dark-goldenrod	#B8860B		#CC9966	Burlywood	#DEB887
Medium-orchid	#BA55D3		#CC9999	Lightcyan	#E0FFFF
			#CC99CC	Lavender	#E6E6FA
Rosybrown	#BC8F8F		#CC99FF	Darksalmon	#E9967A
			#CCCC00	Violet	#EE82EE

TABLE A.21 continued: The Named Colors and the Safe Colors

NAME	CODE	NAME	CODE	NAME	CODE
Palegoldenrod	#EEE8AA	Deeppink	#FF3333	Pink	#FFCC66
Lightcoral	#F08080		#FF3366		#FFCC99
Khaki	#F0E68C		#FF3399		#FFCCCC
Aliceblue	#F0F8FF		#FF33CC		#FFCCFF
Honeydew	#F0FFF0		#FF33FF	Gold	#FFD700
Azure	#F0FFFF	Orangered	#FF4500	Peachpuff	#FFDAB9
Sandybrown	#F4A460	Tomato	#FF6347	Navajowhite	#FFDEAD
Wheat	#F5DEB3		#FF6600	Moccasin	#FFE4B5
Beige	#F5F5DC		#FF6633	Bisque	#FFE4C4
Whitesmoke	#F5F5F5		#FF6666	Mistyrose	#FFE4E1
Mintcream	#F5FFFA		#FF6699	Blanched-almond	#FFEBCD
Ghostwhite	#F8F8FF		#FF66CC		
Salmon	#FA8072		#FF66FF	Papayawhip	#FFEFD5
Antiquewhite	#FAEBD7	Hotpink	#FF69B4	Lavender blush	#FFF0F5
Linen	#FAF0E6	Coral	#FF7F50	Seashell	#FFF5EE
Lightgolden-rodyellow	#FAFAD2	Darkorange	#FF8C00	Cornsilk	#FFF8DC
			#FF9900	Lemonchiffon	#FFFACD
Oldlace	#FDF5E6		#FF9933	Floralwhite	#FFFAF0
Red	#FF0000		#FF9966	Snow	#FFFAFA
	#FF0000		#FF9999	Yellow	
	#FF0033		#FF99CC		#FFFF00
	#FF0066		#FF99FF		#FFFF33
	#FF0099	Lightsalmon	#FFA07A		#FFFF66
	#FF00CC	Orange	#FFA500		#FFFF99
Fuchsia	#FF00FF	Lightpink	#FFB6C1		#FFFFCC
Magenta	#FF00FF	Pink	#FFC0CB	Lightyellow	#FFFFE0
	#FF00FF		#FFCC00	Ivory	#FFFFF0
Deeppink	#FF1493		#FFCC33	White	#FFFFFF
	#FF3300				

INDEX

Note to the Reader: Page numbers in **bold** indicate the principal discussion of a topic or the definition of a term. Page numbers in *italic* indicate illustrations.

Be sure also to see the Appendix, the HTML Master's Reference, for alphabetized guides to HTML tags and attributes, Cascading Style Sheet properties, the components of JavaScript, HTML special characters, and HTML color codes.

SYMBOLS

& (ampersand)
  in JavaScript, 559
  in URLs, 437, 440

* (asterisk) in Perl regular expressions, 449

@ (at sign) in Perl list notation, 417

\ (backslash)
  for escaped characters in Perl, 411–412
  newline character (\n) in Perl, 411
  in Perl regular expressions, 449

^ (caret) in Perl regular expressions, 448

, (comma) in style sheet rulesets, 314

$ (dollar sign)
  in JavaScript variables, 567
  in Perl regular expressions, 448
  Perl scalar variables and, 415

! (exclamation point)
  in HTML comment tags, 7
  in Perl comments, 410

/ (forward slash) in Perl and Unix, 407

( ) (parentheses) in Perl regular expressions, 449–450

% (percent sign) in URLs, 437, 440

. (period)
  in JavaScript, 595
  in Perl regular expressions, 449

+ (plus sign)
  in Perl regular expressions, 449
  in URLs, 440

(pound sign) as comment character in Perl, 407, 410, 414

? (question mark)
  in Perl regular expressions, 449
  in URLs, 437, 440

" (quotation marks)
  in attributes, 91
  escaped double quote (\") in Perl, 412
  in JavaScript, 575–576, *576*
  in Perl list notation, 418

' (quote mark)
  in JavaScript, 575–576, *576*
  in Perl list notation, 418

; (semicolon)
  in JavaScript, 559
  in Perl, 411
  in style sheet rulesets, 314

/ (slash) in HTML tags, 5

_ (underscore character) in JavaScript variables, 567

| (vertical bar) in Perl regular expressions, 448

A

B

G

H

M

O

OSD (Open Software Description) vocabulary, **657**

outerHTML content property, **523**, 524–525, 527–532, 533, *534*

outerText content property, **522–523**, 524–525, 527–532

P

<P> tag. *See* paragraphs

pack function in Perl, **447**

packaging properties and methods in containers, 601, 605

pages. *See* Web pages

PaintShop Pro software, 249

palettes
safe palettes, **203–204, 218–219, 252**
selecting for sites, 208

paragraphs
indenting, **107**, 265–266, *266*, **346–347**
<P> (paragraph) tag, **7**, 12–13, *13*, **97–100**, *99*, 263–264, *265*

parameters in Perl, **410–411**

parentheses ( ) in Perl regular expressions, 449–450

parsed HTML (Server Side Includes), **366–367**

parseFloat() and parseInt() JavaScript methods, 585–587, *587*, 627

parser software, **656–657, 658–659**

password fields in forms, 34–35, *35*

Pepsi site, 61–63, *61*, *62*

percent sign (%) in URLs, 437, 440

period (.)
in JavaScript, 595
in Perl regular expressions, 448

Perl, **371**, **395–418**. *See also* CGI (Common Gateway Interface)
advantages of, 448
case sensitivity in, 415
CGI (Common Gateway Interface) and, **419–421**, *419*, *420*
compiling Perl source code, 406
defined, **371**, **396**, **400–401**
downloading, 405
forward slash (/) in, 407
history of, 400–403, *402*
HTTP and, 398–399, *399*
as an interpreted language, 403–404
lists, **414**, **416–418**
defined, **414**, **416–417**
double quote (") and single quote (') in, 418
naming, 417
at sign (@) in, 417
strings in, 418
syntax of, 417–418
Perl interpreter, **405–407**
installing, 405–406
starting, 406–407
regular expressions, **401**, **444–450**
asterisk (*) in, 449
backslash (\) in, 449
caret (^) in, 448
components of, 448–450
defined, **401**, **444–445**, **448**
difficulty of, 448
dollar sign ($) in, 448
hex function, 447
pack expression, **447**
parentheses ( ) in, 449–450
period character or dot (.) in, 449

Q

R

S

W

X

Y

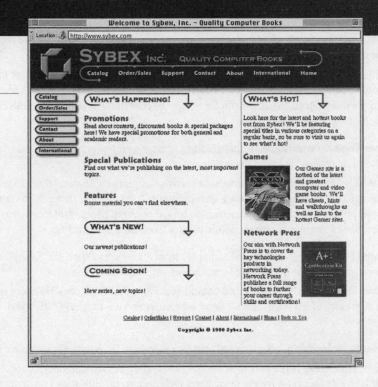

About the Contributors

Some of the best—and best-selling—Sybex authors have contributed chapters from their current books to *HTML Complete*.

Pat Coleman contributed chapters from *Mastering Internet Explorer 4* (coauthored with Gene Weisskopf) and *Mastering Intranets: The Windows 95/NT Edition (coauthored with Peter Dyson)*.

Ms. Coleman is a writer and editor. Formerly editorial director of Microsoft Press and founding editor of the Microsoft Developer Network, she was an editor for *Encyclopaedia Britannica, The Academic American Encyclopedia* (the first encyclopedia published online), and *The World Almanac*.

Peter Dyson contributed a chapter from *Mastering Intranets: The Windows 95/NT Edition* (coauthored with Pat Coleman).

Mr. Dyson is a writer and consultant software engineer with more than 20 years of experience in engineering, software development, and technical support. His computer-related publications include numerous technical research papers and more than two dozen books. Among his recent Sybex titles is *The ABCs of Intranets*.

Vincent Flanders contributed a chapter from *Web Pages That Suck: Learn Good Design by Looking at Bad Design* (coauthored with Michael Willis).

Mr. Flanders is the mastermind behind WebPagesThatSuck.com. He spent two years as a Webmaster for a large Internet Service Provider and has taught HTML and design courses.

Molly E. Holzschlag contributed chapters from *web by design: The Complete Guide*.

Ms. Holzschlag is the author of several best-selling Web design books, including *Sizzling Web Site Design*. A widely recognized Web design consultant and content provider, Molly also develops and teaches design courses for the New School University, the University of Phoenix, Pima Community College, and DigitalThink.

James Jaworski contributed chapters from *Mastering JavaScript and JScript*.

Mr. Jaworski led the development of multilevel secure networks for the Department of Defense. He is the author of *Do-It-Yourself Web Publishing with HoTMetaL* and *The Java Developer's Guide* and has developed secure network applications since 1980.

E. Stephen Mack contributed chapters from *HTML 4.0: No experience required.* (coauthored with Janan Platt Saylor).

Mr. Mack is a Web designer, software trainer, and computer consultant. He has worked with several major companies over the last ten years, written computer articles, and cocreated two best-selling computer books.

Natanya Pitts contributed a chapter from *XML In Record Time.*

Ms. Pitts is the author of several Web-oriented books covering topics such as style sheets, Dynamic HTML, and XML. An experienced Webmaster, she has taught Web design and development at Austin Community College for several years. She works as a technical writer and corporate trainer for a software company in Austin, Texas.

Janan Platt Saylor contributed chapters from *HTML 4.0: No experience required.* (coauthored with E. Stephen Mack).

Ms. Platt has 13 years of experience as a controller and consultant teaching people to use computers. She publishes multimedia poetry, often from her online poetry workshop, Alien Flower.

Deborah S. Ray and Eric J. Ray contributed material from *Mastering HTML 4.0.*

Ms. and Mr. Ray are owners of RayComm, Inc., a technical communications consulting firm that specializes in cutting-edge Internet and computing technologies. Together they have coauthored more than 10 computer books, including *Unix Visual Quickstart Guide, The AltaVista Search Revolution, HTML 4 for Dummies Quick Reference,* and *Dummies 101: HTML 4.* They also write a syndicated computer column, which is available in newspapers across North America.

Joseph Schmuller contributed chapters from *Dynamic HTML: Master the Essentials.*

Mr. Schmuller, a Senior Systems Analyst at Barnett Technologies, is the author of *ActiveX: No experience required.,* also from Sybex. Editor-in-Chief of *PC AI* magazine from 1991 through 1997, he has written numerous articles and reviews on advanced computing technology. He is also a partner at Adcomtek, a firm specializing in Web site design for mass-media organizations, and an Adjunct Professor at the University of North Florida.

Erik Strom contributed chapters from *Perl CGI Programming: No experience required.*

Mr. Strom is an Assistant Managing Editor of the *Denver Post.*

Gene Weisskopf contributed a chapter from *Mastering Internet Explorer 4* (coauthored with Pat Coleman).

Mr. Weisskopf has been involved in the PC revolution since the early 1980s. He has developed software applications for business and science and has taught a variety of classes and training sessions. His articles have appeared in a number of computer magazines, and he has written several books for Sybex, including *The ABCs of Excel 97, Mastering Quattro Pro 6,* and *Murphy's Laws of PCs.*

Michael Willis contributed a chapter from *Web Pages That Suck: Learn Good Design by Looking at Bad Design* (coauthored with Vincent Flanders).

Mr. Willis has been a graphic designer for 18 years and has a successful Web/print design firm.

MASTERING MICROSOFT INTERNET EXPLORER 4

BY GENE WEISSKOPF AND PAT COLEMAN

960 pages
ISBN: 0-7821-2133-0
$44.99

Internet Explorer 4, the popular browser suite, paves the way to Microsoft's Active Desktop, with new features and built-in push technology. Perfect for every user from beginner to advanced, *Mastering Microsoft Internet Explorer 4* provides complete, in depth coverage of all the new features and explains how to get the most out of them. The accompanying CD-ROM is loaded with valuable software, including a fully searchabl customizable electronic version of the book, Web publishing tools, and useful Net utilitie

MASTERING MICROSOFT INTERNET INFORMATION SERVER 4

BY PETER DYSON

944 pages
ISBN: 0-7821-2080-6
$49.99

Mastering MS Internet Information Server 4 is the complete reference for setting up a maintaining an Internet Web site and/or an intranet with IIS and Windows NT Server. Filled with real-world corporate examples, this book provides expert advice about IIS security issues, TCP/IP, Java applications, Web page creation, and Internet eCommerce

WEB PAGES THAT SUCK: LEARN GOOD DESIGN BY LOOKING AT BAD DESIGN

BY VINCENT FLANDERS AND MICHAEL WILLIS

288 pages
ISBN: 0-7821-2187-x
$39.00

Based on the hugely popular, award-winning site (webpagesthatsuck.com), this beau tiful, four-color book effectively uses humor and down-to-earth tactics to teach suc cessful Web design to the masses. You have probably seen authors Flanders and Will all over the place—on TV, on radio, in print, and even in person. They are shameless self-promoters who are quickly becoming Internet gurus. As a bonus, the companion CD is packed with valuable "Software That Doesn't Suck" plus all the HTML from the boo